THE HIGHLAND FURIES

THE HIGHLAND FURIES

The Black Watch
1739–1899

Volume I

Victoria Schofield

Quercus

First published in Great Britain in 2012 by
Quercus
55 Baker Street
7th Floor, South Block
London
W1U 8EW

A CIP catalogue record for this book is available
from the British Library

ISBN 978 1 84916 550 1

10 9 8 7 6 5 4 3 2 1

Text and plates designed and typeset by Ellipsis Digital Ltd

Maps © Jamie Whyte

Printed and bound in Great Britain by Clays Ltd, St Ives plc

*The Highland furies rushed in upon us with more violence
than ever did a sea driven by a tempest.*

Fontenoy, 1745

To the fallen of The Black Watch

Contents

I am delighted to contribute a few words to mark the publication of this first volume of the history of The Black Watch. As this book reveals, my great-great-great grandmother, Queen Victoria, had a special affection for the Regiment. My great grandfather, King George V, was the Regiment's first Colonel-in-Chief; my grandmother, Queen Elizabeth The Queen Mother, was the second – for more than sixty years. When I was appointed by The Queen to be the Regiment's third Colonel-in-Chief I felt enormously proud and honoured, for there can be few with any interest in military or Scottish history who have not heard of The Black Watch and, of them, fewer still who would not want to salute the record and memory of Scotland's senior Highland Regiment.

No-one was more dismayed than I was when the announcement came in 2004 that The Black Watch was to merge with other Scottish regiments and I took no pleasure in knowing that I would there-fore be not just the third, but the last Colonel-in-Chief. Happily, the name continues in the British Army's order of battle and I take immense pride in the achievements of The Black Watch, 3rd Battalion The Royal Regiment of Scotland, of which I am privileged to be Royal Colonel.

The new battalion has already proved itself in two tours of Afghanistan. The officers and men have shown beyond contra-diction that however sad the passing of the old, the new is more than equal to the challenges that they have faced with such skill and fortitude. It gives me particular pleasure to know that this splendid new history of the regiment will not only provide for posterity an authoritative record of the old Black Watch, but will also help to inspire the officers and men serving now and in the future to match and exceed the extraordinary achievements of a very fine Regiment.

Charles

Preface

by Lieutenant General Sir Alistair Irwin, KCB, CBE.

On 28 March 2006 The Black Watch (Royal Highland Regiment) joined the other remaining Scottish infantry regiments to form the Royal Regiment of Scotland. As the last Colonel of the Regiment I had the unhappy duty of attending a parade in Palace Barracks Belfast to mark the moment at which the old became the new. For those who were serving, it was a time to mourn the passing of the Regiment that they had specifically elected to join, but it was also a time to set the eye firmly on the future. For those no longer serving, the day was one of infinite sadness and regret but also one of immense pride in having been part of a legend, part of a regiment that had made its name famous around the world. In the 267 years since its formation in 1739 The Black Watch had played a prominent and gallant part in the unfolding history of the United Kingdom of Great Britain and Northern Ireland, forging a record of service and a reputation of which no one could fail to be proud.

Quite rightly the Regimental Trustees of The Black Watch were determined to do all that they could to ensure that their Regiment's history and legacy should be preserved and honoured. Among the measures they took was the initiation of a project to expand the regimental museum in Perth and to use this as the basis for an educational outreach programme that would serve to inspire future generations of young Scots to live their lives in the spirit of selfless service and ambition to excel that had so characterised the life of the Regiment over the years.

The Trustees also decided to commission a new history of the Regiment, of which this is the first of two volumes (a second volume will appear later). There have of course been many previous histories, each of them with their admirers, but most now out of print. The author, Victoria Schofield, had already produced a fine biography of the most famous of the sons of The Black Watch, Field Marshal

Earl Wavell. The Trustees were delighted when she agreed to turn her attention to the regiment to which that great soldier had belonged. She was invited to produce a book that was at once readable and scholarly. The history of the Regiment was to be set in the context of events beyond the Regiment and the emphasis was to be on the experiences of the officers and men who had served, for it was they who had created the history; the Regiment of itself had no meaning without the men who lived and breathed it. Above all the author was required to ensure that as much as possible of the material she used was from contemporary primary sources including diaries and letters and that these and other sources should be properly noted in the book, something that no previous history from that by Stewart of Garth to the present day has done.

As a result of these stipulations we have been presented with a story that is full of human interest as it traces the progress of the Regiment from its earliest days until, in the case of this volume, the end of the 19th century. The narrative does not pretend to follow every twist and turn of each battle fought, but rather to tell the story of how the Regiment survived the challenges that it faced. This book is about the officers and men, who they were, what they did, what they thought, and how they lived and fought. Periods of peace on garrison duties are as much part of this story as the conflicts; in the process absorbing new light has been cast on the life and times of The Black Watch.

The regimental Trustees dedicate this history to all the officers and men who have served in The Black Watch since 1739 and especially to those many thousands who laid down their lives in the service of the Crown. They hope that members of the regimental family will take pleasure in this record of their beloved Regiment. And they hope that the wider readership will understand why those of us who have served in The Black Watch are so closely at one with Sir George Murray, a former Colonel, who said in 1844: *How high an honour I shall always esteem it to have been for upwards of twenty years the colonel of a regiment, which, by its exemplary conduct in every situation, and by its distinguished valour in many a well-fought field has earned for itself so large a share of esteem and renown.*

Acknowledgements

I should like to thank the Trustees of the Black Watch Regimental Trust for the confidence they placed in me to write the official history of The Black Watch in two volumes. It is both a privilege and an honour. In so doing, the assistance of Thomas B. Smyth, Archivist at the Black Watch Regimental Museum at Balhousie Castle, Perth, has been unstinting and invaluable. I am also grateful to Lieutenant Colonel Roddy Riddell, Secretary, The Black Watch, and his wife Jenny for their tremendous kindness in providing me with a home from home in Scotland.

During my research I have had numerous helpful conversations with retired officers of the Regiment, especially the Chairman of Trustees, Lieutenant General Sir Alistair Irwin, KCB, CBE, who first proposed that I should undertake this work and who has made many useful comments on the manuscript. My thanks also to Brigadier Garry Barnett, OBE, Brigadier Duncan Cameron, OBE, Lieutenant Colonel Stephen Lindsay, Major Ronnie Proctor, MBE, Major General Andrew Watson, CB, and to the staff at Balhousie Castle, especially Janet Telford.

I should also like to thank the Trustees of the Black Watch for permission to cite from numerous unpublished memoirs, diaries, letters and journals of officers, non-commissioned officers and private soldiers held in the Regimental Archives; in selecting the quotations for this first volume, I have done so with the view to illustrate to the reader the life of the soldier in the eighteenth and nineteenth centuries, his sense of duty, the comradeship he enjoyed with his fellow officers and men and the hardships he endured. Above all, I have endeavoured to tell the story of this most illustrious and well-known Regiment through the experiences and words of those who served in it, using, as far as possible, exclusively contemporary regimental sources.

Additional quotations from documents held in The National

Archives are cited with the permission of the Controller of Her Majesty's Stationery Office. I am grateful for permission to quote from Robert, Lord Blantyre's diary held in the National Museums of Scotland, with thanks to Stuart Allan, as well as for permission to quote from a number of documents held in the National Records of Scotland (formerly National Archives of Scotland). Additional letters deposited in the National Records of Scotland are used with the permission of Sir Roderick Campbell of Barcaldine and Glenure, the Earl of Seafield and William A. Stirling Drummond Moray, Esq. The letters of Lieutenant Colonel Frederick Green Wilkinson are cited by kind permission of the Royal Green Jackets (Rifles) Museum Trustees, Winchester; Lord Loudoun's Papers are cited with the permission of the Huntingdon Library, Pasadena, California; quotations from the manuscript transcripts in Macquarie University Library websites 'Under A Tropical Sun' and 'The Lachlan & Elizabeth Macquarie Archive' are cited with the permission of Macquarie University and the State Library of NSW, with special thanks to Robin Walsh for all his advice. John Grant's Journal is cited with the permission of the Alexander Turnbull Library, National Library of New Zealand. The extensive volume of material available in The British Library and The National Library of Scotland both in terms of published works and primary source material has been invaluable in adding to the depth of my research. I am pleased to be the recipient of Carlyle membership of The London Library, whose liberal lending policy and online facilities have been of great assistance. My thanks also to the staff at Marylebone Public Library, City of Westminster, London, who facilitated an interlibrary loan from the National Library of New Zealand.

Illustrations in the book are used with the permission of the Regimental Trustees, with thanks to Emma Halford-Forbes, the Manager of the Museum of The Black Watch, Jill van Milligen, Curatorial Assistant, and John McKenzie, who photographed many of the pictures. The colour transparency of Governor Lachlan Macquarie by Gordon H. Woodhouse is reproduced with the permission of the State Library of Victoria, Australia. Robert Gibb's painting,

Alma: Forward the 42nd, is reproduced on the cover with the permission of Kelvingrove Art Gallery and Museum, Glasgow.

Several friends and colleagues have helped me in terms of offering constructive advice and assistance, in particular, Alison and Robert Allen, Sir Nicholas Barrington, KCMG, CVO, Brian Cloughley, Ruari Halford-Macleod, Major Robin and Pippa Maclean, Brigadier Ian McLeod, CMG, OBE, MC, John Raisman, OBE, William T. Reid, Jane Ridley Thomas, Catherine Tudhope and Brigadier C.W. Woodburn. My thanks to my agent, Sara Menguc, to Richard Milner, Josh Ireland and Bethan Ferguson at Quercus Publishers, and to Jamie Whyte, who drew the maps. I am most grateful to my husband, Stephen Willis, my children, Alexandra, Anthony and Olivia and to my extended family, for their unfailing support in this most challenging and rewarding of literary enterprises.

Black Watch Title Changes and Military Formations

Throughout its 267-year history, The Black Watch has had several 'official titles'. In the narrative the Regiment is referred to by the name appropriate to the period:

1725–1739   The Independent Companies or The Black Watch.

1739–1741   The Earl of Crawford's Highlanders, or the Highland Regiment, listed as the 43rd in order of precedence in the British Army.

1741–1745   Lord Sempill's Highlanders, or the Highland Regiment, listed as the 43rd.

1745–1749   Lord John Murray's Highlanders, or the Highland Regiment, listed as the 43rd.

1749–1751   Lord John Murray's Highlanders or the Highland Regiment, listed as the 42nd.

1751–1758   The 42nd Regiment of Foot, The Highland Regiment.

1758–1861   The 42nd or Royal Highland Regiment of Foot, also known as Royal Highlanders.

1861–1881   The 42nd Royal Highland Regiment of Foot, The Black Watch.

1881–1934   The Black Watch (Royal Highlanders).

1935–2006   The Black Watch (Royal Highland Regiment).

1786–1816   The 73rd (Highland) Regiment of Foot (the former 2nd Battalion 42nd, raised in 1779).

1816–1862   The 73rd Regiment of Foot.

1862–1881   The 73rd (Perthshire) Regiment of Foot.

In 1881 The 73rd (Perthshire) Regiment became The 2nd Battalion, The Black Watch (Royal Highlanders).

In 2006 the Regiment was merged, and became The Black Watch, 3rd Battalion The Royal Regiment of Scotland (3 SCOTS).

For certain periods of the Regiment's history, for both the 42nd and 73rd, there were two battalions, with up to ten companies of about 100 officers, non-commissioned officers and private soldiers, known as 'rank and file.' From 1881 onwards the Regiment consisted of a regimental depot and two battalions; one battalion was intended to remain at home to train recruits, while the other served overseas.

The size or 'establishment' of an army or expeditionary force was regularly increased or decreased by augmenting or disbanding battalions, or by increasing or decreasing the number of companies. New regiments were also raised and although The Black Watch was the first Highland Regiment, others were subsequently formed, The Black Watch frequently fighting as part of 'The Highland Brigade'.

The principal components of an army in the field consist of headquarters; one or two corps, each made up of a varying number of divisions; divisions comprise a varying number of brigades, each of two or more regiments of cavalry or battalions of infantry; in addition to all these is an extensive range of supporting troops, such as the artillery.

Battle Honours

In the Black Watch Regimental Museum at Balhousie Castle, Perth, Scotland, there are several old 'laid-up' stands of the Regimental and Sovereign's Colours; the oldest in the museum is the tattered stand carried throughout the Peninsular Wars and at Waterloo. On the Colours are traditionally embellished the Battle Honours. In addition to the Sphinx superscribed 'Egypt', granted after the Battle of Alexandria in 1801, The Black Watch gained the following Battle Honours:

Guadaloupe 1759, Martinique 1762, Havannah, North America 1763–64, Mangalore, Mysore, Seringapatam, Corunna, Busaco, Fuentes d'Onor, Salamanca, Pyrenees, Nivelle, Nive, Orthes, Toulouse, Peninsula, Waterloo, South Africa 1846-7, 1851–2–3, Alma, Sevastopol, Lucknow, Ashantee 1873-4, Tel-el-Kebir, Egypt 1882, 1884, Kirbekan, Nile 1884–85, Paardeberg, South Africa 1899–1902.

The Great War: Retreat from Mons, Marne 1914, 18, Aisne 1914, La Bassée 1914, Ypres 1914, 17, 18, Langemarck 1914, Gheluvelt, Nonne Bosschen, Givenchy 1914, Neuve Chapelle, Aubers, Festubert 1915, Loos, Somme 1916, 18, Albert 1916, Bazentin, Delville Wood, Pozieres, Flers-Courcelette, Morval, Thiepval, Le Transloy, Ancre Heights, Ancre 1916, Arras 1917, 18, Vimy 1917, Scarpe 1917, 18, Arleux, Pilckem, Menin Road, Polygon Wood, Poelcappelle, Passchendaele, Cambrai 1917, 18, St Quentin, Bapaume 1918, Rosieres, Lys, Estaires, Messines 1918, Hazebrouck, Kemmel, Béthune, Scherpenberg, Soissonnais-Ourcq, Tardenois, Drocourt-Quéant, Hindenburg Line, Epéhy, St Quentin Canal, Beaurevoir, Courtrai, Selle, Sambre, France and Flanders, 1914–18, Doiran 1917, Macedonia 1915–18, Egypt 1916, Gaza, Jerusalem, Tell'Asur, Megiddo,

Sharon, Damascus, Palestine 1917–18, Tigris 1916, Kut al Amara 1917, Baghdad, Mesopotamia 1915–17.

The Second World War: Defence of Arras, Ypres-Comines Canal, Dunkirk 1940, Somme 1940, St Valery en Caux, Saar, Breville, Odon, Fontenoy le Pesnil, Defence of Rauray, Caen, Falaise, Falaise Road, La Vie Crossing, Le Havre, Lower Maas, Venlo Pocket, Ourthe, Rhineland, Reichswald, Goch, Rhine, North West Europe, 1940, 44–45, Barkasan, British Somaliland 1940, Tobruk 1941, Tobruk Sortie, El Alamein, Advance on Tripoli, Medenine, Zemlet el Lebene, Mareth, Akarit, Wadi Akarit East, Djebel Roumana, Medjez Plain, Si Medienne, Tunis, North Africa 1941–4, Landing in Sicily, Vizzini, Sferro, Gerbini, Adrano, Sferro Hills, Sicily 1943, Cassino II, Liri Valley, Advance to Florence, Monte Scalari, Casa Fortis, Rimini Line, Casa Fabbri Ridge, Savio Bridgehead, Italy 1944–45, Athens, Greece 1944–45, Crete, Heraklion, Middle East 1941, Chindits 1944, Burma 1944.

The Hook 1952, Korea 1952–53, Al Basrah 2003, Iraq 2003.

The narrative which follows describes how these Battle Honours were won in the continents of Africa, America, Asia and Europe, the first volume ending before the South African War in 1899 and the beginning of industrialised warfare, the second volume covering the twentieth and twenty-first centuries.

List of Illustrations

Unless otherwise stated all illustrations are from the collection of The Black Watch Regimental Museum at Balhousie Castle.

Illustrations at the beginning of Chapters 1–8, 10–20 by Richard Simkin (1850–1926).

The illustration at the beginning of Chapter 9 is of Norman MacLeod of MacLeod by A.E. Haswell Miller (1887–1979).

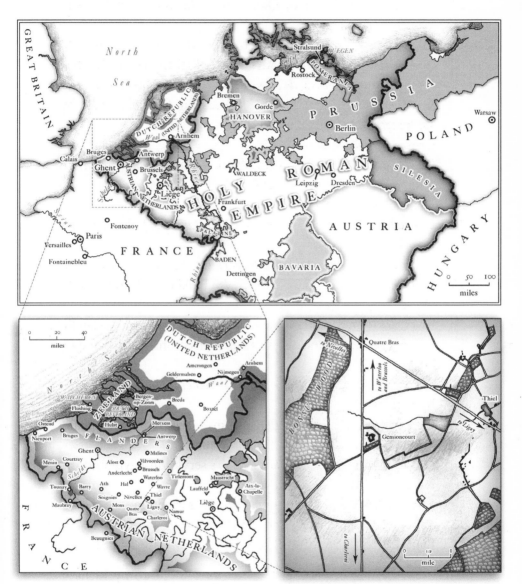

Northern Europe, pre-1815

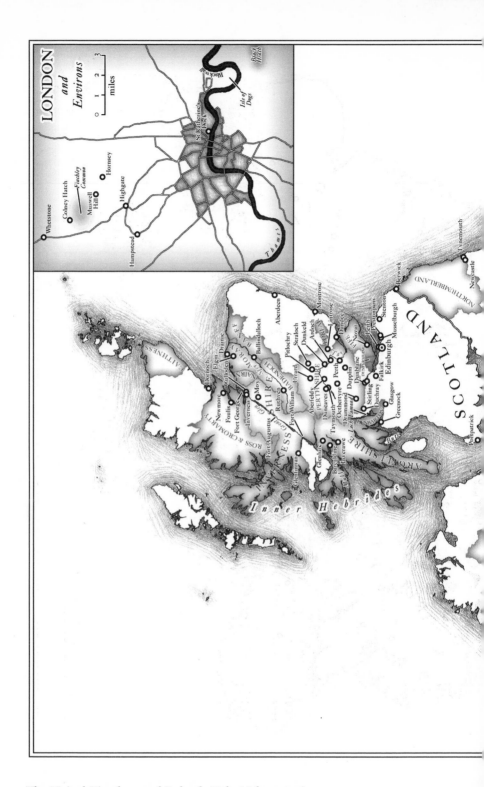

The United Kingdom and Ireland, 18th, 19th centuries

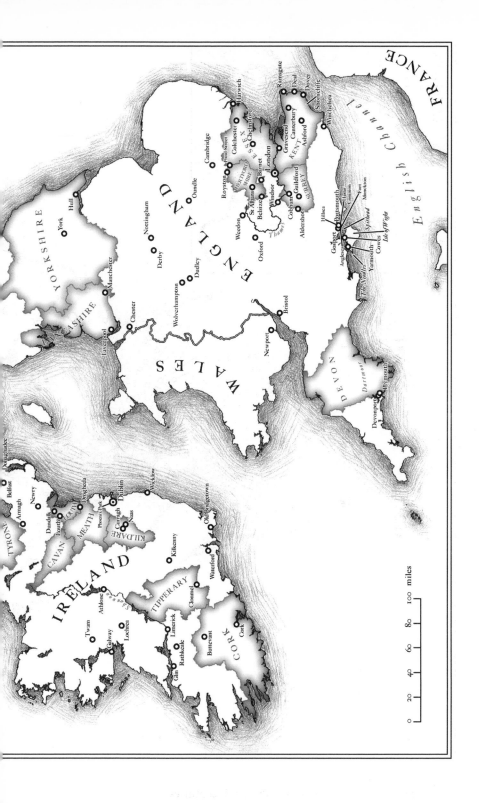

North America, late 18th century

NEWFOUNDLAND

CANADA

s of
nam

St Francis
Mission

Quebec

Taymouth

NEW BRUNSWICK
Nashwaak

Prince
Edward
Island

Charlottetown

NOVA SCOTIA
Cape Breton

Louisbourg

Halifax

Lake Champlain

VERMONT

NEWHAMPSHIRE

MASSACHUSETTS

M A S S

Boston

NEC-
CUT

RHODE ISLAND

Newport

Plymouth

Long
Island

Atlantic Ocean

Bermuda

**NEW YORK and
the HUDSON
and DELAWARE
RIVERS**

Lake Champlain

NEW YORK

Crown
Point

Ft Carillon
(Ticonderoga)

VERMONT

NEW HAMPSHIRE

Ft William
Henry

Lake
George

Mohawk

Ft Edward

Saratoga

Greenwich

Schenectady

Albany

MASSACHUSETTS

CONNECTICUT

Hudson

NEW YORK

PENNSYLVANNIA

Delaware

2   1

New
York

3

New York
Island

Watchung
Mountains

4

6

Long Island

5

8

9

11

12

10

13

14

Staten
Island

15

Sandy Hook

16

17   18

19

Philadelphia

NEW JERSEY

1.	Verplancks
2.	Stony Point
3.	White Plains
4.	Morristown
5.	Newark
6.	Paulus Hook
7.	Jamaica
8.	Flatbush
9.	Springfield
10.	Utrecht
11.	Gravesend
12.	Pisquatua
13.	Princeton
14.	Monmouth
	Court House
15.	Trenton
16.	Valley Forge
17.	Paoli
18.	Chester
19.	Billings Port

CANADIAN
PROVINCES

SPANISH
TERRITORIES

0   25   50

miles

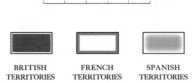

BRITISH
TERRITORIES

FRENCH
TERRITORIES

SPANISH
TERRITORIES

The West Indies, late 18th century

MARTINIQUE

St Pierre
Morne Grenier
Morne Tartenson
Cas des Navires
Fort Segro
Fort Royal

0   5   10   15 miles

GUADELOUPE

Port Louis
GRANDE-TERRE
LA DÉSIRADE
BASSE-TERRE
Arnouville
Ste Anne
St François
Ste Marie
ÎLES DE LA
PETITE TERRE
Basse-Terre
Capesterre
MARIE-
GALANTE
ÎLES DES
SAINTES

0   5   10   15 miles

ST VINCENT

Fort Charlotte   Kingstown
Kingstown
Bay

0   5   10   15 miles

ST LUCIA

PIGEON
ISLAND
Chock
Bay
Ance la Raze

0   5   10   15 miles

The Caribbean Islands

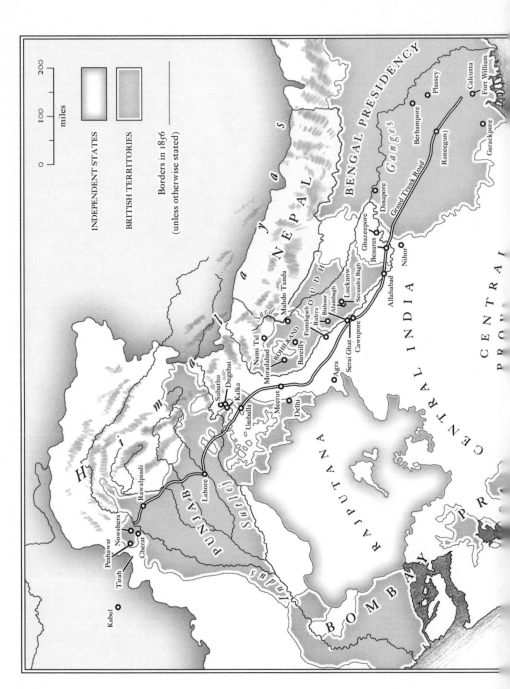

India, mid-19th century

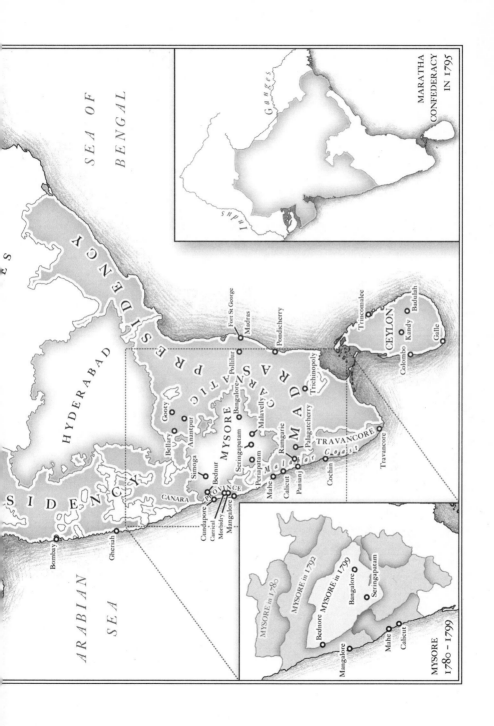

SEA OF
BENGAL

MARATHA
CONFEDERACY
IN 1795

Ganges

Indus

ARABIAN
SEA

HYDERABAD

PRESIDENCY

SIDENCY

CANARA

MYSORE
PROVINCE

Bombay

Gheriah

Cundapore
Cartical
Morbiddy
Mangalore

Simoga

Bednur

Bellary

Anantpur

Gooty

Seringapatam

Periapatam

Bangalore

Malavelly

Ramgurie

Mahe
Calicut
Paniany

Palagatchery

Palamcottah

Pollilur

Fort St George

Madras

Pondicherry

Trichinopoly

TRAVANCORE

Malabar
Coast

Cochin

Travancore

CEYLON

Trincomalee

Kandy

Badulah

Galle

Colombo

MYSORE
1780 – 1799

MYSORE in 1780

MYSORE in 1792

MYSORE in 1799

Bednore

Bangalore

Seringapatam

Mangalore

Mahe

Calicut

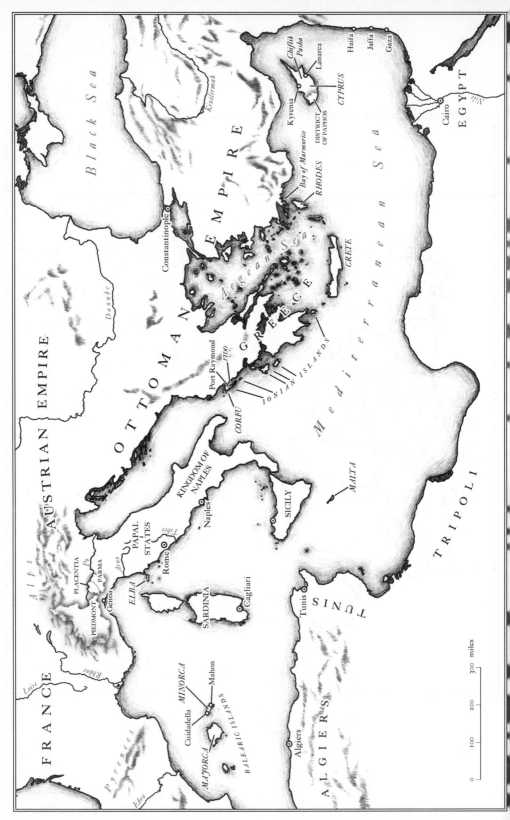

The Mediterranean, mid-19th century

The Iberian Peninsula, early 19th century

Australia, early 19th century

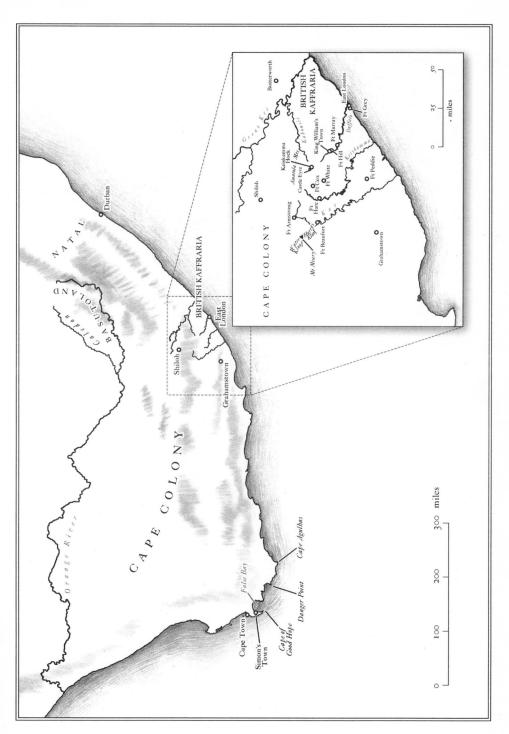

South Africa, mid-19th century

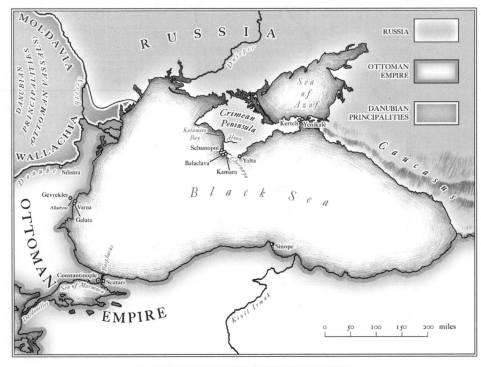

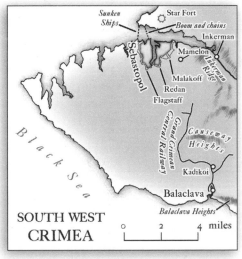

The Crimea, mid-19th century

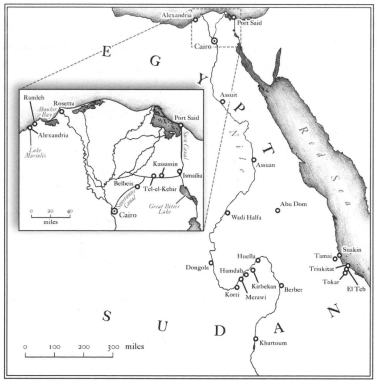

North and West Africa, late 19th century

1.

Raising the Regiment 1739

We're tall as the oak on the mount of the vale,
Are swift as the roe which the hound doth assail,
As the full moon in Autumn our shield do appear,
Minerva would dread to encounter our spear.

Sir Henry Erskine, *c*.1763[1]

1742

Formation

On an early summer's day in May 1740, about seven hundred men armed with muskets and swords and wearing traditional Highland tartan plaids assembled near Tay Bridge, in the field of Boltachan, by the river Tay in the Highlands of Scotland. For the first time in Scotland's history, Highlanders were to be formed into a regiment in the British Army. In 1758 the Highland Regiment was granted the title 'Royal', having famously become the 42nd, or 'forty-twa', usually known by its even better name of The Black Watch, *Am Freiceadan Dubh*. George II's assent to authorise the first Highland Regiment was a leap of faith. Over thirty years since the 1707 Act of Union and over 130 years since the two kingdoms of England and Scotland were united under one monarch in 1603, the Highlanders – known for their fierce fighting spirit and ambivalent attitude to the Crown – were being entrusted to carry arms as part of the British Army on behalf of the Sovereign. The decision could not have been taken lightly. In 1717 all Highlanders had been disarmed, following the 1715 uprising against George II's father by those Jacobites wanting to reinstate the Stuart line on the throne. Only the pressing need to police the Highlands and keep a 'watch o'er the braes' had led to the formation of six 'independent companies' drawn from the pro-Hanoverian clans in 1725.

Independent Companies 1725

The precedent for the formation of these independent companies lay in Scotland's turbulent history, where clans fought each other in a constant battle for power and influence. Since the previous century, George II's predecessors had adopted the practice of raising a rudimentary King's Guard in Scotland.[2] The man tasked with raising the independent companies in 1725 was General George Wade, who had travelled through 'the greatest and most uncivilised parts of the Highlands' the previous year to determine how best this lawless region could be managed.[3] Having discovered that less than half of those capable of carrying arms in the Highlands were loyal to the King, he concurred with the view expressed by Simon Fraser, Lord Lovat, chief of the Clan Fraser, that independent companies should once again be formed. Not only, Lovat had said, were the disaffected clans 'better armed than ever' because the disarming of the Highlanders after the 1715 uprising had been 'so ill executed', enabling them to commit 'Robberies and Depredations', but the clans could also be used 'as Tools or Instruments to any Foreign Power or Domestic Incendiaries who may attempt to disturb the Peace of your Majesty's Reign'.[4] Wade also wished to inform the King how difficult it was for regular troops to operate in the Highlands 'for the want of Roads and Bridges and from excessive Rains that almost continually fall in those parts, which by Nature and constant use become habitual to the Natives, but very difficultly supported by the Regular Troops'.[5]

Acting on Wade's advice, on 31 May 1725 George I had issued a warrant to form six companies 'in the Highlands of North Britain'.[6] A month later Wade, appointed 'Commander-in-Chief of His Majesty's Forces, Castles, Forts, and Barracks in North Britain, &c.', arrived in Scotland and proceeded to Inverness, where the newly raised companies were assembling. There had been no shortage of recruits. As good swordsmen, the right to carry arms was a 'cherished privilege' at a time when there were heavy penalties 'galling to a high-spirited and warlike race' for doing so if not in the King's service.[7] Three companies were to be commanded by captains and three by lieutenants. For his services, Simon Fraser, Lord Lovat was given command of one of the larger companies with a complement of sixty 'effective private men'. One of the smaller companies, with a complement of thirty men, was commanded by George Munro of Culcairn, younger brother of the 6th Baronet and Clan Chief, Sir Robert Munro of Foulis.[8] The other company captains came from the Campbell and Grant clans, also loyal to the Hanoverian dynasty.

An important benefit of serving in an independent company was being able to wear traditional Highland dress, rather than breeches like the regular soldier. This 'peculiar garb', observed Stewart of Garth, The Black Watch's future historian, 'by its lightness and freedom, enabled them to use their limbs, and handle their arms with ease and dexterity, and to move with great speed when employed with either cavalry or light infantry'.[9] To present a degree of uniformity, Wade ordered the colour of the tartan plaid provided by the Company Captains 'to be as near as they can of the same Sort of Colour'.[10] The colour chosen was of 'a dark sett', a sombre black, blue and green, similar to that worn by the Clan Campbell, whose members were commanding three out of the six companies.

Convention suggests that the dark tartan and their policing duties gave rise to the name Black Watch as compared with the redcoats of the regular or 'red soldiers', *Saighdearan Dearg*. It is also possible that the name was acquired because their duties initially involved suppressing outlaws and cattle thieves who indulged in 'black mail'. Another explanation was that the Jacobite clans used the name to insult the pro-Hanoverian clans from which the independent companies drew their volunteers.[11] Despite the grinding poverty of the times, those who enlisted were not all from amongst the poor. Some even arrived with servants, who carried their provisions and weapons, observed Edmund Burt, General Wade's 'chief surveyor'. The captains, he recorded, 'are all of them vying with each other whose company shall best perform the manual exercise'.[12]

After only a few months, William Grant of Ballindalloch, one of the company captains, was being applauded in Aberdeen for being 'indefatiguable in the Service of his Country and Preventing Theifts and Robberies therein' and for having 'recovered a Drove of 28 Cattle, that was stolen from the Braes of this Shire, and returned them to their Owners'. He had also recovered several Horses, 'and by this Means, every thing that has been lost or taken away within his District, since he had his command, has been recovered'.[13] Another report noted that prisons were crowded with thieves brought in by Lovat's company. The independent companies also had to apprehend any

Catholic 'priests or missionarys who attempt to pervert His Majesty's subjects in those parts'.[14]

During the summer months from May to October, Wade was overseeing an extensive programme of road and bridge building – including the construction of a bridge, nearly 400 feet long, across the river Tay, completed in 1733 – undertaken by both the regular soldiers and the Highlanders of the independent companies. In time, over 250 miles of road were built and thirty bridges, enabling the Army to move with greater ease and speed, linking the forts along the Great Glen at Ruthven in Badenoch, Inverness Castle, where there was a fort, known as Fort George, Fort Augustus and Fort William.[15]

Observing the situation in the Highlands was Duncan Forbes, younger brother of John Forbes, the Laird of Culloden, whose family had the support of the powerful Duke of Argyll. Forbes had recently become Lord Advocate of the Court of Session in Edinburgh. In August 1726 'in confirmation' of his health, he visited the 'North Country' on horseback.[16] From Inverness, he reported favourably that: 'the Highlands are at present in full rest, there is not the least complaint of robberys or depredations, and a great stick is become as fashionable an instrument in a Highlanders hand as a broadsword or pistol by his side used formerly to be'.[17] As confidence in the independent companies increased, in early January 1727 the threat of a Spanish landing on the west coast of Scotland induced Wade to increase their collective strength to that of a battalion, numbering over five hundred men.[18] For most of the year, they policed their respective regions throughout the Highlands, but once a year they were brought together to improve their drill.[19]

When, on 11 June 1727, George I died of a stroke in Osnabrück, his son, George II, continued to support the independent companies. Contrary to the belief of later historians such as Archibald Forbes, a descendant of the Lairds of Culloden, who describes the independent companies as performing 'their allotted duties to the satisfaction of the Government',[20] Wade was frequently annoyed at their lack of discipline. In 1731 he was complaining that as soon as he left Scotland at the end of the summer, the men went home. 'I am under a necessity to put them under a better discipline or to free the Country from the charge of near £10,000 per ann[um]. I assembled them at Ruthven to let them know I was no stranger to their ways ... and that they must expect no favour if my orders were neglected for the future.'[21]

Unfortunately, while at Ruthven an altercation between two soldiers resulted in the death of Ensign James Grant, Grant of Ballindalloch's son, who was serving as the adjutant. On hearing two soldiers arguing, Ensign Grant had interceded by taking hold of 'the Muzzle of a Pistole that was held at the Butt end by two or three men to prevent Mischeiff ... it went off and Shott Ensign Grant'. Fatally wounded, he died some days later, the perpetrator being court-martialled and sentenced to transportation for life to America.[22] A trivial dispute, perhaps apocryphal, related to the precedence to be accorded between the drummer and the piper. 'The contention grew exceedingly hot, which the Captain having notice of, he called them both before him, and in the end, decided the matter in favour of the drum; whereupon the piper remonstrated very warmly, "Ads Wuds, Sir," says he, "and shall a little rascal that beats upon a sheep-skin tak the right haund of me, that am a musician."'[23]

By the following year, when reassembled at Ruthven, the *Caledonian Mercury* was reporting that the independent companies, 'all new-cloath'd and well siz'd, made a very fine Shew, and perform'd all the Parts of Exercise to his Excellency's great Satisfaction'. The writer of the column went on to say that 'we of this Country, and indeed all the Highland and Northern Parts of the Kingdom, have substantial Reasons to be well satisfied with them, since of a long time there has not been the least Ground to complain of Disorders of any Kind; which we attribute to the Vigilance of their Officers, and a right Distribution and posting of the Several Companies.'[24]

Misdemeanours, however, continued, one of which was the pock-eting of clothing allowances.[25] 'General Wade came here last night,' Lovat reported in 1738. 'He roars like a lyon and says that the King knows all our tricks and that we must be broke [i.e. disbanded].'[26]

In his defence, Lovat believed that too often Wade believed complaints against them which were 'groundless . . . in which he resembles many great Men who believe The first report, and act according To The impression it makes upon them without further Examination, or giving people time to vindicate Themselves'.[27] But Lovat was wrong about both Wade's and the King's intentions. War was imminent with Britain's maritime rival, Spain. Instead of disbanding the independent companies, George II took the momentous decision to form them into a regiment of the line of foot.[28] The reason for doing so, believed the English author of the Regiment's first contemporary history, known as *A Short History of the Highland Regiment*, was 'to put a final period to the insurrections of the Clans, and to secure their country from any attempts that might be made by the Highlanders in the Jacobite interest'.[29]

The Highland Regiment 1739

The starting date of the Highland Regiment's commission was 25 October 1739.[30] Over the next few weeks, the King's secretary at war, Sir William Yonge, put his signature to several warrants 'by His Majesty's Command', addressed to 'our Right Trusty and Right well beloved cousin John Earl of Crawford', who, aged thirty-seven, was to be appointed Colonel of the new regiment.[31] In addition to the six companies already established, four more were to be raised 'with all possible Expedition'.[32] Another Order authorised Crawford, 'by Beat of Drumm or otherwise, to raise so many Voluntiers in any County or Part of our Kingdom of Great Britain as are or shall be wanting to compleat the said Regiment to the Numbers above mentioned'.[33]

By the beginning of November, a list of officers had been agreed. Contrary to the normal practice of purchasing commissions in established regiments, when a new regiment was raised the Colonel distributed commissions as his patronage, thereby gathering about him captains whose loyalty would not be in question, who in turn would be entitled to recruit the soldiers from their own parts of the country

7

to serve in their companies.[34] Since Crawford was abroad, taking the waters at Baden in Germany, having been severely wounded in the service of the Imperial Army of the Holy Roman Emperor, the responsibility for selecting the company captains went to the Regiment's Commanding Officer, Lieutenant Colonel Sir Robert Munro of Foulis.[35] As with the independent companies, those chosen came from the pro-Hanoverian clans, the Grants, Campbells and Munros. Since Sir Robert's brother George had already commanded an independent company, he could expect to receive a commission. So too could John Campbell of Carrick, the Earl of Crawford's childhood friend, who had also commanded an independent company. George Grant of Culbin, whose brother was the Laird of Grant, was appointed major in the new regiment.

By the end of October, nine out of ten captains had been chosen. The tenth captaincy was later given to Duncan Forbes's nephew, John Munro of Newmore, also related to Robert Munro by marriage.[36] Lovat, now suspected of harbouring Jacobite sentiments, was not among those chosen.[37] As with other regiments in the British Army, young men who wanted a commission as a lieutenant or ensign were usually second sons with little prospect of inheriting the family fortune. According to military custom, the Regiment, numbered 43rd in the order of precedence in the British Army, was known by the name of its Colonel, as 'the Earl of Crawford's Highlanders'.

Once the names of the captains had been agreed, Crawford's warrant was redirected to them so that they could begin the process of recruiting the soldiers. They were under firm instructions 'not to recruit any Irishman nor any vagabond, but such person only as are born or have resided some time in the neighbourhood where you are recruiting'. Only Protestants born in Britain were to be accepted, and 'not exceeding twenty five years of age, five feet seven inches without shoes. They must be straight well limbed and shouldered with good Countenance and no ways disabled or distorted either in body feet or limbs and great care to be taken to guard against ruptures or other hidden sores or distempers.' No seafaring men were to be enlisted. 'Young lads from 16 to 20 years of age if made for growing will be accepted of, tho' they may want one inch of 5 feet 7 inches.'[38] Unlike those who might have joined the independent companies as a more seasonal occupation, those who enlisted were expected to be professional soldiers, and there were severe penalties for desertion. This loss of personal freedom did not prevent men wanting to enlist in preference to eking out a miserable existence as a weaver, mason or farm labourer at the mercy of Scotland's inclement weather.[39] The opportunity for regular pay at 6d per day was also an attractive prospect. Since each company captain was responsible for recruitment, it was more than likely that the soldiers, who mostly only spoke their native Gaelic, would be marching alongside men they had known all their lives from the same village and clan.

The uniform consisted of a scarlet coat, cut short, and a long-sleeved waistcoat, with 'buff facings and white lace'. As with the independent companies, the soldiers were permitted to retain Highland dress, the tartan plaid, twelve yards long, 'plaited around the middle of the body, the upper part being fixed on the left shoulder, ready to be thrown loose and rapped over both shoulders and firelock in rainy weather'. At night the plaid served as a blanket.[40] Contrary to the belief expressed in Stewart of Garth's history, written nearly a century later, that a new tartan was assumed when the Regiment was formed, it appears to have been similar to that worn by the independent companies, although it is doubtful that the colour was as uniform or as dark as it later became.[41]

Another feature was the blue bonnet – a flat cap similar to a beret – with 'a tuft of feathers, or sometimes, from economy or necessity, a small piece of black bear-skin'.[42] Their traditional weapons were a heavy axe known by its place of origin as the 'Lochaber axe', carried by the sergeants, a broadsword, the bayonet, and the 'Brown Bess' long land pattern musket in use since 1722. Those who chose to have pistols and a dirk – a lethal dagger, ten to eighteen inches long – were allowed to carry them, at their own expense.[43] Once recruited, the new Regiment's full establishment numbered 700 private men or 'centinels'.

In early January 1740, Robert Munro travelled to St James's Palace to present to the King, for his approval, 'a Sergeant and a Centinel' – Gregor MacGregor and John Campbell from Duneaves in Perthshire – 'remarkable for their figure and good looks' in their Highland dress. The Highlanders wielded the broadsword and Lochaber axe 'with such Dexterity, that his Majesty ordered them a handsome Gratuity'.[44] Since, in this instance, the men were not as poor as the King supposed, they gave the gift of one guinea to the porter at the gate as they departed.[45]

After the first muster as a Highland Regiment at Tay Bridge, close to what became the town of Aberfeldy, and near where the independent companies had been regularly reviewed, the Regiment remained quartered on the banks of the river Tay.[46] 'They learnt to march by files, by platoons, by companies and in battalion order. They mastered the three motions for resting their firelocks, four for grounding, twenty-one for priming and loading, and nineteen for firing. They were taught to march upon the centre or wheel to the right and left about, to learn each ruffle of a grenadier drum and to obey its tapping permutations without hesitation,' surmised historian John Prebble. 'All this and more to replace the half-naked storm-charge that had been the only military tactic of their ancestors.'[47]

On 25 December 1740, Crawford was appointed Colonel of the 2nd Troop of Horse Grenadier Guards. His successor was Brigadier General Lord Sempill, giving the Regiment the name Sempill's Highlanders.[48] To save money, he reduced the number of shirts issued per year from two to one and cut money for shoes. Ill-advisedly he also ordered shorter plaids.[49] After fifteen months' training, with the onset of winter, the companies were dispersed among the garrisons of the Great Glen.

The 'Flight of the Highlanders' 1743

On 29 July 1742 Sir William Yonge, secretary at war, wrote to General Clayton, Wade's successor as Commander in North Britain, indicating that His Majesty had commanded him 'to acquaint you that it is his intention that the Highland Regiment commanded by Lord Sempill should march into south Britain'.[50] Whatever George II was thinking when he agreed to raise a Highland Regiment, this was an early indication that it would be required to leave Scotland, in all probability to be posted overseas. Already at war with Spain, Britain was being drawn into fighting on the Continent of Europe in what became known as the 'war of the Austrian succession'.

Without a male heir the Habsburg Emperor, Charles VI, made provision for his daughter, Maria Theresa, to succeed him, setting aside the law of Salic succession which excluded female heirs.[51] This 'Pragmatic Sanction' had been accepted by Hungary and the major European powers, including France and Prussia. But, after Charles's death in 1740, the succession was contested. King Frederick I of Prussia had offered his support to Maria Theresa, in return for territory in Silesia. When Maria Theresa refused, the Prussian Army invaded Silesia in December 1740. By the following year, the war had escalated. Hoping to gain the Imperial Crown, Charles Albert of Bavaria invaded Bohemia. France, allied to Bavaria, sent an army to southern Germany. In January 1742, Charles Albert secured his election as Holy Roman Emperor. Although Maria Theresa agreed to cede Silesia to Prussia, fighting continued. George II, who was both King of Great Britain and Elector of Hanover, had sided with Maria Theresa.

At first King George's British army was involved only as an auxiliary to Hanover, but in 1742 a force of some sixteen thousand soldiers was sent to Flanders. In early 1743 Britain's commitment increased and additional troops were sent to the Continent to join the 'Pragmatic Army'. In the summer of 1743 the combined force of about forty thousand men, plus camp followers, was slowly advancing up the Rhine. The intention was that the new Highland Regiment should join it. At least one person in Scotland was apprehensive. About the end of 1742, Duncan Forbes, Lord President of the Court of Session, wrote to Clayton: 'When I first heard of the orders given to the Highland Regiment to march southwards, it gave me no sort of concern, because I supposed the intention was only to see them; but as I have lately been assured that they are destined for foreign service I cannot dissemble my uneasiness at a resolution that may, in my apprehension, be attended with very bad consequences.'

What Forbes feared was that England's military operations in Europe would provoke outright war with France, in which case the French King, Louis XV, might choose to support George II's adversary, James III in exile, the Old Pretender, 'if not seriously to sett him on the throne, at least to make a very important diversion, at the expense of risquing a very few battalions'. Forbes went on to describe the situation in Scotland, where although Jacobitism was 'at a very low pass', compared with thirty years previously, 'yet I will not be so sanguine as to say, that the fire is totally extinguished; that there is none of it lurking under the embers, or even that what lurks may not possibly be blown up into a flame, if France, besides *words*, which she has always ready, will give some *money*, and the countenance of force.' With the Highland Regiment in France, who else was there, he asked, who could go 'through the mountains with any intention to discover such intrigues with safety'?

By removing the Highland Regiment, Forbes suggested that there was nothing to prevent France's agents 'to have their full swing, and to tamper with the poor unthinking people of the Highlands, with as great safety as if there were no Government at all in the Island'.[52] Persuasive as Forbes's letter was, on 5 March Sempill was instructed to hold the Highland Regiment 'in a readiness to march to Berwick'.[53]

Notices of the Regiment's departure had already appeared in the newspapers. 'We hear the Regiment of Scotch Highlanders,' reported the London *Daily Post*, 'are on their march for London, and are in a short time to be reviewed by His Majesty in Hyde Park.'[54] About twenty men, 'more suspicious than the rest, found means of returning to the Highlands'.[55] The majority – nearly 700 men – thinking that they were going to London to be reviewed by the King, prepared to leave Scotland. The march was via Berwick, through Newcastle and York. Wherever they stopped 'they were so hospitably treated, that they continued in perfect good humour,' wrote the contemporary

English author of the Regiment's *Short History*, 'and it was believed that their love of their country was a little worn off, and that they would relish the change pretty well.' But, he continued, as they came closer to London and 'met with the compliments of our true bred English clowns, they grew more gloomy than ever'. What concerned them was 'a silly story they pick'd up in their passage', that they were being sent to the West Indies, considered 'the highest punishment that spared life; and therefore, when these fellows came to think that they were to be sent to Jamaica, it naturally came into their heads, that they had been first used as rods to scourge their own countrymen, and, after their having sufficiently tamed them were now to be thrown into the fire.'[56] By early May they had reached the outskirts of London. Three companies were quartered at Barnet and Whetstone; three at Hampstead, 'Westend', Belsize and Pond Street; one at Coneyhatch (Colney Hatch), Muswell Hill and Hornsey. Two companies were sent to Highgate and one to Finchley. Their baggage was being sent by sea from Inverness to St Katherine's Dock in East London.

'When the Highlanders walk'd the streets here,' noted the *Short History*, 'everybody must be sensible that there was more staring at them than ever was seen at the Morocco ambassador's attendance, or even at the Indian chiefs.' Everything about the Highlanders was different, especially their style of dress. Their shoes were 'a sort of thin pump or brogue, so light that it does not in the least impede his activity in running; and from being constantly accustomed to these kind of shoes, they are able to advance or retreat with incredible swiftness'. Next, 'broad garters under the knee, and no breeches, but his plaid belted about his waist, which hangs exactly like the folds of the Roman garment, which we see on Equestrian statues; the reason of this dress is, to make the leg firm, and to leave the sinews and joints quite free, to preserve the wearer from any thing that may heat or embarrass him, and to afford him an opportunity of extending his limbs with the greatest ease.'[57] But as the *Short History* noted, 'the amazement expressed by our mob was not greater than the surprise of these poor creatures; and if we thought their dress and language barbarous, they had just the same opinion of our manners; nor will I pretend to decide which was most in the right.'[58]

To the Highlanders' disappointment, George II had already left London to take his place with the Pragmatic Army on the Rhine. Instead, on 14 May, in front of thousands of spectators, the Regiment was reviewed by General Wade on Finchley Common. Having drilled the independent companies a decade previously, he seemed pleased with the Regiment. 'The men were of a good size,' Wade noted in his 'Observations', and performed their exercises 'extremely well'. Their old clothes were 'much worn but the new Cloathing is said to be at Sea and daily expected'. The firearms were complete 'and in Good Order, as also the Accoutrements, but about 400 Broadswords are wanting'. The tents and camp equipment were complete 'and in Good Order'. Wade also observed that there were three lieutenants who 'by age and infirmity' were incapable of serving and so they were ordered back to the Highlands to recruit to bring the Regiment up to its full complement of 700 Private men. In his remarks, Sempill certified that the missing swords would be supplied. Finally, the Surgeon, George Munro, confirmed that those men who were marked as Sick were indeed 'unfit for duty and not able to appear in the Field'.[59]

A report was still circulating in the taverns of London: 'that the Regiment was to be sent to some Parts of the West-Indies, and broke or divided amongst the Colonies'. According to the Reverend Campbell, a minister of the Church of Scotland, present in London, this raised amongst the soldiers 'a very great Animosity against their Officers, whom they groundlessly blamed for not informing them truly where they were to go before they carried them from their own Country'. Moreover they were 'disappointed of an Opportunity of settling their private Affairs in a Manner suitable to so long an Absence'.[60] When, after the review, the soldiers were told they were not going home, as they had been assured, but to the Continent to fight, 'they were out of all Patience, and looked upon the Design of sending them to Flanders only as a Blind to get them on board, in order to ship them really for the West-Indies'.

They had another complaint: 'that some small Arrears were due to them'; and that they had been obliged to use their own swords; and that their clothing, 'especially their Shoes and Plaids, were remarkably deficient, these last being not worth Sixpence per Yard; whereas they used to be allowed Plaids of more than double that Value'.[61] For some, the only course of action was to return to Scotland, 'molesting no one who let them pass, and making payment for all they took'. Corporal Samuel Macpherson realised that 'if they travelled with speed and cunning they might outwit the troops sent to restrain them, but if they provoked the hostility and resistance of country folk with whom they had no dispute they could not hope to pass through the southern shires of England'.[62]

Having been informed that the first contingent would march for Greenwich the following morning, on Tuesday 18 May, a meeting was called at midnight on Finchley Common. When Sergeant Alexander MacBean heard what was happening, he told his senior officer, Lieutenant John Menzies of Comrie, but did nothing further, returning to The Horns at Highgate to enjoy his ale. Before midnight men began to gather on the common. Shots were fired, alerting Macbean that something was wrong. Running towards the noise, he saw Private Farquhar Shaw in the shadows and tried to apprehend him, but after a brief struggle, Shaw disappeared. At Barnet, Captain John Munro of Newmore also heard the commotion and went to investigate. Disobeying his orders to remain, a number of men left the camp, taking their weapons with them. Around midnight another group of sixty to seventy men departed. For the next few hours they travelled northwards, hiding in the woods, in the direction of St Albans.

When news of the mutiny reached Lord Sempill at four in the morning, he at once informed Wade, who informed William Yonge. The secretary at war's response was instant. 'You are hereby commanded forthwith to proceed in pursuit of the said mutiniers,' Yonge wrote to William Blakeney, brigadier general of His Majesty's Forces, 'and to disarm them and bring them prisoners to the Tower of London; and you are to use all necessary means for these purposes, and even to repel force with force if you shall find it necessary.'[63] An 'advertisement' to apprehend the mutineers was passed to 'all Justices of the peace, Mayors, constables and other Civil Magistrates to use their utmost endeavours to secure all or any of the said Mutineers and Deserters in some County Gaol or other Prison according to the Direction of the Act for punishing Mutiny and Desertion'.[64] In the final count, two corporals, one piper, and one hundred and nine private men had deserted from all the companies. Sempill had lost fourteen men from his company. With only a few exceptions, most of the men came from clans known to have Jacobite sympathies or to have mounted resistance to authority from the south.[65]

News of the mutiny spread like wildfire. 'What may be the Consequence of the Affair we know not,' mused Mr Wye, the London correspondent of the *Caledonian Mercury*, 'but we hope it will not be so dangerous as some imagine.'[66] By the time the mutineers were apprehended, they had reached Lady Wood (also known as Bareshanks Wood), four miles from Oundle. 'Such was the end of this wild-goose expedition, which sufficiently shews,' noted the author of the *Short History*, 'how little probability there is of succeeding in attempts of this nature. The Highlanders had certainly all the incentives men could have to march briskly, and make the best of their way home, for they were surrounded every where with the kings troops, and had no prospect but that of death, if they were taken. Neither were they very slow in their proceedings, since they were near seventy miles from London, when they were taken.'[67] Transported to the Tower of London, 'these poor men were not suffered to languish long in confinement before a court-martial was appointed for their trial'.[68] While in the Tower, some of the soldiers fell sick, 'occasioned by their close Confinement in the Barracks', and so a request was made for 'Eight or Ten of them at any Time' to have leave 'to walk about within the Walls for the Benefit of the Air, attended by a proper Guard'.[69] The General Court-Martial was held in the Tower of London in early June. While their petitions were heard, as the author of the *Short History* noted, 'there was nothing but the flight of the Highlanders talked of in town'.[70]

The petition of the Mutineers, some of whom spoke only their native Gaelic, was delivered on their behalf by Private William Gordon of the Grenadier Company. Addressing 'His Excellency General Folliot', Colonel of the 1st Foot of the Guards, and the other 'Honourable members of this court martial', the mutineers indicated that they were 'under the deepest concern and Remorse for our most heinous and infamous Breach of Duty. We are sensible that our Crime is too notorious to be deny'd and too gross to be excus'd, and therefore We unanimously plead Guilty, and earnestly beg and implore the Favour and Intercession of this Honourable Court to recommend us to the Mercy and Clemency of our most gracious Sovereign.' To explain their motives, the petition at first protested the Highlanders' loyalty to George II, and absolved the officers from any charge of hardship, once more apologising 'from the Bottom of our Hearts for the Injury and Affront done to them and the whole Regiment by our desperate Behaviour'. In their defence, Private Gordon explained that their 'unhappy conduct' was due solely to their 'Ignorance and Credulity'.

> We had been made believe by the Suggestions (as We are now convinced) of ill-designing persons that We were to be decoy'd on Board of Ships in order to be transported to the West Indies and other remote parts as recruits to different Regiments, and that our Officers were to return to the Highlands to levy other Men in our place. This Separation from our Officers and from one another, We consider'd a terrible Hardship and even an Injustice done to us, especially as We were then fatally impress'd with an Opinion that We were levied only to guard the Highlands, and not to be imploy'd elsewhere.
>
> But this opinion We now utterly disclaim, and acknowledge that We are bound in Duty as much as any other Soldiers to serve wheresoever His Majesty shall think fit to imploy us. And if His Majesty should, by the Intercession of this Honourable Court, graciously condescend to pardon our past Offence, We promise not only to submit in every thing to the Orders of our Superiours, but We will

likewise cheerfully embrace every Opportunity to sacrifice in the service of our Sovereign, the Lives we owe to his Clemency and Favour. In Testimony of which We all subscribe our Names.[71]

With the exception of one man, who had deserted before the review, all were found guilty of mutiny and desertion and condemned to death.[72] As later commentators pointed out, the petition had not sufficiently stressed the point that they believed they had been levied for service only in the Highlands. 'Had evidence been given that the men had, on enlisting, received assurances that they would not be required to service outside the Highlands; and that they had been induced to march for the south by misrepresentations, the finding of the court-Martial would, or should, have been very different.'[73] A similar court martial in early July of three other captured mutineers had the same verdict. 'Great intercession is making here by people of all ranks and both sexes,' recorded a letter in the *Caledonian Mercury*, 'in favour of the unfortunate Highlanders. It is among other things alledged in their Behalf, That a Report was artfully conveyed to them after the Review, of their being sent to Jamaica as Draughts, and that their Officers were to return to Scotland to levy another Regiment.'[74]

When the matter was put before the King, he decided 'that after a publick example shall be made according to law, of a few of the most guilty, the rest His Majesty would have pardoned upon condition of their being sent to our several Colonies in America.'[75] The unfortunate three deemed to be the 'most guilty' were Corporals Samuel and Malcolm Macpherson and Private Farquhar Shaw, who was considered to have forcibly resisted arrest in his struggle with Sergeant Macbean.

Before the sentence was carried out on 18 July 1743, Reverend Campbell was allowed to visit them. In an 'anonymous' pamphlet he later wrote, he highlighted their fine characteristics. 'They all three were Men of strong national Parts, and religiously disposed both from Habit and Principle, the natural Result of a good Example, and early Instruction in the Doctrine and Precepts of Christianity;

for I received from all of them a great deal of Satisfaction, when I examined them on the Grounds of our holy Religion.'[76] Those to whom the King had granted a pardon were ordered to be present 'at the said Execution under a sufficient Guard', and then to be held 'in safe custody until further Order'.[77] Also present to witness the execution were several officers, including Captain John Munro, who had remained for the trial.[78]

Subsequently, upon payment of £5 for 'each man received',[79] twenty-six of the younger men were sent to Gibraltar and Minorca, to be incorporated into the five Regiments of Foot stationed there. Thirty-eight men were sent 'by Lott' to the Leeward Islands, to fill out the ranks of the 38th Foot, under the command of Lieutenant General Robert Dalzell. Finally, thirty-eight men, including the drafter of the petition, Private William Gordon, were sent to Georgia to join Brigadier General Oglethorpe's Regiment, the 42nd Foot. This Regiment, made up of Highlanders who had been induced to migrate to Georgia, was operating as an Independent Company of Rangers to police the frontier between Britain's American colonies and those of Spain.[80]

Provided they returned to their duty, the more fortunate men who had hidden themselves in the Highlands when the Regiment was ordered to march to England, or who had deserted before they had reached Nottinghamshire, were pardoned.[81] To make up the depleted numbers, an order for recruitment was issued, in the language of the times, authorising Sempill 'by Beat of Drum or Otherwise to raise so many volunteers in any county or part of the Kingdom of Great Britain as are or shall be wanting to recruit and fill up the respective companies of the Highland Regiment of Foot under your Command to the numbers allowed upon the Establishment'.[82]

In the years since the mutiny, arguments have been made for and against the contention that the soldiers should have realised that, as a Regiment in the Line of Foot, they would be expected to serve overseas. At the time, the author of the *Short History* believed that 'they always looked upon themselves from the time they were first raised as a corps destined to serve in Scotland or rather in the Highlands, and no where else'. Firstly, he considered that the manner in which the men were raised was sufficient grounds for believing they would not have to leave Scotland. 'The Jacobite Clans were disarmed, to preserve the quiet of the nation, and because the government could never be entirely safe, whilst they had arms in their hands; but to strengthen the security, and to put the peace of the Highlands past hazard, the arms taken from those Highlanders were given to these, whence they inferred that they were to be the guards of the Highlands.' Secondly, the fact that they wore the Highland dress might be a reason for thinking they would remain in Scotland. 'To what purpose, said they, are we cloathed like Highlanders, if we are not constantly to be employed in the Highlands.'[83] As he also noted: 'If, indeed on the breaking of the old corps, and uniting all the Highlanders in a regiment, they had been clothed like the rest of the army; and told, when the Articles of War were read to them, that they were to consider themselves for the future simply as a marching regiment, this had been sufficient to have prevented all that hath followed since.'[84] 'What happened on that occasion,' recorded Donald Macleod, who had first enlisted in Lovat's independent company, 'falls within the memory of many persons now living, and will be long remembered as an instance of that indignant spirit, which justice and broken faith inspire on the one hand, and of that gradual encroachment which executive and military power are prone to make on civil liberty on the other.'[85]

Later historians also excused the mutineers. 'There are grounds for believing that when these men were regimented the measure was represented to them as merely a change of name and officers,' observed Stewart of Garth, 'with the additional benefit of more regular pay and duty, under which arrangement they were to continue, as usual, the watch of the country.'[86] He went on to say: 'That the unfortunate act which threw such a dark shade over the character of a body of brave men was the result of their simplicity, in allowing themselves to be deceived, rather than of any want of principle, was sufficiently proved by their subsequent conduct. But such an occurrence happening among men, of whose loyalty many were suspicious, produced, as may well be imagined, no inconsiderable sensation in the country.'[87] Finally, he considered it impossible to reflect 'on this unfortunate affair without feelings of regret, whether we view it as an open violation of military discipline on the part of brave, honourable, and well-meaning men, or as betraying an apparent want of faith on the part of Government ... from the evidence of eye-witnesses, and of those who wrote and published at the time, it appears evident that the men considered their service and engagements of a local nature, not to extend beyond Scotland, nor even beyond the Highland boundary.'[88]

In the late nineteenth century, despite Duncan Forbes's reservations, his descendant, Archibald Forbes, was less forgiving: 'Nothing is forthcoming to indicate that the enlistment of the men of the Black Watch was other than normal, or that it was accompanied by any other than the ordinary conditions expressed in the Regulations.'[89] Yet, as others believed, the mutiny and the execution of three men was 'a very regrettable occurrence, deeply affecting the whole population of the Highlands, where the men who had been punished were regarded as martyrs to the treachery of the Government'.[90] 'There must have been something more than common in the case or character of these unfortunate men,' observed Stewart of Garth, 'as Lord John Murray, who was afterwards Colonel of the Regiment, had portraits of them hung up in his dining-room.'[91] In 1910 H.D. MacWilliam dedicated the edited 'Official Records of the Mutiny in The Black Watch' to the memory of the 'Brave Highlanders – Victims of Deception and Tyranny'.[92]

Ignorant of what was to be their comrades' fate, the Highland Regiment had followed orders to proceed to the Continent. 'Yesterday nine Wagons with baggage of Lord Semple's Regiment went through the Borough guarded by some of the Regiment,' noted Mr Wye in the *Caledonian Mercury*, 'to be put on board the Transports; and five companies of said regiment crossed the Thames at Blackwall and the Isle of Dogs; the Remainder of the Regiment are to follow Tomorrow, and next Monday they are to go on board and sail first fair wind for Ostend.'[93] The men remained dissatisfied. 'I formed the men under my command this morning on Blackheath,' Robert Munro informed Sempill, 'and I took in writing from each company the demands they made, that the world might see how unreasonable they were.' The soldiers in Munro's own company were demanding that the two pence which Sempill had stopped for their shoes be reinstated and that they should also receive one shirt more each year, 'as the Earl of Crawford gave them'. They all complained that their plaids were 'very bad and very narrow' and not the full length 'and that all or most of the sword belts are worn, being got when regimented'.[94] Despite these complaints, the author of the *Short History* recorded the men as marching 'very cheerfully', suggesting that they were by now 'with the army, where, I daresay, it will quickly appear they were not afraid of fighting the French'.[95]

> *Farewell to Lochaber, and farewell, my Jean,*
> *Where heartsome wi' her I ha'e mony a day been;*
> *For Lochaber no more, Lochaber no more,*
> *We'll may-be return to Lochaber no more.*[96]

2.

Disastrous Fontenoy and the '45

Hail, gallant regiment! Freiceadan Dubh!
Whenever Albion needs thine aid,
'Aye ready' for whatever foe,
Shall dare to meet the 'Black Brigade'!
Witness disastrous Fontenoy,
When all seemed lost, who brought us through?
Who saved defeat, secured retreat?
And bore the brunt? – the 'Forty-Two?'[1]

1742

Flanders 1743

The Highland Regiment landed at Ostend on the north coast of the Austrian Netherlands in modern Belgium. Passing through unfamiliar countryside in the heat of summer, the soldiers reached Brussels on 1 June. They were too late to join the Pragmatic Army, which at the end of June defeated the French at Dettingen, ten miles from Frankfurt, when, for the last time in Britain's history, the King, George II, was present in the field. Over the next few months, pending a call to arms, the Highlanders learnt to adapt to the novel situation of being part of an army of several thousand men, all making demands on the land. Provisions were scarce, and as summer became autumn they suffered from 'severe cold'. Kept busy on drill practice, as the days became shorter and the campaigning season ended they went into winter quarters near Brussels.[2] Quartered in the local inhabitants' houses, the Highland Regiment apparently made a good impression, 'as these men were not only quiet, kind and domestic,' related Stewart of Garth, 'but served as a protection against the rudeness of others'.[3] So well behaved were they that the Elector Palatine thanked George II 'for the excellent behaviour of the regiment while in his territories, and for whose sake I will always pay a respect and regard to a Scotsman in future'.[4]

The tedium of inaction set in. Rather than remain in Europe, Major George Grant had already relinquished his position and accepted an appointment as Governor of Inverness Castle with a salary of £300 a year, a little more than a major's pay and a task less arduous than soldiering.[5] In August 1744, Captain John Munro was complaining to his uncle, Duncan Forbes, that they were losing 'numbers of men by desertion: there is not a regiment but has lost less or more, but the Highlanders, who still keep up their character'. To his frustration, talk of moving did not materialise '& we are to keep this ground till we get our orders from England'. Domestic matters were also in his mind, especially his concern that his sister was being abused by her husband 'in a most bruteish manner and I cannot think but she is in great danger of being murtherid [murdered] if she stays with the monster'.[6]

In December 1744, an order was given to raise three new 'additional' companies for the Highland Regiment, to be based in Scotland, and to raise new drafts of men for service in Flanders. The three men to whom captaincies were offered included Duncan Campbell of Inverawe, who had served in one of the independent companies, and Sir Patrick Murray, 4th Baronet of Ochtertyre, whose mother was related to the Lovat and Atholl families. Although his father had supported the Jacobites in 1715, Sir Patrick had pledged allegiance to George II. The third Captain, Aeneas (or Angus) Mackintosh, had recently become the Laird of Mackintosh following his elder brother's death in 1740. Mackintosh's young wife, Anne, played an active role in raising his company, later earning for herself the name 'Colonel' Anne. Her brother James secured a lieutenancy in Sir Patrick Murray's Company.[7]

While the Pragmatic Army was back in winter quarters, in early 1745, the Highland Regiment experienced its third change of Colonel in less than ten years. When Hugh Sempill was appointed Colonel of the 25th Foot, the position was left open for Lord John Murray, who had been petitioning to become Colonel of the Highland Regiment since 1743. Aged thirty-four and the seventh son of the 1st Duke of Atholl, his family had been closely associated with earlier independent companies which had been raised under the seal of his grandfather, the Earl of Atholl, in 1667. Loyalties remained divided, however, between those who had accepted the Hanoverians and those still loyal to the Stuarts, and his elder half-brother, Lord George Murray, was a staunch Jacobite.[8] Moreover, it was 'a common expedient', noted historian Forbes, 'in order to save family properties, that father and son, or two brothers of the same house, should take opposite sides'.[9] Lord John Murray's appointment on 25 April 1745 coincided with the raising of another regiment of Highlanders, whose Colonel was John Campbell, 4th Earl of Loudoun, the regiment being known as Loudoun's Highlanders.[10]

At the same time a young divinity student, Adam Ferguson, was appointed as acting chaplain since the Regiment's official chaplain, the Hon. Gideon Murray, had not come to France.[11] Although Ferguson was not yet ordained, he was appointed: 'to be a kind of tutor or guardian to Lord John,' related the nineteenth-century historian Thomas Carlyle, 'that is to say, to gain his confidence, and keep him in peace with his officers, which it was difficult to do.'[12] To enable him to take up his position, Ferguson's ordination was accelerated. Meanwhile, five years since the Regiment had been mustered near Aberfeldy, the Highlanders were preparing to fight their first battle against a foreign enemy.

Defeat at Fontenoy 1745

In January 1745, in the town of Warsaw, in the lands of the Habsburg Empire, representatives from the governments of Austria, Saxony, England and the Dutch Republic of the Seven United Netherlands (including the county of Holland) signed the Quadruple Alliance, pitting themselves against France, Bavaria and Prussia. Britain and France had been fighting since 1744 and the Quadruple Alliance formalised a state of warfare that was to dominate the European landscape for at least the next decade. Maurice, Comte de Saxe, recently promoted Marshal of France, had started the campaign by laying siege to Tournai, on the river Scheldt, garrisoned by 8,000 men under General Baron Dorth. By the time the campaign began, the prestigious position of 'Captain-General' of the British Army – only previously given to the Dukes of Marlborough and Ormond – had been given to George II's second son, Prince William Augustus, the Duke of Cumberland. Just twenty-four years old, he had been wounded at Dettingen and promoted lieutenant general. 'Brave, but stupid', his already stout body meant that he had difficulty in mounting a horse.[13]

Towards the end of April, with the French besieging Tournai, Cumberland issued orders for the Pragmatic Army's departure from camp outside Brussels. The instructions were standard for the time, but new to the Highlanders moving in a huge army for the first time. 'The Quarter Masters that go on before to take care that their men commit no disorder, for which they are to be answerable. No officer below the Rank of a Brigadier to lay in Quarters. The Commanding Officers of Corps are to be answerable that no woman, nor children, nor Baggage, be suffered to go in the Waggons, and any commanding officer who permits it shall certainly be put under arrest.'[14] The 'General' – the drum beat indicating to the troops to prepare to march – would be sounded at five in the morning; the 'Assembly' at six told the men they were to be ready to set out – 'always with the left foot first' – half an hour later. Cumberland also ordered that 'the surgeons of the several regiments are to carry their medicine chests and Instruments upon their Batt horses, which are to march at the head of each Corps with their men's tents'. His Royal Highness allowed '1 Waggon for the Sick of each Regiment in Camp, which wagon goes in the rear of the Regiment'.[15]

The first day's march was a distance of eight miles from Anderlecht to Hal. Once in camp, Cumberland's order was for 'nobody to stir out of camp'.[16] The following day, the Quarter Masters were instructed to 'go with the men for wood and straw'. At 2 o'clock the next day, the Highland Regiment was instructed to march with the Quarter Masters 'and to detach 1 Captain, 2 officers and 60 men to secure the General Officers' Quarters, till the General Officers' guards come up'.[17] By the beginning of May, the army was in camp at Soignies, thirteen miles from Hal. 'The whole Army to Forage to-morrow for two days. Guards and Cavalry first, Dragoons next, then Foot and Artillery.' Cumberland's final instructions were for 'all orders relating to the men to be constantly read to them by an officer of each Troop and Company' and for 'whatever orders come as sent by the Marshal' to be obeyed 'as if they came from the Duke himself'.[18]

The Highland Regiment was one of twenty battalions and twenty-six squadrons of British soldiers, supplemented by additional Hanoverian troops.[19] A further contingent of Dutch was under the command of the Prince of Waldeck. Eight squadrons of Austrians were under the command of Field Marshal Konigseg, giving the

Allied army a total strength of 50,000.[20] Later historians had little positive to say about the commanders. Whereas Waldeck was considered as having 'neither experience nor skill', Konigseg was 'once a brilliant soldier but now almost in his dotage'.[21] After two years of waiting, the Highlanders were going to face the enemy, brandishing their broadswords and Lochaber axes. 'This moment I have Advice,' wrote Mr Wye in the *Caledonian Mercury* on 4 May 1745, 'that a general Engagement between the French and the Allied army will soon ensue.'[22]

By 9 May the Allied army was encamped between the villages of Maubray and Beaugnies, not far from the French outposts at Tournai. When Cumberland, together with Field Marshal Konigseg and the Prince of Waldeck, went to reconnoitre the French position, the Highlanders were required to cover them. 'This was a kind of operation which was thoroughly understood by the Highlanders, all of whom were great hunters and were perfectly able to keep up with horses for hours on end,' observed the Earl of Crawford, who was also in Europe with the Pragmatic Army.[23] Having been Colonel of the Regiment, Crawford was amused to note: 'About the time we were reconnoitring, an advanced Highlander observed a *grassin* [sharpshooter] always firing at his post; wherefore, he set his bonnet upon the top of a little stick, on the edge of a hollow road we made them lurk in, moving a little forward, thereby gaining the more at his leisure the opportunity of aiming at the *grassin*, who amused himself still with popping at the Highlander's bonnet he had left behind him as a blind; but which the *grassin* not finding out, gave the Highlander so far an opportunity that he brought him down.'[24]

After the reconnaissance, the detachment returned to the main body of the army. With the cannon brought forward and preparations along the lines, it was evident that the battle would take place the following day. 'A little after four in the morning,' Captain John Munro described to his uncle, Duncan Forbes, 'our cannon began to play, and the French batteries, with triple our weight of mettal and numbers too, answered us.' Cumberland's best option was for a frontal attack on the French line. On the opposing side, Saxe, ill with dropsy and carried in a litter, had drawn up the French army in a defensive position, protected by three redoubts. After inconclusive skirmishing, Cumberland decided to force his way through the French lines, taking up position in the space between the town of Fontenoy and a wood at Barry. 'About five the infantry was in march,' John Munro continued, 'we (the Highlanders) were in the center of the right brigade; but by six we were ordered to cross the field, and attack (I mean our regiment, for the rest of the brigade did not march to attack), a little village, on the left of the whole, called Fontenoy.' As they passed the field, the French batteries began firing, 'but to no purpose, for their batteries being upon rising ground, their balls flew over us and hurt the second line'. The Highland Regiment had been ordered to support the Dutch, whom Munro described as 'very dilatory'. Having got within range of the French batteries, 'we received three full fires of their batteries and small arms . . . Here we were obliged to skulk behind houses and hedges for about an hour and a half, waiting for the Dutch, who, when they came up, behaved but so and so.'[25]

'Sir Robert, according to the usage of his countrymen,' related contemporary historian Philip Doddridge, 'ordered the whole regiment to clap to the ground on receiving the French fire; and, as soon as it was discharged, to spring up, and march close to the enemy, when they were to pour in their fire upon them, and then retreat, drawing up in order.' Regardless of his 'great corpulency', Munro was recorded as being 'every where with his regiment . . . and it is observed, that when he commanded the whole regiment to clap to the ground, he himself alone, with the colours behind him, stood upright, receiving the whole fire of the enemy; and this, because, as he said, he could easily lie down, though his great bulk would not suffer him to rise so quickly.'[26] 'One consequence of the mode of attack,' wrote Stewart of Garth, 'was . . . a great preservation of the lives of the troops; for the loss was trifling, considering how actively the regiment was engaged.'[27] After the battle, Sergeant Donald Macleod related how he had killed a French colonel, called Montard; 'and, in the midst of dangers and death, very deliberately served himself heir to 175 ducats which he had in his pockets, and his gold watch'. As he was doing so, an Irish officer in the French service attacked him, whom he killed 'after an obstinate and skilful contest'. Set upon by several Frenchmen, Macleod was saved by 'a gentleman of the name of Cameron, . . . in the French service . . . His Scotch blood, he said, warmed to his countryman in such a situation.'[28]

Although the soldiers had smashed through the first French line, Saxe, rousing himself from his litter and mounting his horse, established a second line. Having positioned his best cavalry on the flanks, with the infantry in the centre, he ordered a combined charge of cavalry and infantry under cover of the artillery and the batteries in the redoubts. The collective attack was overwhelming, forcing Cumberland to order a withdrawal. 'Our regiment being in some disorder, I wanted to draw them up in rear of the Dutch, which their general would scarce allow of; but at last I did it, and marched them again to the front,' related John Munro, who was acting on behalf of his corpulent cousin in the Regiment's 'more rapid movements'.[29] 'In half an hour after, the Dutch gave way, and Sir Robert Munro thought proper we should retire; for we had then the whole batteries from the enemy's ground playing upon us, and 5000 foot ready to fall upon us.'[30]

Briefly, having withdrawn from the field of battle, as Munro related, the Regiment was ordered to return 'with all expedition, to assist the Hanoverians, who had got by this time well advanced upon the batteries upon the left. They behaved most gallantly and bravely; and had the Dutch taken example from them, we had supped in Tournay.'[31] Concluding his description of the battle, John Munro described how the Highland Regiment covered the withdrawal, 'as the only regiment that could be kept to their duty', Cumberland later congratulating the Highlanders for doing their duty well. 'I cannot fail telling you, that the Duke shewed as much real courage and temper as ever Caesar or Hannibal did.' With France losing over seven thousand men and the Pragmatic Army over ten thousand, Munro believed the action 'will be found to be the bloodiest, as to Officers, that happen'd to the British in the memory of Man'.[32]

Evaluating the Highland Regiment's performance in its first military action overseas, Stewart of Garth credited Sir Robert Munro, who had both 'presence of mind, and a thorough knowledge of his men'.[33] Another figure was recorded as making an unusual contribution. As described by Stewart of Garth and other historians, Munro was surprised to see a chaplain at the head of a column, brandishing a broadsword. 'He desired him to go to the rear with the surgeons.' The chaplain refused. 'Sir Robert at length told him, that his commission did not entitle him to be present in the post which he had assumed. "D—n my commission!" said the warlike chaplain.'[34] Whereupon, he charged forward, fighting 'like a valiant Scotsman during the bloody fray. The stout Munro forgave his insubordination for the sake of his valorous example.'[35] Mistakenly, later historians, starting with Stewart of Garth, assumed that the 'warlike chaplain' was the new acting chaplain, Adam Ferguson. But Ferguson had not yet left Scotland.[36] 'Glorious' as the story of Ferguson at Fontenoy might be, noted Professor Jane Fagg, 'it must be rejected'.[37] Yet, so inspirational was the tale that over 150 years later, in 1897, the artist W. Skeoch Cumming recorded the actions of the 'warlike chaplain' for posterity, showing the likeness of Ferguson, both 'girt with broadsword' and kneeling beside a wounded man.[38]

A possible contender for the role is Laurence Macpherson, who on the title page of a tract published in 1745 is listed as 'Chaplain of the Highland Regiment' and the author of a 'A New Form of Prayer as used (since the Battle of Fontenoy) by the British Troops in the Allied Army in Flanders'. Amidst several paragraphs of exhortations, proclaiming 'Britons' as ever 'thy favourite people', there was a last paragraph 'only for the Highland Regiment'. 'May the Courage and Intrepidity of the brave Highlanders, be a continual Terror to the Enemy, and a distinguished Example to their Fellow Soldiers.' Written soon after Murray's appointment as Colonel of the Regiment, the prayer begged 'that henceforth their Commander may be a Man of Honesty, Humanity, Affability'. In the absence of Gideon Murray, Macpherson perhaps stayed with the Regiment until Ferguson arrived in September.[39]

Back home, disappointment at the news of the defeat was tempered by the knowledge of how well the soldiers had fought. Less than two years after the mutiny, the Highland Regiment received Royal approval. 'The Duke,' John Munro informed Forbes, 'made so friendly and favourable a speech to us, that if we had been ordered to attack their lines afresh, I dare say our poor fellows would have done it.'[40] Another report related how the Duke of Cumberland had been so struck by their conduct 'that, wishing to show a mark of his approbation, he desired it to be intimated to them, that he would be happy to grant the men any favour which they chose to ask, and which he could concede, as a testimony of the good opinion he had formed of them.' In response, the men requested that a soldier 'under sentence of a heavy corporal punishment' for allowing a prisoner to escape be pardoned. 'The nature of this request,' – which was instantly granted – 'the feeling which suggested it,' related Stewart of Garth, 'and, in short, the general qualities of the corps, struck the Duke with the more force, as, at the time he had not been in Scotland, and had no means of knowing the character of its inhabitants, unless, indeed he had formed his opinion from the common ribaldry of the times, when it was the fashion to consider the Highlander "as a fierce and savage depredator, speaking a barbarous language, and inhabiting a barren and gloomy region, which fear and prudence forbade all strangers to enter."'[41]

Out of a complement of less than 1,000 before the battle began, the Highland Regiment had lost two officers and thirty men. One of the officers was the Earl of Crawford's childhood friend Captain John Campbell of Carrick, whose head was blown off by a cannon ball at the start of the battle. 'Possessing very agreeable manners, and bravery, tempered by gaiety,' Stewart of Garth noted, 'he was regarded by the people as one of those who retained the chivalrous spirit of their ancestors.' Three officers and eighty-six men were wounded.[42] One sergeant, James Campbell, had so impressed the Duke of Cumberland by killing nine men before his arm was severed by a cannon ball that the Duke promised Campbell a reward 'of a value equal to the arm'.[43]

When news of the French victory reached Paris, the French were not averse to praising their opponents' gallantry. 'The British behaved well, and could be exceeded in ardour by none but our officers, who animated the troops by their example, when the Highland furies rushed in upon us with more violence than ever did a sea driven by a tempest. I cannot say much of the other auxiliaries, some of whom looked as if they had no great concern in the matter which way it went. In short we gained the victory; but may I never see such another.'[44]

Soon afterwards Robert Munro was honoured by becoming Colonel of the 37th Regiment, following the death at Fontenoy of its Colonel, General the Hon. Henry Ponsonby. His successor was his cousin, John Munro of Newmore. Although not the most senior captain, his appointment as Lieutenant Colonel of the Highland Regiment was perhaps a reward for his 'good conduct' in battle, especially in commanding the Regiment 'immediately under Sir Robert, who, from his extreme corpulency and being on foot, could not move with the rapidity sometimes necessary'.[45] In September the Regiment, based at Vilvoorden Camp, a few miles north-east of Brussels, had the ministrations of its new acting chaplain, Adam Ferguson. Shortly after his arrival he wrote a long excited letter to his friend John Adam, the son of the architect William Adam, describing how, after spending ten days in Antwerp, he came 'forward to the Camp, where I became acquainted with my officers all at once, we here form a body whose interests are all Connected together, and it is the easiest matter to fall into acquaintance. I'm extremely happy in my colonel [Lord John Murray] nor would I change him or his Regiment for any in the Service, I preached to them yesterday over a Couple of Drums, and tho it was my first I had no more fear or concern than if it had been my hundredth and nineteenth time.'[46]

The '45

The Gaels are totally scorched
By this Parliament that torments them;
Without arms, uniform, or hope,
Without the kilt to fit them snugly.[47]

In the autumn of 1745 the Highland Regiment was ordered to return home. During the absence of so many regiments of the British Army, Charles Edward Stuart, James III in exile's elder son and known as the Young Pretender – or, by his supporters, as 'Bonnie Prince Charlie' – had emulated his father's attempt, thirty years previously, to restore the thrones of England and Scotland to the House of Stuart. On 19 August he raised his standard at Glenfinnan, on the west coast of Scotland. Among those who came out in support of him was Lord George Murray, Lord John's half-brother.

While most of the British Army was in Europe, Charles had secured an immediate victory against the forces led by Sir John Cope, Commander-in-Chief in Scotland, at Prestonpans early in the morning on 21 September. In a battle lasting no more than fifteen minutes, among those who fought in Cope's force was Sir Patrick Murray's additional company raised the previous year. Murray was taken prisoner together with Lieutenant James Farquharson – Aeneas Mackintosh's brother-in-law – and Ensign Allan Campbell, later released on parole.[48] Meanwhile Captain Duncan Campbell of Inverawe, in command of another additional company, was in Argyllshire, defending Inveraray Castle. By the autumn, most of the third additional company, commanded by Aeneas Mackintosh, had deserted.[49] Mackintosh, whose loyalty was being courted by both sides, had already started raising new recruits from the Mackintosh clan. His wife Anne, whose father, John Farquharson of Invercauld, had fought for the Jacobites in 1715, favoured the Prince's cause and had also been recruiting men to fight for the Stuarts.

Mindful of the family ties between the Highlanders and the Jacobites, the Regiment had been ordered to remain in the south, being first sent to Kent to guard against a possible French invasion of the south coast, before moving to London. 'Without attempting to throw any doubt on their loyalty,' commented Stewart of Garth, 'a duty that would have called men to oppose their brothers and nearest connections and friends in the field of battle, would have occasioned a struggle, between affection and duty, more severe than any in which they could have been employed against the most resolute enemy.' As historian Forbes affirmed, since an estimated 300 soldiers of the Highland Regiment had relatives taking part in the uprising – including their Colonel's half-brother, Lord George – 'the wisdom and humanity of keeping them aloof from such a struggle between duty and natural affection was obvious.'[50]

After nearly three years away from the shores of Britain, the officers and soldiers of Lord John Murray's Highlanders were different men from those who, somewhat reluctantly, had marched from Perth to London to be reviewed, as they thought, by the King, and for some of whom rumours of service abroad had led to mutiny. Stationed at Camberwell in south London, the acting chaplain, Adam Ferguson, was pointing to the benefits of living as part of a larger whole: 'It is in a State of Society alone that Man can prosper, either in his civil or religious interests,' he averred in his sermon in 18 December 1745. Lest they forget the uprising currently threatening the peace of the land, Ferguson reminded his listeners that 'the Disturbers of its Peace are now advanced into the very Heart of the Kingdom, and would direct their Course towards the Metropolis, which you, with others, are appointed to defend; and I am persuaded, when you have occasion to act, you will not be wanting to your Religion, your King, your Country and yourselves.'[51]

While the Regiment remained in the south, the battle against the Jacobites reached its inevitable conclusion. Lieutenant General Henry Hawley, who had fought at Fontenoy, was sent to replace Cope as Commander-in-Chief in Scotland in December 1745 and the British army was reinforced. Briefly fortune favoured the Prince and his supporters, swelled to almost double with new recruits. To Aeneas Mackintosh's embarrassment, some of those raised by 'Colonel' Anne joined the Prince's forces at Bannockburn, near Stirling Castle, shortly before the Jacobites and Hanoverians fought on the sleet-ridden fields at Falkirk in mid-January. Mackintosh himself had been unwell, being reported 'as sick, present' in the company returns of January 1746.[52] Much to the Hanoverians' surprise, their forces were defeated, Hawley arriving too late on the field of battle to organise the troops.[53]

Among those who fell was the Highland Regiment's first Lieutenant Colonel, Robert Munro, now with the 37th Regiment. Too heavy to run, as his son later related to Duncan Forbes, after being 'deserted, [he] was attacked . . . for some time defended himself with his half Pike'.[54] Another casualty was Munro's brother, Duncan of Obsdale, who came unarmed from behind the lines to assist him, and was also struck down. The following day, Munro was buried 'with honour by the Prince's command, with the Jacobite leaders in attendance'. His brother was interred with him. The inscription on a monument later erected reads: 'As long as the history narrates the Battle of Fontenoy, His courage and conduct that day In command of the Highland Regiment will be remembered.'[55] Prince Charles did not follow up his victory by going south; instead, in the face of desertions, his army withdrew to the Highlands to recruit.

Slighted by the defeat at Falkirk, Cumberland, back from the Continent, had come in person to Scotland. Together with Hawley, he was watching the Prince's progress northwards through heavy snow towards Inverness, currently held by Lord Loudoun and a force of some 2,000 men. After passing through Ruthven in mid-February, the Prince came to Moy Hall, the Mackintosh home, to be welcomed by 'Colonel' Anne. On hearing that Prince Charles was there, Loudoun gathered a force of 1,500 men and marched towards Moy. Aeneas Mackintosh was by his side. Warned of Loudoun's approach, the Prince succeeded in escaping in his nightclothes, his departure assisted by a blacksmith and four companions who had taken up position some distance from Moy. Once the advance guard appeared, the men had opened fire in quick succession; imitating the war cries of the Cameron, Macdonald and Mackintosh clans, they gave the impression of being more numerous than they were, the stratagem earning for 'Colonel' Anne the title of The Heroine and the action dubbed the Rout of Moy.[56] The Prince, accompanied by a few thousand men, succeeded in reaching Inverness. Outnumbered, the defenders of Inverness Castle, including the commander, Major George Grant, formerly of the Highland Regiment, surrendered.

In March, Loudoun's men were surprised in thick fog by the Jacobites at Dornoch. Although Loudoun, accompanied by Duncan Forbes, escaped, Aeneas Mackintosh was put under the custody of his wife at Moy. On reaching Aberdeen, Cumberland and the Hanoverian army marched towards Inverness, where Prince Charles's Highland army was quartered. On 16 April 1746 the armies joined battle at Culloden Moor, where the Jacobites were decisively crushed. None of the additional companies of Lord John Murray's Highlanders was present. Harsh retribution followed, earning Cumberland the name of 'the Butcher', while Hawley was called 'Hangman Hawley'.

The year of 1746 was remembered as *Bliadhna nan Creach* ('the year of pillaging').[57] Once more, an attempt was made to disarm the highlanders and to abolish the heritable jurisdiction of the clan chiefs. Another 'Disarming Act' received Royal Assent on 12 August 1746, dictating that anyone who bore arms after 1 August 1746 was liable to be fined £15; in default of payment, the offender, if fit, would be obliged to serve as a soldier in America; if unfit, to serve a six-month prison sentence. Second-time offenders would be transported to the colonies for life. Concealing arms was punishable by a fine of between £15 and £100. The penalty for wearing 'highland clothing' – regarded as a symbol of disaffection – was 'imprisonment, without bail'.[58]

In honour of Cumberland's victory, *The Glasgow Journal* brought out a special edition recording 'the greatest rejoicings that have been known' in the city.[59] All Jacobite areas were placed under military occupation. Adopting a scorched-earth policy, the intention was to break the power of the clans once and for all. The Highland companies, which had fought alongside the Hanoverians, recorded historian Forbes, were employed 'in a most repulsive service – that of burning the houses and laying waste the lands and property of the unfortunate rebels'.[60] Major George Grant, who had surrendered Inverness Castle to the Jacobites, was court-martialled and dismissed from the Army. Aeneas Mackintosh's rebellious wife did not suffer the same retribution as so many Jacobite sympathisers, retaining her place in society. Her brother, James Farquharson, captured at Prestonpans, retired in September 1745, selling his commission to another officer. Ensign Allan Campbell, also captured at Prestonpans, remained with the Regiment, purchasing his captaincy ten years later.[61] Lord George Murray escaped to the Continent, where he remained. He died in 1760, a week before the death of George II – the King he had fought to overthrow. For a while Prince Charles remained in Scotland, moving from one 'safe' island to another, on one occasion helped to escape his pursuers by Flora MacDonald, who disguised him as a servant girl.[62] But the chance to continue the fight had been lost, and by September 1746 the Prince was back in France.

Flanders again 1746

In June 1746 the British government, under the authority of the Whig prime minister, Henry Pelham, decided to attempt to occupy the vast region of Quebec in Canada, where the French had established a profitable trading business. Lord John Murray's Highlanders were among the nearly 8,000 men who embarked for Cape Breton on the North American coast.[63] Heavy storms in the Atlantic delayed the expedition, and after three attempts they were ordered to attack the French port of L'Orient. On 19 September 1746, a complement of men anchored in Quimperle Bay, but although the town was besieged, French resistance was too strong and British forces were withdrawn. After this venture, the Regiment was ordered for the first time to Ireland, landing at Cork on 15 November, whence they marched to Limerick, in the south-west close to the estuary of the

Shannon river. Hardly had they adjusted to their new surroundings before they were once more ordered for service in Europe.

Throughout 1746, while the British army had been preoccupied with crushing the Jacobites, Marshal Comte de Saxe had been steadily moving towards the frontiers of the Dutch Republic through the Austrian Netherlands.[64] Having reduced Tournai after Fontenoy, the French moved onwards to attack Ghent, Bruges, Antwerp and Ostend. In view of the threat to Britain's lines of communications, in early 1747 an expeditionary force, under Cumberland's command and including Lord John Murray's Highlanders, was dispatched from England. Landing at Flushing on the island of Walcheren at the mouth of the river Scheldt, the Highland Regiment saw some action against the French at the siege of the fortress at Hulst, before its surrender to the French in early May.

While embarking to defend South Beveland, the Regiment again came under attack.[65] 'The Duke [of Cumberland] staid till he saw the troops safely imbarked,' recorded the account of 'Foreign History' in *The Scots Magazine*, 'by which he exposed himself to consider-able danger; for scarce had he got on board when a great body of French came and attacked about 300 of the Highland regiment, who were the last to imbark; but they behaved with so much bravery, that they beat off three or four times their number, killing several, and making some prisoners, with the loss of only four or five on their side.'[66] Writing to his half-brother, James, 2nd Duke of Atholl, Lord John Murray described how: 'As soon as we got under sail, [I] perceived a body of them with horse, which I am since informed ... were about 5000, as they give out, so that had we staid but two hours longer, in all likelihood we had been taken Prisoners.'[67]

With the French controlling all of the Austrian Netherlands to bar further progress into the Dutch Republic, Cumberland had to defend two key positions: north of Liège lay the town of Maastricht on the river Meuse; north of Antwerp was the town of Bergen-op-Zoom (the hill on the boundary) between Brabant and Zeeland. On 2 July Cumberland and his forces were defeated at Lauffeld, near Maastricht. Capitalising on his success, Saxe deputed his lieutenant, General Ulrich

Frederic Woldemar, Comte de Lowendahl, to attack Bergen-op-Zoom, garrisoned by two battalions of the Scots Brigade in the Dutch service and commanded by the octogenarian General Cronstadt. To bolster the defences, Cumberland sent Lord John Murray's Highlanders – with Lord John Murray in person – and the recently arrived Loudoun's Highlanders to join the forces in the lines. During the seven-week siege, the British consul in Flushing, Charles Stuart, was noting 'that wherever the lines were attacked' the Highland Regiments would 'stand the first brush'. By the end of August, the ability of the garrison to hold out was diminishing. During the siege the Highland Regiment lost 'about thirty or forty' men, as well as Captain Malcolm Fraser. The soldiers were also suffering from illness, known as the 'Walcheren fever', the ranks of Lord John Murray's Highlanders being reduced to 375 men.[68]

In early September, Cronstadt ordered the two Highland Regiments, 'who render no service in the town', to Breda, leaving their tents and baggage behind, to be replaced by Dutch battalions. Days later, the French stormed the garrison, thereby gaining control of the length of the river Scheldt.[69] While in Breda, Piper Hugh Ross, who had joined the independent companies in 1728, got drunk and abused a sentry, for which offence he received 250 lashes as punishment. Another soldier, James MacDiarmid, received 500 lashes for theft.[70] As later historians observed, although there was little chance for the soldiers to distinguish themselves, by their presence at least Cumberland's communications on Walcheren and at Flushing had been secured.[71]

While the respective armies went into winter quarters, a Congress of diplomats was preparing terms for a peace treaty to be signed at the 'Imperial Free City' of Aix-la-Chapelle (Aachen). Signed in October 1748, it ended the war which, for the Highland Regiment, had begun with its first action at Fontenoy in 1745 by virtually reinforcing the status quo. Accepted as Queen of Hungary, Maria-Theresa was obliged to recognise Frederick the Great's conquest of Silesia and relinquish some Italian territory to Spain. Britain's commercial rivalry with France and Spain remained an issue for future conflict. One benefit of the Treaty of Aix-la-Chapelle was French acceptance of the Hanoverians as the rightful occupants of the British throne. All Jacobites were expelled from France, including Bonnie Prince Charlie – his father having already taken up residence in Rome, where he remained until his death on Christmas Day 1768. Charles – the Young Pretender – died in 1788.

The end of the war was celebrated with a massive fireworks display in Green Park, for which the composer George Frideric Handel wrote his *Music for the Royal Fireworks*. As the soldiers started arriving home at the end of 1748, Lord John Murray received an order of 'disbandment'.[72] On 1 April 1749 the secretary at war, Henry Fox, informed William Pitt, paymaster-general, that the King 'thought fit' to reduce the Highland Regiment; all the 'reduced' men were to receive three shillings 'in lieu of his sword, all of which swords are to be delivered into His Majesty's Stores of Ordnance, that shall be so disbanded, and that such disbanded Sergeants, corporals, Drummers & private men shall each receive 14 days subsistence as of His Majesty's Royal Bounty to carry them home'.[73] At the same time, the three additional companies, which had never left Scotland, were disbanded, the officers joining the Regiment or obtaining other commissions. Those remaining in the Regiment were to march from Portsmouth to Bristol, for service in Ireland.

While Major Francis Grant was complaining that 'there are neither hamocks nor mattrosses for the soldiers to lye upon' on the transports which were to take them to Ireland,[74] another change occurred. After nearly a decade as the 43rd Regiment in the order of precedence, in April 1749 Oglethorpe's Regiment, which had received into its ranks thirty-eight of the 1743 mutineers, was disbanded; Lord John Murray's Highlanders moved up to take its place as the 42nd. Two years later, on 1 July 1751, a Royal Warrant was issued, regulating the standards, Colours, clothing and rank or number of regiments of cavalry and infantry. Henceforward the Highland Regiment would be also known as the 42nd Foot. For all regiments, the King's Colour was of the Union flag, with the rose of England and the thistle of Scotland united; the Regimental Colour, which for the 42nd was in buff silk, was to have the Union in one corner, and in the centre the number XLII in gold Roman characters, within a wreath of roses and thistles on the same stalk with the crown above.[75]

Ireland 1749–1756

Quartered in Ireland for the next seven years, the 42nd went into barracks at Limerick, before moving to Galway, on the west coast. No sooner had they arrived than a new Commanding Officer had to be appointed following the sudden death of John Munro. His successor, appointed on 24 May 1749, was John (Jack) Campbell of Mamore, grand-nephew of the 3rd Duke of Argyll.[76] When the Hon. Gideon Murray retired as chaplain of the Regiment in 1746, Adam Ferguson was formally appointed chaplain on 30 April and travelled with the Regiment to Ireland. His greatest distress was despairing of finding 'a Wolf Dog, for the Breed is become very Scarce in the Country'.[77] As later historians recorded, 'great regularity was observed in the duties of public worship'. Every day the soldiers would be required to be present for morning prayers, and on Sundays there was divine service morning and evening. 'The greatest respect was maintained towards the ministers of religion. When Dr Ferguson was the chaplain of the corps, he held an equal, if not in some respects a greater, influence over the minds and conduct of the men than was exercised by the commanding officer.'[78]

At this time, the contemporary Company Rolls – detailing the rank, name, country and parish of birth, age, height in feet and inches, as well as hair colour, trade, date of enlistment and service abroad – indicated that the average height of the men was five feet and eight and a half inches, although some were unusually tall at six feet. Their previous occupations were varied. One described himself as a fiddler, others had been masons, blacksmiths, weavers and shoemakers. Out of a total complement of 318 non-commissioned officers and men, over a third came from Inverness-shire, over a third from both Argyllshire and Perthshire; the rest – in diminishing numbers – were from Ross, Banff, Nairn, Caithness, Moray, Dunbarton and Aberdeen, with one coming from England and one from Ireland. More than a third of the men had been with the Regiment since 1740. Many of the sergeants had served in the independent companies. Each company, now averaging thirty-five men, had a drummer, but there were only three pipers – one each for the colonel's, lieutenant colonel's and major's companies.[79]

The 'Black List' of 29 July 1752 showed the crimes for which men would have 'the disgrace of being whipped'. The most common misdemeanours were disobeying orders, being drunk and quarrelling, as well as theft and abuse of another officer. A soldier could also be punished for being absent from the barracks after roll-call or being absent all night or marrying without leave. The most serious crimes were 'concealing and disposing of a sword', being drunk and wounding a soldier, being drunk on duty and mutinous, being drunk and quarrelling in the streets, being drunk at the general review, and desertion.[80] Despite the 'animosities, jealousies, and disputes' which often existed between the soldiers and the local people, there were good relations between the Irish and the Highlanders. 'Perhaps,' suggested Stewart of Garth, 'the similarity of language, and the general and prevailing belief of the same origin, might have had some influence.'[81] While in Ireland, for administrative purposes, the Regiment was on the Irish rather than the British 'Establishment', which meant that the Irish government was responsible for paying the men. Whatever was brought into Ireland was normally subject to duty, but there were exemptions. In May 1751 a note was made that '30 bonnets for officers . . . 21 sergeants' bonnets, 320 privates' bonnets, 21 sergeants' shoulder broadsword belts and buckles, 320 privates' shoulder broadsword belts and buckles' should all be allowed into Ireland duty free. In 1755 there was an order for fifty-six Grenadier caps, again duty free.[82]

During peacetime, in common with other regiments, senior officers were choosing their best options, even if it meant transferring to another regiment, so they could retire with a respectable sum of money, resulting from the pyramid system of selling commissions.

Having commanded the Regiment since 1749, Jack Campbell obtained preferment as Colonel of the 55th in December 1755, later succeeding his father as the 5th Duke of Argyll. As a soldier-politician, day-to-day command of the Regiment had devolved on Major Francis Grant, the fifth, and third surviving, son of the Laird of Grant, who had served in one of the six independent companies before 1739. So anxious were the men that Grant should succeed Campbell that they reportedly raised the necessary sum of money for Grant to purchase the commission.[83] Grant's successor was the most senior captain, Duncan Campbell of Inverawe.

In early 1756 the 42nd was ordered to leave Ireland. Having acquitted itself honourably in the nearly two decades since its formation, the Highland Regiment was to become part of Britain's 'military spearhead of imperial expansion' in Britain's colonies in North America, while being permitted to retain both the Highland dress and 'their *esprit de corps*'.[84]

> *Awake on your hills, on your islands awake,*
> *Brave sons of the mountain, the frith, and the lake!*
> *'Tis the bugle – but not for the chase is the call,*
> *'Tis the pibroch's shrill summons – but not to the hall.*
> *'Tis the summons of heroes for conquest or death,*
> *When the banners are blazing on mountain and heath:*
> *They call to the dirk, the claymore, and the targe,*
> *To the march and the muster, the line and the charge.*[85]

3.

Ticonderoga: The Utterance of the Dead

It was at Ticonderoga
That you met the enemy
And you struck blows in combat[1]

1745

North America

It did not take long after the signature of the Treaty of Aix-la-Chapelle in 1748 for Britain's traditional enmity with France to erupt in North America. As both countries continued to occupy immense tracts of land on the North American continent, it was inevitable that their spheres of interest would collide. The territory at issue was the Ohio valley. Whereas the French had occupied the land to the north of the Great Lakes, Britain had established colonies on the east coast. In early 1755 two British regiments, the 44th and the 48th, had arrived in North America to bolster colonial resistance to France's continuing expansion south into Ohio. In July a force of 1,300 men, commanded by Major General Edward Braddock, set out for Fort Duquesne, constructed by the French where the Allegheny and Monongahela rivers joined to form the Ohio river. While crossing the Monongahela, the column was ambushed by French and Indian forces. Braddock was fatally wounded and his troops were routed, leaving nearly 500 dead. Among the survivors, was a militia volunteer, twenty-three-year-old George Washington.[2]

The French–Indian Wars 1756

When news of Braddock's defeat reached London, the prime minister, the Duke of Newcastle, sought King George II's permission to send reinforcements. Although George II was reluctant to commit additional troops overseas, he agreed to raise a force of 17,000 men. John Campbell, 4th Earl of Loudoun, who had supported the King during the '45, was appointed Colonel-in-Chief of the Royal American Regiment of Foot, 'to be forthwith Revived for Our Service in America'.[3] To bolster the force, two additional regiments were chosen: the 42nd and the 35th, both stationed in Ireland.

Before departing on such a long journey across the Atlantic, a number of administrative procedures had to be followed. First the regiments had to be ordered from Ireland. The Navy Board then had to contract for transports 'and to see that they were properly fitted with beds, victualled, and washed down with vinegar'. The Victualling Board had to buy adequate beef and butter for immediate consumption on arrival. The regiments needed to be augmented to full strength and payment for baggage and forage money authorised. Purchasing of commissions and promotions was accelerated. The apothecary general needed to prepare chests of medicine and the paymaster general had to advance a proportion of one month's subsistence to purchase 'camp necessaries'.[4]

Having marched to Cork from Dublin, in early March 1756 the soldiers took the customary sea route to Plymouth. As news of the departure of the Highlanders to America reached the ears of their kinsmen in Scotland, James Maclagan, a young divinity student, composed a song: 'To the Highlanders Upon Departing for America', with the meaningful couplet: 'Britain and Ireland and all of Europe / Will be scrutinizing the Scottish Gaels.'[5] Maclagan's father was Dr Maclagan of Little Dunkeld, one of the principal clergymen of the Presbytery of Dunkeld, who had ordained the 42nd's Chaplain, Adam Ferguson. Since then, Ferguson had been dutifully ministering to the Regiment's spiritual well-being. 'The importance of what was proper [còir], what was right and just [ceart], what was necessary or obligatory [dligheach] and the need for strict loyalty [dìleas] were all key elements of a preaching military chaplain's ministry.' Clergymen were also adept at using popular Gaelic poetry and songs to propagate their message, and Ferguson could draw on a pamphlet entitled 'A System of Camp Discipline', emphasising the importance of morning prayers.[6] Since being posted to Ireland,

For a while Ferguson unofficially left the Regiment, and went to Europe as a tutor. When the 42nd's departure to North America was known, Ferguson's friends were dismayed. 'I suppose [Ferguson] will be going to America with the regiment in which case we may bid an eternal adieu . . . for he will be slain as sure as he's a highlander.'[7] But

Ferguson did not go to America, eventually resigning at the end of 1757, having 'tired of following a Regiment'.[8]

While the officers and soldiers waited for the long-haul ships for the voyage across the Atlantic to arrive, Lieutenant Colonel Francis Grant had time to order his personal affairs, including sending his brother Ludovic, Laird of Grant, a letter to send to 'a Girl who I left in Ireland, with a young God daughter of yours, Lewisa, by name, and I think with child of another. How soon Lewisa is grown up, I design to give her a little Scotch education, or at least, you must, & if I survive the Indians, I design to give her a portion fit for a Presbyterian Parson.'[9] In mid-April, the first contingent of the 42nd embarked in Plymouth harbour. Loudoun's second-in-command, Major General James Abercromby, another veteran of the Flanders campaign, sailed with them, together with a similar complement from the 35th.[10]

As the Highland Regiment was crossing the Atlantic, recruitment was taking place throughout the Highlands. With high unemployment and the Disarming Act in force since 1746, the right to carry arms in the King's service attracted new recruits. This was their chance, one broadside proclaimed, 'to don "Bonnets blue, with Sword and pistol and warlike Goods" and "chace the Indians thro' the Woods."'[11] Once enlisted, they had a rudimentary two weeks' training on Glasgow Green before being reviewed and passed fit for service in North America.

On 7 June 1756 the second contingent of Highlanders marched to Greenock. Ten days later they sailed from Rothesay Bay, under the command of Major Duncan Campbell of Inverawe, who had stayed behind to oversee recruitment. In stormy seas, the first contingent took over two months to reach North America, dropping anchor in New York harbour on 16 June 1756, the same day as France formally declared war on Britain. The second contingent arrived in early August, although four transports were separated from the main convoy, arriving a few weeks later.

The French too were sending reinforcements, and in early May the Marquis de Saint-Véran, Louis-Joseph de Montcalm, Commander-in-Chief of the French forces in North America, reached the St Lawrence river with two battalions of fresh troops.[12] On arrival, the 42nd was immediately ordered to sail up the Hudson river to Albany, 140 miles due north of New York. A busy port and trading centre, established as Fort Orange by the Dutch, it was strategically located at the junction of the Mohawk and Hudson rivers. A further fifty-five miles north, on the southern end of Lake George – named after George II, but which the Indians called the 'Horican' – the tail of the lake, debouching into Lake Champlain, was Fort William Henry. Built in 1755 by the pioneer trader and Superintendent of Indian Affairs, William Johnson, and named after one of the sons of the Prince of Wales, the fort had a commanding position on what was a natural water highway north to Canada. Here, half of the provincial force was gathered.[13] Additional garrisons were at Fort Edward, on the Hudson river, fifteen miles south-east of Fort William Henry, also named after a son of the Prince of Wales, and at Fort Oswego, an important frontier post for British traders 160 miles west on the shores of Lake Ontario.

When the Highlanders arrived at Albany, as recorded in *The Scots Magazine*, a number of Indians 'flocked to them from all quarters, on which account an interpreter was chosen on either side'. These were the Mohawk Indians – the People of the Flint – whose traditional homeland stretched south of the Mohawk river, eastwards to Vermont, westward to the border with the Oneida tribe and northward to the St Lawrence river. Original members of the Iroquois League, they guarded incursions into their lands from the east. 'From the surprising resemblance in the manner of their dress and the great similitude of their language, the Indians concluded they were anciently one and the same people, and most cordially received them as brethren, which may be productive of effects beneficial to the British interest.'[14]

In a climate far hotter than the soldiers had ever experienced, in early July the 42nd lost its first men, when Major General James Abercromby rode up to the Cohoe (Great) Falls, ten miles north of Albany. With a guard of twenty-four soldiers, as reported in the

Pennsylvania Gazette, one of the first American newspapers in circulation, 'the Weather was extreme hot, hotter than it has been this Year; yet he being on Horseback, the Guard were obliged to march very fast to keep up with them. When they came to the Falls, one of the Guard, a Highlander, was taken Light-headed and imagining he saw an Indian, was going to fire his Gun; but before he could draw his Trigger, he fell down dead.' Two more died of heat exhaustion, while thirteen others fainted, having to be revived 'by being bled. Some of them are still in a bad condition.'[15]

Shortly afterwards, a contingent of fifty Highlanders volunteered to take part in a mission to 'go a-scalping' at the northern end of Lake Champlain where the French had several settlements. Using Mohawk guides and fifty Highland soldiers, they were led by Lieutenant Quinton Kennedy, 44th Foot, a survivor of the massacre at Monongahela, and who had married an Indian squaw 'whose tribe has made him a king'. As the *Scots Magazine* related to the undoubted surprise of its readers, Kennedy 'has learned the language, paints and dresses like an Indian'.[16] Moving stealthily into the French settlements, they burnt several storehouses and a ship-building yard, full of 'a very large Quantity of Cordage, Canvas, and other naval and warlike stores'. When, a few weeks later, the men returned their clothes were 'in rags and [they were] in a starving condition'. From among the Highlanders, the only casualty was Private Stuart, described as 'a drunken fellow', whom they left behind so that he could surrender to the French.[17]

In late July 1756, Loudoun reached North America. Travelling to Albany, he apologised to the Duke of Cumberland for apparent idleness, saying that they were 'at present groping very much in the dark'. He had no Intelligence and 'no part of the Country reconnoitred; few Men to Act'. The fort, he said, was 'ruinous; the Town is palisaded round, these all Rotten'. Barracks, a hospital and storehouses all needed to be built, although he had 'not one shilling to do this with . . . The Expences here, are immense; the Prices of every thing in this Country are dear.'[18] Loudoun was also beginning to realise the drawbacks of his own ignorance in such an alien land:

'the distances are so great, and no way has ever been tried, but by Indians, who are in no shape to be relied on, that we really know nothing at present.'[19] Despite the unusual circumstances of life in North America, with the French having successfully taken Fort Oswego on the Oswego river in August, when writing home, Lieutenant Colonel Francis Grant was less interested in describing what was happening than in requesting news of his family and whether his sister-in-law, Lady Margaret, had been 'brought to bed of a son'. He was also receptive to recommendations from his siblings for commissions for their friends, assuring his brother, the Laird, that he would 'do every thing in my Power for the young Gentlemen'.[20]

To counter French aggression, Loudoun intended to attack Quebec, in the heart of France's North American possessions, by first capturing Louisbourg on the French island of Cape Breton in Nova Scotia, but until his plan was sanctioned he had to wait. Once the weather began to deteriorate, tents were again struck for the army to march into winter quarters. On 25 September the Regiment marched into Fort Edward 'with Drums, trumpets and bagpipes going, sounding sweetly, women and children with them'.[21] Loudoun, however, believed that the 42nd were not yet ready to be left to garrison a fort throughout the winter. As he explained to Cumberland: 'There was a great push made, to persuade me to throw in the 42nd Regiment into the Forts, but as they have very few Men remaining, that were with You in Flanders: great part of those that came from Ireland, new; and five hundred recruits thrown in just now; I dare not trust the defence of those places to them this Winter.'[22] Instead, the Highlanders were to be billeted in houses in Schenectady and along the Mohawk valley, first settled by the Dutch in the seventeenth century. 'They will have most of their Men together, having only two hundred and Fifty men detached, where they are among the Indians, and are likelier to agree with them, than any other of the troops, as the Indians have an Opinion, that they are a kind of Indians.'[23]

Francis Grant, meanwhile, had been sending money back to his brother and was becoming frustrated by not hearing from him. 'You may easily believe that People encamped in a wilderness must long to hear from their friends, and therefore I desire you won't be so lazy as formerly. I have nothing of Consequence to write you but that all your friends are well.'[24] In early December, Cumberland responded to Loudoun's lists of complaints, recollecting the Highlanders' prowess in Flanders: 'As to the Highland Regiment, they have an excellent officer at their head: and if there were but a Couple of Hundred of old Flanderkins in the Battalion I shall look upon it as a pretty good one.'[25]

By the end of 1756, the Highland Regiment had been in North America for six months. The snow was as deep as any the soldiers had experienced in their native Scotland and the weather as cold. In Schenectady their main duty was to mount guards in the town fort and up the river valley as far as a stone house, which Loudoun named the 'Flanderkins' in honour of their work in constructing earthen works and palisades around it.[26] Shortly before Christmas, two private soldiers – John Maguire, 'reported to be an old offender and to have made the grand tour', and John Gordon, 'a sailor on board the transports from Glasgow who to prevent being pressed [en]listed with them at Sandy Hook' – deserted, travelling south to New York. As Abercromby informed Loudoun in New York: 'Two recruits from the Highlanders deserted five days ago, upon which Colonel Grant sent immediately a party after them, who tracked and nabbed them.' Describing their background, Abercromby continued: 'I dare say the verdict of the court will put a check to any further deserters from that Corps.'[27] With swift justice, redolent of the fate of the first mutineers thirteen years previously, the two men were tried and found guilty of desertion. On 29 December the Highlanders formed in a square in the freezing snow to witness their execution, to the beat of the 'Rogue's March', traditionally played when a soldier was stripped of his rank, badges and buttons, before punishment was carried out.

In Britain, a political upheaval was taking place among the King's ministers, news of which did not reach the troops in America until at least two months after the event. In his mid-seventies, George II was no longer taking an active interest in the politics of his country; instead, his Cabinet of ministers were directing policy. In November 1756, Newcastle had been replaced as prime minister by William Cavendish, the Duke of Devonshire. Foreign policy was henceforward directed by the rising politician and paymaster-general, William Pitt.[28] Appointed secretary of state for the Southern Department, in addition to reorganising the Royal Navy and reviving the militia, his responsibilities included the American colonies. While supporting Prussia against France in Europe, Pitt wanted to vanquish the French in both India and North America. This meant sanctioning Loudoun's plan to attack the French in North America.

Louisbourg 1757

Winter was brought to a sudden end with the news in March 1757 that a French force of over 1,600 men, including their Indian allies, had attacked Fort William Henry. Britain's response was immediate. So swiftly had the 42nd mobilised, leaving their billets at Schenectady and up the Mohawk valley, that they had 'marched without Tents, and lay in the Woods upon the Snow, making great Fires, and I do not find the Troops have suffered,' Loudoun later noted in a long letter to Pitt.[29] The French plan to lay siege to Fort William Henry failed and, after burning the storehouses and the sawmill, they withdrew. When writing to Pitt, describing the threat of the French attack, Loudoun took pains to commend the 'alertness and Activity with which each behaved in their different Stations, as well as the Behavior of the Men; Those in the Forts, determin'd to defend them to the last ... and those in the Reinforcements, marched through deep Snow, and lay in it without Tents, with the greatest cheerfulness.'[30]

By the end of April, the 42nd was assembled at Schenectady, ready for Loudoun's expedition against Louisbourg. If successful, the British would gain a strategic foothold at the mouth of the St Lawrence river. 'The Regiment is now assembled,' Francis Grant informed Loudoun, 'and ready to march when your Lordship's pleased to order them.' He also felt compelled to report a quarrel between two ensigns, in which George Maclagan 'behaved in such a manner that all the subaltern officers of the Regiment wrote me a letter, acquainting me they could not roll in duty with him until he cleared his character'. Grant had ordered his arrest, and was now interceding with Loudoun that he should be allowed to resign his commission in favour of a young gentleman volunteer, Peter Grant, one of his relations, 'rather than expose him to the world, which might be a detriment to him in gaining his bread in another way'. Loudoun agreed to Maclagan's replacement, while Grant paid the necessary £50 to send Maclagan home.[31] Writing again to his brother, Grant said that he hoped the troops 'will behave so as to give satisfaction to our Friends and Country', and begged him to remember him 'to all my Friends, but in particular to my brothers and sisters'.[32]

By the end of April, the necessary transports were ready in New York harbour. Once provincial troops arrived in Albany to take over from the three British regiments stationed at Albany, which included the 42nd, they sailed down the Hudson to New York harbour. Briefly stationed at Staten Island, they had to assist in rounding up a number of seamen who had jumped ship and were hiding in New York, without whom there would not be enough men to man the ships.[33] On 23 May 1757 the fleet of some thirty transport ships set sail. Their destination was the town of Halifax, named after Lord Halifax, president of the Board of Trade and Plantations, on the Atlantic coast of Nova Scotia, where in 1749 the British had established a garrison town as a counterweight to the French fortress of Louisbourg. After five weeks at sea, at the end of June, the armada of British ships reached Halifax, one of the finest natural harbours in the world.

During the first few weeks, the men sorted their supplies, cleaned and repaired their weapons. Meanwhile five more regiments were arriving from England, which included two newly raised Highland regiments – numbered the 77th and 78th – commanded by Lieutenant Colonel Archibald Montgomery and Simon Fraser, son of Lord Lovat, executed for treason in 1747.[34] Since their recruitment had been hurried, Fraser was at pains to warn Loudoun that, despite their physical resemblance to the 42nd, 'we shall resemble them in more respects when we are disciplined, for as yet, we have never been four days together'.[35]

Once the summer rains ceased, the men had to contend with exceptional heat waves. They also suffered from mosquitoes and black flies from the swamps. Drinking water was scarce. Loudoun, who was distressed that there was no garden to grow vegetables to prevent scurvy, at once ordered detachments from each regiment to be employed 'in clearing ground for and inclosing a large garden which is to be immediately cultivated, to supply the sick and wounded of the army with vegetables during the siege of Louisbourg, it being intended that the general hospital shall be established here'.[36] Another preparation was the construction of mock fortifications to practise the art of attack and defence, which afforded 'much mirth' to the spectators, but gave the young soldiers some taste of what to expect, as well as rendering 'the smell of powder more familiar'.[37]

By the beginning of August, Loudoun's army was ready to depart. Having loaded artillery, stores and baggage, they set sail for Louisbourg. Valuable time had been lost, however, both in assembling the army at Halifax and in waiting for a fair wind, which confined the soldiers on board ship for a further two weeks. By the time they were ready, Loudoun received intelligence that the French, in a superior fleet, had already reached Louisbourg, which meant the expedition, described as 'more of a summer vacation than an act of war', had to be abandoned.[38]

While the disappointed soldiers were returning from Nova Scotia to New York, Montcalm captured Fort William Henry, which gave the French a strategic advantage with a commanding position of Lakes George and Champlain. Although the departing troops were promised safe passage, about 200 men were attacked by the Indians. In what became known as 'the Fort William Henry massacre', the Indians 'committed all sorts of outrages and barbarities, the French troops averring that they were unable to restrain them'.[39]

In Britain, under the instruction of the Duke of Argyll, an additional nine Highland companies were to be raised, three for each Highland regiment stationed in North America. 'This is to acquaint your Grace that there is to be three additional companies raised for Lord John Murray's Regiment,' Argyll wrote to the Duke of Atholl in July 1757. 'I believe the nomination of the officers will be left to me and consequently to Your Grace . . . The raising the men will be the merit of those who shall desire to be officers and if any can be found who have served in Holland, so much the better . . . I shall speak to Lord John but I will bid him consult you.'[40] Atholl nominated his nephew James as captain of one of the 42nd's additional companies: the second son of the attainted Jacobite Lord George Murray, Commander-in-Chief of Bonnie Prince Charlie's army in 1745, James was also Lord John's godson. In his early twenties, it was believed that if he could acquit himself honourably in America, his actions might go some way to restoring the family honour. James Stewart, Younger of Urrard, in the lands between Blair Atholl and Pitlochry, and Thomas Stirling of Ardoch, north of Dunblane, who had fought in the Flanders campaign in 1747, were nominated as captains for the other two additional companies.[41]

In addition to pledging allegiance to the King, each recruit had to complete a printed form attesting that he was a Protestant, 'and that I have no Rupture, nor ever was troubled with Fits, that I am no-ways disabled by Lameness, or otherwise, but have the perfect Use of my Limbs'.[42] At the end of October the nine additional companies marched from Perth to Glasgow. Proceeding onwards to Greenock, they boarded transports for Cork on 1 December. Violent storms meant that it took ten days to reach Ireland. 'We had a fair wind and good weather until Sunday (when we were past Waterfort on our way to Corck) about eight, there came on one of the most prodigious storms that the sailors said they had ever seen the like before,' James Murray wrote to his brother, John Murray of Strowan, from Ireland. 'The storm abated somewhat Monday morning but it continued bad weather untill Friday evening, during which time we were often in risk of our Lives, especially twice, once being within two yards of a great rock, & the other time when we were in two fathom water going on a sand bank.'[43]

Ticonderoga 1758

The attack on Fort William Henry left the British eager for retribution. Since returning from Louisbourg, Loudoun had been suggesting undertaking a 'secret winter expedition' against the French Fort Carillon, situated on a prominent head of land between Lake George and Lake Champlain and so called to describe the noise of the cascading waters; the local name was Onderoga, or more commonly Ticonderoga.[44] Loudoun wrote enthusiastically to Cumberland: 'If I succeed in this Attempt, I think it will open a Door to get into Canada this Way.'[45] By mid-February, preparations were under way, but delays occurred, firstly with too much snow and then a sudden thaw, and so the expedition had to be cancelled. For Loudoun personally, there was a greater disappointment. On 11 March 1758, HMS *Hampshire* arrived in New York harbour, with a dispatch from Pitt, relieving Loudoun of his command and replacing him by Major General James Abercromby.[46]

The 42nd's major, Duncan Campbell of Inverawe, wondered how far this appointment, and the 'many other changes and promotions in our Military affairs in this Continent may change our Luck I shall not pretend to judge, but we have need of some sort of medicine for that end. We have a prospect of a very warm and vigorous campaign, and I hope it will be successful ... we are all in very good health and compleat for service.'[47]

Personally, Duncan Campbell was worried by his financial affairs, which may have accounted for his attempt the previous November to sell his commission and go on half-pay, assuring him £137 a year or £1,400 in hand. 'The State you sent me of my affairs is not very agreeable nor encouraging,' he wrote home, emphasising that he would not go into detail, 'as letters from this part of the world to yours are liable to inspection and many accidents'. However, not all the junior officers could afford to pay for their respective preferment and Loudoun had vetoed an alternative suggestion for Campbell to retire on a captain's full pay. There was perhaps another reason why Duncan Campbell was apprehensive. A traditional 'ghost' story relates how some eighteen years previously, Campbell had been warned of his impending death by the ghost of his dead cousin, Donald, who appeared three times to reprimand him for having given sanctuary to his murderer. 'Farewell, Inverawe,' the ghost had said. 'Till we meet at Ticonderoga.'[48] At the time, according to the legend, the name meant nothing, but he remembered the warning. Meanwhile, as with many who found themselves in a 'new world', and as an expert farmer, Campbell had become interested in the flora and fauna, having sent home 'two Barrels of the different kindes of Timber tree seeds &c.'[49]

In the same convoy as HMS *Hampshire* were eight out of the nine additional companies, the ninth, under Stirling's command, still on the high seas, having been blown off course. With the addition of three companies to the 42nd Highland Regiment, raising its ranks to 1,300 men, Captain Gordon Graham of Drainie wanted to be raised to the rank of major in addition to Duncan Campbell of Inverawe. His request was endorsed by Lieutenant Colonel Francis Grant, who petitioned Abercromby that 'such a body of men being too numerous to be exercised and disciplined by one Major only, your memorialist humbly conceives, that it would be for the good of His Majesty's service to have another Major added'.[50] Abercromby had no objection but lacked the authority to sanction the request, which had to be passed on to the King.

In preparation for Pitt's ambitious plan – the conquest of Canada – his instructions were for a three-pronged assault against the three French bastions of power in North America: Louisbourg, Fort Duquesne and Montreal. Each Highland Regiment would take part on a separate front. At first, Abercromby intended that the 42nd would become part of the attacking force on Louisbourg; he then decided to send the Regiment to attack Montreal, leaving the 78th to travel by sea to take part in the attack on Louisbourg: 'besides which, Lord John Murray's Regiment, having been all Winter in the back country, and have been fed on salt provisions, several of them were ill of the Scurvy, with which it would not have been safe to have ventured them to sea.'[51] To reach Montreal, the army, under Abercromby's personal command, had to move northwards through the corridor of lakes and land, protected by Fort Carillon at Ticonderoga, and further to the north by the fort at Saint Frédéric, which the British called Crown Point.

During weeks of preparation, a sizeable force had been assembling, numbering over fifteen thousand men.[52] Of the British regulars, the largest regiment was the 42nd. Since much of their journey north was to be along the great waterway of Lake George, a special contingent of 1,600 'battoemen' – expert boatmen – complemented the fighting force. Second-in-command was Brigadier General George Augustus, Viscount Howe, a descendant of the Hanoverian dynasty.[53] Described by William Pitt as 'a character of ancient times: a complete model of military virtue', Howe at once took note of the novel terrain and how ill-equipped the men were, dressed in their cumbersome and tight-fitting uniforms. The infantry were ordered to take off their wigs, cut their hair and wear shorter coats. The forerunners of the 'light infantry', Howe ensured that those men of lighter build than the 'crack' grenadiers became good marksmen, so that with less equipment they could act as skirmishers. Howe's orders to the 42nd were to discard their full plaids while in the forest or working in the camp. Some Highlanders even put on breeches.[54]

As acting brigadier, Francis Grant assumed command of the 2nd Brigade, while, for the duration of the campaign, Major Duncan Campbell of Inverawe was in command of the Regiment. The second senior captain of the Regiment, John Reid, recognised by his colleagues as a talented musician, had fallen ill and was ordered to remain as Commandant at Fort Edward.[55] Reid's replacement was James Murray, one of the additional company commanders. Captain Allan Campbell, commissioned as an ensign in one of the three earlier additional companies in 1744, and taken prisoner at

Prestonpans in 1745, was put in command of the grenadier company. Before departing, the men spent time in target practice, road building and manufacturing powder cartridges. Ten of the 42nd's best marksmen in the new 'light infantry' company were issued with rifles. Twelve men were assigned 'to do duty with the Royal Artillery, & no other duty, till further orders'.[56] At the beginning of June, just as the Regiment was preparing to depart, the last of the additional companies, under Stirling's command, reached Fort Edward. After several adventures, including being attacked by French privateers, Stirling had put ashore on Antigua in the Caribbean, before travelling northwards to New York.

On 16 June 1758 the 42nd was mustered by companies. The Articles of War were read in English and Gaelic. With departure imminent, Francis Grant again wrote to his brother, assuring him that he was 'certain we shall drub the rascals'. In his letter he included a bill for £100 Sterling 'to defray my expences, which I hope you'll take care of'.[57] At first light the following day, the soldiers departed. Each man carried ten days of provisions; eight oxcarts, piled high with tents and extra provisions came with them. Their interim destination was the southern end of Lake George, where they encamped for a further three weeks. While they waited, the 42nd was ordered to provide one of four siege detachments, which would include gardeners, carpenters and masons, 'if possible such as have serv'd in sieges'.[58]

While they waited, the men enjoyed good food. 'The lake abounds in fine trout (the meat of which is red), parch, suckers and several other sorts of fish; there is also plenty of beavers. On the side of the lake there is plenty of Deer but I have not seen any since I came to this country,' recorded James Murray. He also described how he had 'killed rattlesnakes about four feet long and as thick as the small of one's leg . . . when touched they make a great noise with their rattles. Their bite is not so bad as called, for it can be easily cured with oil or salt. They smell exactly like a goat (rather ranker if possible) before they are seized, but afterwards have almost no smell. They make the richest and best soup that can be which I eat of and like much; the meat is but insipid.'[59] At the end of June, Abercromby issued a manifesto reminding the men of the 'massacre' at Fort William Henry and how the terms of capitulation had been 'most shamefully broke, to the disgrace of the French nation'.[60]

On the evening of 3 July 1758, in the setting sun, siege guns were mounted onto the heavy rafts, soon to be loaded with tents, stores, barrels of gunpowder and provisions. On the prows of fifty wide river boats the numbers '42nd' were painted. These special 'battoes' were more unwieldy than whaleboats or Indian canoes, but they could transport larger quantities of materials. Piper Ewen McIntyre, of Captain Allan Campbell's grenadier company, played 'The Menzies' Salute', composed by his ancestor, John McIntyre.[61] After a further day's labours, at dawn on 5 July 1758 Abercromby's army set out. 'At the break of day, tents were struck, and all the troops, amounting to 6367 regulars, officers, light infantry and rangers included, and 9024 provincials, including officers and bateau-men, imbarked in about 900 bateaux and 135 whale-boats: the Artillery, to cover our landing, being mounted on Rafts.'[62]

This huge armada filled the lake 'from side to side, which is a mile and a half at the upper end; and in the narrower Places, they were obliged to form into Subdivision to give them Room to row, they extended from Front to rear full seven Miles; and by the time the rear had left the Shore three miles, there was not any of the Lake to be discern'd except that Part that was left behind.'[63]

In one of the boats sat Captain James Murray: 'There are several small islands . . . all around the lake is very hilly and quite covered with woods, as the most part of the country is, at least what I have seen on't.'[64] As the oarsmen rowed, the pipers played, helping the men to keep their strokes in time. By five in the evening they had reached Sabbath Point, about twenty-five miles down the lake, where they rested, before proceeding onwards through the night to their landing-place, 'a cove leading to the French Advanced guard'.[65] After two hours, the army had disembarked. 'Have met with no opposition,' Abercromby wrote to Pitt, 'landed troops, formed them in four columns, regiments in the centres, provincials in the flanks, and marched towards the enemy's advanced guard, composed of one battalion, posted in a logged camp; which, upon our approach, they deserted, first setting fire to their tents, and destroying every thing they could.' Instead of taking the most direct eastern route to the fort, Abercromby approached on the western side of the La Chute river, which flowed north and then wound eastwards to Lake Champlain. Heavy rainfall meant the water level was higher than expected and the terrain difficult. 'The army in the foregoing order continued their march through the wood, on the west side, with a design to invest Ticonderoga. But the wood being very thick, impassible with any regularity to such a body of men, and the guides unskilful, the troops were bewildered, and the columns broke, falling in one upon another.'

Late in the afternoon, they heard firing in the distance. 'Lord Howe, at the head of the right centre column, supported by the light Infantry, being advanced, fell in with a French party, supposed to consist of about 400 regulars, and a few Indians, who had likewise lost themselves in their retreat from the advanced guard. Of these our flankers killed a great many, and took 148 prisoners, among whom were five officers and three cadets. But,' as Abercromby continued: 'this small success cost us very dear; not as to the Loss of Numbers, for we had only two officers killed; but as to Consequence.'[66] 'Lord Howe was killed at the second shot,' James Murray told his brother, 'and he is very much regretted.'[67] His death, wrote Captain Hugh Arnot, with the Light Infantry, 'seem'd to presage the future.'[68]

Howe's loss was a great blow, both to morale and the future conduct of operations. After the attack, part of the army, including the 42nd, returned to the landing place, while others, including Abercromby, remained in the woods not far from the sawmills, 'a strong Post upon the East side of the Lake (or Narrows) which the Enemy had abandon'd'.[69] Lieutenant William Grant, commissioned into the 42nd after Fontenoy, took up the story: 'The 7th we spent in reconnoitring the French lines before Ticonderoga, and finding out the easiest approaches to them. The engineers, who had been sent out to take a view of the lines this day, reported to the General, that they could be easily forced, even without cannon, if they were attacked with spirit.' Having reconfirmed their assessments, Abercromby held a Council of War, 'where it was unanimously determined to attack the enemy in their lines, covered with the cannon of their fort. The piquets of the army, with the grenadiers, were ordered to begin the attack; and in the mean time the whole army advanced to sustain the piquets and grenadiers.'[70]

What Abercromby did not realise was how strongly, during the interim, the French had reinforced their defences. 'Logs well squar'd and Dove taill'd,' recorded Lieutenant Arnot, 'and from 10 to 6 feet high, had been erected. Besides the space from the lines until about 50 Yards outwards was fill'd with large Logs and limbs of Trees; which retarded our approaching them extreamly; and intirely broke our Line of attack.'[71] Having heard that French reinforcements were on their way, Abercromby had ordered the attack before the heavy artillery arrived from Lake George, while remaining himself at the sawmills.[72] On the morning of 8 July, Sir William Johnston arrived with 300 Indians, who positioned themselves on some high ground in front of the Fort and, related Arnot, 'began a mock Fight with a great deal of whooping and Noise (Indian fashion) in order as it was suppos'd to let the enemy know we had Indians'.[73]

'The attack,' Lieutenant William Grant wrote, 'began a little past one in the afternoon, and about two the fire became general on both sides; which was exceedingly heavy, and without any inter-mission; insomuch as the oldest soldiers present never saw so furious and incessant a fire. The affair at Fontenoy was nothing to it; I saw both.'[74] But Abercromby's plan to have six regiments moving forward to overwhelm the French by their sheer force of numbers was thwarted at the outset by the obstacles in their way. 'The enemy's breastwork was about nine or ten feet high,' noted Grant, 'upon the top of which they had plenty of wall-pieces fixed, and well lined on the inside with small arms.' The barricade of logs not only broke their ranks but 'put it entirely out of our power to advance briskly; which gave the enemy abundance of time to mow us down like a field of corn'.[75]

'If you reflect but a little on these many obstacles thrown in our way,' Grant continued, 'you will easily see, that the forcing of the enemy's lines was absolutely impracticable.'[76] Even so, the men persevered. 'Between one and two we marched up to attack the trenches,' James Murray reported, '& got within twenty paces of them and had as hott a fire for above three hours as possibly could be, we all the time seeing but their hats & the end of their muskets.'[77] So eager were they to fight, that an officer in the 55th commented: 'Impatient for orders they actually mounted the enemy's entrenchments, which, when advancing, and effected, they appeared like roaring lions breaking from their chains: their intrepid courage was rather animated than dampened, by seeing their fellows on every side (whose courage could not resist death) fall a sacrifice, in the cause of their King and country.'[78]

Although at about two-thirty in the afternoon Abercromby ordered the regulars to fall back, the 42nd maintained its position. William Grant concluded his account: 'I have seen men behave with courage and resolution before now but so much determined bravery can hardly be equalled in any part of the history of ancient Rome. They did not mind their fellow-soldiers tumbling down about them, but still went on undauntedly.' Even the dying, he said, 'cried aloud to their companions not to lose a thought upon them, but to follow their officers and charge the enemy and to mind their honour of their king and country. Nay, their ardour was so very extraordinary, that they could not be brought off while they had one single shot remaining. Indeed they paid dearly for their intrepidity. The remains of the regiment had the honour to cover the retreat of the army, and brought off the wounded.'[79]

Observing the battle from the parapet, Montcalm's Chief of Staff, Louis Antoine de Bougainville, noted how the column of 'English grenadiers and Scottish Highlanders returned unceasingly to the attack, without becoming discouraged or broken, and several got themselves killed within fifteen paces of our abatis.'[80] One man in particular caught the French attention: the six-foot figure of Captain Lieutenant John Campbell of Duneaves. In the heat of the battle, with a group of twenty men, he had forced his way over the parapet walls, wielding his broadsword, as he had over a decade previously in front of King George II. But the attack was in vain. Captain Salah Barnard, in command of a company raised by the province of Massachusetts Bay, and who had barely escaped with his life at Fort William Henry, recorded the outcome: 'A part of the Hilanders forcd them Selves within the first lines of ye Enemys Brestwork & But were Soon obligd to quite the Same & Retreat a few yards, Back where they Stood Fast and Faught Like Brave Soldiers with as much Liklyhood of doing Service as if they had discharged so many Rounds into the Lake.'[81] In the attempt, Campbell and several men were killed.

By late afternoon, the battle was over. 'About half an hour before we were obliged to retire,' James Murray informed his brother, 'I received a shot through my thigh, after which I stayed a few minutes, but finding if I stayed any longer my thigh would turn stiff and losing a great deal of blood I with help got into the road.'[82] After one final attempt to attack the centre of the French line, the 42nd withdrew, gaining recognition for having been the only regiment to make such a determined effort. As the eighteenth-century song writer acknowledged: 'You did not get any assistance / In that battle, by yourselves / On the day of agony as your blood was spilt / Gushing out with violence.'[83]

After the withdrawal, Captain Allan Campbell, who had 'eskeap'd without a Scratch',[84] wrote to his brother describing the 'hot Brush at the lines of Ticonderoga where we lost a Considerable number of men and Officers . . . our Regt acquired great Glory by the good behaviour of Both men, and Officers, tho we were unsuccessful.' Explaining that they were now camped at the end of Lake George, he said that he had no time to write more, 'being excessively hurried having no body to assist me in the affairs of my Company having my three L[ieutenan]ts killed or wounded'.[85]

One of the wounded lieutenants was William Grant, who was writing to his family describing how: 'The whole weight of the fire fell upon the regular troops, but our regiment suffered more than any other.'[86] Dragged to safety by his comrades, 'I had myself my fusee broke in my hand by a musket ball,' he recorded, 'and some-time after I was shot through the middle of the thigh a little below the groin. The ball went out behind through the hip, but luckily for me missed the bone. However, it knocked me down and I was carried off by two grenadiers of my platoon.' As he recorded, even Lieutenant Colonel Francis Grant had a narrow escape, being 'shot through the bonnet, and a little after was knocked down by a spent ball, which hit him on the head; but in a moment he recovered, and charged the enemy at the head of the regiment'.[87]

Major Duncan Campbell of Inverawe was wounded. As the ghost story, related above, continued, having told his fellow officers of the ghost's dire warning about Ticonderoga, Campbell was assured that the battle was going to take place at Fort George, not Ticonderoga. But when he realised that they were at Ticonderoga, he announced: 'Today I die.' And so it proved. During the action, his right arm had been so badly shattered that it had to be amputated; he died nine days later. The ghost story became so much part of Scottish folk-lore that Robert Louis Stevenson was inspired to write his ballad 'A Legend of Argyll', which began:

> This is the tale of the man
> Who heard a word in the night
> In the land of the heathery hills,
> In the days of the feud and the fight.
> By the sides of the rainy sea,
> Where never a stranger came,
> On the awful lips of the dead,
> He heard the outlandish name.
> It sang in his sleeping ears,
> It hummed in his waking head:
> The name – TICONDEROGA,
> The utterance of the dead.[88]

Duncan Campbell's second son, Lieutenant Alexander Campbell, who had travelled out to America with his father, was wounded in the arm and later invalided home to Glasgow, dying two years later. Out of a total casualty rate of nearly two thousand, almost a third were from the 42nd: 316 Highlanders had died, including eight officers; 333 were wounded, including seventeen officers, making a total of 649 casualties.[89] Their losses were the worst the Highland Regiment had endured. 'There were more than five hundred / Of the majestic lions there / Laid low without any life in their bodies.'[90] 'How can we recruit,' asked Lieutenant William Grant, 'and when shall we have so fine a regiment again?'[91]

Having withdrawn to the banks of Lake George, Abercromby wrote to Barrington, secretary at war, 'with a Heart full of Grief & Concern', enclosing a list of all the officers and men killed at Ticonderoga and in the skirmish two days previously when Howe had died: 'in both which, the officers, as well as the Men behaved with the greatest Intrepidity'.[92] He wrote a similar dispatch to Pitt, explaining the reasons for their withdrawal: 'Notwithstanding all their intrepidity and bravery, which I cannot sufficiently commend, we sustained so considerable a loss, without any prospect of better success, that it was no longer prudent to remain before it; and it was therefore judged necessary, for the preservation of the remainder of so many brave men, and to prevent a total defeat, that we should make the best retreat possible.'[93]

The Highlanders' fortitude in battle had been well noted by the French. When Bougainville, who had been 'slightly wounded by a shot in the head',[94] reported back to Paris, he recommended that the French government would do well to recruit 'a troop of Scots, even of only sixty men, headed by a MacLean or a MacDonnell, or some of the other tribal chiefs whose names are cherished and respected by all Highlanders'. Aware of the legacy of mistrust between the English and the Scots, Bougainville was keen to emphasise that the Highlanders 'understand very well they are sent to America in great numbers by the British in order to depopulate their lands and even in hopes of seeing some of them killed'.[95]

News of Ticonderoga reached London late on 19 August, when Abercromby's aide-de-camp arrived with his dispatches to Pitt and

Barrington. The British public heard of the defeat at Ticonderoga in *The Gentleman's Magazine*, which pointed to blunders and oversights, poor intelligence as well as 'pannic at the headquarters', and the retreat of an army of 'near 14000 men' from 'an enemy not above 3000'.[96] Given the sobriquet 'Mrs Nabbercrombie', Abercromby's reputation was severely damaged, the Iroquois Indians even suggesting that 'he was an old Squaw that he should wear a petticoat'.[97] Britain's other military objectives met with greater success. Shortly after Ticonderoga, on 26 July, Louisbourg was captured by forces commanded by Major General Jeffrey Amherst. In the third military attack, Brigadier General John Forbes had marched from Philadelphia to Fort Duquesne. Included in his force was the 77th – Montgomery's Highlanders – commanded by Major James Grant of Ballindalloch, grandson of William Grant, Captain of one of the original independent companies. Grant, in an advance party, had been ambushed and captured, although Forbes – in command of the main force – took the fort, which was renamed Fort Pitt, in honour of William Pitt.

Unaware of the 42nd's exceptional losses at Ticonderoga, on 22 July 1758 the title 'Royal' was bestowed upon the Highland Regiment, which had served the Sovereign loyally for nearly twenty years. The Warrant, signed on George II's behalf by Lord Barrington, proclaimed:

> We being desirous to distinguish Our said 42nd Regiment of Foot with some Mark of Royal Favour, Our Will and Pleasure therefore is And we do hereby Direct that from henceforth our said Regiment be call'd and distinguished by the title and name of our 42nd or Royal Highland Regiment of Foot in all commission Orders, and writings.[98]

This distinction meant that the Regiment changed its Regimental Colour, facings, collars, cuffs and drums from buff to royal blue. It was the King's 'further will and Pleasure' that, with the further increase of seven companies (and the three additional companies already in North America), the Regiment should be formed into two battalions to consist of ten companies each. The King also sanctioned the 'addition of a Piper to each of the Two Grenadier companies'.[99] Once again, the Duke of Atholl and his brother, Lord John Murray, were responsible for recommending the new officers: 'I wish you had shown me your list before you left London,' Lord John complained to his 'dear Brother', 'as some were recommended by us both, which was unnecessary.' The officers appointed to command the seven new companies of the 2nd Battalion 42nd included Francis MacLean, aged forty-nine, the oldest and most experienced of the new company commanders.[100] William Murray, son of Lintrose, obtained the captaincy of another company;[101] another was Alexander Reid, whose brother John was in the 1st Battalion 42nd. There was one captain whose appointment Lord John Murray was unhappy with: he was John Stewart, Younger of Stenton, who had opposed the King in 1745. 'I wish you had not named him,' he continued in his letter to his brother, 'as he is the only one of that denomination in the Regiment under my command.'[102]

One of those who gained a commission in the newly raised 2nd Battalion was seventeen-year-old John Grant, whose father had been steward to the Laird of Grant, Francis Grant's brother Ludovic. An orphan and only son, his friends 'obtained for me a Lieutenancy of the Highland Watch under condition of raising 25 men', he recorded. 'Recruiting was somewhat difficult . . . I first got a good piper and then 4 young men, good dancers, [and] established myself at an ale House.' His sergeant made a 'flowery harangue', followed by piping and dancing.[103] Given three guineas 'for each recruit and the Bounty was a Guinea and a crown', Grant soon recruited sufficient men.[104] Within three months, the seven companies had been raised. While the soldiers were 'merely taught to march', the officers enjoyed themselves attending 'plenty of balls'.[105] 'Eighteen Irishmen were enlisted at Glasgow, by two gentlemen anxious to obtain commissions,' related historian Forbes. Since Lord John Murray had said only Highlanders should be accepted, the men – with the names O'Donnel, O'Lachlan,

O'Brien – 'passed muster' by changing their names to Macdonnel, Maclachlan and Macbriar.[106]

As always, equipping an army required organisation. The account supplied by the Regiment's Agent in Perth, William Sandeman, detailed that 'for the 7 companys of the Royal Highland Regiment', the men were to be equipped with 714 plaids for 700 privates & 14 drummers, '30 ditto . . ., being for 27 sergeants 1 sergeant major, 1 piper major and 1 drummer'. They also needed '1428 pairs of hose for private and drums. 60 pairs ditto, for sergeants and majors. 714 bonnets for private & drums, 30 ditto for sergeants & majors, 30 ditto for sergeants and majors, 744 pairs shoes . . . ' Then there were the 1,428 shirts, 714 shoulder belts and 714 broadswords. Another order included a consignment of six yards of 'Drummers Lace'.[107] Each company received one hundred knapsacks, one hundred haver-sacks, one hundred canteens, as well as 106 combs and cases, pairs of shoe buckles and private men's shirts.[108] On 19 November 1758 one Hogs head, Copper Kettles and four chests of Arms were recorded as being received. Francis MacLean noted that he had received forty-one swords, which appeared to be one more than he required 'and for which I am to be accountable'.[109]

Pitt had originally intended to reinforce Amherst's army in North America but, in retaliation for the loss of Minorca in 1756, he decided that the capture of the French 'Sugar islands' of Martinique and Guadeloupe would be of greater benefit. Lacking sufficient trans-ports, only two of the seven companies embarked from Greenock in mid-November. Buffeted by storms in the Bay of Biscay, being 'dreadfully seasick' was a new and unpleasant affliction.[110]

Meanwhile, the 1st Battalion remained in New York State throughout the winter, licking its wounds after Ticonderoga. 'I am recovering pretty well & can walk about,' James Murray told his brother John in August, 'altho' I am much pain'd in my knee.' He also related how the area around Lake George was no longer safe: 'Since the engagement there has been severall people scalpt at different times going up to Lake George, by French and Indian partys, for they have even scalpt women.'[111] Francis Grant was writing to his brother urging him to 'apply, that I might have the command of the Second Battalion, ... which I can't but think, might be brought about upon proper application, considering I have been a Field Officer these thirteen years, ten of which I have commanded this Battalion, and given close attendance to the Regt.'[112]

The 1st Battalion remained in winter quarters until the spring, with the usual guard and drill duties and occasional misbehaviour. 'Complaints being made that several of the Regt go out a shutting [shooting] and that they Break Down the Farmers Fences, its therefore Col. Grant's orders that no man whatsomever Do for the future shutt [shoot] again any fences or go into any inclosers [enclosures].'[113] The men had also developed the habit of being absent 'from Exercise'. Orders were therefore given 'that no man shall be allow'd to be Absent for the future but such as are on Duty, and those who may be Certify'd by the Surgeons to be sick or recovering and not fitt for Exercise'.[114] As custom dictated, unless other arrangements were made, the personal possessions of a deceased officer were sold at auction, as with those of Lieutenant William Baillie, who had died at Ticonderoga. 'The Auction to begin at 3 o'clock in the afternoon,' advertised a Regimental Order in March 1759.[115] Mindful of potential action as spring approached: 'the spare arms in the stores of the different Companys [were ordered] to be Repair'd with the utmost Expedition'.[116]

Those whose wounds after Ticonderoga were too serious for them to remain in the Regiment were sent home. 'Forty-five private men of the Royal Highlanders, disabled at Ticonderoga,' recorded *The Scots Magazine*, 'and lately arrived in England, were conveyed from Portsmouth to Chelsea in wagons, and billeted there, March 17 till they should be admitted on the out-pension.' So distressed was Lord John Murray at their condition, 'lacerated by the slugs and broken nails which the enemy fired', that he took a personal interest in their welfare, arguing on their behalf to make sure the wounded men obtained a pension.[117] 'To two widows he gave a guinea each, and is to settle them on his own estate,' noted a contemporary writer. 'Such kind usage will have the best effect in encouraging others to enlist.'[118]

4

Clipping the Wings of the French

Our affairs on the Continent of America have taken a very Favourable turn this year, and I hope we'll be able this Campain to Clip the wings of the French so as not to be so troublesome to us as they have been formerly.

Captain Allan Campbell, 1759[1]

1745

The West Indies: the 2nd Battalion 1759

Having resolved to attack the French West Indies, a British expedition was fitted out under Major General Peregrine Hopson, described as 'old but inexperienced, thorough rather than active'.[2] Second-in-command was Major General the Hon. John Barrington, the brother of the secretary at war.[3] While the 1st Battalion 42nd remained in North America, the 2nd Battalion was to be part of a force of approximately 6,000 men, divided into three brigades, making its way across the Atlantic to assemble in Carlisle Bay, Barbados, south-east of Martinique. By early January 1759 most of the fleet, under the command of Commodore John Moore, had arrived in the Caribbean.[4] A week later the transports, carrying five companies of the 2nd Battalion, reached Barbados; the remaining two companies, which had set out earlier, were still on the high seas, having been caught in a storm. With no time to practise disembarking from their flat-bottom ships – newly designed to land in shallow waters – Hopson ordered the expedition to leave at once for Martinique.[5]

On 15 January, the British fleet sighted the volcanic cliffs of the island. Once the Royal Navy had silenced the nearby onshore batteries at Fort Negro, the marines landed, the French having left their positions 'with some Precipitation'.[6] By the early afternoon, the fleet had anchored in Fort Royal Bay, in preparation for landing the troops at Cas de Navires, about two miles to the north of Fort Negro and five miles from Fort Royal. Since the French had mistakenly believed the troops would disembark at Fort Royal, Cas de Navires had been left undefended.[7] Once the army had landed, two of the three brigades under Barrington's command, 'with a few Highlanders', marched to Negro Point, forming themselves into an oblong square: 'two Regiments in front and Rear, one on each Flanks, Grenadiers in front – Highlanders and Parties upon Angles; in that Position [we] passed the Night very quietly under a fine Tree in the Centre Sugar Canes and an old Wall in our front'.[8] The third brigade had to wait on the transports until the next day.

At daybreak, the soldiers 'saw the Enemy advancing thro' Woods and Ravins in great Numbers in an irregular Manner, from Woods and Canes'. Hopson at once ordered out the grenadiers. 'At seven in the morning saw the Troops advanced beyond Fort-Negro,' related Captain Gardiner, observing events from the deck of the *Rippon*, 'firing the Woods and clearing their Front towards Port-Royal.'[9] By their irregular manner of fighting they realised that their adversaries were not regular soldiers but the 'mulattoes', the local inhabitants of mixed ancestry. The countryside was impenetrable. One officer described never seeing 'such Country; the Highlands of Scotland for Woods, Mountains, Canes and continued Ravins is nothing to it'.[10] Hopson therefore decided to send in the Highlanders, who were more practised at countering the guerrilla tactics of their opponents.[11] 'At ten,' continued Gardiner, 'saw an English Battery playing from an Hill above the Fort and scouring the woods.'[12]

Around midday, Gardiner saw the soldiers advancing up Morne Tartenson, one of two strategically located hills overlooking the town and citadel of Fort Royal. During the skirmishing which followed, the Regiment suffered its first casualty in the West Indies when Lieutenant George Leslie was wounded.[13] Although 'all appearances seemed to promise Success', Hopson believed that it was impossible to maintain his ground without support from the Royal Navy's guns. Having held a council of war, such support was 'judged to be impracticable' given the risks involved. With the odds against them, the order was given to abandon the attack. At nine in the evening 'when the Moon was well up, the Troops re-imbarked at Fort-Negro, after setting Fire in their march to all the Canes and Country round about them, with little or no molestation from the Enemy'.[14]

An alternative plan to attack the town of St Pierre along the coastline was attempted but abandoned because Commodore Moore believed that, although they might be able to take the town, 'the ships and Troops might Suffer so much as to disable them for any future Attack'. Attention was therefore directed towards the nearby island of Guadeloupe. The failed attempt on Martinique had cost the lives of twenty-two men and one officer; forty-seven men and two officers were wounded. 'The only good reason for attacking Martinique first was that Martinique's fall would have a better effect on public opinion,' noted historian Marshall Smelser. 'A great many persons had heard of Martinique who had not heard of Guadeloupe, since the produce of the latter was shipped to Europe by way of Martinique.'[15]

A week later, the British fleet anchored off Guadeloupe, an archipelago of six islands lying north of Martinique. With a population of about two thousand Europeans and thirty thousand 'negro' slaves, the islands, discovered by Christopher Columbus, were called Alto Guardelupo, 'from the great height of the Cliffs and Mountains on it'.[16] The largest two islands were almost combined into one, with the cartographic impression of a seaborne butterfly whose wings spread north-west and south-east. Separated by mangrove swamps and a saltwater river, the steep volcanic western half was called Basse Terre. The eastern half, Grande Terre, was more suitable for a landing. Planted with tobacco, cotton and sugar, its terrain provided Guadeloupe's wealth. Four smaller islands, Isles des Saintes, Marie Galante, Petite Terre and Désirade, completed the archipelago. The British fleet dropped anchor off the main town, Basse Terre, and bombarded the coastline in a cacophony of cannon fire.

The soldiers could only stand on board their transports and stare at the ferocious naval bombardment, which was so severe that the town was set on fire, which, 'from the Quantity of Rum & Sugar that was in it, occasion'd its total Destruction, with Goods and Treasure to a very great Value,' Commodore Moore later informed Pitt.[17] In the afternoon of the following day, the soldiers were ordered ashore to take possession of the fort, which had been abandoned. The fire meant there was neither plunder nor rum, the only items of real value being 168 slaves.[18] 'Part of the Troops laid upon their Arms all Night upon the rising Ground that overlooked the Town,' recorded Captain Gardiner on board the *Rippon*, 'part of them made themselves Masters of an advantageous Post upon a Hill about a mile to the West, and part enter'd the Town and lined the Streets, which still remained on Fire, and continued burning all Night.'[19] The five companies of the 2nd Battalion 42nd were ordered to the back of the town.[20]

Hopson made his headquarters at the Governor's House, 'or rather the Ruins of it', in Basse Terre.[21] Most of the French and local inhabitants had taken refuge in the hills, their main concentration being in the Dos d'Ane, six miles south-east of Basse Terre, where the French governor of the island, the Chevalier Nadeau du Treil, had fled. To guard against the threat of sniping, a detachment was ordered to seize an advanced post on the plantation of Madame Ducharmey, who had armed her slaves in defence.[22] Lieutenant Alexander MacLean of the 2nd Battalion's grenadier company 'had the honour to begin an attack at the head of twelve Granadiers, supported by 150 men,' he later wrote to Lord John Murray. 'We had a steep precipice to climb in sight of an Enemy, defended by a parapet 8ft high, and within that an entrenchment; within ten yards of this parapet was a slop[e] over a rock, where a man with great difficulty could scramble over without arms.' Having taken the French by surprise, 'we immediately sprang forward with fix'd Baynots, mounted the parapet and drove them like a flock of sheep with push of Baynet before us'.

During the fight, MacLean was wounded in the arm, while 'pushing my baynet into a fellow, who, falling back, drew his trigger; the ball entered at my elbow and came out close to the shoulder, shattering the bone all the way.' Before withdrawing, he saw their opponents 'spitted like Larks, and the place our own'. As MacLean continued in his letter to Lord John Murray: ''Twas [believed] impossible to save my arm, but I was obstinate not to have it cutt off, for I dreaded being put among the Invalids, and besides, as my ambition was pretty great, I considered that all my hopes were blasted, and I much preferred death to life in that situation.'[23] Although Alexander MacLean did not have to lose his arm, he was killed in Germany in 1762, having transferred to another regiment. In his contemporary account, Gardiner described the Highlanders as distinguishing themselves 'greatly'.[24] Madame Ducharmey escaped but some of her female 'companions in arms' were captured.

Unfortunately, another scourge had appeared: on 30 January, in a long dispatch to Pitt describing the campaign and including an explanation of the failed attack on Martinique, Hopson reported that 1,500 men – a quarter of the force – were on the sick list 'occasioned by the very great heat and fatigue that the Troops undergo which is unavoidable, there being so many out Posts necessary to be maintained, and the Labour of carrying the provisions up to them so great that it harasses them very much; The few negroes we have here not being sufficient for that.'[25] As yet no one understood how deadly was the mosquito, which caused the fatal disease of yellow fever or 'yellow jack'. An acute viral infection, affecting all vital organs, it gained its name from the fact that the sufferer became jaundiced; it was known as black vomit, because another tell-tale sign was when vomit contained blood. Bringing nausea and delirium, the illness led to internal haemorrhaging and death.

Meanwhile, Brigadier General John Clavering, 2nd Guards, had been put in charge of a small force bound for the island of Dominica, so called because Columbus had reached it on a Sunday.[26] While at sea, he encountered the two delayed companies of the 2nd Battalion 42nd. As Lord John Murray explained to his brother, the Duke of Atholl, they had parted from the convoy 'in a hard gale' four days after they sailed.[27] After seeing how well the five other companies of Highlanders had fought at Martinique, Clavering considered ensuring that the two companies joined his force. Having called the two company captains on board, as Lieutenant John Grant related, Clavering addressed them: 'Gentlemen, I could not hear a Scotch talk lately – for I got so many wounds from the Highlanders at Prestonpans that I could not bear them. But now I have changed my mind and I would command them sooner than other people, so I order you to join me.' But 'for some reason or other', Grant noted he changed his mind.' Although Grant was not privy to their discussions, Clavering's change of heart arose once he realised the Highlanders had not yet received their firelocks and were armed only with broadswords and dirks.[28]

Proceeding to Basse Terre, the two companies were too late to take part in the city's capture and were kept on board their transports, eventually being assigned to a force of 400 marines under Commodore Moore's command. The intention was for this force to capture Fort Louis on the west coast of Grande Terre, 'to facilitate any Attempts upon the Eastern and more fertile Part of the Island'.[29] On 13 February the attack was mounted on Fort Louis, subjected to heavy shelling by the Royal Navy ships. 'In less than 40 minutes, not a stone was standing,' noted Grant. 'As soon as that was done we and the marines were ordered on to flat bottomed boats to land and take possession.' Grant estimated they were opposed by about 400 French soldiers, who had returned to the battery when, 'for fear of striking us', the Royal Navy ships had ceased firing.[30]

Looking back on his first 'ship to shore landing', Grant recorded an instance of 'highland fidelity'. 'When we were ordered to land my faithful servant, who had enlisted merely to act as my servant, called me aside and said "We are going to land John (such was the familiarity seen in those days) and I trust you will behave yourself like a man and not disgrace your family – don't take amiss what I say. I do it as you are so young."'[31] Getting out of the boat, Grant 'stumbled over a stone and fell forward into the water; my servant, thinking me mortally wounded, seized me and was dragging me on shore, in so doing he scraped my shins . . . we all rushed in pell mell, and the French ran like hares up the hill which rose almost from the water, at the back of the battery, which being covered with brushwood was difficult to ascend.'[32]

When Grant and his companions reached the top of the hill, they found a four-gun battery deserted by the French. Since the battery guns were still loaded, Grant thought they could still be fired. Having turned one gun around, he could not find a match. Turning to one of the marines, he asked him to point the gun, while he fired at it. 'I pulled out the pistol and snapped it in the priming.' The shot bounced and reached the retreating French, 'whose motions it much accelerated'.[33] Looking back, Grant recorded: 'It was my happiest moment as it had been my first *fait d'armes* and had been successful.' He was also pleased because he had had no practice commanding 'men under arms'.[34] By nightfall, the Highlanders and marines had taken possession of the defences surrounding Fort Louis and mounted their pickets. The following day, they encamped near the shore, having retrieved their tents from the boats. After hoisting the British Colours at the fort, 'of this they kept Possession, doing Duty on Shore'.[35]

Disease was still rampant and with the hospitals crowded, Hopson ordered some of the sick to be evacuated to British-controlled Antigua. 'The Surgeons were sent before as usual, to make the necessary Preparations for their Reception, and to buy Water,' noted Richard Gardiner, whose ship, HMS *Rippon*, was detailed to assist in the transportation of six hundred sick and dying.[36] Even Hopson fell ill, and on 27 February he died. His successor was John Barrington, who immediately wrote to Pitt, apologising for what might have 'the Appearance of Inactivity' and explaining their difficulties. 'The Army at present consists, as appears by the returns, of only 2,796 Men, fit for Duty.' Having accounted for those required for relief duty, he believed the only practical course of action was to evacuate from Basse Terre to join Commodore Moore's contingent of marines and Highlanders at Fort Louis.[37]

According to Lieutenant Grant, the forces at Fort Louis had been surviving 'under very unpleasant circumstances, we were too weak to advance into the country and we had no provisions but from the ships. Beef and such bacon which had been in store since the former war and Biscuits full of maggots, so that after endeavouring to clear them of vermin we used to wet them and toast them.' They had no water except from the ships, which was 'so putrid that we could not drink it without holding our noses. I and some other officers got into a large deserted house and made ourselves more comfortable.'[38] Grant became ill, as did the surgeon, Robert Drummond. Evacuated from the beach, they were tended by two Royal Navy doctors on board ship, who 'bled us profusely and would have killed us but luckily their ships were order'd off and we were saved'.[39]

While preparing to leave Basse Terre, and reading through Hopson's papers, Barrington found a letter from Pitt, ordering the commander to send the 'Seven Companies of Highlanders' – in other words the Royal Highland Regiment's 2nd Battalion – to North America after the attack on Martinique. When Barrington responded to Pitt, he protested, indicating that their numbers were already greatly reduced by sickness, death and injury. If he had to send the 2nd Battalion 42nd to North America, he could not hope to continue with a successful campaign. 'This is Sir a very delicate Situation; However I think it of so much Consequence for His Majesty's Service, that it will be absolutely necessary to keep the Highlanders some little time longer to see what can be done on the other side of the Island.' He did, however, promise to send them with an additional draft of a thousand men, requested by the King, once he had captured Guadeloupe. When Pitt received this communication in May, he concurred, although by the time Barrington would have received his assent, the campaign was over.[40] In his correspondence with Pitt, Barrington included a casualty list of the fifty-five killed and 140 wounded during the campaign. Compared with other regiments, the figures for the 42nd were high, indicating, as historian Smelser noted, 'the penalty of merit'.[41]

On 1 March, the batteries in and around Basse Terre were blown up and destroyed, the army re-embarking on board the transports 'without the Loss of a man'.[42] Held up by adverse winds, Barrington reached Fort Louis on 11 March. News of the arrival of a French fleet of warships, however, raised fears of a French counter-attack. To outflank the attacking force, Commodore Moore left with the greater part of the fleet to take up anchorage in Prince Rupert's Bay, in the northern part of Dominica, lying strategically between Martinique and Guadeloupe, whereupon Barrington built up a 'naval army' to fight a 'war of detachments', by attacking several of the island settlements simultaneously, and adopting a 'scorched-earth' policy to force the islanders to capitulate. One detachment, commanded by Lieutenant Colonel Byam Crump, and including 600 men from the 42nd, was ordered to attack the southern coast of Grande Terre, by landing on the beach between the two villages of Sainte Anne and Saint François. The two forces would then divide and advance inland. Although, since they were sailing in full view of their opponents, there could be no element of surprise, the attack was successful. After destroying the towns, they returned to Fort Louis, whose defences Barrington had strengthened, having renamed the fort 'Fort George'. With most of Grande Terre in flames, Barrington returned with the army to Basse Terre. Two ensigns of the 42nd were wounded, both dying later.[43]

On 12 April, a force of over 1,000 men, under Crump's command, and including the 42nd, was dispatched to land at a bay close to the town of Arnouville. Since their rudimentary drill practice together in Scotland, it was the first time that the seven companies would be fighting together. Expecting 'warm work', John Grant recollected that the Highlanders were in the centre of the force, which advanced slowly. 'Not a shot was fired until a masked battery open'd upon us with grape and knocked down almost a whole platoon of the 4th Regt opposed to it, and a heavy fire of muskets opened – We did not fire a shot, but gave a cheer [and] instantly ran on, jumped into the ditch and when we scrambled to the top the whole body of French were retiring or rather running into the sugar cane grounds in the rear of the battery, from which they opened a fire upon us.' When the order was given to set fire to the sugar canes, and with 'the sea breeze blowing, in an instant there was a blaze, this soon dislodged the French and a good many were killed in getting off'.[44] During the encounter, the Highlanders showed their customary impetuosity, drawing their swords and rushing forward against the French.

As the British troops continued their advance, the French kept retreating. By nightfall, twenty-five houses full of sugar cane 'were reduced to ashes and the whole beautiful face of the country was a smoking ruin. We halted for the night in some houses after throwing out the pickets, quite exhausted with our exertions. Our Attack had been so sudden and complete that we found plenty of provisions to regale ourselves with.'[45] The following day, Grant and some members of his company, together with others, were ordered to garrison Petit Bourg and a nearby redoubt. The only remaining town barring entry to Capesterre, to which the French militia had withdrawn, was Sainte Marie. 'This pass they had strongly fortified,' narrated Gardiner, 'but like the rest was ill supported.' Pursued into the town, the French 'quitted the Cannon and fled; upon which the [British] Detachment took Possession of the Town and next Morning broke into the Capesterre.'[46]

Stopped by heavy rains for a few days, on 18 April the British force was assembled at Sainte Marie, while the French withdrew to another entrenched position beyond the town. Once more the British chased the exhausted militia out of their last refuge. The next day the 2nd Battalion 42nd, together with the others, marched into Capesterre, one of the richest districts in the West Indies. The inhabitants, fearing the loss of their valuable crops, sued for peace. 'By private accounts,' Stewart of Garth later noted, 'it appears that the French had formed the most frightful and absurd notions of the "*Sauvages d'Ecosse*;" they believed that they would neither take nor give quarter, and that they were so nimble, that, as no man could catch them, so nobody could escape them; that no man had a chance against their broad-swords; and that, with a ferocity natural to savages, they made no prisoners, and spared neither man, woman, nor child: and as they were always in the front of every action in which they were engaged, it is probable that these notions had no small influence on the nerves of the militia and perhaps regulars of Guadeloupe.'[47]

On 1 May, Barrington and Moore signed Articles of Capitulation with their French adversary, Governor Nadeau du Treil. Soon afterwards, 'shops were opened and the Produce of the Country sold as usual, unmolested by the Troops in Camp or Garrison, where General Barrington caused the strictest Discipline to be observed.'[48] A relieving French force arrived too late to bolster further resistance. The small island of Marie Galante, which was not included in the surrender, capitulated on a show of force from the British. Over the next few weeks the men restored their health.

'We set out and marched through a piece of rich countryside covered with plantations and swarming with slaves, whose lot, tho' pretty well off as to clothing and food [were] treated very cruelly, unlimited power being in the hands of the masters,' observed John Grant.[49] After the campaign, Barrington, with the remaining regiments of the British army who had fought alongside the Highlanders, set sail for England.

The 2nd Battalion 42nd was destined for North America. On 2 July 1759 the seven companies left Guadeloupe under convoy of the frigate HMS *Rye*. During the campaign, from their original complement of over seven hundred men, they had lost nearly two hundred men through fever or in battle.[50] Reporting to his brother, the Duke of Atholl, Lord John Murray described how the newly raised 2nd Battalion 'have gained the greatest applause, and behaved like Veteran Troops'.[51] But Guadeloupe was not Martinique and, as Richard Gardiner on board the *Rippon* realised: 'The Attention of the Publick in England, on this Expedition, being totally swallowed up in the Idea of Martinico, the Conquest of Guadelupe, (as we were told) became little considered by the Generality of People.'[52]

Ticonderoga again: the 1st Battalion

While British forces had been consolidating Britain's position in the West Indies, the defeat the previous year at Ticonderoga had yet to be avenged. The new commander in North America was Major General Jeffrey Amherst; his star had risen after his victory at Louisbourg the previous year, at the same time as Abercromby's defeat at Ticonderoga. Pitt's plan was for Amherst to retrace the steps taken the previous year up Lake George to make another attack there and on Crown Point. Once the forts were taken, the army would continue northwards to join forces with James Wolfe; recently promoted Major General after distinguishing himself at Louisbourg, he had been put in charge of an expeditionary force which was to sail up the St Lawrence river to take Quebec. Included in Amherst's force was the 42nd's 1st Battalion.[53]

On 24 April 1759, the Articles of War were read. The men were ordered to embark on sloops to make the familiar journey up the Hudson river to Albany. While the grenadier and newly constituted 'light infantry' company, each of over 100 men, were allocated one sloop per company, the remainder were to be divided between the available sloops, with 'the Officers of the companys that are to be divided also in the sloops in proportion to the men'.[54] Since the 1st Battalion was still below strength, its numbers were supplemented by the inclusion of the three additional companies raised in 1757. They were now officially part of the 2nd Battalion, although they had not been required to join it in the West Indies. Prior to their departure, all company commanders were ordered to submit a list of women's names 'they intend should receive the allowance for provision this campaign and are to Recommend the first that came with the regiment from Europe if they are willing to be nurses to the General Hospital when required'. General Orders stipulated that they were not to exceed four per company.[55]

Throughout May preparations continued. While in camp at Albany, the non-commissioned officers and men were required 'at all times' to wear their plaids 'except when otherwise ordered'. If any of the women 'whatsoever pretends to pitch a tent near the regiment, the Quarter Master is to order it to be struck and burnt directly'.[56] Their progress towards Lake George was not easy. While heavy rain had made it easier to transport 'all matters up the Hudson as well as Mohawk rivers',[57] conditions were miserable for the men marching from Albany, and when the Highlanders arrived at Fort Edward on 7 June, 'on a most terrible wet blowing day', Amherst reported that the men were 'half-drowned; I sent them under cover to the great block house and sheds on the Island'.[58]

As always, provisioning the army remained a priority: 'if Pease are wanting, half the Quantity of Rice' was to be given, 'or a Pound of Bread or Flouer, or the third of a Pound of Pork, may be received in leu of Pease; if Pease and Rice are wanting, one Pound of Pork, or two Pound 12 Ounces of Flouer may be received in lue of Pease and Rice; if Pease, rice and Butter are wanting, one Pound and a quarter of Pork or three pounds and a half of Bread and Flouer may be received in lue of the Pease, Rice and Butter.'[59] Spruce-beer was to be brewed for the army, 'it is hoped, sufficient for the whole, and will cost the men but a very moderate price'.[60]

While they waited to depart, the 42nd's light infantry company was ordered to practise firing ball 'near the Royal Blockhouse on the other side of the river; the camp not to be alarmed ... whenever there are any firelocks that cannot be drawn, a report is to be made thereof.'[61] On 10 June, both the light infantry company and the grenadier company were brigaded with the other light infantry and grenadiers respectively. Leaving them behind, Francis Grant, appointed 'Colonel in America', marched with the rest of the Regiment, together with American provincials, rangers and Indians, to establish a post at Half-way Brook. Having put up a redoubt, heavy rain impeded further activity.

On 17 June, Amherst was recording that he had intended to send a battalion of the Massachusetts Provincials to join Grant, 'but the weather was so bad I stopped them. The roads broke our carriages very much.'[62] At the end of June he sent a detachment, under the command of Captain Allan Campbell – recently appointed major of the grenadier companies for the forthcoming campaign – on a fishing expedition designed as a ruse to 'draw the enemy in'.[63] Instructed 'to take one day's provisions and to go as light as possible', Campbell was told they were 'not only a covering party for the battoes but to attack any body of the enemie they may find'.[64] On this occasion, there is no record of whether they encountered the French or caught any fish.

In the third week of July – later in the year than the previous expedition – Amherst embarked his force of approximately 11,000 men at Lake George.[65] In addition to the 42nd, the 77th Highland Regiment was part of the expedition, as well as five other British regiments, many of whom had fought at Ticonderoga in 1758. On 22 July the army landed at the northern edge of the lake and proceeded at once to the sawmills, having encountered little opposition. In contrast to their determined defence of the fort at Ticonderoga in

1758, the French had decided to retire down Lake Champlain, leaving only a small detachment of 400 men at the fort. Their orders were to defend the fort as long as practical and then to retire. The following day, as Amherst informed Lieutenant Governor James DeLancey, they continued their march, 'the enemy on our approach having abandoned the lines, some got away in Boats, and a Garrison taken to the Fort, from whence their fire has hitherto done no Execution'.[66]

According to Captain James Murray, while Amherst's army was taking up position, the remaining French troops could not have kept up 'a hotter fire, for I dare say they fired ten thousand cannon shott & five hundred Bombs'.[67] With comparatively few men killed and wounded, as Amherst was about to commence his own bombardment, the remaining French set fire to the fort, making their escape to the Isle-aux-Noix, approximately eighty miles down the lake from Crown Point, at the northern end of Lake Champlain. While the fort at Ticonderoga was burning, Murray, badly wounded the previous year, wrote to his brother from the 'Camp at the Lines of Burning Theanderoga', assuring him: 'that I am in perfect good health.'[68] Allan Campbell wrote to his brother, Duncan Campbell of Glenure: 'I have the pleasure of acquenting you that this morning we have got possession of the lines at Fort of Ticonderoga with very little loss . . . I wish we had been as lucky last year.'[69]

At the same time, Captain Alexander Campbell, wounded the year before, was informing his father, 'our men behavd exceeding well'. Out of the total losses, which Amherst described as 'inconsiderable',[70] three private soldiers from the 42nd were killed, one sergeant and four soldiers wounded.[71] Having taken possession of the fort, Amherst at once ordered its burnt-out buildings to be repaired 'in the utmost Expedition. Each Regiment will immediately send a Return to the Major of Brigade of the Numbers of Carpenters, Masons and Lime Burners they have.'[72]

The sawmills also had to be made operational so that they could start milling much-needed timber. The next challenge was to take Crown Point, 'which is only fifteen miles from us,' Allan Campbell informed his brother, 'if we be able to take that I think we do wonders considering the Difficulty it is to get at them, but our Troops have such Confidence in the abilitys of our present General that they'll get over all Difficultys and with reasons, for he is as good a man as lives and a very Great Officer.' Once this had been achieved, Amherst and his army could sail across Lake Champlain to join Wolfe, who was continuing his advance up the St Lawrence river to Quebec. For the officers and men, the experiences of 1759 had been dramatically different from the previous year. 'Our affairs on the Continent of America have taken a very Favorable turn this year,' Campbell continued in his letter to his brother, 'and I hope we'll be able this campain to Clip the wings of the French so as not to be so troublesome to us as they have been formerly.'[73]

New York to Oswego: the 2nd Battalion

After fourteen days at sea, the seven companies of the 2nd Battalion 42nd reached New York harbour in mid-July 1759, gaining their first glimpse of the coast of North America and the 'fine city' of New York.[74] Compared with the searing heat of the Caribbean, the air was cooler, although more humid than a summer's day in Scotland. After so much illness, the priority was to bring the companies up to full strength, both numerically and physically. Arriving at Albany, the first event the soldiers witnessed was the burial of 'a gallant officer', Lieutenant Colonel Roger Townsend, one of the two officers killed during the successful assault at Ticonderoga.[75] Time was spent sorting out supplies and ordering new clothes. Each item the men received had to be accounted for in the Captain's Orderly book, including requirements for caps, belts, hatchets, swords, pistols and bayonets. On 3 August 1759, Captain William Murray, commander of the 2nd Battalion's light infantry company, recorded that he had received from the quarter master, Lieutenant Adam Stewart, 'twenty Five pairs shoes for the use of my company'. On the same day, Captain Alexander Reid received twenty-four pairs.[76]

Having stopped at Albany, the seven companies of the 2nd Battalion continued along the banks of the Hudson river, pulling their bateaux, crammed with baggage and provisions. Lieutenant John Grant recollected being tormented by mosquitoes while marching through 'splendid forests'.[77] News had already reached them of Amherst's almost bloodless victory at Ticonderoga, which meant that the way was open for the British to move towards Montreal down the St Lawrence river, 'that the Enemy may be pressed and attacked in every Corner, which cant fail of Success'.[78]

Instead of joining the 1st Battalion, as the soldiers expected, Amherst ordered the 2nd Battalion – placed under the command of Major Gordon Graham of Drainie – to retrace its steps to Albany, in order to march to Oswego on Lake Ontario. Having stopped at the Half Moon staging post to draw three days' rations, they travelled up the Mohawk river to Schenectady.[79] Here, as Grant recollected, the Highlanders learnt a severe lesson in survival. 'Highlanders have a great antipathe to Pork and it was the provision issued to the Regts for their march.' Anticipating that they could get alternative provisions at the next town, despite warnings they threw the pork away. 'Ignorant of the country they thought that they could still find other foods, to their consternation however the halt was made at night in an uncultivated spot where nothing could be got, they were ashamed to murmur but, next day when the halt was made for breakfast they could no longer hold out and sent a deputation to the Major telling the circumstances.' After ill-advisedly disposing of the pork, Grant was able to record that subsequently there was 'not a morsel of pork but was cherished with as much care as it had been before regarded with disgust'.[80]

At Fort Stanwix, those men still suffering from fever had to be left behind. Having stocked up with provisions, the diminished group proceeded onwards to Oswego, being caught, on at least one occasion, in a terrible storm: 'rain, wind, thunder and lightning – the scene was terrific, the boldest trembled – trees falling in every direction, deluge of rain'. Afraid of being attacked by the Indians, they took off their bonnets to protect their weapons, 'and thus bareheaded we bore the pelting of the pitiless storm, the water running out of our shoes'. According to Grant, the adjutant was nearly killed by a falling tree.[81]

By the end of August, the men arrived at Lake Oneida: 'we rowed all day along banks where solitude reigned and [there were] large pines and magnificent forest trees.' Landing at night, they had 'a serenade of the bullfrogs and wolves'. Going down to the river's edge and imitating the yelp of a dog, Grant recorded that 'all around rose such a yell as if Pandemonium had broke loose – we were almost afraid of them but as wood was not scarce had rousing fires – we were also obliged to keep a picket of one Officer and 50 men against the Indians.'[82]

Nearly six weeks after arriving in New York, the 2nd Battalion 42nd reached Oswego, where work had already begun on Fort Ontario. 'Each regiment and a regiment of the provincials had a Bastion and a curtain [wall] to finish', which, 'was unpleasant work'. They were 'always on the alert, as we expected to be attacked by the French and Indians'.[83] Food was scarce, their salt provisions occasionally supplemented by 'a duck and sometimes some fish'.[84]

Crown Point and back to New York: the 1st Battalion

While the 2nd Battalion remained at Oswego, preparing for the move northwards, the 1st Battalion was engaged in fort-building at Crown Point, where the French had blown up a part of the original fort before abandoning it.[85] Amherst had assigned about 3,000 men the task of constructing a huge pentagonal fort, with five bastions, enclosing barracks and a six-acre parade ground. Lieutenant Kenneth Tolmie, in charge of four companies of workmen at Ticonderoga the previous year, was put to work as an 'Overseer' of the project. This new fort was to be named Fort Amherst.[86] Ensign John Gregor, the grandson of the well-known Highlander 'Rob Roy' (MacGregor), was appointed Tolmie's assistant.[87] Once completed, it would be the largest British fort in North America.

At the same time, Amherst wanted to continue northwards across

Lake Champlain. The British plan was to destroy the fortifications erected by the French on the Isle aux Noix, whence the French had retreated after leaving Crown Point, leaving the way open to Montreal. Until a brigantine and a sloop were constructed to protect the boats required to transport the army, Amherst had to wait. While the men were kept busy working on the fort, detachments were sent out on a variety of missions. These included bringing up provisions, cutting roads, and mounting exploratory expeditions to map the surrounding areas. At the end of September company commanders were informed that 'as there is a prospect of going upon immediate service' they were to review 'their men & arms and ammunition to be particularly carefull in examining the Locks, and if anything is found out of order to be immediately put in repair. As it is necessary that each man should have two sufficient flints, a return to be made of what will be requisite to compleat them to that number, also of what ammunition there may be wanting.'[88]

To gain information about the surrounding terrain, Amherst had dispatched two regular officers, accompanied by a Ranger and four Indians, with a flag of truce to offer peace to the Abenaki Indians of St François – a settlement of forty wigwams and a small Catholic church, comprising the Saint François de Sales Mission in the village of Odanak. Situated on the eastern bank of the St Francis river, one of the southern tributaries of the St Lawrence, it was approximately 150 miles from Crown Point.[89]

When, in early September, Amherst received news that the two officers had been captured by a hunting part of 'St Francis' Indians, 'this insult exasperated the General to such a degree, that he immediately determined to chastise them with a severity equal to the offence.'[90] He therefore ordered a detachment of over 200 men, commanded by Major Robert Rogers – whose Ranging School at Fort Edward specialised in training men in the less conventional methods of warfare – to destroy 'the St François Indian Settlements and the French settlements on the South side of the River St Lawrence.'[91] Rogers and his men were forbidden 'to use any retaliation against women and children; in a spirit truly becoming an

English enemy'.[92] Among the volunteers were several Highlanders from the 1st Battalion 42nd.[93]

In early September 1759, while Wolfe was besieging the French on the Plains of Abraham just outside Quebec City, and Amherst was still hoping to join him, Rogers's force was sailing down Lake Champlain. The weather was cold and they had to make fires every night, hoping that they did not reveal themselves to the French.[94] After less than a week, Rogers had to send back one-fifth of the force due to injury or illness. 'A man of the Royal Highlanders and one of Montgomerys were brought in by seven Rangers,' Amherst recorded on 19 September, 'this makes 40 men returned of Rogers, two officers included, the two men wounded by a firelock accidentally going off. The Royal Highlander dyed soon after he was brought in.'[95]

Leaving their boats concealed near Missiquoi Bay on north-western Lake Champlain, the men had a long march in swamp and wilderness to reach St Francis. Having reached the west bank of the St Francis river, they crossed. As Rogers related, by putting the 'tallest men up the stream, and then holding by each other, we got over with the loss of several of our guns'. Since these could not be spared, the best swimmers stripped off their clothes and dived for them.[96] After twenty-two days, Rogers and his reduced party reached the village.[97] At dawn on 4 October the attack began: 'the carnage [was] terrible,' recollected Private Kirkwood, 'hardly any of the enemy escaping; those who the flames did not devour, were either shot or tomahawk'd.'[98] As the contemporary historian Thomas Mante related: 'In this short period the English killed at least two hundred Indians, and took twenty of their women and children; but brought away but five. The rest were permitted to go where they pleased. Five English captives were likewise delivered from slavery, and taken under the protection of their countrymen.'[99]

Having accomplished his mission, Rogers began the return journey. Desperately short of provisions and pursued by the French and Indians, the party split up into small groups. Extreme hunger drove them to take drastic measures, which, for some, meant resorting to eating their prisoners.[100] A detachment including Lieutenant George

Campbell – Allan Campbell's nephew, wounded at Ticonderoga in 1758, serving with the 80th Light Infantry – was, at one time, 'four days without any kind of sustenance', related historian Mante. When they came across some of their dead comrades 'not only scalped but horribly mangled', they fell upon them 'like Cannibals, and devoured part of them raw'.[101] Less than half of the men out of the original force made it back to Crown Point. Legend fuelled the macabre stories of cannibalism and how much loot they had carried away from the stricken village.[102]

Meanwhile, instructions were being issued for the army's departure north. The 1st Battalion 42nd was assigned twenty-four boats for the journey across Lake Champlain.[103] The Colours of the Regiment were to be left with the guard of the fortress 'after Retreat Beating'. The surgeons and surgeons' mates were to go with their respective corps, having furnished a list of the sick left behind to the Director of the Hospital.[104] 'The enemy if any should appear is to be received with fixed bayonets.' Finally, the men were instructed to be ready to embark 'on the first notice and to carry as many tents with them as are necessary for their number'.[105] Compared with the 77th, which numbered 609 of all ranks, the 1st Battalion 42nd numbered 536 men of all ranks, around half its full strength. The remainder were detailed either to man the warships or to continue with work on the forts at Ticonderoga and Crown Point.[106]

On 11 October 1759, Amherst and his army were ready to depart. During the intervening time, the necessary naval escort, the brigantine *The Duke of Cumberland* and a sloop the *Boscawen*, had been fitted out. Once embarked on the lake, the men were instructed that 'great care' should be taken to row in turns, 'and those that do not row go to sleep that the armie may be able to proceed night & day if it is found necessary'.[107] Assembled in four columns, the advanced guard was in front in whale boats. The first column of grenadiers and light infantry were on the right, the second column, the 'Royal Brigade', including the 42nd, were next to them. Next in line were the artillery stores, while on the left the fourth column consisted of the remaining British regiments.[108] Both *The Duke of Cumberland*

and the *Boscawen* sailed in front to challenge any French sloops in the vicinity. Also in front was a huge raft (radeau), the *Ligonier*, from which it was hoped the other ships would take their bearings. Unfortunately, as Amherst noted in his journal, during the night 'some of the R. Highlanders mistook & followed a light that they saw either on the Brig or Sloop'. By dawn they had advanced well in front of the rest of the fleet. Before long, Amherst heard gunfire and realised that a skirmish was taking place on the lake. The 42nd had come into contact with some French sloops, which they at first mistook for British ships. Lieutenant Alexander Mackay was taken prisoner, together with a sergeant and ten men.[109]

The calm weather did not last. By the following day 'it blew a storm and quite contrary wind', with the water was running 'as high as some seas in a Gale of wind'.[110] An encounter between the *Cumberland* and *Boscawen* and the three French sloops which had fired on the 42nd resulted in the loss of all three, two of which the French had scuttled, the other being run aground. As Amherst later learnt, the decision to scuttle was mainly due to the captured Mackay's description of the British fleet as being larger than it was. 'That upon report of Said Officer, greatly magnifying our naval Strength, they had Come to a Resolution not to Strike a Stroke but to Sink or Drive their Vessels on Shore and then to Abandon them.'[111] Despite this success, Amherst was unable to make further advance, because the wind continued to blow and the water was choppy, making 'the Lake impassable for boats'. For three days they waited for the storm to abate.[112]

In the meantime, news reached Amherst that, after a three-month siege, Quebec had fallen a month previously on 13 September and Wolfe had been killed. The French commander, the Marquis de Montcalm, Britain's indefatigable opponent at Ticonderoga in 1758, had been hit fatally in the stomach by a musket ball. On 18 September the surrender was signed and the British took control of the city. Soon afterwards, with the onset of the cold weather, the Royal Navy had to withdraw because of the danger of pack ice. As Amherst realised, there could be no immediate follow-up and he would have to withdraw to Lake Champlain. Before starting the return journey, the troops were ordered onshore to make fires and warm themselves. 'I ordered the Troops back to Crown Point to finish the works there as much as possible before we go into Winter Quarters, and we sailed and rowed back to Ligonier bay where we lay all night.'[113] By 21 October, Amherst and the army were back in Crown Point, the grenadiers and light infantry 'at work at their Forts, and the Fortress was going on pretty well'.[114]

On 10 November 1759, in honour of the King's 76th birthday, the regiments in North America 'drank the Kings Health, the Prince of Wales & Royal Family, & Prosperity to His Majestys Dominions in America with a Volley to each, and at Gun firing the Army was under Arms'.[115] A prisoner exchange took place, which resulted in the exchange of Lieutenant Alexander Mackay and his boatload of Royal Highlanders, taken prisoner by the French sloops on 12 October. Towards the end of the month, with frost on the ground, Amherst ordered all remaining regiments, minus the provincials, who had either already deserted or been sent home, to move south. Five companies of the 1st Battalion 42nd were garrisoned at Ford Edward, while individual companies were stationed in the various forts between Fort Edward and Albany to the south and Fort George to the north.[116] At the end of November the 2nd Battalion 42nd arrived in Albany from Oswego. They were joined by the three additional companies, stationed with Amherst's army at Crown Point, bringing the 2nd Battalion up to its full complement.

Winter in North America came 'so suddenly', Lieutenant John Grant wrote, that some of the soldiers 'had their hair and bodys frozen to the ground in their tents'.[117] Grant was one of the more fortunate ones who boarded at a Dutch house. 'We had our parties at our quarters every evening, gambling & dancing and we got stout and Madeira.'[118] Among the several new appointments, James Murray was given command of the 2nd Battalion's grenadier company, 'which Ld John was so good' to have offered him. But, he said, it had cost him 'a deal of trouble' in forming it. Not only were the men 'the smallest body of men ever I saw', but he complained that Albany was 'as extravagant a place as ever I was in'.[119] In Scotland the demand for men to fight in America had not passed unnoticed. James Murray's brother, John Murray of Strowan, had estimated that in the past three years, with the raising of additional companies and new Highland regiments, the Atholl estate alone had furnished between 700 to 1,000 men, 'and there really seems but few middle aged men in the country'. Most recently, he said, three hundred men had been raised for the Royal Highland Regiment 'to make up for the slaughter of Ticonderoga'.[120]

5.

Reduction of the Universe

We have Troops brave enough to attempt the reduction of the Universe.

Lieutenant Alexander Farquharson, 1762[1]

Montreal 1760

1760 signalled Britain's conquest of Canada. After surviving the harsh winter, both battalions of the 42nd Royal Highland Regiment were to be part of Amherst's downriver attack on Montreal from Oswego. Another contingent was preparing to leave Quebec to attack Montreal upriver. A third line of approach was to be along the Richelieu river from Lake Champlain. Stationed in Albany throughout the winter, the 2nd Battalion reached Schenectady at the beginning of May.[2] By mid-June the 1st Battalion was encamped across the Mohawk river. Since the greater part of the journey to Montreal was to be by water, all regiments had to travel with their own heavy boats, dragging them with difficulty in low water, or floating them in the shallow creeks. When they reached Oswego, the ground had to be cleared to pitch their tents. No tree was to be left standing within the encampment 'or so near to it . . . that if the winds should blow them down they can hurt any of the men'. Work also had to be resumed on the fort: 'so essential for the future protection of this country that no time may be lost in effecting it, before the troops are assembled here, at which time the whole will proceed over the Lake, for the reduction of Canada'.[3] In the hot weather those working on the fort did not have to begin work until 2 p.m.[4] On no account were the men 'to drink the water of the swamps but are to get it from the Lake or River which is known to be good water'.[5] All candles had to be out by 9 p.m. and 'no spirituous liquors' could be sold.[6]

By the beginning of August, Amherst had assembled a formidable body of troops at Oswego. Consisting of over 10,000 regular and provincial regiments and over seven hundred allied Indians, it was the largest of the three forces converging on Montreal. Travelling in several hundred bateaux and whale boats, they were to be escorted by the *Mohawk* and *Apollo* sailing vessels. Before embarking, the Indians requested the *Apollo* to be renamed *Onondaga*; when a flag with the image of an Onondagan Indian was run up, the 42nd fired a volley and Amherst broke a bottle on the vessel's bows.[7] On 7 August the advance guard set off, the main body of the army, under Amherst's command, leaving three days later. An early prize was the capture of the French brig *L'Outaouaise*, which Amherst renamed *Williamson*. Lieutenant Richard Sinclair of the 2nd Battalion 42nd was put on board 'to command with a proper crew'.[8] After a day's sailing, Amherst's force reached Fort Lévis. Located on an island in the St Lawrence river, it had been built by the French after the British capture of Fort Niagara in 1759 to guard the 'back-door' approach to Montreal. On 23 August, the attack on the fort began; after a cannonade lasting two days, the French ran out of ammunition and requested a parley. Amherst demanded immediate capitulation, promising that the occupants of the fort would be treated honourably. Unable to enjoy the spoils of war, some of the Indians returned home.[9]

Having taken possession of the fort, renamed Fort William Augustus, the onward journey along the St Lawrence river involved negotiating several dangerous rapids. 'On a sudden I saw the boats ahead of me . . . disappear,' described Lieutenant John Grant, 'and felt the suction of the water, immediately divined the cause, I jumped up, called "a Rapid" and to keep to the right, & to pass the word.' Despite his warning Grant's boat 'whirled about and filled with water – the casks floated & one struck me a blow in the side that almost stunned me. We however got down safe,' the men using camp kettles to bail the water out. Thanks to 'timely notice', he recalled, the boats behind steered a different direction and also 'got down safe'.[10] Writing his journal, Amherst was distressed to record one of the boats carrying men 'of the 1st Batt of the R Highlanders in coming down the Long Seau [Long Sault] & keeping too near the shore was staved & a Corporal & three men drowned'. Several other boats overturned, with the men 'struggling in the eddies below the falls, and calling piteously for help'.[11] Captain Thomas Stirling later wrote to his elder brother William, heir to the baronetcy of Ardoch in Scotland, saying that 'to see fellow creatures floating on the wrecks and you passing them not being able to assist would pierce the most obdurate heart'.[12]

'General Amherst's Army suffered more from the rapid currents & rocks in the River St Laurence than from any opposition we mett with,' Captain Alexander Reid, John's younger brother, informed their father, Baron Reid of Straloch. 'These are not so terrible as they were represented to be, but bad enough in all conscience, & God keep me from returning that way.'[13] To prevent further loss, Amherst 'marched covering Partys on the Shore'.[14] 'We all approached the shore and landed,' recalled Grant, 'leaving some men to direct the boats down the rapids, most the regular boats got safe.'[15] Reflecting in his journal, Amherst noted: 'The Rapids cost us dear, notwithstanding every Corps had a Pilot . . . We lost 84 men, 20 bateaus of Regts, 17 of Artillery, 17 whaleboats, one Row Galley, a quantity of Artillery Stores & some guns that I hope may be recovered.'[16]

After regrouping in the waters below the rapids, Amherst's still impressive army rowed towards the island of Montreal. 'Colours displayed, drums beating, pipes playing, the River was like glass.' As soon as they reached La Chine, on the southern side of the island, the men disembarked. 'The 42nd Regt was immediately ordered to advance. We pushed along at double quick along a narrow path bounded by brushwood and only four abreast. We were afraid of a surpize attack from Indians,' Grant recorded. 'It was 9 miles and in less than two hours we had debouched from it and formed in the plain in front of Montreal.' Expecting to be attacked at any moment, they remained under arms until sunset. 'We had no tents and spent but a miserable night, our bodies heated by our rapid march – and the hot day and the chilly night dew . . . threw some of us with fever.'[17]

Amherst's plan of converging on Montreal from three directions had the desired effect. To the soldiers' surprise, the French governor-general, the Marquis de Vaudreuil, surrendered without a shot being fired. 'I believe never three Armys, setting out from different & very distant Parts from each other joined in the Center, as was intended, better than we did, and it could not fail of having the effect of which I have just now seen the consequence.'[18] As a result, the immense terrain of Canada, stretching across the top of the continent of North America, would eventually fall under the sovereignty of Britain. 'You will no doubt be pleased to hear that our Army arrived here and that with little or no loss, we made ourselves masters of all Canada,' wrote Lieutenant Alexander Farquharson to Mr Jacob Feneik at Albany. 'This seems to be an agreeable fine country and deserves all the trouble it has cost in getting of it.'[19] 'Before this reaches you you'll probably have the agreeable news of the total reduction of Canada,' Alexander Reid continued in his letter to his father. 'It is a very valuable acquisition: &, if confirmed to Britain, it will open up very rich sources of trade.'[20]

Alexander Reid's brother John was also corresponding with their father, informing him that they had 'at last put a period to the War in this part of the world by an entire conquest of Canada. The campaign has been excessively fatigueing to that part of the army immediately under the command of General Amherst, particularly to the first Battalion of our Regt, which has been under my command during the last winter, and the greatest part of the campaign.' Reid was keen for preferment and his father had already been petitioning the Duke of Atholl for a lieutenant colonelcy for his son. Fearing that he might never gain command of the Regiment, 'which ought to be the point in view of every man of spirit', he explained to his father why 'I have been so very earnest with you concerning a purchase.' If successful, he pledged that he would 'in gratitude ... do everything in my power to serve His Grace during the whole course of my life'.[21]

Although Reid was unsuccessful in his request, he at least lived into old age. His younger brother, Alexander, had barely two more years to live.[22] Others were disappointed at missing out on the chance to distinguish themselves in a better-known theatre of war. After twelve years in North America, Captain Thomas Stirling was hoping the Regiment would be sent to Germany, 'for I am heartily tired of this Country as is every officer in it'. As he wrote to his brother: 'Long may Peace reign here, for sure God never intended any war should be carried on by any other besides the natives for the soldiers are wrought like horses & the officers can acquire no honour in a Country where as the New England people says, every Tree is a fort and every man a Gen[era]l.'[23]

Meanwhile, Amherst, promoted Military Governor of Canada, was making the necessary dispositions for the army to survive another winter. Both battalions of the 42nd were billeted in Montreal, 'a place of some consequence', observed John Grant.[24] 'As we are to continue here for the winter, I will have occasion for my baggage,' Farquharson wrote in his letter to Jacob Feneik, who had been looking after his belongings. 'You will therefore please give the bearer the large chest & small box I left at your house with the bag & mattress.'[25] Unlike Quebec, which had been destroyed during the bombardment, Montreal's buildings were untouched and provided more comfortable accommodation. In early November, unaware that King George II had died on 25 October, they celebrated the King's seventy-seventh birthday.[26] Up to their knees in snow, to ward off the cold the men wore leggings of 'greencloth like the backwoodmen . . . We were badly off for vegetables, they have none but onions, garlic and cabbages, and but little of them.'[27] Beer was the most common drink and the men enjoyed dancing. 'But priests forbade the young women from joining the quarters where the officers were, but still they shirked the Priests.' With few books, time was 'very heavy'.[28]

Before the next campaigning season, Amherst had to heed instructions from the new King, George III, whose accession was proclaimed on 17 January 1761.[29] His grandfather, George II, had been on the throne of Britain for thirty-three years, the longest-reigning monarch in England since Queen Elizabeth over a century earlier, outliving his eldest son, who had died in 1751 after being struck by a cricket ball. For most of George II's reign, William Pitt and the Whig faction had dominated foreign policy, forcefully pursuing wars abroad. George III, aged only twenty-two, did not favour his grandfather's old adviser. Instead he had a new favourite, James Stewart, the Earl of Bute, who urged a less belligerent foreign policy. The King's directive to Amherst was that the regiments in North America should be reduced in numbers. Although Amherst was notified on 20 March 1761, the order was to be retroactive to 25 December 1760.

Thus when the two battalions of the 42nd reassembled after the winter, they could expect changes in their ranks. Since the grenadiers and light infantry companies were going to be reduced, the surplus men would be sent back to the 'bonnet' companies.[30] The swords of the supernumerary grenadiers were to be lodged in the Regimental store 'and the men are obliged to keep the scabbards in repair'; 'the supernumerary tomihawks, powder horns and shot bags' belonging to the light infantry were also to be put in store.[31]

Those who remained in the Regiment could look forward to new clothing: 'The Taylor to be employed in altering the men's wistecoats according to the pattern of last year, but to make them longer in the body and the button holes broader in order to correspond the better with the lace on the new cloathing.' Those who had spare waistcoats were to have theirs altered first, 'afterwards as the season grows warmer', those with one waistcoat 'may more conveniently spare them, as they will be altered in one day. Such men who have no sufficient wiste-coats of any kind, must wait till the Arrival of the Cloathing in order to have their old coats converted into wistecoats.'[32]

Crown Point 1761

By early spring the vegetation of Canada appeared 'in full vigour'.[33] On 4 June, in honour of the new King's birthday, there was to be a grand review; the 'm[o]urning' that the officers had been wearing in respect of George II's death the previous October was 'to be left off'.[34] In the first contemporary mention of feathers being worn, officers were specifically ordered 'to provide themselves with black feathers for their bonnets, which for the future [are] to be Regimental'. Non-commissioned officers were to wear bearskin tufts.[35] At noon, on the day of the review, the Royal Highlanders were to fire three volleys in response to 'three Royal Salutes from the Artillery in honour of his Majesty's birthday'.[36] The 1st Battalion 42nd was to be formed up one hour in advance, 'the men to be in their new clothing, to be powdered and perfectly clean and well dressed, the arms to be bright as possible and the brass to be well scoured'. Since there were too few new plaids to show the Battalion off at its best, the 'Centre Rankmen' of each company were to wear the old plaids, with the new plaids worn by the front and rear ranks. Yet again the order was repeated for the officers to use black feathers for their bonnets 'in order to be uniform with the Battalion who are to have Tufts'.[37]

After the parade, together with other regiments, the 42nd received marching orders: 'the regiment will embark in their Battoes [bateaux] at the rate of nine men in Each Battoe, and will have as many artillery boats as they can.'[38] Provisions and baggage were to be loaded 'at day light and the officers to have their baggage ready pack'd this evening, that they may be no hinderance on that account'. The boats, they were ordered, 'are always to row two in a breast where the river will admit and are to keep as close to one another as possible'.[39] Having crossed the St Lawrence river, the soldiers would have to march for three days to reach the Richelieu river, before proceeding onwards in larger boats to Crown Point. Twenty-five men were assigned to each bateau with provisions for four days. As an escort, they were accompanied by a row galley and the sloop *Boscawen*, loaded with heavy equipment, including tents. Realising that those in the sailing ships would have a less tiring journey than those in the battoes, the companies drew lots.[40] Francis Grant, the Lieutenant Colonel, led the small fleet in a captured French schooner, followed by the battoes.

Once at Crown Point, they had to continue work on the massive fort. 'We worked for six weeks at the Fort, very unpleasant on acc[oun]t of the heat,' noted Lieutenant Grant. 'We were forced to be out at 5 o'clock.'[41] Strict discipline had to be maintained. No wheelbarrows, tools, timber 'or anything belonging to the Fort' was to be removed without permission. 'Firing of Arms in the Camp is Contrary to orders.'[42] All men not on duty were to be employed 'from 5 o'clock till sun sett' in clearing the encampment of logs and tree stumps so that the men could pitch their tents.[43] 'When the men refuse the Task offered them, the officers and non-commissioned officers as well as the Overseers are not to suffer these men to sit Down.' Furthermore, no one was to work 'in big Coat while the weather is good – as complaints have been made this morning that several of the men quit their work almost as soon as they begin'.[44] At every location, muster rolls, listing who was absent on leave or due to illness were rigorously kept and checked by the 'Muster Master'.[45]

While at Crown Point, a check was also made on the number of women accompanying the Regiment, the maximum permitted being three per company, 'such as are most serviceable to the men in washing'.[46] They were to be encamped 'out in front of the Regiment near the Lake'.[47] All the 'useless women of each Corps' were to be sent 'down the country'.[48] Boats would be made available to carry them to Ticonderoga. 'If any of them presume to Remain after this order, or Return to Crown Point,' they could 'depend on being Drum'd out of the Regiment'.[49] Those who 'absconded' and did not depart when they were supposed to 'must depart tomorrow morning at sun rising with there baggage, their husbands to be acquainted that if they again disobey, that their names will be put in orders discharging them for ever from the Regiment'.[50]

Officers had been advised to send away 'by every opportunity' any unnecessary baggage. 'The men also to be requested of the same thing, and to be assured that from henceforth they will not be allowed to have a chest or a Box on the march or more Baggage than they can conveniently carry in their knapsacks.'[51] An order was also passed for the Quarter Master of the 2nd Battalion 42nd 'to build imme-diately a Regimental Hospital for the use of their sick according to the dimensions that will be given by the Surgeon'.[52] As sustenance during their stay, they could expect 'fresh beef on one day and salt pork for 2 days'.[53]

After six weeks working on the fort, the 2nd Battalion continued the journey to Albany, passing by Ticonderoga and Saratoga.[54] Before the 1st Battalion could leave, a final effort was made to complete the fort, the soldiers encouraged to be 'Diligent at Work' and informed that the reason for bringing so many troops to Crown Point 'is solely to Execute the work of the Fort. The most Essential Service they can do their King and Country during their stay there is to give their Labour Cherefully.'[55] On 12 July the 1st Battalion was ordered to be ready to march the following day. Tents were to be struck 'at gun firing'. The men were to be dressed in kilts and their old clothing, with all their most valuable 'things packed up this evening which they are to carrie on their backs'.[56] Since part of the journey was by road, wagons were needed to transport the tents, baggage and the sick. Once they reached Albany, they could proceed in sloops, which would make the journey quicker.[57]

Glorious Successes 1762

Throughout the hot humid New York summer and autumn of 1761, both battalions of the 42nd were encamped on Staten Island in New York harbour with ten other regiments.[58] Francis Grant, Lieutenant Colonel of the Regiment for the past six years, was appointed Commandant of the Staten Island camp.[59] Discipline was strict and there were numerous court martials for petty offences: 'no officers or soldiers were to stir off the Island without Colonel Grant's Especial Leave in writing and Guards are to be posted at the different Ferrys for that purpose – In order to preserve health of the troops, the Regiments to be out at exercise twice a day.' No soldier 'on any account' was permitted to rob the garden or an orchard; the men were also prohibited from using fences for firewood, 'as they may depend on being severely punished and make good the damage'.[60] The order was given with good reason. John Grant's landlord had complained to him that 'soldiers used to come and steal his vegetables'. Frequent patrols were sent round the camp and women's encampment and all soldiers 'whome they find disorderly or in liquor' were to be confined so that they could be appropriately punished. 'They are also to see that all the Lights both in the men and womens tents are extinguished before 9 o clock at night.'[61]

Amherst had already received orders to send a force back to the

West Indies, but first the dangerous hurricane season had to pass. The army, consisting of some 8,000 men divided into five brigades, was under the command of Major General Robert Monckton, Wolfe's second-in-command, and who had been seriously wounded at Quebec in 1759.[62] Francis Grant was put in command of the 2nd Brigade, which included the two battalions of the 42nd, mustering over 650 men each. On 19 November, the fleet set sail.[63] 'We sailed on smoothly enjoying the change of climate,' noted John Grant, who recorded that 'a tremendous hurricane' delayed the transport he was in, separating it from the rest of the fleet.[64] Arriving at Bridgetown, Barbados on Christmas Day 1761, over the next few days the soldiers practised boat loading and unloading drills.

A late arrival was the transport in which John Grant was travelling. Having been given up as lost, 'some hopes of promotion were blighted by our appearance'.[65] A minor inconvenience was that they could only enjoy their Christmas dinner 'the day of our arrival at Barbados'.[66] Mindful that the men were campaigning in extremely hot conditions, Monckton issued a General Order, instructing the commanding officers to order 'the linings to be ript out of the men's coats, the lapels taken off and the skirts cut shorter. The General recommends to them, providing their men with something that is thin, to make sleeves for their waistcoats, as the troops may be ordered to land in them.'[67]

In early January, the fleet of eighteen ships, under the command of Rear Admiral George Rodney, set out for Martinique. 'It is a fine picturesque Island,' noted Grant, who had not been part of the attempt to take the island in 1759.[68] Monckton disembarked at their former landing place, near Cas de Navires. As previously, their first objective was to take Fort Royal, defended by the two fortified hills, Morne Tartenson and Morne Garnier. At daybreak on 24 January, the attack was made on Morne Tartenson. As Brigadier Hunt Walsh, Lieutenant Colonel of the 28th Foot and commander of the 5th Brigade, explained, since the 95th Foot, which was to have joined his Brigade, had not yet arrived from South Carolina, 'the first battalion of Royal Highlanders was ordered to me'.[69] Morne Tartenson was swiftly taken, but 'no decisive result could be obtained without gaining possession of the sister eminence of Garnier, which,' noted historian Forbes, 'from its loftier elevation, enabled the enemy holding it to annoy and oppose the British forces.'[70]

Three days later, while the women were washing clothes and preparing an evening meal, 'about four o'clock in the evening, the French attacked our Light Infantry and the 1st Brigade,' related Walsh.[71] John Grant recorded that three French shells burst over their tent lines and 'we saw our adjutant who had been at head-quarters rushing down the hill and calling "Turn out Highlanders."' Immediately taking hold of their muskets and powder horns, they were confronted by a 'large body of French' on the opposite hill – Morne Garnier. 'We instantly gave the Indian Halloo, part of our Backwoods aquirements,' which Grant believed encouraged the soldiers of the 60th who were in the immediate firing line to stand their ground.[72]

The precipitate action by the French in coming down from Morne Garnier to engage the British advance posts gave the British force an advantage. When the French began to retire 'The Highlanders, drawing their swords, rushed forward like furies,' related the *Westminster Gazette*, 'and being supported by the grenadiers under Colonel Grant and by a party of Lord Rollo's brigade, the hills were stormed, the batteries were seized and numbers of the enemy, unable to escape from the rapidity of the attack, were taken.'[73] Having gained possession of both Morne Tartenson and Morne Garnier, the British turned their firepower towards Fort Royal. Before starting the attack, the French governor, Louis-Charles Le Vassor de La Touche, *sieur* de Trouville, sued for peace.

Some of the fighting to take Martinique had been fierce and there were a number of casualties. Lieutenant George Leslie of the 42nd's 2nd Battalion – wounded on Morne Tartenson in 1759 – was again wounded storming the same hill. Captain James Murray, wounded in the leg at Ticonderoga in 1758, was shot in the chest. Unable to write one of his regular letters to his brother, he deputed Lieutenant Sandy Farquharson to write on his behalf, describing

how 'during a warm attack on the enemy's battreys and entrenchments', James Murray had received a wound 'with a musquet ball,
which entered at the left breast and was cut out below the right
shoulder, & consequently pass'd thro' the Lungs. The surgeons and
every body else were at first of opinion that the wound was mortal,
but on proper examination it has happily turn'd out to be quite
otherways.' Informing John Murray of Strowan that 'he is just now
in a fine way, & in great spirits', Farquharson urged Murray's brother
not to have any 'uneasiness on his account, or believe any vague
reports that you find mentioned in the public papers or otherways. He is certainly out of all danger, and in a little time will be
able to walk about.'

Farquharson, commissioned as an ensign into one of the three
additional companies raised in 1757, aged about nineteen, described
'the glorious successes we have had since our landing on this Island,
which I hope we will soon be entire masters of'. He also uttered the
enduring sentiment, so essential for soldiers who daily faced the
prospect of their own mortality: 'We have Troops brave enough to
attempt the reduction of the Universe. Nothing can or dare withstand us.'[74] James Murray went on to make a good recovery, 'considering the badness of the wound'.[75] Invalided home to Scotland, he
spent the next six years on sick leave. 'He was never afterwards,
however, able to lie down,' recorded Stewart of Garth, 'and during
the thirty-two years of his subsequent life, he slept in an upright
posture, supported in bed by pillows.'[76]

While Monckton's forces were preparing to assault St Pierre, in
the north of Martinique, French emissaries arrived to arrange terms
for the surrender. The death toll for the expedition was estimated
at 500 officers and men killed and wounded. Of these, fifteen men
of the 42nd died; eighty-four were wounded, including Captains
James Murray and Thomas Stirling. Major John Reid, so anxious
for promotion after the fall of Montreal, had been struck twice, but
the impact of one almost fatal bullet near his waist had been stopped
by 'a bunch of keys and some Spanish Dollars' in his pocket.[77] Of
the seven wounded lieutenants, Peter Grant, the Gentleman

Volunteer, who had taken the quarrelsome George Maclagan's place as an ensign in 1756, and had also been wounded at Ticonderoga, died soon afterwards. John Reid's cousin, Lieutenant John Robertson of the 2nd Battalion, had been wounded storming the same ridge on Morne Tartenson in 1759 and was wounded again.

After Martinique, Captain James Stewart of Urrard, whose 'Orderly books' were to provide future generations with detailed information on the life of a soldier in North America, sold out to Lieutenant James Abercromby, the son of the unfortunate General Abercromby ridiculed as 'Nabbercrombie' after the defeat at Ticonderoga in 1758.[78] Death through illness took a severe toll. 'The yellow fever raged in the town and many of the men and officers died of that terrible disease,' recorded John Grant, who also fell ill. 'There was 8 officers ill in the house with me, 4 of them died.' Describing himself as cured 'by vomits of tartar & milk', he was so 'reduced' that he could not move for a month. Ordered to go as an 'invalid' to North America, Grant preferred to chance his luck and recuperate on board ship.[79]

Havana: 'Pearl of the Antilles'

They fought boldly in Havana,
Light-stepping, agile, purposeful.
A smooth musket, arrayed with blades,
With a belt on every man's side;
Fearless in the face of mortal danger.[80]

While British soldiers had been engaged in the campaign against Martinique, George III and his counsellors had been planning another operation: the conquest of Havana, capital of the island of Cuba, controlled by the Spanish since Christopher Columbus claimed the island for Spain in 1492. During the intervening time it had become 'the greatest emporium of the Western hemisphere and the depot of the precious metals of Mexico and Peru before their final dispatch to Old Spain'.[81] In early January 1762, following news of a secret alliance between France and Spain, Britain declared war on Spain. Since then preparations had been under way for the campaign against Havana (as well as against Manila in the Spanish islands of the Philippines). It fell to the King's uncle, the Duke of Cumberland, to select the operation's commander. His choice was thirty-eight-year-old Lieutenant General George Keppel, Earl of Albemarle, Colonel of the 3rd Dragoons. Having been Cumberland's aide-de-camp at Fontenoy in 1745, he had remained loyal during Cumberland's period of disfavour at the end of George II's reign.[82] Second-in-command was Major General George August Elliott. According to Lieutenant John Grant, when Albemarle arrived at Fort Royal with reinforcements from England, seeing how ill so many of the men were, 'he began to be alarmed and he enquired into the state of the medical staff,' who he discovered were 'chiefly London apothecaries and the mates were merely their apprentices'.[83]

Admiral Sir George Pocock, with over forty years' service, was in command of the British fleet. Second-in-command was Albemarle's brother, Commodore the Hon. Augustus Keppel. Another brother, the Hon. William Keppel, was placed in charge of siege operations with the rank of acting major general. By the end of May 1762 a considerable armada – described by Grant as 'one of the greatest expeditions that ever sailed from England' – had assembled off north-west Hispaniola within reasonable striking distance of Cuba. Over the next few months, reinforcements came from the West Indies and North America.[84]

To gain an element of surprise, Pocock chose to approach Cuba by a more direct, less well-known but more dangerous route known as the 'Old Channel of Bahama', which would enable the fleet to reach Cuba more speedily from the north, with the trade winds at their backs. 'We knew of no large ship that had ever taken it,' recorded Captain David Dundas, Albemarle's ADC, 'and certainly no such fleet as ours had ever attempted it.'[85] At night, during the passage, a signal was hoisted to shorten sail and all the fleet closed in. Admiral Pocock, 'like a hen', recollected Grant, 'gathered us under his wings'.[86]

Their passage through the channel took a week, and 'not one vessel was lost, the only accident that occurred was the running down of one small sloop . . . It was never found out who did it, but the vessel was missing and no accounts was ever heard of her.'[87]

By early morning on 6 June, the fleet was off the coast of Havana, anchoring 'off the mouth of the harbour about a mile from the land'. At first sight, the island appeared 'mountainous and but little cultivated'.[88] With a fine deep-water port – 'a noble inner basin where more than a thousand ships might anchor, sheltered from every wind' – Havana, under the command of the governor, forty-six-year-old Don Juan (de) Prado Malleza Portocarrero y Luna, was protected by a bastioned wall around the city limits and large forts on both sides of the harbour entrance. La Punta, the smaller of the two forts, protected the western side, while El Morro, overlooking the city and harbour – and which the British called the Moro – guarded against an attack from the sea. 'We had started with very inaccurate and indistinct intelligence, and no tolerable plans of the place,' Dundas noted in his Memorandum. 'An English trader who had long lived there, a sensible man, but who had never looked with a military eye, was the only person we had who possessed a personal knowledge of the place and country.'[89]

From what they knew, it was decided to land either to the east at Coximar (Cojimar) or to the west at Chorera. Since El Morro had such a commanding position of the city and harbour, the Chief Engineer advised that it should be taken first before attempting to take the town, a view with which Albemarle concurred.[90] One advantage was that the heights of La Cabana were unfortified. As Dundas also recorded: 'All accounts agreed in the perfect dominion that the heights of La Cabana had of the town, of the command that El Morro gave those heights, of the small dimensions and imperfect state of El Morro as a fortress, but to none occurred or were known the peculiar difficulties that must attend the attack of it.'[91]

As the men prepared to land, Lieutenant Sandy Farquharson, on board the *Felicity* transport, made a will. His elder brother, George, had already died at Ticonderoga. There was no paper to hand and so he wrote on the blank page of a small 'Hutchins' almanac, a popular guide for soldiers containing gossip, advice and humour, as well as astronomical and horological predictions, and in which Farquharson had been keeping a brief diary. 'I desire in the case of my death, my shirts and whatever else of my clothing is found, may be delivered to William Simpson my servant. My other effects to be disposed of for the behalf of my family or for the pay of what debts It may be found to be due.' On the flyleaf he wrote a quotation from 'Spring' one of James Thomson's celebrated set of four poems, *The Seasons*: 'Fruits and blossoms blush'd / In social sweetness on the self-same bough.'[92]

Having dispatched Commodore Keppel to take sufficient ships to protect the transports, Pocock sailed to the west to make a diversionary landing at Chorera, enabling the main landing to be made between the Coximar and Bacuranao rivers, about six miles to the east of El Morro.[93] About midnight on the night of 6/7 June, the troops were put into boats, rowing to shore at first light. Among the first to be sent in were some 300 Highlanders.[94] An intense naval bombardment reduced the onshore defences to rubble. Surprised by the strength of the attack, the Spanish deserted their redoubts. 'We landed to the eastward of the town without opposition,' recorded John Grant. By the afternoon of 7 June, the whole force had landed and encamped for the night. 'We halted and bivouacked that day in low hilly ground covered with brushwood. The next day at daylight we marched forward in the direction of El Morro. We met with no opposition, the occupants having fled from the few scattered houses into the towns.'[95] Reconnaissance parties were sent out 'and having found a footpath which led through it to the open country at the distance of 2 and a half miles, a broader communication was immediately prepared for our march next day'.[96]

The first objective was to take up position at the village of Guanabacoa, through rough countryside, about six miles to the north, which required cutting a road 'through the woods to a large plain, at the extremity of which the above village is situated'.[97] Assembled in two corps, the army advanced inland, sighting for the first time the 'full and noble view of the Havana, and of the extensive fertile and open country that surrounds it'.[98] As they marched, the Spanish cavalry attacked. 'In an instant [they] were in front of the troops, who, with the greatest steadiness and presence of mind had faced about, wheeled forward, were in 2 lines, and in readiness to give them a fire of 500 light infantry at a distance of 60 yards,' recorded Dundas. 'This checked their career, they ceased to advance, the troops reloaded, recommenced a fire, and the enemy went back as fast as they came.'[99] Having beaten off this first attack, Albemarle's force occupied Guanabacoa, prior to operations against El Morro. Having reconnoitred the fort, the force marched forward, encamping in the woods between the Coximar river and the fort. A detachment of troops was left at Guanabacoa, where there were supplies of cattle and vegetables.[100] There was no fresh water: the only available supplies had to be carried from Coximar.

To defend El Morro, the Spanish had begun to construct a redoubt on the unfortified heights of La Cabana. Before they could complete it, Albemarle marched the main army from Guanabacoa and camped in the woods, preparatory to an attack. Plagued by mosquitoes, John Grant was on piquet duty the night before the battle. 'The night was lovely . . . one could scarce imagine that the stillness around was to be soon disturbed by the thunder of war.'[101] Before daybreak he was rudely awakened by an orderly, informing each company to prepare for an assault on the unfinished redoubt of La Cabana. 'As we advanced some shots were fired from the redoubt, which tore the ground but without effect. We had just reached the dangerous pass and there was a moment's hesitation, a dash was made by the head of the column and the same moment a salvo from the Moro sent 5 poor fellows beyond the column, shattered corpses, no time was to be lost.' Rushing onwards before the Spanish could reload their guns, Grant found that the ground was 'tangled and difficult . . . The Spaniards now changed their mode and kept on a running fire, so that we all had to pass the ordeal. I never made better use of my legs, which were much lengthened by the hiss of a twenty-four pounder over my head.'[102]

While they were advancing Grant heard a drummer call out from behind that he had been shot. With the only firing coming from the front, Grant ridiculed him on the grounds that the bullet 'must have passed thro' my body to reach him'. After the firing had finished, the drummer came 'lurching into the redoubt. I again taxed him with falsehoods' but he pulled down his breeches 'about the hip and showed it was true. Upon examination, the ball had made a circular move around his body and remained under the skin. I cut it out with a penknife; upon looking at my own dress, I found the mark of a ball right through my kilt a little above the knee.'[103] Unable to withstand the British attack, the Spanish retreat from La Cabana was 'so rapid that they were out of fire and under the Moro before we could reach them'.[104] Having successfully taken the redoubt, the British had a commanding position not only of El Morro, but also of La Punta, the harbour and the city of Havana.

The next objective was the great fortress of El Morro, commanded by Captain Don Luis (de) Velasco.[105] As Albemarle observed, the fortress was protected by the gulf of a dry moat cut out of solid rock, more than sixty feet deep, and, in places, more than 100 feet wide. Only a knife-edge of rock had been left to keep out the sea. At first Albemarle determined to destroy El Morro by naval bombardment, at the same time as launching attacks from the land batteries. His brother, the Hon. William Keppel, was given charge of operations. Preparations in the boiling heat, with insufficient water, were arduous. At dawn on 1 July, the naval bombardment began, but El Morro remained relatively unscathed, while the Royal Navy ships suffered considerable damage to masts and rigging from the Spanish batteries. On the second day of the bombardment, the British 'Grand Battery' consisting of eight powerful twenty-four-pounder guns and two mortars caught fire. Since it had not rained for two weeks, the dry timber used to construct the emplacement also caught fire. Without water, the best the soldiers could do was to attempt to extinguish it by piling on dirt.[106]

Short of fresh water and living on a diet of salted pork and rum, disease spread rapidly, and the Spanish remained hopeful that if they could exhaust their adversaries through fever and fatigue, the hurricane season at the end of August might cause the British to abort the attack.[107] Even Albemarle, able to sleep in more comfortable quarters on board ship, was suffering from malaria. 'The hardships which the English troops sustained in forwarding their approaches against the Moro, are altogether inexpressible,' observed assistant engineer Thomas Mante. 'It was necessary to bring them water from a great distance; and so scanty and precarious was this supply, that they were obliged to have recourse to water from the ships. Roads of communication were to be cut through thick woods, and the artillery was to be dragged for a vast way over a rough rocky shore. Several of the men on these services, dropped down dead with heat, thirst, and fatigue.'[108] Already an estimated five thousand soldiers and three thousand seamen were 'laid up with various distempers'.[109] By the third week of July, the surgeons and their mates of both Battalions of the 42nd were listed as 'Ill in Camp'.[110] To make matters worse, the expected reinforcements from North America were delayed, and so Albemarle was obliged to withdraw the troops stationed at Guanabacoa to help in the attack on El Morro.

After nearly three weeks, the fortress had been sufficiently battered to enable an approach to be made. Since El Morro had been built on solid rock, the normal procedure of digging trenches was impossible.[111] The only option was to build a line of breastworks and barricades to the edge of the ditch under El Morro's right bastion, where the narrow ridge, preventing the sea from flooding the moat, crossed the ditch. On 20 July Army sappers began to mine the right bastion's wall. Watching events from Havana, Governor Prado realised the need to counter-attack. But although a few thousand Spanish soldiers climbed the hills in an attempt to disrupt the British positions, they were repulsed. The 42nd were amongst the defending force, Keppel himself marching with them.[112] After a brief truce to bury the dead, 'the firing was renewed on both sides with the utmost vigour,' recorded Mante. 'This was the last effort made by the city for the relief of the Moro, which yet held out with a sullen resolution, and made no sort of proposal to capitulate.'[113] By the end of July, the mines were ready to be sprung and a narrow breach in the bastion was made. Keppel lost no time in ordering an assault across the breach which the Spanish could not resist.[114] Don Luis de Velasco was mortally wounded, and 'fell offering his sword to his conquerors'.[115] His second-in-command, the Marquis (de) Gonzales, was killed while attempting to rally his men.

Although sickness was still raging through the British army, Albemarle could not claim victory until the city of Havana was taken. This meant expanding the beachhead eastwards at Chorera, where Albemarle moved his headquarters from Coximar. In addition to remounting the guns on El Morro, guns were mounted on La Cabana to bombard the city and the fort at La Punta. These operations were assisted by the belated arrival, at the end of July, of over 3,000 reinforcements from North America. On 11 August, British guns opened fire on the city of Havana. Having already cut the city's main water supply, concerted efforts were made to block the roads leading into the city. One company of the 2nd Battalion 42nd was assigned the task of blocking one of the routes. Positioning themselves in a large sugar house as a barrack, as related by Grant, they took position 'to the westward of the town on the main road to prevent provisions entering'.[116]

Short of food themselves, the soldiers were also sent on foraging expeditions. The fleeing inhabitants had left a number of mules so, Grant noted, they had 'no lack of cavalry'. On one excursion, he noticed some beehives; while he was searching in a nearby house for a suitable container for the honey, some Spanish soldiers appeared. Dropping his prize of honey, Grant ran to the front door. 'I saw six armed men close to it, so quickly returned back, but saw a man within the house levelling a musket at me. He fir'd and the house was filled with smoke. I instantly thrust in his direction with my fusee which had a small bayonet attached.' Realising that his bayonet had found its mark, having pinned his opponent to the wall, 'whilst his face glaring with rage and pain was close to me, I wrenched my piece from him by a violent effort and darted out of the house'. This was not the end of his adventures. 'New danger awaited me.' Two other men were firing at him. 'Unless I could clear a deep ditch at the end of the house which surrounded the garden, I was a dead man or a prisoner.' Having successfully cleared the ditch, Grant rejoined his party of men. They proceeded to shoot several cattle grazing in a nearby field, using the mules they had purloined to transport the carcasses back to their position. 'All this was very agreeable to a youth.'[117] Although, during their forays, they were instructed not to plunder 'in a wanton manner but merely to take necessaries', Grant could not resist taking some 'excellent shirts' and some 'stacks of chocolate'.[118]

Having made a desperate attempt to withstand the British bombardment on the city and the smaller fort, La Punta, the Spanish could not compete with superior British firepower. The surrender of Havana and the island of Cuba to Britain was signed on 13 August 1762.[119] Compared with Spanish losses, whose men were either shot, bayoneted or drowned while attempting to escape, there were relatively few British battle casualties. 'This important conquest', recorded Mante, 'cost the English, in killed, wounded, and prisoners, including those who died, two thousand seven hundred and sixty-four men.'[120] What had decimated their ranks was 'putrid fever'. The shortage of water had also taken a severe toll.[121]

Six soldiers of the 42nd were killed and thirteen wounded during the campaign; those who died through illness were estimated at nine officers, two drummers and seventy-one soldiers, their decline having begun on the voyage to Havana when, 'being close stowed and the heat being intense, their spirits sunk'. Then, 'during the long siege in that sultry climate, the labour was so great and so constant that it was impossible to be supported; and the greatest number died of mere fatigue.'[122] 'The poor Highlanders died in numbers,' Albemarle wrote to Pocock on 8 August. 'I wish you could spare a frigate to send them to North America; it would perhaps be the only means of saving the remains of these poor people.'[123] Sandy Farquharson, who had had the foresight to write a will, had died of fever on 25 July, aged twenty-four. George Leslie, still recovering on a hospital ship from the wounds received at Martinique, died of fever in early

August. Captain Alexander Reid, John Reid's brother, had also died at the beginning of August. Whereas the two surgeons recovered, the chaplain, Lachlan Johnston, died of fever. As an interim, Adam Ferguson, now Professor of Natural Philosophy at Edinburgh University, was reappointed in Johnston's place, although he did not go to America. Ewen McIntyre, 'Piper Major' of the 2nd Battalion, who had stood playing the 'Menzies Salute' before the first assault on Ticonderoga in 1758, also died.[124] Amongst the senior officers, John MacNeill was promoted Major when, in early July, Gordon Graham succeeded as Lieutenant Colonel to replace Francis Grant, who was promoted Colonel of the 90th Foot. When, MacNeill died of fever on 15 August, just after the capitulation, Alan Campbell of Barcaldine succeeded in his place.

Once Albemarle had overseen 'the articles of capitulation punctually performed', the defeated Spanish embarked for Spain.[125] The 42nd Royal Highlanders were ordered to New York. 'The 17th, Royal Highlanders [42nd] and the 77th are so reduced by sickness,' Albemarle informed Amherst, 'that I am obliged to send them to a northern climate in hopes that the change of air may recover them.'[126] Between 7 June and 18 October, from an army of 16,000, over a third had died.[127] 'It will be scarce credited by future ages, that an army of Europeans persisted,' Mante recorded, 'for two months and eight days together, in the siege of a fortress situated in the hottest climate of the torrid zone, and during the hottest season of that climate.'[128] The value to the British Crown of conquering Havana was estimated at three million pounds. While Albemarle's share of the approximately £737,000 allotted to the victors amounted to just under £123,000, private soldiers received just over £4, or eleven Spanish dollars. Battle Honours for *Guadaloupe 1759*, *Martinique 1762* and *Havannah* were not granted until 1909.[129]

For all the Highlanders' gallantry, some ill-feeling against the Scots remained in England. On 8 December 1762, the diarist James Boswell, recently arrived from Scotland, was at Covent Garden watching Isaac Bickerstaffe's new comic opera *Love in a Village*. Before the Overture, two Highland officers entered. 'The mob in the upper gallery roared out, "No Scots! No Scots! Out with them!"' Seeing them pelted with apples, Boswell described how his heart warmed to his countrymen, and his Scotch blood 'boiled with indignation'. Jumping up on the benches, he roared out: 'Damn you, you rascals!' Approaching the officers, he found that they belonged to 'Lord John Murray's [Highlanders], and that they were just come from the Havana. "And this," said they, "is the thanks that we get – to be hissed when we come home."' According to Boswell, the English 'soon gave over' their taunts. Joining his countrymen in the gallery he was 'really well entertained' by the opera.[130] Despite such personal insults, there was perhaps some compensation in the accolade given by the rising political theorist Edmund Burke: 'It [Havana] was without question the most decisive conquest we have made since the beginning of the war, and in no operation were the courage, steadiness, and perseverance of the British troops and the conduct of their leaders more conspicuous.'[131]

They were distinguished in America,
And did not depart from their custom:
They were spectacular and victorious,
Fierce, fiery, dealing expert blows,
Full of flames, sparks and lightning,
With lead and gunpowder,
Making the Indians repentant,
Just as the presence of the sun
Makes dew disappear from the grass.[132]

6.

Every Tree is Become an Indian

Driving the rout like a northern wind,
Or a hawk, is the speed of the kilted men . . .
Who will deliver the serene peace
From the Mountain to them.[1]

Serene Peace

While British soldiers were recovering from the exertions of 'reducing the universe', British politicians were negotiating peace terms. Having wrested prized possessions from France and Spain and assured British naval supremacy, the rising cost of the war encouraged the prime minister, the Earl of Bute, to reach a settlement with Britain's erstwhile enemies. In November 1762, preliminary peace terms between Britain, France and Spain, with Portugal's agreement, were signed in London. The people could well rejoice at the end of seven years of war, but for officers whose livelihood depended on fighting for King and Country, peace meant potential reduction onto half-pay. Although they were under no obligation to leave the Army and could well find an alternative commission in another regiment, years sometimes passed between commissions, resulting in severe economic hardship.

In North America, General Jeffrey Amherst had been assessing the future of the 42nd Royal Highland Regiment, spending the winter in familiar quarters in and around Albany. 'The numbers of the Royal Highland Regiment being greatly reduced by Deaths,' he wrote on 2 October 1762 'I am come to a Resolution to Draft the Men of the 2nd into the 1st Battn and to Send the Officers and non-commissioned officers Home in Order to Recruit.' Those whose 'private Affairs' required their presence in Britain could request 'leave to exchange with any officer of the 2nd that may be willing to Remain . . . No Officer is to take a Servant with him that belongs to the Regiment.'[2] At the end of 1762, the depleted 2nd Battalion departed for home in convoy, together with twenty-four women and seven children. Lieutenant Colonel Gordon Graham of Drainie also went on leave to England. During Major John Reid's absence, command of the 1st Battalion devolved onto the junior major, Allan Campbell of Barcaldine.[3]

On 10 February 1763, the Treaty of Paris was signed. By its terms, most of the conquered territories were restored to their pre-war administrators, although Britain made some significant territorial gains. Since France wished to retain control of Guadeloupe, Louis XV was prepared to cede Canada to Britain and any claims France might have to territory east of the Mississippi river which included the Ohio valley; France retained Martinique and Saint Lucia, but ceded Tobago, Grenada, Dominica, Saint Vincent and the Grenadines, the chain of islands lying between Saint Vincent and Grenada. Spain gave Florida to Britain (later receiving New Orleans and French Louisiana from Britain) in exchange for Cuba's return. Britain also regained control of Minorca. Other clauses related to British and French possessions in Africa and India.

Plans were also being made for a further reduction of the British Army. Instead of undertaking further recruitment, as the officers of the 2nd Battalion anticipated, on 11 March 1763 George III signed 'orders for disbanding the 2d Battalion of Lord John Murray's Regt of Foot'. Care was to be taken, 'that each Non Commissioned Officer and private man hereby to be disbanded be permitted to carry away with him his cloaths, belts & knapsack which he now wears'. Private soldiers, corporals and drummers were to be paid three shillings for their swords. Non-commissioned officers and privates were to receive fourteen days' subsistence 'as of Our Royal Bounty to carry them home, payment is to be made of the same to each of them respectively out of such monies as shall be advanced for that purpose'.[4] The order, received while the officers and non-commissioned officers were stationed in Guildford, was addressed to Lieutenant Colonel Gordon Graham. At the same time a number of officers were ordered to be reduced.[5] News travelled slowly across the Atlantic and it was not until a few months later that the full impact of disbanding the 2nd Battalion was felt in North America.

Pontiac's War 1763

As soon as peace terms were announced, British forces began to occupy the military posts garrisoned by French troops in the Ohio valley. The only post they could not immediately reach was on the east bank of the Mississippi river, south of St Louis, near present-day Prairie du Rocher, Illinois, where in 1720 the French had built Fort de Chartres. The most direct route to the fort lay through Indian territory, controlled by the powerful confederation of Ten Indian Nations, whose lands were centred in Illinois and around the Great Lakes. Just as the British were preparing to send an expedition to Fort de Chartres, they were faced by rebellion, later known as 'Pontiac's War' or the 'Conspiracy of Pontiac', led by Pontiac, Chief of the Outewa (Ottawa) and Chippewa Nation. Angry at Amherst's policy of reducing the amount of gunpowder and ammunition allocated to the Indian population, Pontiac and his fellow chieftains hoped to revive the more lucrative French–Indian alliance by driving the British out of the forts they were occupying. Believing that their adversaries were 'weak and enfeebled' by the war against the French, all Indians were invited 'to take up the Hatchet, or to rise and attack the English all at the same time'.[6]

The offensive began by attacking posts between Fort Pitt, built near the site of the old French Fort Duquesne, on the junction where the Allegheny and Monongahela rivers joined the Ohio. In early May, Pontiac laid siege to Fort Detroit on Lake St Clair, blockading it with between 500 and 1,500 Indians, 'which is a vast body to keep together, considering they wholly subsisted by precarious and uncertain hunting'.[7] John Rutherfurd, a seventeen-year-old, captured by Chippewa Indians in May 1763 while on an expedition to investigate the lakes and rivers around Detroit, was warned by his captors that the fort was so blockaded 'that nobody could come in or go out, and that in a few days there would not be an Englishman left in it alive; whereupon I found it absolutely necessary for my safety to affect to relish their savage manners, and put on an air of perfect contentment, which I had often heard was the way to gain the affections of the Indians'. Every day, he recorded, 'there were captures and scalps brought into the camp'. Having been traded back and forward between the Chippewa and Ottawa Indians, he later escaped and was commissioned into the 42nd in New York in 1764.[8]

At the beginning of June, Amherst ordered the Swiss-born 'soldier of fortune' Lieutenant Colonel Henry Bouquet to take command of a force made up of the light infantry companies of the 17th, 42nd and 77th Regiments.[9] Since Reid was still absent, command of the three regiments (later reduced to two, when the 17th was dispatched to relieve Fort Detroit) was given to Major Allan Campbell. 'They shall proceed Directly to Execute such Orders as I shall think proper to give Major Campbell,' Amherst directed, 'according to the Advices I may receive from you, of the further proceedings of the Savages.' Judging the force 'more than Sufficient to Quell any Disturbances the whole Indian Strength could Raise', he was still thinking 'this Alarm will End in Nothing more than a Rash Attempt'.[10]

Amherst was mistaken. With attacks on several other posts including Presqu'Isle on Lake Erie, he was forced to admit to Bouquet a few days later that 'the Affair of the Indians appears to be more General than I had Apprehended'.[11] Campbell was therefore ordered to march at once, taking with him three days' provisions. No time was to be lost in retaking the captured garrisons 'and securing them so that we may keep Entire Possession of them', Amherst wrote to Bouquet, whilst suggesting that if necessary he should proceed towards Fort Pitt 'that you may be the better enabled to put in Execution the Requisite Orders for Securing the communication and Reducing the Indians to Reason'.[12] By 19 June, Amherst had decided that the entire 42nd Regiment 'should advance to Philadelphia, to be available, if necessary'.[13]

Worse news was to come. On 22 June, emboldened by their success, the Delaware and Shawnee Indians laid siege to Fort Pitt. By the end of June, Bouquet had reached Carlisle. 'There appears to be few Savages yet on these frontiers, but every Tree is become an Indian for the terrified Inhabitant,' he informed Amherst.[14] By mid-July, Allan Campbell, who had returned to Staten Island to take command of the remaining companies of the 42nd, had rejoined Bouquet at Carlisle.[15] Proceeding onwards, Bouquet's 'little army', as the detachment of over 400 men was called, reached Fort Bedford. While they were there, Campbell heard the news – publicised in

March in London – that the 2nd Battalion had been disbanded. Those to be reduced included Campbell himself, as well as two captains and nine lieutenants, all of whom were on active service in America. Writing at once to Amherst, he explained that the reduced officers 'think it hard upon them, to be employd in an Extensive and fatiguing Service, and only to have half pay'. In what manner, he asked, are they 'to be Subsisted, if continued in the Service', since, as he said, the Paymaster had been ordered not to advance them any more money. 'The officers of the regiment have beg'd of me to lay before your Excellency the great Expence they have been at, in providing horses and Equiping themselves for this Service, to make them the usual allowance of Ball and forage money.'[16] News of the reduction reached Lieutenant Henry Timberlake on the same day he received his commission. Having travelled to New York to see Amherst, he returned to Virginia 'after spending between twenty and thirty guineas to no purpose'.[17]

Having made his complaint, Campbell had no alternative but to follow orders and continue on the march. It took five days to get the wagons over the Allegheny Mountains, reaching Fort Ligonier, fifty-five miles from Fort Pitt, at the beginning of August. With no news coming from Fort Pitt because all the agents Bouquet had sent out had either been killed or obliged to return, Bouquet ordered the provisions and supplies to be unloaded and stored at Ligonier. The flour necessary for the onward journey was packed into bags, and loaded onto over 300 packhorses.[18]

From Bushy Run to Muskingum

By 5 August, having passed through Fort Ligonier, Bouquet's 'little army' had reached Edge Hill, twenty-six miles from Fort Pitt and a mile from the Bushy Run Station. Accounting for his movements to Amherst, Bouquet described how he had intended to halt at Bushy Run to refresh the men and horses, before continuing onwards. 'But at one o'clock this afternoon, after a march of 17 miles, the Savages suddenly attacked our advanced guard, which was immediately supported by the two light infantry companies of the 42nd Regiment, who drove the Indians from their ambuscade & pursued them a good way.' When the Indians returned to the attack, Bouquet and his forces made a general charge to dislodge them from the heights, 'in which attempt we succeeded, without obtaining by it any decisive advantage; for as soon as they were driven from one Post they appeared on another, till, by continual Reinforcements, they were at last able to surround us and attacked the convoy left in our Rear'. Marching back to protect the rear, 'the Action became then general, & though we were attacked on every Side and the Savages exerted themselves with uncommon Resolution, they were constantly repulsed with the Loss. We also have suffered considerably.'[19] More than sixty officers and men were killed or wounded.

The action was not conclusive and they expected 'to begin again at day break'. Lest worse befall in their next encounter with the Indians, Bouquet had thought to write to Amherst: 'I fear insurmountable difficulties in protecting or transporting our Provisions being already so much weakened by the losses of this Day in Men, and Horses.' The situation of the wounded, he said, was 'truly deplorable'. Above all, he wished to acknowledge the 'constant assistance' he had received 'from Major Campbell, during this long action', as well as expressing admiration 'of the cool and steady behaviour of the Troops, who did not fire a shot without orders, and drove the Enemy from their Posts with Fixed bayonets. The conduct of the officers is much above my Praises.'[20]

In preparation for the next day, Bouquet and the advanced guard took up position on a 'commodious piece of ground', leaving the wounded protected by the bags of flour they had brought with them. 'The Savages surrounded our camp at the distance of about 500 yards, & by shouting and yelping quite round that extensive circumference thought to have terrified us with their numbers.' Although the British soldiers stood firm, Bouquet realised how difficult it was to inflict sufficient losses on the Indians, 'who always gave way when pressed, and appeared again immediately'. The soldiers were also very tired from the action the day before, 'and distressed to the last Degree by a total want of water, much more intolerable than the Enemy's fire'. Unable to move, lest they expose the convoy of wagons '& our wounded to all a Prey to the Savages, who pressed upon us on every side', they had to stand their ground. Bouquet therefore planned a manoeuvre 'to intice them to come close to us, or to stand their ground when attacked'. Ordering two light infantry companies to move backwards as if withdrawing, he ordered another company and the grenadiers of the 42nd to move up in support.

'This manoeuvre Succeeded to our Wish,' he related. 'The Barbarians mistaking these motions for a retreat, hurried head-long on, and advancing upon us with the most daring intrepidity galled us excessively with their heavy Fire; but at the very moment that certain of Success, they thought themselves Masters of the Camp, Major Campbell at the head of the two first companies Sallied out, from a Part of the Hill they could not observe, and fell upon their right Flank. They resolutely return'd the Fire, but could not stand the irresistible shock of our Men, who rushing in among them, killed many of them and put the rest to flight.'

After the battle 'scarce a Scalp was taken, except by the Rangers & Pack Horse Drivers'. Having made litters for the wounded and destroyed the flour they could not carry with them 'for want of Horses', the army marched 'without molestation' to the camp at Bushy Run. 'After the severe Correction we had given the Savages a few hours before, it was natural to suppose we should enjoy some Rest; but we had hardly fixed our camp when they fired upon us again: this was very provoking!' Dispersed by the light infantry, Bouquet concluded his long dispatch by expressing the hope that they would be 'no more disturbed, for if we have another action, we shall hardly be able to carry our wounded. The behaviour of the troops on this occasion speaks for itself so strongly, that for me to attempt their Eulogism would but detract from their merit.'[21]

With his letter, Bouquet enclosed a return, listing their losses. The 42nd had suffered most, having had killed two officers and twenty-seven men; two officers and thirty-two men were wounded, compared with the 77th, who had five soldiers killed and seven wounded.[22] Among the items lost by the 42nd alone, Allan Campbell recorded: fifty-seven plaids, 267 shirts, 114 pairs of shoes, eleven pairs of hose, two haversacks and three canteens, costing a total of £316 and 5 shillings. Lest any blame be attached, Bouquet certified that, on the first day of the action at Edge Hill, 'I ordered the Troops to drop their packs to charge the Enemy, and that after the Engagement which lasted till night, I was informed that many of the packs could not be found. As that loss did not happen by the fault of the men, who are much distressed by it, I humbly recommend the sufferers to His Excellency the commander in chief.'[23]

The battle at Edge Hill was perhaps more successful than Bouquet at first realised. Having broken off the siege to attack Bouquet's force, the Indians did not return to Fort Pitt, and although they 'kept whooping round us with their odious death halloo', recorded Private Kirkwood, 77th, they did not appear again, 'being terrified with their defeat'. Two days later – on 10 September – Bouquet reached Fort Pitt. Amherst later described the battle, later known as the Battle of Bushy Run, although it had taken place at Edge Hill, as 'a fine Check to the Savages'.[24] 'No Troops under the Sun could Behave better than the Little Army under Colonel Bouquet has Done.'[25] Writing to Bouquet, he conceded that the convoy they were accompanying was 'too Essential an Article to be Left Behind, otherwise the pursuing of the Savages when once they gave way, would have been the surest method of making the Advantage you had gained Decisive'.[26]

Having reached Fort Pitt, Bouquet instructed Allan Campbell to return to Ligonier with a detachment to escort the convoy of stores and provisions, which had been left behind, and to bring it safely to Fort Pitt. 'The Women, Children and useless People are to go under your Escort, and you will please to forward them, from Ligonier to Fort Bedford under the Escort of thirty militia men.' They were to be given provisions as far as Fort Bedford, 'but no meat which is very Scarce'. Once at Ligonier, 'not a moment' was to be lost in putting the flour into Bags, 'leaving only Six thousand Weight of it for use of that Garrison. Every Part of the Waggon's Load that can possibly be carried by Horses must be taken from the Waggons, such as Powder, and Lead &c.' Finally Campbell was instructed to return by 'the best Road, and carry Tools to clear & repair it so as to bring the Waggons on'. He was also told that 'it would be proper to have our dead buried, a duty we could not pay them, for want of Tools. If any broken Arms should be found, they might be put in the Waggons.'[27] In terms of continuing the fight against the Indians, to Bouquet's 'great mortification' he had to tell Amherst that he could not continue onwards to relieve Presqu'Isle, on Lake Erie. Not only were the men tired after the 'fatigue of long marches' and having to sleep on the ground without tents, but several had fallen sick.[28]

At the same time, the impact of the reduction of the 42nd was being felt. The day after Bushy Run, Amherst had written to Bouquet from New York giving further instructions regarding the officers to be reduced: 'You may allot the Eldest according to the new Establishment, it being His Majesty's pleasure that the Youngest Officers of each Rank shall be reduced Without regard to the Battalions to which they belonged, as the 42nd Regt has always been Considered as one Corps tho' divided into two Battalions.'[29] Bouquet was also ordered to complete the 42nd by the 'best men you can find from the 77th'. Each company was to consist of forty-five men, with permission for an extra two supernumerary men.[30]

To compensate for the stoppage of four pence from the soldier's pay, Amherst pointed out the 'several advantages a soldier may now have in this Country, by cultivating some Ground where he may happen to be in quarters, or Providing himself with Fish, Game etc.'[31] One of those who was 'entertained' from the 77th into the 42nd was Private Robert Kirkwood.[32] John Peebles, the only Volunteer with the 77th, 'dangerously wounded' at Bushy Run, gained a commission in the 42nd as an ensign.[33] Having informed Bouquet that his wound 'was Still in a precarious condition', he requested permission to go downcountry to recuperate, lest 'the Severity of the Winter may be much prejudicial to my recovery'.[34]

Instead of being reduced onto half-pay, Allan Campbell would have liked to purchase the senior major's commission from John Reid, who had still not returned to the Regiment. On 17 August, he wrote again to Amherst, requesting either to be relieved of 'a most fatiguing, disagreeable and expensive service', or to be allowed to take Reid's place.[35] Amherst responded sympathetically: 'I sent to Lt Colonel Reid and Acquainted him with the contents of your Letter, which I really think is in part very Reasonable & Just . . . He will by this occasion, give you an Answer; so that I have only to say, – that whatever may be agreed upon between yourselves, regarding the Majority; I shall Readily come into, as I wish to serve you both, as far as the service will permit me.' Amherst also wanted to assure Campbell that 'I can't suppose the officers can be considered as on Half pay, until the Reduction actually takes place, being persuaded His Majesty would not Allow any of His Officers to suffer by their being necessarily employed on Service; so that you cannot be said to be Doing Duty on Half pay.' Amherst concluded his long letter by assuring Campbell that 'the commendations which Colonel Bouquet has given of the whole Corps & particularly of yourself in the late actions give me the highest satisfaction as such behaviour reflects great honor on his Majesty's Arms & ought upon Every occasion to be Encouraged.'[36]

Reid, who soon after the 1759 victory at Ticonderoga had married a wealthy American of Irish descent with substantial landholdings around Crown Point, was busy organising his personal affairs and was quite happy to resign his commission. But, as Campbell informed Amherst, he wanted him to pay the difference 'usually given from the half for full pay, which I cannot possibly do, as I have not the money'. In addition, Campbell considered that his health was 'so bad at present' that he did not feel able 'to undergo the fatigue that the service of this country necessarily requires'. He therefore chose 'to retire on my half pay, being perfectly happy that my small service has met with your Excellency's approbation which is the thing in the world I most Desired'. Campbell returned to Britain in late December. In 1770 he transferred to the 36th Foot, ending his service with the 42nd which had begun with his capture at the Battle of Prestonpans in 1745.[37]

At the same time as countering Pontiac's rebellion, the British government in London had been discussing boundaries. On 7 October

1763, by Royal Proclamation, George III agreed to demarcate Britain's new North American Empire, having 'taken into Our Royal Consideration the extensive and valuable Acquisitions in America, secured to our Crown by the late Definitive Treaty of Peace'. By the terms of the proclamation, a boundary was created – known as the 'Proclamation Line' – along the Appalachian Mountains, demarcating Britain's thirteen American colonies and the land ceded to Britain by France but on which the Indians lived, known as the Indian Reserve.[38] All settlement west of the line was prohibited 'on Pain of our Displeasure' without 'our especial leave and Licence', which effectively gave the British Crown a monopoly on any further westward expansion. Although the aim was to effect a supervised move westward, and stabilise the relationship between the American colonists and the Indians, the colonists objected; not only because they resented the monopoly which the terms of the Royal Proclamation gave to the British government to grant land, but also because a number of people had already settled west of the Proclamation Line.[39]

By the beginning of December, Bouquet had made the necessary disposition for the soldiers to go into winter quarters at Fort Pitt, Ligonier, Bedford and Carlisle. The winter of 1763 in North America was 'excessive hard', recollected Kirkwood. 'The snow falling deep, we were obliged to shovel it away every night to make our beds and fires; every man being provided with a hatchet to cut wood, and a shovel for the snow.'[40] During this time, following Adam Ferguson's second retirement on 15 June 1764, a new chaplain was appointed: James Maclagan, author of the rousing song 'On the Highlanders departing for America', written when the Regiment left for North America in 1756. Since first composing the song, he had added several verses.[41]

It was not until September 1764 that Bouquet began to assemble the necessary troops for a further expedition against the Indians. The objective was to advance against them in a show of force inside the 'Indian Reserve', penetrating into the heart of Ohio and if necessary destroying the Indians' villages unless they agreed to surrender their European prisoners. Setting out at the beginning of October, Bouquet's force of approximately 1,500 men, drawn from the 42nd and 60th, and from the Pennsylvania and Virginia militia, moved slowly westwards. Second-in-command of the expedition was Major John Reid. 'We cross'd the river Alleganey, then proceeded down the Ohio about 30 miles,' recorded Kirkwood. When the Indians 'saw that our force was considerable, and that in all probability we would destroy their country entirely, all their courage forsook them'.[42]

On 13 October the army reached the Tuscarawas, a tributary of the Muskingum river in northern Ohio. Proceeding to the forks of the Muskingum, Bouquet positioned his forces so that he could strike, if necessary, at the main Indian villages which surrounded his position in a twenty-mile radius. The soldiers immediately started fortifying each of the four corners of the camp, as well as constructing store houses and a meeting house, where they could receive the Indians, and a reception area for prisoners. Faced by such a powerful force, a delegation of Indians indicated that they were ready to sue for peace, promising to return their English captives, as Bouquet had requested, if only the army would spare their villages. 'They came to the following agreement,' noted Kirkwood. 'viz. That the Indians should lay down their war-hatchet, and restore all the white people they had prisoners amongst them since the beginning of the war. And that when we received them we should return.'[43] By 9 November, Bouquet counted over 200 men, women and children who had been returned, even though some of the liberated children 'had to be dragged screaming from their adoptive Indian parents, to be reunited with blood parents they no longer recognised, and whose language they no longer spoke'.[44]

Although some captive Europeans remained to be brought in, Bouquet had to order a withdrawal before winter set in. Having taken hostages, the detachment returned to Fort Pitt, arriving in late November. Yet again the 42nd went into quarters at Fort Pitt, Ligonier and Bedford. One half-company of men was posted at Fort Cumberland, formerly the westernmost outpost of the British presence in America, until the construction of Fort Pitt. Another half-company was at Fort Loudoun, south of Bedford and Carlisle. This effectively meant that the 42nd Royal Highland Regiment was holding the British frontier in North America.

Fort de Chartres 1765

Before the formal end of 'Pontiac's War', but with Indian resistance to the British presence weakening, General Thomas Gage, Amherst's successor as Commander-in-Chief in North America, considered it was time to turn his attention to the relief of the garrison at Fort de Chartres. An expedition set out from New Orleans up the Mississippi river in February 1764. Within a month, after being attacked by Indians, the convoy was forced to return. Since part of the problem was the easy target the British presented to the Indians by having to row slowly against the current up the Mississippi, Bouquet suggested that a force moving down the uncharted Ohio river from Fort Pitt might have the advantage of taking the Indians – and any residue of hostile French – by surprise.[45]

There was to be a two-pronged advance.[46] Major Robert Farmer and a contingent of the 34th would approach up the Mississippi from New Orleans. At the same time, Gage had agreed to send the proposed downriver expedition from Fort Pitt. Since the 42nd were still at Fort Pitt, a detachment of approximately 100 men was chosen, led by Captain Thomas Stirling. Having been wounded in the West Indies, he had only just returned to North America after a prolonged home leave. Stirling's party consisted of Lieutenant John Smith, who was second-in-command, Lieutenant James Eddington and Lieutenant James Rumsey, formerly of the Independent Company of Free Negroes, acting as the supply officer.[47] There was also the Surgeon's mate, James Murdoch, four sergeants, two drummers and ninety-six men, as well as five artillery men and two interpreters. To accomplish the 1,000-mile voyage, they were provided with seven 'battoes'.[48] Like the boats used to travel up Lake George for the assaults on Ticonderoga, the boats were more unwieldy than whaleboats or canoes but could carry large quantities.[49]

Eight Indians of the Mingo tribe were prevailed upon to accompany them, but Stirling considered they were of 'no account among themselves'.[50] In addition to ammunition, provisions of pork, beef and flour to last them two months were loaded onto the boats, as well as a few spikes, pickaxes, hatchets, oakum – a tarred fibre essential for packing (or caulking) the joints of the timber boats – as well as caulking irons. 'Thus equipped we set out in the morning of the 24th August 1765 and after dining with some friends, who gave us a convoy we lay at the mouth of Beaver Creek that night, 24 miles from Fort Pitt,' Stirling recorded in a memoir 'occasionally' dictated to Murdoch, the Surgeon's mate, while they were rowing down the Ohio river.[51] That night they had their first and only casualty: 'One of our Sergts in taking leave of his comrades had drunk too freely, fell out of his boat & was drowned, tho' every assistance was given to save him.'[52]

During the journey, Stirling marvelled at 'noble trees' and a 'diversity of colours in the Leaves of the different trees on the Banks, points & hills', gliding over water which seemed 'like a looking glass', all of which 'formed to the eye one of the most delightful prospects'. 'The suniness of the weather, the vistas of the country, the smoothness of the noble piece of water with diversity and delightful prospect we had feasted our eyes, than which nature herself cannot exhibit a finer, made an impression which can never be erased. The plenty in which we then abounded made it appear a real party of pleasure rather than a duty.' However, as Stirling realised, 'all these gay scenes were darkened with the reflection on the Service we were sent upon; a handful of men to go fifteen hundred miles through a Country most of which was inhabited by a very Treacherous and subtil enemy who had shewn themselves such and with whom no steps had been taken to reconcile them to us & to our coming into their country.'[53]

To be ready for any eventuality, Stirling ordered the soldiers to keep their cartridge boxes near by with their firelocks, 'the lock kept carefully dry'. They always chose 'advantageous ground' for camping 'by having creeks swamps or Rivers to cover our flanks & good ground in front'.[54] Fortunately, as Private Kirkwood recorded, the anticipated resistance from the Indians did not materialise: 'We were told that we should meet with the great resistance from the Indians in our passage down the Ohio, so were thus prepared to give them a reception; but Providence left little for us to do.'[55] Even without attack, the journey was not easy. As another diarist (believed to be Lieutenant James Eddington) recorded, since the river was low 'our Battoes every Day struck several times either on sand bards, Rocks or large Logs of Timbers, which, at most Seasons, particularly the Spring, we should have gone over without the least encumbrance.'[56] A welcome change from their rations was provided by 'excellent wild yellow plums' as well as plentiful turkeys and buffalo.[57] 'This Country abounds with large mouses or overgrown deer, Buffalos and Panthers,' recorded Kirkwood. 'We had good pastime in killing the Buffalos which were then in their Prime fatness.'[58]

On 11 September, the expedition reached the Ohio Falls (at modern-day Louisville). Since the water was low, the men had to empty the boats so they could be floated in the few inches of water which covered the rocks on the south side of the falls, while others carried their provisions and equipment along the bank. The work was exhausting, and once past the falls Stirling ordered a halt to let the men rest and repair any damaged boats and equipment. 'We took this opportunity of giving our Indians a Frolic, on their having promised to be on their good behaviour for the future. Indeed they had given me great uneasiness & retarded us exceedingly by repeated sulky fits.' Feasting on venison, buffalo, bear and turkey, provided by the Indians, 'I furnishing rum for the feast, a Large Fire was kindled and a kettle put on with all the different kinds of meat . . . We concluded the night with all the festivity & joy the plain company & cheer could afford by singing dancing &c.'[59]

As they continued their journey, a Frenchman with a group of apparently hostile Indians appeared out of the woods. Outnumbered by the waterborne British, they agreed to parley with Stirling and his superior force. As Stirling related, it appeared that the main grievance of the chief Indian of the party, Corn Cob of the Shawnee tribe, was that he feared, following Bouquet's Muskingum expedition, that his white wife would be taken from him. To placate Corn Cob, Stirling told him that he could keep his wife, so long as the convoy could pass unhindered to Fort de Chartres. He also recorded Corn Cob's resentment, which typified Indian hostility towards the white man: 'You are a greedy & encroaching People. When the first of you came upon our Coast you were naked & you were hungry; a mere handful. We took compassion upon you & gave you venison to eat and skins to cloath you, as you could not follow the beasts of the forest. You asked a little land to plant corn on. We gave it you and supplied you with everything we had to spare. You asked for more land. We gave it.'

Even so, Corn Cob, continued, the Europeans were not content and penetrated further into Indian hunting grounds. 'You even envy us our woods, for you never see a fine tree but you look up at it and cry, I wish I had it in England.'[60] Listening to the Indian chief, Stirling was forced to concede the truth of what he said: 'I could not help smiling at this part of the speech, and, looking upon the spot we then sat on, was at the foot a remarkable fine Oak.'[61] According to Kirkwood, 'The Indian Chief gave his opinion for our returning immediately and threatened that he would never suffer us to pass in safety . . . however we were too far embarked in our expedition, for his remonstrances or threats to have any weight.'[62]

The verbal confrontation ended with an offer of an exchange of goods, leaving Stirling and his detachment of the 42nd free to continue on their way. When they reached Fort Massac (near Metropolis, Illinois), built by the French but now abandoned, Stirling decided to send a party of men overland to inform the French garrison at Fort de Chartres of their impending arrival and to request guides. In charge of the group was the supply officer, Lieutenant James Rumsey. At the end of September, Stirling and his party reached the junction of the Ohio and Mississippi rivers, their journey made more arduous by having to row upstream. They also had to stop frequently to fell trees and make oars, to replace broken ones. By 6 October, the expedition was close to Fort de Chartres, but with no word from Rumsey.[63]

After travelling over 1,000 miles in just over six weeks, on 9 October 1765 Stirling entered Fort de Chartres. To his relief the commandant, Louis St Ange, Sieur de Bellerive, handed the fort over peacefully. 'The men being all properly dress'd, we got under Arms about 10 o'clock and marched to the Fort with our Drums beating,' recorded Eddington.[64] Stirling at once wrote to Gage: 'I have the Honour to Acquaint Your Excellency of my Arrival at this Post, with the Detachment under my Command on the 9th Instant, after having been Forty Seven Days on the way, the lowness of the Ohio made the Navigation Extreamly difficult and tedious, and tho' I made the utmost Expedition, it was not in my Power to do it Sooner.'[65] At the fort, Stirling also encountered the half-starved Rumsey, who had got lost and only just arrived.[66]

Since the main British force under Major Farmer and the 34th was still on its way, Stirling had to wait, garrisoning the fort with what armaments the French had left. 'The Indians have not been accustomed to have troops among them since the Peace, so that they have been quite Masters here,' he informed Gage. 'I have made some few Regulations with Regard to that, I have not been able to get an exact Account yet of the Numbers of Inhabitants, but shall transmit that or anything else I may learn by the first Opportunity.' After describing the various actions he had taken to ensure that the inhabitants took an 'Oath of Fidelity' to the King, Stirling was at pains to describe 'the disagreeable Situation I am in here without an Agent or Interpreter for the Indians, or Merchandize for presents to them which they all expect. I bought a few things from Fort Pitt, but they were neither sufficient nor proper and I have been obliged to take up some Goods from the French merchants at a dear rate.'[67]

Farmer and the 34th reached Fort de Chartres at the beginning of December, and so Stirling was able to depart, taking the route down the Mississippi to New Orleans. 'The season was far spent,' explained Private Kirkwood, 'and the rivers frozen in such a manner, that we could not go by the Ohio.'[68] Travelling down the Mississippi, yet again, the men marvelled at the novel countryside. 'Turkies are everywhere, in the woods & plains in prodigious numbers,' noted Eddington in his journal. 'A sort of small partridge is very common, as likewise Wood pidgeons and Turtle Doves. There are Millions of all kinds of Water Fowl in the little Lakes and Marshes everywhere that water is to be found . . . There are likewise Herons, Cranes, Snipe, woodcock &c; there are Likewise Eagles and Hawks of different kinds . . . They have cattle and horses, the same as in Europe . . . In their gardens they have all kinds of vegetables and Roots, and in their orchards are most of the European Fruit Trees.'[69]

On 21 December, Eddington was noting in his journal: 'Cloudy, rainy weather, which cleared up with a N. wester in the afternoon occasioning a considerable swell in the River. We pass'd several French Battoes that were hunting for Buffaloes.'[70] On Christmas Day they halted 'to hunt and eat' their Christmas dinner. Unfortunately Rumsey, who went 'out a hunting', got lost again for three days.[71] After just under three weeks, they reached New Orleans on 5 January 1766, having taken twenty days to achieve what it had taken the 34th Regiment 'about six months to accomplish owing to the rapidity of the stream, against which they sailed, where as we went along with it'.[72] Received by the governor of New Orleans, Monsignor d'Aubrie, 'we were treated by him and the rest of the French Officers and Gentlemen there with the utmost Hospitality and politeness during our stay,' recorded Eddington.[73]

At the end of January they resumed their return journey. 'About six leagues down the river is a very narrow pass call'd *detour aux Anglis* where the French us'd to have a strong Battery of Cannon on each side of the river,' Eddington continued. 'When we pass'd it was all in ruins and the guns dismounted . . . The Master of our Transport thinking he could take the Vessel down himself, to the Balise [fort] without a pilot, had the misfortune to run aground. The wind was Fair and all the Vessels that then lay at anchor at the Balise got over the Bar to the roadsted before we could get off the shoal. So we lay at anchor inside the Balise waiting for a wind till near the later end of February.'[74] Eventually they set sail for Pensacola, on the coast of

Florida, but another misfortune awaited. 'Our Master thought that the land we made was to the westward of Pensacola. He ran to the Eastward as far as Lake Blaire before he discovered his mistake. This was due to the strong current that set on all the Coasts in the Gulph of Mexico just off their Capes. About three leagues from land we ran over a shoal amongst the breakers, so shallow that we thought the ship would strike the ground every instant.' So fearful was the Master that he called to the sailors 'to stand by to let go the anchor, and the Carpenter to set up his axe to cut away the Masts'. Luckily, as Eddington recalled, they sailed clear. 'We afterwards ran into some very blowing squally weather and finally arrived Safe at an anchor in Pensacola Harbour on the 13th of March.'[75] Arriving in New York in June 1766, Stirling and his detachment, which had travelled in places where no other members of the Royal Highland Regiment had ever ventured, marched to Philadelphia.

At the same time, a general peace with the Indians was being agreed. Among those listed as participating in the peace talks with the Shawnee, Delaware and Iroquois Indians in June at Fort Pitt was the 42nd's chaplain, James Maclagan.[76] On 25 July 1766, Chief Pontiac travelled to Oswego to meet Sir William Johnson, still British Superintendent of Indian Affairs; a formal end to 'Pontiac's War' was effected, which appeared to be peace 'almost' on Pontiac's own terms. 'We were not to build any forts within his Nation or his Allies, nor was any European to come into his Country without his consent.'[77] Lieutenant Colonel Henry Bouquet did not live to see the fruits of his labours against the Indians, having died of fever on 2 September 1765 on board ship in Pensacola Bay, shortly after Stirling had set out on the expedition to relieve Fort de Chartres. Pontiac, whose relationship with the British was envied by rival tribes, was killed by a Peoria Indian of the Illinois Confederation on 20 April 1769.

Stirling's achievement in reaching Fort de Chartres and person-ally claiming the Illinois country for Britain marked a new phase of British colonial expansion, giving Britain physical occupation of territory in the heart of the North American continent. It also marked the furthest west that the Royal Highland Regiment ever served in its entire history. For the next decade, although little settlement took place, Britain not France held sway over this prized landscape.

Ireland 1767–1775; Scotland 1775–1776

You will return to your residences
Going across the ocean with rhythmic pipe music
With merry rejoicing in your fleet.
There will be thousands of beautiful mermaids
And fish dancing around your bagpipes.[78]

In the summer of 1767, the 42nd Royal Highland Regiment was ordered to leave North America. Some chose to forsake the Highlands of their birth in preference for a life in the 'New World', transferring to other regiments or leaving the Army. Those who remained sowed the seeds of a generation of Americans with Highland traditions. As part of a policy to secure the empire, the British government permitted half-pay officers and soldiers to settle on land to the north of Albany in the state of New York. On 11 July 1764, Major Allan Campbell had been granted 'a tract of land lying in the country of Albany between Ticonderoga and Crown Point on the West side of the River or Waters which empty out of Lake George into Lake Champlain, beginning at a black Oak Tree . . . containing 5,000 acres of Land'.[79] Major John Reid remained with the Regiment but left the Army in 1770 and returned to America, hoping to enjoy a peaceful life on his property near Crown Point. The outbreak of hostilities with the American colonists led to his eviction from his lands by the rebel Americans.[80] Reid's first cousin, John Small, had gone on half-pay in 1763 before enlisting with the 21st Foot. He too decided to stay in America, having acquired lands in Nova Scotia.

When Private Kirkwood boarded the transports, he observed that only six or seven men per company were returning home.[81] 'Last Sunday evening the Royal Highland regiment imbarked for Ireland,' noted the correspondent for the *Virginia Gazette*, 'which regiment, since its arrival in America, is distinguishable for having undergone most amazing fatigues; made long and frequent marches through an inhospitable country, bearing excessive heat and severe cold, with alacrity and cheerfulness; frequently encamping in deep snows, such as those who inhabit the interior parts of this province but rarely see, and which those who only inhabit the northern parts of Europe can have any idea of; continually exposed in camp, and on their marches, to the alarms of a savage enemy, who in all their attempts were forced to fly.' Referring to the period when the Regiment was stationed in Philadelphia, he continued: 'Besides our thanks for having thus secured our peace, they receive our thanks for that decorum in behaviour, which they kept up during their stay in the barracks of this city; giving an example, that the most amiable behaviour in civil life is not inconsistent with the character of the good soldier.'[82]

As the Regiment arrived in Cork in October 1767, Lord John Murray marched in full Highland dress with his broadsword, pistol and dirk to meet the soldiers. Since their numbers were so diminished, the first priority was to send recruiting parties to Scotland. By May 1768, when the Regiment was reviewed, the establishment was complete, 'and every man in it, with two exceptions born north of the Tay'.[83] While quartered in Ireland, the 42nd was used to help the civil power against 'miscreants' and robbers. There were also disputes between Catholics and Protestants and between landlords and tenants.

On 19 December 1768, by Royal Warrant, the Royal Highland Regiment was authorised to bear on the Colours the King's cipher within the Garter with the Crown over it in the centre; under it was the figure and cross of St Andrew with the motto of the Most Ancient and Most Noble Order of the Thistle, *Nemo me impune lacessit* (No one provokes me with impunity). In the three corners of the Regimental Colour was the King's cipher and crown. The caps of the grenadiers were emblazoned with the King's crest and St Andrew, as on the Colours. The Regiment's original Colours were deposited in the Tower of London in the Grand Store House.[84]

The men were badly in need of new uniforms: 'The jackets,' Stewart of Garth noted, 'were of a dull, rusty-coloured red . . . Economy was strictly observed . . . the old jacket after being worn a year was converted into a waistcoat, and the plaid, at the end of two years, was reduced to the philibeg [kilt]. The hose supplied were of so bad a quality, that the men advanced an additional sum to the Government price, in order to supply themselves with a better sort.' It appears that no provision was made for obtaining the feathers, prescribed as Regimental in 1761, 'instead they were allowed only a piece of black bearskin; but the men supplied themselves with ostrich feathers, in the modern fashion, and spared no expense in fitting up their bonnets handsomely'.[85] A sympathetic observer in Ireland described the men as possessing 'the attractive beauties of a soldier; sunburnt complexions, a hardy, weather-beaten visage, with a penetrating eye, and firm, expressive countenance, sinewy and elastic limbs, traces of muscles strongly impressed, indicating capacity of action, and marking experience in service'.[86]

In 1769, the 42nd was posted on 'Dublin duty'. While fighting in North America they had forgone conspicuous decorations to their uniform; their coats were now brightened with gold lace. The Colonel also supplied them with white waistcoats and buff leather purses, 'deemed an improvement on the vests of red cloth, and the purses made of badgers' skin'.[87] Sergeants wore silver lace, provided at their own expense. The heavy Lochaber axes were exchanged for carbines (fusils). In 1775 the soldiers were issued with new muskets, shorter than those already shortened at the start of the Seven Years War.[88] In 1770 the Regiment was transferred to Donaghadee and Belfast. Three companies were stationed in the Isle of Man. In the same year, Lieutenant Colonel Gordon Graham of Drainie retired – he died the following year. His successor was Thomas Graeme of Duchray, who had joined the Regiment in 1741 and been wounded at Bushy Run. He remained in command for less than a year, retiring in September 1771; his place was taken by Thomas Stirling.

In 1771 an event occurred, which was potentially disastrous for the Regimental history. When moving from Dublin to Donaghadee, 'the baggage was sent round by sea'. The ship was wrecked and most of the cargo and baggage lost, but 'the portion saved, especially the Regimental books and records, was much injured'.[89] Throughout 1772 and 1773, the Regiment was occupied in suppressing riots in Galway, then moving back to Dublin in 1774. A minor power struggle was taking place between the Lord Lieutenant of Ireland and Lord John Murray, who was resisting the introduction of southern officers into the Regiment. Murray's inclination was to give commissions to men from the Highlands, 'well aware how greatly their influence would avail to procure men from the hill-country, and sensible also of its possessing officers who understood the dispositions and character of the men'.[90] As related by Stewart of Garth: 'The influence of the Lord Lieutenant prevailed.'[91]

Nearly twenty years after leaving the shores of Britain, in 1775, the Regiment returned to Scotland, landing at Portpatrick. 'Impelled by characteristic attachment to the soil of their birth,' recorded a later historian, 'many of the old soldiers leaped on shore with enthusiasm and kissed the earth which they upheld in handfuls.'[92] Throughout this extended period of service abroad, the 42nd Royal Highland Regiment had retained its particular identity, recognisable by its Highland dress and having gained a reputation as fearless and trusted soldiers. 'Their attachment to their native dress, and their peculiarity of language, habits, and manners, contributed to preserve them a race of men separate from others of the same profession,' noted one of Stewart of Garth's 'respectable and intelligent' friends, who served in the Regiment at this time, 'and to give to their system of regimental discipline a distinctive and peculiar character'.[93]

In April 1776, the Regiment was pronounced 'complete to establishment, and so unexceptionable that none were rejected'.[94] Soon afterwards, the soldiers were retracing what were becoming well-worn footsteps from Glasgow to Greenock. The decade of peacetime soldiering was at an end. Twenty years after the 42nd had first crossed the Atlantic to fight the French in North America, the Regiment was ordered to return. This time their adversaries were the provincial Americans, beside whom they had so recently fought and died.

> *The King's reward and the gratitude of the land,*
> *And eternal fame will be yours forever*
> *For protecting your land from the despoiler's greed*
> *And proving the Gael's great worthiness.*[95]

7.

America: the War of Independence

Hard is the fate of many who suffer indiscriminately in a civil war.

Captain John Peebles[1]

No regiment was more exposed to danger, – underwent more fatigue, – or suffered more from both.

Lieutenant Colonel Charles Graham[2]

1780

Open Rebellion

The catalyst which led Britain to wage war on the American colonies was an argument over taxation. In the decade following Britain's successful struggle against France in North America, George III – no longer the young man who had ascended the throne in place of his grandfather – had drawn up 'measure after measure designed to bind American colonists to the motherland, only to see the rift widen'.[3] In April 1775, General Thomas Gage, Commander-in-Chief in North America, had been ordered to suppress 'open rebellion' among the colonists 'by all necessary force'. Three major generals, William Howe, brother of George, who had died at Ticonderoga, Henry Clinton and John Burgoyne, were appointed to command the King's 'Royal' Army. Howe's brother, Admiral Richard Lord Howe, was placed in command of the Royal Navy.[4] By the end of May some 23,000 Americans had taken up arms. On 10 June, George Washington, the wealthy plantation owner who had fought alongside the British a decade previously, was appointed commander of the 'Continental Army', whose forces were besieging Boston.

In November, George III appointed a new secretary for the American Department, Lord George Germaine, who favoured a swift war by applying maximum force.[5] Once the authority of British arms had been asserted, Germaine believed the Loyalist Americans would affirm their allegiance to the British Crown. A key priority was to bolster the forces in America with regiments from Britain, which included the 42nd Royal Highland Regiment, under the command of Lieutenant Colonel Thomas Stirling.[6] While the transports waited for a fair wind to set sail, the soldiers busied themselves 'finishing the cloathing, making cartridges & completing our Sea Stores', recorded Lieutenant John Peebles, who had fought with Bouquet at Bushy Run before receiving a commission in the 42nd.[7] On 28 April 1776 the 'Blue Squadron' comprising eleven ships with the Royal Highlanders on board weighed anchor, followed by the 'White

Squadron' carrying Fraser's Highlanders, the 71st.[8] Sailing in summer, the weather was mostly 'fair' with light winds; but, after only a few days at sea, a gale scattered the fleet. The *Oxford* transport, carrying Captain John Smith's company, was attacked by an American privateer. Having thwarted the attempt to take the ship, they proceeded across the Atlantic, sailing up the James river in Virginia to Jamestown, only to find the town was in the hands of the Americans. 'We came up with her,' recorded a young rebel American, 'and took her without any engagement. There were on board about one hundred and twelve Highlanders.' Promised military promotion and the grant of land if the men would change sides and support the American cause, they refused and were kept as prisoners in Williamsburg.[9]

Meanwhile, the rest of the fleet had made a record crossing in six weeks. Their destination was Boston, where it was believed Howe was waiting to be reinforced before opening the campaign against the Americans. But, even before the convoy had left England, Howe had been forced to evacuate Boston in March and sail for Halifax, Nova Scotia, to await supplies.[10] Obliged to wait for Howe's return, the newly arrived troops had to remain at sea until the beginning of August, eventually disembarking on Staten Island, New York harbour. On 4 July 1776 the American Congress had passed a 'Declaration of Independence', signed by all thirteen states, declaring that 'these United Colonies of America are, and of right ought to be, free and independent States, that they are absolved from all allegiance to the British Crown . . . ' Symbolically, the huge leaden equestrian statue of George III was knocked from its plinth in Bowling Green, New York City. Reportedly, it was melted down and turned into over 42,000 'patriot' bullets.[11]

As soon as the 42nd was on dry land, Stirling started training the soldiers 'in the manner of fighting practised in the former war with the Indians and French bushmen, which is so well calculated for a close woody country'.[12] The grenadier companies were formed into a Grenadier Battalion. The light infantry companies were also brigaded together.[13] The remaining eight companies of the 42nd were formed into two battalions. An immediate disappointment was the withdrawal of the pistol and broadsword; regarded as 'impeding the progress of the men through the thick woods which abounded in North America', they were replaced by the bayonet and musket.[14] Writing fifty years later, Stewart of Garth thought this was a shame: 'I have been told by several old officers and soldiers ... that an enemy who stood for many hours the fire of musketry, invariably gave way when an advance was made sword in hand. It is to be regretted that a weapon which the Highlanders could use so well, should together with the pistol, which is peculiarly serviceable in close wood countries, have been taken from the soldiers, and, after the expense of purchase had been incurred, sent to rust and spoil in a store.' Although the broadsword ceased to be an official weapon, a number of officers continued to purchase it privately.[15]

The British army, composed of seven brigades under the command of Hugh Percy, 2nd Duke of Northumberland, amounted to 30,000 men. The 42nd was placed in the Reserve, commanded by thirty-three-year-old Charles, 2nd Earl Cornwallis.[16] A brigade of Guards and several thousand German (Hessian) mercenaries, commanded by General Wilhelm von Knyphausen, complemented the force.[17] In 1775 John Small, formerly of the 42nd, had raised a battalion, incorporated into Colonel Allan Maclean's Regiment of Royal Highland Emigrants, the 84th, whose kilts and plaids were of 'government tartan' – the same as worn by the 42nd.[18] One young recruit was Maclean's relative, Lachlan Macquarie, who had come to America with his uncle, Murdoch, with supplies, guns and ammunition.[19] Against the formidable British and European soldiery was arrayed the 'Continental Army' of Patriots led by George Washington.

Long Island and New York Island (Manhattan) 1776

Having endured the humiliation of the evacuation from Boston, Howe's objective was to launch an attack against the outer defences of New York Island. On 22 August the British army landed on Long Island, encamping in front of two villages, Gravesend and Utrecht. The Americans, under General Israel Putnam, the architect of the first major engagement of the war at Bunker Hill the previous year, were at Brooklyn (Brookland), having crossed over from New York. Like Washington, Putnam had fought alongside the British against the French, and was present during the successful 1759 campaign against Ticonderoga and at Montreal.[20]

The most direct route to attack the Continental Army lay through a pass beyond the village of Flatbush, held by Clinton and the 4th Battalion Grenadiers, in which Lieutenant John Peebles, recently appointed Adjutant, was serving. On the evening of 26 August, the main body of the army advanced towards Putnam's lines, intending to occupy a pass on the heights, near Bedford. The 42nd was ordered to march along the coast towards the 'Narrows', to the left of Gravesend Bay, to strike Putnam's right, while a second column attacked the Americans' left. Washington's Continental Army was no match against the combined British and Hessian attack. 'The Hessians and our brave Highlanders gave no quarter,' recorded an anonymous diarist, who favoured the British cause, 'and it was a fine sight to see what alacrity they dispatched the rebels with their bayonets after we had surrounded them so that they could not resist.'[21]

Over two thousand Americans were killed or taken prisoner, including one of Washington's trusted generals, William Alexander, who claimed the title the 'Earl of Stirling'.[22] British losses were fewer and those of the 42nd negligible: one officer and nine soldiers were wounded. The British did not follow up their advantage; 'the cautious Howe', recorded Archibald Forbes, 'would not permit his troops to attack the enemy's position, although he must have seen both the spirit animating his own people and the despondency of the Americans.'[23] After Brooklyn, Washington ordered the Continental Army to withdraw back across the East river to New York Island. Throughout the night, the demoralised Americans, numbering approximately 9,000 men, moved so secretly and silently with their guns, ammunition and stores that it was not until the following morning that Howe realised they had gone.

Operations were resumed two weeks later, on 15 September, when, supported by the Royal Navy, the Reserve crossed the East river to New York Island, overrunning American positions at Kip's Bay, and enabling Howe to occupy New York City. The British army then moved northwards to engage the Americans at 'Harlem Heights'. During the encounter, Major William Murray of Lintrose was nearly captured by an American officer and two soldiers, 'but saved himself by his strength of arm and presence of mind', defending himself 'for some time with his fusil, keeping them at a respectful distance. At last, however, they closed upon him, when unluckily his dirk slipped behind, and he could not, owing to his corpulence, reach it. Observing that the rebel officer had a sword in his hand, he snatched it from him, and made so good use of it, that he compelled them to retreat, before some men of the regiment, who had heard the noise, could come to his assistance.' According to Stewart of Garth, he wore the sword 'as a trophy throughout the campaign'.[24]

Over the next few weeks, the 42nd was involved in a number of actions, on one occasion in support of the light infantry, to 'dislodge a hostile force which had possessed itself of a wood facing the British left'.[25] 'This, although only an affair of outposts,' recorded Stewart of Garth, 'was one of the briskest engagements on a small scale during the war; but no proper account of it was ever published.' A sergeant and five soldiers from the 42nd were killed; and fifty-three officers and men were wounded.[26]

Washington, meanwhile, had withdrawn the Continental Army to White Plains in upstate New York. In mid-October 1776, the British marched to meet the Americans. 'After some time spent in reconnoitring the Ground, a Cannonade began which came on to be very brisk on our side,' recorded Peebles, who was now in the 3rd Battalion Grenadiers since, due to illness, the 4th had been disbanded. As the British moved down the hill, the Americans rushed towards them 'in great numbers & began a very heavy fire upon them as they pass'd the River . . . but the steadiness & intrepidity of our Troops beat them from their strong grounds where they had taken the advantage of fences & stone walls, & made them retire back on the remaining body that was posted on the hill.'[27] Although

Peebles described the Americans as running off 'in great confusion',[28] the posts the British had taken were not close enough to permit an attack on the American camp.

Having claimed to have routed the 'Rebels', Howe retired without a general fight. When news reached a Lowlander in Scotland that the British army had left White Plains without fighting, Stewart of Garth recorded his response: 'Surely the 42d was not there – *they* would not turn their backs on an enemy without fighting.'[29] From the soldier's point of view, the terrain presented an additional challenge: 'This Country is remarkably strong & very Hilly,' noted Peebles, '& the Enemy have taken the advantage of it by posting themselves on the tops of the Highest hills which they are indefatigable in fortifying.'[30]

Howe's primary objective was an assault on Fort Washington, south of White Plains, to open lines of communication between New York and the area east and north of the Hudson river. While the main attack was to be carried out by Knyphausen and the Hessians, supported by Percy and the Reserve, the 42nd was ordered to make a diversionary attack on the fort's eastern side, where the ground was so steep and rugged 'that the enemy, thinking its summit inaccessible, had taken no measures to secure it'.[31] At sunrise on 16 November, the army halted in fields near the Harlem river, '& the 42nd Regt. cross'd Harlem River . . . where they were opposed by a considerable body of the enemy Posted on those steep hills who began their fire upon them before they landed.' Despite 'every difficulty' Peebles recorded that 'they push'd ashore unsupported, mounted the Hill & drove them quite across the island killing & taking a good many, & clear'd the way in a great measure for Lord Percy's Brigades to advance.' By mid-afternoon, the British 'were in possession of all the High Grounds in the environs of Fort Washington, having taken & killed a good number between 3 & 400 of the Enemy & driven the rest into the Fort.'[32]

'Thus the Highlanders, with their characteristic impetuosity,' recorded Stewart of Garth, 'turned a feigned into a real attack, and so contributed greatly to the success of the day.'[33]

Yet again Murray of Lintrose's corpulence deserved a mention. Due to his size, he needed help in the ascent. 'The soldiers eager to get to the point of their duty, scrambled up, forgetting the situation of Major Murray, when he, in a melancholy supplicating tone, cried, "Oh soldiers, will you leave me?" A party leapt down instantly, and brought him up, supporting him from one ledge of the rock to another till they got him to the top.' Their success was not without cost: eleven men of the 42nd were killed; two officers and seventy men were wounded. Of these, Lieutenant Norman Macleod's injury was nearly fatal: illustrating the steepness of the ascent, the ball had entered the back of his neck and made its way down his ribs before lodging in the lower part of his back. He recovered, but left the Regiment in 1779.[34]

After Fort Washington, which secured British control of both Long and New York (Manhattan) Islands, Howe turned his attention to taking Fort Lee, on the opposite side of the Hudson river. Cornwallis, with the Reserve, was once again part of the attacking force. Landing in New Jersey on 18 November, eight miles from Fort Lee, as the Americans fell back, retreating in confusion, 'hundreds of cannon, muskets by the thousand were lost, huge stores of ammunition, along with tents, blankets, tools and clothing'.[35] Cornwallis pursued the rebel Americans to Elizabeth Town, Newark and Brunswick, where the British army halted, 'to the great relief of the enemy, who were flying before him, unable to make the least resistance'.[36] While Cornwallis was at Brunswick, Howe had moved forward to Princeton (Prince Town), which the British had occupied 'an hour after it was evacuated by General Washington, who calculated with such exactness' that his rearguard retired from one end of the town while the British entered the other.[37]

Meanwhile in New York, on 17 November, Peebles, with the 3rd Battalion Grenadiers, was recording how 'things [are] getting ready for a secret expedition, we remained this Camp about a week & then embark'd for the Lord knows where'.[38] Three weeks later, they landed at Newport, Rhode Island. 'The Rebels having a few Guns on t'other side fired some round shot at us, but did no hurt – we lay upon our arms in a field about 3 or 400 yards from the ferry till eveng. & then went into the adjacent Houses & barns some of which were inhabited and others not – the Enemy have drove off as much of the live stock as they possibly could & many of the Inhabitants have left the Island either from fear or Disaffection.'[39] With the onset of winter, the weather was 'rather too cold for field business' and the men spent their time going on parade and foraging, firewood being particularly scarce. There were 'some flagellations on account of irregularity'.[40] They regularly attended Divine Service, the sermon on Christmas Day 'inculcating peace among men'.[41]

'At this time the enemy were greatly dispirited by their late reverses,' noted Stewart of Garth. 'The advance of our troops, although hitherto slow, had been successful, and, if continued with spirit, would probably have reduced the Americans to the last extremity.'[42] During the respite, Washington not only improved the discipline of his army but he was also devising a bold plan of attack. On the evening of 25 December, as Peebles was remarking that it was 'pretty quiet considering it is christmass', Washington was moving his forces stealthily across the Delaware river in icy conditions. Their target was the garrison force of Hessians at Trenton. Making their attack at dawn the following day, they took prisoner almost two-thirds of the 1,500 strong garrison.[43] 'Tis said,' wrote Peebles on 3 January, '900 Hessians are taken prisoners by the Rebels in the Jersey.'[44]

Cornwallis, who was in New York, about to return to England on leave, immediately ordered an advance on Trenton. With Washington and his army on high ground, the two opposing sides began a general bombardment, with some skirmishing between the advanced guards. But, since one detachment of his troops was unable to cross the river, rather than fight and lose, Washington ordered a withdrawal in the middle of the night, 'leaving large fires burning to deceive their adversaries'.[45] Making a wide arc around the sleeping British army, the Americans headed north to attack in the rear near Princeton. The psychological impact of the American offensive, showing that irregular troops could defeat regulars, especially the battle-hardened Hessians, was tremendous. New recruits flocked to join the Continental Army.

The Turning Point 1777

While Washington was achieving his second victory over the British by marching on Princeton, in early January the 42nd Royal Highlanders were sent to Pisquatua, an important staging post on Britain's line of communications. In freezing conditions, and with too few homes to accommodate them, officers and men were billeted in barns and sheds, sleeping in their clothes to keep warm.[46] On one occasion, in February, while out foraging, there was 'a very smart engagement with the rebels'. According to a contemporary account, the 42nd Grenadiers 'got into the hottest of the fire'; it was the most 'fatiguing . . . foraging party . . . we were out fourteen hours, and never had time to sit down five minutes, and had neither rum, biscuit, or pork to refresh us.'[47]

As spring approached, the fighting season began again in earnest, with severe consequences for the 42nd. On 10 May 1777 American soldiers attacked the garrison at Pisquatua. 'Advancing with secrecy and being completely covered by the nature of the country,' related Stewart of Garth, 'their approach was not perceived till they rushed forward on a small level piece of ground in front of the picquets.'[48] Peebles, who had been relating that 'nothing extraordinary' had happened for some days, immediately noted the event in his diary: 'About 1500 or 2000 of the Rebels collected from their different Quarters with an intention to cut off the 42d.' Although 'a heavy fire ensued', with the light infantry companies and the 28th Regiment turning out in support, the Americans were routed.[49] During the fighting, three sergeants and nine private soldiers from the 42nd were killed and over thirty were wounded, making the attack on Pisquatua the worst the 42nd faced while in North America.[50] The wounded sergeant, Macgregor, had 'that day put on a new jacket with silver lace', noted Stewart of Garth, 'having besides, large silver buckles in his shoes, and a watch, [which] attracted the notice of an American soldier, who deemed him a good prize'. Since the

American did not have time to strip him where he lay, he dragged him to a more convenient location. By this time, Macgregor had sufficiently regained his strength to react. Drawing his dirk, he grasped the American by the throat 'and swore he would run him through the breast, if he did not turn back and carry him to the camp. The American, finding this argument irresistible, complied with the request and, meeting Lord Cornwallis and Colonel Stirling, was thanked for his care of the sergeant.' When the American confessed that he was only bringing Macgregor back to save his own life, Cornwallis permitted him safe passage.[51] Another officer, Lieutenant William Stewart, was 'shot thro' the thigh, bone brok[e]'.[52] The son of William Stewart of Garth – and David Stewart of Garth's nephew – he was 'disabled for life'.[53]

As always, the officers were assessing their prospects. John Peebles had his sights on a captain lieutenancy; but if, as Stirling suggested it meant giving £50 in excess of the 'regulation' price to the serving captain lieutenant, Valentine Chisholm, Peebles was not interested. 'I thought it was too much, and am of opinion that Mr Chisholm should either sell or serve . . . if he sold the regulation price was as much as he could expect in the present situation of affairs.'[54] While Peebles deliberated on his future, eventually obtaining preferment in the autumn, a new disposition of the British army had been agreed. Instead of the original seven brigades, in June 1777, the army was organised into five brigades of eighteen regiments. The 42nd, which had been joined by a detachment of 170 recruits from Scotland, was now in the 3rd Brigade under the command of Major General Charles Grey, a veteran of the 1762 siege of Havana.[55]

Pennsylvania: the Brandywine River and Paoli Tavern

Unable to vanquish Washington in New Jersey, Howe changed the theatre of operations to Pennsylvania, for an attack on the American rebel capital of Philadelphia. At the same time, a combined force of British, Hessian and Canadians, commanded by General John

Burgoyne, was advancing from Quebec towards Albany to retake the Hudson valley, lost to the Americans the previous year, including the hard-won fort at Ticonderoga. In terms of overall strategy, a 'slip-up in London' meant that orders to Howe to march from New York to assist Burgoyne did not arrive until after he had committed forces to Pennsylvania.[56] In late July the soldiers embarked for Chesapeake Bay. The voyage down the coast from New York took seven weeks, and it was not until 25 August that the army disembarked at Elk Ferry, at the northern tip of Chesapeake Bay. Far from gaining Loyalist support, as Howe had hoped, the British found that the inhabitants had 'almost all gone off & carried everything with them they could'.[57] Joining Howe, Knyphausen marched with a contingent of troops on the south side of the Elk river. Together they proceeded via Newark before once again separating forces south of the Brandywine river.[58] While the British army had been making the lengthy journey by sea, Washington had marched cross-country, in order to block Howe's progress towards Philadelphia.

On 11 September, Howe and the British army reached the Brandywine river, only to find that the Americans had already erected batteries at Chad's Ford, where they assumed the British would cross. Leaving Knyphausen at Chad's Ford, Howe and Cornwallis, in command of a second column, succeeded in circumventing the Americans and crossing the river higher up at Jeffrey's Ford, which gave them the advantage of surprise in attacking the Americans' right flank. Pursuing the Americans 'thro' the woods & over fences for about 3 miles', recorded Peebles, they sustained 'a warm attack'. Eventually, the approaching night 'prevented any further pursuit & saved thousands of the Rebels'.[59] In the general rout which ensued, Washington withdrew to Philadelphia, leaving the British army in possession of American positions on the Brandywine Creek. 'The Army laid this Night on the Field of Battle,' Howe informed Germaine.[60] But, 'in this disastrous war it was the ill-fortune of the British army that its successes led to no important consequences'. Instead of pursuing Washington's broken army, observed Stewart of Garth, Howe let the Americans reassemble 'and replenish his stores at his leisure'. The 42nd in the Reserve sustained no loss.[61]

To counter the British army's onward progress as they approached Philadelphia across the Schuylkill river, Washington had left a detachment of troops, under the command of General Anthony Wayne, in woods at Paoli Tavern, near Valley Forge. Having received intelligence of Wayne's presence, Howe ordered an attack on the American camp. Towards midnight on 20 September, a force of some 1,200–1,500 men, light infantry, dragoons as well as the 42nd and 44th Regiments commanded by General Grey, moved forward against about 2,000 Continental Army troops. 'The most effectual Precaution being taken by the General [Grey] to prevent his Detachment from firing,' Howe later reported to Germaine, 'he gained the enemy's left about one o'clock, and having, by the Bayonet only, forced their out Sentries & Pickets, he rushed in upon their encampment, directed by the Light of their Fires.' Having killed and wounded 'not less than' three Hundred Americans and taken between seventy and eighty prisoners, only 'the Darkness of the Night' saved the remainder of Wayne's force.[62]

After the action known as the Battle of Paoli Tavern, Grey gained the nickname 'No-flint Grey' because he had ordered the troops to remove the flints from their muskets to maintain the element of surprise. The battle was also called the Paoli 'Massacre', following allegations of butchery. 'A severe and horrible execution ensued,' James Murray, a contemporary British historian, wrote. 'The British troops as well as the officer that commanded them gained but little honour by this midnight slaughter.'[63] Contrary to the claim that the British were instructed to give 'no quarter', Grey's aide later confirmed that 'Seventy One Prisoners were brought off; forty of them badly wounded.'[64] Later historians put the battle in context: 'American propagandists succeeded in whipping up anti-British sentiment with false accusations that Grey's men had refused quarter and massacred defenceless patriots who tried to surrender,' recorded Mark Boatner, pointing out that the allegation that the British gave 'no quarter' was refuted by the number of prisoners taken. 'The "mangled dead" is explained by the fact that the bayonet is a messy weapon.'[65]

This action, bloody as it no doubt was, enabled Howe to enter Philadelphia, from which the Americans had withdrawn. 'The streets [were] crowded with Inhabitants who seem to rejoice on the occasion, tho' by all accounts many of them were publickly on the other side before our arrival,' noted Peebles.[66] Undaunted by his recent losses, having reinforced his troops, on 4 October Washington went on the offensive, making a surprise attack on German Town, on the road to Philadelphia, where the British army was assembled. 'In this attack which was the most spirited I believe they ever made on the British Troops, we have lost above 500 killed & wounded.'[67] Fierce fighting continued until Grey arrived with reinforcements and the Americans withdrew. Meanwhile the 42nd had been sent to attack the Americans at Billings Port, on 'the Jersey side' of the Delaware river, having crossed the river at Chester. As usual the Americans had already evacuated the position, having spiked their guns and burnt the barracks. 'Lieutenant Colonel Stirling pursued them about two miles,' Howe reported to Germaine, 'but to little purpose, as they retired with the utmost Precipitation.'[68]

To the north, Burgoyne was marching south, having successfully retaken Ticonderoga. Lacking support from Howe and also that of a relieving force from the west along the Mohawk valley which the Americans had blocked, Burgoyne halted at Saratoga. On 16 October, the Americans forced his surrender, Peebles gloomily noting in his diary that the Americans had fired a *feu de joie* at their victory.[69] It was a disastrous defeat for Britain, and recriminations followed, mainly criticising Howe's plan to take Philadelphia rather than sending reinforcements to Burgoyne from New York.

By early December 1777, the weather had turned cold and frosty. 'A pair of mitts [is] given out to the men & blankets to those that wanted.'[70] After what had been a difficult season's campaigning, 'the winter passed without any remarkable occurrence'. There was one incident which Stewart of Garth wanted to record. When a Highland soldier encountered an American in the woods, neither had his musket loaded. 'Each flew behind a tree to cover himself while loading.'

Fearful of leaving the safety of the trees, they remained 'till at last the Highlander, losing patience, pushed his bonnet beyond the tree on the point of his bayonet. The American shot his ball through its centre, when his opponent starting forward, made him surrender instantly.'[71]

Enter France 1778

The new year did not bode well for British fortunes. On 6 February 1778, France, encouraged by the news of Britain's capitulation at Saratoga, recognised the Americans' 'independence'. Still hoping that the rebellion could be quelled through negotiation, Prime Minister North introduced a 'Reconciliation Bill'. Howe, annoyed at criticism emanating from London of his conduct of the war, had resigned as Commander-in-Chief. Clinton had also asked to be recalled. Meanwhile, the soldiers were assessing their needs. 'The arms in General not good order & wanting some repairs,' noted Peebles at the end of January. 'The new Bonnets are cock'd & on, – The men wear Philibegs yet, made of their old Plaids.'[72]

During the respite between campaigns, the opposing armies interacted so that they could help their respective prisoners, sometimes without success, if safe passage was not assured. Grimly, Peebles recorded that if any prisoner was 'detected in making their escape they are to be put to death, – poor devils they suffer enough, & many of them are dying in Gaol'. For entertainment, once or twice a week a play was put on at the Playhouse in Philadelphia. 'The performers are gentle[me]n. of army and navy & some kept mistresses – the gentle[me]n. do their parts pretty well, but the Ladies are rather deficient.' Every Thursday there was a ball, 'the Expense defray'd first by a subscription of two days pay from every officer of the British & half a guinea for Ball Tickets'.[73]

At the end of February, the 42nd undertook an operation across the Delaware river together with the Queen's Rangers, formed from amongst the Loyalists and named in honour of Queen Charlotte, the wife of George III.[74] Their orders were to take a particular village, which the Americans were occupying, to prevent the inhabitants selling their supplies to the British soldiers. As so often happened, by the time the British arrived, the Americans had gone. 'The Village contains about 40 families,' recorded Peebles, 'mostly Quakers who seem to be heartily tired of this Contest.'[75]

While the soldiers waited for a new offensive and the British government was still trying to negotiate, the Americans were unyielding in their demands. Their response to North's 'Reconciliation Bill', 'on which they have made some very shrew'd & haughty remarks', was that they would not enter into negotiations with Great Britain 'till the fleet & army are withdrawn, or their Indipendency expressly declared'.[76] In late April, Howe handed over command to Clinton, who had reluctantly agreed to remain. In Howe's honour, before he left, a 'Grand Entertainment' was held; called a Meschianza or medley, it included a regatta, a tournament, a triumphal procession and a *fête-champêtre* – an elaborate garden party. 'The Regatta proceeded down the River with musick, they landed at the lower most wharves & proceeded up to the ground where the tournament was to be.' After the tournament, which involved the traditional throwing down of the gauntlet, the assembled gathering retired to drink 'tea coffee &ca. &ca. after which they went to dancing and about 9 a handsome sett of fire works were played'. The evening ended with 'a very Elegant Supper & a variety of the best wines, after supper they danced & drank till day light'.[77]

With France's 'espousal of the American Cause', and declaration of war, Clinton's instructions were to withdraw from Philadelphia to attack French possessions in the West Indies. With 'a great deal of vague News flying about',[78] one arrival from Britain was the Regiment's former chaplain, Adam Ferguson. Now in his mid-fifties, he had come to America as secretary of a new Commission, instructed to hold talks with the rebel Americans.[79] 'I am told that everything but Independence is offer'd to the Americans;' Peebles recorded on 10 June. 'Alas Britain how art thou fallen.'[80] While the politicians and senior commanders attempted dialogue, plans for evacuating Philadelphia continued. Departing for New York, 'strict orders' were given against plundering.[81] Ignorant of exactly what was happening, the morale of the soldiers was low. 'Many of the Hessians deserting & some of the British,' recorded Peebles, 'owing it is said to the prevailing opinion that we are going to abandon this Country.'[82]

At the end of June, Washington mounted an attack on Clinton's rearguard, as it marched through Monmouth Court House (modern-day Freehold Township) in New Jersey. As part of the 3rd Brigade, having already undertaken 'a very quick & fatiguing march of six or 7 miles', the 42nd 'came upon a Scatter'd Body of the Rebels', which they pursued in the midst of a heavy cannonade. So exhausting was the chase through woods and swamps, that 'a great number of the several Corps died upon the Spot'.[83] The Battle of Monmouth was the last major battle in the north. Although a tactical victory for Britain, it was regarded as an American victory because the Continental Army was left in possession of the terrain. In extremely hot weather, the soldiers marched onwards until, on 30 June, they reached Sandy Hook, enabling them to embark on Royal Navy ships for the safety of New York and Long Island.

At the beginning of September, the 42nd was involved in an attack on a number of privateers lying at New Plymouth. Under General Grey's direction, the grenadiers, light infantry brigade and the 42nd sailed towards the Acushnet river. Landing on the banks of the river on 5 September, they destroyed 'a good many large Vessels & some houses'.[84] In general the fighting was desultory, 'carried on by petty expeditions, unpleasant and fatiguing in themselves and productive of little honour or satisfaction either to the officer or soldier'.[85] Meanwhile, Clinton and Admiral Lord Howe were in New York, anticipating Britain's proposed attack on the French in the West Indies. But the arrival of a French squadron off the coast hampered operations. By October, the weather had turned clear and frosty, and at the end of the month another exchange of prisoners took place, 'mostly Hessians, the 42d. got 44. More coming – poor creatures they have been often ill used & mostly in jails all the time.'[86] To counter the cold, the soldiers were given 'brown trowsers of dona-tion cloth'.[87]

In early November, the army went into winter quarters. Whilst Clinton remained preoccupied with the need for reinforcements, Britain's weakening position affected the soldiers' well-being. 'There seems to be a want of that care of & attention to the Troops that is necessary, & that we used to experience, matters & things seem to [be] conducted & carried on in a very unsteady manner, in this army,' Peebles noted in late November.[88] In early December, an abortive attempt was made to rescue the British troops captured at Saratoga. 'The purport of this Clintonian expedition was to have intercepted Burgoygne's people, whom the Rebels were marching to the Southward, but they cross'd the North River at Kings ferry two days before we got there, so we came back again.'[89]

Southern Strategy 1779

While Peebles was recording that New Year's Day in North America was 'a very fine mild day & warm for the Season', the 42nd remained in winter quarters, the inhabitants of Newton, where they were billeted, grateful 'for their good behaviour'.[90] The officers spent time playing cards, eating and drinking. They attended the occasional ball, which was sometimes more expensive than they would have liked. 'They say this Stupid inelegant Ball will cost us £5. each, pox take 'em all,' grumbled Peebles.[91] On another occasion, he complained there were 'about a dozen Ladies, none of them handsome, some old ugly & fat women, nothing very tempting to go above two miles & spend your money for amusem[en]t to others.'[92] While the men waited for action, they could at least take solace from the reports of British offensive operations in the West Indies. In early February news came through of 'a smart action' in which the British had captured the French island of St Lucia.[93] In the southernmost state of Georgia, the tide of British fortunes had improved with the capture of Savannah at the end of 1778.

As the war dragged on, the 42nd remained either in quarters or undertaking small expeditions. Towards the end of February, together with the 33rd and a Guards' light company, the Regiment was sent to the Jerseys near Elizabeth Town, where they burnt the barracks and some stores. Chased by the rebel Americans and unable to return their fire, they returned to the boats, having had killed or wounded about thirty men: 'neither fun nor credit there', observed Peebles, noting that Stirling's 'humane and genteel behavior' at Elizabeth Town was 'highly extoll'd' in the American newspapers.[94] Shortly before this action, on 19 February, Thomas Stirling had been honoured with the appointment of 'Aide-de-Camp' to the King and promoted Brigadier General.[95]

At the end of April a detachment of 200 men from the 42nd embarked on board small craft to go to Monmouth County to destroy some magazines of ammunition. The outcome was disappointing and, after skirmishing with the Americans, they returned with about thirty prisoners '& some plunder'. A day later, the 42nd was under orders to embark 'for some secret expedition'.[96] Their destination was Portsmouth, Virginia, by way of Chesapeake Bay, to attack some fortifications, enabling them to take possession of ships and stores including 'a great quant[it]y of tobacco'.[97] In late May, the 42nd Grenadiers were ordered to be ready to march 'at the shortest notice'. While the officers' heavy baggage had to go to the regimental store in New York, they took with them tents, bedding, 'portmanteau' and a canteen box.[98]

Clinton's battle plan for 1779 was to draw Washington and the Continental Army into a decisive encounter along the Hudson river. In early June, British troops captured Verplancks and Stony Point, interrupting American lines of communication across the Hudson. Washington refused, however, to be drawn into a general engagement and Clinton's forces were still not strong enough to go on the offensive. While he waited for reinforcements, the Americans counter-attacked. To compound Britain's misfortunes, a French fleet was preventing the British fleet from reaching the safety of New York harbour after its successes in the West Indies. On Sunday 4 July, Peebles was noting some firing 'about noon' to the north 'which we take to be the Rebels commemorating the anniversary of their independence'.[99] By the beginning of August, 'nothing' was going on, although there was more talk of transports getting ready for an expedition.[100]

When reinforcements finally arrived, they were too few to mount the sort of operation Clinton was proposing. He therefore withdrew the army, weakened by fever, into the fortified regions of New York. The 42nd 'fell back on Greenwich, in the neighbourhood of New York', while the grenadier company went back to their 'old ground near the English Church, in Jamaica, Long Island'.[101] After this disappointment, Clinton refocused attention on restoring British authority from Georgia through the Carolinas to Virginia. By late September 1779 he was making preparations to sail to South Carolina. Before departing, he heard that the French had arrived off the coast of Georgia and were helping the American rebels in their counter-attack against Savannah. It was not until November that Clinton learnt the 'great news from Georgia of our having repulsed & defeated the combin'd attack of the French & Rebels at Savannah'[102] and that the French had sailed onwards to the West Indies. On 26 December, after months of planning, a fleet of over 100 square-rigged ships set sail from New York for South Carolina. Among the chosen detachments were the 42nd Grenadiers; the remainder of the Regiment stayed in winter quarters in New York, enduring what came to be recorded as the most severe winter in living memory.[103]

A 2nd Battalion

Throughout the American War, recruitment was taking place in Britain. For the third time in the Regiment's history, a 2nd Battalion was raised.[104] It was authorised by George III on 30 July 1779, thirty-four years after Culloden. Those who signed up came from both sides of the former political divide of loyalist Whigs and dissenting Jacobites. The Commanding Officer of the 2nd Battalion was

Lieutenant Colonel Norman MacLeod of MacLeod. In comparison with other regiments, the 42nd, the oldest Highland Regiment, with its title 'Royal', had gained a certain prestige, and recruiting agents sometimes encouraged potential recruits to think they were signing up for the 42nd, only to find themselves drafted into other regiments. A celebrated case in 1779 resulted in another 'desperate mutiny, by which many lives were lost' when recruits, thinking that they had enlisted to join the Royal Highland Regiment and Fraser's Highlanders, were ordered to join a 'Lowland' regiment.[105] Having arrived at Leith, they were ordered to board transports for Glasgow. But: 'none of them would move . . . the Fray began by two of the Fencibles [army officers] forcing a man of the 42nd on Board, when another of the 42nd pushed his bayonet but misjudged [?] the men and on this the two Companys fired, and killed eight men of the Seventy-first Regiment.' Seventeen men were put in hospital, three died in the night and eight were 'mortally wounded and a man had his leg cut'.[106]

Two of those involved, Archibald Macivor and Charles Williamson, were brought before a court martial, charged with being guilty of a mutiny at Leith. Protesting that they only spoke Gaelic and had only ever worn Highland dress, they were sentenced to death. King George, however, gave them a free pardon and the two men were allowed to join the newly raised 2nd Battalion 42nd.[107] News of the mutiny reached North America some months later. 'Strange mismanagement of Recruits at home,' noted Peebles in August, 'hurtfull to the Recruiting business, & productive of mutiny & desertion.'[108] Following this incident, the new battalion was embodied at Perth on 21 March 1780 in ten companies, quartered in Dundee and Fort George. Instead of going to North America, the 2nd Battalion was ordered to be part of an expedition, fitting out at Portsmouth, to fight the French in South Africa.[109]

The end of the American War

On New Year's Day 1780, most of the British army in North America was at sea, heading towards South Carolina. But strong winds dispersed the ships and a journey that could have taken ten days took six weeks. In New York State the ground remained covered in snow so deep that roads and fences were buried; it was so cold that the Hudson river froze, providing an unexpected means of communication from the Jerseys, where the Americans retained their foothold, and the British garrison on Staten Island, where approximately 1,800 men were garrisoned, including the 42nd, under the overall command of Thomas Stirling.

On 15 January, the Continental Army and New Jersey militia, led by Washington's General 'Lord Stirling' (captured in 1776 and released in a prisoner exchange) mounted an attack on Staten Island. Travelling in 500 sleighs across the frozen landscape, 2,500 soldiers and New Jersey militiamen attacked British outposts, forcing them to retire. 'They [the Americans] formed the line,' reported General Knyphausen, who had been put in charge of all forces in New York State during Clinton's absence, 'and having made some movements in the course of that day, withdrew in the night, after having burnt one house, pillaged some others, and carried off with them about 200 head of cattle.'[110] Subsequently, a combined force of Hessians and British army soldiers, including a detachment from the 42nd, successfully attacked 'a rebel post in the Jerseys'. 'By these little enterprises,' Knyphausen reported to Lord Germaine, 'during the winter, as far as we can ascertain, we have made 320 prisoners, and killed about 65 of the enemy.'[111]

Meanwhile, having reached John's Island, thirty miles from Charleston, on 11 February, it took until the beginning of April for Clinton to assemble his force in South Carolina, by which time the American forces, under General Benjamin Lincoln, had successfully dug themselves in for a long siege. Realising that he would need more troops, in view of those lost or captured at sea, Clinton ordered a detachment of the 42nd Royal Highland Regiment and the Queen's Rangers to come from New York. Spared the delays of the original force, they left New York at the end of March, reaching Charleston on 18 April. For much of the time, they were engaged in opening up a secure route across the Ashley river, which bounded Charleston on its southern side. After less than six weeks, on 12 May, the besieged Americans surrendered: 'the British flag was immediately hoisted at the Gate as the Rebels march'd out & a Salute fir'd of 21 Guns.'[112]

The capture of Charleston was Britain's greatest success. Clinton had forced the surrender of 6,000 soldiers, taken 300 cannon, four warships and one of the most important southern cities. During the fighting, the 42nd lost one officer and twelve soldiers; fourteen men were wounded, including Lieutenant Alexander Grant. 'The wound of Lieutenant Grant was remarkable for its apparent severity,' recorded Stewart of Garth. 'A six-pound ball struck Mr Grant on the back in a slanting direction, near the right shoulder, carrying away the entire scapula with several other bones, and leaving the whole surrounding parts in such a state, that he was allowed to remain on the ground, the only care of the surgeons being to make him as easy as possible for the short time they believed he had to live.' To their surprise he survived and 'served many years in perfect health', dying in 1807.[113] Having secured this victory, at the beginning of June, Clinton relinquished command in South Carolina to Cornwallis and returned to New York with the bulk of the army, including the 42nd.

Almost immediately on arrival at Staten Island, the 42nd was ordered to take part in what became known as General Knyphausen's 'Springfield Raid': a concerted attempt to invade New Jersey. Their route took them through Elizabeth Town, in order to capture a strategic pass through the Watchung Mountains in northern New Jersey, which would bring them to Washington's headquarters in Morristown. During fighting near Elizabeth Town, Stirling was severely wounded 'by some skulking rascal from behind a house; his thigh bone broke, & very ill' related Peebles.[114] Serious as Stirling's wound was, he refused to have his leg amputated.[115] As Knyphausen's forces continued to move forward, the Americans made a determined stand at the small village of Springfield, forcing a withdrawal. The attempt to reach Morristown signified Britain's last incursion into New Jersey. While more decisive battles were being fought in the south, from the American point of view the Battle of Springfield became known as 'the forgotten victory'.[116] Throughout this period, the strain of war was taking its toll on British troops: on 21 June there was a court martial for drunkenness and irregularity, 'of which there are a good many instances, & some too of the 42d'.[117] During the autumn of 1780, the 42nd was stationed in different parts of New York. Although their ranks were supplemented by another draft of 100 recruits, 'all young men in the full vigour of health and ready for immediate service', after Springfield the Regiment did not see active service again.[118]

Although Cornwallis had achieved two minor victories at Camden near the North Carolina border in May 1780 and at Guildford Court House in March 1781, he could not secure the territory and the troops were hungry and tired. After he moved the army to Yorktown, his position became untenable. Promised reinforcements by Clinton and instructed to occupy the peninsula of land known as Williamsburg Neck, overlooking York river, Cornwallis and his army became trapped by a combined French and American force. The failure, in early September, of the Royal Navy at Chesapeake Bay in preventing the French fleet from blockading Yorktown sealed Cornwallis's fate.

In a belated attempt to provide assistance, on 12 October Clinton ordered a detachment of the army to start embarking on board Royal Navy ships at New York for the journey south down the coast to Virginia. As the troops departed, they marched past George III's son, Prince William Henry, third in line to the throne. Aged sixteen, he had recently arrived in America as a midshipman on board the *Prince George*. 'The Prince being arriv'd he was posted near the beach on the ground where the 42d. were Encamp'd, and the Troops according to their order in line, march'd past by half Company's & the Officers Saluted the Young Prince,' recorded Peebles. 'He was in a plain Midshipman uniform, look'd cheerful, & took off his hat with good grace.'[119] While Peebles and other members of the Regiment might be admiring the young Prince, they were unaware of the impending disaster at Yorktown. The fleet did not set sail until 19 October, by which time Cornwallis had already asked for capitulation terms and were surrendering to their adversaries. As the soldiers lay down their arms, the drummers were reported to have played the song: 'The World Turned Upside Down.'[120]

Back in New York and not comprehending that the surrender at Yorktown was the prelude to Britain's defeat in North America, the soldiers went into winter quarters. To celebrate St Andrew's Day on 30 November, Prince William Henry visited the Regiment for a formal dinner, hosted by Clinton. 'Having dress'd & mounted a St Andrews X', the officers went to their headquarters at four o'clock in the afternoon. The Prince was already there 'with his green Ribbon and Star on'. He was received by a Captain's Guard of the 42nd with 'Colours &c.'. 'The Company were near an hour in collecting & it was past five before we sat down to dinner.' Once the Prince – together with the generals – was seated: 'Every body sat down as they happened to come in, about 45 in number.' 'A very good dinner' was served, 'with Several Scotch dishes such as Sheepshead broth, cocky licky, a Haggies &ca'. After dinner, several toasts were given and then 'the Band of Musick & the Pipes of the 42d. play'd alternately, & the little Prince being highly pleas'd with the Piper gave him a bumper after every tune, & behaved himself so properly that he was admired by every body there.'[121] By the end of the year, the 42nd Royal Highland Regiment was spending its sixth Christmas in North America, with the ground covered in snow '& the sleighs flying about'.[122]

Peace Preliminaries 1782

1782 dawned with no prospect of reasserting Britain's authority in North America. The 42nd Royal Highlanders continued to be ready for active service. In early January, a detachment of fifty men from the 42nd together with another fifty from the 40th and 100 Light

Infantry was ordered to Brunswick to destroy some boats 'that were said to be getting ready there for hostile purposes'. During the action, several men were killed or wounded, including the captain commanding the detachment, although they successfully destroyed 'two or three boats'.[123] While the men waited for orders, they distracted themselves with cockfighting, horse racing and sack races.[124] Dinners in the Mess passed the time for the officers.

In early 1782 Cornwallis, taken prisoner at Yorktown, had been exchanged for a prisoner of equal rank and returned to Britain. Although criticised by his opponents for his actions in North America, he retained the confidence of George III, who was still encouraging the soldiers to pursue the war 'with Vigour'.[125] On 20 February, realising that the war was nearing its natural conclusion, North resigned as prime minister. His successor, the Marquess of Rockingham, had no alternative but to open negotiations with the Americans. Britain's successful defence of Gibraltar against Spain and display of British naval supremacy in the West Indies against the French strengthened the government's bargaining power. During the negotiations, the Americans agreed to forgo any claim on Canada in the belief that the British presence there would prevent France or Spain asserting any claim. Britain was, however, obliged to cede lands west of the Mississippi, previously incorporated into the province of Canada under the terms of the 1774 Quebec Act.[126]

Peebles was one of several officers who wanted to return to Britain. Since arriving in America, he had been corresponding with his future wife, Anna Hamilton, the daughter of Charles and Isobella Hamilton of Craighlaw (Wigtownshire), waiting for 'pacquets' to arrive so that he could dispatch or receive letters. Having sold his captaincy in February 1782 to Lieutenant William Dickson, he took his leave of the Grenadier Company he had commanded: 'I very much regret my leaving so respectable a Regt. & Corps as that to which I belong, & the Company I have the honour to Command, with whom I have served so long with satisfaction and pleasure to myself.' Since he was going home at once to Scotland, he offered to take any letters 'or anything that I can do for you there I will do it with pleasure'.[127]

Unusually, before his departure Peebles found himself taken into confidence by General Clinton. 'I found his Ex[cellenc]y busy en deshabille just finishing some Letters, he then opene'd a conversation relative to the Letters betwixt him and Lord Cornwallis on the affairs of the Chesapeak[e].' Anxious to explain that the debacle which had led to Cornwallis's surrender at Yorktown was 'not so subject to blame as might be implied', he wished to deflect the growing criticism he was receiving for not having come to Cornwallis's assistance, 'as,' he claimed, 'it depended on the Fleet'.[128] What use the departing Peebles made of this information is not known. 'He then wished me well & a happy Voyage, I bowed & took leave.'[129] After over twenty-five years, Thomas Stirling, already back in Britain recuperating from his injury, left the Regiment. He had been in command for eleven years – the longest to serve in that position to date – and the King now appointed him Colonel of the 71st – Fraser's Highlanders. The 42nd's new Commanding Officer was Charles Graham of Drainie, whose father, Gordon Graham of Drainie, had been Lieutenant Colonel two decades previously.[130] For the first time (but not the last) in the Regiment's history, a father was later followed by his son in command.

During the negotiations for peace, the British army began to reduce its presence in North America. On 11 July 1782, British troops evacuated Savannah, Georgia. At the end of November, preliminary Articles of Peace were signed. On 14 December, British troops left Charleston, South Carolina. Nearly a year later, in September 1783, the treaty document was signed at the Hotel de York in Paris by John Adams, Benjamin Franklin and John Jay, representing the United Colonies (States) of America, and by King George III's representative, David Hartley, later renowned for being the first Member of Parliament to move a resolution for the abolition of the slave trade. Britain signed separate agreements with France, Spain and later the Netherlands relating to overseas possessions to be retained or handed back. The American Congress of Confederation ratified the treaty on 14 January 1784. Britain did so in April and the ratified versions were finally exchanged on 12 May 1784, well over a decade after the spirit of rebellion against British authority in North America had first become apparent.

For the soldiers who had come to America to fight and win, the loss of the American colonies was a bitter blow. The reputation of the 42nd Royal Highland Regiment became yet more celebrated, leading future historians to overlook any possible misdemeanours. Although drunkenness and misbehaviour occurred in other regiments, asserted historian Archibald Forbes, 'in this regiment it was otherwise: not a man deserted, and of more than a thousand men of whom the corps consisted there was but one man punished during the whole of those five years. One man who had been refused leave of absence went away, settled his business, and returned to the Regiment. For this defiance of orders he was tried and punished.'[131] Once the war had been lost, there was an admission of standards slipping: 'While the regiment was quartered at Paulus Hook a marked deterioration was unfortunately evinced,' Forbes continued, 'and some occurrences took place which were equally unexampled and disgraceful.' One such was the desertion of a young soldier, who was caught, tried and shot.[132] Total losses for the Regiment were recorded as eighty-five killed and 287 wounded.[133]

After the American War, nearly 450 men from the 42nd took their discharge.[134] Lieutenant Dugald Campbell, a descendant of the Campbells of Argyll, secured a grant of 11,343 acres on behalf of himself and 111 others in Nova Scotia. The land was located on the Nashwaak river, stretching from Taymouth (named after the river Tay in Scotland) to the mouth of the Cross Creek Stream – near where many Loyalists had settled.[135] Corporal Angus McBean and Donald MacDonald, taken prisoner when the 42nd were attacked at Pisquatua in 1777, went to New Brunswick. Still speaking their native Gaelic, the Highlanders created further generations of Scots in North America. MacDonald was recorded as being the last living member of the 42nd on the Nashwaak, dying in 1850 aged ninety-five.[136]

Nova Scotia 1783

In October 1783, the 42nd Royal Highland Regiment was ordered to board transports for Halifax. Reduced from ten to eight companies of fifty men, the officers of the 9th and 10th Companies were retained as supernumeraries to fill up vacancies, avoiding the hardship of being put on half-pay. Other regiments were disbanded, including the 71st – Fraser's Highlanders – some of whom joined the 42nd. Their addition to the ranks fuelled a story relating to the wearing of red feathers in their bonnets (rather than black as ordered in 1761).[137] Reportedly, during the skirmishing of 1776 and 1777 the 71st's Commanding Officer, Lieutenant Colonel Maitland, had informed Washington, whose friendship pre-dated the war, that his men 'would be distinguished by a red feather in their bonnets, so that he could not mistake them, nor avoid doing justice to their exploits, in annoying his posts, and obstructing his convoys and detachments'. When Maitland died of fever in 1779, in his memory the men continued to wear a red feather in their bonnets; those who transferred to the 42nd kept the tradition.[138]

On 1 January 1785 the 42nd Royal Highland Regiment was awarded new Colours to replace the 'ragged, but honorable remains' of the old ones. 'These Colours are committed to your immediate care and protection,' stated the Commander of the British army in Nova Scotia, Major General John Campbell, 'and I trust you will, on all occasions, defend them from your enemies, with honor to yourselves, and service to your country, with that distinguished and noble bravery which have always characterized the Royal Highlanders in the field of battle.' Campbell went on to remind his listeners 'that being a national and reputable corps, your actions as citizens and civil subjects, as well as your conduct as soldiers will be much observed, – more than those of any other regiment in the service.' Praising the Regiment's 'decent, sober, and regular behaviour in the different quarters you have hitherto occupied', which had rendered them 'the distinguished favourites of their respective inhabitants', he urged the soldiers not to allow their morals to be corrupted by associating 'with low, mean, or bad company'. He concluded by emphasising the importance of Christian virtues: 'So that if it should be your fate hereafter to fall in the Field of Battle, your acquaintances and friends will have the Joyful consolation of hearing you leave an unspotted name, and of being assured, that you rose from the bed of Honour to the Crown of Immortality.'[139]

Winters in Nova Scotia were harsh. By the end of October the soldiers were permitted to wear trousers 'any day after the last of this month that the Commanding Officer may think proper to order'.[140] 'The severity of the frost rendering the freezing over of the harbour more than probable,' noted an order dated 21 January 1786, 'in such a manner as to render the communication with the Eastern Battery difficult and of course the subsistence of the Detachment on duty there from hence precarious, the General therefore directs that the Commissary cause a fortnight's hard bread, and 4 weeks provisions of all other species to be lodged in charge of the Commanding officer to be in readiness for the use of that Detachment whenever the regular supplying them is prevented from Halifax.'[141]

Pastimes such as pigeon-shooting were strictly forbidden. 'It having been reported to Major General Campbell that a practice prevails among a certain description of the Army under his command of shooting lame pigeons whenever a sly opportunity offers. The General indignant at such disgraceful conduct, wishes first to endeavour reforming in principle by representing the meanness of an action that demonstrates treachery, injustice, and a want of dignity and pride in a Soldier, as he thereby exposes himself to the ignominy & shame of public punishment.' Those 'delinquents' who continued the practice would be considered 'a disgrace to the Corps', as well as suffering 'the penalty prescribed by the civil law'.[142] Deserters were warned that after a general court martial they 'must expect certain . . . execution of sentence', the penalty being death.[143]

In May 1786, two companies were dispatched to Charlottetown on nearby Prince Edward Island, while six were sent to Cape Breton.

As usual, detailed instructions accompanied their movements. 'The 42nd to deliver over the Barrack bedding etc in regular manner to the Barrack master,' the departing companies were informed, 'after which [they are] to receive back one blanket per man for bedding for the voyage.'[144] When Campbell reviewed the Regiment in early June, he expressed his 'high pleasure and satisfaction' at 'the soldier like appearance & satisfactory performance of their Exercise and Manoeuvre', while praising 'the discipline and dress of the Corps'.[145] According to General Orders, the Espontoon – or wooden baton – was replaced by 'a strong substantial uniform Sword, the Blade of which is to be straight and made to cut and thrust to be one inch at least broad at the shoulder and thirty two inches in length. The hilt if not of steel is to be either gilt or Silver according to the colour of the buttons on the uniforms and the sword knot to be crimson and gold in stripes as required by the present regulation.'[146]

On 18 May 1787, Lord John Murray died, aged seventy-seven. With so much of the Regiment's service overseas, he had seen little of the soldiers whose interests he had promoted for forty-two years.[147] 'Till Lord John Murray was disabled by age,' noted David Stewart of Garth, who was commissioned as an ensign in the autumn of 1787, 'he was the friend and supporter of every deserving officer and soldier in the regiment.'[148] The new Colonel was Major General Sir Hector Munro of Novar, an ancient branch of Clan Munro of Foulis.[149] According to family folklore, as a young man he had saved the life of a lady whose horses had bolted with her. In return she secured his commission in the Army. Having started his military career in Lord Loudoun's Highlanders in 1747, he had spent over twenty years in India. Now in his sixties, after returning to Britain in 1782 he had been appointed Barrack Master General in North Britain.

After thirteen years in North America, the 42nd Royal Highland Regiment returned to Britain in 1789. Landing at Portsmouth in October, the soldiers marched north via Guildford and Finchley Common, 'where numbers flocked to see them, no Highland corps having been in that neighbourhood since the year 1745'.[150] In the

interval since the Regiment's first military action in France at
Fontenoy, its reputation had been established as a celebrated fighting
force whether, as at Ticonderoga in 1758 and throughout the
American War, the battle was eventually lost, or, as in Canada and
the West Indies, British force of arms prevailed.

> *The sad, ill-fated war of the Revolution*
> *Began without reason, in order that people might be hurt . . .*
> *Between Great Britain and yonder America,*
> *About some trifling tax or other that*
> *Forced the Army to go to preserve peace in every place*
> *And to battle the Indians to protect them.*[151]

8.

Revolutionary Wars

Wad Bonaparte land at Fort-William
Auld Europe nae langer should grane;
I laugh when I think how we'd gall him,
Wi' bullet, wi' steel, an' wi' stane.[1]

1799

The Year of the Sheep

While unprecedented revolution was consuming neighbouring France, the 42nd Royal Highland Regiment was spending the winter in Tynemouth, Northumberland. In May 1790 the soldiers resumed the march north across the Scottish border. But, as Stewart of Garth could personally testify, in Scotland, as well as in England, their reception was only 'warm and cordial . . . in America the service was far less brilliant, and the interval that had elapsed between the war and their arrival rendered the recollection of their services less vivid.'[2] Following the turmoil in France and a 'misunderstanding' with Spain, the British Army was once more increased. Since a great many of Scotland's youth were lying dead or had been wounded in America, recruitment in Scotland was less easy. To augment the numbers who wanted to sign up, advantage was taken of Ireland's consent for recruitment to take place there. 'I think it right to apprise you,' Sir George Yonge wrote from the War Office to the Regiment's Colonel, Sir Hector Munro, 'that if you judge it expedient, you may cause parties to be sent thither, without delay and to report their arrival to the Lord Lieutenant, under whose directions they will receive Beating Orders, and every necessary assistance for carrying on the Recruiting Service in that Country.'[3] Pardons were given to deserters so that those who were 'able bodied men and fit for the Service' might re-enlist.[4]

In Scotland the practice was once more adopted of encouraging the recruitment of independent companies through the various clans. An additional relaxation to the rules was made when the minimum height for recruits, previously set at five feet seven inches, was reduced to five feet six inches, 'men of which stature, not exceeding thirty years of Age, may be enlisted, till further orders'.[5] In October 1790, the twenty-year-old George Gordon, Marquis of Huntly, had received a Letter of Service from the King authorising him to raise an independent company. Having done so, he chose a commission in the 42nd as Captain of the grenadier company, bringing with him the men he had recruited, and giving rise to the popular jingle: 'Cock o' the North, my Huntly braw / Whaur are ye wi' the Forty Twa?'[6] Reportedly, Huntly was so proud of his uniform that he wore it when presented at Court. His mother, the Duchess of Gordon, equally attracted by the tartan design, introduced tartan in silk, which became the rage of London society, and she was famously caricatured as the 'Tartan Belle'.[7]

By November 1790 the Regiment was back in the familiar quarters of Edinburgh Castle. Despite augmentation, the 'Effective Size' of each company was thirty-six rank and file, including sergeants and corporals. Among Huntly's recruits, all of whom came from Scotland, there were weavers, carpenters and a gardener. Tailors and bakers enlisted in other independent companies being raised.[8] In October 1791 the men marched north, the various companies being sent to Fort George, Dundee, Montrose, Banff and Aberdeen. At about this time, instead of the black leather belts traditionally used for the bayonet, the men were supplied with white buff belts and the officers' epaulettes were enlarged. A general overhaul of standards in the Army was instituted: no 'useless ornaments' were to be worn; 'superfluous expense in dress of every kind' was recognised as being 'heavy drawbacks' on the soldiers' pay. The idea behind the reforms was for the men 'to discharge their duty on all occasions, with alacrity, diligence, and contentment and [to] be left without any inducement or excuse for Desertion, a crime in itself of the most heinous nature and which hereafter will be punished with the utmost and most exemplary severity'.[9]

In the spring of 1792 the Regiment reassembled at Fort George, before marching further north. After so many years fighting in foreign wars, their duties reverted to their former role of keeping a 'watch' in Ross and Cromarty, where large tracts of the Highlands were undergoing a rural transformation. Landowners, competing for the rich pasture land, had been forcibly dispossessing crofters and farm workers of their farms in what became known as the 'Highland Clearances', so that the land could be converted into pasture.[10] In

1792, the year of the 'Terror' in France, and known as 'the year of the sheep' in Scotland, the people protested.

One of the oligarchy of landowners who had joined forces to defeat them was the Regiment's Colonel, Sir Hector Munro, who had leased a large tract of his land for sheep farming, resulting in the eviction of many small tenants and the curtailment of cattle-grazing rights. When the protest movement, known as the 'Ross-shire Sheep Riot', came to a head, three companies of the 42nd were ordered to quell it. As in the days of the '45, countering insurrection called for loyalty to King and Country, as opposed to sympathy with kith and kin. David Stewart of Garth – 'a very young soldier at the time' – realised the predicament he and his fellow officers and soldiers were in and sympathised with the people. 'The manner in which the people gave vent to their grief and rage when driven from their ancient homes,' he later wrote, 'showed that they did not merit this treatment.' Fortunately, by the time the 42nd arrived at the expected scene of protest, he was able to record that 'the people had separated and disappeared of their own accord'.[11] After only a few weeks on what could have been an objectionable task had the soldiers been called to fire on their countrymen, the Regiment was ordered south.

At War with the French Republic 1793

In the early 1790s, the revolution which had overthrown the French nobility, starting with riots in Paris and the fall of the French state prison, the Bastille, in July 1789, had provoked a new belligerency with France's neighbours. The underlying cause for the breakdown in relations with Britain was the 'Decree of Fraternity' issued on 19 November 1792 in which the French Republic promised to help all those nations who 'desired to overthrow their kings'. In 1792 Austria and Prussia had invaded France to suppress the revolution and restore the deposed King Louis XVI to his throne. Their action resulted in a backlash against the aristocracy. France was declared a Republic, the monarchy abolished and the King and Queen imprisoned. Louis was executed in January 1793; Marie Antoinette went to the guillotine in October. Fearful of revolutionary fervour spreading across the Channel, Britain had joined with Austria, the Dutch Republic, Spain, Prussia and Russia to form the 'First Coalition' of European countries against France.

As a result of the French declaration of war on Britain on 1 February 1793, the 42nd was ordered to assemble at Montrose, the War Office having proposed a further increase in soldiers.[12] Two independent companies, raised by Captains David Hunter of Burnside and Alexander Campbell of Ardchattan, joined the 42nd.[13] In May, the Regiment left Montrose for Musselburgh, embarking on transports to take the soldiers around the coast to Hull. 'In that town the appearance of the Highlanders occasioned much interest and surprise, as no plaids or bonnets had as yet been seen in that part of Yorkshire,' noted Stewart of Garth. 'The people showed them great hospitality, and were so well satisfied with their conduct, that, after they embarked for Flanders, the town of Hull sent each man a present of a pair of shoes, a flannel shirt, and worsted socks; a very seasonable supply for a November encampment.'[14]

Their destination was Ostend, which they reached in early October 1793, joining the British army already encamped around Menin, under the command of Prince Frederick, the Duke of York and Albany, George III's second son.[15] No sooner had they arrived, than the 42nd (with other regiments) was ordered to return to Portsmouth for passage to the West Indies and an attack on the French. As they were waiting to depart from Ostend, the French laid siege to the town of Nieuport; orders were therefore given to disembark and to march 'with all possible expedition' towards the town, garrisoned by the 53rd and a small battalion of Hessians. Under fire from the French throughout the night, the following day they received the 'agreeable intelligence' that the French were retiring.[16]

In early November, the 42nd – minus one sergeant who died of his wounds and five wounded soldiers – embarked again at Ostend.[17] Once more, their destination was changed and they were ordered to proceed to the coast of France to assist a group of French Royalists.

At the end of November the expedition set sail. Having put in at Guernsey, the British contingent was again recalled to Portsmouth once it was discovered that the French Royalists had failed to secure the coastline necessary to enable the British to land.

In June 1794 the 42nd was ordered back to Flanders; during the journey another misfortune befell the regimental records, traditionally carried on the Regiment's various postings. The books had already been badly damaged during the shipwreck off the coast of Ireland in 1771. Now, after disembarking the men at Ostend, the transports carrying the records were ordered around the coast to Helvoetsluys. 'But the vessels had not been long there, when the enemy invaded Holland in great force, and entering Helvoetsluys, seized on the transports in the harbour.' Since the soldiers had only disembarked with their knapsacks, all the baggage including 'a well-selected library, and, what was more to be regretted, all that remained of the historical records of the regiment, from the period of its formation till the year 1793, fell into the hands of the enemy,' recorded Stewart of Garth.[18] As a result, all contemporary record of the Regiment's formation in 1739 and its subsequent service was either lost or destroyed.[19]

Meanwhile, oblivious to the whereabouts of the Regiment's history and not yet feeling the impact of the lost baggage, the soldiers continued on the march. Their destination was Malines, where the Duke of York remained encamped. Passing through the market place in Alost in early July, Private McDonald of the 42nd was wounded defending a basket of provisions 'when a French trooper rode up to him and inflicted a sabre-wound on his arm; McDonald instantly threw down his burden, and attacked the dragoon with his bayonet, and the Frenchman rode off at speed.'[20]

After 'a fatiguing march', the 42nd and other regiments joined forces with the Duke of York, taking part in a series of minor skirmishes. The 42nd was attached to the Reserve under Major General Ralph Abercromby, who had fought in the French–Indian wars.[21] For perhaps the first time the soldiers heard the name of the 3rd Brigade's Commanding Officer, Lieutenant Colonel the Hon. Arthur

Wesley (later Wellesley), the younger brother of the 2nd Earl of Mornington, Member of Parliament in William Pitt the Younger's government. With news that the French were occupying the town of Boxtel, north-east of Antwerp, the 3rd Brigade and the Reserve were ordered to force an evacuation. Since the French were in too strong a position, Wesley was also obliged to withdraw – the first time the future 'Iron Duke' came under fire.[22] As summer became autumn, the weather was miserable. The campaign was arduous, with the men fighting in bitter cold up and down the Rhine, making sorties across the icy waters. The main centre of the fighting was at the ancient city of Nimeguen (Nijmegen), where Abercromby was wounded. The men's discomfort was increased by the fact that 'clothing for the year had not been received' and, unlike other regiments, the 42nd did not have greatcoats.[23]

Geldermalsen 1795

Towards the end of 1794, a British force commanded by Major General David Dundas and including the 42nd was occupying cantonments on the river Waal. 'So intense was the frost' that the French had crossed the river on the ice.[24] 'We drove the French across the River on the ice,' recollected Sergeant Cameron, 'and [maintained] a position on the banks of the river till the evening of the 3rd [January].'[25] Next day the French crossed the river a second time. Having taken Thuyl, they attacked the pickets, which withdrew to Geldermalsen, where Dundas was encamped. 'The 11th Light Dragoons were stationed in front of the village,' recorded Cameron, 'to cover the retreat of the picquets with their two field-pieces.'[26]

Private Andrew Dowie, another witness to the ensuing action, continued: 'The French being very superior in numbers pressed the 78th so hard that they were obliged to give way, the cavalry also gave way leaving their guns which the enemy turned upon us.'[27] According to Cameron, instead of resisting the French, the Light Dragoons retreated 'at a furious pace to the rear of the village, leaving their guns in possession of the French cavalry who commenced dragging them off'. At this stage, said Cameron, the 42nd's Commanding Officer, Major George Dalrymple, was ordered to advance. In his account, Dowie recalled that Dalrymple was told: 'Forty Second for God's sake and for the honour of your country, retake these guns!', at which two companies of the 42nd moved forward. 'The guns were then dragged in by the Corps as the harness had been cut and the horses disabled,' concluded Cameron.[28] Writing in later life, Dowie recorded having heard General Dundas say: 'Forty Second, the 11th [Light Dragoons] shall never wear the Red Plume any more, and I hope the 42nd will carry it so long as they are the Black Watch.'[29] 'There was no notice taken of the affair at the time, as all was bustle and confusion,' noted J.S. Keltie in his history, repeating the account.[30]

Although this narrative was to form the basis of a longstanding belief concerning the Red Hackle – the red feather plume – worn by the 42nd in their bonnets, Dundas made no mention of the retrieval of the abandoned guns in his report, written on 6 January, merely stating that 'after a great deal of Musquetry firing for above an hour, [the enemy] were every where repulsed by the steadiness of the Troops'. He concluded by praising 'the Infantry that was engaged'. In particular he recognised that by the 'firm and cool behaviour of the advanced Companies of the 78th, the progress of the Enemy's Cavalry was first checked'.[31]

After this encounter, during which one soldier from the 42nd had died, short of provisions and in freezing conditions, 'destitute of every material necessary for preparing against a siege or Bombardment', the British troops continued to withdraw.[32] At Beuherua, the 42nd, together with the other regiments, rested for a few days at the palace of William, Prince of Orange, the future King of the Netherlands. In hot pursuit, on 14 January the French attacked British lines from Arnhem to Amerongen, forcing the army once again to retire. 'In this dreadful winter, they had to traverse barren and extensive wastes, and to encounter the hostility of the country people, who could not be softened to the least kindness by the sight of any degree of misery, however extreme,' recorded Stewart of Garth.[33]

The dreaded Walcheren disease was rampant, with sickness continuing 'to an alarming Degree particularly in General David Dundas's Corps in which there are Battalions reduced by it and their losses before the enemy to 150 Men for effective Duty'.[34] The 42nd was luckier than most, losing only twenty-five men in deaths from sickness and battle – 'a small number, considering the length of the service, the fatigue they underwent, and the severity of the weather to which they had been exposed'.[35] By the beginning of February 1794, the 42nd was recorded as having 103 men out of 508 sick and 'wanting 239 to complete'.[36]

In early April, the Regiment reached the port of Bremen in Hanover, where the hospitality they received 'formed a noble contrast to the conduct of those through whose country they had marched'.[37] After landing at Harwich, the soldiers marched to Chelmsford. By June the horrors of the winter were behind them and the Regiment remained encamped with other regiments in Essex, under the command of Lieutenant General Sir William Medows, recently returned from India.[38]

On 4 June 1795 a ceremonial parade was held at Royston to celebrate the King's birthday. At the parade, according to Sergeant Cameron, the 42nd Royal Highland Regiment received the distinction of being permitted to wear a 'Red Vulture Feather'. 'After firing 3 rounds in honour of HM George 3rd's birthday, a box containing the feathers arrived on the common, and which were distributed to the officers, and men.' In his opinion, the honour of wearing a specifically red feather was conferred on the 42nd Regiment 'for their gallant conduct on the 4th January 1795'. He then described how both officers and men 'placed the Feathers in their bonnets and marched into Royston, and in the evening of the 4th June were paid the arrears due for eighteen months, with a caution to keep close to their billets and be regular.'[39]

As time passed, the narration of these events, based on Cameron and Dowie's accounts, added to the belief that the presentation of the 'Red Hackle' was because of their actions at Geldermalsen. 'For this spirited action,' noted Allan McAulay in the *Military History of*

Perthshire, published in 1908, the 42nd was awarded 'as a special badge the Red Hackle or vulture's plume, to be worn as a memento of the occasion'.[40] The accounts of Cameron and Dowie, on which the supposition is based have now been discredited. 'It appears that neither was written until many years after the event,' observed the Linklater history published in 1977, 'and in Colonel Stewart's history, published in 1822, there is no mention of the affair.'[41] 'Most telling of all,' wrote Colonel the Hon. David Arbuthnott in 1982, 'who ever heard of a Ministry of Defence Dress Committee taking a decision stemming from a battle in January in time for a parade the following June!' What can be accepted is that the wearing of feathers of varied colours had been common practice for many years, with the early attempt in 1761 to make them uniformly black. For reasons which are not clear – even in the present day – the 42nd Highland Regiment became the only regiment to have the exclusive right to wear red feathers. So memorable was the account of the action at Geldermalsen that, in 1919, 5 January came to be celebrated as Red Hackle Day.[42]

The West Indies 1795–1796

In October 1795 the Regiment embarked in transports as part of a large force bound for the West Indies, under the command of Major General Sir Ralph Abercromby, recently knighted for his services in Flanders earlier in the year and appointed Commander-in-Chief of British forces in the West Indies. Second-in-command was the Regiment's former Commanding Officer, Charles Graham of Drainie, promoted major general in February 1795, the Regiment now under the command of Lieutenant Colonel William Dickson.[43] For the first time in Regimental history, the men were issued with a complete set of tropical clothing. 'The evils sustained in the late unfortunate expedition to the Continent made Government sensible of the necessity of providing the soldier with a proper equipment, and with articles adapted to the climate and the service in which they were to be engaged,' observed Stewart of Garth, who was serving in the Regiment as the events he was describing were taking place.[44]

To protect the soldiers against the cold nights, they were issued with flannel underclothes. They were also given a style of linen trouser known as duck pantaloons. The reasons appeared well founded: 'The yellow-fever having been very destructive in the West Indies during the two preceding years,' observed Stewart of Garth, 'many precautions were taken to guard the soldiers against its effects by a change of clothing and other measures.' Potatoes and other vegetables were made available to supplement their diet and 'filtering stones' were provided to purify the water. While some favoured the measures, others argued that the linen pantaloons, when wet, would stick to the men's legs and thighs and never have an opportunity to dry, so that 'rheumatisms and various other diseases would be generated'. Critics believed that the new round hat, which was to be of coarse felt, would be like a damp sponge in the rain and afford no protection against the sun, whereas the traditional bonnet, 'being of woollen cloth stuffed with materials of the same substance, and covered with feathers, formed a complete protection against the effects of a vertical sun'.[45]

No sooner had the huge armada of ships, 'calculated to impress the mind with a just idea of British wealth and British power',[46] cleared the Channel than 'there arose a most tremendous storm, which scattered the fleet and seperated them from one another,' recorded Private John Simpson. 'The ship on which I was aboard with 5 companys of the 42nd regiment broke open our instructions and found we was bound for Barbados which caused us to make the best of our way to the place of our destination.'[47] Caught in the Bay of Biscay for four weeks, when they reached Madeira the weather improved, enabling them to catch the trade winds across the Atlantic.[48] The other five companies, with Lieutenant Colonel Dickson, returned to Portsmouth. Instead of attempting to cross the Atlantic, this detachment was ordered to the Rock of Gibraltar, captured by the British in 1704 and established as an important fortress guarding entry into the Mediterranean. There the soldiers remained, equipped with the duck pantaloons and round hats they no longer needed.[49]

The five companies of the Royal Highland Regiment whose transports were not diverted reached Barbados in early February 'in such a state of health, that only two men, with slight bruises, were on the surgeon's list'.[50] In time, the remainder of the fleet arrived, and the army was deemed ready for action against the French. The original objective had been to take Guadeloupe, captured in 1759 with the participation of the 2nd Battalion 42nd, but handed back to France by the Treaty of Paris in 1763. Since the force was not as large as originally planned, Abercromby was instead ordered to take the smaller island of St Lucia, captured by Britain in 1778 but again returned to France. The 42nd was placed under the command of Brigadier General John Moore, who had first seen action in 1778 as a lieutenant in the 82nd during the American War of Independence.[51]

St Lucia and St Vincent 1796

The landing on St Lucia was to be undertaken in four places. The 42nd was detailed to land in a bay close to Pigeon Island, while other contingents would attempt landings at Longueville Bay, Chock Bay and Anse La Raye. As soon as the ships came to anchor, the 42nd went into battle 'while the ships of war engaged in silencing the battreys on Pidgion Island, and they succeeded in making the French run from their guns, they not being able to stand by them,' recorded Private Simpson. As a result, the landing was completed without opposition.[52]

After this initial success, they halted 'for the purpose of getting our field guns landed, as we could not advance with safety without them'. As Simpson described, 'a warm action took place in which their was a few wounded on both sides and the French defended themselves with great bravery.'[53] Unable to sustain their position, the French retreated to a high hill about two miles away. On 27 April the British and accompanying German riflemen moved forward, the

42nd 'evincing the same forward gallantry and contempt of danger for which the regiment had always been distinguished', noted Cannon's *Historical Record*, whereupon the French fled.[54] 'We emeidetly took possession of the high ground covering that part of the bay where the main division of the army intended to land.' By sunset, the entire British force had landed 'with ease'.[55]

Marching in the footsteps of the retreating French, 'it being the heat of the day and the men wanting water were very much fatigued. They were falling down in faints with their tongues hanging out of their mouths and their comrades were obliged to bring them to their sense by their own urine in place of water; their being none to be got.'[56] After a month's pursuit through the wooded countryside of St Lucia, during which the British razed virtually every house to the ground, the French garrison surrendered. Casualties from the five companies of the 42nd were slight. One officer and two soldiers were wounded.[57]

Immediately after St Lucia, the five companies of the 42nd formed part of the expedition against nearby St Vincent, arriving in Kingston Bay on 4 June 1796. Four days later they disembarked 'and marched to a plantation a little above the town of Kingston and lay their that night in an old barn and the next day at 12 o'clock we took our march along the sea side for the distance of 9 miles and lay that night in a field of sugar cane.' The following day, they caught up with the French, who had fortified a ridge of hills with four redoubts. 'We began a brisk fire, from a wood that lay near the highest of them, and continued a hot fire upon them,' recorded Private Simpson, 'without doing any good; they having very good breast works, and our men having no cover, suffered very much from the well Dericted fire of the enemy.'[58]

As a result, Abercromby decided to attack the first redoubt, which was 'stronger by the natural difficulties of the approach, than by the art displayed in their formation'.[59] The 42nd, together with five companies of the 3rd Regiment, was ordered to advance, 'when a signal should be given by firing 3 guns from the place where the commander-in-chief was stationed'. At midday the signal was given, which surprised the French, 'it being the heat of the day'. After ascending the hill, '[we] gave 3 cheers and put the enemy to the point of the bayonet; we kept close at the heels of the enemy till we put them out of the first, second and third [redoubts].'[60] When they reached the more strongly fortified fourth redoubt, they were reinforced by three more regiments, having brought up additional guns 'with which we began to play upon them'. By early afternoon, the French sent out a flag of truce, offering capitulation terms. 'The Detachment of the 42nd was ordered to advance close to the draw Bridge at the entrance of the battery and remained their all night,' recorded Private Simpson, 'and the next morning the French marched out with Drums beating and Colours flying and passed the English Army who stood with presented Arms. They consisted chiefly of Negroes and the nake[de]st set of ratches [wretches] ever was seen . . . after passing us, they laid down their arms according to agreement, and were marched prisoners to Kingstown and embarked.'[61]

During the fighting, the 42nd lost fourteen men, including two officers; thirty-two soldiers were wounded.[62] 'The fall of three soldiers of the Forty-Second, named Farquharson, – two of them brothers and the other an uncle's son, who were killed by the same volley, was much regretted,' noted Cannon's *Historical Record*.[63] While storming the redoubts, Lieutenant Stewart of Garth witnessed the bravery of a soldier's wife 'standing with her clothes tucked up to the knees, in the heat of the battle; "Well done my Highland lads," she exclaimed, "see how the Brigands scamper like so many deer!"' When Stewart asked others about her conduct, he heard that 'she had been in the hottest fire, cheering and animating the men, and when the action was over, she was as active as any of the surgeons in assisting the wounded.'[64]

Despite the surrender, 'about six hundred men broke the capitulation and escaped to the woods, to join their friends at the farther end of the island'. Whereupon ensued 'a trying and harassing' type of warfare against the local population, the Caribs.[65] 'We sent small partys from each post close to the woods,' Simpson noted in his memoir, 'for the purpose of taking and destroying as many of the Carabes or Indians as we could, for they were in great number in the woods and still committing depredations on the plantations.'[66] During one encounter, the 42nd's former Commanding Officer, Charles Graham, was stunned senseless. Stewart of Garth recollected directing him to be carried to a military post, but, since there were no surgeons available, he was tended by the 'Amazonian' soldier's wife.[67]

So 'annoyed' were the troops by the constant night attacks, that: 'anxious to put a stop to this teasing kind of annoyance, and to discover the post of camp whence those nightly parties came', Stewart of Garth related how he gained permission 'to select a party, consisting of a sergeant and twelve Highlanders and entered the woods at nine o' clock at night, guiding myself by the compass.' Using short cutlasses, the men cut their way through the undergrowth. Seeing signs 'of people having lately passed through the woods', Stewart went forward with the sergeant, leaving the men to rest. 'We had not gone five hundred paces, when on a sudden we came to an open spot, on which stood a man with a musquet, apparently as a sentinel. The instant he saw us he presented his piece, when a small spaniel, which followed me, sprung forward and seized him by the foot. In the agitation of alarm or pain, the man discharged his musquet at the dog, and, plunging into the woods, was out of sight in an instant, and before the sergeant, who attempted to cut him down with his sword, could get near him.'

Looking over the edge of a precipice, Stewart saw a small valley 'with a crowd of huts, from which swarms of people sprung out when they heard the report of the musquet'. Having found the location from whence the attacks on their camp were coming, the detachment began retracing its steps. 'But we had not marched half way, when we were attacked on both flanks and rear by the enemy, who followed the party.' Since they were 'excellent' climbers, the Caribs were mounting their attack from the trees. 'The woods was in a blaze, but not a man was to be seen, all being perfectly covered by the luxuriant foliage.' Stewart of Garth then related how he directed the men to keep under cover if possible and 'to retreat from tree to tree, firing at the spot where they perceived the fire of the enemy, who followed with as much rapidity as if they had sprung like monkeys from tree to tree. In this manner we continued retiring till we got clear of the woods.' During the encounter, seven men were killed and eight wounded, 'though not one enemy had been seen, so completely were they concealed by the thickness of the woods'.[68]

Unable to catch the Caribs, Private Simpson related how they adopted 'a different plan, by sending partys as far into the woods as they could, and destroyed all the fruit and roots they could come at; we continued sending out partys, every day, for a considerable time till we at last got them reduced to a state of starvation.' The next stage of the plan was to offer the Caribs 'good encouragement if they would come in and give up their arms'. But, Simpson noted, 'it was for some days before any of them could be prevailed upon to come in, although we every Day left bottles with letters of terms hanging to trees at open places of the wood, where the roads led through.'

Finally, overcome with hunger, one of the chiefs came to parley with Abercromby, 'with whom he had the honour to sit at Dinner, although he was naked'. After dinner, Abercromby allowed him to depart with mules loaded with provisions, promising the other chiefs the same treatment 'if they would come in peaceable'. The following day, more chiefs arrived, promising that 'they would bring in the whole of the Carabes under their command but they could not promise to get the Brigands in with them, as they were not under their charge, but did not doubt but they would follow their exemple, as they were in a worse state than the rest, not being acquaint[ed] where or how to get provisions in the woods.' According to Simpson, the second day after the tribal leaders returned to the wood 'we observed about sunrise a party of them coming out of the woods, about 5 hundred in numbers With a white flag flying in front of them.'[69]

Having taken St Vincent, the British occupied the island, the soldiers being put into barracks, 'which was the first time we had been into a house since our arrival in the West Indies. It appeared very comfortable to us although we had no beds nor bedding but our camp blankets.'[70] On St Andrew's Day – 30 November – Simpson was relating how 'every man of our five companys got some money on account to hold the day with and liberty from all duty on purpose to hold them selves merry'. The men also received the balance of 18 months pay, 'it being the first settlement we had got since we came to the country, we got 3 days liberty to spend our money.' For a while they remained at Fort Charlotte, a fortified citadel with a commanding view of the bay. But a shortage of water meant that they had to go to Kingston 'twice a week to wash our cloathes'.[71] The improved climate meant there were fewer deaths through fever, 'which did not exceed one-third of their number', noted Stewart of Garth, recently promoted captain lieutenant, whereas at St Lucia, out of a total complement of 3,890 men, only 470 were fit for duty at the end of thirteen months.[72]

The 42nd remained on St Vincent until April 1797, when they received orders to march to Kingston, ready for embarkation. Their destination was the island of St Kitts, where the army was forming 'to compose the expedition under the command of Sir Ralph Abercrombie against the Spanish island of Portorico'.[73]

Porto Rico and Martinique 1797

In the middle of May 1797, Abercromby's force reached the island of Porto (Puerto) Rico, literally the 'rich port', located by Christopher Columbus on his second journey across the Atlantic in 1493 and under Spanish control ever since. In addition to being at war with France, Britain was also at war with Spain, so attacking such a valuable possession was an obvious military objective. 'As soon as we came to anc[h]or, we had orders to land the next morning, but their arose such a surge that it was impossible for us to land,' recalled Simpson. The next day, they landed under heavy musketry fire 'from the enemy who lay in ambush in the woods close to the sea side'.

After disembarking, the men lay on the sand until the field guns and ammunition had been brought on shore, 'after which we moved forward keeping a good distance between each file, on purpose to make the enemy think that we had a great force on this advance; we was very much fatigued with the extreme heat'. Yet again, in the heat of the day, Simpson complained of the lack of fresh water. 'We met with no opposition all the way, the enemy still keeping out of our reach.'[74]

As the men found, the town and citadel of Porto Rico were strongly fortified on an island separated from the mainland by a narrow stretch of water. When Abercromby heard that the occupying Spanish had assembled a force of 25,000, 'this was very bad news for us, who would not be a mouthful for the Enemy. The whole of our force,' recorded Simpson, 'did not make a strength of 5000.'[75] Abercromby therefore decided to withdraw, 'and the whole to be under arms as soon as it was dark, with every article belonging to them, and not to take down any of the tents or carry off any of the licquer on pain of death, the few prisoners we had, we was ordered to take with us, when it got dark we took the retreat towards the Bay where we landed at, we sent in a party to destroy all the provisions and stores which were landed.' After spending the night on the beach, the British troops re-embarked, 'the enemy not knowing that we had retreated, seeing our camp standing kept up a constant fire on our works and camp'.[76]

The ruse gave the British the necessary time to weigh anchor. By sunset of the following day, the fleet sailed into Fort Royal, Martinique, in whose capture the 42nd had assisted in 1762. Handed back to the French in 1763 after the Treaty of Paris, in 1793 the island had again come under British jurisdiction pending restoration of the French monarchy. 'We disembarked at the town of Fort Royal and was put into an old French Cottage cleaned out for the purpose. It was full of all kind of dirt and vermin and neither bed nor bedding,' recorded Simpson. The only positive aspect was the supply of water, which 'came in pipes to the very doors of the house'.[77] Throughout this time, death and disease was 'lamentably great'.[78] To fill the depleted ranks of the 42nd, soldiers in the 79th, who had already spent two years in the West Indies and were returning home, were permitted to volunteer for the 42nd. Even so, as Private Simpson related, the addition 'did not make us up to the strength we were when we came to this destructive country'.[79]

Gibraltar 1797

On 21 June 1797, the five companies of the 42nd embarked on board the *Carron of Bombay*, one of the four East India trading ships transporting the army back across the Atlantic. Also on board each ship were 200 prisoners, as well as captured brass guns and mortars. Over five weeks later, on 2 August, they sighted 'the land end of England; we sailed up along the coast with the wind foul, the 3rd the wind being still the same, we was off Plymouth at which place some of our passengers went on shore.' On the morning of 5 August they passed through the Needles. 'Our ship the *Carron* got aground, but was got off again in a short time.' Anchoring at Spithead, they had to hoist the Quarantine flag to await medical inspection. 'Finding us all in good health, the doctor ordered the Quarantine flag to be taken down ... that same day all the French prisoners we had in charge was sent onboard the prison ships.' The following day, they disembarked at Portsmouth.[80]

After being reviewed at Hillsea Barracks, the first thing the men could look forward to was receiving (and spending) the balance of their pay due 'from the 24th Dec. 1796 to the 24th Sept 1797'. Soon after their return, at the end of October, they re-embarked on board transports to sail to Gibraltar, where, after two years apart, the five companies which had served in the West Indies were reunited with the other companies of the Regiment. 'On our arrival on the Rock we were put into old store Houses in different places of the town, it being in the cold time of the year we were very cold coming out of so warm a climate and when it rained the houses were so old that the rain came through them – The third day after our arrival in the Garrison we were put to the Kings works, not having uniform Cloathing with the rest of the Regiment to do duty. This work was very sore on our men not being accustomed to carrying loads in that form.'[81] Only when, after two weeks, their new clothes arrived in Gibraltar could they do garrison duty with the rest of the Regiment, presenting 'a splendid appearance on parade'.[82]

One of Lieutenant Colonel Dickson's duties was overseeing the 'voluntary' contributions which the Regiment was expected to subscribe 'towards the prosecution of the present War'. On 28 March 1798 he signed an order confirming that commissioned officers had subscribed £204 15s 2d. Non-commissioned officers, drummers and privates subscribed one week's pay each, amounting to £216 7s 11d, giving a total subscription from the 42nd of £421 3s 1d.[83]

While in Gibraltar, the men were often unwell, which the Governor, General Charles O'Hara, attributed to poor provisions. Writing to the home secretary, William Bentinck, Duke of Portland, in December 1798, the gist of his letter was that the French and Spanish had gained the upper hand when it came to getting supplies, because of the 'ascendency' they had gained over the Emperor of Morocco, 'by putting large sums of money in the pocket of his Minister, Ben Ottman, formerly Ambassador in Spain'. As a result of 'valuable presents' sent by other European countries, the Emperor was using this as a pretext to complain that he was being neglected by Britain. 'Your Grace is the best judge,' he continued, 'whether in a political view no less than for the partial benefit of His Majesty's Troops and other subjects inhabiting this garrison, it might not be advisable at the present crisis to renew the ancient Treaties with Morocco and to endeavour to bring the Emperor into the views of the Grand Signor against the common Enemy, to which he is strongly solicited by every consideration that Mussulmen hold sacred.'[84]

The year that the 42nd Royal Highland Regiment spent in Gibraltar was not recorded as one of its best, due to the presence of 'indifferent characters' and 'the cheap and free indulgence in wine'. In a fit of rage, one soldier killed one of the local inhabitants with his bayonet, leading to his trial and execution. Two soldiers deserted to the Spanish Army.[85] 'We continued in Gibraltar doing duty and working at the Battreys till the 12th October 1798,' recorded Simpson, 'when there was a fleet arrived at Gibraltar with the 68th Regiment on Board.' Once the relieving regiment had arrived, the 42nd was ordered 'to hold themselves in readiness for embarkation on the shortest notice'.[86] Four regiments, including the 42nd, had been chosen to take part in a secret expedition.

Minorca 1798–1800

'When we set sail,' recollected Simpson, 'we did not know where we was bound for, it being kept secret, we steered to the eastward but the wind was against us; on the 21st [October] we were behind the rock of Gibraltar and was obliged to remain off and on behind the rock, the wind blowing from the eastward till the 23rd when it turned in our favour.'[87] Their destination was Minorca, the second-largest of the Balearic Islands in the Mediterranean, off the coast of Spain. Captured by the British in 1708 and ceded to England by the Treaty of Utrecht in 1713, it had been recaptured by the Spanish in 1782 and retained when peace terms were agreed the following year.

In early November 1798 the British force disembarked and advanced towards the capital, Cuidadella. 'The state of the roads, and the multitude of high and strong stone inclosures,' recorded Stewart of Garth, 'rendered the progress of the army as slow as in a mountainous country.'[88] 'On the 16th, the army was drawn up in line in front of the walls of the garrison, thinking by that means to draw the enemy out upon us but they did not appear willing to engage us,' related Private Simpson.[89] Working parties were there-fore set up to make a breach in the wall 'that we might storm the place, and scaling ladders were getting ready for that purpose'. But the next day the Spanish commander sent out a flag of truce, 'that they could give up the place if they would agree to the terms which were proposed'.[90]

As noted in Cannon's *Historical Record*, due to a clever stratagem of placing troops on various eminences 'leaving only a few light infantry in the valleys, and causing numerous fires to be kept burning during the night ... the Spanish garrison was impressed with a belief that the place was invested by ten thousand men, and that resistance would be useless.' As a result, when the surrender took place, 'prisoners were more numerous than the invading army'.[91] British troops then went into winter quarters. 'The inhabitants were very kind to us and provisions of all sorts were very cheap,' noted Simpson. 'We could get a bottle of good wine for two pence but we had not been long in the Island till it rose to six pence owing to the great quantity which was used by the English army.'[92]

Throughout this time, the Regiment had been wearing tartan trousers rather than kilted plaids. In early June they received their new clothes. 'The inhabitants were very much surprised at seeing us put on our Highland dress,' related Simpson, 'as they had never seen the like before.'[93] While stationed on Minorca throughout 1799, they practised using 'field pieces', even taking part in sham fights between regiments. Gone was the intemperate behaviour observed by Stewart of Garth in Gibraltar: the Regiment's 'old habits and conduct were in a great measure restored by the excellent discipline of Brigadier General [Hildebrand] Oakes, under whose immediate command they were for several months placed'.[94] On one occasion the men were rewarded with half a pint of wine from the Commanding Officer's pocket. Having received orders to 'pouder at all parades', the men economised by using a 'white kind of free stone'. Fearing the harmful effects to the men's sight, Oakes ordered that they should only 'pouder when for duty and on Sundays and any man found to be using that stone was to be punished'.[95]

To counter a possible incursion by the French or their Spanish allies in neighbouring Majorca, working parties were sent to the various bays around the coast tasked with making roads so that big guns could be mounted against a seaward attack. 'We accordingly had men posted on every hill that commanded a view of the sea to make signals of the approach of the enemy's fleet.' They built 'very strong Towers' as observation points. In addition, working parties were sent 'to make roads for Carriages to run on, whereas before we took the Island, the inhabitants had only mules with the Burden on their Backs, but in the course of 6 months we had a road between Cuidadella and Mahon the distance of 28 miles, as good as any in England'.[96]

Throughout the past decade, the 42nd had been fighting on the periphery of the French Revolutionary Wars, either in the miserable terrain of northern Europe in winter or in the fever-ridden islands of the West Indies. As the new century dawned, the soldiers would find themselves both in the heart and heat of battle.

It is over the mountains and over the main
Through Gibraltar to France and Spain
Get a feather tae your bonnet, and a kilt abee your knee
An' list bonnie laddie an' come awa' wi' me.[97]

9.

The East Indies and the Tiger of Mysore

Great Mars, the God of War, did never see such men before,
Nor Alexander fight like us at Mangalore;
At Seringapatam we fought and Tipu Sahib we slew.[1]

1786

India

Britain's continuing enmity with France meant that, while the 1st Battalion 42nd was still fighting in North America, in January 1781 the newly raised 2nd Battalion 42nd, commanded by Lieutenant Colonel Norman MacLeod of MacLeod, had been ordered to the Cape of Good Hope.[2] After a month at sea, the fleet, comprising some forty ships, put into Port Praya in the Cape Verde Islands. As they were taking on fresh provisions, a French squadron attacked. 'Our ships had been permitted to anchor as they pleased, and were consequently all mixed and in no regular order,' recorded Lieutenant James Spens, who had been commissioned into the Regiment as an ensign in 1778. 'Many of the seamen from the ships of war were on shore getting off water, livestock, and other necessaries. The decks therefore were loaded and encumbered, and all was in confusion.'[3] Ill-prepared as they were, they repulsed the French, whose ships sustained more damage than the British.

Before reaching the Cape of Good Hope, news came that a French fleet had already reached the Cape and reinforced the Dutch garrison, so the attack had to be abandoned. While Commodore George Johnstone, in command of the British fleet, returned home, General Sir William Medows, in command of the military force, was ordered to proceed to India. To pass the tedium of the sea voyage, the soldiers read books and played deck games. Lieutenant John Oswald devoted his time to studying Greek and Latin.[4] But, as Spens noted, the men developed scurvy 'to an alarming extent'. At the beginning of September they put in to Joanna, one of the Comoro Islands in the Mozambique Channel, to get fresh fruit and other provisions 'which were cheap and plentiful'. After three weeks, the men had sufficiently recovered, although those who had been allowed to sleep on shore carried with them the 'Joanna fever', which killed Major Patrick Graeme, four other officers and sixteen non-commissioned officers and private soldiers.[5]

As they continued their passage to India, an adverse monsoon forced the fleet to put in at Morebaut Bay, on the Arabian coast. Four ships, including the *Myrtle* transport ship, carrying Lieutenant Colonel MacLeod and three companies of the 2nd Battalion, were driven downwind, arriving at Kissen Bay, near the Strait of Bab el Mandeb, at the junction of the Red Sea and the Indian Ocean. There they remained for six weeks. 'As the natives and we did not speak each other's language, and had no interpreter, it is surprising how we contrived to communicate reciprocal wants, and to get them mutually supplied,' noted Spens. 'They were highly delighted with the music of our bagpipes and much amused at our Highlanders dancing reels.'[6] In MacLeod's absence, command passed to twenty-eight-year-old Major John Campbell, who had been commissioned the previous October, having served in Fraser's Highlanders during the American War.[7]

The Second Mysore War

At the same time as defeating the French in North America in the French–Indian Wars, the British had been victorious in India. The authority of the East India Company had been established in the 'Presidencies' of Bengal, Bombay and Madras. Each Presidency maintained an army, composed of Indian sepoys, the battalions staffed by British officers. In time of need, additional regiments were brought from England. The challenge now was to retain control against warring Indian chieftains, some of whose loyalties remained with the French. One such was Hyder Ali, who had risen to become commander of the army of the Rajah of Mysore, Khasa Chamaraja Wodeyar II. When the Rajah died in 1766, Hyder Ali assumed guardianship of his young heir. Having taken control of the state, 'he soon evinced decided hostility to the British interests in India'. Since France had entered the war against Britain in support of the American colonists, Hyder Ali became a natural ally of the French.[8]

While reinforcements – including the 2nd Battalion 42nd – were on the high seas, the army of the East India Company was fighting against Mysore in the second of four wars fought against the kingdom in the eighteenth century, the first war having been fought in the late 1760s.[9] Hostilities were precipitated by Britain's seizure of the French port of Mahé, when in July 1780 Hyder Ali, in alliance with the French, had launched an attack on the Carnatic (Karnataka), bordering the Madras Presidency. His famed second-in-command was his son, Sultan Fateh Ali Khan Shahab – better known as Tipu Sahib, the Tiger of Mysore.[10] In September, British troops were forced to surrender to Hyder Ali at Pollilur, having sustained considerable losses. Among the prisoners held in Seringapatam, capital of Mysore, was Captain David Baird, 73rd (MacLeod's) Regiment.[11] As fighting continued, British troops recovered some lost territory.

In early March 1782, the troops under Medows' command landed at Calicut on the Malabar coast, where they joined a force under the command of Lieutenant Colonel Thomas Humberston of the 78th. To induce Hyder Ali to withdraw part of his army from the Carnatic, an attack on Palagatcherry was planned. Considered one of the strongest fortresses in India, 'the mountains bounding the pass which it commanded were covered by thick forests through which there was no passage, and the plain below, a long and wide extent of deep rice-grounds was cut and intersected, like a chess-board, by the Panianj River,' noted historian Charles Macfarlane.[12] Humberston's force consisted of four companies of the 2nd Battalion 42nd, a contingent of the 98th, the 100th and a detachment of artillery, together with various battalions of Indian troops.

The attack on Palagatcherry had to be postponed because of the monsoon. For European soldiers, unused to the extremes of a tropical climate, the torrential rain was an ordeal. Many succumbed to the painful illness 'cramp', affecting the limbs and body. Once the rains stopped, Humberston continued operations, setting out from Calicut in early September. Major John Campbell of the 42nd was placed in command of the flank corps. By the end of the month they had only reached the fort at Ramgarie. 'In this fort,' related Spens, 'was found a considerable quantity of rice, which turned out of much comfort to our Highlanders, as a number of *querns* [handmills] were also found nearly of the same construction, and on the same principle, as the *querns* of their native country. They were made not of stone, but of a hard kind of wood. These were a great prize to our men, who immediately put them in use.' While they remained at Ramgarie, scones and bannocks became their staple fare.[13]

On one occasion, Spens recorded some officers going to shoot wild bullocks. 'Just as this party had ascended a little hill, they saw advancing towards them a party of the enemy's irregular horse, about twenty in number and brandishing their drawn scimitars. The little party immediately formed, determined to sell their lives dearly; and the captain gave positive orders that one-half only of his party should fire at a time, and that the other should reserve their fire till the first had re-loaded.'[14] This plan worked and the attackers fled.

When the British army reached the outskirts of Palagatcherry on 19 October 1782, they found that the fort was too well fortified and so Humberston had to withdraw to Ramgarie. In recognition of Campbell's action in covering the retreat, he was mentioned in Humberston's General Orders. A month later, the army marched again from Ramgarie, pursued by a force led by Tipu Sahib. Yet again, the 42nd covered the withdrawal, on this occasion Campbell having his horse shot from underneath him. By evening they had reached the Panianj river which was swollen by rain. The soldiers succeeded in crossing it by tying 'their cartridge boxes on their heads; and each fixing his arm in his comrade's (as is practised in the Highlands on similar occasions) they resisted the force of the current, and all crossed without loss'. The following morning, Spens recalled, Tipu's army 'were greatly surprised and disappointed at finding us gone, and crossed to follow us, but we had the start of them so fully that they could not overtake us.'[15]

By late November they were at Panianj, 'the sea making our Rear secure, we had only the Front and Flank to defend,' noted Campbell. Here, Lieutenant Colonel Norman MacLeod, who had at last reached India, resumed command of the 2nd Battalion 42nd. Having been separated from the main squadron, MacLeod's transport, the *Myrtle*, had made its way to St Augustine's Bay, Madagascar, the appointed rendezvous place in case the transports separated. After waiting for some time, the *Myrtle* proceeded to Madras 'long after having been given up for lost'.[16] Meanwhile Tipu Sahib had pursued the British to Panianj. 'The Enemy kept at a respectable distance, without attempting to bring any Guns near us, in this peaceable situation we remained for five days, when before day light in the morning, a serious attack was made upon our Posts, the Principal push was against mine, they quickly drove in all the Picquets who retired to the Post (a small Pagoda).'[17]

During fierce fighting the Indians were eventually overcome.[18] Among those Norman MacLeod commended in his General Order was John Campbell 'in flying to the attack on the first alarm, the coolness and boldness with which he repeatedly charged the columns of the enemy, his perseverance in the field after being wounded, and the zeal with which he continued to perform every duty in that situation'.[19] After this defeat, Tipu Sahib agreed that Panianj would form the barrier between the Kingdom of Mysore's sphere of interest and that of the British.

In early January 1783, the 2nd Battalion 42nd joined the Bombay army, commanded by Brigadier General Richard Matthews. Following rumours that Hyder Ali had died in December, Matthews had been instructed to take a force down the Malabar coast. Passing through the Ghats, the immense barrier of mountainous land which separated Mysore from the Malabar coast, he was to take possession of Bednur, which Hyder Ali had renamed Hyder Nagur or the Royal City of Hyder. Apart from the prestige of taking Bednur, now under the authority of Tipu, proclaimed the new Sultan, its capture was seen as a strategic necessity. Surrounded by hills, it was not only a natural fortress but the depository for the 'treasures collected by the late Hyder Ali, as well as the grand magazines of his arms and military stores'.[20] On 27 January Matthews entered Bednur.

John Campbell was placed in command of the flank brigade, which was detailed to take the fort of Anantpur, on the Seringapatam road, east of Bednur. Having erected a battery against Anantpur, a breach was made in the walls, and on 15 February the fort stormed, with considerable loss of life to those inside. When news of the attack reached Britain, reports circulated of 'revolting acts of cruelty and inhumanity' against the local Indians.[21] John Moodie, the Royal Artillery's surgeon, denied the allegations, as did Spens, sent by Campbell 'to prevent further effusion of blood, to grant protection where necessary, and to restore order as far as possible in such a juncture'.[22] The next offensive in which the 2nd Battalion 42nd took part was against Tipu Sultan's forces at Simoga, thirty miles from Anantpur. 'It was designed to take them by surprise, and a forced march was therefore necessary,' recollected Spens. 'Accordingly, we moved with scarcely any baggage, and with no bazaar, which gave rise to a most unpleasant privation. For several days we lived on broth and beef without salt, one of the most annoying of the lesser miseries of human life.'[23] After the attack on Anantpur, the 42nd was detailed to occupy two mud forts at Carrical and Morbidry, at the bottom of the Ghats.

On 9 March the fort at Mangalore fell to British troops. Situated on the Malabar coast, about 100 miles from Seringapatam, its possession was an important asset in Britain's continuing bid for supremacy against Mysore. British lines of communication were already badly stretched, and the following month Tipu recaptured Bednur, taking into custody several officers including Matthews, relieved of his command pending an inquiry into the recent conduct of the war.[24] In his place, Lieutenant Colonel Norman MacLeod was appointed Brigadier General and John Campbell took command of the 2nd Battalion 42nd.

Siege of Mangalore 1783–1784

Having retaken Bednur, at the end of April Tipu Sultan launched an offensive against Mangalore. Towards midnight on 6 May, Campbell and the 42nd, who were part of the occupying force, marched from the fort to surprise him. Attacking at daybreak, they routed Tipu's forces, taking possession of his artillery. Highly prized were the bullocks: 'to the number of 180, large fine animals', noted Spens, 'as we could no longer get any supplies of cattle for the commissariat, the country being overrun and in possession of the enemy'.[25] Eager to retaliate, on 19 May Tipu Sultan's formidable army – estimated at 100,000 infantry and cavalry, assisted by a French infantry battalion commanded by Colonel David Charpentier de Cossigny – reached within four miles of Mangalore.[26] Besides guns, many of which were 18- and 24-pounders, there were seven large mortars, out of which, instead of shells, the Indians discharged what Spens described as 'ponderous stones . . . the damage done by these engines was considerable and most annoying, as it was generally only during the night that they were kept in continual play.' Shells, he explained, would perhaps have been more destructive, 'as more might have been killed and wounded by their explosion; but of those who were struck by the stones, scarcely any recovered, such was the shock given to the frame. They forbade rest and sleep and destroyed our roofs, which were not bomb proof, and which we had no means of repairing, a sad grievance during the rainy season.'[27]

On the morning of 23 May, Tipu Sultan's forces attacked one of the outposts. Two battalions of sepoys immediately gave way and three European subalterns were captured, as well as a number of Indian officers and sepoys. After this setback, all other outposts were evacuated, except a circular stone 'Ram' Tower and the Cask Battery, built of casks filled with earth: both had embrasures and guns, and were so near the fort at Mangalore that they were covered by its guns. At this juncture, the strength of those fit for duty inside the fort was recorded as 1,883 men. When the siege began, they were 'under many disadvantages', recalled Spens. 'There was want of safe hospitals, of barrack accommodation and of provisions, medicines, wines, spirits etc and the troops were exposed to all the inclemencies of the monsoon.'[28]

While Campbell was withstanding the siege at Mangalore, Brigadier General Norman MacLeod, accompanied by Colonel Humberston and Major Shaw of the 100th, were proceeding down the Malabar Coast, when they were attacked by Marathas from the fortress of Gheriah, a centre of piracy. Shaw was shot dead and Humberston died of his wounds. MacLeod, who was shot through the lungs, was fortunate to recover.[29]

Meanwhile, events in India were being determined by what was going on elsewhere in the world. In North America, Britain's war with the American colonists was nearly at an end, and peace terms were being discussed with the kings of France and Spain, who had supported the American cause. In faraway Mangalore, Tipu Sultan could no longer rely on France's support against the British in India. On 2 August 1783, articles of cessation of arms were signed and exchanged through the mediation of Monsieur Piveron de Morlay, envoy from the court of France at Tipu Sultan's Court. Henceforward in Mangalore, 'the siege may be said to have been turned into a blockade,' noted Spens, 'during which, we incurred less personal danger and risk of falling into the enemy's hands'. But their 'various privations increased daily, and our situation became every moment more melancholy and distressing'.[30]

On 13 August Campbell had an audience with Tipu Sultan. 'The prince gave him a most polite and gracious reception, and paid him many high compliments,' recounted Spens, also present, 'which the Colonel returned in kind, in the same oriental style, acquitting himself on the occasion with great propriety and éclat.' What also 'excited the Sultan's admiration' was the officers' Highland garb. Presented with shawls, Tipu Sultan sent Campbell 'a very fine horse, which, in our great scarcity of provisions, we afterwards killed and ate'.[31] Other British officers were less fortunate. In early September, Matthews and several other captive officers were poisoned in retaliation 'for some loss Tipu had sustained on the Malabar Coast'.[32] No doubt aware how precarious his position was, Campbell continued to act with caution. At one stage, one of Hyder Ali's old favourites, Mohammed Ali, who was a general in Tipu's army, had offered to betray the Sultan if Campbell would send out a detachment of men to assist in his capture. Not only did Campbell doubt Mohammed

Ali's sincerity, but he also realised that dispatching any men would weaken the garrison, and so he refused. The conspirators were captured and hanged, with the exception of Mohammed Ali, whose sentence was commuted, his fate remaining unknown.[33]

By Christmas Day 1783, provisions in the fort were almost finished. In addition to horsemeat, they were reduced to eating 'rats, mice, frogs, snakes, and carrion-birds'.[34] Scurvy, dysentery and fever had taken their toll. Although some supplies came by sea, the provisions were 'by no means adequate to our wants; nor did they, from their kind and quality contribute much to our comfort, or prevent much sickness'. As Spens related, on several occasions they saw ships of war, but were 'cruelly disappointed' that they did not attempt an assault, because, with negotiations for peace not yet finalised, 'it may be presumed, that the public authorities were most anxious to avoid infringing the terms of the armistice'.[35] According to historian Macfarlane, MacLeod committed the 'monstrous absurdity' of trusting Tipu's word that supplies would be made available to the besieged men, although what was provided was either overpriced or unfit to eat – 'so fetid and foul that the very dogs would not eat them'.[36] Informed of Tipu's 'duplicity', MacLeod sent a letter accusing him of breaking his word and offering to fight the Sultan on the beach, each with 100 men. According to a contemporary account, dictated by Tipu, he rejected the Highland challenge, called MacLeod a 'Nazarene' idolater and asked him to 'taste the flavour of the blows inflicted by the hands of the holy warriors, and behold the terror of the religion of Mohammed'.[37]

With peace negotiations still in progress, by 23 January 1784 Spens was noting that the garrison was 'in such a diseased and famished state, that our excellent commander [Campbell] saw the necessity of assembling a council of war to consider our sad situation and consult and advise as to what was to be done'. Since the majority believed that 'it was unavoidably necessary to propose terms of capitulation', these were duly prepared and submitted to Tipu Sultan, and were 'with a few trifling exceptions, accepted by him'.[38] The garrison had held out for nine months. Of the 1,883 men recorded as fit for duty the previous May, the 'General Return for his Majesty's Troops belonging to the Mangalore garrison' counted twenty-four officers and 208 private soldiers, of which sixteen officers and 153 soldiers were from the 2nd Battalion 42nd. Another survivor was the surgeon who had been the only doctor for the entire complement inside the fort.[39] On 30 January the half-starved defenders of Mangalore departed. In recognition of their courage in withstanding the siege, Tipu Sultan permitted them to leave with the full honours of war.

What mattered for the subsequent history of events was the knowledge that the besieged men had held up Tipu Sultan's army outside Mangalore, preventing him from joining forces with the French. 'The defence of Mangalore, for such a length of time,' recorded Spens, 'with its attendant circumstances, may be justly considered as one of the most important events of that war with Tippoo and the French, which ended in the peace of 1784.' At such a point in time, he said, compelling him to withdraw most of his forces from the Carnatic and retain them on the Malabar coast 'was accomplishing an object of the greatest importance'. Had Tipu Sultan remained in the Carnatic, 'there is no saying how disastrous the result might have been'.

Explaining his reasons for the surrender, Campbell wrote: 'It was with the utmost reluctance I found myself under the disagreeable necessity of evacuating so important a Post as Mangalore, but the situation of the Garrison in every respect called aloud for relief from some Quarter or other the immense number of Sick who were dying by 12 and 15 of a day merely for want of proper nourishment.' On 11 March 1784 a 'treaty of perpetual peace and friendship' was signed in Mangalore between Tipu Sultan and representatives of the East India Company. All prisoners were to be released; among them Captain David Baird and his companions, held for nearly four years in Seringapatam.[40]

During the months spent at Mangalore, Lieutenant Colonel Campbell had fallen gravely ill. When the siege was raised he was in the last stages of consumption. On 23 March 1784 he died, having arrived in Bombay 'feeble and exhausted . . . greatly fatigued in body and mind'.[41] Later, by order of the Court of Directors of the East

India Company, a monument was erected in the Church of Bombay 'to the Memory of Lieutenant-Colonel Campbell, for distinguished services at Mangalore'. In recognition of the struggle, the government of Bombay ordered a gratuity of two months' full pay to be given to all sergeants, drummers and private soldiers who had been at Mangalore; the total sum given to the 2nd Battalion 42nd was £462 9s 2d.[42] Throughout the period of their shared occupancy of the fort at Mangalore, the 2nd Battalion 42nd was recorded as being 'on the most cordial terms' with the 8th Battalion, Bombay Sepoys, who called themselves 'the third Battalion Royal Highlanders', which the soldiers of the 42nd 'in all good humour' permitted them to do.[43] Those who had defended Mangalore became known as 'Mangaloris' or the 'Old Mangalores'.[44]

The 73rd Highland Regiment 1786

While the 2nd Battalion 42nd was engaged in the fight against Mysore and the 1st Battalion was in Nova Scotia, a general correspondence was taking place in Britain in relation to reduction on half-pay. As previously expressed, the War Office's opinion was that junior officers should be reduced in both battalions. Given the economic hardship this would cause to those officers so reduced, representations were at once made by both battalions. From Nova Scotia, Lieutenant Colonel Charles Graham highlighted the fact that 'no Regiment was more exposed to danger underwent more fatigue or suffered more from both' than the 42nd. The newly raised 2nd Battalion 42nd, he said, had no 'other Relation, Connection or Interference with the 42nd whatever – not one officer of the old to be justly considered as such was promoted in the new or had even an option proposed to him of serving in it'.[45] George Yonge received another letter from the officers of the 2nd Battalion, signed by Captains James Drummond and Colin Campbell and Lieutenant Alexander MacGregor, arguing that both Battalions were 'one and the same Regiment'. To impose the hardship of reducing officers on half-pay 'while the youngest officers in the first Battalion are kept standing, is what they do not conceive that you, Sir, would wish to countenance'.[46]

This was not an uncommon problem where a Regiment had two battalions, and to adjudicate the matter, Yonge sent both memoranda to Sir Charles Gould, the Judge Advocate General, for consideration by the 'Board of General Officers'. Keeping with precedent, they decided in favour 'of reducing the junior officers of each Rank throughout the Regiment generally'.[47] Yonge later informed Gould that: 'His Majesty has been pleased to approve the decision of the Board, "that under all the circumstances of the case, it will be most expedient for the Service, as well as most consonant to Justice, that upon the Disbandment of the said Battalion, the Junior Officers in each Rank throughout the Regiment should be reduced" and directions will be given accordingly'.[48]

The following year the concern that the officers of both Battalions had expressed was allayed, when in April 1786 George III 'thought fit to order that the Second Battalion of the Royal Highlanders should be regimented and named the 73rd (Highland) Regiment of Foot'. The 73rd Regiment of Foot (MacLeod's) – which had been fighting in India – was given the number of the 71st, left unassigned following the disbandment of Fraser's Highlanders at the end of the American War.[49] Henceforward, the two battalions would be two separate Regiments with two separate Records of Service. Whenever their paths crossed in their various postings, they would recognise each other as members of the British Army but, as time passed, as not necessarily having formed part of the same regiment.

The first Colonel of the new Regiment was Sir George Osborn, former Lieutenant Colonel of the 3rd Regiment of Foot Guards. After a few months he was succeeded, on 11 August 1786, by Sir William Medows, under whose command the 2nd Battalion 42nd had travelled to India, and who had been appointed Commander-in-Chief and Governor of Madras.[50] Norman MacLeod of MacLeod became the new Regiment's Commanding Officer. As a 'Highland' Regiment, the soldiers continued to wear Highland dress with the same dark 'government' tartan, but since it did not have the title 'Royal', the facings were green instead of blue.[51]

In March 1787, while the new Regiment remained at Dinapore, Richard, Lord Mornington, member of Parliament and lord of the treasury under Prime Minister William Pitt the Younger, obtained an ensigncy for his younger brother, the Hon. Arthur Wesley, in the newly regimented 73rd. Not yet eighteen years old, as his biographer Elizabeth Longford points out, he was 'not too young to appreciate that "since I have undertaken a profession I had better try to understand it"'.[52] He later denied that it was while he was with the 73rd that he had 'a private soldier & all his accoutrements & traps separately weighed' to give 'some insight into what the man had to do & his power of doing it'. Although he confessed to having 'frequently calculated the weight of each of the articles which the Soldier carried', he did not recollect making 'this calculation on the day I joined a regiment or ever said that I had made it at that period'.[53] Wesley remained only a few months in the 73rd, being promoted lieutenant in the 76th on 25 December 1787, by which time the 73rd had moved to Cawnpore, in the Kingdom of Oudh (Oude), bordering Nepal, bounded by the massive mountains of the Himalayas.

The Third Mysore War

Peace with Tipu Sultan did not last long. The next *casus belli* was a dispute over the neighbouring Rajah of Travancore's acquisition of two fortresses in Cochin, which traditionally owed allegiance to Mysore. In December 1789 Tipu Sultan attacked Travancore. Since, according to the Treaty of Mangalore, Travancore was an ally of the East India Company, the Rajah appealed to the Company for assistance. Earl Cornwallis, appointed Governor-General in 1786, at once ordered the Madras army to punish Tipu Sultan for his 'wanton violation of the peace against one of the Company's allies'.[54]

Medows, Commander-in-Chief in Madras, at once issued an order

FARQUAR SHAW
Belonging to the Highland Regiment who was Shot in the Tower 18 July 1743 for desertion. Sold by R. Halton the Corner of Pall-Mall

MACDONNEL.
Piper to the Highland Regiment was Tried in the Tower for Deser-tion in June 1743 & sent to Georgia. Sold by B. Halton at corner of Pall

1. Private Farquhar Shaw, one of three members of the Highland Regiment executed after the 1743 Mutiny. Reverend Campbell, who visited the condemned men, described them all '*of strong national parts and religiously disposed*'.

2. Piper Donald Macdonald (Macdonnel), one of over a hundred mutineers pardoned by King George II, provided they served in '*our several colonies in America*'. He was sent to the Leeward Islands.

3. *The Battle of Fontenoy, 11 May 1745*, by W. Skeoch Cumming. Although defeated by the French, the Highland Regiment was praised for its bravery. The Commanding Officer, Lieutenant Colonel Sir Robert Munro of Foulis, was recorded as being '*every where with his regiment*'.

4. Objects relating to the Early Years of the Regiment. The powder horn was commonly used for carrying gunpowder in North America, where the 42nd served between 1756–1763 and 1776–1786.

India for Ever!

5 *Shillings a Day, and a Black Servant,*

God prosper the **73**rd, or Old Mangalore Regiment.

All Lads of Spirit and true Courage desirous to push their Fortunes, have now a glorious opportunity, by entering from the Militia into the Old

Seventy-third.

The First Battalion is at present on its Passage from New South Wales to the

EAST INDIES,

and the Second Battalion has been particularly selected by His Majesty to do the honourable Duty of the Tower of London, from whence they will follow their First Battalion when completed by the true generous Spirit of the

Militia Volunteers.

NOW is your time, brave Lads of the Militia, hasten and enrol yourselves among the *Old Mangalores*. The 73rd is so called from its great and glorious Services at Mangalore, at Seringapatam, and every other Part of India, for which reason, and their particular knowledge of the Country, The Commander in Chief has been pleased to send them now to the East.

Brave, bold, and undaunted young Heroes of the Militia, whose Hearts beat high at the warlike sound of a Drum, this is the Moment. Do not lose it. Remember your Pay in India, *Five Shillings a Day, and every Man a Black Servant.*

Hasten to the Tower, where you will be welcomed, and received into the Ranks of the 73rd, the *flashing, flaming, fighting, Old Mangalores.*

5. *India Forever!* After the siege of Mangalore 1783–1784, the 2nd Battalion 42nd became known as the 'Old Mangalores'. In 1786, the Battalion was regimented as the 73rd Highland Regiment.

6. *The Glorious Conquest of Seringapatam, 1799* by John Vendramini. The 73rd was part of the attacking force against Tipu Sultan's capital in Mysore. '*The Breach was good, and the men got forward in great style*,' related Lieutenant Charles MacGregor.

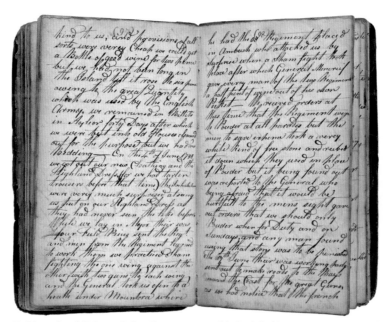

7. Memoir of Private John Simpson, 42nd '*The inhabitants were very much surprised at seeing us put on our Highland dress*,' he recorded when the Regiment was in Minorca in 1799 '*as they had never seen the like before*'.

8. *Attack of the French Chasseurs at the battle of Orthes, 1814*
by Ensign Thomas McNiven, 42nd.

9. *Passage of the Garonne, 1814* by Ensign Thomas McNiven, 42nd. *'Everything directed that a great battle was impending,'* he wrote in his journal. He was wounded at Toulouse in April 1814, later having *'a quiet reflective survey of the battle field'*.

10. Lord John Murray. '*He was the friend and supporter of every deserving officer and soldier in the regiment,*' observed Stewart of Garth.

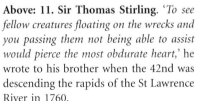

Above: 11. Sir Thomas Stirling. '*To see fellow creatures floating on the wrecks and you passing them not being able to assist would pierce the most obdurate heart,*' he wrote to his brother when the 42nd was descending the rapids of the St Lawrence River in 1760.

Above Left: 12. George Gordon, Marquis of Huntly. He was so proud of his highland dress that he wore it when presented at Court.

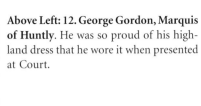

Left: 13. Sir Duncan Cameron. '*With his white head, & stern cast of countenance,*' wrote Ensign Peter Halkett in 1853, he seemed '*the very beau ideal of a commanding officer*'.

14. Sir Robert Henry Dick, described by his fellow officers as *'a generous courteous and considerate commander, a gallant and devoted soldier'*.

15. David Stewart of Garth, author of the celebrated *Sketches of the Character, Manners, and Present State of the Highlanders of Scotland*, describing the Regiment's history until 1815.

16. Lachlan Macquarie, by Gordon M. Woodhouse, *'the father of Australia'*.

17. Sir John Chetham McLeod, *'a good man and well liked by the Regiment,'* noted Private Archibald McIntosh in 1868.

18. *Les Ecossais à Paris*, cartoon sketch from Genty illustrating universal interest in what Highlanders wear under their kilts!

19. *The Highlanders' Farewell* or *The Soldier's Widow* by Hugh Cameron. '*It is needless to describe to you the pangs of parting with friends,*' Lieutenant Henry Antill wrote to his family when leaving for Australia in 1809, '*let me ask you why a soldier should be denied the luxury of a tear! Is his heart to be harder than another's because his way of life is so?*'

indicating that if 'the fortune of war' put Tipu Sultan into their hands, he was to be treated humanely. He also made clear that the severest example would be made of any men who disgraced the Army and that plunderers would not be shown 'the smallest mercy'.[55] The 73rd was placed under the command of Major General Robert Abercromby, younger brother of Ralph. Although eventually less illustrious, he had already fought alongside the 42nd in both the French–Indian and the American Wars.[56] In March 1790 the 73rd moved to Fort William in the Bengal Presidency. The following year, the main British force advanced under Cornwallis in person and took Bangalore, threatening Seringapatam. In retaliation, Tipu's forces adopted a 'scorched-earth' policy, which denied the East India Company's army and their allies vital resources, and deprived the animals of fodder.

In addition to fighting, the 73rd had been assisting in the construction of roads and bringing up provisions across the Ghats. Recognising that the troops were 'worn down by sickness and fatigue and exposed to incessant rains which then deluged the western coast of India', Cornwallis called off any further attack on Tipu Sultan.[57] During the next campaigning season, their fortunes changed. In February 1792 – the year of the Terror in France – Cornwallis was ready to take the offensive again, having ordered Abercromby (and the 73rd) to march from Periapatam (Periyapattinam), where the Bengal army had spent the winter. 'The power of the Sultan being greatly reduced, and preparations for the siege of his capital having been commenced, he sued for peace,' noted the 73rd's Record of Service.[58]

By the terms of the Treaty of Seringapatam, half of Tipu Sultan's vast kingdom in Mysore was ceded to Britain. A large sum of money was to be paid, all prisoners were released; Tipu was obliged to hand over two of his sons as hostages to the agreement. So ended the 'Third Mysore War' and the first military engagement of the 73rd Highland Regiment.

No sooner had the East India Company secured its position in southern India than Britain once more found itself at war with France, whose revolutionary National Convention declared war on

Britain and the Dutch Republic on 1 February 1793. News of the French declaration of war reached India in May and the 73rd was immediately ordered to be ready for active service. This time the soldiers were to march against the French town of Pondicherry (Pondichéry) on the coast of Coromandel. Marching through the Indian countryside in severe heat, as part of a brigade which included the 72nd and 74th Regiments, together with the East India Company's 3rd European Regiment, they were under the command of David Baird, who, after being a prisoner in Seringapatam, was now Lieutenant Colonel of the 71st. The siege against Pondicherry began in early August. The army was encamped in a thick wood 'where tigers were so numerous, that the natives durst not travel in the night'.[59] After a brief skirmish, British troops stormed the town. Three officers and seven soldiers of the 73rd were killed and three soldiers wounded.[60]

The 73rd's next action was in the island of Ceylon (Sri Lanka), off the southern tip of India. In 1795 the Dutch Republic had been annexed by France, becoming the Batavian Republic. This meant that the Dutch settlements in Ceylon were potential enemies. Now under the command of James Spens, one of the survivors of Mangalore, the soldiers embarked on transports bound for the port of Trincomalee on Ceylon's north-eastern coast. The siege was begun as soon as artillery and stores were landed. On 26 August a breach was made and the garrison surrendered, with a total of eight Europeans killed and thirty-six wounded, although no one from the 73rd was killed.[61] Over the next year, the Regiment continued operations against the Dutch until all the settlements were brought under British control. Finally, in February 1796, the Governor, John Geraud Van Angelbeck, surrendered and the fortress at Colombo fell into British hands. Since the inhabitants of the interior had remained independent from Dutch control, the Record of Service noted that 'they were not interfered with by the British so long as they preserved a peaceful demeanour'.[62]

While the Regiment was in Ceylon, after ten years as Colonel, Medows became Colonel of the 7th Dragoon Guards. The 73rd's new Colonel was Major General Gerard Lake, who had served in the American War under Cornwallis and had also been taken prisoner at Yorktown.[63] On Lake's request, the King granted that the word *Mangalore* should be borne on the Regimental Colour and Appointments 'in consideration of the gallant conduct displayed in the defence of that place'.[64]

The Fourth Mysore War

Tipu Sultan's power had been diminished, but he was not vanquished. War in Europe, with the rise to power of a belligerent Napoleon Bonaparte, had given him an opportunity to reassert his authority, leading to the final Anglo-Mysore War. In 1798 he entered into an agreement with the Governor of the Ile de France, the island of Mauritius and sent an embassy to Zaman Shah, the king of Afghanistan, encouraging him to attack British possessions. To pre-empt an attack, Lord Mornington ordered a British force to strike at the heart of Tipu Sultan's dominions. Having served in Europe, Mornington's brother, Arthur Wesley, had returned to India in 1797 as Lieutenant Colonel of the 33rd, changing his name back to its traditional spelling: Wellesley.[65] Due to his brother's patronage, he was given the additional command of chief adviser to the Nizam of Hyderabad, Asaf Jan II. Recognising the growing authority of the British, the Nizam had been the first to accept Mornington's doctrine of 'subsidiary alliance' which was to form the foundation of Britain's future relations with the princes of India. In return for protection, the Nizam had to permit a British Resident at his court and agree to expel all non-British foreigners from his state – in other words the French – as well as keeping and paying for British forces in his state.[66]

In command of British troops, reinforced by the Bengal army, was Lieutenant General George Harris, who had fought in the earlier campaigns against Tipu Sultan.[67] Towards the end of March, the army reached Mallavelly, near Tipu Sultan's encampment. When his forces attacked British pickets, a battle ensued which left one thousand of Tipu's soldiers dead and resulted in their immediate withdrawal to Seringapatam.

A month later, the general attack began. The 73rd in the 2nd Brigade, commanded by thirty-five-year-old Brigadier John Coape Sherbrooke, was one of six European infantry regiments – a total of 4,608 men – in a 'Grand Army' of over 20,000.[68] Captain Michael Moneypenny, commanding four companies of the 73rd and four companies of Bengal Volunteers, was ordered to turn the right flank of Tipu Sultan's army. The centre column, composed of six companies of the 73rd and four of Bengal Volunteers, under Brevet Lieutenant Colonel the Hon. George St John, was ordered to create a diversion, which – if appropriate – was to become the main attack. Another column to the right was to turn the enemy's left flank. 'The enemy's resistance was unavailing and the several attacks were completely successful,' noted Cannon's *Historical Record*.[69]

By the end of April, having established an adequate breach in the walls, the assault on Seringapatam began. Advancing in two columns, the 73rd was in the right column of attack, instructed 'to move along the south Rampart of the Fort, leaving such parties as may be thought necessary'. If possible, both columns were ordered to attack the fortress at the same time, but if 'the road or breach are too narrow the left Attack is to move on first. The leading companies to use the bayonet principally and not to fire but in cases of absolute necessity.'[70] Lieutenant John Lalor, commissioned as an ensign in the 73rd in 1792, led the columns into position. Baird, who had been given the senior brigade command, led the storming party.[71]

On 4 May the assault commenced. 'The soldiers were all in the greatest spirits; about half past eleven o'clock General Baird ordered each man a dram and a biscuit,' related Lieutenant Charles McGregor, 33rd, 'and at 1 o'clock he ordered the troops to advance, the passage across the river was bad; [there were] sharp rocks and some parts [were] nearly four feet deep. The Breach was good, and the men got forward in great style.' Within two hours, they had taken the fort, but with severe casualties. 'About 27 officers were either killed or wounded, and about 200 Europeans; at least 9,000 of the enemy were killed, the slaughter was immence all over the Fort; in some passages, the dead were five and six deep laying on one another, many women were unavoidably killed,' noted McGregor, conceding that the British victory cost many innocent lives.[72]

By comparison, the 73rd emerged from the fighting relatively unscathed. Only one officer, Lieutenant Lalor, who had been leading from the front, was killed in addition to several private soldiers. Among the wounded was Ensign Henry Antill, whose father was an American Loyalist and had fought on the side of the British during the American War. After the battle, Baird took possession of the Palace and went in search of Tipu Sultan's body, reported as having been killed in a gateway crammed with dead. 'It was after a long search discovered, and brought to the Palace, a servant that was lying wounded beside him, discovered the body to us, or we should not have found it.'[73] Tipu Sultan, aged forty-eight, who had relentlessly fought the British for over twenty years, was buried in the mausoleum which he had built over his father's tomb. British Colours were raised over the fortress. The victory gave Britain control over the lands of Mysore 'and extinguished a power in India which had proved itself a formidable enemy'.[74] As a souvenir, the 73rd acquired one of Tipu Sultan's ornate long staffs, made of wood with an engraved silver top and with the bottom encased in silver.[75]

Having heard 'the official detail of the glorious and decisive victory obtained at Seringapatam', Mornington offered 'his cordial thanks and sincere congratulations to the Commander-in-Chief, and to all the officers and men composing the gallant army which achieved the capture of the capital of Mysore on that memorable day'. He went on to say that he viewed with admiration 'the consummate judgment with which the assault was planned, the unequalled rapidity, anima-tion, and skill with which it was executed, and the humanity which distinguished its success'. Finally he pointed out that the 'lustre of the victory' could only be equalled by 'the substantial advantages which it promises to establish, in restoring the peace and safety of the British possessions in India on a durable foundation of genuine sincerity'.[76]

Once assured of victory, what especially interested the officers and men was their share in the prize money, assiduously counted by the East India Company's paymasters. The local currency was the pagoda – thus, after the fall of Mysore, subalterns received 1,080 pagodas, a captain 2,160, a major 4,000, lieutenant colonel 6,000, colonels 10,000, major generals 15,000 and the Commander-in-Chief 150,000 pagodas in cash – as a first dividend. Since the Nizam of Hyderabad had supplied troops to help, he too was given a financial reward.[77] Once the fighting was over, traders and merchants came from Madras 'with all kinds of supplies', noted Lieutenant McGregor, who took the opportunity of exchanging from the 33rd into the 73rd 'for a difference of £150'.[78] In the General Orders issued by General Harris, the gallantry of Lieutenant Colonel Moneypenny and the Hon. George St John were particularly recorded. In 1818, the 73rd was given Royal Authority to bear 'on its Colors and Appointments . . . the word *Seringapatam* in commemoration of the distinguished gallantry displayed' in the storming and capture of that fortress.[79]

After Tipu Sultan's death, the Kingdom of Mysore was again reduced. The East India Company retained control of an extensive area of the state, while another part was given to the Nizam of Hyderabad in thanks for his assistance and another to the Marathas; the remainder of the state continued as an independent state under Mummadi Krishnaraja Wodeyar, descendant of the Rajah whom Tipu's father, Hyder Ali, had deposed decades ago. On 30 June, the new King of Mysore 'was this day placed on the throne, General Harris and all the staff was present, the ceremony took place at the old town of Mysore,' recorded McGregor, noting that he was 'but 4 years of age'.[80] Wellesley, appointed Governor of Seringapatam and Mysore, embarked on reforming the tax and justice systems. 'Thus was the hostile combination against England confounded, the British territory extended, and its power and revenue increased.'[81]

The 73rd remained in Mysore throughout the summer of 1799. 'The Garrison begins to get pleasant,' noted McGregor. 'We have frequent amusement, Deer hunting generally twice a week with the chieters, a kind of Tyger or Leopard trained to this.' On another occasion they had 'a grand entertainment' at the young King of Mysore's palace. There were regular races. Although the markets were well supplied 'with everything there is', accommodation for the soldiers and officers was not good. As the monsoon season approached with heavy rains, the stench was 'simply insufferable in the middle of the day, when the bodies are buried'.[82] In November, the 73rd was ordered to garrison Seringapatam, where they celebrated 30 November by giving 'a Grand Ball'. As McGregor noted, 'this has always been a custom among the Regiment every year on St Andrews Day, all the officers of the Regiment were present, and the things went off astonishingly well'.[83]

At the beginning of 1800, the 73rd were still in Seringapatam. On 14 February, with Gerard Lake's promotion to Commander-in-Chief in India and Colonel of the 80th Regiment, General Lord Harris was promoted Colonel of the 73rd, Moneypenny remaining as the Regiment's Lieutenant Colonel. When not on active service, the garrison was 'very pleasant. There are two very comfortable messes established [for the] 33rd and 73rd and we have a very good coffee room and two Billiard tables, and the officers have many of them built comfortable quarters for themselves. There are now three European ladies in Garrison and we have now and then dances, etc. Colonel Wellesley makes himself very popular, he regularly dines, twice a week the two public days they have here for strangers, with his Regiment the 33rd.'[84]

A residue of opposition persisted amongst the Indians and in February 1800 McGregor was recording in his journal how there was 'a little conspiracy among the natives to lay hold of Colonel Wellesley and to carry off the Princes too, several Black fellows are confined on suspicion'.[85] On 17 March 'there was a great disturbance amongst the natives this day and most of the Madras servants were concerned'. From what McGregor understood, the dispute was between various lower castes of Indians. 'They proceeded this year to very great lengths, got armed and took possession of a hill near us, they were not properly dispersed until Colonel Wellesley ordered them to be fired at.'[86] When the soldiers were not involved in policing the locals, the troops benefited from 'plenty of all kinds of shooting – many Tygers are seen here at times'.[87]

One of their more arduous operations under Wellesley's command, involving both the 73rd and the 77th, was capturing a rebel chief, Doondiah, who had escaped from prison in Seringapatam and had assembled a large force against the British. While the countryside was 'fine', forage was scarce. Unaccustomed to the heavy rainfall of tropical climates, they had swiftly to adapt: 'in the part of this country we are in,' observed McGregor, 'we find the monsoon is only setting in, we have rain almost every night and as we shall most probably have some rivers to cross, we have determined on carrying boats along. This is a most laborious undertaking; the common basket boat of the country will take at best 35 men to carry and this is the only mode of carrying them from here, being so awkwardly made.'[88]

Throughout July and August, they were constantly on the move, travelling between four and fourteen, sometimes twenty miles a day, occasionally encountering 'the enemy'. As usual, they suffered as much through illness as they did through military encounters. 'Twenty men are obliged to be carried in Doolies,' observed McGregor on 18 July, commenting that the 77th Regiment had more than double the number of sick than the 73rd.[89] Heavy rain continued to impede their movements: 'it rained incessantly all this day and our camp is in a complete swamp, it is impossible to stir out of our tents without being knee deep in mud – our Bullocks are dying fast, from the great rain and there being no corn and for want of forage.' As they resumed their march, even the 200 camels were beginning to 'fagg' and the elephants which were required to carry their tents 'look bad'.[90]

On 10 September, Wellesley and the combined contingent of cavalry and infantry – in all about 1,100 strong – encountered Doondiah, who, as McGregor related, had at least 5,000 of his best horse. 'Doondiah had taken up a good position, a village on his right and on the left some rocks and strong broken ground, in his front a deep nullah, a water course, and all rotten cotton ground, full of holes. After forming in two lines, the Colonel charged the enemy and met with complete success – there was at first some appearance of a recharge from the enemy, they stood undecided for a short time, while our gallopers were firing, but after our cavalry got amongst them they all gave way, about 1000 were left dead and the same number or more wounded on the field. Our loss was not great, two Europeans killed and 11 wounded, with about 60 horses.' Doondiah was killed: 'he fell after receiving 11 wounds; sometime after his wife – a girl that was attached to him – tried to carry off the body, and was taken prisoner in the attempt.'[91] Wellesley took pity on Doondiah's orphaned son, Salabut, and paid for his future upkeep.[92]

After the battle, the cavalry 'got a great deal of plunder, about 300 camels were taken, some elephants and a number of horses'.[93] Inevitably, discipline had suffered, and in October McGregor was obliged to record that 'the sentence of a General Court Martial was this day put in execution at 6 o'clock in the morning.' Two of the 73rd Regiment were hanged, one 'a foreigner for desertion to the enemy'; the other was recorded as being an Englishman who had fired at an officer. Another soldier of the 73rd was sentenced to death, 'but drew lots with another man and [was] saved'. Two more men of the 73rd were flogged.[94]

Throughout 1801 the 73rd was involved in skirmishes against local Polygar chieftains who challenged the East India Company's authority; as usual, in addition to jungle warfare, they had to deal with the extremes in climate. 'A great deal of rain fell during the night and the days are still very hot,' McGregor recorded in May 1801. 'Our tents are very bad indeed and we were altogether very uncomfortable.'[95] At the end of the year, an attack on a Polygar fort left a number of officers wounded, including Lieutenant Colonel Moneypenny. Major James MacDonald was so seriously wounded that he requested a pension for his wounds and was granted a year's pay as a major.[96] Three other officers were wounded and seventy-three soldiers killed. Eventually they succeeded in taking the place 'by storm after breaking the walls without the loss of a man'.[97]

Lieutenant John McGregor, who had described the Regiment's activities in detail, had fallen so ill that he was obliged to return to Europe, concluding his diary – found in a Hindu temple in 1891 –

in early 1802. Having failed to sell his lieutenancy to pay for the £200 passage, he had to borrow the money. One of those whose help he requested was the 73rd's surgeon, Dr Pulteney Mein, who offered a loan. 'This was a most handsome thing of the Doctor, but as I had already arranged all matters I returned him his order with thanks,' McGregor noted on 16 March.[98]

For the remainder of the 73rd's service in India, fighting against the Polygars continued. British troops were also involved in fighting against the Maratha Confederacy, whose rulers still controlled large areas of northern India and guarded their independence jealously. In October 1801 the 73rd was sent to Gooty, formerly part of the kingdom of Mysore, before being posted to Bellary, returning to Gooty in July 1803 and then moving to Pondicherry, where the Regiment remained for a year. The 73rd's final year in 'the East Indies' was spent at Fort St George in Madras. The East India Company's overthrow of the Polygar chieftains resulted in the suppression of the influence of the local leaders. The war against the Marathas continued until 1805, erupting again in 1817–18 and resulting in the cession of yet more territory to the East India Company. After over twenty years in India, the events of which the soldiers were undoubtedly most proud were those for which, in time, they received the Battle Honours of *Mangalore*, *Mysore* and *Seringapatam*.

10.

Egypt: the Honours of Battle 1801

'Highlanders! Remember Egypt!'

Sir John Moore at Corunna[1].

1802

The Army of the East

While the 42nd Royal Highland Regiment was fighting the soldiers of France and Spain in the West Indies and the Mediterranean, and the newly regimented 73rd was in India, the armies of the French Republic had been triumphant in Europe. Having temporarily abandoned a plan to invade Britain, in 1797 Napoleon Bonaparte had turned his attention towards Egypt, intending to challenge Britain's supremacy in India. By establishing a presence on the shores of North Africa, he aimed at forging an alliance with Britain's enemy in southern India, Tipu Sultan. After capturing Malta in June 1798, and eluding pursuit by the Royal Navy, on 1 July, Napoleon and his 'Army of the East' arrived in the harbour city of Alexandria. Three weeks later, he defeated the Mameluke Sultans of Egypt in the Battle of the Pyramids, capturing Cairo and driving them into Upper Egypt.

Soon afterwards, on 1 August – in the Battle of the Nile – the Royal Navy fleet, commanded by Admiral Lord Nelson, surprised the French fleet, anchored in Aboukir Bay, and destroyed or captured all but two ships. This defeat left Napoleon literally stranded on the shores of Egypt. In early 1799 his forces invaded the Middle Eastern lands of the Ottoman Empire, storming the coastal towns of Gaza, Jaffa and Haifa. With his army weakened by bubonic plague, Napoleon's attempt to besiege Acre was repulsed by the Turks, assisted by British troops. Returning to Cairo in May 1799 – at the time of Tipu Sultan's defeat and death at Seringapatam – Napoleon escaped to France. On 9 November – 18 Brumaire, Year VIII under the French Republic - he staged a *coup d'état* against the 'Directory' which had ruled France since 1795, and appointed himself the French Republic's First Consul. In June 1800 he secured a decisive victory against Austrian forces at Marengo in Piedmont.

To counter France's expansionism, Prime Minister William Pitt agreed to send a detachment of British forces stationed in Minorca to Italy. Relieved of garrison duty and recognised for its 'excellent

228

discipline' and 'orderly conduct' the 42nd Royal Highland Regiment left Minorca on 31 August 1800.[2] 'Next morning by Break of Day we stood over to the Island of Majorca but the wind being westerly we was beating up against it and making little way of it till the 12 of Sept. when we got a fair wind and on the 14th we came in sight of Gibraltar and came to ancor in the Bay,' recorded Private John Simpson.[3] The original order was to embark on transports to relieve the Republic of Genoa, on the Italian coast. But once Genoa had fallen to the French, the order to land in Italy was rescinded and the Regiment was ordered to make for Gibraltar.

Fresh instructions were then given for the 42nd to be part of an expedition to attack Cadiz. Since 1797, France had been enforcing a naval blockade against Spain to prevent the Spanish from sending supplies to their South American colonies. Yet again the British action was suspended, when news came that the Spanish were proffering a flag of truce because of 'a pestilential disease raging with great violence in the city at the time'.[4] 'The object of this communication,' explained Stewart of Garth, 'was to deprecate any attack upon a town and people already suffering under the ravages of a pestilence, which had carried off thousands.'[5] The British fleet, with the soldiers on board, was still at sea in November; separated into two squadrons, 'one [was] Bound for the Island of Minorca and the other for the Island of Malta', retaken from the French in 1800 after their unpopular occupation. 'Our ship the *Inconstant* belonged to the Malta Squadron,' noted Simpson, 'and the remainder of our Regiment belonged to the Minorca one so that the Regiment was divided which made us believe that it would not be long before we should meet again.'[6]

Britain's new strategy was to expel Napoleon's 'Army of the East' from Egypt, and the 42nd was to be part of this great enterprise. 'This intelligence was joyfully received,' noted Stewart of Garth, who was serving with the Regiment. 'All were elevated, both by the prospect of relief from the monotony of a soldier's life on board a transport, and by a debarkation in an interesting country.'[7] Having anchored in the harbour of Malta, 'in the evening we hauled in close to the

Beach,' recorded Simpson. 'It's one of the best harbours in the world surrounded with a high ridge on each side covered with fine building[s]; as soon as we came to ancor we were suppleyd with every article we stood in need of, and the next day the whole fleet was suppleyd with good fresh Beef from the Island of Cisily and Vegitables of all kinds was very cheap, wine of the best Quality . . . while we lay here the Taylors were employd in making the new Cloathing in the Town of Vilitta [Valetta] and the men was sent ashore everyday to walk two or three miles for Exercise.'[8]

After leaving Malta, the fleet sailed to the Bay of Marmorice, north of Rhodes, 'a fine bay where 7 or Eight Hundred ships may lay in at a time in perfect safety, it being surrounded on all sides with a high ridge of mountains, and a long narrow entrance into it with high land on each side.' It was, Simpson recalled, in the same bay where the French fleet had been concealed before Nelson came upon it in Aboukir Bay. 'In this bay there is plenty of good water to be got very easy and wood in abundance, the whole time we lay here there was strong working partys sent to cut wood for the use of the fleet for which they had half a pint of rum each man.'[9] There they remained throughout the winter months, collecting provisions and horses for the forthcoming expedition to Egypt. In early February 1801 there was 'a tremendous storm of rain and hail, which was as large as musket balls with loud claps of thunder and a great deal of lightning'. Safe as their anchorage was, the ships could not hold their anchors, 'and ran foul of each other so that their was a great deal of damage done to the shipping'. Fortunately, there were no rocks in the Bay, otherwise the damage would have been greater.[10]

Alexandria

On 22 February 1801 the Royal Navy – carrying an army of nearly 15,000 men – set sail: 'the greatness of the armament,' noted Cannon's *Historical Record* of the 42nd, 'containing the disposable force of England, and its destiny affecting the dearest interest of the country, was a scene calculated to excite impressive reflections.'[11] After a six-day journey from the Turkish coast, the fleet appeared off Alexandria, dropping anchor in Aboukir Bay. The 42nd Royal Highland Regiment formed part of the Reserve under Major General John Moore, who had distinguished himself in the American War and in the West Indies under Sir Ralph Abercromby.[12] Under Lieutenant Colonel Dickson's command, the 42nd was detailed to be part of the landing force, comprising over 5,000 men. 'But the sea ran so high and so large a surf that it was impossible to land,' noted Simpson. After waiting a week for the storm to abate, giving the French 'full time to get every thing ready for giving us a warm reception', over a hundred boats made for the shore.[13] As they approached, they were met by 'a tempest of bullets which cut the surface of the water into deep furrows, and sank several of the boats'.[14] 'Every discharge,' recalled Simpson, 'was answered by a shout from the seamen, and all seemed insensible of danger and when within musket shot, the enemy commenced a smart fire from at least 3000 troops.'[15]

Once in shallow waters, the soldiers made for the beach, 'rushing up the steep ascent rendered difficult by the loose sand in the face of the fire of a battalion of infantry and two guns'. Having gained the summit, they closed in on their opponents with their bayonets.[16] 'As soon as we had formed,' recorded Simpson, 'we charged the enemy and the reserve Brigade on the right ascended the height and took eight pieces of Canon which the enemy seeing, they then retreated with the loss of one half of their Artillery.'[17] When the French soldiers withdrew to form a second line, the British forced another retreat. In the annals of the official history, it was 'a victory almost without parallel'.[18]

Their success was not without cost. From the ranks of the 42nd, thirty-one soldiers were killed. Eight officers, seven sergeants, four drummers and 140 soldiers were wounded.[19] Among the wounded officers was Lieutenant Colonel James Stewart and Captain Charles Macquarie, who had transferred to the 42nd from the 116th Foot in 1795. Macquarie had received a serious wound to his head, which caused him pain and dizzy spells for the rest of his life.

Coincidentally, his brother Lachlan was in Egypt, serving as Deputy Adjutant General to an 8,000-strong contingent of the army from India, which had come to Egypt under the command of Major General David Baird. The two Macquarie brothers had not met for over ten years, and most of their time together was spent discussing the purchase of land on the island of Mull, in the Inner Hebrides, where they had been born.[20] The major losses were sustained while the men were in the boats and climbing the heights in order to silence the French batteries.

David Stewart of Garth witnessed a strange incident while watching the burial of some of the dead soldiers. 'I stept up to one of them, and touching his temple, felt that it retained some warmth. I then told the soldiers not to bury him, but to carry him to the surgeon, as he did not appear to be quite dead.' Once the soldier regained consciousness, 'in six weeks he was able to do his duty. He lived many years afterwards, and was most grateful for my interference.'[21] Having secured their presence on Egyptian soil, the 42nd encamped near the fort of Mandora.

On 13 March the British army made its first attack on the French troops, who had taken up position 'on an advantageous height with his right to the canal of Alexandria and his left to the sea'.[22] 'The army marched in two lines by the left, with an intention to turn their right flank. The troops had not been long in motion before the enemy descended from the heights on which they were formed, and attacked the leading Brigades of both lines,' noted Simpson.[23] With the French falling back on their entrenchments before Alexandria, the British army followed them 'till the line had come within point-blank range of the hostile batteries'. But the French fire was too 'murderous' and Abercromby, who had had a narrow escape when his horse was shot from under him, ordered a halt.[24]

The 42nd in the Reserve, under Moore's command, were positioned on high ground, close to the sea, four miles from Alexandria 'with our right to the sea and our left to the lake Mariolis'.[25] Although they had not been in the forefront of the fight, a French bombardment in their midst had caused several casualties in addition to the losses already sustained. Three soldiers were killed. Their Commanding Officer, Dickson, had been wounded, together with two other officers and several soldiers.[26] 'The first duty incumbent upon us was to bury the Dead as we had possession of the field of action, it took up the most part of the night in compleating this Duty; and getting dark their was some of the wounded lay all night on the ground. We sent out strong Picquets and guards in our front and sent a great many men to work to raise Battreys to strengthen our position, it was found necessary to plant some heavy guns before the tower of Abokir.'[27] For a week the two armies faced each other, strengthening their defences. 'The 19th the Tower of Abokir surrendered after a siege of 6 Days and the Prisoners marched out to the number of 200,' recorded Simpson.[28] Every morning before daybreak the soldiers had to be under arms, lest the French attack.

On the night of 20 March, as usual, the men had lain 'according to orders, with our Blankets, Haversacks, Canteens, and Accoutrements on our Back all night'.[29] After being woken at dawn, 'half an hour afterwards the fire of musketry and artillery on the left announced the approach of adverse forces and every eye was directed in anxious expectation towards the gloomy atmosphere which concealed the approach of the enemy.'[30] The French military commander, General Abdullah Jacques-François de Menou, Baron de Boussay, had issued orders 'to attack the English tomorrow morning the 21st. All the troops will therefore be at three o'clock in the morning precisely in order of battle without beat of drum and without making any kind of noise 200 paces before the present camp.'[31]

As soon as the attack began, at 'about 4 o'clock', the left wing of the 42nd advanced under Major James Stirling's command to fill the open space left by the 28th Foot – later renowned as the 'Glorious Glosters' – which had taken up position in line with the ruins of Queen Cleopatra's Palace.[32] Finding that the element of surprise had been lost, the French 'set up a tremendous huzza and set all their Drums to work and trumpets and rushed on with fury, the noise they made caused the Elements to Echo'. As Simpson continued, although their plan 'to put us in Confusion' was good, they were up against the 'best troops that England could produce'. 'Just as they came up with the Battrey, they were met by the 42nd Regiment, who had just come up in time to hinder them from gaining the Flank of the Battrey in which the 28th Regiment was posted.'

Recalling the details of the battle in his journal, Simpson realised that if the French had succeeded in getting possession of this battery, 'the whole British army would have been ruined as it commanded all the other posts in our Possession'.[33] Continuing his account: 'When the enemy found that they were opposed by Troops on each flank of the Battrey No. 1, they made a stand and commenced a regular fire which they supported for a while but finding that they could not make us retire and being exposed to a heavy fire from us, they retired under the cover of the raising ground on which the Battrey was formed.'

The French then formed 'a Strong Column of their Cavalry on Purpose to make a Charge and put us in Confusion; they accordingly came on us at full speed at the time we were keeping up a constant fire on the Infantry and but too well succeeded in their plan; owing to the Darkness and the softness of the sand the Cavalry were never observed till they made their way through the 42nd Regiment by cutting down all that came in their way, which put them in confusion for a minute.' But, as Simpson was anxious to point out, the Highlanders 'soon formed again and the Cavalry in returning to follow their stroke were disappointed when they found a strong compact line faced about'.[34] The British 'steady and well-directed fire' forced their opponents to retire.[35]

Simpson also noted that the British had an unintended advantage: 'When we first came on the ground, we had no tents, and each Mess of six men digged a hole in the sand. These Holes were in general six feet deep and descended by steps; they were of a large enough size to hold the Mess of six men to shelter them from the night Air which was very cold. These holes which the 28th Regiment had made were in the rear of our Regiment the 42nd.' When the French cavalry charged, they had broken through the ranks 'exactly in front of these holes, and before they could stop tumbled into them so that they were full of mess and Horse some of which lay under their Horses till the Action was over'. Although the French field cannon kept up a 'continuous roar', they failed to turn the British right flank, 'which was their plan'.[36]

As the fighting continued, Napoleon's 'Invincible Legion' – the Bons Grenadiers, about 1,300 strong – advanced. 'They got round the left of the 42nd Regiment in a Close Column, through a hollow piece of ground that lay between the left of the 42nd Regt and the height on which the Brigade of Guards were Posted. There was about a Quarter of a Mile in that place without any troops being Posted,' related Simpson.[37] When they first appeared in the rear of the 42nd, the commanding officer thought they were the Brigade of Foreigners, comprising mainly the Minorca Regiment, who were coming up to reinforce the British. But, observed Simpson, 'upon closer examination they were found that their Dress did not consist of the same as that of the Foreign Brigade'.

Whereupon, Major James Stirling, who had taken command after Dickson was wounded, ordered the men to open fire; when they returned the fire, he 'ordered the left wing to face about and gave the word Charge with fury which was done. The Enemy being at this time in Close Column and hearing this rush coming on them, they set off thinking to defend themselves inside the ruins of Queen Cleopatra's palace which was not far distant, on the right of the Battrey and rather to the rear; the 42nd pursued them and kept killing the rear of their column with the Baynot and when the head of their Column reached the old walls of the palace great was their surprise to find that in place of defending themselves in that place there was two regiments posted their, Viz. the 23rd and 58th Regiments of Foot.'[38] In hot pursuit came the 42nd, which left the Invincibles no way of escape. 'It was on that spot that the most of that fine Regiment fell all but about 150 who was not hurt, were marched Prisoners and Embarked on board of the fleet.'[39] Having captured the Invincible Legion's standard, Stirling entrusted it to Sergeant James Sinclair.

No sooner had they destroyed the Invincibles and reformed line than the French cavalry charged.[40] 'The Cavalry came on at the full gallop but they received a very hot fire and was received with a firm Baynot.' Lacking support from their infantry, and not realising what had happened to the Invincibles, they withdrew, having lost 'a great number of both men and Horses'. According to Simpson, 'the Enemy seemed insensible of danger they having drank a great Quantity of spirits each man which was given to them no doubt to "inspire" them in their cruel design. The field of action and inside of the old walls where the bayoneting of the Invincibles took place smelled more like a spirit shop than anything else.'[41]

In the general melee and with the action having started in the dark, there was confusion on the British side. According to Cannon's *Historical Record*, when the French infantry came forward there was not enough time to complete their formation.[42] Abercromby's instruction to the 'brave Highlanders' was to 'remember your country, remember your forefathers!'[43] Rushing forward 'with heroic ardour', the Highlanders had succeeded in driving back the French infantry. But when Moore saw the growing numbers of French cavalry preparing to charge through the lines of the retreating infantry, he ordered the 42nd to desist from pursuing the infantry and to prepare to repel the cavalry. The order to fall back, repeated to Stirling, was 'only partially heard by the regiment, owing to the noise from the firing; the companies which heard it fell back, and the others remained in advance'. Even so, 'in this broken state', the 42nd succeeded in inflicting serious loss. Unfortunately, during the fighting, Sergeant Sinclair of the 42nd, to whom care of the Invincibles' standard had been entrusted, was stunned. When he recovered, the standard had gone, later to be recovered by Private Anthony Lutz of the Minorca Regiment.[44]

'By this time our great gun shot was run out, and the 42nd regiment had no ammunition. We were firing stones from the great guns in place of shot, but we soon got a supply.'[45] Fortunately, the Foreign Brigade came up 'to fill up the vacant ground which was between the reserve Brigade and the Brigade of Guards'. Another French cavalry charge was unsuccessful. As Simpson later reflected, 'It was the Orders of the Day for the Enemy to put the front line of the English army to the Baynot and after they had accomplished it they were to form again, on purpose to attack the rear line. They expected to find the reserve brigade all getting up out of their sleep and in confusion, but we had too vigilant a commander to be took in that situation.'[46]

The intense fighting which had begun at 4 a.m. continued throughout the day, 'and it was night time before the Enemy retired. About 12 o'clock the Enemy formed in different columns and took the retreat, when our Battreys and Field guns gave them a grand salute.'[47] Finally, the 'great guns' of the English ceased firing and the soldiers marched to their different encampments. 'The French left upward of 5,000 laying on the field besides prisoners and what wounded they carried along with them, which was supposed to be a great number. The English army lost considerable in this engagement but nothing in proportion to the French.'[48] Of the over one thousand men wounded and nearly two hundred and fifty killed during the 21 March battle, the 42nd Royal Highland Regiment lost four officers and forty-eight private soldiers. Major James Stirling, seven other officers, six sergeants and 247 private soldiers were wounded.[49]

The Regiment's future historian, Captain David Stewart of Garth, was among those wounded, although when writing his history he did not mention his own part in the battle nor the nature of his wound. One of the dead officers was Brevet Major Robert Bisset, who had transferred to the Regiment as a captain in 1793, and whom Stewart of Garth recorded as having 'the character of the soldier, the gentleman, and the man of the world'.[50]

During the battle, Abercromby, astride his horse, had been attacked by two French Dragoons. 'At this moment a corporal of the 42nd seeing his situation,' narrated Stewart of Garth, 'ran up to his assistance, and shot one of the assailants, on which the other retired.' Abercromby's wound was serious. As was later discovered, a musket ball had entered his groin and lodged in his hip joint. 'A soldier of the Highlanders,' continued Stewart of Garth, 'seeing that he had some difficulty in dismounting, assisted him, and asked if he should follow him with the horse.' Abercromby's reply was sombre: 'I don't think I will require him any more this day.' Despite his wound, for the rest of the day he continued to observe the battle. 'He betrayed no symptoms of personal pain, nor relaxed a moment the intense interest he took in the state of the field; nor was it perceived that he was wounded, till he was joined by some of the staff, who observed the blood trickling down his thigh.'[51] Abercromby's death a week later on board HMS *Foudroyant* in Aboukir Bay 'was greatly lamented by the Soldiers of the whole army in Egypt', noted Private Simpson in his memoir.[52] 'Though a rigid disciplinarian, when rigour was necessary, such was the general confidence in his judgment and in the honour and integrity of his measures, that,' observed Stewart of Garth, 'in the numerous armies which he at different periods commanded, not a complaint was ever heard, that his rigour bordered on injustice, or that his decisions were influenced by partiality, prejudice, or passion.'[53]

Abercromby's successor was Major General John Hely-Hutchinson, who commended the stand taken against a superior French force. 'The Reserve, against whom the principal attack of the Enemy was directed, conducted themselves with unexampled spirit; they resisted the impetuosity of the French Infantry and repulsed several charges of Cavalry . . . the 28th and the 42nd Regiments acted in the most distinguished, and brilliant manner.'[54]

While the soldiers were enjoying much-needed rest and refreshment, assisting the wounded and burying the dead, intelligence came from a deserter 'who informed our General that it was reported in Alexandria to be the intention of General Menou to attack the English Army for three successive days; accordingly on the night of the 22nd the whole of the Army was marched to their alarm posts and remained under arms all night.' General Orders stipulated:

> Should any attack take place, it is hoped the greatest order, silence, and regularity may be observed. The troops must be fully conscious of the glory they have already acquired and of their superiority over an enemy whom they have so often beaten. But at the same time providence and discipline, must be strongly recommended and with a little caution, the British Army in Egypt will find they are Invincible.[55]

But no attack came. The following day another deserter 'gave the same account as the one that came in the day before, and said that the whole of the troops in Alexandria were marched to the outworks at night on purpose to attack our army (not having any hopes of Victory) but to cripple our Army so that they could not act on the offensive.' When they reached the outside of the works, the troops 'showed a disposition to go no farther'. When asked the reason, 'they said they would defend the Garrison to the last drop of their blood, but they might as well be took to a slaughter house as engage the English army again.'[56]

With the French army withdrawn into the city limits of Alexandria, the British remained on the outskirts, digging themselves in. Their position was strengthened by the arrival of the Turkish fleet, anchored in Aboukir Bay, with reinforcements. 'On the whole our circumstances in Egypt are much more favourable than could have been hoped for,' Hely-Hutchinson noted on 1 April. 'The difficulties we have had to encounter, particularly the physical ones, have been much fewer than was at first imagined, we have found water almost everywhere in the peninsular, provisions abound, the troops continue still healthy, and we have not yet experienced any great heat, every precaution is taken to prevent Drunkeness amongst the soldiers, which I am confident is the real, and efficient cause, which renders British Armies so unhealthy in warm climates.' He also conceded there were still obstacles to be overcome: 'The French are probably nearly as numerous as we are, much more inured to the Climate, to every sort of fatigue and to the privations, which in war are unavoidable; they are besides, in a position out of which it is impossible to drive them unless we receive a very considerable augmentation of force indeed. It is dangerous in this country, to make detachments, because it is extremely difficult to keep up the communication with the main body of the Army.'[57]

French resolve was not yet broken. 'On the 10th April the enemy erected four flagstaffs on the heights in front of Alexandria and hoisted French, Spanish, Russian and Genoese Colours, thereon and in the height of their pride fired a Royal salute letting us see the

239

nations that were in alliance against us,' recorded Simpson. 'They never took down these flags night or day.'[58] Undaunted, the British army settled down for a siege, whilst contriving to flood the low ground around Alexandria by breaching the canal which crossed the country from the Nile. 'This plan of cutting the canal and over-flowing the low country was of great service to the British army who was not strong enough to hem the enemy into the garrison, so that they might not get any supplys from the country, but once we got them surrounded by water their was gun Boats sent upon the place where the Enemy used to draw all his supplys of Provisions from the Country.'[59]

On 19 April 1801 the French gave up Rosetta, on the coast east of Alexandria, following a Turkish attack, 'but [since] the most of the Army had retreated before they capitulated, their was only a very few men left in the place,' observed Simpson.[60] 'You will find by my publick dispatch that we are now masters of the town and Castle of Rosetta, and consequently of the entrance of the Western branch of the Nile,' Hely-Hutchinson informed his superiors back home.[61] As Simpson realised, with most of the British army having advanced to Cairo, they had to remain alert 'in case of any alarm, and the whole had orders to turn out and be under arms every morning at 3 o clock, without the sound of Drum or Trumpet as it was most probable the Enemy would make an attack upon us'.[62] Having heard that the French were continuing to gain provisions from a specific location, the order was given for the flank companies of the Reserve Brigade, with a squadron of horse and some field officers, to march in search of the place; 'they accordingly proceeded on this Service to the other side of the Lake to the Post where all the French embarked all their supplys of Provisions and water, but the Enemy stationed at the place had got information of their coming and had fled into the interior of the Country'.[63] After destroying what they found, the flank companies returned to camp.

In early June, in sweltering heat with limited supplies of water, the 42nd and the 28th were ordered to march with a company of artillery to join the main British army in front of Cairo. 'We marched the next morning at 3 o'clock and got all across the cut which was made in the Canal before day break, and lay on the opposite side while the Baggage was getting over which took a long time.' By the time they had finished transporting the baggage, 'the Day became very warm; we marched along the banks of the Canal till we came to the place where the Enemy had the Post for Collecting provisions to carry across for the use of the Garrison' – about ten miles from the camp before Alexandria. 'Their was some of our Troops stationed at this place and fresh water to be found, but we did not halt we went on for the distance of two miles farther, till we came to a small pond of water, where we halted and piled arms.' The men ran immediately to the pond to drink the water, 'regardless of the dirt which they made by treading amongst the mud, but still worse the water was brakish and of a bad taste, but the men being all in a fainting condition, with the extreme heat and warm winds which came of the deserts, in spite of all the endeavours of the officers to keep the men back from drinking too much, the most of them quenched their thirst with that bad water'.[64]

Marching onwards, it did not take long before the men began to suffer the ill-effects of the water, 'for the most of the men was attacked with sickness according to the Quantity they had drank, they who had drank to satisfy their thirst was in great agony, the men was falling down every step.' When they arrived at their camp for the night, the locals – realising their predicament – were 'very kind when they found the situation of the men, they came along the road and sold them good water, which they brought from a great distance, as well as cucumbers water melons & which refreshed them very much'.[65]

Bolstered by a Turkish force, the British army had begun to besiege the French garrison at Cairo, held by a force under the command of General Augustin Daniel de Belliard. Hardly had the siege of Cairo begun than, on 27 June, Belliard sent out a flag of truce, requesting that the French army be permitted to return to France. Having captured the capital of Egypt, the British army returned down the Nile to invest Alexandria. Reaching Aboukir Bay, they marched 'on the sand Beach which was all strewed with dead Bodys, some wanting legs and arms, strewn out upon the shore', recorded Simpson, who surmised 'from the decayed state of some of them [that it was] as if they had lain since the Engagement that was fought between Lord Nelson and the French fleet in that Bay 3 years before, others were perfectly fresh sewed up in Hammocks and Blankets who had died of their wounds on Board of the Hospital ships.' Having been thrown overboard, 'the Ballast giving way or being too light which was entended to keep them at the Bottom was the cause of so many of the Corps being cast on shore. This however was put a stop to by an order being given that any who died on Board the fleet should not be thrown out into the Bay but be carried on shore and interred.' As Simpson continued in his journal, 'it was a shocking sight to see so many of our Countrymen's Corps laying exposed to the sight of every savage who might chance to come that way; or curiosity might draw thither to gaze on the dead Bodys of those Brave men who had lost their lives in fighting for their King and Country.'[66]

With the French entrenched in Alexandria, the British force advanced to the outskirts of the city. The 42nd was involved in making a diversionary attack on the eastern side so that other regiments could attack from the west. 'On a signal being made when the troops in the boats were ready to land we were to advance and commence a false attack on our side which was to be the time they were to take advantage, and land on the desert coast on the west side of the garrison; accordingly at 12 o'clock the whole of the army advanced and attacked the enemy outposts and drove them in, the enemy then opened all the cannon that would bear on that side, thinking it was a serious attack.'

Meanwhile, the main army under General Eyre Coote – another veteran of the American War – went ashore; 'the army on our side kept the enemy in play till it was thought that a landing had been made and day being near we were ordered to retreat, we came off with little loss as the whole of the army was kept under cover, only a few who went in front to alarm the Enemy. Had the army been exposed to the fire of the enemy for a few minutes they must have done us a deal of damage for their was such a number of guns opened upon us that they tore up the ground in every place that they could bear upon.'[67]

Once again, short of supplies and suffering illness, the French capitulated. On 26 August a gun was fired, the four flags previously hoisted were hauled down, and General Menou ordered a white flag to be run up in their place. 'We received orders that afternoon,' Simpson recollected, 'that the Army was not to turn out before day break as their was a capitulation going on with the French garrison of Alexandria, and that no man was to go into the French lines without a written pass from the Commander in Chief.'[68] By the end of August the terms of what became known as 'the capitulation of Alexandria' had been agreed and British troops were ordered to prepare to take possession of the city's outworks. On 2 September, noted Simpson, the French pulled down their colours and soon afterwards the flank companies marched from the camp in four columns 'with a band of music and two field guns at the head of each column'.[69]

With Alexandria secured, orders were given for ten regiments, one of them the 42nd, to be ready to embark at short notice. 'There was a great deal of baggage sent on board from the reserve brigade in the course of the day which made us in high spirits thinking it would come in our turn to embark in a short time for we was afraid that we should be left in the country.' Before they departed, they received the thanks of their commanding officers 'for their Gallant conduct in all the services they were called upon under their command since they landed in Egypt'.[70] The following day the Regiment was mustered, 'which had not been done for a good while before and our number was but small besides what they were when we left Minorca'.[71]

On 6 October, together with the 23rd and 90th Regiments, the 42nd marched through 'very heavy' sand the ten-mile distance from the camp before Alexandria to Aboukir. 'As soon as the whole had got on board the signal was made to sail early the next morning,' recorded Simpson. 'When we lost sight of Alexandria, the French flag was still flying on the works on purpose to decoy any of the Enemys Ships into the Harbour who might not be informed of the surrender of the place.'[72] Since arriving in Egypt, 173 men of the 42nd had been killed or died from their wounds; twenty-one had died of natural causes.[73]

During the journey home, by way of Malta and Gibraltar, a warship came alongside and 'informed us that peace was made between France and England; when the men heard of this there was great cheering and noise . . . I thought they would have knocked the decks of the ship in.'[74] On 4 November, they thankfully came to anchor off Spithead. After raising the Quarantine flag, the doctor came on board. Finding all the men 'in good health', they disembarked at Southampton. 'Thus we were once more landed in England after experiencing a good many hardships.'[75] On arrival in England, the 42nd Royal Highland Regiment marched to Winchester.

In recognition of services rendered to the Ottoman Empire, the Grand Seignior established an order of Knighthood and the senior officers were presented with large gold medals. Among those who received the medal were the two lieutenant colonels, Dickson and Stewart, both of whom had been wounded. A smaller medal was given to the surgeon, John Erly, who had been with the Regiment since 1797, tending so many of the dying and wounded men.[76]

At Home; a 2nd Battalion raised; Gibraltar and Ireland

Peace between France and Britain – negotiated under the authority of Pitt's successor, Prime Minister Henry Addington, 1st Viscount Sidmouth – was agreed at Amiens in northern France on 25 March 1802.[77] According to the terms of this 'Definitive Treaty of Peace', Britain agreed to give up all conquests except Trinidad and Ceylon. Malta, taken by Napoleon in 1798 and recaptured by Britain in 1800, was to be returned to the Knights of St John, although remaining under British administration. Egypt was to be restored to the Ottoman Empire; France agreed to withdraw from Naples and the Italian states. George III confirmed renunciation of the somewhat anomalous title of King of France, retained on official documents since

William the Conqueror crossed the Channel in 1066. The treaty marked the end of the Second Coalition which had been fighting Revolutionary France since 1798. But, as subsequent events were to prove, the 'definitive' peace lasted barely one year.

In May 1802, 'the King having expressed a wish to see the 42nd Regiment, they marched to Ashford, and were reviewed there by his Majesty ... accompanied by the Prince of Wales and the Duke of York.' Soon afterwards, the Regiment marched over familiar ground to Edinburgh, 'exciting on the road less curiosity and surprise at their garb and appearance than on former occasions, when the Highland dress was rarely seen'.[78] On parade in Edinburgh at the beginning of December 1802, the 42nd was presented with new Colours. They were the first to show the Second Union – enacted in 1801 to include Ireland – which meant the addition of the Cross of St Patrick and the shamrock to the Union wreath. For services in Egypt, by Royal Authority the Regiment was given permission for the 'Sphinx' and the word 'Egypt' to be added to the Colours.[79]

Lieutenant General Vyse, Commander of His Majesty's forces in North Britain, addressed the Regiment, reminding the soldiers that the standards were 'not only revered by an admiring world, as the honourable monuments and trophies of your former heroism, but are likewise regarded by a grateful country, as the sacred pledges of that security, which, under the protection of Heaven, it may expect from your future services'. Vyse concluded his address by warning that if 'the restless ambition of an envious and daring enemy, again call you to the field, think then that you behold the spirit of those brave comrades who so nobly, in their country's cause, fell upon the plains of Egypt, hovering round these standards.'[80]

As historian Forbes pointed out, the honour was the first the Regiment had received since its formation. 'During the long period from 1739 unto 1801, it had taken part in but one pitched battle, that of Fontenoy.' Although the Regiment had earned 'immortal renown', the actions in which it had fought could not be classed as battles. 'It was the misfortune of the regiment, not its fault, that it should have been for the most part skirmishing and bush-whacking on and beyond the confines of civilisation, when more fortunate comrades were stirring the nations by such memorable victories as Minden, Louisbourg and Quebec.'[81]

The old Colours were presented to the Colonel, Sir Hector Munro of Foulis, who mounted them in his ancestral home of Novar in Ross-shire, 'never to be removed from it while one stone of the house remains above another', and where they are still on display.[82] The Highland Society of London – founded in 1778 – honoured the Regiment when its members unanimously resolved 'to vote the thanks of this Society to the British Army in Egypt for their gallant achievements, in which our countrymen the Highland regiments maintained in so conspicuous a manner the warlike character of their ancestors, and more especially to that old and long-distinguished corps, the Forty-Second or Royal Highland Regiment'. Subsequently the vote was added to Regimental Orders and read to the Captain of each Company. The Highland Society also decided to bestow on the Highlanders 'some mark of their esteem and approbation'. Having collected from amongst its members the sum of fifteen hundred pounds, medals were struck with the head of Sir Ralph Abercromby 'and some emblematical figures on the obverse. A superb piece of plate was also ordered.'[83]

Unfortunately a contentious issue was raised. While the medals, designed by the renowned artist, Sir Benjamin West, and the piece of silver were being made, the Society held a meeting, when the Scottish politician and economist, Sir John Sinclair, 'with the warmth of a clansman', mentioned Sergeant Sinclair as having taken possession of the French standard. 'Sir John being at that time ignorant of the circumstances, made no mention of the loss of the ensign which the sergeant had gotten in charge.' This resulted in attention being focused on the role played by Lutz in rescuing the colours from the stunned Sinclair. When challenged by the Highland Society, whilst explaining the story as they knew it, the officers of the 42nd were surprised 'that the Society should imagine them capable of countenancing any statement implying that they had laid claim to a trophy to which they had no right. This misapprehension of the Society's meaning brought on a correspondence, which ended in an interruption of further communication for many years.'[84]

While the Regiment was stationed at Edinburgh 'several fell under the notice of the police, and helped in no small degree to lower the corps in the esteem of the inhabitants, who expected to find them as quiet and regular in quarters as formerly.'[85] Ordered to march south, having embarked from Leith at the end of May 1803, they landed at Harwich, taking up quarters at Weely (Weeley) Barracks, in Essex. Having had over half the Regiment's complement of men discharged the previous year, private soldiers numbered less than four hundred men. Brigaded under the command of Major General Sir John Hope, the son of the Earl of Hopetoun, 'all the bad effects of the festivity and hospitality of Edinburgh disappeared'.[86]

As the reality of peace with France proved an illusion and invasion scares became rife, Britain's military establishment was increased. In 1803 the Additional Forces Act was passed; this provided for fifty of the ninety-three regiments in the British Army to raise a second battalion to be known as the Army of Reserve; the intention was for the men to be raised by ballot, on condition that they only served in Britain or Ireland 'with liberty to volunteer into the regular Army, on a certain bounty. In Scotland, those men were, in the first instance, formed into second Battalions to Regiments of the line.'[87] A home-based Militia was also to be raised by ballot, whose members could volunteer to join the regular Army; finally, the British government was placing reliance on a record number of volunteers, who were to be instructed in waging guerrilla warfare once the anticipated invading French forces landed. By the end of 1803 Britain could boast an unprecedented combined military force of 615,000.[88]

With recruits coming from Perth and the counties to the north and west, including Elgin (Morayshire), Caithness, Argyll and Bute, the 2nd Battalion 42nd was placed on the establishment on 9 July 1803. Once raised, orders were received to leave Fort George to join the 1st Battalion under Hope's command at Weely. 'I liked well enough our marching in England,' recollected a young private soldier,

John, who had joined the militia before transferring to the 42nd. 'And I was greatly amused by the difficulty our Highlanders had to understand the common people with whom they talked; and reciprocally, the astonishment of the English at the speech of the Gael, furnished matter of amusement: in fact some of my comrades knew no language but the Erse, and you may thence judge of their hardships.'[89] As John discovered, there was never any question of retaining the bounty of twenty pounds given him for enlisting: 'I was rich: a lawful prize to the sharks. The old soldiers thought they had got a fine catch, when they met a young one in the barrackroom with so much money. Every one has then his friend, and I had mine, ready enough to assist me in getting rid of such troublesome stuff.'[90]

At Weely, the 1st and 2nd Battalions had 'drill plenty and two brigading days a week'.[91] The selling of 'spirituous liquors within the barrack Grounds' was a problem and General Orders passed on 28 May 1804 warned that if it continued, the Commanding Officer assured the men 'any of their wives detected disobeying this order, they will be immediately turned out of barracks'.[92] A few days later, married soldiers were being advised 'to provide themselves with hutts as in the course of next week it will become necessary to make some arrangement on account of the increasing heat of the weather, when only one woman will be permitted to remain in each Barrack room. The Officers to wear thin Blue Pantaloons till further Orders. The company will give in Returns to the Q[uarter].Master tomorrow morning for the number of Feather Hackles & Cockades they want to complete, the number of bonnets lately issued to the Company for the Recruits.'[93]

In September 1805 the 1st Battalion 42nd marched to Portsmouth, bound for Gibraltar to relieve another regiment in garrison. The Rock of Gibraltar at the southern tip of Spain, noted another private soldier, James Gunn, in memoirs he wrote in his eighties for the benefit of his grandson, was 'a wonderful place as well by Nature as by art – on the Mediterian Side a perpendicular height of a mile on the North Side a Declivity but where the town is build is a Narrow

Strip within the Battery so that it was well termed Impregnable by Nature as well as by art.'[94] The Regiment's Commanding Officer was James Stirling. Having enlisted as a volunteer in 1774, he had participated at every engagement in which the 42nd had taken part since the American War, most recently at the battle of Alexandria.[95]

At the same time, the 2nd Battalion left Essex to be quartered in Ireland, whose inhabitants were regarded as being 'infused with a spirit of French Republicanism' and with a coastline 'calculated for the landing of an Enemy'.[96] The new Lieutenant Colonel of the 2nd Battalion, appointed in September 1804, was Robert Blantyre, the 11th Baron, who had been serving with the 17th Light Dragoons.[97] Embarking at Liverpool, their march seemed more 'like a party of pleasure, rather than a military movement, part of it being on foot, and part in boats on a canal'.[98] Arriving at Dublin, the soldiers set out for Tuam. 'This march occupied us ten days, and it was by no means agreeable, on account of the bad quarters on which we were billeted; but I must say that the kindness of the inhabitants compensated for the wretchedness of their cabins: their means were limited but their hands were open,' noted Private John.[99]

Without military action, boredom set in, alleviated by playing cards. 'It occupied my whole leisure, and for two years I was the slave of chance.'[100] After several months in Tuam, the 2nd Battalion moved to Lochrea: 'here our regiment got the full highland dress, bonnet, plaid, kilt, hose and purse.'[101] A brief stay at Arcourt was followed by orders to proceed to a large camp in the Curragh of Kildare, under the command of Lord Cathcart, Commander-in-Chief in Ireland since 1803. 'Our march thither was in the style of a flying camp. The whole camp was formed on the same day, and the troops might be in number from fifteen to twenty thousand men. There could not be a finer piece of ground for an army than this . . . we had enough of exercise, marching and marshalling, for we were constantly at drill, from six o'clock in the morning, till sun-set, except an hour or so at mid-day.'[102]

During this time, 'a general order was issued for the army to discontinue the tying of the hair, and to have it cropped. Never was an order received with more heartfelt satisfaction than this, or obeyed with more alacrity, notwithstanding the foolish predictions of some old super-annuated gentlemen, that it would cause a mutiny in the army,' remarked James Anton, a young soldier serving in the militia in Scotland, and shortly to join the 42nd. 'The tying was a daily penance, and a severe one, to which every man had to submit; . . . the soldier who looks back to the task with the painful remembrance of the punishment he suffered every morning, daubing the side of his head with dirty grease, soap, and flour, until every hair stood like the burr of a thistle, and the back was padded and pulled so, that every hair had to keep its due place . . . indeed, it was no uncommon circumstance for us, when on the guard-bench and asleep, to have the rats and mice scrambling about our heads, eating the filthy stuff with which our hair was bedaubed.'[103]

Meanwhile, relations between Britain and France were again hostile. Crowned Emperor and King of Italy in the summer of 1805, having annexed the states of Parma, Placentia and Piedmont, Napoleon Bonaparte turned his attention towards vanquishing his neighbours in the Third Coalition of countries ranged against France, which included Austria, Britain, Russia and Sweden.[104] Although Britain's victory off Cape Trafalgar on 21 October 1805 ensured British naval supremacy, on land Napoleon remained triumphant, securing a decisive victory in early December against Austria and Russia – in a battle known as the Battle of the Three Emperors - at Austerlitz.

At the end of 1805, a new Colonel of the Royal Highland Regiment was appointed. General Sir Hector Munro had died in Ross-shire on 26 December after nearly nineteen years as the Regiment's fourth Colonel. He was 'a brave officer and possessed of a firm mind', but Stewart of Garth considered that 'he did not interest himself much about his regiment, nor seemed to regard them with that feeling which might have been expected from a countryman of their own.'[105] Munro's successor was George, Marquis of Huntly, who a decade before had raised an Independent Company for the 42nd, proudly wearing his Highland dress in London society.

In 1806, an order came for 120 men of the 2nd Battalion to join the 1st Battalion in Gibraltar, leaving the remainder to return to

Scotland to recruit. Private John was one of those who volunteered: 'I cared not whither I went, north, east, south, or west; my regiment was home, my company my friends in the second battalion, and I expected to find the same or better in the first battalion of the 42d.'[106] When he reached Gibraltar he considered 'duty on this rock is very hard; two nights in bed and one on duty; and king's works every third day. There was no time here for cards; no room for diversion.' Provisions were 'good and cheap, and plentiful. We had four days salt beef, and three days fresh meat, and coffee every morning. The wine too was cheap.'[107] The 'king's works' – for an extra nine pence a day – involved making a safer anchorage for the ships of the Royal Navy. For work at the artillery stores they received an extra shilling and sixpence.[108] It would not be long, however, before both battalions of the 42nd were enduring greater hardships than either had known.

11.

Australia: a Place So Little Known

Here's Forty Shillings on the Drum,
For those that Volunteers do come,
With Shirts, and clothes, and present Pay
When o'er the Hills and far away.[1]

New South Wales

After over twenty years in India, in September 1805 the 73rd Highland Regiment of Foot – the 42nd's former 2nd Battalion – received orders to return to Britain. Of the complement of men who might have come home, over five hundred had remained, transferring to other regiments.[2] Of those who had served in the 42nd, Norman MacLeod, the 73rd's first Commanding Officer, had died in 1801. James Spens, who had succeeded him, had retired by sale in 1798, before Seringapatam. The Regiment's new Commanding Officer was Lachlan Macquarie, whose brother Charles, a captain in the 42nd, had been seriously wounded at Alexandria in 1801.[3] Promoted Lieutenant Colonel of the 73rd in May 1805, it was not until 1807 that he joined his new Regiment, by which time it had returned from India, where he too had been serving. Disembarking at Greenwich at the beginning of July 1806, the soldiers stayed in quarters throughout the autumn until the winter cold of November, before returning to Scotland. As with the 42nd Royal Highland Regiment, while the war against France continued new recruits were required and recruiting parties were sent out throughout the country. From Stirling Castle, the Regiment moved to Glasgow and then Perth, receiving new Colours from the Colonel of the Regiment, Lieutenant General George Harris, in 1807.[4]

After only two years in Britain, in December 1808, the 73rd was again posted overseas. 'This order as being wholly unexpected,' related Lieutenant Henry Antill, one of the wounded officers at Seringapatam, 'created not a little surprise and some anxiety in my mind, as I fully expected we should have been exempted from foreign duty for some time to come as the Regiment had but two years before returned from the East Indies.' Antill believed that the Regiment was 'still very weak and unfit for service, and was uncertain what destination they could intend us for . . . I shall not dwell on the regret I felt at leaving Glasgow. It is needless to describe to you the pangs of parting with friends we love and esteem; mine were sufficiently acute to draw a tear even from the eye of a soldier; you may both smile at the Idea, but let me ask you why a soldier should be denied the luxury of a tear! Is his heart to be harder than another's because his way of life is so?'[5]

The 73rd's destination was New South Wales – further than any soldier of either the 42nd or 73rd had yet travelled. Founded as a penal colony in 1788 after Lieutenant James Cook RN took possession of the eastern coast of the continent of Australia eighteen years previously, successive governors had been sent to preside over Britain's growing presence. Most recently Governor Captain William Bligh, of *Bounty* fame, had fallen foul of powerful free settlers, some officials and the New South Wales Corps. This Corps, which became known as 'The Rum Corps', was formed in England in 1789 as a permanent regiment to relieve the sailors who had accompanied the 'First Fleet' of eleven ships which had come to Australia with the first contingent of prisoners. Due to the remoteness and unpopularity of the posting, the New South Wales Corps was composed largely of officers on half-pay and soldiers on parole from military prisons, as well as those who hoped to make a life for themselves in the new colony. Sailors who wished to remain in New South Wales were also recruited.

This new generation of 'Australians' had become used to running the colony themselves and chafed under Bligh's authoritarian and somewhat confrontational style. When Bligh, instructed by Lord Castlereagh, secretary of state for war and the colonies, attempted to stop the barter of rum and other spirits, the settlers resented the government's interference in their activities.[6] In an action later known as the 'Rum Rebellion', Bligh was deposed in January 1808. The rebels, supported by the New South Wales Corps, installed their own administration, urging Bligh to return to England. Refusing to do so, he failed to gain support from the small penal colony at Van Diemen's land – renamed Tasmania in 1856 – for a counter-coup. Throughout 1809 he remained effectively imprisoned on board the storeship HMS *Porpoise*.[7]

In Bligh's place, the British government appointed Brigadier General Miles Nightingall, who had served as Cornwallis's military secretary in India. The 73rd was ordered to accompany him.[8] 'You may naturally suppose my dear friends,' recorded Antill, 'that my reflections were not the most agreeable at the prospect of so distant a voyage of upwards of sixteen thousand miles to a place so little known; my regrets were, I think in some degree natural, but as I was determined to dwell upon the subject as little as possible, I was resolved to be thankful it was no worse, and to look forward with hope to a future day however distant, when I might return to my Native Country.'[9] Lieutenant Colonel Macquarie was not pleased at such a distant posting, which was unlikely to advance his career; he therefore wrote to Castlereagh requesting appointment as lieutenant governor, to which Castlereagh agreed. Embarking at Leith, winter storms meant that the passage round the coast of Britain took a month. 'We were twice very near lost, the wind blowing mostly from the S. W. in strong Gales with very cold weather.'[10]

On arrival at Gravesend, the men learnt 'with much satisfaction that the Government had thought proper to give us a second Battalion,' noted Antill, who benefited by being promoted captain in what would now be the 1st Battalion 73rd.[11] William George Harris, the son of the Colonel of the Regiment, was put in command of the 2nd Battalion; while serving with the 74th he had fought alongside the 73rd at Seringapatam, being one of the first to enter the breach, and had been with the 73rd since 1804.[12] By the terms of the 1803 Additional Forces Act, permitting recruits to come from the militia, the 73rd received 'a very considerable augmentation of force by volunteers, particularly from the Irish militia'. Thirty-three men from the Staffordshire militia volunteered, 'a circumstance totally unexpected, from the dislike English soldiers were known to entertain to the Highland uniform'.[13]

The new 2nd Battalion, raised in Nottingham, was to consist of four companies; when they were completed to one hundred private soldiers, it would again be augmented to six companies, 'and so on in succession, until the establishment was increased to one thousand'.[14] The following year, to encourage additional recruitment throughout Britain, and as an indication that the 73rd had already become less of a purely Scottish regiment than when it had been first raised as the 2nd Battalion 42nd, the wearing of Highland dress was discontinued. Henceforward, the men were ordered to wear 'breeches & leggings' as worn by the other regiments. 'Only the battalion's piper, Hugh McKay, was permitted to wear the kilt, a privilege he retained until his discharge in 1817 aged 59.'[15]

While waiting to depart for Australia, Nightingall fell ill with a violent rheumatic attack, requiring him to relinquish his position as Governor, whereupon Macquarie again wrote to Castlereagh offering his services as Governor, which Castlereagh approved.[16] Antill, who had been pleased to be appointed ADC to Nightingall, retained the position under Macquarie.[17] In place of Macquarie, Lieutenant Colonel Maurice Charles O'Connell took command of the 1st Battalion 73rd. O'Connell, who had entered the British Army as a captain in the Irish Brigade in 1794, had seen action in the West Indies before transferring to the 73rd in October 1806.[18] Nearly six months after leaving Scotland, 'on Sunday May 7th the Regiment being assembled on the parade at Colville Barracks marched down to Yarmouth, on the Isle of Wight,' recorded Antill. As he related, a total of fifteen officers, 451 soldiers, ninety women and eighty-seven children embarked on board the HMS *Dromedary*. A similar complement of ten officers, 406 rank and file, and ninety-seven women and children boarded HMS *Hindostan*: both 'large roomy' ships. Over the next two days, the baggage was loaded, and the two ships set sail for Spithead. 'We had hardly got half way before we struck on a place called Old Castle Point, but fortunately soon got off again without receiving any damage, and came to anchor in the evening.' The next day they anchored at Spithead.[19]

For the next two weeks, 'nothing material happened except a disorder of the eyes which broke out among the soldiers,' recorded Ensign Alexander Huey, who was travelling on board the *Dromedary*.[20] On 21 May the ships weighed anchor, to be joined in the afternoon by Lachlan Macquarie and his wife Elizabeth, accompanied by the Judge Advocate, Ellis Bent, and his wife, their respective servants and baggage. 'We received him,' recorded Huey, 'in all the state circumstances would allow; the Guard consisting of 40 men on the Quarter deck and the Band was stationed on the Poop. The moment the Governor came on the Quarter deck the Band struck up, the Guard presented arms and the officers took off their hats.'[21] So, related Antill, they departed 'from Old England perhaps to be absent from it for some years'.[22]

For seven months, the men became accustomed to following the Ship's Standing Orders: 'At 8 o'clock pipe to breakfast, at 12 o'clock to dinner, the grog always to be served at 1 o'clock and at half past four in the evenings.' 'No Cloaths', the men were firmly instructed, were to be hung to dry in the rigging; and they were ordered to divide themselves into messes.[23] Having realised that the number of men, women and children on board the *Dromedary* meant 'that we were too much crowded, application was in consequence made and 39 men were sent on board the *Hindostan*,' recorded Antill. Two officers, fifty private soldiers and forty-one women and children were offloaded at Portsmouth to take passage with the first convict ship to follow on.

'Every day during the voyage before 8 o'clock in the morning every man's Hammock was brought upon deck and stowed away in the netting, the decks were washed and scraped and no person permitted to remain below when the weather would allow their remaining upon deck. We regulated the men likewise into three watches, each watch commanded by an officer who took his rotation of duty on deck with the watch he belonged to.'[24] When, barely a week after setting sail, six private soldiers of the 73rd were discovered sleeping on watch, Antill noted that they were punished in order 'to make an example at the beginning of the voyage to prevent a repetition of it in future'.[25]

A common sight throughout the journey was 'a strange sail'. Sometimes the Captain thought it was worth giving chase; on one occasion it was discovered that the ship was a Swedish vessel, in French possession for five years, 'and was therefore lawful prize'. Laden with rice and cotton, her cargo was estimated to be worth about £45,000. 'Captain Pasco put a lieutenant with a party of sailors on board of the prize and sent her to England the next day.'[26] On 4 June a determined effort was made to celebrate the King's birthday 'in as great a style as possible', and the band was ordered to play 'God Save the King' on the quarterdeck; but, wrote Huey, 'they had scarce played the first half of the tune when the ship gave a lurch which sent them all rolling to the lee side, to the great amusement of the sailors.'[27] Having stopped at Madeira, 'watering and procuring what little refreshments could be had',[28] they caught the north-easterly trade winds. 'The wind since our departure from Madeira had been quite fair and the passage had hitherto been very pleasant,' recorded Huey. 'The band performed on the Quarter Deck every evening at 6.00 o'clock. At 8.00 the drums and fifes began to play and the soldiers and sailors danced till 10.00.'[29]

Taking the same route as if they were travelling to India, the ships stopped at the Cape Verde Islands, where the men enjoyed abundant supplies of pineapples, plantains and pumpkins as well as oranges, lemons, limes, cocoa nuts, bananas and apples. 'Poultry is so plentiful here,' observed Huey, 'that for an old cocked hat or belt you will get 20 turkeys or hens. A pair of monkeys sell here for 1/- or an old hat.'[30] Antill considered Port Praya to be 'a most wretched place. The Town, if it can be called such, consists of one wide Street with a row of miserable huts on each side, situated on the brow of a steep bank leading down to the sea. The appearance of the inhabitants corresponds with the Town, and partakes of the battered condition of their habitation, they are so badly off for all kinds of Clothing, that you have here an excellent market for all your old cast-off Cloths.'[31] Before departing, the *Dromedary* took on board thirteen bullocks and fresh vegetables for their onward journey.

While at sea, 'Divine Service' was held 'every Sunday when the weather would permit'.[32] On 5 August 1809 the fleet anchored in the harbour of Rio de Janeiro, capital of the Portuguese settlements since the Portuguese first arrived on 1 January 1502. Here the men found an 'abundance of fruit and other vegetables . . . especially oranges'.[33] They reached Rio de Janeiro at a time when the Portuguese royal family, evacuated from Portugal following Napoleon's invasion in 1807, was in residence. On one occasion, Huey saw one of the Princesses on a balcony, and felt it necessary to record that he could see her legs 'as far up the thigh', and that 'she had no stockings on'.[34] He was pleased to note that the fresh provisions and oranges with which they were supplied daily were 'at the Prince Regent's expense'.[35] This was John, later João VI the Merciful, who ascended the Portuguese throne in succession to his mother in 1816.[36]

While at Rio, Antill and Huey went together to visit a monastery. 'Two Monks met us and very politely took us through the whole place, even into the Sanctum Sanctorum.' Huey also recorded how, when two officers went ashore in their kilts, it was 'to the great wonder and admiration of the Portuguese, who flocked from all quarters to see them'.[37] During their stay, Sir James Gambier, the English Consul, entertained the officers at a ball.[38] Before they departed, two soldiers who were prisoners deserted. 'They got ashore at the west end of the harbour, and made into the interior of the country,' never to be seen again.[39]

On the morning of 23 September, the ships came in sight of the Cape of Good Hope, 'the land distant about 30 miles, and came to anchor at noon with the small Bower in Table Bay in 7 fath[om]s water about 2 miles from the Town. The Town is handsome,' recorded Antill, 'regular and well built and kept remarkably clean, the streets wide and airy'.[40] Together with Mr Shippin, the gunner, Antill climbed to the top of Table Mountain: 'we were the only two belonging to the ships that would venture the journey.'[41] 'While we lay at the Cape of Good Hope,' recorded Huey, 'two ambassadors arrived from the King of the Caffrees. They wore rings on their arms made of the teeth of the elephants they had killed. They were dressed in the compleat Caffri style, with tiger skins on their shoulders and buskins, armed with asagays and shield. They performed some of their war manoeuvres in presence of Governor Macquarie and Lord Caledon [the Governor].'[42]

Before departing, Antill was pleased to note that they had 115 live sheep on board to augment their supplies.[43] As they continued their journey in the southern hemisphere, the weather got warmer. 'This day was so hot,' recorded Huey on 14 October, 'that it was almost impossible to remain on deck above half an hour.'[44] By 2 November, using two tons of water a day, they had only 150 tons of water remaining. 'Allowance of fresh water was one quart a day for each man. No water to be taken from the scuttle butts unless for the Sick Bay and the Officers and that before sunset.' Having assessed that they had started the voyage with forty-one children, Huey remarked that the number had risen to fifty-one. At least the weather 'was now pleasant. We scudded along at 5 and 6 knots.' But, after enjoying relatively calm seas, the ill effects of a sudden squall brought water 'into our beds in the gun room through the seams of the gun deck, which had been worked open by the constant rolling of the ship'.[45]

To break the tedium of the journey, Captain Pasco, on board the *Hindostan*, amused himself shooting a strange new flying bird, the albatross. 'We bore away for fear some of his shot would come aboard us,' recorded Huey on board the *Dromedary*.[46] Throughout the journey, numerous people fell ill. On 1 December, he was recording thirty-seven soldiers on the *Dromedary*'s sick list; for a while, both Captain Pritchard and the Judge Advocate, Ellis Bent, were very ill. Every so often a message would be passed between the *Dromedary* and the *Hindostan*. 'How is Mr Bent? ... Can you spare me any more firewood?' to which the reply came back: 'Mr Bent is better. I can spare you no more firewood and Captain Pritchard is very ill.'[47] To add to their discomfort, only salt provisions were now left, 'our stock of sheep and pigs being all consumed'.[48]

On 15 December, the ships at last sighted land. 'It is impossible to describe the sensations this sight occasioned to all hands on board, after a Passage of seven months from England and nine weeks from the Cape thus to have the hopes of a speedy termination to our long voyage in health and safety,' recorded Antill.[49] On 25 December: 'This being Christmas Day served out an extra allowance of grog to the Soldiers and ships company, the Ladies and Gentlemen of the Cuddy [Cabin] dined with us, our Fresh Provisions being quite expended for some time past, nothing to give them for dinner but salt Beef and

Pork, and part of an old goat which was killed for the occasion.'[50] 'This day,' recorded Huey, 'the soldiers were paraded with their new clothing, arms and accoutrements complete. They made a very fine appearance and gave great satisfaction to the Commanding Officer.'[51]

After nearly eight months since leaving England, on 28 December they dropped anchor in Port Jackson, a large harbour just north of Botany Bay, New South Wales. Unfavourable winds meant that they had to wait before proceeding to safe anchorage up harbour at Sydney Cove. On a typical hot midsummer's New Year's Day, 1810, the men got onto dry land. 'The debarkation of the 73rd Regiment took place in the forenoon,' reported *The Sydney Gazette and New South Wales Advertiser*. At midday, the troops formed into a square on the Grand Parade. On one side the New South Wales Corps was lined up.

> On the arrival of the Governor and Suite in the centre of the Square, HIS EXCELLENCY was received by a general salute from the troops. His Majesty's Commission was then opened by the GOVERNOR himself, and given by HIS EXCELLENCY into the hands of the Judge Advocate, by whom it was unfolded. The Great Seal of the Territory was then displayed; on which part of the ceremony the Troops again saluted, by presenting arms, Officers saluting, and the Music playing 'God Save the King!'[52]

Until the New South Wales Corps, designated as the 102nd Regiment, was ready to vacate the barracks, the 73rd had to camp at Grose Farm, about two miles from the town, Ensign Alexander Huey noting in his diary that they had had 'nothing to eat this day but potatoes'.[53] As the days passed, their food improved: 'In the course of a week, we could procure bread and coffee or tea. Bread was very dear – 1/- for a 2d loaf.' Not long afterwards a ship arrived from India 'laden with wheat and India goods'.[54] No longer wearing kilts, the continued presence of the thistle on the cross-belt plates and buttons gave the Regiment a 'Scottish flavour'.[55]

One of the new Governor's first actions was to make a series of proclamations; first he made known the King's displeasure 'at the late proceedings in the colony'; second, all the actions of the interim governors since Bligh's deposition were rendered void; the third proclamation gave Governor Macquarie the authority to act as he saw fit with regard to the future. Magistrates, Jailors and Constables were given 'full and free Indemnity from all prosecutions and suits at law whatsoever, that might be brought against them, for all Acts, Orders, Warrants, Commitments, Fines, Punishments, and Proceedings whatever, that have been performed, ordered, executed, or imposed by them' since Bligh's deposition.[56] In return, Macquarie had to affirm that he did not follow the Roman Catholic doctrine of transubstantiation, a reminder that Catholics still suffered discrimination. The situation was even more sensitive in Australia, since many of the convicts were themselves Roman Catholics.[57]

On 17 January 1810 Commodore Bligh, embittered at his recent experiences and now aged fifty-six, arrived at Sydney. 'The 102nd,' recorded Huey, 'was drawn up on the wharf to receive him, but he refused to come on shore and said he would not be received by those who had so lately threatened to cut his throat.'[58] Next day he came on shore 'and was received by our flank companies, who had marched into Sidney for that purpose'. Later Macquarie presented the Regiment to the former Governor. Huey recollected Bligh addressing them with the following words: 'Gentlemen, I congratulate you on your safe arrival. This is a very fine climate. I hope you will be happy.'[59] On 27 February an additional detachment of thirty men and four officers, including Captain Archibald Maclaine, belonging to the 73rd arrived on board the *Ann*, as well as 200 convicts.

In April, over three months after the 73rd's arrival in Sydney, the 102nd began embarking on the *Dromedary* and the *Hindostan*, eventually setting sail in May for the long journey back to England. The 73rd was at last able to march into barracks, their tents 'being all rotten with the incessant rain which had fallen at Grose Farm Camp', recorded Huey.[60] In preference to returning to England, a number of former officers and soldiers of the 102nd chose to join the 73rd. One young man who transferred was Charles Whalan.[61] At the age of fourteen, he had been sentenced to transportation for seven years for catching a fish on private property. On arrival in New South Wales, having learnt to read and write, he secured a job in Government Stores. After receiving a certificate of pardon on condition he joined the 102nd, he married a servant who worked in Government House. When Bligh became Governor, Whalan served as his Orderly Sergeant, rising under Macquarie to become Sergeant of his Bodyguard.[62]

Since the age limit for transferring from one regiment to another was thirty-five, Macquarie proposed the formation of an Invalid or Veteran Company: 'of one hundred Rank and File with the usual proportion of Sergeants and Drummers to be under the Command and Charge of an Officer of the 73rd Regiment until I shall receive orders from home respecting it'. Pointing out that, quite apart from enabling 'old' soldiers to remain with their families 'and in a Country they are so much attached to, the Measure will be a very Considerable Saving to the Crown as from their great Length of Service, most of them having served between twenty and thirty Years, they would be entitled to very high Pensions on their arrival at home (in Britain) and being discharged for very few of them would be found fit for Service in a Cold Climate.'[63] Once embodied, the Royal Veteran Company was attached to the 73rd and similarly dressed, except with dark blue, distinguishing its status as a Royal Corps, rather than dark green collars and cuffs.

One of the Regiment's earliest causes for a celebration was the marriage on 8 May 1810 of forty-two-year-old Lieutenant Colonel Maurice Charles O'Connell to Captain Bligh's twenty-seven-year-old daughter Mary, whose first husband had died of tuberculosis in November 1807. A splendid dinner was held in their honour by the Macquaries at Government House, followed by a display of fireworks. As later historians observed, Bligh was distressed that his daughter was not returning with him to England, but she was 'a headstrong woman'. Subsequently, while her dresses, by their transparency, had shocked the more conservative members of society, 'her hostility to her father's enemies in the colony soon embarrassed Governor Macquarie'.[64] Ellis Bent, the Judge Advocate, was less than flattering about the Lieutenant Colonel's new wife: 'very small, nice little figure, rather pretty but conceited and extremely proud. God knows of what! . . . I regret this marriage for I dislike her and in the next place it crushed any hopes I had formed of seeing compara- tive harmony restored to the colony.'[65] Four days after his daughter's wedding, Bligh sailed for England, never to return to the southern hemisphere which had made his name so famous. After six months in New South Wales, the young diarist Ensign Huey was sent back to England with dispatches from Macquarie for the British govern- ment. He never returned, leaving the Army to become a painter of miniature portraits.[66]

From Sydney, detachments of the 73rd were sent to Norfolk Island, the small island in the Pacific Ocean which Britain had attempted to colonise in the late 1780s to prevent it falling into the hands of France and used as a penal colony. In the early 1800s the process of transferring convicts to the less remote Van Diemen's Land, at the tip of south-eastern Australia, had already begun and detachments of the 73rd were sent to the Derwent river and Port Dalrymple in Van Diemen's Land to supervise convict work parties. Other detach- ments went to the penal settlement of Newcastle, which supplied Sydney with coal, lime and cedarwood. They were also required to hunt down 'bushrangers' – outlaws who preyed upon local inhabi- tants using highwayman or rudimentary guerrilla tactics – as well as providing for the colony's defence against any external attacker. To help with law and order, soldiers of the 73rd formed the nucleus of Australia's first mounted police force.[67]

The presence in Australia of a British regiment just over two decades after the penal colony was established began a tradition which lasted sixty years. The soldiers' existence was in marked contrast to what their comrades in arms were facing, still fighting the armies of Napoleon in Europe. In the open spaces of Australia, far from the crowded streets of European cities, the men could look forward to a varied outdoor life. In October 1810 they joined some local inhabitants in arranging Sydney's first-ever 'race meeting', proudly announced in *The Sydney Gazette*. A track was prepared on what is today Hyde Park and attendance was recorded as being 'the largest ever collected in the Colony'. The following year, another three-day race meeting was held in mid-August. Although not cavalrymen, the 73rd were responsible for training some of the winners and O'Connell became a Steward of the race course. One year, his horse Carlo won the Ladies Cup.[68] But the races were not without incident. In 1811, Macquarie's secretary, John Thomas Campbell, severely wounded Captain John Ritchie in a duel having quarrelled after the races.[69]

During Macquarie's tenure as Governor, he oversaw an expansive programme of development to rebuild a society where 'the whole population was depressed by poverty; there was neither public credit nor private confidence; the morals of the mass of the population were debased; public worship had been abandoned'.[70] Some 265 public works were undertaken to replace dilapidated buildings or create new ones. New army barracks were completed at the end of 1810. A new hospital was built by the Surgeon, D'Arcy Wentworth, whose son was commissioned into the 73rd. Among other duties, in early 1811 the 73rd was detailed to build a road from Sydney to South Head which helped to develop the eastern suburbs of the growing city. Originally cleared as a public way in 1803, and roughly running along the line of the present-day Old South Head Road/Oxford Street, twenty-one soldiers of the 73rd worked on improving the road, providing access down the hillside towards Watson's Bay. A monument still stands near Watson's Bay waterfront, inscribed:

This Road made by Subscription Was compleated in ten Weeks from the 25 of march 1811 By 21 Soldiers of His Majesty's 73 Reghment. VIII Miles from Sydney.[71]

In the same year an expedition under Captain Archibald Maclaine, 73rd explored the hinterland beyond Sydney. Public morality was high on Macquarie's list of priorities and he spoke out against people living together before marriage. He was also anxious to provide convicts with the opportunity to be rehabilitated into society. One of these was Francis Greenway, deported to New South Wales for forgery, whose architectural skills designed some of the most significant buildings.[72] Another was Andrew Thompson, a reformed burglar who had served for many years as an efficient chief constable, and whom Macquarie appointed as a magistrate, the first emancipist to be appointed to such a position.[73] Although Macquarie's approach was not appreciated by the government at home, it paved the way for what had originated as a penal colony to develop as a free settlement and flourishing economic asset to the British Empire through trade, whaling and wool-growing. As part of his programme of humanitarian reform, assisted by Antill, who shared his ideals, Macquarie organised a school for Aboriginal children and an orphanage for the hundreds of children abandoned by their unmarried parents.[74]

During the 73rd's service in New South Wales, the behaviour of some of the soldiers became lax. 'The effects of the fiery East Indian rum, the cause of so much disorder among the New South Wales Corps, became apparent,' noted historian Peter Stanley, 'while the officers were bored and dissatisfied and complained of the expense of colonial life.'[75] In December 1810 Private John Shea of the 73rd had murdered a prisoner, William Maher. In his defence, Shea argued that Maher had 'by intrigue and artifice deprived him of the affections of a wife who had been the mother of his children'. Found guilty, Shea was sentenced to death.[76] In March 1812, John Gould of the 73rd was executed for murdering a fellow soldier's wife, 'the immoderate use of Spirituous Liquors' being blamed for having 'excited his Passions'. Reflecting on the circumstances which had led to this incident, Macquarie published in 'Government and General Orders' an exhortation to the 73rd:

> SOLDIERS! You once by Valour obtained the honourable Badge of "MANGALORE". You have been selected on Account of your long and justly established Character for Gallantry *in the Field*, and Regularity of Conduct *in Quarters*, for the Purpose of protecting the peaceable and well-behaved Inhabitants of this Country! The still higher Honor of being called the *Defenders* of Peace and good Order in New South New Wales awaits you! – It only rests with you to obtain it by steady and soldier-like good Conduct.[77]

A less drastic misdemeanour was the contraction of 'matrimonial or less proper connexions with the Women of the Country', which led them to 'lose sight of their military duty and become ... identified with the lower class of inhabitants'.[78] One liaison among many was that formed by Private Alexander (Sandy) Mackenzie with Anne Clarke, from Liverpool, who had arrived in New South Wales in September 1810, having been convicted of stealing some printed cloth. Although they never married, and he fathered only one of her four children, Mackenzie returned to live with her in Australia after completing his term of service with the 73rd; all four children were listed with his surname in the 1819 population muster.[79] At least one man, Peter Geary, deserted from the ranks of the 73rd, becoming a bushranger until he was caught and executed in August 1817.[80] Macquarie was also obliged to remove an officer from the position of Commandant of Hobart Town in Tasmania when it was discovered that he had been using labour gangs to build his mansion instead of road building.[81]

When two officers, Lieutenants Archibald McNaughton and Philip Conor, were sentenced for the brutal murder of a soldier, Private William Holness, Macquarie once more lectured the 73rd in morality, expressing 'in the strongest Terms, his Indignation at an Occurrence so disgraceful to the Military Character; and he trusts, with Confidence, that the high Sense of Honor which so eminently characterizes the British Army in every Quarter of the World, and which the 73d Regiment in particular has possessed a most flattering Portion of, will induce them to look to this lamentable Event as a Beacon set up to guard them, against the fatal Consequences attendant on a life of, Drunkenness, Debauchery, and Riot, which inevitably tends to the Debasement and Degradation of the upright and manly Character of a British Soldier, and necessarily induces the Contempt and Indignation of all brave and honorable Men.'[82]

The deteriorating reputation of the 73rd was exacerbated by the lingering antagonism between O'Connell's wife, Mary, and those who had supported her father's deposition. In 1813 Macquarie wrote to Earl Bathurst, secretary of state for war and the colonies in Lord Liverpool's government, requesting the 73rd to be withdrawn, 'for the peace of the colony'. Instead of returning home to Britain, its next posting was Ceylon, where the Regiment had last served in 1795. Although, by the terms of the 1802 Treaty of Amiens, the coastal regions, formerly under Dutch authority, had become a British Crown Colony, the Kingdom of Kandy in central and eastern Ceylon had retained its independence and a power struggle had broken out between the local chiefs and the King of the Malabar dynasty from southern India, drawing the British into military operations; the first war had been fought between 1803 and 1805, an uneasy peace now prevailing.

As the 73rd prepared to depart, Macquarie praised the Regiment, masking the rift which had developed. Recognising that the posting in New South Wales 'has not afforded the usual field for military glory', he said, 'in as far as the industrious exertions of those non-commissioned officers and privates, who could be spared from military duty, have been exerted, this colony is much indebted for many useful improvements, which but for the soldiers of the Seventy-Third regiment, must have remained only in the contemplation of those anxious for its civilization for a length of time.'[83] The first detachment which left on 24 January 1814 included three companies under Major George Gordon's command on board HMS *Earl Spencer*. Two months later, O'Connell departed on board HMS *General Hewitt* with additional companies. A third detachment left Sydney Cove on board HMS *Windham* on 14 April 1814.

Among those who remained, creating a new generation of men and women with Scottish antecedents, was Henry Antill, promoted major in 1811, and who had been so distressed at having to leave his family in Scotland in 1809. As the Governor's ADC, he had been Macquarie's companion and adviser for over three years.[84] He married in 1818, later becoming a Justice of the Peace and continuing to share Macquarie's interest in the welfare of orphans and aboriginals. He died in Australia in 1852.[85] After serving as the Regiment's Commanding Officer for twenty-five years, O'Connell, knighted in

1834, returned as commander of the forces in Australia in 1838, dying in Australia a decade later.

Another officer who distinguished himself was Captain Richard Lundin, when returning to Britain on leave of absence at the end of 1812. Having been entrusted with dispatches from Macquarie, he was travelling on board the *Isabella* by way of Cape Horn, 'which though in distance considerably greater than by way of the Cape of Good Hope, is always preferred, because of the strong westerly winds which prevail in these latitudes.' On 8 February 1813, the ship foundered on one of the uninhabited islands of the Falkland Islands. Together with five others, in a journey lasting thirty-six days, Lundin sailed in the ship's seventeen foot longboat to Buenos Aires to seek help for the remaining crew and passengers left on the island. After returning as a guide on board HMS *Nancy* to the site of the wrecked *Isabella*, Lundin eventually arrived in England in early December 1813, later joining the York Chasseurs.[86]

The most illustrious member of the 73rd was Lachlan Macquarie, although his command of the Regiment was short-lived. His position as Governor, which he held for twelve years, enabled him to make such a lasting contribution to Australia's administration and development that he is now regarded as its first statesman. Having resigned as Governor in 1821, following criticism of the alleged extravagance of his building works, and claims that the colony was failing in its role as a place of punishment, he returned to Britain in 1822, dying in London in 1824 aged sixty-three.[87] Virtually unknown in Britain, his name has lived on in Australia. With Macquarie University, Hospital, Bank in Sydney, a dictionary, Sydney's most impressive street, a river and a harbour in Tasmania, a sub-Antarctic Island, and several locations – including a lighthouse, pier, port and numerous hotels – throughout New South Wales all named after him, the inscription on Lachlan Macquarie's tomb on the Island of Mull in Scotland aptly reads 'the father of Australia'.[88]

Kandyan Conflict 1814–1818

While the Allied armies of Europe were continuing to fight against Napoleon, the 1st Battalion 73rd embarked on a different kind of warfare in Ceylon. Having left Australia in January, on 25 March 1814 the *Earl Spencer* sailed into Colombo harbour. The men were 'in good health after a pleasant passage', Lieutenant D'Arcy Wentworth informed his father, 'having lost but one man and two women'.[89] Surveying the new arrivals, the Governor and Commander-in-Chief, Lieutenant General Robert Brownrigg expressed surprise that they were 'very much encumbered with Women and Children, which in this part of the World is attended with distressing consequences but which to the utmost of my power I will endeavour to shield them from'. To accommodate the new arrivals, Brownrigg informed Bathurst, secretary of state for war and the colonies, that he would 'order comfortable Huts to be constructed for Married Soldiers within the Forts of Colombo and Galle, in the hope of being able to control the vicious habits of European Soldiers'.[90]

Soon after the arrival of this first contingent, the 1st Battalion 73rd was caught up in renewed hostilities with the Kingdom of Kandy. 'Upon our arrival at this place the King of Candy [Sri Vikrama Rajasinha] and his Adigar [Prime or First Minister] was at variance,' Wentworth wrote home.[91] Instead of obeying a summons from the King, the prime minister had put himself under British protection. Wary of reprisals from the King, British and Ceylonese troops were ordered 'to hold themselves in readiness to march at a moment's warning . . . our regiment was not to go till the last on account of their not being sufficiently inured to the climate which is very unwholesome in the interior. People have been known to have gone up the country only for a day and to have returned with the jungle Fever, which is never got rid of without change of climate and then not always.' But, because of the onset of the monsoon, the expected call to arms did not happen; 'thus were all our hopes blasted.' At least the men could be thankful to remain in Colombo, which was 'considered to be most healthy Part of the Island', although the heat was 'excessive at times and it is even dangerous to go out'.[92]

Bad behaviour in the ranks of the 73rd was continuing to cause problems. One offender was Lieutenant Thomas Atkins, who was 'continually drunk on Parade and would sit down in company with any blackguard who would give him a glass of grog', Wentworth told his father. Having been cautioned three times by Major Gordon, 'notwithstanding this and the repeated cautions given by myself and others he still persisted[.]' Returning to quarters one night, Wentworth heard a noise in a nearby ditch; further investigation revealed Atkins – on duty as Officer of the Day – 'so drunk that it was with the greatest exertions I was able to get him out and I have not the least doubt had I not providentially passed by at the time but that he must have been drowned[.]' When these 'repeated irregularities' reached the ears of the Commandant, he ordered Atkins to be brought before a Court Martial. As Wentworth admitted, this was not the only instance. 'We have had great trouble with the Detachment since our arrival. Several men have been tried by General Courts Martial'.[93]

So bad was the 73rd's conduct that Brownrigg felt compelled to inform Bathurst in London that their behaviour 'has been in the most culpable degree disorderly and mutinous and in some instances outrageous'. Having pardoned two privates convicted of assaulting their officers and sentenced to death, in 'the hope as it was the first offence in the Detachment of so atrocious a nature that an act of mercy would have a good Effect on their minds', worse behaviour meant that Brownrigg had felt obliged 'to carry the Law into Effect in the instance of John Stevenson who suffered Death by Military Execution on the 13th of last month'.[94] Brownrigg blamed their behaviour on the plentiful arrack and the loss of discipline in New South Wales, when the men had been required to undertake 'avocations foreign to and not very compatible with Military duty', as well as having contact 'with the Convicts whose profligacy they cannot but be expected to imbibe'.[95]

When, after Stevenson's execution, behaviour improved, Brownrigg felt 'warranted' – in celebration of the Prince Regent's birthday – 'to try the Effect of a remission of all punishment then depending, to withdraw some restrictions which I had been obliged to impose on the liberty of the men and to grant them the usual indulgence of liquor to join with their comrades in celebrating the day'. He also improved the allowance of provisions to wives and families. 'The heavy burden of these numerous Families no doubt led to and furnished some kind of Excuse or at least an Extenuation of the practice of smuggling so prevalent amongst the women of the lately arrived Detachment.'[96]

Meanwhile, in mid-August the *General Hewitt* with Lieutenant Colonel O'Connell and three more companies of the Regiment had arrived, 'after a very circuitous voyage round New Guinea, New Britain, and through the Molucca Islands.' The third contingent on board the *Windham* reached Ceylon in early November.[97] A fourth detachment sailed on board the *General Brown(e)*, arriving in Ceylon on 2 March 1815, by which time British troops were engaged in fighting 'the Second Kandyan War.'[98]

At the end of January 1815, the British force advanced inland to Kandy. 'At length our long expected expedition has taken place,' D'Arcy Wentworth informed his father on 30 January, 'and the Division to which I belong is at the moment advanced, upwards of fifty miles into the interior of the enemy's country, without meeting with the smallest opposition. The Army is divided into eight Divisions, which have entered the Country at different points. To ours has been allotted the most difficult route, tho' we have hitherto met with few obstacles in the road, at least we think little of them, compared with those which our guides inform us we have to encounter.' As noted by the Record of Service, 'the soldiers underwent great fatigue in crossing mountains morasses & rivers, and traversing regions inhabited only by wild beasts of the forest.' By the middle of the month they had overcome the opposition. On 18 February the King, who had fled with 'a small number of his Malabar adherents', was captured by his own subjects, 'who' affirmed the Record of Service 'showed the utmost detestation of the tyrant'. Following discussions between Brownrigg and the chiefs of Kandy, the Malabar dynasty was deposed and, by the terms of the Kandyan Convention, the provinces of Kandy were joined to British Ceylon. All forms of torture and mutilation were abolished. A detachment of troops was left to garrison the newly acquired territory, while the 73rd returned to Colombo, where the Regiment remained throughout 1816.[99]

In September 1817 the British authorities heard that some chiefs 'hostile to British interests' were preparing to support a new claimant to the Kandyan throne who had arrived from mainland India. In late October, all British regiments in Ceylon were again ordered into the interior.[100] At this time the 73rd's ranks were supplemented by a detachment of the 2nd Battalion 73rd, which, after fighting amidst the victorious Allied armies in Europe, had been disbanded in 1817. Among those who arrived was William Morris, who had fought against Napoleon, with his brother Thomas, at Quatre Bras and Waterloo.[101] At the end of the year, the Regiment marched north to the natural harbour of Trincomalee to relieve the 19th Regiment, which supplied 172 volunteers to the 73rd before returning to England.

The 'long and desultory war' against dissident Kandyans was 'extremely harassing to the parties engaged in it', recorded Morris. 'Frequent attacks were made upon the enemy, who although they fought bravely, and had plenty of the munitions of war, were yet obliged to retire from their intrepid assailants, who were steadily and securely advancing towards the capital.'[102] As Morris discovered, the 'mode of warfare' in the British Empire was very different from Europe. 'In Ceylon, for instance, a thousand men, in their advance against the enemy, would be accompanied by, perhaps two or three times their number of supernumeraries, so that a small force of fighting men assumes a very formidable appearance, attended as they are, by numbers of the finest elephants, for which this island has been so celebrated.' In the jungle a soldier had to 'pay his respects' to snakes and serpents, which often crossed his path: 'and occasionally a boa constrictor will present himself, of such immense size as to be capable of swallowing and digesting anything which should come in his way, from a buffalo to a rat.'[103] 'The want of surgical aid was severely felt,' noted the Record of Service, and so the officers were obliged 'with the assistance of manuscript instructions' to give out medicine and dress wounds. On occasion, they performed 'trifling operations'.[104]

One instance of bravery was singled out in the Record of Service, which described how 'a very small party' of the 73rd 'in charge of Lance Corporal Richard McLoughlin was furiously attacked'. When two men were killed, instead of leaving their dead comrades, the soldiers divided themselves into two groups, 'part remained in charge of the bodies, and the other portion, at an equal risk, proceeded to Badulah [Badulla, southeast of Kandy] a few miles distant and returned with a reinforcement, that enabled them to carry off their deceased comrades.' This they did, 'in spite of the exertions of the enemy to the contrary' costing three more lives. In recognition of their bravery, medals were struck by the Ceylonese government. Among the dead was McLoughlin, a veteran of Waterloo.[105]

By the end of November 1818, the 'Third Kandyan War' was over. Known as the Uva rebellion since it had begun amongst the nobility in the region of Uva, Britain's victory, using 'scorch and burn' tactics, signalled the end of the four-hundred-year-old politically independent Kingdom of Kandy. Not realising the impact their conquest made on the social and cultural traditions of the local people, the soldiers believed they were doing their duty in support of creating a more humane society. 'Our objects are not simply aggrandizement, coercion, and robbery, but to civilise, ameliorate, and improve, as far as practicable; seeking, of course, by the extension of commerce and improvement of trade, to make it conducive to the interest of the mother country,' noted William Morris.[106]

After the end of the war, the 73rd spent two more years in Ceylon, but there was little fighting and one of Morris's least pleasant occupations was making coffins 'for our poor fellows, who were dropping off regularly from cholera, fever and diarrhoea'.[107] While in Ceylon, ten officers and 366 soldiers of the 73rd had died, but only one officer and about twenty soldiers had been killed during active service, the remainder dying of illness due to the climate. The officer killed was Lachlan Macquarie's young cousin, Lieutenant John Maclaine, whom Macquarie had appointed as his ADC when Antill was promoted brigade major in 1812. Having returned to England in 1814, and fought against Napoleon, Maclaine arrived in Ceylon in 1816. He was shot in the head on 13 January 1818 while leading a detachment of men through jungle terrain.[108]

Others died through misadventure or misconduct. In January 1817, three ensigns, recently arrived from England, died on board the *Iphigenia*, when the ship foundered. On 27 October 1817 Private John Jenny was executed, having been found guilty of striking his superior officer, Major Haddon Smith. 'The Troops were formed into three sides of a square (the fourth being open to the Sea) in the centre of which, the unhappy man being placed, prayed devoutly for a few minutes & the Death Warrant being read, he underwent the awful Sentence of the Law; the Scene was solemn & impressive & appeared to have its due effect on the minds of the Soldiery.' [109]

In time, after surviving the hardship of their lives as soldiers, some returned to Australia. One such was Lieutenant William Thomas Lyttleton, a talented artist who recorded and published some of the earliest British views of Kandy and Trincomalee, including aquatints of the royal tombs at Kandy, destroyed in 1850. Having married Ann Hortle, the daughter of a private soldier in the New South Wales Corps, he returned to Van Diemen's Land (now Tasmania) in 1825. Returning to England in 1836, he died three years later.[110]

D'Arcy Wentworth returned to Sydney in 1829, dying in Tasmania in 1861, his remains interred in the Wentworth family tomb in St John's Cemetery, Parramatta, on the outskirts of Sydney, where other 73rd veterans were buried: of these Sergeant John Baxter had arrived in Australia on board the *Dromedary* (together with Huey and Antill) in 1810 and died in 1862; Sergeant Daniel Humm had enlisted with the 73rd while it was stationed in New South Wales and died on 14 June 1842. According to the inscription on the headstone of Humm's grave, having served in the 73rd 'during a period of 27 years he returned to his Native land rewarded with a pension for his services but with such an emaciated body worn and wounded that it sank shortly after his return.' There is also a family vault with the remains of Charles Whalan, described by Macquarie as 'peculiarly correct, honest, honorable and faithful,' during his service as Sergeant of the Governor's Bodyguard.[111]

> And lo! – within this Austral zone,
> In regions unexplored, unknown,
> Till time has into dotage grown,
> An infant state appear.[112]

12.

The Peninsular Wars

So, at Corunn's grand retreat,
When, far outnumbered by the foe,
The patriot Moore made glorious halt,
Like setting sun in fiery glow.
Before us foam'd the rolling sea,
Behind, the carrion eagles flew;
But Scotland's 'Watch' proved Gallia's match,
And won the game by 'Forty-Two!'[1]

The Peninsula

The French defeat at Trafalgar in 1805 brought Britain only temporary respite. Napoleon's victories against his European adversaries had made him master of the Continent. He now turned his attention towards destroying Britain's commercial empire. The Berlin Decree, issued in November 1806, forbade any of France's allies to trade with Britain. To reinforce the 'Continental Blockade', Napoleon determined to close the Atlantic ports on the Iberian Peninsula to British shipping. When the Portuguese government refused to agree to the blockade, in November 1807 a vast army, commanded by Marshal Jean-Andoche Junot, crossed through Spain and invaded Portugal.[2] The Portuguese royal family fled to Brazil, where they were in residence when the 73rd stopped at Rio de Janeiro en route to Australia.

In response to Napoleon's aggressive manoeuvres, which had included installing his elder brother, Joseph-Napoleon Bonaparte, on the Spanish throne, the British prime minister, William Cavendish Bentinck, Duke of Portland, ordered an expeditionary force to embark for the Peninsula.[3] Lieutenant General Arthur Wellesley, recently returned from India, was chosen to lead the British force. Sailing from Cork in July 1808, with an army of less than 10,000 men, he disembarked at Mondego Bay. To bolster the force, additional troops commanded by Lieutenant General Sir John Moore were ordered to depart, among them the 42nd.

1st Battalion 42nd

On 14 August 1808 the 1st Battalion 42nd embarked from Gibraltar 'in a sailing transport, no steamers in those days', related Private James Gunn in his memoirs. 'We were very merry aboard, the sea being unrippled as a pond; our officers always kind to their men.

There was no less than a few Reels Danced in the Cool of the evenings.'[4] Before they landed in Portugal, news arrived of Junot's defeat by Wellesley at Vimeiro on 21 August. According to the generous terms of the Convention of Sintra, the French were permitted to evacuate their troops from all the towns and forts they had occupied without further attack.[5] 'Soldier-like, we then fancied we had nothing more to do, so little did the common soldiers of the 42d know the immense force Buonaparte had scattered in swarms over the Peninsula.'[6] Landing north of the river Tagus, the 42nd was ordered to Quilla Camp, 'about three leagues' from Lisbon. Before long a number of men died 'with a severe turn' of diarrhoea, 'in Defiance of all our Good Colonel and his Medical men could do'.[7]

In early October, active operations were resumed, the intention being for the British army, cooperating with disaffected Spanish troops and Portuguese, to march into Spain to challenge Napoleon in person, joining up with a force under the command of General Sir David Baird, who, like Wellesley, had returned from India. Lacking sufficient intelligence, and as historian Stewart of Garth narrated, 'believing it impossible to convey his artillery by the road through the mountains, it was judged necessary to form the army in divisions, and to march in by different routes'.[8] 'We accordingly marched by regiments through Portugal,' related Private John. 'At all the towns and villages through which we passed, the inhabitants received us with great joy, as the saviours of their country.'[9]

Entering Spain by the frontier garrison town of Ciudad Rodrigo, they continued to Salamanca, where Moore intended to assemble his forces. 'In this city the British army assembled; but of the various regiments that composed it, there was not one so much admired as the 42d,' recollected Private John. 'We were a novel race of beings – our dress, except the red coat, bore no resemblance to that of the other regiments.'[10] Quartered in a convent, as Gunn recollected, and 'at a loss as to speaking the Spanish Language', they encountered some Irish students who printed a small book with the names of necessary articles they might want to purchase in Spanish and in English, 'which proved very useful'.[11] While Moore was waiting for the army to assemble, on 23 November news came of the defeat of the Spanish armies and Napoleon's approach to Madrid. Having first thought to retire through Portugal, Moore decided to help the beleaguered Spanish by advancing northwards against French lines of communication. In early December the British army set out to Sahagun, joining forces with Baird's column, which had come from Corunna. After the fall of Madrid, Moore determined to make good his presence by attacking what he believed was an inferior French force under the command of Marshal Nicolas Jean-de-Dieu Soult, encamped near Sahagun.[12] When news was received that the French army, under Napoleon's personal command, was advancing in great strength from several directions, Moore's only option was to order a withdrawal.

Corunna January 1809

'Everybody has heard of that retreat; the ground was covered with snow,' related Private John.[13] For two hundred and fifty miles, the soldiers, wives and camp followers marched 'along roads covered with snow, over mountains and rivers, and through narrow defiles, with a numerous enemy following in full career, and frequently skirmishing with the rear-guard'.[14] As Private Gunn recalled, it had been an 'unusually severe winter for Sunny Spain', and now that the thaw had set in, the roads were 'very bad'.[15] Having passed Villa Mañana, they reached 'a rather formidable river that had to be forded'. This was the river Esla, which they reached on Christmas Day. Ordered to take off their kilts and cartridge pouches and belts, 'and lay them on the top of our Knapsacks at the Back of our heads no doubt to keep the powder dry', as Gunn recognised, 'the Caution proved to be a necessary one.' With ice floating in the river, a 'Generous Dragoon' helped him across the river, without which 'assuredly I would be carried away'.[16]

During the march, discipline broke down. According to Private John, 'a great many of the 42d got drunk, and some of them lagged behind in the line of march, and became prisoners to the French. When our day's march was over, there was a drum-head court-martial held, and 24 tried and flogged.'[17] At Astorga they encountered some Spanish troops, recently defeated by Soult: 'this was all we saw of that Great Spanish army that was to support us or Rather us to support them against Bonaparte's Rule,' recollected Gunn. As they left Astorga 'it came on to snow but we travelled all night, coming in gray daylight we halted for about an hour. I mind it well. This was the first Severe Hunger I ever felt.'[18] By 30 December the main French army had begun crossing the river Esla in anticipation of encircling the British before they could reach the mountains of Galicia. Fifteen miles still separated the two armies, and it was not until New Year's Day 1809 that the French reached Astorga, hard on the heels of the British. Napoleon then retraced his steps to France, leaving the army under Soult's command.

By this time the British army was 'in a wretched condition, from the want of provisions, shoes and blankets; and insubordination began visibly to show its capricious front in more brigades than ours,' Private John related. 'When we got upon the mountainous roads we found them covered with deep snow; and our march that day was very long and fatiguing. When we halted, neither barracks nor convents offered us an asylum; the earth was our bed, the sky our covering, and the loud winds sang us to sleep.' Served out with a pound of beef per man, they had 'neither wood nor water to cook it', until, using the wood from some derelict houses for firewood and the snow for water, they managed to get a fire going to boil the meat. 'We sat on our canteens and knapsacks by the fires all night, for we could not lie down on the fields of snow.'[19]

As the men marched onwards, often barefoot, they saw the miseries of those who had gone before them. 'It was the most shocking sight to see the road that day after the army had passed. Dead horses and mules and asses, and wagons, and baggage of all descriptions lay at every step, and men and women and children that were not able to keep up with the army implored our aid, or, in the bitterness of their soul, cursed their hard fate, or lay dying beside the dead.'[20] As

Gunn admitted, much as the men suffered, the women fared worse. Unable to keep up with the army, they were often compelled to march with the French Advance Guard, 'who treated them kindly ... strange to relate my pay Serjts wife was safely delivered of a daughter on this retreat and was as kindly treated as the Circumstance could allow and suffered to join her husband in Corunna.'[21] On one occasion, after thinking they might have to fight the French, 'nothing came of it, for at night we bade our foes a silent adieu and got a night's start of them'.[22]

The next big town was Lugo. By the time the 1st Battalion 42nd arrived, all available billets had been taken and so the men had to find quarters 'where we could in the adjacent country houses. The house I was in,' recalled Private John, 'was in poverty, the inhabitants having got everything out of the way before we arrived; it was well for them, assuredly we should have plundered them; yet, in all this we were only acting on a small scale, and by the direst necessity, what an Alexander or a Caesar would have done; – nay, what they did, – what is done every age by great generals and ambitious monarchs.'[23] While they were settling down to enjoy their scanty provisions, a sudden French attack meant that 'the bugle was sounded to turn out the whole. Then the scramble commenced, tearing the half-boiled beef in pieces, every one catching what he could, and gobbling the wine.' As the French cavalry appeared, the soldiers ran to protect the pickets. 'Our quarters being hard by the point of attack, we were the first on the ground, to the support of the pickets; when our brigade was formed, the French fell back.'[24]

While at Lugo, as Moore wrote in a dispatch home, he decided that Vigo, where he had initially thought to embark the army, was too far away 'and offered no advantages to embark in the face of an enemy'. He therefore decided that the best place to head for was Corunna, which he believed offered a good defensible position.[25] By this time, Private John was recording that there was no officer left to carry the Colours: 'All fell behind: but while a man was left, the 42d's colours would be where they were safe. This shews what the retreat to Corunna was. I have not language to express what hardships I endured.'[26] Since leaving Astorga, an estimated 3,000 men had died, with five hundred left in hospitals there and at Villafranca.[27] Having had no provisions since Lugo, at Britanzes (Betanzos) there were 'all sorts of stores . . . I had a pair of shoes served out to me before I mounted guard. I had been a poor miserable being before, trailing my musket after me, and drawing one leg after the other for many a long league; and I felt in shoes, as no monarch ever felt on a throne.'[28]

On 11 January 1809, the men had their first sight of Corunna: 'when we came in sight of the sea, we fancied all was well. When I saw the vessels in the harbour, I was so rejoiced, that in a few hours I was a new man again. What is man made of that he can endure all this?'[29] But, as they soon discovered, the transports had not yet arrived, 'which,' recollected Gunn, 'disappointed us not a little'.[30] Over the next few days, while they waited, the French caught up. On 14 January the transports arrived and the sick and wounded were evacuated.

In the meantime the French artillery had arrived; to cover the evac- uation Moore positioned the army on a ridge blocking the road to Corunna, while Soult's army took up position on a range of heights facing them. The 1st Battalion 42nd, in Baird's Division, was posted near the village of Elvina. On 16 January, around midday, shots were fired from the French battery. 'Some of their balls fell among our huts, and we were then very soon under arms,' recollected Private John. 'We had two field pieces at the right of our brigade. The enemy was then seen advancing, in two very large compact columns, down on our brigade. . . . Our artillery fired a few shots, and then retreated for want of ammunition. Our flankers were sent out to assist the picquets. The French columns soon formed their line, and advanced, driving the picquets and flankers before them, while their artillery kept up a close cannonade on our line with grape and round shot.'[31]

Some of the 42nd were killed outright, others wounded; Baird's arm was shattered by a musket ball, and so Moore took personal command of the Division. 'On the advance of the French to the village of Elvina, Sir John Moore allowed the enemy to deploy,' recollected Lieutenant Colonel James Stirling, 'and form their line at half-musket-shot from us. He then gave me orders (about half-past two o'clock) to advance and charge with the Forty-Second, accompanying that order with the words, "Highlanders, remember Egypt!"'[32] 'The sound of the voice of the general officer,' noted Cannon in the *Historical Record*, 'under whose command they had conquered at Alexandria, animated the soldiers, and they rushed forward, over-powering all opposition.'[33] 'Sir John came in front of the 42d,' recorded Private John. 'He said, "There is no use in making a long speech; but, 42d, I hope you will do as you have done before." With that he rode off the ground in front of us. Sir John did not mention Egypt; but we understood Egypt was the meaning of his expressions, as Buonaparte's Invincibles were the last the 42d was engaged with.'[34]

Victory was not assured. 'The ground, on which both the French and British were, was very bad for making an engagement,' Private John continued, 'being very rocky and full of ditches, and a large valley between the two positions . . . our colonel gave orders for us to lie on the ground, at the back of the height our position was on; and whenever the French were within a few yards of us, we were to start up and fire our muskets, and then give them the bayonet.'[35] 'As soon as the regiment had given their fire,' related Stirling, 'and drove the enemy with the bayonet to the bottom of the ravine, Sir John directed me to halt the corps, and defend that position.'[36] Within moments of giving the order, as Stirling turned round, he saw Moore 'struck to the ground off his horse, and I immediately sent a party to carry him from the field.' Hit by a cannon ball, Moore's injury was fatal. Since Baird was already wounded, command passed to Lieutenant General Sir John Hope, who later described events to Baird: 'The troops tho' not unacquainted with the irreparable loss they had sustained, were not dismayed but by the most determined Bravery not only repelled every attempt of the Enemy to gain Ground but actually forced them to retire altho' he had brought up fresh Troops in support of those originally engaged.'[37]

'The confusion that now ensued baffles all my powers even of memory and imagination,' recalled Private John, 'pell-mell, ding-dong . . . and many of us skivered pairs, front and rear rank: to the right about they went, and we after them.'[38] 'The Enemy finding himself foiled in every attempt to force the Right of the Position endeavoured by numbers to turn it,' Hope continued in his letter to Baird. But 'a judicious and well timed Movement' by the Reserve prevented them from doing so.[39] 'We pursued them more than half way taking a few prisoners of whom we were very careless,' narrated Gunn.[40] To their surprise, 'the fellows whom the poor weak 42d put to the rout, were ten times our numbers, yet they fled like a mob of women and children.'[41] According to Stirling, in the heat of the battle, the Grenadiers and 1st Company did not hear his order to halt and 'continued the charge a little in advance, as did the Light Company also', remaining 'in close action with the enemy, until night put an end to the contest'.[42]

With the French repulsed, the British army embarked under the cover of night, leaving a small contingent behind 'to keep up large fires that we had kindled to deceive the French'.[43] The body of Sir John Moore, who had survived long enough to know that the French had been defeated, was buried, wrapped in a military cloak on the southern ramparts of the town. According to Private John, he did not hear any of the soldiers in the Regiment talking about the burial, 'therefore I conclude none of our men attended it'.[44]

Eager to get off Spanish soil, the men were formed on the beach 'where boats were awaiting us', recalled James Gunn, 'and as we came forward, stepped in to a boat until told to stop. The boats filled was ordered off to such a transport no. until word was brought back that such a no. was full.'[45] Having left their position 'about Ten at Night with a degree of order that did them Credit', Hope informed Baird that 'the whole of the Army was Embarked with an Expedition which has seldom been equalled'.[46]

On 18 January, the rearguard departed. Hope issued General Orders, congratulating the soldiers: 'On no occasion has the undaunted valour of British troops been more manifest.' Together with the 4th and 50th Regiments, the 1st Battalion 42nd was recognised for having 'sustained the weight of the attack'.[47] The 42nd had lost one sergeant and thirty-six soldiers. Six officers, one sergeant and

104 soldiers were wounded.[48] Ninety-nine men were listed as 'missing' 'from the toils and privations of the retreat from the interior of Spain'.[49] In 'consequence' of the 1st Battalion's 'distinguished gallantry', it later received the Battle Honour *Corunna*.[50]

Arriving at Plymouth, the officers and men disembarked: 'a poor dejected miserable looking set of soldiers as ever landed in England; some with bonnets and others without, some with shoes and others bare-footed; some with fire-arms, and others defenceless, as nature made them; our clothing in rags; our hair and beards overgrown'.[51] But, as Gunn recollected: 'the good English dinners we got in our billets soon restored us to our former selves, only speaking of the poor Fellows we left behind in Spain to be taken prisoners'.[52] From Plymouth, the 1st Battalion took up quarters at Shorncliffe, in Kent. 'In one town through which we passed, all the people came out to meet us; there was a feast for us; and casks of beer paraded in the street to treat the few of the 42d thus wandering on to head quarters. Next morning we had a hearty breakfast from them, and they placed boughs of laurel in our bonnets or hats'.[53]

With fears of a French invasion 'gaining ground in the minds of the British public', drills at Shorncliffe 'were devoted to learning how to fire down on the beach either standing or lying down, and in repelling imaginary attacks from the French flotilla'.[54] Having shared the ordeal of retreat to Corunna and the action on 16 January, the soldiers found the officers 'were far more like brothers and friends, than men employed in a military command'. One welcome perk was coffee. 'We had, besides, plenty of fine porter and ale, so we recruited very fast, and soon forgot the retreat to Corunna'.[55] While at Canterbury, the soldiers decided to present Lieutenant Colonel James Stirling, who was relinquishing command, with a sword 'for his goodness, and in token of our high opinion of his bravery'. To pay for it, every soldier subscribed a day's pay and every non-commissioned officer two, which 'purchased a very handsome sword'.[56]

Walcheren 1809

In July 1809 the 1st Battalion 42nd was ordered to Walcheren as part of an expeditionary force of 40,000 men to attack Flushing and destroy French arsenals and ships at Antwerp. 'This was the grandest spectacle I ever witnessed,' observed Private John, 'to see so great a number of soldiers and sailors leaving England at one and the same time, the sea covered with ships, all sailing along with a fine fair wind.'[57]

Having landed at South Beveland, where their predecessors had served two and three decades previously, 'the 42d then marched some six miles, to a small village, upon the inhabitants of which we were quartered, as we had no tents to encamp in its neighbourhood'. Their duties were light, but within a short time, the men began to fall ill.[58] 'Now our Sorrows began not from powder and ball but the Walcheren Fever and ague. On its first appearance our Company alone had 20 attacked at once which caused no small consternation, having never known anything about the Disease before,' Private Gunn recollected. 'Water was blamed and ordered to be boiled. Fruit, of which there was abundance was prohibited, Milk also, but the Disease increased Strange to say.'[59] With the army so debilitated, the attack on Antwerp had to be abandoned.

In September 1809 the 1st Battalion 42nd returned to England to be stationed at Canterbury. 'Here we stopped for some months, the malady increasing. Strange the Medical Department did not know how to treat it effectually.'[60] The fever lingered until the following spring. 'We are all here jogging on doing nothing but looking after the sick,' Major Robert Macara was writing to Robert Henry Dick, the junior major of the 2nd Battalion in March 1810. 'We have lost about 130 since the Regt returned from Walcheren, have only about 200 fit for duty, and even those looking as yellow as a Kite's Foot.'[61]

In July, 'the regiment being still very unhealthful, the Marquis of Huntly, our Colonel, it was said, petitioned to have us sent to Scotland;

the request was granted.'[62] Stationed at Musselburgh Barracks, outside Edinburgh, every man was given leave 'at the conclusion of which (though some stayed away double their time) we all returned vastly improved in health,' recollected Gunn, 'much to the gratification of our dear old Colonel, who was well entitled to his nickname of "Daddy" as he looked on us all as his own family.'[63] Reflecting on the Walcheren expedition, Private John commented: 'There was scarcely a man in our regiment who did not think the Walcheren expedition a very foolish thing. We were a fine army of men sent to an unhealthy climate to do nothing, except the few troops who were engaged at Flushing.'[64]

Return to the Peninsula 1809: 2nd Battalion 42nd

The retreat from Corunna did not mean that Britain's fight with France was over. In April 1809, having avoided a near disastrous shipwreck, Wellesley returned to the Peninsula. Arriving in Lisbon, where a contingent of British troops had remained, he gained an immediate victory against the French at Oporto on 12 May. Soon afterwards, the 2nd Battalion 42nd, quartered in Ireland, under the command of Lieutenant Colonel Lord Blantyre, received orders to be ready for foreign service.[65] On arrival at Lisbon in early July, the Regiment remained encamped for nearly a month before travelling by road and boat up the river Tagus to Nisa.[66] Meanwhile Wellesley had crossed into Spain, to join forces with the Spanish General Don Gregorio de la Cuesta in an attempt to march on Madrid.[67] In late July the combined British and Spanish armies had engaged the French at Talavera. For what was regarded as 'a brilliant but severe Battle', Wellesley was ennobled, assuming the title of Viscount Wellington of Talavera and of Wellington.[68]

The strategic advantage, however, remained with the French. Since Soult was believed to be threatening to cut the British and Portuguese lines of communication, Wellington withdrew the army into Portugal. 'This sudden & Rapid retreat proved afterwards not to have been from apprehensions of the Enemy,' explained Blantyre, 'but entirely from the state of actual starvation in which the Portuguese Army was & we were ordered to retreat that they might fall back upon what little supply of Bread & Biscuits we had been able to collect.'[69] With no immediate fighting, Wellington's army remained 'idle'. In Blantyre's opinion the Battalion and other regiments of the Brigade were 'worse off in every respect than any other Brigade', because they were encamped on the banks of the Guadiana river, which had 'the character of being very unhealthy'. By mid-October, he was reporting 'the Army extremely sickly & a contagious fever carrying off great numbers of them daily. There died during these two months upon an average not less than between 300 & 400 men every week. Our Regt suffered much having buried in that time 70 men, most of them the stoutest men we had.'[70] In early December they left the Guadiana; 'our numerous sick, which ought to have been taken away before, moved with us'.[71] Having left one Division at Abrantes, Wellington established his headquarters at Viseu, south-east of Oporto, where the army went into winter quarters.

Busaco September 1810

Heavy rains in early 1810 meant that the men were short of supplies and living 'almost entirely upon bad English biscuit' in a mountainous region of Portugal where 'the inhabitants say they have nine months of winter'.[72] As in other campaigns, uniforms became tattered and worn. When Captain John Swanson took charge of the 42nd's sick, he reported that 'most of the men had made down their kilts into trowsers, some had kilts & others wore coloured trousers'. To make the men appear 'somewhat decent', he ordered the kilts to be cut down. 'If I have acted wrong,' he pleaded to Major Dick, in command of the Battalion, while Blantyre was commanding the Brigade, 'it was from the best motives I gave such orders, indeed I was perfectly ashamed to see them going about in so many different dresses.'[73]

Having received intelligence that the French, under Napoleon's brilliant field commander Marshal André Masséna, were reassembling to besiege Ciudad Rodrigo on the Portuguese frontier, the army began to move out of winter quarters. 'The French force continued to collect in our front in large numbers and were busily employed in preparing for the siege of Ciudad Rodrigo,' recorded Blantyre in his Journal in mid-June.[74] When it fell in July 'after a most gallant resistance of three weeks',[75] Masséna advanced into Portugal. By the end of August, the fortress of Almeida had fallen. Wellington was having to fight a delaying battle, and positioned the army along a high ridge, which extended from the Mondego river northwards, with his headquarters in the convent of Busaco.

'There was some smart skirmishing on the 25th & 26th [September]' continued Blantyre, '& we saw the whole of the French Army take up its ground opposite us – amounting as was supposed to 80,000 men.' Using the tactic of occupying the reverse slope out of sight of the enemy, which was to become the hallmark of Wellington's battles, Blantyre described how, to encourage Masséna to attack, Wellington: 'concealed the British Troops as much as possible, & only shewed the Portuguese. The consequence was that Masséna conceiving that we had not above 10,000 British (as we afterwards learnt from French Officers taken Prisoner) and also not supposing that the Portuguese Troops would stand – attacked our Position at day break on the morning of the 27th in two points.' They were repulsed on both sides, 'with great slaughter'. The Brigade, which included the 2nd Battalion 42nd, was brought up in support 'but were not required'.[76] Whereas French losses of killed and wounded were estimated at 4,400, those of the British and Portuguese numbered 1,250. Since the Battalion had remained in reserve, only two sergeants, one drummer and three soldiers were wounded, compared with a total of 560 British soldiers killed, wounded and missing.[77] *Busaco* as a Battle Honour was granted a century later by Army Order in 1910.[78]

At daylight the following day, they awoke to find that the French had moved off and were making for the road towards Oporto.

Although 'nothing of consequence took place except some little skirmishing in the afternoon,' Blantyre was writing on 13 October, 'we were kept however constantly on the alert & under Arms – Weather still rainy.'[79] The army then fell back on the Lines of Torres Vedras, whose ranges of rocks and mountains protected the approach to Lisbon. With the French unable to penetrate Wellington's stronghold around Lisbon, despite intermittent skirmishing, for the rest of the year, 'both Armies remained perfectly quiet & stationary – without giving each other the smallest annoyance of any sort,' recorded Blantyre. 'Some of our Officers were even invited by a Flag of Truce to go to their Opera in Santarem, promising them a safe escort back to our Lines.'[80]

As the weather became colder, in early January 1811 Dr Dick was writing to his son, Major Dick: 'We are in hourly & anxious expectation of hearing from you ... Your mother & myself have been in misery lest the late severe cold has reached you among the mountains of Portugal, where you must be but very badly sheltered from the inclemency of the weather – God grant that you may be able to stand such severe trials to your constitution – & that you may enjoy many happier New Years than the present could have been.'[81] Two weeks later, Dr Dick was telling his son that a new Regimental jacket and boots were being sent, as well as a shirt, made by his mother, '& we shall put two or three flannel shirts in with them – but how to get them sent is more than I can possibly find out at present'.[82]

When the army moved out of winter quarters, following in the footsteps of the French, they found 'every house & village totally gutted & destroyed. The Inhabitants who came in from the mountains (where they had hid themselves) on our Approach were in a most miserable & pitiable state. In the villages we found many dead bodies who had perished either from want, or been murdered by the French, and indeed the French had not been at the pains of burying their own dead – but left them in houses or on the road just as they died. No country in short could afford a more shocking scene of desolation.'[83]

Wellington's strategy for the 1811 campaign was to attack the French on two fronts, one at Badajoz and the other at Almeida. The 2nd Battalion 42nd formed part of the force, under Wellington's personal command, that besieged Almeida. Dick, whose duties alternated between being in command of the Battalion (when Blantyre took command of the Brigade) or of the Battalion of light infantry companies of the Brigade, received special commendation from an unknown commentator: 'During Masséna's retreat he was constantly in advance with his Corps – on the 15th March [1811] he was warmly engaged for upwards to two hours with the Light Division in driving the French from a ridge of Hills across a River in which a number of the French were drowned. On that day fourteen of his men were killed & wounded – & he was grazed in the hip with a musket ball – but did not report himself wounded.'[84] 'We lay that night,' recorded Blantyre, 'on the Field of Action, very uncomfortable, for it rained, & our Baggage was not allowed to come forward. We had also no Provisions, indeed we had been two days without Bread.'[85]

As they continued their pursuit of the French across the river Alva, the 2nd Battalion 42nd was ordered in front to cover the Headquarters. 'As soon as our Army made its appearance on the heights above the Alva, we saw the French begin their retreat from the opposite side with their accustomed hurry, & confusion.'[86] When the British reached the river 'dreadful confusion' ensued 'in passing the river in the dark; it was eleven at night before our Regt. which was in the rear got over'. That night they lay 'on a base, wet piece of ground', without provisions 'or without the means of cooking, if they had [had provisions], as none of our Baggage came up till next day'.[87] On 11 April Blantyre was recording that the men were now 'three days in arrear of Biscuit, & no Supplies coming up, the Commissaries were obliged to purchase bread from Spain at 1 shilling per pound to issue to the soldiers'. When the market did get 'tolerably' supplied with the 'common necessaries of Life', including bread, salt, cheese, chocolate and bad wine, everything was 'exorbitantly dear'.[88]

Fuentes d'Onor May 1811

At the beginning of May 1811, the opposing forces met at the town of Fuentes d'Onor. 'After daylight,' recorded Blantyre on 3 May, 'after a good deal of marching & countermarching we took up a Position about 11 a.m. on the heights above & in the rear of Fuentes d'Honore . . . we saw the French Army coming towards us, & it halted on the plain on the other side.' The two armies were separated by a small river running through the village. 'About 2 in the afternoon the Enemy formed & moved on to attack Fuentes which was occupied by the Light Companies of our Brigade under Major Dick of the 42nd . . . a very heavy fire ensued & our people were hard pressed by superior numbers.'[89] Once reinforcements arrived, 'the Enemy were driven completely out of the village . . . the business lasted till near 8 at night – & the loss on both sides was considerable.' The following day, Blantyre was recording how 'the French Officers and Soldiers came down & talked to us, & both parties washed their Linen in the river together as if comrades of the same nation – They also brought our dead from their side of the river, & asked to take theirs out of the village which they were allowed to do.'[90]

On the morning of 5 May, fighting resumed when the French 'commenced a sharp attack on our right with their Cavalry & Infantry – & certainly for some time had the advantage, & handled our Cavalry very roughly . . . the attack then extended towards our part of the line & the village of Fuentes – & a most heavy cannonade was kept upon us for two hours – from which our line suffered considerably. About 11 a.m. our skirmishers were pressed in front & the 42nd Regt was ordered forward to support them.' Hardly had they got in position, when the French Cavalry 'dashed forward among our skirmishers, who made off towards our Regt which was in a hollow & not perceived by the Cavalry, nor they by us till we were very near each other'. As soon as the French saw the 42nd they 'made directly towards us. We were formed in Line, & allowed them to get within twenty yards before we fired. The men were perfectly steady & we then poured in our fire upon them so effectually that they immediately wheeled round, & made off in the greatest confusion – nor did they attempt to come near us again the whole day.' In Blantyre's opinion, the 42nd's action saved not only the light companies but also a regiment of Portuguese. 'Not a man of them could otherwise have escaped.'[91]

French losses were estimated at 5,000 men, compared with 1,800 from the British and Portuguese side. 'Our Brigade alone lost 340 men and 14 Officers,' recorded Blantyre, although casualties of the 2nd Battalion 42nd were relatively light, with the loss of six men. One officer, two sergeants and twenty-seven soldiers were wounded.[92] Another Battle Honour, *Fuentes d'Onor*, was later given to commemorate 'the steady valour of the second battalion on this occasion'.[93] Dick's father was delighted with the outcome: 'I believe few troops were ever put to so severe a trial, & for so many hours as you were in that Village, & you all deserve immortal honour for it – you were almost all Highlanders engaged in it – & certainly no troops ever behaved better ... as matters turned out, I am glad you had the command of the light companies then – but I would rather in future you should continue in the command of the 42nd for the other was a service of constant danger.'[94]

After the battle, the French began to withdraw to Ciudad Rodrigo. The French garrison at Almeida had also managed to escape, leaving Blantyre to record that 'there was not a Frenchman now in Portugal except Prisoners'.[95] Almost immediately afterwards Wellington made for Badajoz, where severe fighting took place, although the fortress did not fall. Throughout the summer, with the weather 'dreadfully hot, & the men without shade',[96] the soldiers were constantly on the move. In late September, during an attempt to prevent the French supplying Ciudad Rodrigo, Blantyre was noting, for the first time, the use of what he called 'fireballs among our Troops which scorched many of them terribly & blew up some of their Pouches of Ammunition'.[97] Although the French greatly outnumbered the British and their Portuguese allies, it soon became evident that 'they never had any intention of bringing us to a General Action, & that their only object was to amuse us & keep us off while they got their convoy quietly into C. Rodrigo – after accomplishing which they immediately retired.'[98]

Back in Britain, in August 1811 the 1st Battalion in Scotland received 'the anxiously looked, and longed for, order to move south', recorded Lieutenant Donald Mackenzie, who had joined the Regiment in 1807.[99] Proceeding from Leith in 'sailing smacks', they reached Gravesend, from where they marched to take up quarters in Lewes in Kent, where they remained throughout the winter of 1811/1812.[100]

1812: 1st and 2nd Battalions 42nd

By the beginning of 1812, Wellington had decided to attack Ciudad Rodrigo. 'The weather was very cold, boisterous, & snowy.'[101] The soldiers were engaged in breaking ground and constructing trenches. 'We carried on the works with wonderful quickness so much so that on the evening of the 14th our Batteries opened upon the Place with 30 Pieces of Heavy Artillery,' noted Blantyre. By 19 January, 'two practicable breaches' had been made. Having heard that General Auguste de Marmont, Masséna's successor after the French setback at Busaco, was marching to relieve the fortress, Wellington at once determined to storm it. The 2nd Battalion 42nd was not chosen to be part of the storming party, the honour falling to 'the Division on duty the day the breach became practicable'.[102] Dick's confession to his father that he would have volunteered to lead the storming party elicited a stern reprimand: 'I have no idea that your prospects are so hopeless as to render it necessary to volunteer for desperate service for the chance of getting a Brevet Rank if you should escape. Let those do that who have no possible chance of succeeding otherwise – you are not very old – nor will you be when the regular promotion will bring you in.'[103] Casualties of the 42nd were light. 'Our Regiment lost in all 15 Men,' recorded Blantyre.[104]

After Ciudad Rodrigo, Wellington turned his attention to Badajoz. Once more, the 2nd Battalion 42nd was part of the besieging army. 'We all marched on the morning of the 16th [March] & we crossed the Guadiana [river] by a pontoon bridge about 4 miles below Badajoz,' related Blantyre, who was once more in charge of the Brigade, consisting of the 42nd and 79th. 'The night of the 17th was dreadful both from rain & wind – & we had no cover whatever not even of a Tree.'[105] By 6 April, three breaches had been made in the walls of Badajoz and the fortress was captured by storm. Losses were considerable. 'It's importance must be great indeed if it be worth the tenth part of the lives lost in taking it,' observed Dr Dick, thankful as always that his son's name was not among the list of the dead.[106] Future historians hoped – although could not be sure – that the soldiers of the 42nd were not part of the orgy of looting which took place after the British victory either in Ciudad Rodrigo, where the 'heroic troops' turned into 'a horde of drunken maniacs', or at Badajoz.[107]

In the spring of 1812, the 1st Battalion, stationed in Kent since the previous summer, received 'the welcome order' to proceed to Portugal. 'Our most noble Colonel, the Marquis of Huntly,' related Lieutenant Donald Mackenzie, 'ever anxious for the happiness and well-being of his Regiment, arrived from London and saw the last division on board.'[108] Sailing in three frigates, 'the weather proved stormy and the wind for some days contrary; while in the Bay of Biscay, we experienced the tossings for which it is notorious.' Having landed in Lisbon in late April, they marched along the river Tagus to Nisa. 'We passed through a fine country where the richness of nature was seen to profusion; villages were everywhere scattered over the landscape but these also had been plundered, either by the enemy or our own soldiers, who, during retreats, cannot always be restrained from marauding.'[109]

At Gavião, north-east of Santarém, the 1st Battalion met up with the tired 2nd Battalion, whose officers were returning home to recruit. 'On our arrival,' noted Private Gunn, 'our Second Battalion was Broke up, the Staff went home and the Rest Joined us which brought us up on Strength to above 1,200.'[110] The 1st Battalion's Commanding

Officer was Robert Macara, who had joined the Regiment in 1803, having recently purchased the lieutenant colonelcy from John Farquharson, much to the disappointment of Major Dick's father, who wanted the position for his son.[111] Wellington's commendation of the departing 2nd Battalion was generous: 'On every occasion it conducted itself in a manner worthy of the Distinguished Regiment of which it forms a part.'[112]

Salamanca July 1812

After the capture of Ciudad Rodrigo and Badajoz, the road was open for Wellington to march into the heart of Spain. By the beginning of July the Allied army was close to Salamanca, 'and at length were gratified by a view of this ancient city from the heights above it, the River Tormes flowing below and on which the town is situated,' noted Lieutenant Mackenzie.[113] 'Our Army advanced on Salamanca which we found to be held by the enemy, their main body being about two leagues away, and in order to deceive us they had placed dummy sentinels on the walls, these were made of straw and dressed in French uniforms,' related Private Gunn, who, having fought at Corunna, believed this was a payback for Britain having slipped its troops away at night.[114]

The soldiers, however, were unaware of the precise situation in which Wellington and the army now found themselves. Having formed their respective battle lines, the French, under Marmont's command, created a diversion by crossing the river Douro (Duero) at Tordesillas on Wellington's left, hoping to create the impression that this was where their main attack would come. On the night of 17 July, the French pulled back; having destroyed the bridges, they marched east to threaten Wellington's right. According to Mackenzie, 'there was some fighting with a loss of 700 to 800 each day.' Wellington resisted a full engagement and for a while both armies faced each other separated only by the Guarena river. 'During the whole of the 19th we marched in a parallel line with, and in sight of, the French.

We continued retreating and reached the ford on the [river] Tormes without much hurt.'[115]

The march of both armies, numbering approximately forty thousand men, on occasion separated by only a few hundred yards, constituted the famous 'parallel march' of the Peninsular War. With the French still 'shouldering' the British force, 'we found they had forded the river higher up, which caused us to cross also'.[116] Having gained possession of a hill which covered their withdrawal, at night, Mackenzie described how they were caught in a 'dreadful' storm, with thunder, lightning and hail 'making us most wretched creatures. We were drenched to the skin, the sleet driving in our faces, no fire, nothing to eat and sitting in ploughed land. That night I lay without a cloak or shelter of any kind, and with a starving horse tied to my leg.'[117]

The following day, 22 July, the two armies at last engaged. The 1st Battalion 42nd in the 1st Division was on the far left of Wellington's line of battle and did not see action until nightfall. 'I will not attempt to describe the different movements and brilliant charges, in some of which we participated but only to such a limited extent that this engagement does not appear on our Colours,' recalled Mackenzie.[118] When representation was made to Wellington, he promised that the Regiment would have a chance to distinguish itself at the next battle. Out a total of 3,176 British soldiers and men killed, wounded and missing, only three soldiers from the 42nd were wounded. The French lost considerably more, with an estimated six thousand dead or wounded and seven thousand taken prisoner.[119]

Flushed by the victory at Salamanca, the Allied army pursued the French to Madrid. 'The weather was very trying, the heat during the day being excessive, while at night the dews were heavy and cold.'[120] At the beginning of August the 1st Battalion 42nd was ordered to Cuellar, where the soldiers remained for a few weeks, 'and this rest was most beneficial', noted Mackenzie who had fallen ill with fever and dysentery. Others were suffering from swollen legs 'and other results of the exposed and ill-fed life we had lately been living'.[121] In late August they received orders to march to Madrid, which Wellington had entered on 12 August to great jubilation, being handed the keys of the city. Created Earl and then Marquess, the forty-two year-old Wellington was given command of all Allied armies of Spain. The 42nd did not enter the city, but instead returned along the road to Valladolid, where they 'were received with much joy, especially by the female part of the community'.[122]

Burgos September 1812

Marching northwards, Wellington's plan was to attack the French army while it was still weakened from their losses at Salamanca. His next objective was the town of Burgos, fortified by a castle, which stood as a bulwark, impeding further progress across Spain. 'Our Division consisted of our own Brigade,' related Gunn, 'a Brigade of Germans, and a Brigade of Guards, or "Wellington's Pets" as they were called.'[123] But since the castle of Burgos stood on 'a piece of table land about half a mile long and a quarter of a mile broad, and as there was no high ground near it, it was impossible to bring our guns to bear on it'.[124] In a rare example of misjudgement, Wellington had left most of the heavy guns in Madrid. So short were they of ammunition that any soldier who picked up a French musket ball, which they were throwing 'so plentifully', was rewarded with nine pence.[125]

Before attempting to storm the castle, a detachment of the Battalion, under Dick's command, was ordered to take part in the attempt to storm the large hornwork which fortified the hill of San Miguel (Fort St Michael) near the castle, linked together by a causeway running across a deep gorge. Responsibility for capturing the hill was given to the Portuguese, assisted by the 42nd, who were to carry the scaling ladders. 'The evening was clear,' recalled Mackenzie, 'but our prospects were gloomy, for we were going to attack walls and ditches whose strength could not be ascertained.'[126]

Another detachment was ordered to make a diversionary attack in the gorge beneath the castle. Unfortunately the moon, or what Private Gunn referred to as 'the Queen of Night', was shining brightly, which gave the French the advantage. 'Off we went and soon reached the level ground close up to the walls,' Gunn continued. 'It was our business to draw the attention of our cunning opponents away from the scaling party as much as possible for it is no child's play to be going up a scaling ladder with a nimble French man disputing your right to be there. We pretended to be moving very stealthily, just to draw their attention towards us, and they appeared to use just as much cunning in never letting on that they saw us.'[127]

The French were waiting and every soldier who reached the top of the ladder was bayoneted. As he fell, he knocked down those who were following up behind him. 'The enemy, who had their walls thickly manned, fired, killing and wounding half the party,' related Mackenzie, whose friend, Lieutenant Dugald Gregorson, was killed. 'I had him by the hand as we cheered, and the next moment I was bespattered with his blood.'[128] As was soon apparent, the attack was doomed: 'four of the seven ladders were rendered useless by the first fire, and the others were too short.'[129] Joined by the 79th, after fierce fighting they forced the entrance at the gorge and captured the works, 'but we could never have done so had not the attention of the besieged been partially withdrawn and occupied by the attack on the centre'.[130] In his dispatch after the assault on Fort St Michael, Wellington praised the 42nd, among other regiments, for having 'distinguished them-selves'. The Return of Killed, Wounded and Missing listed from among the 42nd, two lieutenants dead, one sergeant and thirty-two private soldiers; three captains, two lieutenants, one volunteer, ten sergeants, one drummer and 153 private soldiers had been wounded.[131]

For the next month, the British soldiers battled against the French under siege in the castle. 'The making of fascines was the most of the employment we had. These things are made of brush-wood and filled with sand or earth,' recorded Private John, who, like Gunn, had returned to the Peninsula.[132] As time passed, the weather deteri-orated 'and the parties that would be up at the works all night came home in the morning in a dreadful plight. The trenches were in such a state, with mud, you would hardly know the colour of the soldier when he came to the camp in the morning; he was all over clay.'[133]

But they 'never got any nearer the castle than the second line, from which we were repulsed, or which our officers abandoned, from the impracticability of getting nearer the castle, . . . for it was Tom Thumb work, to undertake the siege of such a place as Burgos with small arms, I may say: you might as well have sent the boys of the grammar school to take the Castle of Edinburgh with pop-guns and two-balls.'[134]

On 22 October 1812, Wellington ordered a withdrawal. 'Our artillery could not get near enough to make any adequate impression, on account of the superiority of the enemy's guns, and at last our army had to beat a retreat, as the French were again coming down on us in force,' related Mackenzie.[135] Passing close under the walls of the castle, to avoid being seen by the French, 'the greatest silence being enjoined, and having the Artillery wheels muffled with straw, we had twelve hour's start of our pursuers. But the French, being very strong in cavalry, were bold, and pushed our rear guard much, and there was hourly hard skirmishing.'[136]

Losses during the storming of Fort St Michael and the attempt on Burgos were more severe for the 1st Battalion 42nd than in previous battles in the Peninsula. A total of forty-nine men were killed and 248 wounded (nearly as many as those wounded during the American War).[137] Some casualties occurred when a shell fell in a trench. As described by Private John, although most men fled, 'one stupid body' remained, trying to smother the fuse with handfuls of earth, 'but in an instant he was blown to pieces. I threw myself flat down on the earth where I was, about four yards from the active shell.' One officer and a sergeant were killed by the explosion: 'my musket was wrested out of my hand by another splinter, and broken into a hundred pieces.'[138]

No Battle Honour was granted for Burgos, since no honours were given for battles lost, however hard they had been fought. It was small comfort to know – when the men heard the news – that 1812 was proving Napoleon's nemesis. His ill-fated campaign to Russia had resulted in a retreat which was more disastrous than any experienced by an army previously. While total British losses after Burgos were estimated at just over 2,000, the retreating French army's losses in Russia were at least 300,000. Looking back on what had been Wellington's first major setback, even the young soldiers were critical of the decision to besiege Burgos. 'I think,' recalled Private John, 'this was as foolish a piece of work as ever I saw Wellington encounter to begin the siege of Burgos without shot and without a battering train. All we had were two eighteen pounders, and three howitzers (that had been taken from the French, I believe), a species of guns not adapted for a siege.'[139]

Retiring to Salamanca, 'the roads were miserably bad'. Rations were not served out regularly. 'Some days we were without altogether; and soldiers are not priests, to make up by meditations the gnawing pains of fasting.'[140] Having crossed the river Arlanson in the dark at Torquemada, the men bivouacked 'in the greatest confusion', related Mackenzie. To make matters worse, 'the soldiers had stumbled on the well stocked wine vaults of the town and we found them in the morning in such a disorderly and disorganised condition as cannot be described: it is said that 10,000 to 12,000 men were in a state of helpless inebriety . . . Had the French known and attacked us, we could have made no stand.'[141] The only plentiful food was beef, which 'was marched alive with the army, and whenever we halted, a certain number of bullocks were killed for the brigade, by the butchers of the different regiments'.[142] But as Private John related, the bullocks were generally slaughtered on the ground and the flesh became 'so full of sand and grass, that it was impossible to clean it; and when this was done at night, it was still worse'.[143]

After a rest on the banks of the river Duero, the withdrawal towards Salamanca continued. 'We had no tents during this campaign. When we staid a short time at a place, we erected huts; when we were advancing or retreating, the cold clay ground was our bed, and the dews of heaven refreshed us.'[144] On 15 November they crossed the river Tormes, 'where the two armies were in full view of each other, but Lord Wellington, calculating his opponents too strong for him, continued to fall back on Portugal. At this time the weather was dreadful; rain fell in torrents; the roads were knee deep with mud;

men, women, children and horses were lying about dead or power-less,' recorded Mackenzie. 'I lost three animals and all my baggage; the poor animals stuck in the mud from want of nourishment, and had to be left to their fate.'[145] 'Our privations were on occasions beyond description,' he continued, 'and we often longed for, and would have been glad could we have had, the meal and potatoes we knew were daily distributed to the farm animals at home.'[146]

After a march of over 300 miles across Spain and Portugal, Wellington's army went into winter quarters. The 1st Battalion 42nd was stationed in the small town of Ceia, 'by no means comfortable, yet the spirit of contentment came to our aid and we were glad that our toils were over for a time,' wrote Mackenzie.[147] 'We had no beds; the floor of the house was the bed of the poor soldier: each man had a blanket. We rolled down on the floor, and usually lay by fours, if there were four in a house. We had always straw to lay on, when we could get it, and the cavalry needed it not; here we could get none.'[148] Under stern discipline from Major Robert Henry Dick, several men were flogged for offences ranging from drunkenness to murder. Private John, who had been given his corporal's stripes at Burgos, lost them when a soldier in his section was found wearing trousers instead of a kilt. 'Dick gave me a great deal of abusive language; telling me, among other speeches, he would have me tried by a drum-head court martial, and broke for not being alert on my post, and for having my guard improperly drest . . . I did not much mind being reduced to a private, as I was fit for all duties a soldier could be called to; but I regretted the loss of the extra pay.'[149]

A particularly serious offence took place at Ceia when Corporal McMorran shot the officer in charge of his company, Lieutenant Alexander Dickenson. According to Private John, 'everything that McMorran did was a fault in his officer's eye'. At issue was McMorran's relationship with a young Portuguese girl. When he appeared late for a parade, Dickenson reprimanded him, whereupon, musket in hand, McMorran shot his superior. Condemned to death by hanging, his body was tied to a tree and left to rot 'as an example to all'.[150] According to the Adjutant, Lieutenant John Innes, part of the problem was because the Commanding Officer, Macara, 'hardly commands common respect from the private soldiers'. Having served in the 2nd Battalion, under Blantyre, Innes was surprised at finding the 1st Battalion 'in a worse state of discipline' than he expected. 'They appeared to be under no command, and when they turned out, they looked more like a flock of sheep than a Regiment of Royal Highlanders.' Every officer, he said, does as he pleases and the sergeants and corporals 'are commanded by their men'.[151]

Vittoria June 1813

At the start of 1813, the 42nd had been serving in the Peninsula almost continuously for over four years. 'This year,' noted Private John, 'the army was greatly reinforced, both in infantry and cavalry; and Lord Wellington having got us in a very fine condition for the advance, we were all provided with tents, three for each company.'[152] Having been part of the 1st Division, the 1st Battalion 42nd was transferred to the 6th Division, commanded by Major General Sir Henry Clinton, under whose father the Regiment had served in the American War.[153] Having benefited from a period of rest and reorganisation, when they again took the field in May 1813, 'although not very strong', noted Private Gunn, 'we were ready for the March and recruited our Strength daily'.[154] Marching in two divisions, the route taken was via Burgos towards Vittoria (Vitoria). 'We had immense difficulty in marching this road, for the country was very mountainous, and in some places we were compelled to halt and cut roads for the guns. And we were only eight days on the march when the rations began to grow scarce ... language cannot paint the fatigue and hunger we endured'.[155]

Finding that they were being pressed both north and south of their lines of communication, the French withdrew from Burgos. Having destroyed the castle, they took up position across the river Ebro, running almost parallel to the Pyrenees mountains and the border with France, a hundred miles to the north-east. In place of

Marmont, who had been wounded at Salamanca, General Bertrand Clausel had taken command of the French army, with Napoleon's brother Joseph in supreme command. Once more the Allied armies went in pursuit, crossing the Ebro above French lines and forcing the French to fall back on Vittoria. 'The country the Army marched through on the upper Ebro is the wildest I ever beheld, nothing in the Highlands of Scotland to be compared with it,' Macara wrote. 'It was with great difficulty the Artillery were brought on, on many occasions the cattle were obliged to [be] unyoked, and the guns drag'd by Hand.'[156]

On 21 June 1813 the combined Allied forces occupied the valley of Vittoria, attacking French positions there. When the fighting began, the 1st Battalion 42nd was still on the march. 'We moved in two forced Marches which just brought us within hearing of the Action of the 21st,' Macara wrote.[157] 'We distinctly heard firing going on, and, although we pushed on as rapidly as possible, did not manage to be forward in time to take part in the glorious engagement,' recalled Mackenzie.[158] The victory was decisive. Joseph Bonaparte, recorded as having invited the ladies of Vittoria to watch 'how he would pommel the English', lost not only his throne but also his treasure and all his heavy baggage.[159]

When the soldiers reached the 'dreadful' scene of the battle, they saw 'the road and the fields round about the town were covered with guns of every description, ammunition wagons, and baggage'. They were not too late to share in the spoils of war. 'I got a superfine blue coat, and a pair of trowsers the same, both new, and about four pounds of tobacco, and six or eight pounds of good flour: this I thought as much of as if it had been gold dust, as I had nothing to eat for two days before,' recorded Private John. 'Some of the 42d got lots of money, and some got articles of silver manufacture, and others got boxes of jewels and clothing of every description, plenty of flour, tobacco, and fine French brandy.'[160] 'Ammunition, treasure, everything fell into our hands,' recorded Mackenzie. But the scene was grim. 'As the French dead were not buried, nor the wounded removed, you can believe we saw many painful spectacles. In the heat of the action one does not think of the death and havoc going on around, but, when the contest is over, there is time to look at its horrid results.'[161]

Chased out of Spain, Joseph Bonaparte fled to France before the road was cut off by the victorious British, leaving the remaining French forces to retreat to the town of Pampeluna (Pamplona), capital of Navarre. Following hard on their tracks, Wellington halted to besiege the fortress of San Sebastian, as well as mounting a blockade on Pampeluna, 'the key of one of the entrances into France'.[162] 'We had a good deal of severe marching by night as well as by day some-times,' recalled Mackenzie, 'after which we directed our course towards Pampeluna, which was strongly garrisoned by the enemy and block-aded by our troops, and here we were engaged for some days in throwing up redoubts.'[163] 'I dare say this was the greatest sight I got during the war,' remarked Private Gunn, 'the place was like an amphitheatre, sloping hill[s] all round and a plain in the centre. About 2 o'clock in the afternoon the French was in motion and moved forward on the road by sections in as good order as if they were going to an ordinary field day, but our Division, on their left, hurriedly fell in and moved down on them and engaged [them].'[164]

As usual in war, there were moments of calm when opposing sides forgot they were enemies. 'There was a field of potatoes between us,' Gunn continued. 'Shortly after our men entered the one End and did the French the other, digging with their Baynots . . . shortly after it became dark both parties withdrew to their Respective Sides . . . Daylight appearing, we were on foot again and the same work of potatoes hoeing resumed.'[165] Thinking back on the shared pleasure of potato digging, Gunn asked future readers of his memoir: 'What is war? Is it Natural to man as to Beast or is it what a French soldier said to me it might be that it was Me that wounded you and you that wounded me But it was neither of our Faults but of our Grandies.'[166]

Pyrenees

On 12 July 1813, the soldiers were relieved from trench work and ordered to the mountains of the Pyrenees. After 'a few difficult marches', they reached Sanostian, 'on a rapid stream falling into the Bidassoa, the boundary between France and Spain. The country there was wild and beautiful; the houses appeared large and clean, the women tidy, and the men, who were well-made, wore chapeau or "bonnets" similar to those used in the south of Scotland,' observed Mackenzie.[167] To secure the region, they had to occupy 'a great extent of country, containing a range of bold and precipitous mountains, intersected in every direction, but more particularly from north to south, by deep passes, ravines, and valleys, which, in a confined space, afforded the best means of defence,' noted Stewart of Garth. A distance of some sixty miles separated San Sebastian and the pass of Roncesvalles. 'To command every pass, therefore, was impossible.'[168]

Towards the end of July, having consolidated the army after the defeat at Vittoria, Marshal Soult, in supreme command after Joseph Bonaparte's flight, intended to relieve Pampeluna, before swinging the army to the north-west to relieve San Sebastian. First he ordered an attack on Allied positions on the Pyrenees at the passes of Roncesvalles and Maya to the north, leading to severe British losses. On 26 July the 6th Division – including the 1st Battalion 42nd – was ordered to thwart the attempt to relieve Pampeluna. 'After a few days of extreme fatigue our Division [the 6th] succeeded in getting between the enemy and Pampeluna, not an hour too soon either, as three days before, the Marshal had forced the pass of Maya, cut to pieces the regiment defending it, and was now driving our 3rd and 4th Divisions before him.' This countermove by the British foiled Soult's attempts to relieve Pampeluna and San Sebastian, and he withdrew northwards. 'We continued following up the French until they entered their own country, having daily skirmishes with them.' As the men marched onwards through the Pyrenees, enveloped in a fog, they could not see more than a few yards in front, nor 'ascertain where we really were'.[169]

By early August they were at the Maya Pass, the scene of the previous battle on 25 July, and where, as Mackenzie witnessed, 'the dead were still unburied'.[170] 'The position is naturally so strong,' noted John Home, the Paymaster, 'and we have added so much to it by our working parties, which are employed every day from sun rise, till sunset, constructing field works, that I think, if they should make another attempt at this point, they will have a warm birth of it.'[171] However, until what Home called 'that infernal place San Sebastian' fell, the British army could not proceed, because it was only by that route that the artillery could advance. Much to the soldiers' disappointment, as Home informed Dick, back in Scotland with the 2nd Battalion, 'the Royal Highlanders have had very little share in the glories of the late campaign'. As a result their losses were 'very trifling; from this circumstance, and our having been uncommonly healthy of late, I trust we will soon be respectable again as to numbers'.[172] Fresh troops were also arriving at Passages, on the northern coast of Spain, 'all in high health and spirits', remarked a new arrival, Lieutenant John Malcolm, 'to which the crowds of sick and wounded men hourly arriving from the army, pale and emaciated, and on their return home, exhibited an appalling contrast'.[173] Another new arrival was Sergeant James Anton, who thought 'it better to hazard life and limb in the army abroad . . . than remain at home with no other prospect before me, but poverty and hard labour'. Recently married, he had brought his wife with him.[174]

The arrival of reinforcements coincided with the raising of the siege of San Sebastian on 31 August in an assault lasting five hours. 'Our troops were drawn up along the ramparts,' recorded Malcolm, 'and in a short time we perceived the French garrison, headed by their commander General Rey, slowly advancing from the castle, and wending down the side of the rock in long serpentine lines, by its only narrow pathway. Upon arriving in the town, immediately below the place where we were stationed the garrison threw down their arms with an air of indignation; and at that moment a feu-de-joye was fired from the battery at the termination of the trenches.'[175] General Rey and Wellington's second-in-command, Lieutenant General Sir Thomas Graham, then shook hands. When the Allied troops entered San Sebastian, Malcolm was shocked: 'It exhibited a scene sufficient to blanch the hair and to wither the heart. Many of the streets were blown up into hills of rubbish: not a house was left entire: not a living thing was to be seen – not a sound did I hear but the echo of my own footfalls through the lonely streets. Or the wind as it moaned away through that city of the dead which stood in all the blackness of recent ruin.'[176]

Having secured San Sebastian, the besieging forces were ordered to join the main body of the army, encamped in the Pyrenees. 'We commenced our march on a sultry day in September,' Malcolm recalled. 'The heat being so excessive that numbers of the men dropt down along the line of march.'[177] For the next few weeks, the Allied army of British, Spanish and Portuguese surveyed the French lines, separated by the Bidassoa river. As Malcolm related, each evening they paraded, 'their arms glancing in the setting sun, and the martial or mournful strains of their native lands, performed by their bands of music, rising amid the calm and mellowed by the distance, came floating up the mountain glens like strains of Fairyland.'[178] After nearly seven years in the Peninsula, the Allied army, with the 42nd in its midst, was poised to attack the French on what Marshal Soult called the 'sacred territory' of France.[179] To commemorate the 'gallantry displayed' by the 1st Battalion, another Battle Honour was later granted: *Pyrenees*.[180]

Baltic Detour 1813–1814: Gorde, 2nd Battalion 73rd

In May 1813, while the soldiers of the 42nd were chasing Joseph Bonaparte out of Spain, the 2nd Battalion 73rd was on its way to Pomerania, a dominion of the Swedish Empire on the coast of northern Europe in modern Germany and Poland. Having remained in England since the Battalion was first raised in 1809, the soldiers had served in Derby, Ashford and Deal, before being posted to the Tower of London in 1812 and then to Colchester. Much as Britain's concerns had been mainly in the Peninsula, Napoleon's exploits elsewhere determined where British soldiers served. As explained by Thomas Morris, who together with his elder brother William had enlisted in the 73rd: 'To account for our being sent so far north at this particular time, it may be necessary to state, that Buonaparte having so signally failed in his gigantic invasion of Russia the year before . . . had ordered the remains of his armies to concentrate at Dresden, where he rejoined them with large reinforcements of French, as well as auxiliary troops.' Opposed to Napoleon was a powerful coalition of grand Allied armies, consisting of Russians, Prussians and Austrians, 'commanded in person by their respective monarchs', later joined by Bavarians and a contingent of Swedes.[181]

The 2nd Battalion 73rd, with five other regiments, was to become part of this multinational infantry force, ranged against an estimated 200,000 Frenchmen, assembled between Dresden and Leipzig. Under Lieutenant Colonel William Harris's command, the 2nd Battalion embarked at Harwich.[182] By late August 1813 they had reached Ruegen, where they disembarked and the troops marched to Stralsund. Morris was part of the fatigue party detailed to remove the baggage from the ships, which took a day, 'and we had to remain there during the night, and the next morning to remove the luggage to smaller vessels to convey it up the river to Stralsund, which would have been considered a very delightful trip if the wind had been fair'.[183] Once at Stralsund, their first task was to repair the fortifications and batteries. Their duties, noted Morris, were 'excessively severe, continually on guard, picket, or at work at the fortifications, and every morning under arms an hour before daybreak, until (in military phraseology) we could see "a grey horse a mile"'. Billeted on the local inhabitants, the men had their own rations and were forbidden to take anything from their hosts without payment.[184]

Proceeding through Germany in forced marches 'of about thirty miles a day, and as we had not commissary with us, we were obliged to trust entirely to chance for our daily supplies'. As Morris related, the people had not seen English troops before 'and strove with each other, as to which should have the honour of entertaining us'.[185] While Napoleon was at Dresden, those loyal to him were occupying positions between Dresden and Leipzig, 'ready to act singly, or to co-operate with their master as circumstances might require'. As the 2nd Battalion advanced, Morris realised they might easily fall in with the French, 'as we had no exact information of their position'.[186] Bivouacking in the woods, they lived off such potatoes and fruit as they could find.

In early September 1813, the 2nd Battalion 73rd was detached 'in obedience to the orders of His Royal Highness the Crown Prince [of Sweden]' to join Lieutenant General Ludwig von Wallmoden-Gimborn and his army of 20,000 men, who were about to attack the French at Gorde (Göhrde), a village near a small castle 'which had heretofore been the favourite retreat of George II'.[187] 'On our left was the French army drawn up, with their right near the road through which we had just passed.' On their right centre was a little hill, occupied by French infantry, about a thousand strong, and two pieces of cannon. On 16 September, having been instructed to take the hill, Harris addressed the troops, reminding them of their position amongst a vast contingent of foreign soldiers: 'Now, my lads, you see what we have to do; we are the only English regiment in the field; don't let us disgrace ourselves and our country,' whereupon the men gave 'a hearty cheer'.[188]

The Battle of Gorde was France's first sighting of the 2nd Battalion 73rd's Colours. 'Our colours, which were quite new, and had been covered up with oil-skin cases, were now unfurled, and the exhibition literally frightened the enemy from their position; so that as we came to the charge with increased speed, we saw the enemy making the best use of their legs in getting away.'[189] Elsewhere on the field of battle, the French either had to withdraw or were defeated. Compared with the bigger battles to come, losses were less than 1,000 on each side. 'Our regiment had none killed and but few wounded,' observed Morris. 'But the prominent part we had played made us afterwards not a little proud of our maiden battle, and fully recompensed us for the hardships we had suffered.'[190]

Having collected some of the prisoners under their charge, and after tending to the wounded, the soldiers encamped for the night. 'And miserable indeed was our position; the rain continued all night, increasing the suffering of the wounded, and rendering our own situation anything but pleasant.'[191] Making their way back through Germany, Morris related how the soldiers were cheered by their Piper, Hugh McKay, who 'would fall back to the extreme rear, and then striking up one of his lively tunes, and at the same time pushing forward at a brisk rate, he would soon have the whole regiment about him like a cluster of bees'.[192]

Meanwhile, the Allied armies were preparing for what they hoped would be their final encounter against Napoleon at Leipzig, resulting in a 'glorious victory' over the French in the largest battle of the Napoleonic wars.[193] Napoleon withdrew to Paris. By this time, the 2nd Battalion 73rd was assembling at Rostock, where 'great rejoicings took place for the recent victories, and to celebrate the release of Germany from the ambition and thraldom of the French emperor'.[194]

At the end of October 1813, the soldiers marched to the Gulf of Lübeck to board transports for England. Delayed due to storms, they sheltered in the harbour of Gottenburg, where they remained 'frozen in for three weeks'. With the men suffering from dysentery, the smell below decks was so bad that the fitter men preferred to stay on deck throughout the night. Having arrived at Yarmouth, only the women and children were permitted to disembark. With orders to sail to the Netherlands, under French control, 'with a due proportion of medical officers and stores',[195] Morris described the distress 'to our married people to be thus suddenly separated; the women and children to be cast adrift in a strange place, perhaps hundreds of miles from their homes and no resources'.[196]

On arrival off the Dutch coast, many were so ill that they had difficulty in getting ashore. Compared with the other regiments, the 2nd Battalion 'cut rather a miserable appearance', related Morris.

Their uniforms 'were in such a shattered condition that many of the red coats had (new) sleeves made out of the (old) gray trousers, there being no possibility of getting red cloth for the purpose'.[197] To compound the 'unpleasantness' of the march, the French had opened the sluices, 'inundating the country to a very considerable extent', obliging the soldiers to wade through layers of ice, 'of which the top surface not always being sufficiently strong to bear, we would go down to the next, wading through the water sometimes two or three feet deep'. Once on dry land, their trousers froze, which made them 'anything but warm and comfortable appendages'.[198] Their destination was Antwerp, to cut lines of communication between Antwerp and Bergen-op-Zoom.

While the 2nd Battalion 73rd spent the winter of 1813/1814 in villages 'tolerably secure' from a surprise attack, the 1st Battalion 42nd remained embedded in the frozen foothills of the Pyrenees.[199]

13.

The Road to Toulouse

It is an unfortunate thing for the relatives of those who fell at Toulouse that this news [of Napoleon's abdication] did not reach us some days sooner, and the battle might have been in that case saved.

Ensign George Gerard[1]

The South of France

After over five years in the Peninsula, Wellington's ponderous Allied army was poised to enter France. In early October 1813 the order was given to move from the Pyrenees. John Malcolm had yet to experience the 'fiery ordeal' of battle, and the night before they left was 'the most momentous evening of our lives . . . A host of long slumbering recollections came crowding over me. I thought of my home, and of the friends I might never see again, – of the scenes of death in which a few hours would see me engaged – and that I might be among the number of those who were taking their last hour of earthly rest.'[2] In the early hours of the morning, the soldiers descended from the hills in silence, marching alongside 'ravines skirted with woods' towards the Bidassoa river. 'Along the Spanish side of the Bidassoa was erected a line of defence, consisting of a broad and pretty high wall of turf, having a ditch behind it. Upon this wall the Spanish sentries continually walked to and fro, as did the French ones on the opposite side of the river.'[3]

As daylight came, after a tremendous storm, 'a thick cloud hovered beneath us,' recollected Sergeant Anton, 'and hid the country from our view.'[4] Knowing that the French army lay below, shrouded in the morning mist, every man was 'full of anxiety to view the contest below'.[5] Once the French realised their adversaries were crossing the river, they rallied, appearing 'in great force upon a range of hills'. As the soldiers marched onwards, the French poured a deadly round of shot and shells, which 'did considerable execution'. The French soldiers did not wait for the charge, 'but fled with the utmost celerity, leaving us in possession of the range of heights, and several pieces of cannon'.[6]

After this first encounter, having occupied a 'strong position' in front of St Jean de Luz, the British and their Iberian allies pitched their tents. Separated from the French by about a mile, 'in this situation both armies remained quiet for about a month,' noted

Malcolm. 'During this period of inaction, we formed frequent little convivial parties in our tents, though we had then little else than our rations to subsist on . . . a certain modicum of rice, rum, hard biscuit and beef of the most wretched quality.'[7] 'Cold and despair occasioned much desertion,' observed Lieutenant Donald Mackenzie, 'and it was supposed about 2,000 to 3,000 left us. I know the 42nd lost 40 men.'[8] With the French offering promises of protection and passports to their country of choice, Wellington found it necessary to disabuse the soldiers of 'these delusions . . . informing the men that instead of ease and leisure they would be sent to labour at the various works and fortifications in the interior'. His pronouncements seemed to have 'the desired effect', since, according to Malcolm, desertions eventually ceased.[9] Instead of sharing a communal tent, Sergeant Anton had made a habit of building his own hut to give himself and his wife some privacy. 'I now became a complete Robinson Crusoe in my daily labour, when regimental duties permitted.' When his hut was finished, he and his wife enjoyed it for two weeks before receiving orders for camp to be struck. Whereas others who had built similar huts burnt them, Anton left his 'with too much regret to become its incendiary'.[10]

Nivelle November 1813

The next barrier into France was the line of fortifications on the hills beyond the river Nivelle, on which Soult had built a series of redoubts, stretching for twenty miles from the mountains behind Ainhoa at the Roncesvalles Pass to the sea. 'But,' as recorded in the 42nd's *Historical Record*, 'the soldiers who had chased the famed legions of Napoleon from the gates of Lisbon to the boundary of the Spanish dominions, were ready to assault these stupendous works of art, and carry their conquering arms into the interior of France.'[11] Heavy snowfall and rain delayed the assault until early on the morning of 10 November. 'Not a musket was yet fired . . . no voice was heard, save that of command,' recalled Anton. After crossing the river and passing through a wood, they reached the bottom of a steep hill which marked the heights of Ainhoa, 'the face of which presents long ridges of formidable breastworks behind which the enemy keeps up a heavy fire of musketry'.[12]

Having distributed troops along the whole of the French line, Wellington's plan was to make diversionary attacks to the right and left to draw off Soult's reserves, while the main attack would aim at the centre in order to dislodge the French from their fortified position. 'We were enfiladed by a fire from some other batteries and entrenchments, and lost some men,' related Lieutenant Malcolm. 'By a variety of masterly movements and desperate attacks, the villages and entrenched positions occupied by the enemy's centre were successively carried'.[13] The Regiment, said Mackenzie, 'took a very active part. I fortunately escaped without more damage than being knocked down, and well sprinkled with the earth thrown up by grape-shot ploughing the ground as we advanced'.[14] 'With no little pride,' recalled Private Gunn, 'we encamped on French soil, with strict orders not to injure any of the inhabitants, a wise and just order, for if we in our turn should be compelled to retire they could doubly revenge themselves if so inclined.'[15] 'Night closed the battle,' recorded Malcolm, 'and two lines of watch-fires indicated the positions of both armies, and showed that the British troops occupied the last range of the mountains, and that the French were driven into the plains below.'[16]

'This was the first engagement I was in,' recollected Anton, 'and I considered myself no longer a recruit. I had now smelled the enemy's powder, as the old soldiers boastingly exclaimed; I had heard his bullets whistling past my ears, seen them dropping harmless at my feet, and burrowing in the ground.' As he realised, during the battle there were 'many shifts in the game of war' when victory could have been turned into defeat, depending on the orders given and the risks taken. 'It is, therefore, not much to be wondered at, that a soldier thinks less about the points of attack than he does of the vigour with which they should be attacked, and of the leader's abilities to push forward, so as to hold fortune fast when within his grasp.'[17]

During the fighting, one private from the 1st Battalion 42nd was killed, while two officers, two sergeants and twenty-three soldiers were wounded.[18] As at Vittoria, victory was accompanied by a night of plunder, or, as the soldiers called it 'reconnoitering' for extra provisions.

Wellington had already issued orders against 'any irregularities in the neighbourhood of our camps or cantonments or of offering any violence to the inhabitants'. Commanding officers were therefore again called upon 'to enforce a strict compliance with these orders', related Anton. To check on their whereabouts, there were hourly roll calls, by day and night. 'This was a very harassing system, but it tended not a little to prevent plundering.'[19] After bivouacking in a field for the night, 'morning dawned at last,' recalled Malcolm, 'but we remained stationary for some time afterwards in consequence of a thick fog, which rendered it impossible to reconnoiter the enemy's position in front.' When the mist cleared, they advanced up a hill 'which the enemy had rendered so formidable by redoubts and batteries; but not a gun was fired'. As they soon realised, the sentries were made of straw, 'left as a decoy, presenting to us the most undaunted and soldier-like attitudes'.[20] Below them was St Jean de Luz.

'With torn shoes and lacerated feet, we advanced,' related Anton, 'under a heavy fall of hail and snow, the first of winter's stormy blasts which threatened to obstruct our progress.' Having frequently to stop because of 'the obstacles thrown in the way of our advance by the enemy, who were making good their retreat to the Nive,' their progress was slow.[21] 'The weather was very bad, snow falling heavily which soon covered the mountains, the cold was intense,' recollected Private Gunn. 'We had to post double sentries, one to watch the front whilst his comrade walked about to keep warm.'[22]

Passing through St Jean de Luz, with the approach of winter, quarters had to be found. The 6th Division went into cantonments near Ustritz. 'After remaining a few days longer in camp, under torrents of rain, we received orders to strike our tents, and to occupy certain detached houses and villages,' recollected Malcolm.[23] Much as the men wanted rest, they were kept 'constantly employed by day, always ready by night, and at our alarm posts every morning before daybreak'.[24] With meagre rations, salt was 'a most desirable article'.[25] During a period of inactivity, Malcolm recollected time passing 'pleasantly enough in shooting excursions – convivial parties, and visits to St Jean de Luz, where Wellington had established his head-quarters, and which was a scene of the greatest gaiety. There might be seen the officers of the guards, and all the aristocracy of the British army, dashing about through the streets, bedizened with gold and silver.' On one occasion, they saw Wellington 'lounging about and looking at the markets, calm and unconcerned, as if he were merely a passing traveler, having nothing to do but amuse himself'.[26]

Nive December 1813

With the British occupying St Jean de Luz, the French had with-drawn first to the village of Bidart and then encamped near the town of Bayonne on the Bay of Biscay, their front 'defended by an impass-able morass'.[27] Since the French were in too strong a position for a direct attack, Wellington resolved on a movement to the right to threaten their rear. First they had to cross the river Nive. To confuse the French, and give the impression that the British were still in their quarters, the drummers beat the reveille. Instead, they were already forming in line, hidden by the morning mist. Crossing the river by a pontoon bridge at Ustritz, most of the following day's action was carried out by the light infantry companies skirmishing with the French.

During the fighting, Captain George Stewart and Lieutenant James Stewart, 'connected by kindred ties'[28] were killed. When George Stewart fell, 'a favourite little spaniel, which had been his companion from Scotland', recollected Ensign Thomas McNiven, recently arrived with a detachment at Santander, 'was beside him, and when consigned to his lonely grave, in his full uniform, his attached dog continued for three days and nights, scraping at the ground until forced away and consigned to the care of his cousin Roger Stewart'.[29] 'It always happened somehow that it was young officers who met their death,' observed Mackenzie, whose company had been sent in advance with the light infantry companies. 'Whether they were braver or more reckless than their seniors I don't know.'[30] Bad weather meant that the soldiers returned to their quarters in Ustritz, only to find that the occupants had returned 'and considered us rather unwelcome guests', recorded Anton, who described how they had 'to rest satisfied with less accommodation than we had had'.[31]

The respite was short-lived. On 10 December, Soult attacked on Wellington's left flank, forcing back the Allied outposts. 'We had now had three days hard fighting without intermission,' recollected Malcolm, 'and were quite exhausted with fatigue and want of sleep, when darkness once more brought a temporary respite to the work of death.'[32] Having made another unsuccessful attack on the Allied left, on 13 December, Soult changed his strategy by attempting to break through the centre and right. When the 6th Division reached the heights overlooking Bayonne, their orders were to support the left flank of the 2nd Division, which was bearing the brunt of the French onslaught. But, Anton complained, when the Brigade Commander, General Pack, ordered the 1st Battalion 42nd to advance to the main road to intercept a retiring French brigade, Macara 'led us into such a brake of furze, thorns, and brambles, that it would have been impossible to have taken our bare thighed regiment through its impenetrable meshes'. By the time they had found an alternative route, the French were locked in combat with the 92nd. With numerous dead, the victory of the British was 'dearly bought'. The 42nd lost two officers; eleven soldiers were wounded.[33]

As the weather deteriorated 'with unusual inclemency',[34] the army went into winter quarters between Villafranque and the heights overlooking Bayonne, which Soult had fortified. Lieutenant Mackenzie was occupying a 'mansion' with ten other officers and two hundred men: it was, he said, 'stripped of everything, not even a partition was left, all having been consumed as firewood by the enemy'.[35] 'Our mode of cooking was very simple,' recalled Anton, 'not a single blade of vegetable was to be had to put into it, our supply of rice was curtailed, and the only thickening for it was the crumbs and dust of the ship-biscuit. The lid of the camp-kettle served for a carving dish.' The nights 'passed off pleasantly in singing songs, and telling tales, until sleep overpowered all and our dreams were of better times on our native shores. Every man lay down fully accoutred, as when on the campaign, and turned out before the beating of the reveille in the morning.'[36] At Villafranque, a market was established and although, noted Anton, articles were 'extravagantly dear, yet they were to be got, which was considered no small advantage to those who had the money'.[37]

Orthez February 1814

Once the winter rains of early 1814 had ceased, Wellington went on the offensive. Having left two divisions to blockade Bayonne, on 14 February the Allied army started to mobilise. A week later the cantonments were broken up. 'My poor wife was busily employed washing when the order arrived, and was thus under the necessity of bundling up the wet linen along with her other articles, and following in the best manner she could, under a heavy burden,' recollected Anton, who later retraced his steps to help her.[38] 'At this time,' recalled Ensign Thomas McNiven, who was carrying the Colours, 'everything directed that a great battle was impending.'[39]

Wellington's objective was to dislodge the French army from its position on the heights above the Gave de Pau river at Orthez (Orthes), east of Bayonne. 'From morning's dawn of the twenty-sixth [February], endless lines of French artillery were seen, some entering the town, and others going towards the heights,' recorded McNiven. Towards midnight the march began, 'the night proving clear, with the milky way in the celestial dark blue sky finely marked, and French fires blazing away'.[40] Feeling sleepy, and carrying the Colours, McNiven thought he might fall down 'perhaps [into] some neighbouring ditch, for it was impossible to see anything beyond a few yards, and our only security seemed to be, to keep well linked together'.[41] After 'slipping quietly and cautiously along' for about ten miles, they found themselves 'in the grey of the morning, under a clear sky, the beams of day, gradually ascending from the east', near the river, where a pontoon bridge had been constructed. Looking back, McNiven could see 'column after column, emerging from the west, north and south, toward the bridge, with dense masses of cavalry, crowning the distance eminences. The sight was grand in the extreme. It was a moment of striking magnificence.'[42]

By the morning of 27 February, the Allied army was on the outskirts of Orthez. 'On ascertaining our advance,' recorded Lieutenant Mackenzie, 'Soult quitted Orthez and took up strong ground above the town.'[43] Unable to turn the French right flank, Wellington planned a frontal attack, with Lieutenant General Sir Thomas Picton leading the 3rd and 6th Divisions against the French centre. 'The light companies, which had preceded the brigade, were keeping up a sharp fire upon the enemy's skirmishers,' recorded Anton, 'and our grenadier company was ordered to take post along the bank overlooking the ravine, and commanding a narrow road below.'[44]

'Both cavalry and infantry came out to oppose us,' recalled Gunn. When a French cavalry regiment charged the Portuguese detachment in Pack's Brigade, it had remained in line 'manfully', and repulsed the attack. 'We were in support, and our picquets soon let us know that the enemy intended to try their strength with us.' As Gunn continued: 'They got a reception such as I have never seen before, men and horses tumbling over one another dead and wounded. We next advanced just as their infantry was getting ready to attack us, but just as we were forming into line to receive them for some unknown reason they went to the right about without firing a shot, we of course giving them a parting salute; we then got into open column, and it was here that I being the second from the right in the rear rank received a bullet which struck me in the leg, just below the kneecap.' Retiring to the rear to seek medical assistance, Gunn 'passed through the poor fellows that had received our volleys and were now lying dead or wounded, many of them crying out for water which, crippled as I was I could not get them, even had I known where to get it, which I did not'.[45]

Mackenzie had 'two personal encounters', when a French officer 'singled me out and he and I had a very determined hand-to-hand combat. He was a nice looking youth of 21 or 22, and while not much older than myself, I had the advantage in weight and agility, so after a time succeeded in disarming him and sent him a prisoner to the rear.'[46] Mackenzie's next opponent was more formidable. 'He was a very superior swordsman, and evidently determined on mischief.' Mackenzie saved his own life by enacting a 'feint' which he had learnt in Scotland: 'I put my left leg forward to tempt my adversary with its exposed position. This it did and on his making a cut at it, I suddenly drew it back and brought the full weight of my claymore on his head – with what result I leave you to imagine; had I not done so his fate would have been mine.'[47]

During the battle, the 1st Battalion 42nd was ordered to drive the French from a nearby village. The bearer of this order was Pack's acting brigade major, Lieutenant John Innes, commissioned into the Regiment in 1804. 'He might have retired after delivering the orders, without throwing a blot on his good name, but his heart was with the regiment, and he advanced to the charge in person.' Although British arms prevailed, as Anton recorded, 'it was amidst the animating shouts which arose around him, that the last hostile and fatal bullet pierced his brain, and laid him in the dust'.[48] In addition to Mackenzie and Gunn, there were ninety-four wounded. Five soldiers died.[49] Even Wellington had been badly bruised and unhorsed when a canister shot hit his sword hilt.

The night after the battle, the army bivouacked in columns on the fields. 'Night, after a battle, is always glorious to the undisputed victors,' recollected Sergeant Anton, 'They draw close to one another to hear and tell of the hazards of the day, while some show the petty prizes snatched off the field.'[50] The next day, they continued along the road leading to St Sever. 'Our cavalry [was] in front, pursuing and harassing the enemy's rear, and making a number of his stragglers prisoners,' recorded Anton. 'Many of these were deeply gashed by sabre-wounds, and being unable to get on so fast as the escorts urged, they fell down by the road-side, faint from loss of blood, or panting with thirst, frequently soliciting a little water to cool their parched tongues.'[51]

On 1 March, the army passed St Sever. By this stage, 'the clothing of the army at large, but of the Highland brigade in particular, was in a very tattered state,' recorded Anton. 'The 42d, which was the only corps in the brigade that wore the kilt, was beginning to lose it by degrees, men falling sick and left in the rear, frequently got the kilt made into trowsers, and, on joining the regiment again, no plaid could be furnished to supply the loss; thus, a great want of uniformity prevailed.' Their greatest discomfort was lack of shoes. 'As our march continued daily, no time was to be found to repair them, until completely worn out; this left a number to march with bare feet, or, as we termed it, *to pad the hoof.*' To prevent the men falling out and marching irregularly, those without shoes were formed into a separate group and permitted to march in the rear of the brigade, on softer ground. A partial remedy was found by giving the hides of slaughtered bullocks to the men to make into shoes.[52]

Marching by day and camping by night, 'unfavourable' weather meant that in early March they were ordered into cantonments. The Highland Brigade was quartered near the town of Ayre (Aire), where they remained for nearly two weeks until ordered to cross the Adour at Ayre, encamping two miles to the west. On 17 March the 1st Battalion was joined by a draft of men from the 2nd Battalion as well as a number of men from hospitals in the rear. The following day, they advanced through Pau. Meanwhile, in a separate action, Bordeaux had been taken. Inching their way across the French country-side, 'many were the annoyances and miseries which we suffered,' recorded Malcolm. 'Scarce a day passed without some skirmishing betwixt our advanced and the enemy's rear guard.'[53] And, as Stewart of Garth pointed out, as Soult was pushed back closer to the centre of France, he was nearer his supplies, 'while the allies, on the other hand, had receded to a proportional distance from theirs'.[54]

'Our movements,' recorded Anton, 'were now directed towards Toulouse.'[55] First, the Allied army had to cross the Garonne river, swollen by the recent rains and melting snow. 'In the course of two hours, the bridge was thrown over upwards of twenty boats broad,' described Private John. 'The rifle brigade, and part of the cavalry, with a few guns of flying artillery, crossed first; then the 6th Division.'[56] Temporarily, those who had crossed first, including the 42nd, became separated from the main army when the bridge collapsed and had to be rebuilt. Soult, however, did not attack, fearing the risks of losing his own men.[57] Meanwhile, after a month on the march, Ensign George Gerard, who had missed the passage to Spain, met up with the 1st Battalion; having travelled 'often thro' the most horrible roads and in the worst weather, frequently deprived of every comfort and almost starving'. But, as he remarked in his journal: 'All however is now forgot, and so long as I continue with the regiment I fear nothing.'[58]

Toulouse April 1814

In the early hours of Easter Sunday morning, 10 April 1814, tents were struck and the army moved closer to Toulouse, 'from whence we had a distinct view of the enemy's position on the ridge of hills,' observed Malcolm.[59] A chain of five redoubts, mounted with artillery, had been erected on a range of hills. 'Their position is naturally very strong being on the top of a hill,' Gerard noted, 'and I am afraid it will cost us many men to take it; God only knows to whose lot it may fall.' But, he said, 'Primaeval Hope' whispered 'to every one that he shall be one of those who are fortunate enough to escape'.[60] As the soldiers marched forward in silence, 'all nature seemed to enjoy repose, save our moving columns on every side, and the bullfrogs, that gave their loud unharmonious croaking to the midnight breeze'.[61] Briefly they caught sight of Wellington, 'accompanied by his staff, riding back from the front at a hard trot. Some of the men called out, "There goes Wellington, my lads; we shall have some hot work presently."[62]

When the sun rose over the hills, it glistened on thousands of French bayonets on the heights where Soult had assembled his force. As Private John described, Pack had ordered Macara 'to form the regiment by wings, or half battalions, in a ploughed field on the side of this road. We were to march by wings on the works. Whenever we were formed, our orders were to charge the breast-works and the redoubt in front of us.'[63] 'The drums then beat to arms,' recorded Malcolm, 'and we received orders to move towards the enemy's position.'[64] According to Private Gunn, lest their Spanish allies 'attempted to play us false' by withdrawing, Wellington had broken up the pontoon bridge over the Garonne, and placed the Spanish troops in the front line of his attacking army.[65]

Describing the battle as 'a bloody day for the Royal Highlanders', Gerard recorded how they ran on under a heavy cannonade 'over very difficult ground in a line parallel with the enemy's position until we came opposite the right of it when we formed line and prepared to charge. As soon as they saw us in line and advancing they sent out a column of infantry by a road immediately in our front to charge the skirmishers who very coolly retreated on their point of formation in front of our left.'[66]

'The enemy came down upon us like a torrent,' recorded Malcolm; 'their generals and field-officers riding in front, and waving their hats amidst shouts of the multitude, resembling the roar of an ocean.' The Highlanders' instinctive reaction was to take off their bonnets and wave them in the air, returning the French soldiers' greeting with 'three cheers', whereupon a 'deathlike silence ensued for some moments, and we could observe a visible pause in the advance of the enemy.'[67] 'When they were formed, the French column, which till then had come down very resolutely, began to hesitate,' recorded Gerard.[68] Malcolm continued: 'At that moment, the light company of the 42d regiment, by a well directed fire, brought down some of the French officers of distinction, as they rode in front of their respective corps. The enemy immediately fired a volley into our lines, and advanced upon us, amidst a deafening roar of musketry and artillery.'[69]

The battle was intense. 'It was shocking to see the carnage that was made on this spot. Macara could hardly get the right wing formed; it was mostly all cut off before the men got to the works, although the distance was only 200 yards,' recorded Private John. 'I belonged to the right wing; it was, for all the world, like a target to the enemy; for we received their first fire; and it raged most dreadfully. The smoke and fire obscured the sky: the cannon and musketry roared like thunder; and many a hero fell to rise no more.'[70] 'We now ascended at double quick time,' described Anton, 'and the whole of the division crowned the eastern summit of the heights. Here we were exposed to a destructive fire of round shot, shell, grape, and musketry, while we had not as yet got up one gun, owing to the numerous obstructions that lay in our way. The ground we occupied sloped towards one of the main roads that runs over the hill to the city, and the fields on the opposite side of the road were in possession of the enemy, and extremely broken and intersected by deep cross-roads, breastworks, and redoubts.'[71]

By the time they were nearly at the top of the hill, they had overtaken the Portuguese troops. Having reached a road which ran over the hill to Toulouse, they halted and Gerard enjoyed some brandy with a friend in the 79th. 'After resting here for some time, during which they gave us all the annoyance in their power by throwing shells and by a gun which they brought to rake the road and which did some execution, the 42nd received orders to storm the redoubt by wings.' The order, he said, 'was immediately executed by our scrambling up the bank on the side of the road, forming such a line as the nature of the fire we were under would admit of, and rushing forward to the charge of their works. The instant they saw us mount the bank they redoubled their fire of grape and round, and of musketry from a large convent which they had loop holed to the very top, and from the redoubts which were full of men.'[72]

Private John felt that he had no hope of leaving the field alive.

'The shot was whizzing past us like hail; most of the right wing that were killed and wounded received two, three, and some several shots at once. The man on my right hand received six grape shots in his body, and fell like a log; and his brother, on his other side, was wounded at the same time.' When they were about fifty yards from the redoubt, he received a shot through his right arm, and had to stop. 'I was almost sure of receiving another before I could get under cover. I went to the rear a few yards.' Weak from loss of blood, Private John was given a drink of wine by a passing artillery man. Sufficiently revived, he was able to make his way to the surgeons' depot, but 'it was full two hours before the surgeons could look at my arm; they were amputating legs and arms so fast, and so many, it was very lamentable to be two hours the spectator of this sight'.[73]

The redoubt in their possession was an old country farm cottage. But, as Anton remarked, 'it cannot be for an instant supposed, that all this could have been effected without very much deranging our ranks, and as the enemy had still a powerful force, and other works commanding this, time would not permit of particularity, and a brisk independent fire was kept up, with more noise than good effect, by our small groups upon our not yet defeated enemy. Our muskets were getting useless by the frequent discharges, and several of the men were having recourse to the French pieces that lay scattered about.'[74]

Numbers were decreasing. Both Lieutenants Mackenzie, who received a bullet through his left hand, and Malcolm were wounded.[75] 'I received a blow,' Malcolm recorded, 'as if from a huge club on the elbow. A musket ball had passed through the upper part of my arm, and splintered the bone. I felt stunned, and, in a few moments, became faint, and dizzy, and fell.' As he lay by the roadside, two French soldiers fell upon him. 'They immediately began to rifle my pockets, and one of them was in the act of tearing off my epaulet, when an officer came up, sword in hand, and drove them off, to my great relief.' In danger of being fired upon by the advancing British troops, Malcolm tried to escape but was again apprehended by two French soldiers; they took him to the town of Toulouse, 'which exhibited such a scene of confusion as I ever witnessed. Almost the whole

French army occupied the streets . . . all was terror and excitement.'[76]

Anton had some narrow escapes: 'A musket-ball struck my halberd [axe] in line with my cheek, another passed between my arm and my side and lodged in my knapsack, another struck the handle of my sword, and a fourth passed through my bonnet and knocked it off my head; had the ball been two inches lower, or I that much higher, the reader would have been saved the trouble of perusing this narrative.'[77]

As he believed, only two officers of the 1st Battalion's right wing and sixty soldiers remained without a wound. The Colours were in tatters, stained with blood. 'The standard, cut in two, had been successively placed in the hands of three officers, who fell as we advanced; it was now borne by a sergeant,' related Anton.[78] 'Nothing however could withstand the bravery of our lads and we drove them out at the point of the bayonet without firing a shot,' recorded Gerard, who had 'escaped with only an ugly knock from a spent ball on the right knee, which however did not prevent my going on with my regiment'.[79]

'We were by this time something short of 100 men,' Gerard continued. When the French saw their weakened force, 'they made a most desperate effort to regain the works we had taken by sending up two strong columns, one on the right and another on the left of the redoubt where the shattered remains of the 42nd were. No support being at this time up (for what reason I cannot divine) we were ordered to retire from the redoubt, into a road which connected it with the convent, and the 79th meeting us there, we again rallied our men on them, and charged, when the enemy retreated with the greatest precipitation.'[80] With another line of redoubts to storm, the Spanish, 'who had shamefully run off in the beginning of the day', were brought up. Assailed by the British artillery, 'the enemy retreated and by the evening we were in possession of the whole of the position which he [the French] had occupied in the morning'.[81] Cannon's *Historical Record* was effusive in praising the 42nd, noting that 'the steady and determined bearing of the regiment excited universal admiration: when the soldiers reached the redoubts, they leaped into the trenches with the most heroic bravery, capturing the works at the point of the bayonet.'[82]

That night the men lay on their arms on the field overlooking Toulouse. Since Macara had been severely wounded in his hand, command had passed to Captain John Campbell. Together with the other regiments, the 42nd was recognised as having lost at Toulouse 'considerable numbers, and were highly distinguished throughout the day'.[83] Fifty-four officers and men of the 1st Battalion 42nd were killed. One ensign was missing and 358 officers and men were wounded. The total loss on the Allied side was less than 600 killed and over 4,000 wounded; French wounded and killed were esti-mated at over 3,000. 'On the whole I believe the regiment never did anything more worthy the name of Royal Highlander than their conduct yesterday,' Gerard wrote in his journal.[84]

As the men surmised, the French were not yet beaten. 'Early on the morning of the 12th it was discovered that Marshal Soult had retreated from Toulouse,' Gerard recorded in his journal, 'and we were making ourselves happy with the idea of being allowed to rest ourselves for some days in the town, when we received orders to march in pursuit. We had not even the satisfaction of marching thro' the place, as we were obliged to keep, for a considerable distance, on a cross road to the left of it, in consequence of General Soult having blown up a bridge on the main road.'[85] From what the soldiers were told, Soult had held a council of war, proposing to fight for the town of Toulouse. 'This they unanimously opposed,' recorded Gerard, 'saying it would only lead to another defeat, and the total destruction of the town, the consequence of which was, that he had no alternative left but to retreat, as he did.'[86]

The news that peace had been proclaimed was received 'with every demonstration of joy', related Anton. 'We now retraced our way, marched through Toulouse, so lately the scene of carnage, and took up our quarters about a league beyond it, at a large farmhouse, and extensive wine-store, in which we had been quartered on the 3rd and 4th of the same month, before crossing the Garonne.'[87] Entering Toulouse, they found a number of wounded and men who had been taken prisoner. Gerard also observed 'great quantities of military stores, guns, etc. etc.'[88] He noted that the wounded were doing 'as well as could be looked for, but from the severity of the wounds, many of the cases are very doubtful. Our surgeon told me that he never saw anything like such a proportion of *severe* wounds as at the battle of Toulouse.'[89]

Anton was particularly distressed when Lieutenant Donald Farquharson died, since he had earlier helped him by giving him a blanket for the hut he had built for himself and his wife in the Pyrenees. Having been wounded as the soldiers were entering a redoubt, 'it was impossible to render him any assistance at the time, we were so closely engaged; but when the action closed, I returned and found him where he fell.' His thigh had been badly broken and, as Anton related, having been 'for a few minutes in the power of the enemy', he had been stripped of 'his sash, sword, epaulettes, and money, but no other violence had been offered to him. I got him conveyed to a house which was enclosed in another redoubt, and now filled in every place with our wounded. From this he was removed, on the morning of the 12th, to Toulouse, where he died of his wounds.'[90] Gerard was the one who carried Farquharson in his arms, describing how he behaved 'with uncommon gallantry'.[91]

Ensign McNiven, wounded in the early stages of the fighting, had endured 'three days of suspense' in a farmhouse before knowing the outcome. On the morning of 13 April, carts and carriages with straw in them arrived 'in great numbers, as well as various saddled cavalry horses, for those of the wounded, who were able to ride, but as my case would not permit of this mode of conveyance, I was carried out by four men. Being stiff and cold, I was not a little glad to escape from the corner of the room, where I had lain constantly on my back, during my three nights sojourn.'[92]

On 16 April, Gerard was recording in his journal news of the momentous events in Paris which led to Napoleon's abdication 'and of the French senate having called Louis 18th to the throne'. Since Napoleon had already lost Paris in March and had been forced to abdicate unconditionally on 6 April, he considered that it was 'unfortunate' for the families 'of those who fell at Toulouse that this news did not reach us some days sooner, and the battle might have been in that case saved'.[93] Recovering from his wounds in hospital, Private John described how the head surgeon came to tell him that 'peace had been made before the battle was fought. I cannot tell you how this news affected me. I was sick and wounded and I thought on the thousands who had fallen a few days before.'[94]

Even as the men rejoiced, on 17 April Gerard was recording how 'unsettled' was the life of a soldier. 'When I last wrote I thought all further advance of the British into France was stopped. Soult it seems however, has refused to give credit to the new order of things being established in France and in consequence Lord Wellington has moved his army, altho' it is not thought that we shall have any more fighting, but only that we have been moved for forms sake until Soult gets some official information of the revolution.'[95] By the next day, 'everything' had been 'put to the rights between Soult and Lord Wellington', and the soldiers were on the march again, heading for the town of Auch, 'where it is said we are to go into barracks until arrangements are made for our leaving the country'. On the way, Gerard was recording how they passed over 'the field of battle on the 10th and the peace and stillness which reigned over it at this time formed a striking contrast with the murderous scene of confusion, of which it had been the theatre but a few days before'.[96] Having recovered sufficiently from his wound, McNiven had decided to have 'a quiet reflective survey of the battle field'. Passing through the redoubts and field works, 'their areas bore a crimson line, from the blood of many brave men, who had been buried in swarms, in the wet ditches which encircled these field fortifications'.[97]

In April 1815, a general honour for the *Peninsula* 1810–14 was granted to all the regiments which had fought in the war, including both battalions of the 42nd. In time, as detailed in subsequent Memoranda, the individual Honours which the Regiment was permitted to bear 'on its Colours and Appointments' were: *Busaco,*

Fuentes d'Honor, Salamanca, Pyrenees, Nivelle, Nive, Orthes and *Toulouse*'.[98] Although criticised for his leadership, Macara was 'honoured with the dignity' of Knight Commander of the Order of the Bath (KCB).

While stationed at Auch, McNiven noted how the 'balls and other gaieties, taking place presented a very strong contrast to the multitudes of wounded, crippling about the town, with many of the French dragoons walking about for exercise, with their arms and faces, poor fellows, bandaged up, their eyes scarcely visible, – all in the way of war and glory'.[99] After spending five weeks at Auch, in early June 1814 the 1st Battalion 42nd was given orders to proceed to Bordeaux, 'which exhibited a scene of great mercantile bustle; the opening of the port to British shipping and colonial produce, which had for a number of years been interdicted, invited an immense number of traders, while the demands of the army gave a stimulus to the agriculturalist, the merchant, and the mechanic'.[100] On 21 June the soldiers embarked on transports at Pauillac on the Garonne river. 'While on the salt sea,' recalled Private John, 'sailing to Ireland, I was pensive enough, remembering all I had gone through; the want, cold fatigue, and danger, in which I had my share with the regiment, since I joined it, especially since we came into Spain, first and last.'[101]

By the terms of the first 'Treaty of Paris', signed at Fontainebleau, the boundaries of France were limited to where they had stood in 1792. Britain was to keep Malta, Tobago, St Lucia and Mauritius but to restore the Dutch colonies, except Ceylon, Cape Colony and part of Guiana. The new King of France was Louis XVI's fifty-eight-year-old brother, who became Louis XVIII; the Dauphin – Louis XVII after his father's execution in 1793 – had died in prison in 1795.[102] In London, the city was illuminated in celebration. 'Scarcely could the popular exultation have been less,' recorded *The Times* newspaper, 'if it had been our own country which had been liberated from the yoke of tyranny, instead of a nation with which we had been twenty years at war.'[103] Napoleon was given sovereignty of the island of Elba, off the coast of Italy near his place of birth, Corsica.

Permitted to keep the title of Emperor, he spent the early months of his exile creating a small army and navy and developing Elba's iron mines.

Landing at the Cove of Cork in mid-July 1814, the soldiers were 'in good health and high spirits'.[104] 'Whilst at Kilkenny all those who had been taken prisoners during the retreat to Corunna, and in the campaign in Spain rejoined us,' noted Gunn.[105] Those who had completed their term of service were discharged, some with pensions 'but most without any reward for their perilous services'.[106] With the war over, all arrears – often six to ten months – were to be paid. 'This appeared to be a most Herculean task to our pay-sergeants,' recorded Anton; 'for they had always a most decided aversion to paying money'.[107] The reason, he continued, was that 'a most detestable practice had crept into the regiment (I may say into the army), of allowing the pay-sergeants to serve out shirts, shoes and other necessaries'. Soldiers often fell into debt. 'It was therefore, no wonder that he was backward in paying money, when he had so much interest in withholding it'.[108]

2nd Battalion 73rd

In northern Europe, having survived the winter, in early 1814 the 2nd Battalion 73rd, in a force of two divisions and cavalry, took part in the action against the French in the village of Merxem, two miles from Antwerp. After an initial success, the French rallied, although Lieutenant General Sir Thomas Graham, who had come from the Peninsula to take command, wanted to assure the politicians at home that the action had been conducted 'with all the zeal & intelligence possible'. Included in his appreciation was Major Dawson Kelly in the 73rd for the 'distinguished manner in which these corps attacked the left and centre of the village, forcing the enemy from every strong hold'.[109] An unsuccessful attack in early March on Bergen-op-Zoom, in which the 73rd did not take part, was repulsed.

Once Paris fell, Graham could negotiate the evacuation by the French of both garrisons at Antwerp and Bergen-op-Zoom. Billeted in a country house, Sergeant Thomas Morris recorded how, during the fine July weather of 1814, they enjoyed their meals 'under an avenue of trees at the back of the house, where the table groaned beneath a profusion of the most substantial fare; and in the interval, between the meals, those who were not for guard, had the privilege of strolling through the extensive and tastefully laid out grounds'.[110] Moving into Belgium, they went first to Ghent and then Tournai, which 'has had its share of the vicissitudes of war'. Inexplicably, the men were attacked 'by a disease of the eye', its symptoms 'an intolerable itching at night, when inflammation would take place, and in the morning the eyes would be completely closed'. So serious was the affliction, believed to originate from stagnant water outside the citadel walls, that some men were blinded. Moving to Courtray, south-west of Ghent, 'the prevalence of the small pox rendered it imperative that those who had not had the disorder in its natural state, should submit to vaccination'.[111]

Aside from illness, one feature of the 73rd's stay in Belgium was the less frequent use of flogging as a punishment. According to Morris, the locals regarded it with such disgust that the Colonel was persuaded to try alternative forms of punishment. 'Solitary confinement was awarded for the more serious crimes, and extra guard and punishment drill for the common offences.' The experiment proved so successful that crime diminished and henceforward flogging was used only 'in special cases, and under special circumstances'.[112] The winter of 1814 was spent 'very agreeably . . . with good quarters, abundant rations, and light duty'.[113]

Aftermath

Throughout the concluding stages of the war in Europe, the officers of the 2nd Battalion 42nd had remained in Scotland. When Blantyre went on half-pay on 6 May 1813, Sir George Leith took command, coming from half-pay. For a brief period, following renewed hostilities with the United States of America in 1812, it was thought that the 1st Battalion 42nd might sail to America, where fighting had been taking place around the Great Lakes, in the Atlantic and in the southern states. Although negotiations with the Americans had begun in August 1814, news travelled slowly. 'I was sorry to hear that you were under Orders for America, but if you do go I think it will be in the command of the Regt.,' Blantyre wrote to Dick in September, ever concerned about his friend's prospects. 'I feel much interested about you in particular, as well as about the old Corps in which we served so long together, & spent so many happy days, for I never was happier than during the three years we were in Portugal & Spain notwithstanding all our fatigues etc.'[114] The orders were rescinded and the 1st Battalion remained in Ireland.

At the same time, the British Army was again reduced. In October 1814 the 2nd Battalion was disbanded, its men transferred to the 1st Battalion in Ireland. By the end of the year, as far as the officers and men of the 42nd were concerned, the 'French Revolutionary Wars', which for many had included seven gruelling years on the Peninsula, were at an end. Since 1793, 263 officers and men from the Regiment had been killed, well over a thousand wounded.[115]

> *And art thou fallen with the brave,*
> *All hopes and fears and doubts of thee*
> *Concentre now in glory's grave;*
> *And honour seals the destiny.*[116]

14.

1815

The last time France stood British fire
'The Watch' gained glory at its cost;
At Quatre Bras and Hugomont,
Three dreadful days they kept their post.
Ten hundred there, who form'd in square,
Before the close a handful grew;
The little phalanx never flinched,
Till 'Boney' ran from Waterloo.[1]

One Hundred Days

The year 1815 began with little expectation of the momentous battles in which the 42nd and the 73rd would fight. The 42nd – reduced to one battalion – was still in Ireland, the 1st Battalion 73rd was in Ceylon and the 2nd Battalion 73rd had remained in northern Europe. With 'vague rumours' of 'something strange that was about to happen', in March the soldiers were ordered to Tournai. At Ath, they heard 'that more work was likely to be cut out for us by the return of Buonaparte'.[2]

On 26 February Napoleon had escaped from Elba. Three days later he was marching on Paris. Having assembled what Loyalist forces he could, Louis XVIII issued a Royal Proclamation, promising to redress past grievances. But, with news of Napoleon's return electrifying his compatriots, the French King soon fled to Ghent. Among those who switched allegiance was Marshal Michel Ney, commander of the troops dispatched by Louis to arrest Napoleon. 'The Bourbon troops, sent by the King to capture him [Napoleon] on his way to Paris, were won over by his undaunted courage and confidence,' recorded Lieutenant Donald Mackenzie. 'The French people might have been tired of war, still they only half liked, and acquiesced in, being made over to a King, however respectable in a way, who had been set on the throne by the arrangement of so many of their enemies and conquerors.'[3] 'From the Pyrenees to the Alps, from the Mediterranean to the Atlantic, all were in motion,' recollected James Anton. 'The sovereigns of Europe beheld with astonishment this man of boundless ambition, with whom no obligations were binding, no oaths sacred and no promises regarded.'[4]

On 13 March, the 'Great Powers', meeting at the Congress of Vienna to determine Europe's future following Napoleon's first abdication, declared him an 'outlaw'. Four days later, with the formation of the Seventh Coalition, the Grand Allied Army was reconstituted, with Great Britain, the United Kingdom of the Netherlands and Prussia pledging to put a vast army into the field of battle. Under the supreme command of the Duke of Wellington, and numbering 92,000 men, the army was divided into three corps: 1 Corps, consisting of two British divisions, as well as the 2nd Dutch–Belgian Division, was commanded by the twenty-four-year-old Crown Prince of Orange, William Frederick, eldest son of King William I of the Netherlands.[5] 2 Corps was commanded by General Rowland Hill, veteran of the Peninsula. In the Reserve, under Wellington's personal command, were two more British divisions, a corps of Brunswickers commanded by Frederick William, Duke of Brunswick, and contingents of Hanoverian, Dutch and Nassau troops. Marching to join them from the Lower Rhine was the Prussian army, 121,000 strong, under the command of seventy-two-year-old General Gebhard von Blücher, who had defeated Napoleon at the Battle of Leipzig in 1813. To make a pre-emptive strike at this formidable coalition of armies assembling to invade France, Napoleon planned to cross into Belgium.[6]

In late April 1815, the 42nd Royal Highland Regiment was ordered to leave Kilkenny, where the soldiers considered they had been 'employed more as a set of police officers in keeping the inhabitants quiet, than as soldiers'.[7] Arriving at the Cove of Cork in early May, 'no time was lost in preparing for active service,' recorded Anton; 'all our old and apparently debilitated hands were invalided and left behind; four women to each company were permitted to accompany us, and the rest were sent to their respective homes or parishes.'[8]

'We embarked here on board 5 small vessels with miserable accommodation,' recorded Lieutenant John Malcolm, complaining that there was 'not a single cot or hammock on board'.[9] 'The misery we endure on board this cursed tub is most complicated,' recorded Gerard, on board the *Flora*.[10] A greater privation was the reduction of women. 'As we were stepping on board,' recollected Anton, 'an order was received, importing that only two women would be allowed to proceed with each company. This was a great disappointment, and no small cause of grief to those who had to return, without any preparation for such an unexpected separation, or any provision, but that which the liberality of their country might allow, or the hand of charity present, to carry them to their distant home.'[11]

Bad weather meant that the full complement did not disembark at Ostend until 24 May. After marching for two miles, they came 'to a fine canal where we found 2 large barges waiting to take our 4 companies on board', recorded Malcolm. 'We started about 10 OC [lock] at night in these barges lashed together drawn by 2 horses & arrived at Ghent on the 25th where we joined the head Quarters of the Regt who had been lying there for nearly a week – the country we passed between Ostend & Ghent was much finer than our gardens are in general.'[12] Passing by Bruges, where they breakfasted for 'the small sum of one franc', Gerard observed that 'the inhabitants certainly have not gone too far when they have named their country the "Granary of Europe."' In Ghent, the soldiers were aware of the deposed French King's presence: 'he makes very little show of Royalty, except when going to Mass on Sunday.'[13] Although Gerard was confident that Napoleon would be 'ultimately crushed', he confided to his sister that 'when the English papers tell you that there is a popular feeling in France in his [Louis XVIII's] favor, they deceive you grossly.' Billeted with the local inhabitants, the soldiers enjoyed claret at 2 shillings and sixpence a bottle and champagne for five shillings. 'The country is astonishingly rich and provisions cheap, notwithstanding the immense consumption of the army.'[14]

The Regiment arrived in Brussels on 28 May, 'after a most unpleasant march occasioned by the scorching heat and dust'.[15] The Highlanders, known as *les petits Ecossais*, were 'the theme of affectionate praise among the Flemings', related Walter Scott, travelling in their footsteps a year later. 'They were so domesticated in the houses where they were quartered, that it was no uncommon thing to see the Highland soldier taking care of the children or keeping the shop of his host.'[16] Some were tempted to increase their drinking money by selling their newly provided blankets. When the fraud (which consisted of selling one blanket and reducing two in size to make a third) was discovered, a court martial was held and the defaulters punished. 'The man who would attach blame to our colonel, for this prompt but severe decision, knows little of military affairs,' noted Anton; 'had he winked at their proceedings, he might have led a half-naked regiment out of Brussels; and instead of seeing us comfortably covered in our night's bivouac, beheld us shivering under useless shreds of blankets and himself called to account by the general for the curtailment.'[17]

On 28 May, Gerard was noting: 'Everything now begins to look like war.'[18] Whilst wandering through the city, he learnt that 'the Belgian soldiers were not to be trusted, as the greater part of them had served under Bonaparte to whom they were much attached.' Astonished that they should form part of the Allied army, he surmised that 'it may be however that the Duke of Wellington wishes, by giving those who are traitors at bottom an opportunity of deserting before hostilities commence, to secure the fidelity of those who remain when he shall have occasion for them.'[19] By 8 June, Gerard was feeling 'completely in the dark with regards to our future motions. We are each day inundated with thousands of different reports which are completely falsified by those of tomorrow and in such a contradictory mass it is totally impossible to distinguish the probable from the improbable. One of the most ridiculous of those in circulation yesterday was that Bonaparte had left France and taken refuge in London !!!'[20] On 13 June, he wrote a long letter to his sister, Keturah, in Scotland. 'We have expected the order to advance every day since our arrival here, but it is now said that the 15th is the earliest day on which the army will move.'[21]

Quatre Bras

On to battle, on to fame, on to preserve our glorious name;
On to death, if die we must, but reach the foe a parting thrust.[22]

On the night of 15 June, the Duchess of Richmond was hosting a lavish ball in honour of the Duke of Wellington, later described as the 'most famous ball in history'. The Duchess's husband, the 4th

Duke, was commanding a reserve force in Brussels, ordered to protect the city in case Napoleon proved victorious.[23] Attended by Belgian, British, Dutch and Prussian nobility, among those present at the ball was Brevet Lieutenant Colonel Henry Dick and Lieutenant Donald Mackenzie of the 42nd. 'The sight of so many gorgeous uniforms,' wrote Mackenzie 'and the splendid toilets of the ladies, not to mention such a galaxy of beauty created a scene never to be forgotten.'[24] A few soldiers from each of the Highland Regiments had been invited to dance reels. But 'alas at two o'clock in the morning, everything that could make a noise in the way of a drum or bugle to assemble' sounded. Thinking that they were being turned out for an ordinary 'Brigading day', recollected Private James Gunn, it was only when 'the Road we travelled was Rather Long' that they realised they were 'on the way to meet Bonaparte'.[25]

Although Wellington had first received news in the afternoon that Napoleon had mobilised his forces and was crossing into Belgium, he did not know his route. It was not until the early evening that he drafted orders for the Allied army to mobilise, thinking that the French attack would be through Mons. Later, having heard that the reported French movements around Mons were a diversion and that Napoleon was marching through Charleroi, he ordered a 'general movement of the army' towards the east, as far as Nivelles.[26]

'After marching for 13 or 14 miles through a forest,' recorded Lieutenant Malcolm, 'we were halted in the edge of it for a few hours and march[ed] on through a fine open country for some miles when we began to hear a heavy fire apparently only a few miles in our front.' As part of the 9th Brigade, the 42nd was under Sir Denis Pack's command, in the 5th Division, one of the two divisions in the Reserve.[27] 'Our Brigade was formed on the left of some houses & the whole moved forward for a short distance in open column of Companies.'[28]

Napoleon's plan was based on the belief that, having stolen a march on the Grand Allied Army, he would find Wellington unable to move forward in sufficient strength to counter his forces, provided he could first defeat Blücher and the Prussians and prevent them from joining Wellington's force. Ney, in command of Napoleon's left flank, marched to take the strategically located crossroads near the village of Quatre Bras, which commanded the roads between Nivelles and Namur and between Charleroi and Brussels. Once Quatre Bras was secured, Ney could join up with the centre forces and march on Brussels. Anticipating an easy victory, Napoleon waited at Charleroi.

Meanwhile, Wellington's army was continuing to assemble. Having left Ath, the 2nd Battalion 73rd had reached 'a pretty village', three miles from Soignies. As part of the 5th Brigade, commanded by Major General Colin Halkett in the 3rd Division, they too had been ordered to march.[29] 'On the 15th of June, 1815,' Thomas Morris related, 'some of our officers and men were engaged playing at ball against the gable-end of a house in the village . . . when an orderly dragoon was seen rapidly coming down the declivity which led to the village; and on being directed to our commanding officer, he presented a letter, which, at a single glance, informed the colonel [which] was the "route" [we were to take]. The men were scattered about variously engaged, but the roll of the drum and the tones of the bugle soon brought them together in heavy marching order.'[30]

Reaching Soignies, they found it 'filling fast with troops; there was evidently something extraordinary in this sudden movement, but no one knew anything further than that we were ordered to fall in. We had billets here, but had strict orders not to go to bed. At Twelve o'clock we received further information, but still nothing definite.' Morris continued: 'On quitting the town of Soignies at midnight [on 15/16 June], we plunged at once into the wood.'[31] Their progress was slow. 'By eight o'clock in the morning we had not accomplished more than ten or twelve miles. After an hour's rest we again started, and fell in with other troops, all marching in the same uncertainty as ourselves, but all animated by the best feeling and anxious to meet the foe.'[32]

Having reached Nivelles, the men enjoyed some rest, eating their hard biscuits and salt meat. Foraging parties were sent out for wood and water. 'The camp kettles were put in requisition, the meat put on to boil, and we began to fancy that we should settle down here for the night.' But before the meat had time to cook, with the sound of cannon in the distance, a horseman rode up, urging them to 'Fall in!' 'The bugles were set to work to call in the foragers, and all was bustle.'[33] As Morris and his companions soon realised, Ney was moving to occupy Quatre Bras, where the Prince of Orange had sent forward his 2nd Brigade. Since Ney's forces were far superior, the Dutch needed reinforcing. 'We fell in and commenced our march,' recorded Morris, 'the men full of ardour, full of excitement. We were going to battle; and it is impossible for anyone who has not experienced it, to conceive of the amount of enthusiasm, which prevails at such a time. The regiments, in passing, bandy compliments, and salute each other by the names they have on their colours; and this has the effect of producing an esprit-de-corps, which renders the men almost invincible.'[34] Meanwhile the Prussians, pursued by the French right flank under Marshal Emmanuel de Grouchy, had fallen back on Ligny.[35]

'On the morning of the 16th June, before the sun rose over the dark forest of Soignies,' related Sergeant Anton in the 42nd, 'our brigade ... stood in column, Sir Denis Pack at its head, waiting impatiently for the 42d, the commanding-officer of which [Macara] was chidden severely by Sir Denis for being so dilatory. We took our place in the column, and the whole marched off to the strains of martial music, and amidst the shouts of the surrounding multitude.'[36] 'We had a long and hurried march,' Mackenzie recalled, 'but as time was everything we pushed rapidly forward.'[37] Entering the forest of Soignies, south of Brussels, Anton described how the columns of soldiers 'moved on in silent but speedy course, like some river confined between two equal banks. The forest is of immense extent, and we continued to move on under its welcome shade, until we came to a small hamlet, or auberge, imbosomed in the wood to the right of the road. Here we turned to our left, halted, and were in the act of lighting fires, on purpose to set about cooking.'[38]

Like the 73rd, they were 'flattering' themselves they might rest until the following day and they were at once ordered to march.

Having passed through the town of Waterloo, the village of Quatre Bras came in view: 'the frightened peasantry came running breathless and panting along the way. We moved off to the left of the road, behind a gently rising eminence,' recorded Anton; 'a beautiful plain appears in view, surrounded with belts of wood, and the main road from Brussels runs through it'.[39]

By the time the 5th Division arrived at Quatre Bras, the Prince of Orange's troops were heavily engaged with the numerically superior French. The area over which they were fighting 'with alternating fortune' was roughly three-quarters of a mile either side of the Charleroi–Brussels road.[40] Near by was the farmhouse of Gemioncourt, which the Dutch and Belgians had been struggling to retain. A 'luxuriant crop of grain' hid from view 'the contending skirmishers beyond, and presented a considerable obstacle to our advance'.[41] Thinking they might rest on their knapsacks, the men began to lie down, but Pack rode past at once and ordered them to fix their bayonets. 'We were all ready and in line,' related Anton. ' "Forward!" was the word of command, and forward we hastened, though we saw no enemy in front. The stalks of the rye, like the reeds that grow on the margin of some swamp, opposed our advance; the tops were up to our bonnets, and we strode and groped our way through as fast as we could.'[42] Having made it through the field, as the Prince of Orange's troops fell back the Highlanders went in pursuit of the French. 'Those who had so proudly driven the Belgians before them, turned now to fly, whilst our loud cheers made the fields echo to our wild hurrahs ... We drove on so fast that we almost appeared like a mob following the rout of some defeated faction.'[43]

According to Anton, seeing the Highlanders advance, Ney ordered the lancers 'to bear down upon us'. Unfortunately, from a distance, the soldiers thought they were the Duke of Brunswick's troops, 'coming to cut up the flying [French] infantry; and as cavalry on all occasion have the advantage of retreating foot, on a fair field, we were halted in order to let them take their way.'[44] Realising their mistake when a German orderly dragoon galloped past, shouting

'Franchee! Franchee!', Macara immediately ordered the soldiers to form a square, 'in doing which two companies were left out, or were rather in the act of falling in, when they were pierced by the lancers'. The number of the 42nd killed was considerable and included Macara, hit by a lance on his chin, which penetrated upwards to his skull, killing him instantly, whereupon Dick took command, although already wounded in the shoulder by a musket ball.[45] Having rallied the men, he formed them into a 'diminished' square until, weak from loss of blood, he had to be carried from the field, 'the gallant remnant of the men' eventually 'putting the lancers to flight'.[46]

Command then passed to Brevet Major George Davidson, but he too was wounded.[47] Brevet Major John Campbell, who had replaced the wounded Macara, again took command. 'Thus in a few minutes, we had been placed under four different commanding officers,' noted Anton.[48] During the fighting, Mackenzie had been 'slightly' wounded twice: 'a bullet struck one of the buttons of my jacket, which it indented, thus however turning the direction of the ball which ran along my breast, cutting the skin and escaping through my clothes on the right side'. He was knocked down, but since no bones were broken he remained, believing that 'one should always stick to their post while able to be useful'.[49] To their right and left, others suffered a similar fate: 'the superiority of the enemy in cavalry, afforded him a decided advantage on the open plain, for our British cavalry and artillery had not yet reached the field.'[50]

In a final attempt to resist the French cavalry, the 42nd, under Campbell's command, again formed a square: 'in the centre were several wounded French soldiers, witnessing our formation round them: they doubtless considered themselves devoted to certain death among us seeming barbarians, but they had no occasion to speak ill of us afterwards; for as they were already incapable of injuring us, we moved about them regardful of their wounds and suffer-ings.'[51] When the square was formed – 'so far as unequalised compa-nies could form a square' – the cuirassiers again attacked. But, as Anton related, a momentary pause, when Pack – in command of the Brigade – raised his hat to return the salute of his French adversary, gave them the advantage, enabling them to open fire on the lancers before they charged: 'riders cased in heavy armour, fell tumbling from their horses; the horses reared, plunged, and fell on the dismounted riders; steel helmets and cuirasses rung against unsheathed sabres, as they fell to the ground; shrieks and groans of men, the neighing of horses, and the discharge of musketry, rent the air, as men and horses mixed together in one heap of indiscriminate slaughter.'[52]

Also on the field of battle was the 3rd Division, including the 2nd Battalion 73rd. They too came upon the field of rye, 'of such an extraordinary growth (seven feet height), that we were prevented from seeing the force to whom we were likely to be opposed'. As they soon realised: 'we were not advancing unobserved, a body of the enemy's cuirassiers came on us by surprise, and having no opportunity to form square, we were compelled to retire as rapidly as we could out of the corn-field. When we rallied the cuirassiers wheeled off to the left, coming in contact with the 42nd by whom they were roughly handled; not, however, before they had committed great havoc in the Highland ranks.'[53] The 73rd's timely withdrawal saved them from the fate suffered by the 69th, also in the 3rd Division, whose ranks were decimated by the French cavalry.[54] For a while, the 73rd had fought alongside the Brunswickers who, 'under their brave Duke', had driven 'before us a vast body of the enemy, when the Germans and ourselves parted company. We were now considerably in advance, and as the shots were whistling thickly around us, we were ordered to lie down to avoid the favours intended for us.'[55]

By nightfall, the French had been driven back, leaving their adversaries in possession of Gemioncourt and the south of the wood of Bossu. In a desperate last attempt, Ney had called for the French I Corps, under the command of Jean-Baptiste Drouet, Comte d'Erlon.[56] Deliberately positioned between Napoleon's forces at Ligny and Ney's three miles away at Quatre Bras, the intention was that d'Erlon would assist whoever's need was greatest. Without informing him, Napoleon had called on d'Erlon to march to Ligny. When Ney attempted to recall him, it was too late. At Ligny, the

French offensive against Blücher had been intense. Eventually the Prussians had to retire, enabling Napoleon to claim his last victory. Ney lost an estimated 4,000 men to Wellington's 4,800, leaving historians to wonder whether the outcome would have been more decisive had the French I Corps under d'Erlon been engaged at Quatre Bras, and, had they prevailed, whether there would have been a battle at Waterloo.

'The day's contest at a close,' recorded Anton, 'our attention was directed to the casualties which had occurred in our ranks.'[57] Losses for the 42nd at Quatre Bras were considerable. Four officers, including Macara, and forty private soldiers had been killed. Davidson died later in Brussels. Ensign George Gerard was killed. The long letter he had written to his sister three days before the battle remained unsent in his suitcase, to be found later by his brother Arthur.[58] Fifteen officers, including Dick and Mackenzie, were wounded, as well as fourteen sergeants and 213 men.[59]

Shortly before the 42nd retired from the field of battle, Lieutenant John Malcolm had been hit in the left arm by a musket ball. 'But as we were completely surrounded at the time I had no alternative but to remain with the Regt until they retired.' Having lost a lot of blood, and feeling faint, he found the surgeon, Dr Stewart, on the road leading to the village where the men had assembled '& had the ball cut out'. As a result of his injury, Malcolm played no further part, spending 'a very uncomfortable night' in a house reserved for the wounded.[60] An especially short private soldier – five feet high – captured by the French, was later returned 'dressed in the clothing of a French grenadier, and was saluted by the name of Napoleon, which he retained until he was discharged'.[61]

Losses for the 2nd Battalion 73rd were around fifty dead and wounded of all ranks. 'We were glad of the opportunity, when the firing had ceased, to lie down with the dead and dying,' recollected Morris after the battle.[62] 'I was awakened at midnight, and while sitting meditating on the events of the past day, I thought of the poor fellows we had lost, and wondered whose turn would come next. The corn, which had covered the field in the morning, was now trodden down, and I had an uninterrupted view. The scene by moonlight was grand, but awful.'[63]

In his dispatch relating the day's events, Wellington gave 'a mark of approbation' to the 42nd.[64] Other accolades followed: 'Every man fought with desperation which no language can describe,' recorded writer and essayist William Mudford in his historical account of the campaign. 'The fine brigade of Highlanders suffered much. They were everywhere in the hottest of the fight, and well did they maintain their warlike renown.'[65]

The next day, around midday, after tending the wounded and dying, the Allied army retired towards Brussels. 'To retreat is always disagreeable to British soldiers,' recorded Mackenzie, and so 'gloom and doubt were apparent in the faces of officers and men.'[66] While on the march, there was one accidental death in the 2nd Battalion 73rd when Private Jeremiah Bates's rifle went off, killing Lieutenant Joseph Strachan. 'From the enquiry which was made,' related Morris, 'it would appear that a portion of the corn which had been trodden down, had resumed its upright position, and some of it getting entangled with the trigger, had caused the explosion.' In the early afternoon the sky darkened and it began to rain heavily. 'We had some very steep hills to descend, and the rapidly accumulating rain came down with such inconceivable force, that it was with the greatest difficulty we could keep our footing.'[67] Their destination was the plain of Waterloo, south of Brussels, where Wellington had chosen to make a stand against Napoleon. Its main feature was a ridge, sloping towards a 'sunken' road: 'about thirty feet wide, with on either side a high mud-bank', recalled Morris. 'On this road the troops were closely wedged together. The artillery and cavalry in the middle, the infantry on either side.'[68]

'The afternoon and night of the 17th were dreadful,' recorded Mackenzie, 'thunder, lightning, rain and hail, accompanied by wind, poured down on the Army, making us wretched and uncomfortable in the extreme.'[69] While the storm continued, the French were continuing to take up position, making Morris think that 'they seemed at times half inclined to attack us that night; but the heavy rain probably made them defer it till the next morning. Their artillery, however, had opened on us perhaps with the view of feeling their distance, but one of their shots killed two of our light company; one of them it hit on the cheek, and the other was killed just as suddenly and effectually by the wind of the passing ball.'[70]

Although the men were told to pile arms, no one was allowed to leave his position. Their only sustenance was the remnant of biscuit served out the night before. It was impossible to lie down in the mud, 'and to stand half up to the knees in mud, almost equally so; but at last we hit on a middle course'. Collecting armfuls of the corn, they placed it on the ground and sat on it, holding their blankets over their heads to keep off the rain and cold night air. 'Silence prevailed,' recollected Anton, 'and wet although we were, we were falling asleep sitting round the fires, or stretched on scattered branches brought for fuel.' When a false alarm was given of a French attack, 'in an instant each man of the brigade stood by his musket; the bayonets were already on the pieces, and these all loaded, notwithstanding the rain. We stood thus to our arms for nearly an hour, sinking to our ankles amongst the soft muddy soil of the field.'[71]

Those unable to sleep passed the night 'chatting over the events of the last two days, and in speculative discussions as to the issue of the next day's fight', recollected Morris. 'We also indulged in the relation of anecdotes of bygone times.'[72] Major Archibald John Maclaine related stories of his service in the East Indies with the 1st Battalion 73rd, having fought and been wounded at Seringapatam and served in New South Wales. He was 'much beloved', noted Morris, because he had suggested discontinuing the practice of flogging. When thinking about the battle to come, 'it seemed to be the general opinion, that the contest on the morrow would be a most severe one; . . . on the part of Napoleon an empire; and, on the part of Wellington and his allies, to secure repose to Europe.'[73]

Waterloo

Now for our second battalion, to give to them their due,
They fought like British heroes on the plains of Waterloo:
With General Harris at their head, who nobly drew his sword,
Crying 'Death or glory now, my boys, for the loyal 73rd.'[74]

By daybreak on 18 June 1815 the rain had stopped. The men could forage for firewood and warm themselves. Recollecting that it was Sunday morning, Thomas Morris shaved and put on 'a clean (though not dry) shirt'.[75] To give the Allied army maximum advantage, 'having the village of Waterloo a mile or two in our rear',[76] Wellington's defensive position was along the crest of a ridge in front of the farm of Mont St Jean. As in previous battles, where possible he positioned the troops on the reverse of the slope, taking advantage of the sunken road, to conceal his full strength from his adversary. On the right of the British line was the chateau and orchard of Hougoumont, commanding the road to Nivelles and eventually Paris. On the centre right, in front of the Sunken Road, was the farmhouse of La Haye Sainte. Further to the left was the village of Papelotte, which commanded the road to Wavre, along which Wellington had ordered the reassembled Prussians to march to reinforce his left flank. Wellington had positioned himself on rising ground behind La Haye Sainte by an elm tree on the crossroads of the Sunken Road and the road leading from Quatre Bras to Brussels. From this vantage point, seated astride his horse, he could survey the progress of the battle.

'The line of battle was formed alternately of British and foreign troops,' recorded Morris; 'where the British were in front, they were supported by German cavalry; and where the Germans or Belgians were in front, they were supported by British cavalry.'[77] The British Foot Guards were on the right, nearly opposite Hougoumont. As part of the 5th Brigade in the 3rd Division, the 2nd Battalion 73rd was positioned in a square with the 30th. 'The ground in our locality was covered with corn, and of so loose a nature, owing to the heavy rains, that we were literally knee deep in mud,' recollected Morris.[78] To the left of the Brussels–Quatre Bras road was Lieutenant General Sir Thomas Picton's 5th Division, which included the depleted 42nd in Pack's Brigade. 'Our line, being on the slope next to Waterloo, was hidden from the enemy. Being all arranged in the manner pointed out by our immortal leader,' related Anton, 'we piled our arms, kindled fires, and stood round the welcome blaze to warm ourselves and dry our dripping clothes.'[79]

About three-quarters of a mile away, the French army had taken up position on another series of ridges, parallel to those of St Jean. In the centre of the French position was the farmhouse of La Belle Alliance, which Napoleon used as one of his headquarters. On the right (or the British left) was I Corps, under Comte d'Erlon; on the left was II Corps, virtually opposite Hougoumont; the centre was occupied by troops in the Reserve and the Imperial Guard, under Napoleon's personal command. Marshal Ney was put in command of troops in the battlefield. Unless and until Blücher and the Prussians arrived, in terms of guns and men, Wellington was outnumbered. Aware of the saturated ground, which did not favour his heavy cavalry and artillery, Napoleon did not draft his General Order to advance until around 11 in the morning. Within the next hour, the battle had begun.[80]

Before taking up their respective positions, Thomas Morris bade farewell to his brother William, serving with the 2nd Battalion 73rd's light infantry company, 'as we did not suppose it likely, that both could be preserved through such a battle as this promised to be'.[81] Recollecting the day's events, Morris related how, not realising the battle was about to begin, some commissariat wagons had entered the field, 'with a supply of biscuit and spirits; and a fatigue party of each regiment was sent for it. I was one of these, and had about half a mile to go, when we came to two wagons.' One contained biscuits, the other, three barrels of the popular strongly flavoured gin known as 'Hollands', 'standing on end, with the top end knocked out, that it might be delivered with the greater speed'. While they were getting their supplies, the signal for battle had been given in the French centre 'and immediately their whole line of batteries opened simultaneously on us, and the cannon balls were flying by us in rapid succession'.[82]

Returning to where the 2nd Battalion 73rd was positioned, the men 'had to exercise a great deal of ingenuity and dexterity' to avoid being hit. By the time Morris got back, he saw that they had already suffered some fatalities, 'being too much exposed on the ridge'.[83] To avoid being hit during the cannonade, Morris recollected being ordered to lie down. Surprisingly, he slept 'for nearly an hour, as comfortably as ever I did in my life'.[84] Meanwhile, once the smoke from the French artillery fire dissipated, the French heavy cavalry advanced to attack Hougoumont, which the Guards converted 'into a strong little fortress',[85] resulting in heavy fighting throughout the day.

At the same time, the French were advancing on La Haye Sainte. To the left, the first line behind a hedge – manned by the 95th Rifle Brigade – was made up of soldiers from the 2nd Dutch–Belgian Division; the second line comprised Picton's 5th Division. 'France now pushed forward on the line of our Belgic allies,' related Anton, 'drove them from their post, and rolled them in one promiscuous mass of confusion through the ranks of our brigade, which instantly advanced to repel the pursuers, who came pushing on in broken disorder,' until they were stopped by the hedge. The 42nd might have forced themselves through, 'but our bare thighs had no protection from the piercing thorns'. As they opened fire, the French did likewise; one of the British casualties was Picton, the most senior officer to be killed on the Allied side.[86]

At this critical moment, the Earl of Uxbridge, who famously lost his leg at the close of battle, ordered a charge of the 1st and 2nd Cavalry Brigades. As the 42nd opened ranks to let the 2nd 'Union' Brigade – under General Ponsonby's command – gallop through, ' "Scotland for ever!" bursts from the mouth of each Highlander, as the Scots Greys pass through our ranks,' recalled Anton with pride.[87] 'What pen can describe the scene?' he continued graphically in his memoir. 'Horses' hoofs sinking in men's breasts, breaking bones and pressing out their bowels. Riders' swords streaming in blood, waving over their heads and descending in deadly vengeance. Stroke follows stroke, like the turning of a flail in the hands of a dexterous thresher.'[88]

To their right, La Haye Sainte had become 'one pool of blood; against it Napoleon's artillery incessantly play, and columns of infantry are urged on to drive the brave defenders out. But these meet them with fire and steel and repel them with determined resolution.' Hougoumont was 'no less a scene of slaughter'.[89] Having failed to take the chateau, the French cuirassiers 'made their appearance on the rising ground in our front', recalled Morris, 'taking the artillery stationed there and riding down upon us. Their appearance was well-calculated to inspire a feeling of dread – none of them under six feet, defended by steel helmets and corslets made pigeon-breasted to throw off the balls. Thus armed and accoutred they looked so truly formidable that I thought we should stand no chance against them.' Fortunately, with the square holding firm, they were stopped by firing from the rear, leaving the front ranks, to pay 'them a similar compliment'.[90]

Throughout the day, Wellington kept visiting the front line. According to Morris, when he was with the right flank some French cuirassiers, 'who had evidently recognised the Duke, made a dash forward to secure their prize. Wellington had the option of riding to the rear, but he took the more dignified course of riding into our square, – the best proof he could give of his entire confidence in the bravery of his men,' continued Morris, who recorded the Duke's parting words: 'Well done my lads,' before he returned to his position in the centre.[91] On the cuirassiers' next advance, they 'brought up two light field-pieces and poured grape-shot into us, watching the havoc they were making; and, whenever they saw an opening, they rushed up, but before they could reach us, our dead were thrown outside and the wounded removed to the inside, the ranks immediately closing in. As our ammunition was nearly expended we could only act on the defensive.'[92]

During one deafening cannonade, Morris witnessed the men on either side of him go down: 'the poor fellow on my right got a bullet through the thigh, which proved mortal; and on looking round I saw my left-hand man get a ball in his left eye; the blood rushed out, and he fell forwards.'[93] Soon afterwards a live shell fell near the front line, where Morris was standing, 'and while the fuse was expending itself we were wondering if any of us would escape'. When it burst seventeen men were injured, including Morris, who received some metal in his cheek. The injury was not serious enough for him to retire, but 'the blood ran copiously down inside my clothes, and made me feel somewhat uncomfortable'. One soldier, badly wounded in the head, thought he was going to the rear, when instead, he was rushing into the line of fire, and was cut down by the advancing French.[94] For a brief period, with their ranks depleted, the soldiers retired under a bank. Here, Morris met his brother William. 'He had been taken prisoner in the early part of the day, but got away and made his escape to one of the Guards' squares, where he remained until the coast was somewhat clear, when he again joined his company; but, as we were in different faces of the square, we had no opportunity of seeing each other till now.'[95]

On the left, the 42nd had retained its position. 'All day long,' recorded Mackenzie, 'we had masses of infantry hurled against us, varied by cavalry, and, as our Division held the key of the position, the whole force of the enemy was directed against it. Again and again after receiving the French with a volley, and repelling them with the bayonet, we had scarcely time to form a square before dragoons were upon us.'[96] On one occasion, unable to regain the square, Mackenzie ordered the men with him to lie on the ground and let the horses pass over. 'This we did, but it required some nerve to be perfectly still and be thus ridden over.' Later, Mackenzie succeeded in unhorsing a French officer, 'and thought myself justified in appropriating his steed, which I sent to the rear with a wounded man. This horse I named "Waterloo," after the battle in which he was captured and he served me for many years.' Although Mackenzie received 'several wounds' he considered none were 'sufficiently serious' for him to retire.[97]

Late in the afternoon, Blücher's Prussians arrived from Wavre. Delayed by 'roads turned into quagmires by the appalling weather,'[98] an assault could now be made on Napoleon's right flank. Meanwhile, the 73rd had remained in relative safety by the bank. 'About half-past six or seven o'clock the Duke of Wellington rode up,' recollected Captain John Garland, 'and asked who commanded the square. I replied Colonel, now Lord Harris, who happened at that moment not to be so near his Grace as myself. He then desired me to tell Colonel Harris to form line, but should we be attacked by the Curassiers to re-form square. I delivered these orders to Colonel Harris and we formed line.'[99] Soon afterwards Garland was severely wounded in the thigh by a musket ball, and was carried back by the Morris brothers to the shelter of the bank.[100]

Having taken La Haye Sainte, at around seven thirty in the evening Napoleon sent his Imperial Guard into battle. His objective was to attack the Allied army in the centre and then swing round to attack the Prussians. 'All now depended on this fine body of men, who were never brought into action except under the most desperate circumstances and then they had generally been successful,' recorded Morris. 'As they commenced their onward movement, the artillery, which at the beginning of the action had been placed on the right of the Guards, brought their right shoulder forwards, and opened a tremendous fire obliquely against the columns of the Imperial Guard; but, although they saw their ranks literally mowed down, still they pressed forward.'[101]

As even Marshal Ney realised, the Emperor was now fighting a losing battle. 'I saw four regiments of the middle guard, conducted by the Emperor, arriving. With these troops, he wished to renew the attack, and penetrate the centre of the enemy. He ordered me to lead them on; generals, officers and soldiers all displayed the greatest intrepidity; but this body of troops was too weak to resist, for a long time, the forces opposed to it by the enemy, and it was soon necessary to renounce the hope which this attack had, for a few moments, inspired.'[102]

When, after trying to break through, the Imperial Guard began to withdraw, panic set in among the French army. Seeing the disorder, Wellington ordered a general advance against the retreating French.

'From right to left the welcome word flew over the field; the forest of Soignies echoed to its farthest bounds the loud shouts of the elated army. The guns cease their thundering roar,' recorded Anton in his poetic account. 'The charge is given from right to left, and all Napoleon's columns and lines, foot and horse, in one mingled mass of confusion, fly over the field, while on our left the hardy Prussians come in to share the toils of the hard-fought day, and push the disorganized enemy over the face of the country.'[103] 'We were marching and at a comparative Ease but the Prussians pursuit of the French troops was as the Locust in the Green Fields,' Private Gunn wrote, recollecting the day's events.[104]

To the right, the 2nd Battalion 73rd, 'on forming line, cut but a sorry figure'. Since the Battalion was 'in such a shattered state', related Morris, they did not take part in the pursuit of the French, instead taking up a position near where they had been fighting.[105] In the remaining daylight – it was nearly midsummer – Morris went among his wounded comrades, 'rendering them all the assistance in my power, binding up some of their wounds, and placing them in more easy positions. All their cry was for water; but, alas! We had none to give them. We were ourselves suffering the most intolerable thirst, from salt provisions and the heat of the weather, together with the excitement and exertion we had had.'[106]

With the rout of the Imperial Guard and the retreat of the French, Wellington's victory was assured. That night the men lay on the ground near where they had fought, amidst the thousands of dead and dying. 'After all was over,' related Mackenzie, 'I slept soundly within a few yards of where Napoleon had stood during the day.'[107] At daylight, the field of battle presented 'a most awful appearance, the ground being literally strewed with bodies, and hundreds of the poor fellows who had been severely wounded, had to remain for many hours before they could be removed, or even attended to; and thus many valuable lives were lost which might, with prompt attention, have been restored,' recorded Morris. 'The appearance of the dead was really frightful, as most of them had been reduced to a state of nudity.'[108]

Total losses of the Anglo-Allied army at Waterloo were recorded at 15,000, those of the Prussians 7,000, while the French losses were estimated at 25,000 dead and wounded and 8,000 prisoners taken.[109] Thousands of horses were dead or helpless. Compared with Quatre Bras, the 42nd sustained relatively few losses: five private soldiers were killed and forty-four of all ranks wounded.[110] Macara's death at Quatre Bras meant that Robert Henry Dick had at last gained the Lieutenant Colonelcy his father had been wanting to purchase for him. 'I congratulate you sincerely upon your escape,' Blantyre wrote in early July, 'as well as upon your having got to the head of the 42nd Regt. & it must be much more gratifying to yourself to have *fought* your way to that station, than to have got it by purchase.' Mindful that many of his old friends in the 42nd had suffered at Quatre Bras, he suggested that Dick would have 'a small tho' an honourable command to march into Paris with'.[111]

The losses sustained by the 2nd Battalion 73rd were the worst they had experienced. Out of 558 men, forty-seven officers and men were killed, while twenty-three died of their wounds. Sixty-two were so badly wounded they had to be pensioned off, and eighty-two were wounded but continued to serve.[112] Major Archibald Maclaine died of his wounds; Lieutenant Colonel Harris had been wounded in the shoulder by a musket ball, 'which afterwards subjected him to a long and painful confinement'.[113] Captain John Garland, who had been carried off the field of battle by the two Morris brothers with a fractured thigh bone, was told that amputation was 'indispensable'; but, 'objecting to the loss of a limb, by the most assiduous and eminent skill, in a twelvemonth he was sufficiently recovered to be removed, he being the last wounded officer who left Brussels'.[114] He lived for another thirty-five years. Morris, wounded in the cheek with a piece of metal, had it removed the following evening.

Sergeant Major William Ballam was killed instantly when a bullet struck him on the nose. As Morris related, with men falling so fast throughout the day, Ballam, who had fought in the Peninsula with another regiment, had turned to Colonel Harris, saying: 'We had nothing in Spain like this, Sir.'[115] Ensign and adjutant Patrick Hay, former assistant surgeon, was 'dangerously wounded' in his left arm.[116] A surprising survival was William Robinson, who had enlisted with the 2nd Battalion 73rd in 1813 and been present at the siege of Antwerp. According to Morris, when he saw Robinson shot in the eye, he had assumed that he was dead. 'Judge then my surprise when he joined us at Paris! The ball was still in his head, and could not be extracted. He was not fit for duty, and was sent to England.' Contrary to Morris's earlier claims that he died 'a few months later', he lived until 1880, dying at the age of eighty-five.[117] Another notable survivor was the Jamaican-born 'man of colour' and former slave George Rose, who had earned his freedom by enlisting in the 2nd Battalion 73rd in August 1809. Having fought in the campaigns of 1813 in Germany and 1814 in the Netherlands, where he was first wounded, he was severely wounded in the right arm at Waterloo.[118] The longest-lived British veteran who fought at Waterloo was believed to be Private Maurice Shea of the 73rd, who died in 1892 in Canada aged ninety-seven.[119]

Victory in Paris

Leaving the field of battle around midday on 19 June, the victorious soldiers found that 'the road for miles bore traces of the horrors of war'. Marching about thirty miles each day, they headed towards Paris. As Morris pointed out to future readers of his memoir, 'it was of importance that we should reach Paris before the scattered French troops could have time to rally'.[120] But the French did not rally. Instead, with the Grand Allied Army on the doorstep of Paris, the Chamber of Deputies surrendered. On 24 June 1815, Napoleon abdicated for the second time. As far as Robert Blantyre – the 2nd Battalion 42nd's former Commanding Officer – was concerned, if Napoleon 'had had a proper degree of spirit, he ought to have died on the field of Battle at Waterloo – rather than live to recount his own disgrace to the Chambers in Paris'.[121] Louis XVIII was once more reinstated as King of France. 'The caricatures more or less offensive towards the Princes of the House of Bourbon,' noted the French *Journal de l'Empire*, 'which the dealers in prints have been in the habit of displaying, have now nearly all disappeared.'[122]

Having reached the outskirts of Paris, the victors encamped on the banks of the river Seine. 'Indeed,' noted Gunn, 'we were enjoying the luxury of Bathing here.' According to Morris, no British troops were quartered in Paris, 'that privilege being reserved for the Prussians', who had reached Paris first. Instead they were camped in the Bois de Boulogne, just west of the city. 'We had been through three campaigns, and never till now had we the privilege of sleeping under tents, excepting such as we had formed with our blankets.'[123] Allowed to visit Paris in groups, 'we went into a wine house of course where a number of French men was also enjoying themselves. The manner of drinking there is every Man having his own tumbler instead of saying "to your good health", he touches your glass with his; in going to drink mine I said as I best could "Vive Napoleon"; there then were such a touching of tumblers and a free offer of their contents as did credit to their owners for their can be no doubt but the French loved their Emperor.'[124] 'No doubt, you will amuse yourself well at Paris,' Huntly, the Regiment's Colonel since 1806, wrote to Robert Henry Dick in August. 'Remember me kindly to all the Officers and tell them as well as all Highlanders, that I am going to build on a high hill near this a Monument to the Memory of the brave highlanders who fell at Waterloo.'[125]

To conclude the victory celebrations there were several 'grand reviews' attended by European royalty.[126] A Field Day was held to resemble the recently fought 'Battle of Waterloo'. 'The Prince of Orange, with a vast number of distinguished persons, were present, and the affair went off with the greatest éclat,' recollected Morris.[127] On parade, Gunn observed the 'smart, active-looking' Prussians: 'I never did see any men marching with such precision. Indeed compared with [us] they might well [be] called Giants but I hope that it might and still be said of the British soldier what was said of Rob Rorison's bonnet that it was not the bonnet but the head that was in it – that it was not the size of his body but the soul that was in it.'[128] 'Returning to our Camp, our band struck up "The Downfall of Paris".' But, said Gunn, the music was ill-timed 'and our Colonel was not pleased at it, the French knowing the tune well and we were now on the eve of bidding farewell to Paris and pretty France'.[129]

In October, as the weather turned cold, the British camp in the Bois de Boulogne was broken up. Some regiments returned to England, while the remaining troops went into quarters around Paris. One task which the 73rd undertook was supervising the removal and return of four bronze horses, dating from classical antiquity, which Napoleon had taken from the Basilica San Marco in Venice in 1797.[130] In November 1815 the 42nd began the return home, via Calais. The first day's march was to St Germain. 'Here we were quartered in a large brick building, said to be our King James's palace, built by the French for him and said to be haunted,' recalled Gunn. 'The men diverted themselves by making a noise and saying "Here comes the Stuarts back again."'[131]

The 2nd Battalion 73rd remained a month longer as part of the Allied army garrisoning France. Stationed at St Rémy, Sergeant Thomas Morris was sent on detachment to a nearby mill. 'Our duty here was very light, as we had only to furnish a regimental and a beacon guard, the latter on the top of a very high hill, thickly studded with trees and bushes on the sides, but the top having a large flat surface, and there the beacon was erected.' As he related, a sentry was ordered to stand near by, 'with instructions to keep his eye on a similar object in the distance; and if he saw that one fire, he was to call out the guard, and the non-commissioned officer would set fire to his beacon, which would then be perceived and answered by some on the other side of us. Any insurrection or outbreak would have been thus immediately communicated to the proper authorities.'[132] In late November there was heavy snow: 'the beacon guard was not the most pleasant position to be placed in for twenty-four hours; and the journey to and from it, through the snow, was both difficult and dangerous.'[133]

In early December 1815 the 2nd Battalion 73rd received orders to return home. Marching via Versailles, St Denis and Abbeville, they met 'great quantities of Napoleon's disbanded troops'.[134] At Calais, on the morning of 23 December, they took passage to Dover, but bad weather meant they landed at Ramsgate. Morris and many like him were well pleased at the prospect of peace: 'Oh! How sweet the name of home, and how pleasant the hope of again seeing those from whom we had been separated, and whom the changes of war had rendered it at times extremely doubtful if we should ever see again.'[135] Having arrived back in England just before Christmas, the Battalion marched from Ramsgate to Colchester to join the depot. Throughout 1816, it was quartered in Nottingham, Weedon and Colchester. In the same year, instead of being known as the 73rd Highland Regiment, the order was given for it to be known only as the 73rd Regiment of Foot. In May 1817, while stationed at Chelmsford, the 2nd Battalion 73rd was disbanded.[136]

Despite the heavy losses on all sides, Morris considered they had fought a 'just and necessary war; there being no other means of restoring the balance of power among the continental nations, and of bringing about an honourable peace'.[137] By Royal Authority, both the 42nd and the 2nd Battalion 73rd, together with other regiments, were permitted to bear the word *Waterloo* on their Colours. As pointed out by historian Forbes, since the 42nd was not as heavily engaged at Waterloo as at Quatre Bras, the award of *Waterloo* on the Regimental Colour 'commemorates the gallantry it displayed at Quatre Bras'.[138]

Each subaltern officer and soldier present on the field of battle was permitted to count two years' additional service to his record. Between 1816 and 1817, 39,000 commemorative silver medals were struck. Known as the 'Waterloo Medal', on one side there was an impression of the Prince Regent, the future King George IV. On the reverse side was the figure of Victory, holding a palm in the right hand and an olive branch in the left. The word 'Wellington' was inscribed over Victory's head, with the words 'Waterloo! 18th June, 1815' at the feet.[139] It was the first medal given to all those who had served at Ligny, Quatre Bras or Waterloo, and the first medal to be awarded to the next of kin of those killed in action.[140] Among the thousands who received the Waterloo Medal were the two Morris brothers who, despite their worst fears, had both survived.[141]

15.

The Long Peace

The braw Red hackle honours badge
And emblem of the brave
That proudly leads the way where er
Their dark green tartans wave.[1]

'A Grateful Country'

In Europe, the events of 1815 marked a watershed. The Napoleonic Wars were the last time Britain and France fought on opposing sides. For those accustomed to a generation of warfare, there was now the prospect of 'the long peace'. Having left France in November 1815, the 42nd Royal Highland Regiment reached Scotland the following spring. 'Our reception in Edinburgh was extraordinary,' recollected Private James Gunn, 'the crowd on Castle Hill being so dense that several of our men were carried off their feet.'[2] 'We entered the city amidst the loud cheering and congratulatory acclamations of friends,' recorded Anton; 'while over our heads, from a thousand windows, waved as many banners, plaided scarfs or other symbols of courtly greetings. We entered the castle, proud of the most distinguished reception that ever a regiment had met with from a grateful country.'[3]

For officers and soldiers, peacetime meant a change of uniform, which became more elaborate, appropriate for parades and guard duty rather than active service. Anton was not pleased. 'The plaid at one time consisted of eight yards of tartan, and served instead of a great-coat or blanket; it now consists of a yard and one quarter, a useless shred of cloth, like a child's pinafore reversed, and pinned to the back of the shoulder.' The bonnet, mounted on a wire cage, and covered in feathers, had an opening at the right side known as a 'craw's wing', leaving soldiers 'grinning and cursing at their ineffectual struggles to keep their heads covered'.[4] By 1817, according to historian Forbes, for active service the kilt 'seems to have fallen into disuse, for the officers of the 42nd wore sky-blue trousers laced with gold, and these with the feather-bonnet! . . . the officers' coatees were very richly laced, and officers of all ranks wore heavy bullion epaulettes', later exchanged for 'wings'.[5]

After a year in Edinburgh, the Regiment moved to Glasgow, where there was frequent rioting by the working classes because of the harshness of their lives, unemployment and rising food prices. Instead of listening to the demands of the groups demanding reforms, the government's response was to crush the dissent militarily. 'About the commencement of 1817,' recalled Anton, 'the spirit of disaffection began to assume a more offensive aspect than for some weeks previously; and, excited by itinerant orators and delegates, from kindred associations at Manchester and other manufacturing towns, it seemed to feel secure in the strength of its numbers, and in the stability of its widely spreading ramifications.'[6] In addition to quelling riotous gatherings, another duty was dispersing 'meal mobs', when starving groups of people would attack the carts carrying oatmeal into town. 'There being no properly organized police force, the Military were often called upon to assist the weak Civil authorities.'[7]

Meanwhile, thanks to the mediation of Prince Frederick, Duke of York, President of the Highland Society (and under whose command the 42nd had fought in Flanders in the 1790s), the feud over the 'Invincible Standard' was set aside. On 21 March 1817 – the sixteenth anniversary of Alexandria – having praised the Royal Highlanders' services since 1739, the Duke had the 'delightful duty' of presenting a massive silver vase, weighing nearly fifty pounds, to the Marquis of Huntly, the Colonel of the Regiment, 'in acknowledgement of the high sense entertained by the society of the brilliant achievements of that distinguished corps'.[8] Like the medal, struck to commemorate the Battle of Alexandria, it had been designed by Sir Benjamin West.

Supported on a triangular plinth, the vase had a fluted bowl, decorated with thistle foliage, 'encircled with laurel and supported by an ancient and modern Highlander with appropriate emblems'. For men like Major Mungo Macpherson, who had fought at Alexandria, there was special meaning: on one face was a replica of Abercromby's head, with the inscription 'Abercrombius Dux in Egypto cecedit victor [Abercromby, Commander in Egypt, the victor has fallen], 21 Mar. 1801.' On another face was the reverse of the commemorative medal, representing the taking of the Invincible Standard, which bore the inscription: 'Na tir a chaisin buardh san eiphart [The lads who gained glory in Egypt] 21 Mar. 1801.' The third face was inscribed with the words: 'O'Chummum Gaidheulach d'an Threiadan Dubh na 42nd Regiment [From the Highland Society to 42nd Regiment].'[9]

On 1 May 1817, while the Regiment was in Glasgow, John Wheatley, not yet seventeen, enlisted as a private soldier. Even in peacetime, the process of becoming a soldier was rapid. A young recruit, he noted, 'might be enlisted on Thursday, attested on Friday, and find himself at drill in kilt, shoes with buckles, and next day out seeing his friends displaying his feather'd bonnet, etc.'[10] Another new recruit – although veteran soldier – was the Jamaican, George Rose, who had served with the 2nd Battalion 73rd. Although, when the Battalion was disbanded in 1817, most had joined the 1st Battalion in Ceylon, Rose transferred to the 42nd, serving for another twenty years and earning a place in Regimental history as one of the 'very few men' known to have served in both the 73rd and the 42nd.[11]

Disturbed Times: Ireland

The 42nd 1817–1825; the 73rd 1823–1827

After nearly two years in Scotland, the 42nd was sent to Ireland during a period of strife known as the 'disturbed times'.[12] Agrarian unrest, prevalent in the previous century, had not abated. Crops in 1816 were bad; famine and sickness created misery among the poor. The secret society of the 'Whiteboys', farmers in their white smocks, who had resorted to violence to defend tenant farmers against rich landlords, was still active. The 42nd's destination was Armagh, requiring 'three long marches', a distance of nearly sixty miles. Detachments were sent throughout Ireland, to Newry, Donegal and Tyrone. Food for the soldiers was even scarcer than in Britain. 'Such was the high price of provisions that the Irish Government had to add three pence a day to the pay of the soldiers serving in the Ulster district, as temporary relief.'[13] As a young soldier, Wheatley found it tiring marching in the heat of summer, carrying the heavy 'Brown

Bess', 'never having had one drill with arms'. Not least of his complaints was wearing the new bonnet, 'rounded the shape of no human head ... without a chin strap', which, on a windy day, rendered 'the long day's march a perfect misery. Only imagine a youth of not 16 and a half year of age toiling under such an equipment, encouraged by the Old Soldiers, hardy Peninsular and Waterloo men.'[14]

Like his predecessors, Wheatley discovered that virtually every soldier ended up in debt to the pay sergeant due to the continuing system which left him as the middleman in any transaction. Even if men got out of debt, 'many of them again drifted into it in a very short time, and continued going on in the same way, until they became poor emaciated creatures unfit for service, and discharged without, or on very small pensions'. In general, spare money was spent 'in dissipation'. If a young recruit was 'detected eating at an unusual time, [he] was very apt to be hailed with a volley of not the most elegant language as to "why he did not spend his pay like a soldier," the meaning of which was in drink.'[15]

At Armagh, on 18 June 1817, the second anniversary of Waterloo, the Highland Society Vase was presented to the Regiment.[16] 'The parade was in review order, in side arms, and a square of two deep was formed. On a table in the centre was the vase, covered, and several small kegs of Highland whisky, brought over from Scotland for the express purpose.' After Dick addressed the officers and men, 'the casks of whisky were broached, and the cup filled'. The 'day of the Cup' was long remembered 'as to the quality and quantity of the whisky'.[17] During this time Dick undertook to reconstruct the Regimental history, damaged in 1771 and lost in 1794. The person he turned to was Brevet Colonel David Stewart of Garth 'to supply him with some notices on the subject'. 'After some hesitation and delay, I commenced; but merely with the intention of noting down as much as would cover about thirty or forty pages of the record book,' Stewart noted, 'but as I proceeded, I found that I knew more, and had a better recollection of circumstances, than I was previously aware of, although, in the multiplicity of facts I have had to state, some inaccuracies may afterwards be discovered.'[18]

An unpopular duty in Armagh was guarding a magazine of ammunition, where 'with barely a separation, not even a wall, [there] was a burying-ground, with monuments and grave stones fully in view, and great was the terror to have the magazine allotted as a nightly post, particularly from 11 to midnight or the next relief, one to three, and it was often afterwards admitted that it lay heavy on some minds the fear of that post,' especially for the younger men who believed in 'ghosts, and other nightly spiritual visitants'.[19] Another hardship was the cold. One instance of discomfort was duty at Omagh Gaol. Situated on an exposed height in midwinter, 'little attention was paid to the comfort of the men, always with the thin hose, and long quartered shoes and buckles, whereas they might well have been in greatcoats, trews, and gaiters, in such an out-of-the-way place as Omagh, but such was the zeal of some of the Sergeants of the Guard, that the greatcoats had to be donned by the reliefs at 7 o'clock in the morning and the full dress kept on until 7 in the evening. Anything more stupid in such a place and during such a winter can hardly be imagined, yet it was more the fault of the system than of the individuals.'[20]

So afraid was the sergeant major or corporal of being reduced to a private that he would rarely, if ever, risk taking responsibility for changing established procedure. The barracks were 'always crowded to excess with 21 men, and three or four women, the latter in the corner under berths, with single men above, and next to them below'. The berths amounted to 'wooden erections made for two men to sleep together below, and two more above'. In general men preferred the upper berth 'because the lower had to put up with the dust etc., that came from above'.[21]

In late June 1818, the Regiment moved to Dundalk, 'the assize or chief town' in County Louth, where it appears new Colours were presented, although no record remains of their presentation, and where another grisly assignment awaited the soldiers.[22] The detachments from Dundalk were to do duty over the gibbeted bodies of the culprits hanged for the 'Wild Goose Lodge' murders – an episode resulting in the conviction of several men for setting fire to a farmhouse containing thirteen 'souls beneath a blazing roof, supplicating cries of mercy'. If the soldiers found the posting at the ammunition magazine near the cemetery at Armagh 'a trial', recollected Wheatley, 'sentries posted at the dead hour of night over gibbeted bodies was if anything more horrible'.[23] Most soldiers were illiterate and consequently superstitious. 'Neither books [n]or newspapers were ever seen in a barrack room. A very few men might at times be seen reading their bible, but it would hardly do to record the almost general opinion regarding them, and farther it is an established truth that children and young people brought up under the influence of "ghost" and "fairie" stories have ever after a dread about them, about the midnight hours and in lone places, which is not to be overcome, however far they may reason on the subject, therefore the detachment where the gibbets were, were held in much dread.'[24] While the Regiment remained in Dundalk, trials for the murders continued. 'Unhappy Ireland,' Wheatley commented in later life, 'the number of executions in Ireland at this time would hardly be believed by the present generation.' The gibbeted bodies, which became skeletons 'creaking in their chains', were not removed until 1820.[25]

In July a detachment was sent to Drogheda, south of Louth, 'in consequence of some rioting at an election', but on arrival James Anton recorded that 'all was as quietly disposed as could be expected at a contested election'.[26] Wheatley considered it 'a favourite quarters, provisions cheap, and duty moderately easy, notwithstanding gaol and custom house guards'.[27] Old Bridgetown (Oldbridge) – the scene of the famous Battle of the Boyne – was three miles west of Drogheda 'and was a pleasant walk, often made during the summer'.[28]

In December 1818 the Regiment moved to Newry. Sent in detachments around County Cavan, as Wheatley related, 'there being no barrack at any of those stations, the men were in private houses in parties of from 2 to 5 – the inhabitants glad to have them on account of the small allowance of two pence a day for each man for fuel, and 6d per week for lodging; small as it appears in a poor country town where fuel was cheap at the end of the quarter it came to what was looked upon as something considerable by people in poor circumstances.'[29] While in County Cavan, their responsibilities included keeping the peace between the Protestant 'yeoman' Orangemen and the Roman Catholics. 'In those places,' recollected Anton, 'many connexions were formed, and our female followers increased considerably.'[30]

Posted to Dublin the following year, on 29 May 1819 the garrison assembled in the large expanse of Phoenix Park, north-west of Dublin, to fire three rounds to mark the 159th anniversary of Charles II's restoration to the throne of Britain, on his thirtieth birthday in 1660, following nine years in exile. Celebrated as Oak Apple Day, it was a public holiday. While on parade, Dick noticed that the firing was irregular; he therefore ordered the soldiers' firelocks to be examined to determine which soldiers – eager to save themselves the trouble of cleaning their muskets after the parade – had not fired. Those who were found to have clean muskets had to miss dinner, being 'kept on the parade ground until 15 rounds per man was brought from the Magazine'. As Wheatley recounted, 'it stood as a warning for many years'.[31]

'Dublin duty' required even stricter adherence to 'the etiquette of dress and formality, than any other garrison on home service', recorded Anton. 'Each regiment of infantry, and there are generally six in the garrison, furnishes in rotation the colours and band of music that accompany the guard from the parade to the castle; and, on these occasions, the musicians are expected to appear in what may be called their state dress.'[32]

While in Dublin, directions 'considered in future as the Standing Orders of the Regiment' were issued. 'Loose habits,' the men were informed, 'take almost always their source at the private Parades and Inspections when Officers are apt to forget themselves and never to consider what infinite mischief arises to the general correctness of the Regiment by slovenly habits.'[33] A particular offence, warranting immediate arrest, was for an officer to be seen 'in Dublin Streets in plain clothes'.[34] A 'breakfast mess' was established. Previously the soldiers had eaten what they wanted. 'Bread and water satisfied some, while others indulged themselves according to their taste, or ability, to procure what was agreeable to them.' But, observed Anton, the breakfast mess was 'no great blessing' since it prevented soldiers' widows from earning 'a scanty subsistence, by selling coffee ready prepared, together with a slice of bread, if wanted'. Once introduced, the breakfast mess became 'almost indispensable'.[35]

At the beginning of 1820, Huntly retired after fourteen years as Colonel of the Regiment. The new Colonel was fifty-four-year-old General John Hope, now 4th Earl of Hopetoun and who had taken command at Corunna when Moore was killed and Baird seriously wounded.[36] Receiving news of Hopetoun's appointment, Dick wrote approvingly, saying the Highlanders felt 'very sensibly the Honor His Majesty has been pleased to confer' and assuring 'their conduct will always be such, as to meet your approbation'.[37]

In August – after fourteen months in Dublin – the Regiment marched to Kilkenny, the main town in Tipperary. Five companies were posted to Clonmel. At this time, noted Wheatley, 'the unseemly "craw's wing"' of the bonnet disappeared, to be replaced by foxtails, previously only worn by sergeants, bandsmen and drummers, 'and cheerfully the men paid the thirty to thirty five shillings which each bonnet cost. How the hideous article existed so long was a wonder to many, it was the laughing stock of the other highland regiments.'[38] For the first time a white jacket was worn with the kilt, which at first was considered strange.[39]

A resurgence of 'Whiteboy' activity meant that in October 1821 the Regiment marched to Rathkeale, eighteen and a half miles from Limerick. 'This march was made in heavy roads, it may be said in winter, and without any falling out, no squad bags at this time, each man carried his all ready to be sent anywhere.'[40] The trouble had begun because of the 'firmness, or possibly ill-timed severity' of a land agent, recorded Wheatley. 'His son was shot on the highway in noon day, the houses of gentlemen were forcibly plundered of arms, money extorted, and the owners sworn not to prosecute, and the servants warned on their lives not to come forward as evidences.' No action could be taken against the offenders, 'although a reward of one thousand pounds was offered – such was the terror by which the minds of the peasantry was influenced'.[41] Part of the problem was that, under the prevailing laws, the 'Whiteboys' could not be prosecuted unless they were found with weapons.

In 1822 the Insurrection Act was passed, imposing, amongst other provisions, a curfew on certain districts; public gatherings in places where 'malt liquors and spirituous liquors' were found were forbidden. Most importantly, authorisation was given to seize 'any Arms or Ammunition, or Pike, Pike Head, Spear, Dirk or any other offence Weapon of any kind whatsoever, concealed or otherwise'.[42] Once the act became law, Wheatley described the effect on the state of the country as 'wonderful in a very short time'.[43] Despite the Army's strong measures, he recorded that good feeling was shown towards the Regiment due to the 'charitable kindness of Colonel and Mrs Dick at Rathkeal[e]; whose indefatigable assistance to the poor was continued during the entire winter, and it has been stated on undoubted authority that even when opportunities offered, they, the Whiteboys, have remarked "them are Colonel Dick's, let them alone."'[44]

In July 1822, after numerous sorties against the Whiteboys, the 42nd was ordered to Limerick. 'Being fine summer weather and the country more tranquil, it was with some regret that the banks of the Shannon were departed from.' Several decades later, Wheatley returned to the town of Glin, 'a nest of Whiteboys', and 'the most miserable of villages, a mass of poverty and squalor', where his company had been on detachment. 'It was the same dilapidated, miserable place or if anything worse as time had shown its marks on many of the houses.' Standing 'full of thoughts of the past', Wheatley spoke with two old men, who remembered how the Highlanders had occupied a particular house 'in the disturbed times'. Describing the 'Peticoat men' as 'nice', Wheatley was pleased to hear his Regiment complimented, without having given 'even a hint of any discription' that he had been one of them.[45]

While at Limerick, news reached the Regiment that, from a direction in the newly introduced Army Dress Regulations, some of the other Highland Regiments believed they too had a right to wear a 'red vulture feather'. Mindful of the honour believed to have been granted to the 42nd on the King's birthday in 1795, the Royal Highlanders remonstrated, which elicited a memorandum signed by the Adjutant-General: 'The Red Vulture Feather, prescribed by the recent Regulations for Highland Regiments is intended to be used exclusively by the 42nd Regiment: – other Highland Corps will be allowed to continue to wear the same description of Feather that may have been hitherto in use.'[46] Making his own inquiries, Lieutenant Colonel Dick, who himself thought that the distinction of wearing a red feather had been gained 'for taking or defeating a regiment of Grenadiers', wrote to the Regiment's former commanding officer Major General James Stirling asking for his version of events. Stirling's response, making no mention of Geldermalsen, was a variation on the belief, described by Stewart of Garth in his history, recently published, concerning the introduction of the custom of wearing a red feather during the American War for Independence.

'The origins of their wearing this feather,' he responded, 'commenced early in the American War of 1776 when the Regiment was Brigaded with the Grenadiers and a light infantry of the army under the command of the late Marquis Cornwallis. At this period there were no regulation feathers. The Grenadiers wore White Feathers, the first battalion light infantry wore Green. The second battalion wore Red, and to make the whole uniform, General Sir William Howe, ordered the 42nd to get Red feathers.' Stirling attributed the official authorisation not to the parade at Royston in 1795, but to 1802: 'When the Regiment arrived in England from Egypt they were reviewed by His late Majesty and Colonel Dickson who then commanded them asked His Majesty's permission for the regiment to wear the Red Feather, in which his Majesty graciously granted.' With this correspondence, the extent of inquiry has rested, its true origins still unknown. 'Sadly,' Colonel the Hon. David Arbuthnott wrote in 1982, 'there is no short and glamorous answer to the question "How did The Black Watch get the Red Hackle?"'[47] Whatever the reasons, the Red Hackle remains a powerful inspiration to the men who proudly wear it.

While Dick was inquiring about the Red Hackle's origins, the Regiment had remained in Ireland. 'Winter and spring passed over, witnessing innumerable patrols of infantry perambulating the half-flooded face of the country,' recorded James Anton, 'alarming the peaceable and annoying the turbulent by repeated nocturnal visits. Summer at last brought fair weather.'[48] In July 1823 the Regiment marched to Buttevant, in northern County Cork, and afterwards 'occupied many detached stations in the county of Cork', where, asserted the *Historical Record*, 'it preserved its high reputation for correct discipline, and for general efficiency'.[49] But, recollected Wheatley, there was 'much unnecessary duty of patroles, and every day parades'.[50]

Meanwhile, in 1821 the 73rd Regiment, in Ceylon since 1814, had been ordered home. All those fit for service in a tropical climate could volunteer to join Regiments already in Ceylon or to any Regiment 'in the territories of the East India Company'.[51] Arriving at Gravesend, the Regiment, reduced to eight companies, went first to Weedon, from where detachments were sent to Wolverhampton, Dudley and Chester. It then served in Hull, with a detachment in Northumberland, before being ordered in June 1823, for the first time since 1809, to take up quarters in Edinburgh Castle. In December the soldiers embarked at Portpatrick for Ireland, where the 42nd was still stationed. The 73rd remained in Athlone until July 1825, when it was posted to Naas with detachments at Wicklow and Drogheda in County Meath.

In 1825 all Regiments of the Line were increased to ten companies. When abroad, these were divided into six service and four reserve companies. When the 42nd returned to Dublin in July 1825 its four 'depot' companies embarked for Scotland. The six service companies proceeded to Gibraltar. Before embarking at Cork, the Regiment was issued with new weapons to replace those in use since the Peninsular War, 'and dreadful old things they were,' commented Wheatley. 'It was quite a common occasion for a quantity of the powder to get down the lock from the pan (priming place) and on the triggers being drawn to have the lock blown off from the stock.' In place of these antiquated weapons, the soldiers were supplied with what Wheatley called the 'Long Land Tower': 'instead of a polished lock they were bronzed, but it was heavier and particularly unwieldy for short or very young soldiers.' As he surmised, the issuance of more modern weapons was thanks to the influence of the Regiment's Colonel, Major General Sir George Murray, who was Master General of the Ordnance and had replaced Hopetoun as Colonel in August 1823. 'The same arm as was in use by the Guards only at this time.'[52]

In November the 73rd moved to the Royal Barracks at Dublin, recently vacated by the 42nd. There the Regiment remained until May 1826, 'when in consequence of riots in the manufacturing towns in Lancashire and Yorkshire' it returned to England. Once the situation was quiet, the 73rd returned briefly to Dublin and then back to Naas. At Waterford, in 1827, new Colours were presented by Lieutenant Colonel O'Connell's wife, the 'headstrong' Mary, daughter of William Bligh, who had died in 1817.[53]

Mediterranean Routine:

Gibraltar: the 42nd 1825–32; the 73rd 1827–29
Malta: the 42nd 1832–34; the 73rd 1829–34
Ionian Islands: the 42nd 1834–36; the 73rd 1834–38

While the 73rd Regiment remained in Ireland, the 42nd was travelling to Gibraltar. As always, a journey by sea in cramped conditions had its discomforts. Before long, half of the soldiers 'were prostrated with sea sickness. The violent movements of the ship deranged everything,' Wheatley recorded. 'None of the sick men were able to appear till induced to crawl up to see the Coast of Spain.'[54] In mid-December they reached Gibraltar. Anton, with his literary flair, described their arrival: 'The sun was rising on the horizon, as our vessel, borne on the rippling stream, first caught a view of the gray rock for which we were bound. Not a breeze ruffled the face of the wide opening bay.'[55] Once on shore, they proceeded to Windmill Hill Barracks. Their first casualty occurred when 'a fine young man of the Light Company, attempting to get off Windmill Hill, being refused to go out at the barriers, being drunk, fell over the Rock and was killed on the spot'.[56]

Six regiments were stationed in Gibraltar. 'The rations rather astonished us new arrivals, six days salt meat, Beef or Pork in the week, only one day of fresh meat – many of the salt meat barrels were marked 1812 and 14, and something could be made of the Pork but the Beef was what the men named "The Mahogany." As to the fresh [meat] it was so blubbery and it shook so, that it would hardly lye on the hand barrow carrying it [to] the cook house.' As the men discovered, the reason for the poor-quality meat was that there was an epidemic in North Africa and a strict quarantine was being enforced on all vessels. Since most of the meat came from North Africa, 'good beef was seldom seen in the market'.[57] After some time, fresh meat days were increased to two per week and the quality of the meat improved.[58]

New arrivals had to buy 'three mules, three carts with harness, two asses with pack-saddles and cross-trees, and about fifty water kegs, each holding about five gallons'. As he explained, this constituted the Regiment's 'watering establishment'. Depending on the price of the animals and the chance of taking the place of another regiment, the cost was 'about two hundred pounds'. To defray expenses, 'every soldier is charged about five pence per month, and the officers in proportion to the number of kegs required'.[59] In 1826 white gaiters or 'spats' came into use, and the sergeants still wore silver lace until 1830.[60]

Having briefly been in Ireland together, the paths of the 42nd and 73rd crossed again when, in September 1827, the 73rd arrived in Gibraltar. Both regiments were among those who suffered the following year from another severe outbreak of yellow fever. 'In the end of July,' recorded Anton, 'or about the beginning of August, 1828, the Swedish vessel *Deigden*, from Havannah, entered the bay, was placed in quarantine, and notwithstanding that some of the hands had died on the voyage, the master had, by some means, got sailors to fill up their place on the ship's books, and no apparent cause existing to keep her from port, after a few days she was admitted.'[61]

The epidemic was sufficiently serious for the Spanish authorities to place a *cordon sanitaire* around the Rock. Provisions were placed on 'the neutral ground', a strip of land between the Spanish frontier and where British authority began. 'The bargains struck, and a bawling traffic it was, the articles carried away and the money put down on the same spot, but not touched by the Spaniards, but with a pair of tongs passed through a bucket of vinegar and then handed to the owner – this traffic for fruit and all description of vegetables commenced daily at day-break and was the amusing resort of the officers and men for hours.'[62] 'The articles brought for sale, were chiefly provisions of all sorts usually brought to market, vegetables, provender for cattle, and fuel,' Anton recorded.[63]

'In the cemetery, the grave was always ready,' recollected Wheatley, 'a long deep reach, in which all were laid, nor were any honours paid to officers or private, all funeral parade was stopped. Not a soldier accompanied the coffin. The wagon driver was the only mourner from the hospital to the grave.'[64] 'As the contagion increased,' noted Anton, 'the gloom became more apparent, those in health took copious draughts, either of medicine or brandy, as antidotes.' Surprisingly, those who died were 'the strongest men' and very few women and children.[65] During the epidemic, one ensign, six sergeants and fifty-three soldiers of the 42nd died.[66]

The 73rd was likewise affected, although fatalities were fewer, the 'talents' of the surgeon George Martin being acknowledged 'in the most public manner'. Out of the nine officers and 196 soldiers who fell ill, two died, including the assistant surgeon, John Gordon Fraser, 'who fell a victim to his zeal for the service', and thirty-five soldiers.[67] After over two years, the 73rd left Gibraltar for a posting in Malta, the soldiers praised for 'their regular and orderly conduct'.[68]

Meanwhile, a further directive was issued regarding the soldiers' bonnets and cockades of all Highland Regiments in response to the suggestion that, in addition to paying for the regular bonnets and cockades, the Colonels should also be expected to pay for the ostrich feathers with which Highland Regiments had become accustomed to dressing their bonnets. Although, as the Adjutant General pointed out, recruits on first joining would have to defray the additional expense, this was only a 'temporary inconvenience' since ostrich feathers were 'calculated to last many years'. He therefore believed that the arrangement which had already been in practice, whereby the soldiers themselves paid for the ostrich feathers, should be continued![69]

In November 1828, after over thirteen years, Lieutenant Colonel Robert Henry Dick went onto half-pay. The new Commanding Officer of the 42nd was the Hon. Sir Charles Gordon, who came from being on half-pay with the 93rd. According to Wheatley, realising the boredom of life on the Rock, Gordon 'commenced a correspondence relative to the soldiers being permitted, with passes to go to Algeçiras and San Roque for the day, dwelling strongly on the monotonous life of the men kept for 12 or 14 years within the compass of the Garrison. Not even the Sergeant Major could pass out at Waterport or Bayside without producing a pass signed by the Town Major.'[70] The reason for such strict procedure was that once a British soldier set foot on Spanish soil he might refuse to return. Instead of forcing them to return, 'the Spanish guards would turn out for their protection. They were often fired at by our own guards, but "Old Brown Bess" was next to useless after 150 or 200 yards, therefore they always escaped.' To Wheatley's knowledge, three members of the 42nd reached Madrid. Having crossed the Pyrenees, they went to Bordeaux and finally to England. 'Two of them afterwards surrendered themselves at home, and were sent back with a draft and tried by a Court Martial at Gibraltar.'[71]

Gordon's proposal for the men to go on leave in Spain was approved for a trial period, although a number of soldiers did not return and the privilege was withdrawn. 'If a man repented of the step he had taken and was still at Algeçiras, by taking him before the English Consul and his declaration being taken that he wished to return to Gibraltar, he was permitted to do so, and many were recovered in this way. There were instances when individuals said that they would not go back, of the party purposely making him drunk, under the plea of friendship in parting, and lugging him to the boat.'[72]

In July 1830, Gordon and the Adjutant, William Macfarlane, went on leave for a year, leaving the Regiment under the command of Major Hugh Andrew Fraser of Milford. As Wheatley related, the period was called the 'reign of terror' by both officers and men, 'and in naming it so, was no far-fetched idea'. During his command, there were numerous episodes of 'intemperate behaviour, violent language and threats by the Major that the morale of the regiment was greatly impaired'.[73] In Fraser's defence, Wheatley noted that 'he had seen much service in the Peninsula and at Waterloo and was frequently wounded, one severe wound in his loins was always open, and was said as the cause, in a great measure, of the irritability of his temper. Such may have been the case, but from whatever his bad temper arose, from constitutional or otherwise, he was the cause of much unhappiness.'[74] A happier recollection was Gordon's patronage of the formation of the 'famous Regimental Library, which was kept up, always in good order, until the month before the embarkation for the east in 1854'.

Having failed in his proposal for the men to be given passes to go on leave in Spain, Gordon then suggested a 'Mediterranean routine system' so that, instead of remaining indefinitely in one location, with its attendant boredom, service abroad was divided between Gibraltar, Malta and the Ionian Islands.[75] In late 1831, after over six years in Gibraltar, the 42nd was ordered to embark for Malta, one thousand miles to the east, arriving 'safely' in January 1832. Having spent nearly seven years in Gibraltar, the soldiers were put into quarantine lest there was any residual yellow fever. In Malta their appearance in kilts aroused the customary local interest. 'Great was the excitement . . . Heard of, but never before seen in Malta by the present generation.'[76]

Already present in Malta was the 73rd. In 1830 Lieutenant Colonel O'Connell was promoted major general, which meant bidding farewell to 'a corps, endeared to him by all those sacred ties which bind the members of a family together, and which have, in their fullest sense, existed between him and the regiment for a period of nearly twenty-five years'.[77] His successor was James McNair, who had fought at Waterloo in the 52nd.[78] The Regiment's Colonel, General George Lord Harris, had died in May 1829, aged eighty-two. His successor was Major General Sir Frederick Adam.[79] When Adam subsequently transferred to another regiment, he was succeeded by Harris's son, Major General William George Lord Harris, the Regiment's former Commanding Officer, who had fought at Waterloo.

Having served for fifteen years in the 42nd, on 20 July 1832 Wheatley received his commission as an ensign and was appointed adjutant. Without referring directly to his status in his memoirs, he indicated the 'great change' caused by the promotion of a non-commissioned officer. 'It may be truly said that his entire ideas of social life are, or require to be changed much, as he may have before seen of the Officers, he at once finds himself in a hitherto unknown state of society. All is different from what he came from, if observant, and observant he ought to be. He will soon appreciate his new life, and it only requires to be somewhat retiring and unobtrusive for a time, indeed perhaps always, to be well-received and happy in his new line of life.'[80] Shortly afterwards, Sergeant James Anton was discharged from the Regiment on the grounds of ill-health. In 1841 the story of his 'military life' was published, making it one of the first contemporary accounts of the 42nd's history in the Peninsula and at Waterloo.[81]

In July 1834 the 42nd was ordered to Corfu, the main island of the Ionian Islands, where a few months previously the 73rd had been posted, remaining until 1838. An outbreak of cholera delayed the 42nd's departure and the Regiment did not arrive until December.[82] 'If the natives of Malta were surprised at the appearance, to them, of the singular costume of the Regt.,' commented Wheatley, 'the Greeks were more so, although less demonstrative, because the Greek prides himself on his stoicism, whereas the Maltese are somewhat impulsive.' But when the Greeks actually saw the Regiment in its full dress parade, their stoicism gave way, 'and the report of the strange sight was carried all over the Island'.[83]

The change 'from the almost barren island of Malta to the well-

wooded Corfu (all olive trees)' was welcome.[84] There was no comparison with what was available in the markets. 'On the evening of the
landing, three bottles of wine of different colours and qualities were
put on one's table, with a dozen of oranges, ripe and fresh from the
tree *for a shilling*!' recorded Wheatley.[85] The 42nd remained at Port
Raymond Barracks for three months, before moving to the island
of Vido in the harbour, where the men worked on erecting 'an extensive fortification, which, with the Citadel opposite Vido, was to make
the Harbour impregnable'.[86]

In July 1835, Lieutenant Colonel Gordon again went on leave. 'He
had been in the habit at Gibraltar and Malta of going to the Continent
or home to escape the hot season,' recollected Wheatley. Expected
back in early October, the soldiers received the unexpected news that
he had died of brain fever in Geneva on 30 September, aged forty-
five. 'It was a day of regret and gloom amongst all ranks, for, if ever
an officer in command of a Regiment was sincerely beloved, it was
the courteous, affable, gentlemanly Sir Charles – and the term *good*
may be added to his other qualities.'[87] Major William Middleton, 'an
old and experienced officer', who had joined the Regiment in 1803,
became the Regiment's new Commanding Officer.[88] The following
year the 'order of readiness' was received by the 42nd to return home,
their departure regretted by the locals, 'for both officers and men
were very popular with all the inhabitants, the good conduct of the
men was universally admired and spoken of'.[89]

As they lined up along the Esplanade, prior to embarkation in
June 1836, the Lord High Commissioner, Major General Sir Howard
Douglass, assured the soldiers that their conduct had given him 'the
highest degree of satisfaction ... The Highest professional obligation of a Regiment is so to act as to render itself dreaded as well as
respected by enemies. This the 42nd Regt had heretofore nobly and
effectually done ... Forty-Second farewell.'[90]

Shortly after departing on board the *Prince Regent*, Piper Alexander
Macdonald fell overboard. Although he was picked up out of the
water, such was the shock that he became 'insensible' and died. 'His
remains were committed to the deep during a calm,' recorded

Wheatley. He had been seventeen years in the Regiment, 'of quiet and inoffensive manner and much respected'.[91] During the voyage, there was 'a more formidable enemy' than what Wheatley called 'meager accommodation': an infestation of bugs in one of the cabins. 'The active marauders must have discovered the chance of fresh victims to pounce upon and such was their determination to avail themselves of the fresh blood that sleep was impossible.' So, said Wheatley, an attempt was made 'to route the enemy into the adjacent cabin by liberal applications of turpentine'. This treatment lasted for a day, until the next-door occupants adopted the same method 'and sent them back. It then became a fair fight for many days, for each cabin to get rid of them.' As they left the Mediterranean, the temperature dropped and the bugs disappeared.[92] At the end of August 1836, after two months at sea, the *Prince Regent* reached Portsmouth, the 42nd embarking at once in transports for Leith. On arrival, the Regiment marched to Edinburgh Castle, where they remained throughout the winter of 1836 and 1837, having been absent from 'Auld Reekie' – Old Smoky – as Edinburgh was called, for twenty years.[93]

Home and Away: the Mediterranean Again

Britain: the 42nd 1836–38; Ireland: the 42nd 1838–40; Ionian Islands: the 42nd 1841–42; Malta: the 42nd 1842–47

On 20 June 1837, William IV, the 'sailor king' whom the 42nd Regiment had encountered during the American War over fifty years previously, died. He had spent only seven years on the throne, having succeeded his brother George IV in 1830. Their niece, eighteen-year-old Alexandrina Victoria, was now Queen.[94] In June, as the new Queen was being proclaimed, the Regiment left Edinburgh for Glasgow. 'I was very much knocked up the first day,' recollected a new recruit, John Drysdale, 'it being my first days march carrying all my necessaries, but a day or twos rest put me all to rights again.'[95]

After less than two years in Scotland, the soldiers returned to Ireland in 1838, travelling by steamship to Dublin, where Lance Corporal Drysdale was recording his duties as 'very pleasant, every thing being so regulated that we could almost tell what we had to do from Sunday to Saturday. Every day a detachment of cavalry and infantry was required to mount a guard at the castle gateway, with the Colour of the Regiment on duty planted in the centre of the square.'[96] On 7 March 1839, Lieutenant General Sir Edward Blakeney, Commander-in-Chief in Ireland, presented the Regiment with new Colours to replace those used between 1818 and 1839. With the soldiers lined up in the square of the Royal Barracks in Dublin, Blakeney reminded the Regiment that 'there is only one sure means by which their Honor can be upheld and that is by the maintenance of your present discipline'.[97]

Much to Drysdale's disappointment, while in Ireland he was ordered to Glasgow for recruiting duty in the north of Scotland. 'The recruiting service is a very unpleasant duty, being obliged to take all the sneers and abuses which any person wishes to give you.' By the time he returned – promoted effective Corporal – in early 1840, the Regiment had moved to Limerick. Among those duties considered as 'severe' was escorting civilian prisoners to jail. On one occasion, Drysdale was sent to Newcastle, two days' march from Limerick. As he described, a sergeant and four privates had gone ahead to prepare the billets. While enjoying some refreshment at the local inn, they left their muskets unattended. When they returned, three were missing. 'The sergeant and the two men who had lost their muskets were tried by a Garrison court martial; the sergeant being sentenced to be reduced and the privates one months confinement each, and to pay for the muskets.' Not prepared to let the situation rest, the Regiment's Commanding Officer, Lieutenant Colonel George Johnstone, wrote to the local priest, who warned his parishioners that the stolen muskets were to be returned. Four days later the priest brought the muskets in person to Limerick. Although the punishment given to the sergeant and the soldiers was remitted, the offence remained on the record.[98] At the end of 1840, the 42nd marched to Cork, to embark again for the Ionian Islands.

Returning to the Mediterranean, Drysdale, in the troopship *Atholl*, was as critical as his predecessors of the conditions: 'What a scene presented itself on board of that ship, every part of the Deck being crowded with sick men, women vomiting below, children screaming, their mothers not being able to take care of them, sailors swearing at the soldiers, they being in their way. Some [were] standing with tears in their eyes taking a farewell look of Britain, and to many of us the last one, it was an awful scene.' So bad were their circumstances that Drysdale believed that the scene was 'calculated to disgust young men with the service, and prejudice them against their country, we being huddled together seemingly with no care whether we lived or died'. Since Drysdale was now a sergeant, he admitted he was better off than most, but the men were 'miserable'.[99] When the rough sea conditions abated, they had a 'splendid' passage, reaching Corfu in twenty-five days.

As the *Atholl* entered the harbour on 8 February 1841, the band was playing 'The Garb of Auld Gaul', while those of the companies who had preceded them on another transport cheered from the ramparts. As previously, duties involved improving and strengthening the batteries and building new barracks and accommodation for the troops. To guard against any seaborne invasion, powerful guns were mounted. In April 1842 the Regiment was increased from ten to twelve companies in two battalions, the 1st and the Reserve, the latter formed from the depot companies which had remained in Scotland. Numbers of private soldiers were increased from 800 to 1,200 men. In August, the Reserve had the privilege of supplying the Guard of Honour at Dupplin, Taymouth, Drummond and Stirling Castles for Queen Victoria, who made her first visit to Scotland, beginning an attachment which lasted a lifetime.

After over two years in the Ionian Islands, in late December 1842 the Regiment sailed for Malta. Yet again, Drysdale complained that a journey which should have taken four days took fifteen, 'but what could we expect of a transport nearly falling to pieces with age?' To break the monotony, the men amused themselves 'by keeping the band and pipes playing the Highland Fling'.[100] For the next three years, the Regiment, including the Reserve Battalion which had arrived from Scotland, remained in Malta, whose inhabitants Drysdale believed, if 'properly educated', would be 'a very fine people but their ignorance makes them dishonest'.[101] The 1st Battalion was now under the command of Lieutenant Colonel Duncan Cameron, commissioned as an ensign in 1825.[102] On 15 January 1844 the Colonel of the Regiment, Sir George Murray, was succeeded by Lieutenant General Sir John Macdonald, former Adjutant General of the Armed Forces. Before leaving, Murray wrote to Cameron, expressing 'how high an honour I shall always esteem it to have been for upwards of twenty years the colonel of a regiment, which, by its exemplary conduct in every situation, and by its distinguished valour in many a well-fought field has earned for itself so large a share of esteem and of renown'.[103]

Removed both from Britain and Asia, the soldiers were untouched by the catastrophe which had befallen British soldiers in Afghanistan in 1842 when an army of nearly 4,000 European and Indian soldiers and 12,000 camp followers had been annihilated in the passes while withdrawing in midwinter from Kabul to British India. Instead, their only excitement was visits from itinerant monarchs and other dignitaries. On one occasion, in mid-1844, the King of Naples, 'a stout fat man with little intelligence in his countenance', visited the island. Received by a Guard of Honour of the 42nd, the King inspected both battalions. The Queen created a more favourable impression, having 'a very smart little body with red hair. She admired the pipers very much and had them playing highland reels to her for an hour after the Reveille was dismissed.' During the Regiment's four-year stay in Malta, they were visited by four sons of the King of France, Prince Oscar of Sweden, Prince Henry of the Netherlands and Grand Duke Constantine of Russia, as well as by two German Princes, the Pasha of Egypt, 'and I don't know how many Generals'.[104]

Malta's strategic location dictated who came and went: 'owing to it being a middle stage to India and a Rendez vous for the squadron, it is never at anytime free of strangers and a great many invalids resort to it in winter for the benefit of health as the air at that time is very pure.' The soldiers had likewise benefited from the climate, on average losing only seven men each year, mostly from dysentery. When, in December 1846, they were ordered to leave the Mediterranean for service across the Atlantic in Bermuda, Drysdale was not sorry, feeling it necessary to record how the 'religious accommodation' was 'not good', since they had to attend divine service in a red school, where they felt only tolerated. 'The Regiment which I belonged to being strict Presbyterians, no minister of our persuasion was ever furnished by [the] Government. The Free Church kindly sent us out some of her very best men. One of them I will never forget. Mr Baillie he was truly a servant of his Glorious Master. No tongue can describe what he did for the 42nd Regiment. Besides preaching to them 3 sermons every Sunday he had three lectures during the week, one in each barrack and one in the Scotch church.'[105]

Bermuda: the 42nd 1847–51

In early 1847, HMS *Vengeance* arrived to transport the Regiment to Bermuda. Discovered by Juan de Bermudez in 1505, the British had begun to settle the island in the early seventeenth century, making it the oldest of Britain's overseas territories and a valuable base. With 560 men on board and 'about' thirty women and sixty children, Drysdale described their accommodation as 'very bad'. More fortunate than most, since he had recently married and had been given 'a large berth fitted up for myself and wife', conditions generally for the women and children were 'most wretched'. While at sea a 'fine child was born almost amongst the men's feet and the poor creature had nothing but the ship's deck to lay upon and a scanty blanket to cover her – surely this is not known in the proper quarter or it would not be allowed.' To make matters worse, measles broke out. 'No sick bay or any other comforts was afforded to the children.'[106]

On the morning of 16 April 1848 they reached Bermuda. Three companies were sent to Ireland Island, the most north-westerly of the island chain; the headquarters and the remaining companies went to the island's capital, Hamilton, to be joined at the end of the month by the Reserve Battalion.[107] When the men received their arrears of accumulated pay, 'it was nothing but a scene of drunkenness for some days'. Drysdale's first impression of Bermuda was that 'it was a most beautiful place having come from the barren rock of Malta'. Within a month of the Regiment's arrival, a 'fine officer', Lieutenant Samuel Douglas Abercromby, died of pleurisy. As a result, Drysdale was promoted ensign and sent to do duty as acting adjutant at the mile-square Ireland Island, where some 2,000 convicts, kept in floating jails, were employed improving the dockyard. Although the soldiers were not required to oversee their work, they were 'barracked at a convenient distance to awe them into good order, when any of them are punished a sufficient strong guard, armed and loaded are present – but they are in general very quiet, and a guard of 1 subaltern 1 sergeant, 5 corporals and 30 men mount everyday in the dock yard ready at once to check any mutiny.'[108]

As the soldiers realised, especially in remote locations, there was always the risk of a mutiny. When Private David McAusland, who had enlisted in the 42nd in June 1848, was travelling to Bermuda to join the Regiment, he and a draft of fifty men were accompanying over three hundred convicts. As he recorded, during the long passage it was customary to allow the prisoners on deck for some fresh air. On this voyage 'they took it into their mind they could take the ship to themselves and get their liberty'. They formed a conspiracy to attack the Sergeant of the Guard when he was letting out the two convict cooks in the morning, but another prisoner, acting as the Doctor's servant, told him of the plan. The ringleader was caught and placed in irons until they arrived in Bermuda, to be handed over to the Superintendent of the dockyard. 'May I tell you that the convict that gave the information got a free pardon.'[109]

On 1 April 1850 an order was passed to amalgamate the 1st Battalion 42nd with the Reserve, forming a regiment of ten companies of 1,000 men. The following year, six service and four depot companies were formed. Having spent three years in Bermuda, the Regiment was under orders to leave, the Governor noting that throughout the 42nd's service 'the urbanity and affability of the Officers, the steady and upright conduct of the Men' were 'eminently conspicuous'.[110] As the men were about to experience, the 'long peace' was soon to become intensive war.

> *Wha saw the 42nd*
> *Wha saw them gang awa'*
> *Wha saw the 42nd*
> *Sailin' doon the Broomie Law*
> *Some o' them had rusty rifles*
> *Some o' them hid nane at a'*
> *Some o' them had boots an' stockin's*
> *Sailin doon the Broomie Law.*[111]

16.

Frontier Wars

Oh that I could forget what I saw that night. I would not pass such another. It is an awful sight to see despairing men fighting for anything to support them in the water.

Ensign Gould Lucas, HMS *Birkenhead*, 1852[1]

1840.

The Canadas 1838, Britain 1841: the 73rd

By the early 1840s, with the 42nd engaged on its peacetime routine, the British government was beginning to reassert its authority against those countries which might threaten its presumed strategic and economic interests. A supposed tilt towards Tsarist Russia by the King of Afghanistan and China's belligerent reaction to an unwanted glut of opium loomed large on Britain's list of concerns. In Canada, trouble had broken out in both 'Lower' and 'Upper' Canada, named with reference to the headwaters of the St Lawrence river and collectively called the Canadas.

The Lower Canada Rebellion in the north-east arose out of French and English disaffection against the British colonial government. The main instigator was Dr Robert Nelson, who in June 1837 had established a new association, *Fils de la Liberté*, Sons of Freedom, supported by French-Canadian students and young professionals. Joined by unemployed artisans and apprentices, their goal was 'to emancipate our country from all human authority save that of the bold democracy residing in its bosom'.[2] On the assumption that the Canadians wished to emulate the American War of Independence and form a republic, a secret group known as the Hunter Patriots, based in the United States, determined to help them. The rebellion in Upper Canada, the land bordering the northern shores of the Great Lakes, was against the ruling elite: known as the Family Compact, and comprising members of the Executive and Legislative Councils, who advised the Lieutenant Governor, their influence meant that the elected Legislative Assembly had very little authority, which caused friction. In 1837 the disaffection had come to a head when, following a bad harvest, the banks called in their loans. By early 1838 the rebellion had been contained, but, supported by the Hunter Patriots, attacks continued to be made from the United States, where many of the rebels had taken refuge.

Having spent four years in the Ionian Islands, in early 1838 the

73rd left Corfu with orders to proceed to Gibraltar. Instead of returning to Britain, as originally ordered, on 10 April four companies of the 73rd, augmented by an additional draft of men, left Gibraltar on board the *Talavera* and sailed for Halifax, Nova Scotia. A month later, two more companies arrived on board the *Madagascar*. Their destination was Montreal. In early November, information was received that the inhabitants of St Charles Island were collecting arms. 'The Rebels suddenly having appeared in great numbers on the Richelieus,' noted the Record of Service, 'the Regiment was suddenly ordered to St John's [Saint Jean de Richelieu] on that river, and proceeded in two divisions.'[3]

From this vantage point, the 73rd was part of an expedition marching in pursuit of the rebels in neighbouring towns. As it later transpired, the timely action in sending the 73rd to St John's 'foiled' Nelson's plan to set fire to the town.[4] By the time the Regiment was back in Montreal on 16 November, the Hunter Patriots had been decisively defeated at Newport in an action known as the Battle of the Windmill. Several of the Hunter Patriot leaders were executed, the remainder transported to Tasmania.

The 73rd Regiment was then sent to Toronto in response to a request for reinforcements by Lieutenant Governor Sir George Arthur. Having taken up quarters in Brantford, on the Grand river in Southern Ontario to the north of Lake Erie, in June 1839 the Regiment moved westwards to the town of London. It was a bitter cold posting, on a virtually unknown frontier. Confined to barracks during the winter, with very little opportunity for exercise, the Regiment remained in Upper Canada until May 1840, when it returned to Montreal. Before it departed, addresses were presented by the inhabitants 'expressive of their regret at its departure and kind wishes for its future'.[5]

After the military defeat of the rebel Canadians, the 1840 Act of Union, proclaimed by the Crown in February 1841, merged Upper and Lower Canada into one united Province of Canada. Responsible government was later established for all British North American provinces. Life reverted to garrison duties and the large force which had been increased to over 10,000 infantry and 500 cavalry was gradually reduced. In June 1841 the 73rd was ordered home, receiving new Colours at Gosport in November; the old Colours – presented in 1827 in Ireland – had seen no active service.

After North America, the Regiment's next posting was in the north of England, 'in consequence of disturbances in the manufacturing districts' in Yorkshire and Lancashire.[6] From there, it went to Wales, the first and last time either the 73rd or 42nd served there. Based at Newport, detachments had to undertake 'harassing' night marches throughout the region, countering disturbances known as the Rebecca Riots, caused by poor harvests and protests by agricultural workers against a new system of tolls. Once these were pacified, in August 1844 the Regiment proceeded to Ireland, where it remained for a year.

For over ten years Lieutenant General Lord Harris had been Colonel of the Regiment. Having never fully recovered from the wound he received in the shoulder at Waterloo, he died in 1845.[7] His successor was Major General Sir Robert Henry Dick, the 42nd's Commanding Officer for over thirteen years, and who had married Harris's sister Eliza. Having been on half-pay, Dick had gone to India in the early 1840s, serving in both Madras and Bengal. In December he was appointed to command the 3rd Infantry Division of the 'Army of the Sutlej', formed to challenge the rising power of the Sikhs in the Punjab.

At the end of September 1845, the 73rd, under the command of fifty-four-year-old Lieutenant Colonel Charles Vander Meulen, and the 45th, embarked at the Cove of Cork on board HMS *Apollo* bound for South Africa. Britain's presence dated from the previous century. To prevent the strategically important Cape of Good Hope, settled by the Dutch in the early seventeenth century, falling into French hands during the Revolutionary Wars, British forces had occupied the region, taking control of Cape Colony in 1806. The presence of both British and Dutch settlers, had created tensions with the amaXhosas, the indigenous inhabitants of the rich grazing lands to the north and east of the Cape. During the nineteenth century, Britain fought nine 'Frontier Wars'.

The 73rd was to form part of the relieving force of those regiments already there. 'We was all very busy in getting our things packed up in berths and getting our sea kits,' recorded Private John Rich, who had enlisted in the 73rd in 1844 when it was stationed in Wales, 'and making ourselves snug for the voyage.'[8] As usual, the route taken to the Cape of Good Hope was across the Atlantic to Rio de Janeiro before catching the westerlies to South Africa. As soon as the ship began to pitch, 'the sea sickness commenced; men, women and children were all nearly sick together, and such a mess as there was for 7 or 8 days, I never saw before.'[9]

South American Detour 1845

In November 1845, the *Apollo* reached Rio de Janeiro, where Vander Meulen received an urgent message from William Ouseley, the British minister and plenipotentiary in Montevideo, capital of the recently established country of Uruguay. His request was for the *Apollo* to continue south to Montevideo, where Argentine forces were laying siege to the capital in support of the deposed president, Manuel Oribe.[10] Once arrived in Montevideo, Vander Meulen found it impossible to leave.[11]

Lacking instructions from either the Cape of Good Hope or from London, he was anxious to avoid being drawn into the fighting. As he made clear in several letters he sent to London, although 'repeatedly urged' by Ouseley, who was trying to negotiate for the withdrawal of the Argentine forces, he had refused to take part in the skirmishing, 'nor have the British Troops been in any way mixed up with these parties. I have held no communication with their Military commanders.'[12] But he did feel constrained to mention to the government back home that their prolonged stay was taking them into the winter; as a result 'a heavy expense has been incurred in procuring accommodation for the two Regiments'.[13] The only circumstances in which the troops would turn out, he said, was 'in case I should be called upon to protect British subjects or their property. I declined acting on the request of Mr Ouseley to parade the Troops as a demonstration preferring to act with effect or not at all.'[14]

The men were short of food. 'I was in a very weak state,' recollected Rich, 'being so long on board of ship and half starved, was I not a fine soldier to stand against an enemy and fight the battles of my country in that state?' Rations, he said, were not 'of the best kind'; there was no fresh meat, since it had to be brought from Rio de Janeiro, and by the time it reached them, 'it was very poor indeed'.[15]

While preoccupied in South America, after only eight months as the Regiment's Colonel, Sir Robert Henry Dick was killed fighting the Sikhs at the Battle of Sobraon on 6 February 1846. The new Colonel was Major General Sir John Grey, who had likewise served in India.[16] It is doubtful that the soldiers ever saw their deceased Colonel, nor knew of his exploits in the Peninsula with the 42nd and subsequently in Ireland. By those who did know him, he was much mourned, a monument erected at his 'parish church', Dunkeld Cathedral, praising him as 'a generous courteous and considerate commander a gallant and devoted soldier'.[17]

In Montevideo, as time passed and no instructions were received, Vander Meulen became more anxious: 'Things are now quiet,' he wrote again in April, after the massacre of the 'unfortunate' Captain of the Port and his party of men, '– but how long they may remain so is doubtful. Rivera must have money to carry on the war, but, as he is too well known to be trusted it may bring matters to a crisis – myself, I have no faith in any of their authorities or parties, they are replete with treachery, and would turn round upon us if it suited their purpose.'[18] A month later, as the civil war in Uruguay continued, he repeated his concerns to the Adjutant General: 'I am most anxious for instructions from home, at present I have managed to keep clear of collision with any party; and have acted upon my own judgment, and discretion, tho' not exactly in accordance with the opinion of others' – by which he meant the British minister, William Ouseley. Civilians, he said, 'know nothing of military questions, and are not agreeable people to act in concert with'. In his dispatch, Vander Meulen complained that both the regiments were 'sickly'; the meat was bad and gave no nourishment. 'The winter is now setting in here and weather becoming very cold and changeable. We require clothing.' They also needed stores 'of all kinds'.[19]

When, after several months, the ageing Duke of Wellington – Commander-in-Chief of the British Army – heard that the 73rd had been delayed in South America, mindful of the fate of the British soldiers in Afghanistan, his immediate concern was that British soldiers might once again sustain a humiliating reversal. Writing angrily to William Gladstone, secretary of state for war and the colonies, he wished to recollect 'the disastrous events' in Afghanistan, 'occasioned principally by the exercise of the detailed command of the movements of the Troops being entrusted to a Gentleman undoubtedly highly respectable and meritorious, who had not been educated in the military profession and was not accustomed to the direction of the movements of Troops in the detailed operations of war'.[20]

South Africa 1846

After eight months in South America, the 73rd and 45th re-embarked on board the *Apollo*, making a swift journey of twenty-one days across the Atlantic to the Cape. Their troubles were not yet over. Having disembarked the women and children, the sick and supplies at Simon's Town, they proceeded to Waterloo Bay. A storm blew up and 'there was nothing for us to expect but that the ship would be foundered to pieces on the rocks but just at the last moment, a land breeze sprung up, and it pleased the Lord to spear our lives, when all human power and skill had failed,' related Rich; 'and the ship got out to safe[ty] by slipping all her anchors and leaving them behind, so we had to go back to Simon's Town for anchors as there was not one left on board.'[21]

By the time the 73rd arrived in South Africa in September 1846, British troops had become engaged in their seventh frontier war in what became known as the 'war of the Axe' or the 'Amatola' War; it had begun in March when the escort accompanying an amaXhosa prisoner charged with stealing an axe was murdered. The British retaliated and war was declared against several related tribes. The chief adversary was King Mgolombane Sandile Ngqika, the 'Great son and heir' of the Paramount Chief, Ngqika Gaika, founder of the Ngqika or Gaika Tribe, who had died in 1829. British forces had already been fighting Sandile's half-brother, Maqoma, Regent since their father's death until Sandile came of age in 1840. Renowned for his distinction as a warrior, the British accused Maqoma of cattle-raiding and had forcibly evicted him from his lands.[22] In May, a British column sent to challenge Sandile was attacked in the Amatola Mountains, resulting in the loss of military supplies. Soon afterwards, a force of amaXhosas armed with guns attacked the British garrison at Fort Peddie. Although the British prevailed, nearly 4,000 cattle stampeded at the sound of the gunfire. On 7 June, the amaXhosa were decisively defeated on the Gwangu river near Fort Peddie.

Having joined the 2nd Division, the newly arrived 73rd marched towards the Great Kei river; crossing the Keiskamma and Buffalo rivers, they encamped on Christmas Day 1846. By the beginning of 1847, most of the tribal chiefs had made peace; one of the first to do so was Maqoma. A British military presence, however, was still considered necessary. On 2 January a patrol of 1,500 men, including 300 of the 73rd, marched to the Butterworth mission station. Having taken a large herd of captured cattle, they returned across the Kei river. Their hardships were 'very great indeed', soaked by continual rain, 'without a change of clothes, no tents, no blankets, or camp kettles and only 6 days allowance of Biscuit per man'. Without having had the excitement of seeing an enemy or firing a shot, the soldiers were also lamenting the loss of 'a fine young officer', Lieutenant the Hon. Walter Chetwynd, of the 14th King's Regiment of Light Dragoons, killed in an ambush 'after a most gallant resistance in which many of the Kaffir fell'.[23]

Throughout 1847, contingents of troops were on constant patrol. In September, when Lieutenant Colonel Vander Meulen retired, Major Frederick Pinckney, with the Regiment since 1825, took temporary command, although formally the command of the Regiment passed to Lieutenant Colonel William Eyre.[24] Engaged in 'harassing and fatiguing marches' inland from King William's Town, they went out on 'numerous patrols of one to four days'. The primary occupation was rounding up herds of cattle and goats, which had been taken by the local amaXhosas. 'A considerable number of Kaffirs were killed and the tract of country in that direction, as far as the Kei completely cleared,' noted the Record of Service.[25] Another loss of men occurred when six officers, five of whom belonged to the 73rd, were killed in November 1847 while out on an expedition to visit a mountain on the banks of the Kei. The dead men included the 73rd's recently promoted Major William Baker, the surgeon, Neil Campbell, and Ensign William Burnop. 'Punishment followed close on the perpetrators of this sad tragedy,' who had incriminated themselves by wearing the dead officers' clothes and stealing a horse and gun.[26]

In late 1847, Lieutenant General Sir Harry Smith arrived as Governor of Cape Colony. Smith, who had previously fought the amaXhosas in the sixth war in the 1830s, had since served in India and fought against the Sikhs at Sobraon. On behalf of the British government, on 23 December 1847 Smith extended the borders of Cape Colony northwards to the Orange river and annexed the area between the Keiskamma and Kei rivers as a Crown dependency, known as 'British Kaffraria'.

With the region nominally pacified, all the chiefs were ordered to submit before the new Governor. 'On the 21st December the march commenced for King William's Town, where the Regiment arrived on the 23rd, and which day His Excellency Sir Harry Smith, also arrived there, and having previously ordered all the Kaffir Chiefs to a conference, he declared them to have submitted to her Majesty, and the war to be at an end, an announcement which gave great pleasure to all[,] the operations having been conducted against an implacable enemy, in a savage and deserted country and under circumstances of privation and hardship seldom surpassed but which beyond the immediate sphere of action, is unknown.'[27]

Sandile, who had been captured, was released and given land for the amaXhosa people in British Kaffraria. But the humiliation of having to prostrate themselves before the British Governor caused resentment, and, in the months to come, Corporal John Rich heard 'continual rumours of the breaking of the Kaffirs'.[28]

While Smith was preoccupied with relations with the Dutch farmers, the Boers, the 73rd remained at Cape Town, with one company at Simon's Town, until the beginning of December 1850. The amaXhosas resented their loss of independence and they were inspired to further rebellion by the teachings of Prophet Mlanjeni, who assured his listeners that they would be immune to British bullets. As the rebellion gained momentum, large numbers of the local police – recruited to guard against cattle theft – deserted. On the assumption that the tribal chiefs were responsible for encouraging Mlanjeni, Smith travelled to meet them. 'The Governor, Sir Harry Smith, proceeded to the Frontier and made a hasty circuit of it, and to all appearances had put a stop to all difficulties by removing from his chieftainship, Sandilla [Sandile], the Paramount Chief,' wrote Rich. In his place his mother, Sutu, was made Regent together with Mr Brownlee, an English magistrate, who, somewhat incongruously, was temporarily installed as chief of the Ngqika tribe.

Sandile and a band of several thousand armed followers were still at large and to counter the threat to British authority, the 73rd was ordered to Simon's Town. As Rich recollected, at 'about 11 o'clock at night the bugle was sounded for orders'. Four companies embarked on board the *Hermes*. 'Notwithstanding the little time we had to pack up and get ready, and drawing field equipments, ammunition, and in the night, we marched off exactly at the hour named.' Unfortunately for Rich, he was a prisoner 'going on board of the steamer for being drunk on the line of march'.[29] After a passage of a few days they reached East London: 'a heavy surf breaking across the bar, it was rather a hazardous piece of business to land troops.'[30] With the exception of one boat, all were landed safely.

'It was a great mercy we was not all lost,' recalled Rich in the foundered boat. 'I lost everything I had, only what I stood in. One of the men that was a prisoner with me was washed out of the boat ... I had hold of the surf-line and got hold of him, and held him till he recovered a little, or he must have been lost, and then brought him on shore . . . As soon as they found I was on shore all right, they marched me and him to the guard tent, wet as we came out of the sea, and had to lie down on the cold ground in my wet clothes all night. Not one of my comrades brought me as much as a dry shirt, and they all had dry shirts by then. That is the way with the world; . . . the best friends leave when trouble comes.'[31] Thanks to the belated intercession of his comrades, instead of being tried and flogged, Rich was released and able to rejoin his company. From East London, the soldiers marched to King William's Town, alongside the Buffalo river, stopping at Fort Grey, where they camped for the night. The following day they marched nearly thirty miles to Fort Murray, within reach of King William's Town. 'We were all terribly beat up after such a long march as we had had no marching since the previous war, which made it the harder on us.'[32] Arriving at King William's Town, they camped at Fort Hill to await further orders.

Soon afterwards, three companies of the 73rd, under Eyre's command, together with a contingent of Cape Mounted Riflemen, composed of local Africans commanded by white officers, were sent to the Kabousie valley, 'a most beautiful country. [Our camp was] at the most eastern angle of the mountain range, called Kabousie Nek through the Keiskamma and the Boomah Pass and Mount Kemp.' From there, the way led to Fort Cox and the Amatola Mountains, stronghold of the rebellious amaXhosas. On 25 December 1850 'we kept up Christmas day. We had a merry day, foot racing and other games, but in the evening our sports were suddenly brought to a close; strange rumours were giving about that there was treachery in camp.'[33] As was immediately discovered, a conspiracy was being hatched by a group of Cape Mounted Riflemen to hand the British camp over to the amaXhosas. Five men were arrested and the plot failed.

More serious was the news received the following day that Colonel George Mackinnon, who had been sent with a force of 650 men to arrest Sandile, had been ambushed two days previously in the Boomah Pass and forced to retreat to Fort White, losing forty-two men. This action signalled the start of the eighth Frontier War. Encouraged by their successes, the amaXhosas, led by Maqoma, Sandile's elder half-brother, surrounded Fort Cox, where Sir Harry Smith was stationed. From Kabousie, the 73rd were ordered to fall back on King William's Town. 'The whole of the Cavalry was now to make their way to Fort White and endeavour at all hazard to rescue the General.' After 'a desultory skirmish with the enemy', noted Rich, Sir Harry 'arrived in King William's Town safe'.[34]

At the same time, the Khoikhoi tribe, who lived around the Kat river, rebelled. Led by Hermanus Nguxkumeshe Matroos, a half-Khoi, half-Xhosa chieftain, at the end of 1850 they captured Fort Armstrong, west of Kaffraria. When, in January 1851, Hermanus and his followers launched an attack on nearby Fort Beaufort, recently strengthened as a military frontier post, they were repulsed and Hermanus was killed. In the weeks that followed, his supporters were driven out of Fort Armstrong towards the Amatola Mountains.

Throughout this period the 73rd was on patrol in Kaffraria, assisting in continual attempts to resupply the garrisons at Fort Cox, Fort White and Fort Hare. 'From the 30 January the Regiment was almost constantly in the field, with only a day's rest in between each patrole, and was altogether 31 days on Patrole between the 30 January and 31 March,' noted the Record of Service.[35] 'Started from King William's Town on patrol with two companies of the 73rd . . .' wrote Lieutenant Alfred Knox in his diary, describing their march to reach Fort White. 'Halted for breakfast . . . a troop of C[ape] M[ounted] rifles was sent off on the right on the flats to cut off a herd of cattle, but the Kaffirs got them safe in the bush with the exception of 10 cows and a calf which they captured. Killed three Kaffirs and wounded one.'

When they arrived at Fort White, having travelled eighteen miles from King William's Town, they found the 'water very bad and a scarcity of wood'.[36] Having realised that the amaXhosas had already left their kraal (homestead), they returned to King William's Town. 'The Kaffirs fired on our rear the whole afternoon till we halted for the night.' According to Knox 'the only casualties on our side during the day's operations were one 73rd Regiment and one levy man wounded'.[37] Soon afterwards, a contingent of the 73rd was ordered to form part of an escort to Fort Cox, safeguarding forty wagons of supplies. Although they arrived safely, the return journey was treacherous. With about 400 amaXhosas gathering on the hills, Lieutenant Knox's company was ordered 'to skirmish the whole bush through the valley and also the drift in front of the wagons . . . we fired six times from the big gun, which I believe killed a great many. There were a lot of Kaffirs concealed to attack the rear. We attacked them and drove them from their position and killed a great many.'[38]

By early March 1851, they were back in King William's Town. 'Nothing doing all day; rain in the afternoon; everybody very tired after the patrole.'[39] The respite was never long. 'Started on patrole for three days with five companies 73rd,' Knox wrote again in April. 'Left King William's Town at 1.30 a.m. and marched till 12.30 without stopping over the most infernal country any Christian ever went before. While breakfasting the Kaffirs fired two shots.'[40]

Either on the veldt or back in King William's Town, the men had to deal with the extremes of climate peculiar to Africa. Having experienced a drought throughout 1850, in May 1851 the rains came. 'Very heavy rain and wind last night, a great many of the tents thrown over. I was up four times fastening mine, raining heavily all day, very wet and cold.'[41] Food was scarce: 'I have been in that state with hunger and hardship that I have wished the next ball that came to blow my brains out,' recollected Rich, 'as my life was a misery to me. This is part of the life a soldier gets in wartime, and him braving every danger for his country, There is very few poor mothers knows what their sons may come to when they joins the Army, after raising tenderly.'[42]

In late June 1851, the 73rd was taking part in a joint movement on the Amatola Mountains from King William's Town, Fort Hare, Fort Cox and Shiloh, in the north under the command of Colonel Mackinnon. Fearful of ambush, during breakfast 'great caution was observed. One subdivision of each company remained dressed and by their arms.' As Rich noted, having been ambushed at the Boomah Pass in 1850, 'Col Mackinnon evidently was determined that the

Kaffirs should not catch him napping this time.'[43] In parallel with the Keiskamma river, the Division proceeded up the valley towards Keiskamma Hoek. 'The Kaffirs, from rocks, commenced firing on the column but without effect, we giving them a fire that soon made them leave that. They were now seen gathering in a large force in front.' Invariably, when an attempt was made to engage the amaXhosas, they 'fought shy, some of them followed us about half a mile . . . firing at us, but keeping too far away from us to run them down'.[44]

The march was an ordeal: 'Strict orders were issued that no man was to make any delay in crossing the river, and no time to be allowed for taking off boots or socks, which was far from being pleasant on a bitter cold morning. I thought I should never get the use of my limbs any more, kept standing so long after crossing each drift with our wet boots and stockings and trousers on. We was standing long enough to take off forty pairs of boots if we was allowed to do so, but in place of that we was kept standing in our wet things for hours.'[45] After 'fifteen or sixteen hours without so much as tasting food', when they lay down to sleep they could look forward to 'the cold wet ground and a stone for a pillow, each night in the full expectation of a night attack'.[46] Another sortie resulted in 'some skirmishing, killed a few Kaffirs . . . Some Kaffirs appeared, but kept at a distance.'[47] Arduous as their lives were, there was some enjoyment. 'All dined together,' Knox noted on one occasion: 'We had a hell of a dinner, singing songs and playing the fiddle all the evening.'[48]

Despite constant patrols and the use of a favoured tactic – 'corncutting' – destroying the amaXhosas' cornfields – an enclave of revolt remained around the forested region of Water Kloof. Having gained a natural stronghold on Mount Misery, between Water Kloof and Harry's Kloof, Maqoma continued to harass British forces. In early November 1851, Lieutenant Colonel John Fordyce, 74th Regiment, was killed.

As a result of mounting casualties, Governor Smith requested reinforcements. With too few soldiers in the Cape, a draft was ordered to come from Ireland. In command was Major Alexander Seton, who was to take Fordyce's position in command of the 74th. Although they were joining British regiments, most of the new recruits were young Irishmen who had enlisted to escape the grinding poverty and famine in Ireland. One of the two largest contingents of seventy-one men was detailed for the 73rd. Among them were Lieutenants Audley Henry Booth and Charles William Robinson and nineteen-year-old Ensign Gould Lucas, fifth son of the Rt Hon. Edward Lucas, a former under-secretary for Ireland.

Danger Point and the Birkenhead 1852

In early January 1852 the draft of men set out from Cork on board a 1,900-ton paddle steamer, one of the early iron-hulled ships, Her Majesty's Troopship *Birkenhead*, captained by Robert Salmond, RN. On board were 638 men, seven women and thirteen children. No longer dependent on sail, they travelled via Madeira, Sierra Leone and St Helena, dropping anchor at Simon's Bay, twenty miles south of Cape Town, on 23 February. Two days later, the *Birkenhead* weighed anchor, heading towards East London across the expanse of water known as False Bay. It was evening and the ship's company fell into the routine of a sea voyage. 'We got well out of the Bay before dark,' Lucas later wrote to his father. 'I turned in at 9 o'clock as I was to have the watch on deck from 4 to 6 o'clock ... I slept like a top and knew nothing of what happened up to the time I was awakened by three distinct shocks. It immediately struck me that we were on a rock.'

Lucas went on deck to find that the *Birkenhead* had indeed hit a rock off Cape Agulhas – South Africa's most southerly point and popularly known as Danger Point – which had ripped through its forward keel. Below decks, water was pouring in, drowning men in their hammocks as they slept. On deck, 'the ship was rolling at this time so much that it was with great difficulty that anybody could stand. We had nine horses on board; they were kicking and plunging furiously; several had fallen down ... It was pitch dark (the ship having struck at 2 a.m. exactly as the bell was struck,) except when a flash of lightening lighted up the ship.'[49] The Captain's order to bring the engines astern, in the hope of enabling the ship to come clear of the rocks, had the reverse effect. 'The starboard bilge buckled upwards, and water rushed in through the ruptured plating, drowning several stokers.'[50]

Of the available lifeboats, some were useless because of rotten tackle, and it soon became clear that only three boats could be launched. According to twenty-two-year-old Bernard Kilkeary, appointed sergeant major of the 73rd for the journey, he was detailed to help the seven women and thirteen children. As he later recollected, the Commanding Officer, Seton, had ordered him to 'disembark the women and children into a quarter-boat and take charge of the occupants'.[51] The other two boats were soon filled with sailors and soldiers.

Lest the men for whom there were no boats hurried after them, Seton was recorded as encouraging them to: 'Stand fast! I beg you, do not rush the boats carrying the women and children, You will swamp them.' As later commentators wrote: 'The unflinching courage shown by the officers and men on board Birkenhead passed into naval lore as the Birkenhead Drill – a legend now recalled whenever the strong are called upon to succour the weak at sea.'[52] As Lucas recollected, once the ship forward of the mainmast had broken off, those for whom there were no boats were ordered by Captain Salmond 'to jump into the sea and save ourselves if we could. Almost all the officers were congregated on the poop at that time. We were now sinking very fast.' Lucas was afraid the ship would go down 'with a rush by the head, for her stern was so much raised that one of the men swimming saw the heel of the rudder. Indeed it was very difficult to prevent oneself slipping on the deck. I had just taken off my clothes and got over the bulwarks ready for a jump, and was making up my mind to dive head first when I thought that, should I ever get ashore, I should be roasted by the sun in the day. I once more got over the bulwarks and groped for my shirt on the deck and put it on.'

Still afraid of jumping, 'as the water was full of men below me – many drowning as fast as possible, a sad sight', Lucas heard his servant, Collins, calling to him. 'He asked if he was to follow. I knew he could not swim, so I advised his getting as high up as he could in the rigging. He said "All right, Sir! But I have brought your purse up from your cabin; you will want it when you get ashore." I never saw the faithful fellow again.' Lucas waited until the poop deck was about two feet from the water, then jumped off, and 'struck out as quickly as possible to get out of the suction of the ship. When I turned my head to look, I saw nothing but the mainmast and yard, the rigging was crowded with men.'[53]

Lucas swam for about a hundred yards before catching hold of a piece of wreck on which he was able to rest. He then managed to reach an overturned paddle-box boat, to which five soldiers and a sailor were already clinging. 'We were now in comparative safety, but we were much afraid of being carried out to sea instead of to land which we could see; it looked about 9 or 10 miles off.' After twelve hours, with the help of an oar which Lucas had managed to retrieve, they were within 300 yards of the shore. 'It was a most odious coast . . . a seaweed grows along the coast called "sea bamboo". These weeds grow about 15 or 16 feet long, so that for several hundred yards from the shore where these weeds were, it is nearly impossible to swim along them, for being all matted together, they catch the legs. We were now surrounded with these sea bamboos which held the boat, preventing her getting nearer the shore. The breakers were washing us off.' Having abandoned the boat, they made their way through the bamboos to shore.

Since Lucas was the only surviving officer present, the men insisted he should take command. 'Two of the men carried me whether I would or not, saying I had got so far and they would never leave an officer behind to die.' Nursed back to health by a local Dutch farmer, Lucas later joined the Regiment.[54] Those on the boats were picked up by the schooner *Lioness*, which was in the vicinity. According to Kilkeary, who had escaped with the women and children, he suggested to the *Lioness*'s captain that 'our quarter boat and one of his boats should proceed to the scene of the wreck. This he gladly assented to, and it resulted in the rescue of some forty or fifty men who were found clinging to the rigging. These were also brought on board the *Lioness* whose captain treated us all with the greatest kindness.'[55]

Although all the women and children were reported as saved, Lucas believed that a baby was lost when the infant was accidentally dropped into the sea by its mother, reaching out to assist her husband.[56] Of the nine horses on board, eight survived. Having swum to shore, one horse, belonging to Cornet Bond, 12th Lancers, appeared two days later outside the stable in Cape Town, having travelled a distance of some 125 miles. The horse's unexpected appearance was one of the first indications of the tragedy.[57] When news of the wreck reached England, it was described as 'a catastrophe of the most disastrous character ... out of 638 souls on board, only 184 have been saved'.[58] The greatest loss was from the draft of the 73rd: both Lieutenants Robinson and Booth died, as well as fifty-four soldiers; the 74th and 91st came a close second.[59]

Continuing Warfare

After the ordeal, the survivors rejoined their respective regiments and the war against the amaXhosas continued. In March 1852 Smith was replaced as Governor by Sir George Cathcart, who had fought in the Canadas. Lieutenant Knox was still writing his diary, commenting on the details of his life, whether on patrol, sometimes shooting ostrich and partridge, or back in King William's Town, playing billiards and going to divine service. He also took note of the 73rd's losses and those of other regiments. 'On March 17, St Patrick's Day: orders to march at daylight; raining hard; march postponed till tomorrow.' Two months later, the 73rd was 'encamped close to Fort Hare. Rain, thunder and lightning. Road very wet; halted for breakfast.'[60]

By August 1852 a force had been assembled for a final push against the amaXhosas across the Kei river, and in September the 73rd marched from King William's Town to take part in the operations under Cathcart's personal command. On 15 September, a simultaneous attack was made on Water Kloof from all quarters. Under Eyre's command, the 73rd took the same route along the Niland's Pass, 'passing seven skulls of poor 74th fellows that were killed'.[61] 'The Heights were gained without opposition and the "Iron Mountain" hitherto looked upon by the enemy as impregnable was stormed by the 73rd Regiment without another casualty than one man severely wounded.'[62] But Sandile was still at large, and 'with the object of allowing the enemy no rest', the 73rd joined a large force to track him down. 'So closely was the enemy pursued from place to place that the paramount chief of the Gaiah [Gaika] tribes was on the point of being captured by a detached patrole under Major Pinckney 73rd Regt.' The 'notorious Chieftain Sandilla' escaped by 'plunging into the jungle'.[63] Once they believed they had cleared the Amatola Mountains, patrolling ceased and the Regiment marched into Fort Hare in early November, having been 'served out' with new clothing.[64]

Another expedition, against the Basuto chief Moshesh, was mounted soon afterwards. The 'Sovereignty' force, consisting of one cavalry and two infantry brigades, included the 73rd. 'Ascended a very high mountain which took the wagons some time to get up,' Rich wrote on 19 November. 'We had a very hard job to get anything to boil a drop of coffee, as there was not a morsel of wood of any kind to be seen.'[65] Marching through Basutoland, by the beginning of December they reached the Caledon river. 'Crossed, and our Colonel [Eyre] would not allow a man to get a drink of water, and we was nearly up to our bellies in crossing the river. Most of the men was near dropping with thirst, but, such is the life of the soldier.'[66] On 13 December they reached the village of Plaatberg, where Chief Moshesh had been ordered to bring in a fine of several thousand head of cattle. Although some cattle were brought in, fighting broke out. 'The Kaffirs assembled by thousands, all mounted, and fought us hard from about half-past three to eight p.m.,' related Knox. 'We started at 4.a.m. and never eat a thing till 8 p.m., after an awful day's march; men were regularly done up.'[67]

As Rich related: 'The enemy kept up a heavy fire until dark, and charged us repeatedly, but we lay down with our bayonets fixed on the brow of the hill, and out of it they could not move us. Just at dark they made a desperate charge.'[68] Yet again superior weaponry prevailed, and by nightfall the battle was over. Back in camp, Knox bought a captured pony for £1 10s.[69] During the fighting Captain Faunce, Deputy Assistant Quarter Master and 'a valuable officer', was killed.[70] In an earlier accident, Eyre had been severely hurt when his horse fell down a hole and rolled over him.[71] Once peace terms with the Basuto were agreed, the force left Plaatberg on 24 December and returned to King William's Town.

The following year, Maqoma, famous for keeping Sir Harry Smith 'boxed up' in Fort Cox between Christmas and New Year 1850, sued for peace. Sandile fled (reappearing to fight the British again in the ninth Frontier War and dying in an ambush in 1878). In Cathcart's General Order, issued in March 1853, he pointed to the dangers they had faced for two years, which at one time had assumed 'the character of a war of races', had it not been arrested by the 'gallantry, perseverance and unparalleled exertions' of the regiments involved.[72] With hostilities at a temporary end, Cathcart adopted a 'blockhouse' policy, requiring the construction of eight towers between the Keiskamma and the Kei rivers. Only one was ever built – Castle Eyre – named after the 73rd's Commanding Officer, Lieutenant Colonel William Eyre, and built on the outskirts of Keiskamma Hoek. Gould Lucas, who had survived the wreck of the *Birkenhead*, had been promoted lieutenant in October 1852. Two years later he was sent to Natal as district and garrison adjutant, attached to the 45th Regiment. He died in 1914. Sergeant Kilkeary remained with the Regiment, completing thirteen years' service, and spending another twenty in the militia; he died in 1907.

After the formal peace was agreed in 1854, the 73rd moved to Cape Town, with detachments remaining at King William's Town and returning to the Frontier whenever the 'Kaffirs' appeared 'restless' or 'threatened disturbances'.[73] Pinckney, promoted lieutenant colonel in May 1854, briefly returned to Britain to assume command of the depot companies before taking command of the Regiment the following year when Eyre retired on half-pay. In 1856, the soldiers were armed with the new Lee Enfield rifle, with its improved range and accuracy. Medals were awarded to all those who had served since 1846 in the 'Kaffir Wars'.

Canada and Britain: the 42nd

While the 73rd was serving in South Africa, the 42nd had moved from Bermuda to Nova Scotia, where it had last served in 1786. Arriving in Halifax in 1851, detachments were sent to Prince Edward's Island, Cape Breton and Annapolis. After less than a year, in the spring of 1852, as the 73rd was recovering from the shock of the sinking of the *Birkenhead*, the 42nd returned home after an absence from Scotland of over fourteen years. The following year, in April 1853, the Regiment was travelling south to Weedon, where the soldiers encamped with a number of other regiments, before moving to Chobham in Surrey. While they were there, 'one of the first attempts that had been made to gather troops together for manoeuvres in our own country' took place, recalled a new officer, Ensign Peter Halkett, who had just transferred from the 81st.[74] During manoeuvres, the Highland Regiments – the 42nd and 93rd – made 'quite a sensation & cut out the Guards entirely, as such regiments had not been seen before by the country yokels, nor by the Londoners, who used to come in crowds by rail to see the field days'.[75] For the young Halkett, who came from Pitfirrane, Dunfermline, 'everything connected with a Highland Regiment was quite new to me'. Impressed by the men's height, 'and the swagger of both men & officers, which the kilt and feather bonnet unconsciously gives', he thought the officers were 'such a distinguished set of fellows, which no doubt the dress has something to do with'. Lieutenant Colonel Duncan Cameron, 'with his white head, & stern cast of countenance, seemed the very beau ideal of a commanding officer'.[76]

From Chobham, in July 1853, the Regiment went to Gosport, Portsmouth. With headquarters at Haslar Common, three companies were based across the Common at Fort Monckton. 'Our rooms looked out on a piece of lawn with guns & heaps of shot, & below the parapet was the sea, the Isle of Wight close off to the right, Portsmouth to the left, & the "needles" in front,' recorded Halkett.[77] They drilled on Haslar Common, 'a fine open English common with clumps of furze', through which Drysdale – who had been appointed adjutant – 'used to delight to make us march'. Since 'drill order' required the men to wear white jackets and kilts, 'it was no joke going through a fine old healthy furze bush'. As Halkett noted, it was the fashion at the time for the young subalterns of Highland Regiments 'to wear mufti kilts after parade, & of course the MacPhersons, Campbells, Camerons & Frazers had all their own clan tartan'.[78]

During their free time, with 'nothing in the world to do', the young officers enjoyed visiting Portsmouth, 'where there was a Theatre, & all sorts of amusements going on'. Accompanied by another ensign, Francis Scott, Halkett recollected that they kept a rowing boat '& could row ourselves round & up the harbour, instead of walking across the common to Gosport & then having to hire a boat to cross the harbour'.[79]

On one occasion they were lucky to escape with their lives: 'One night I was coming back in the boat quite late, the night being dark & squally & a strong tide running into the harbour.' Accompanied by Lieutenant 'Jock' Campbell, the senior subaltern, who had enjoyed 'sundry hot toddies', they told him to remain still and steer the boat, 'which he did by sending her straight up against the walls of the Block House Fort at the entrance of the harbour'. Since the tide was strong, they were in danger of being swamped. When Campbell tried to shove the boat off with his stick, it bent in half and he fell into the sea. 'The night was dark, & such a swell on, we couldn't see him at first, but I managed to get a hold of his head, & Scott of his arm and at the risk of upsetting the boat we succeeded in lugging him in, swearing at us for having as he said, pushed him in! We hit him on the head with an oar to keep him quiet & had to row back to Portsmouth & get him put to bed in an Hotel.' Looking back, Halkett realised how fortunate they were, 'for we didn't know much about boating, & the tides were dangerous, so that it is marvelous how we managed to escape having drowned in these evening expeditions.'[80]

Even as the officers and soldiers of the 42nd Royal Highland Regiment were drilling and manoeuvring in southern England, and the 73rd was marching on the plains of South Africa, in the distant lands of the decaying Ottoman Empire an argument had arisen between the Turks and the expanding power of Tsarist Russia. For Britain, their quarrel would lead to another war.

17.

Invading the Crimea

O'er the perilous edge of yon iron-crowned height,
Roll the sulphury fire-clouds of War;
Where the Gaul and the Briton their legions unite,
To tread on the neck of the Czar.[1]

1853

The Road to Conflict

The dispute between Russia and the Ottoman Turks related to guardianship of the Holy Places in Jerusalem. Nicholas I, Tsar of Russia, was claiming the right to protect all Christian subjects in those regions bordering the river Danube under Ottoman rule. In early July 1853 the Russian army occupied the Turkish principalities of Moldavia and Wallachia. On 4 October the Sultan of Turkey, confident of support from Britain and France, declared war on Russia. At the end of November, when Russia attacked and destroyed the Turkish fleet at Sinope, there was an outcry in both Britain and France, whose leaders saw Russian expansion in the declining Ottoman Empire as a threat to their interests in the Middle East. Over the coming months, the 'Eastern Question' dominated political debate in London and Paris. In early 1854, the British prime minister, the Earl of Aberdeen, presiding over a coalition government, bowed to pressure from his Cabinet and agreed to send an expeditionary force to Malta.

Almost as soon as the force departed, Britain's military commitment increased, when both the British and French governments agreed to make a combined attack on the fortress of Sebastopol (Sevastopol) in the Crimea, headquarters of Russia's Black Sea fleet. On 1 March 1854 the 42nd was ordered to prepare for active service. 'I look forward to everything even to see a Turkish cat, the fun of the voyage, the meeting of Regiments,' Captain Frederick Green Wilkinson wrote at once to his sister.[2] On 28 March, Britain and France formally declared war on Russia. 'I am sure there was not a town in the country more full of a martial spirit than Dundee,' recollected a young handloom weaver, Sandy Robb, who instantly signed up. 'War was in every one's mouth. In the saloons and public houses nothing but war songs were to be listened to.'[3] Since the 42nd had supplied recruits to the 93rd for the Malta Expeditionary Force, their numbers were increased by recruits from other regiments. 'Never will I forget the day we marched to the warlike sound of the bagpipes out of the ancient and famous town of Stirling,' recollected Private Walter Robertson, 'the windows and streets were filled with townspeople, the waving and adieus from little white hands and snowy handkerchiefs, the pretty eyes straining from every window, taking the last looks of the lads in kilts and bonnets.'[4]

At Portsmouth the new recruits were fitted for their uniforms. 'When we had gone through setting up and marching drill,' recollected Robb, 'we were formed into one squad, to learn what was called firelock drill, and it was the old Brown Bess that we were served with.'[5] The Regiment remained at Anglesea Barracks until early May. 'A great many of the parents of the officers who were ordered out, and who had sons in the Regiments at Portsmouth, came there and took houses to see the last of them; in many cases it *was* the last,' recalled Ensign Halkett. 'The Regt was then nearly 1000 strong & made a fine appearance on parade; many of the men having been 12 & 15 years or more in the Regt & very tall & big, & on Sundays with the feather bonnets, belted plaids hanging from the left shoulder, & red & white diced stockings without gaiters, & shoes with large brass buckles, they did look very well indeed.'[6]

Writing with hindsight, Halkett continued: 'No one knew what was to be the result of the expedition, though most people thought the great display of Naval & Military power by England & France would oblige the Emperor of Russia to accede to our demands without actual fighting.'[7] After a final inspection, Lieutenant Colonel Duncan Cameron 'slow walked his horse down the Ranks, & then riding out to the front, gave the word "42nd fours right" "quick march" the Band struck up and we emerged into the street through such a crowd I never saw & we had actually to push our way along for nearly a mile to the dock gates, such cheering, men & women running out of their houses with pots of beer for the men, girls hanging on to the arms of soldiers, their husbands or lovers.'[8]

Whereas the French and Turks conveyed their troops in warships, the British had chartered special transport ships.[9] 'We are very comfortable indeed in this ship and have made a very good passage,'

Lieutenant Thomas Henry Montgomery wrote home on board the steam transport *Hydaspes*, in which eight companies had embarked on 19 May. 'I cannot say so much for the poor men's accommodation, they are very crowded . . . The band of course play on the poop every day and often pipes play for the men to dance in the evening only it is getting too hot now for that. They sing a good deal in chorus.'[10] Halkett remembered how 'at 12 o'clock every day, the bugle sounded for "grog" & a glass of Rum was served out to each man & boy.' To prevent any attempt to give away or sell his tot, 'each man had to swallow it there & then'.[11] After a stormy passage in the Bay of Biscay, the weather improved: 'Bathing parades took place each morning before 8 o'clock, a large sail was suspended by the four corners, from a boom projecting from the ship's side, allowing the centre of the bagged sail to be in the sea, so that it formed a large swimming bath, safe from sharks, and from drowning.'[12] On one occasion a shoal of porpoises provided pistol practice.[13]

In early June 1854, after 'a delightful run', the *Hydaspes* reached Malta;[14] the anchor was dropped and coal taken on board. 'The letters and newspapers told us that in every likelihood there was to be war to the knife,' recalled Robb.[15] The journey was pleasant, 'for everyone on board was in the best of health and spirits. We were served out with plenty of wholesome food and fresh water.' During the day, they read books or played games; 'and the band did its share to make the time lightsome'.[16] Wilkinson was longing 'to get into marching trim', considering himself 'fat and groggy from lolling about and eating all sorts of luxuries'.[17] Passing through the Dardanelles and the Sea of Marmora, 'a squall came on that caused some stir among us, knapsacks flying here and there'.[18] At Scutari, 'the camp equipage of the Regiment was at once landed,' the Regiment disembarking the next day.[19]

The three Highland Regiments – the 42nd, 79th and 93rd – were brigaded together as the Highland Brigade in the 1st Division, under the command of sixty-one-year-old Brigadier General Sir Colin Campbell, who, in the 9th Foot, had fought in the Peninsular and Napoleonic Wars.[20] The other brigade consisted of three battalions of Guards – the Grenadier, Coldstream and Scots Fusilier – whose men were reportedly less healthy and in whose footsteps, by order of precedence, the Highland Brigade would have to tread. The 1st Division was under the command of Queen Victoria's cousin, Prince George, Duke of Cambridge, grandson of George III. The Light, 2nd and 3rd Divisions made up the British force.[21]

Having disembarked on the Scutari side of the Bosphorus, where there was a large Turkish barracks and a hospital, the men spent their first day getting their baggage on shore and erecting their tents. 'Our knapsacks were our pillows,' noted Robb, 'the bare ground our feather bed, and one blanket our bedclothes.'[22] 'Our first taste of camping now began, by the officers receiving the same rations as the men & everything for both men & officers was cooked in the open air,' Halkett recollected; 'all this being new to the men, they were some time before they got into the way of making the ovens & cooking properly & we had a small ration about 1½lbs of meat & 2lbs of biscuit with a small quantity of cocoa & brown sugar served out to last, the latter at least, for two days, & I had nothing very handy to keep my sugar in, so I put it in a nice clean skull, that I found in the cemetery & found it very convenient.'[23]

The 'field kit' which the soldiers had to carry, related Robb, consisted of 'two shirts, two pairs of socks, two hard towels, and a hold-all complete, and a pair of hoses, with the makings of a pair of soles, heels, and welts, and, as we wore the kilt we had to carry a pair of trousers – all that inside our knapsacks, while our greatcoat was rolled on the top, and a blanket folded on the back'.[24] According to Montgomery, 'so much good feeling' existed between the regiments of the brigade, 'we are just like one regiment'.[25] But he was annoyed by the instructions before they left. 'They told us at home that subalterns were only to have a horse between them and so of course my brother sub and I left England with a pair of bullock trunks between us, now we find that each of us can have a horse and of course our baggage won't fit well having nothing to counterbalance the one trunk.'[26] Robb remembered being told 'that we were to be on friendly terms with the French' – camped near by, under the command of

Marshal Armand-Jacques Leroy de Saint Arnaud, who had distinguished himself in the French Foreign Legion before rising to become
France's minister of war – 'that in no case were we to refer to past
wars, and that we were to pay the same compliments to the French
officers as we did to our own'. It was, he said, 'a common sight to see
a Frenchman and a kilty walking together, and perhaps two sheets
in the wind, although they did not understand what they were saying
to each other'.[27]

By the time the British and French armies arrived in the Bosphorus,
the Russian army had crossed the Danube and was laying siege to
Silistria, in north-eastern Bulgaria, still part of the Ottoman Empire.
Before attacking Sebastopol, the Allies turned their attention to
supporting the Turks, which meant landing at Varna, on the western
rim of the Black Sea. On 13 June, the Regiment again boarded the
Hydaspes, disembarking two days later at Varna, by which time the
siege of Silistria had been raised. 'The news from the seat of war is
very satisfactory,' Montgomery wrote home, 'the Russians getting
beat by the Turks.'[28]

For two weeks, the soldiers remained at Varna. 'Sir Colin Campbell
used to have the Brigade out nearly every morning,' related Halkett;
'the sun got very hot early in the day so the parades were generally
about six o'clock and over by 8.'[29] 'The row in Camp is awful,'
Wilkinson wrote to his mother, 'neighing of horses, breaking loose,
kicking each other. I like it all in spite of everything. But just imagine,
no vegetables, sour bread, no milk, only eggs and cocoa or tea, your
rations not the best, and to get anything in the town you are cheated.'[30]
'There are lots of snakes and centipedes here,' observed Montgomery.
'One has always to shake ones clothes and boots before putting them
on as very likely a reptile of some kind has taken French possession
of them for the night.'[31]

At the beginning of July, there was an outbreak of cholera and the
camp was moved inland to Alladyne, 'a fine large plain,' recorded
Robb, 'with plenty of springs of good water, and plenty of old rotten
trees that supplied good cooking wood'.[32] 'Hang it,' complained
Wilkinson soon after their arrival, 'the Duke [of Cambridge] has just

sent to say we must all shave. Now I am so proud of my moustache and beard you would not believe how the sun brings out one's beard. It is an inch long and thick and strong but of course looks dirty till it is longer.'[33] 'I bathe in the lake everyday before dinner it is such a luxury after the heat of the day,' Montgomery informed his sister Helen.[34] 'We are always obliged to ride out in uniform which is a great bore both for the heat and to us having to carry such a great long heavy sword which is not calculated for riding in and comes greatly in the way of geese, ducks, baskets of eggs, etc which are generally hanging from our saddles, to say nothing of the thumps ones side received from the hilt causing it to become black and blue.'[35]

Despite the move inland, cholera was still prevalent. 'Nothing is so depressing to troops as the constant burying parties,' recorded Halkett, '& sound of the "Dead March" from morning to night; & the deaths soon became so frequent, that no music was permitted, & the soldiers were only followed to their graves by a few men of their companies.'[36] So devastating was the outbreak that, at the end of July, they again moved camp, to Gevrekler, 'and the change was for the better. There were fewer deaths, and we got more cheery,' recollected Robb.[37] 'We are on the whole healthy and the rations are very fair,' Captain Joseph Grove wrote to his uncle, 'the Mail comes in very regularly and we have nothing at all to complain of except idleness, which we feel greatly. Everyone wishes to meet the Enemy.'[38] Lieutenant John McLeod was worrying about his prospects, enquiring from his grandfather about the possibility of borrowing money: £1,100 was the price for purchasing a company.[39]

In mid-August, the 1st Division was ordered to return to Varna, camping at nearby Galata. 'No one knows what we are going to do,' mused Montgomery to his sister. 'A great many say we are to attack Sebastopol this year or at least to land on the Crimea, I shall not believe it till we are fairly off.'[40] 'Won't we astonish the rascally old Czar,' Wilkinson wrote to his mother. 'I hear all the Russians collect in the Crimea, and are very gay indeed, and it is the Isle of Wight of Russia.'[41] As they prepared for their departure, they were told to get flannel linings for their coats, because 'on landing we take no tents, no baggage, no change, and have to sleep each night on the ground'.[42]

Having been delayed by a serious fire in Varna which destroyed valuable supplies, at the end of August a 'magnificent' armada set sail for the Crimea, 'the number of troops embarked being about 26,000 English, 24,000 French and about 10,000 Turks,' recorded John McLeod.[43] 'Talk of other Wars and read what you like,' Wilkinson enthused, 'there never was such a force collected or such numerous vessels. Before we sail we expect some grand signal from the Fleet, like old Nelson did, in short I am in glorious spirits and do nothing but laugh when I ought to feel rather melancholy . . . consider you ought to be proud of having a son in so good a Regiment, and going to do his duty *at last*.'[44] 'So we are now fairly in for some tough work; I shall be glad if we do it and get it all over,' remarked Montgomery, adding: 'the orders are out and we start in a few days to "invade the Crimea", these are the words used. The Light Division land first and ours next. No opposition to our landing expected.'[45]

During the journey across the Black Sea, more outbreaks of cholera reduced their ranks. 'When it was dark a boat would be lowered, and the dead bodies of our comrades, sewed up in their blankets, would be put into it,' recalled Robb. 'The boat was rowed some distance from the ship, so that we might not hear the splash when the bodies were committed to the deep.'[46]

'This ship life is dreadful, one does nothing but eat and drink and little exercise,' Wilkinson was complaining again. 'I cannot feel as I ought before such a grand affair as this will be. I feel much more as if I had left a beastly unhealthy school, and I was going home for the holidays, but I suppose a few 68 pounders grazing ones nose will cause me to consider ones real position.'[47] The grandeur, he said, was almost beyond description. 'If I could only paint, you never saw such a lovely sight, the blue sky and sea and splendid vessels with the glorious old English flags flying in all directions. It is more splendid than anything I ever saw, and particularly knowing our object so good.'[48] Keeping their spirits up, the officers and men danced together to Highland tunes played by the band. 'Everybody employed his spare moments now in writing home,' recalled Halkett, 'as a mail would leave immediately the forces had made a landing – there was no telegraph, then, further than Trieste – so news was a long time reaching home.'[49]

Their landing place was Kalamita Bay, north of Sebastopol. 'The weather continuing favourable, the disembarkation of both armies commenced at once (the French about 2 miles south of the English) under cover of the guns of the Line of Battleships and steamers.'[50] As Robb recorded: 'The fleet sailors did their work nobly; at the landing of us they were up to the waist, some of them carrying us on their backs to dry land in line of march order.'[51]

The first night on shore was 'very wet and uncomfortable', Montgomery told his sister.[52] 'We were without tents,' Halkett recollected, '& lay in wet pools or in mud – our blankets heavy & clinging cold with water.' The following morning, they had to search for firewood, 'but little could be had for so many, though we found some driftwood on the shore which served to make a smoky miserable heat just enough to warm our cocoa, into which we broke the ration biscuits & made a sort of pottage – the only fresh water I got that morning to make my cocoa & wash my face, was in the wheel marks of an artillery wagon, which had filled with rain.'[53] 'It was here we burned the boards of our knapsacks to cook with,' recorded Private John Bryson.[54]

Unopposed by the Russians, they marched inland. 'We had fresh provisions yesterday and very good they were, the beef here is very good and much preferable to Bulgarian, a ration of rum is served out everyday also,' Montgomery told his sister. 'The inhabitants here are very good to the soldiers and give them all sorts of things; it is our policy to conciliate them and no stealing or pilfering is allowed, everything is paid for. The French do not go on the same principle, their soldiers are allowed to go about the country in all directions.'[55]

Alma September 1854

'On, Highlanders, on,' the old General cries –
'And you'll grant me one favour, I know –
Lads! Fire not a shot, though your Highland blood rise,
Till you stand but a yard from the foe!'[56]

On the morning of 19 September, the British force, under the supreme command of sixty-six-year-old Fitzroy Somerset, 1st Baron Raglan, began the march towards Sebastopol.[57] 'The weather was very warm, and as the march was pursued under the full blaze of the autumn sun, across a flat level plain, loaded as we were, we felt it very exhausting and were tormented by a burning thirst which there was no means of alleviating, no water being found on the route,' related Sergeant Edward McSally.[58] 'After a march of about 9 or 10 miles,' Montgomery wrote, 'our horse artillery had a shot or two at some outposts of the enemy which was returned, also the cavalry had some little skirmishing with the Cossacks.'[59]

'When we halted for the night strong outlying pickets were posted,' recalled Robb, 'and our brigade was formed into one square round the field guns, hospital staff, and commissary. We piled our arms, took off our knapsacks, unrolled our blankets, and down we went. Some were soon asleep, but others fell to talking about what they had to do. It was kept no secret that we were soon to be engaged, and the best of friendship was kept up among us, the older soldiers cheering up the spirits of the young ones.'[60] 'It is not surprising,' recollected Halkett, recently promoted lieutenant, and who was carrying the Queen's Colour, 'that sleep did not overcome me till near daybreak, in the first place having charge of the colours I had to take care that the sentry pacing up & down in front of where they were piled across rifles with bayonets fixed close to where I lay, was alert.' He was also thinking of home '& all one's loved friends & relations, whom in all probability, would never more be seen –

every scene of my life seemed to pass before me like a panorama'.[61] Eventually, Halkett fell asleep, to be woken before daybreak by the bugles sounding reveille: 'All were quickly in the ranks & standing in columns silently waiting for day. After it had been reported by the outlying pickets that no movement of the enemy had taken place during the night, we were allowed to fall out for breakfast. That meal consisted of biscuit, salt pork & cocoa.'[62] 'Before marching a shattering fire of musketry was heard in [the] rear,' recollected McSally. 'At first we thought it was some skirmish with the Cossacks, but we soon found out that it was cattle being killed for the day's ration, each man getting his allowance of flesh warm and quivering.'[63]

'A Gun was fired as the order to move off about 8.00 in the morning,' related Private Charles Wilson. 'I think every Band in the Allied Armies struck up a tune when this grand march commenced on this great flat plain towards the river Alma, a beautiful clear sky above, with the sun out and the wind blowing and all the Regimental standards uncovered flying to the wind.'[64] After marching a few miles towards a rolling hillside, they saw the Russian army, under the command of sixty-seven-year-old Prince Alexander Sergeyevich Menshikov, 'strongly posted on a range of heights extending as far inland as we could see', recollected McSally.[65] 'When we came in sight of the high ground where the Russians were, our [Lieutenant] Colonel, D.A. Cameron, gave the order for the pipers to play up,' recalled Private Bryson, 'they played "March to the Battlefield the foe are on before us." The Duke [of Cambridge] rode over and asked our Colonel what the pipers were playing and when told, he said "Very appropriate."'[66]

The position occupied by the Russians was one 'of great natural strength', with the left and right flanks positioned on the heights surrounding a 'great amphitheatre or Wide Valley'. Halfway down the slope was a trench extending for about a hundred yards; on the right was the Russian battery of heavy guns. Artillery had been posted to prevent passage across the river. On the slopes, the Russian infantry was lined up, with the reserve positioned on the heights, amounting to between 45,000 to 50,000 men: 'such was the formidable position of the Alma'.[67] 'It was a pretty and interesting sight to all of us, the commencement of the action,' continued McSally. 'It was begun by the ships far to our right throwing shells into the left of the Enemy's position. The day was warm, with a light westerly breeze, and a beautifully clear atmosphere through which the graceful curve of smoke, left by the shell in its flight, could be plainly distinguished.'[68] 'The noise became tremendous,' Wilkinson recorded, 'and about 40 or 50 guns of the enemy opened upon our troops, the Heights one mass of smoke . . . I thought now Master Fred your hour's coming . . . We kept advancing and lying down, and each time lying down in a spot I had seen a shell or cannon strike.'[69]

With the 42nd under fire for the first time since Waterloo, 'the artillery men on both sides were plying their guns as fast as they could,' recorded McSally, 'while a continuous fire of Musketry was kept up.'[70] 'We had to lie down with the shot and shell coming in amongst us,' Montgomery wrote, confessing 'that is the only time I felt afraid and flinched at every shot.'[71] As McSally recollected, the men were very thirsty; when they came to a vineyard 'the vines hung with grapes that looked cool and inviting. Everyone stopped, and plucked and ate them, although grape-shot and shell were being showered down by the enemy. Pushing across the vineyard we came to the river.'[72]

In front of them, the Light Division crossed first, but, as Raglan later reported to the secretary of state for war, the Duke of Newcastle, the banks of the river were 'extremely rugged, and in most parts steep; the willows along it had been cut down in order to prevent them from affording cover to the attacking party, and in fact everything had been done to deprive an assailant of any species of shelter'.[73] 'On ordinary occasions,' McSally continued, 'when a man is wounded and falls, he has a chance, indeed is certain, to be picked up and taken care of, but in a river, he is more likely to be drowned. Our good luck hitherto, did not, however, desert us here, and we all got over safe.'[74] Halkett, 'encumbered' with the Colour, was given a hand up.[75] Having forded the river, Colin Campbell halted the Highland Brigade under a bank, sheltered from the Russian guns, so the regiments could take up formation. He then spoke 'a few straightforward soldierly words':

Now men, you are going into action. Remember this: whoever is wounded – no matter what his rank – must lie where he falls till the bandsmen come to attend to him. No soldiers must go carrying off wounded comrades. If any man does such a thing his name shall be stuck up in his parish church. The army will be watching you; make me proud of the Highland brigade!

Riding to the front of the soldiers in line, Campbell gave the memorable command: 'Forward, the Forty-second!'[76] According to McSally, when Campbell shouted 'Come on Forty-Second,' no one moved. Waving his hat, Campbell repeated the command. 'The first few paces were taken rather unsteadily. We had never previously stepped off at the Brigadier's command, and waited for the Colonel giving the word, but he did not do so. On Sir Colin repeating his command and so earnestly we saw that he wished us to move off at once, and we accordingly did so at the centre, but the flanks, not hearing his words or noticing his gesture, were late in stepping off.'[77]

'Up the hill we went,' related Montgomery. 'We were well into the thick of it then and thought of nothing.'[78] 'We were now about to meet the hard, square, grey, columns, we had seen from the plain, and many an anxious eye was cast right and left, to see that all were advancing, none hanging back,' recalled McSally. These were the Vladimir and Kazan columns, which had re-formed after an early assault by the Guards. 'With a feeling of pride', the 42nd passed through the ranks of the Light Division, 'and found that no body of British troops was interposed between us and the enemy'.[79] 'I had now some trouble & anxiety,' related Halkett, carrying the Colours, 'as when in advancing in line, the whole Regt "dresses" upon the Colours, which are in the centre of the line.' As he recollected, Ensign Forth – Malcolm Drummond, Viscount Forth, the son of the Earl of Perth – was carrying the Regimental Colour, but he 'kept hanging back, requiring me constantly to keep on saying "come on with you, you're putting out the whole line."' At one stage, Major Thomas Tulloch rode up and 'pitched in to him'.[80]

As they marched forward, Campbell's horse was shot from under him, the men at first thinking he might have been killed. With orders to fix bayonets, one young Highlander dropped his and went back to retrieve it. Thinking that he was deserting, Tulloch gave the order for him to be shot as a coward. Fortunately, he picked up the bayonet and rejoined his comrades before the order was carried out. 'I wasna' runnin' awa', sir,' he exclaimed.[81] At least one straggler was bringing up the rear. 'I was by this time some distance below my regiment, and the musket balls were falling very thick around me,' recollected Robb, 'so I got up as hard as I could to my company, who were on the top of the heights, and were advancing, now keeping up a brisk fire. As I was going up to it I went through plenty of killed and wounded Russians.'[82] 'As our advance continued with its original rapidity,' McSally related, 'we were closing fast on them when their determination to resist so sternly seemed at last to give way, and no wonder. More than half their number were killed or wounded, and they hurried off as quickly as they could, still facing about to fire at us.'[83]

'About this time the battle was to us a most exhilarating sight,' he continued. 'We knew we were the most advanced regiments of the British Line. The enemy were flying before us, our men were cheering and firing, and getting up the hill almost at a run, a few moments more and the Russians passed the crest of the hill disappearing from our sight after leaving at least three-fourths of their number on the hill-side.'[84] Briefly, the soldiers thought the Russians were going to regroup. 'The enemy's column again retreated until it was a short distance up the opposite hill, when they halted and faced in our direction. We could then see Officers with drawn swords passing to and fro along the front of the Companies. After a while the column began to advance towards us at a slow pace, but, in a few moments seemed to think better of it, and turned to the rear again.'[85] Lest the Russians change their minds, a salvo in their midst destroyed them. 'It was terrible to see the effect of the shells bursting in the middle of a great square of infantry,' recalled Halkett. 'The explosion seemed to open out the whole column, but they quickly closed up again & resumed the retreat in perfect order.'[86]

Removing the wounded during the battle had its own dangers: 'the Bandsmen had to go into as heavy a fire as that which threatened ourselves, they had to remain tough under it, without the excitement incident to fighting, and with nothing to sustain them but their feelings of humanity and devotion to their duty.'[87] Being firmly established on the heights of Alma, 'the fortune of the day was decided'. That night the British army bivouacked 'on the enemy's ground'. Having been under arms since six in the morning, and in action since one o'clock, it was four in the afternoon by the time fighting ceased.[88] While British troops had been attacking the Russians' left, the French had attacked their right, 'which ended in the total defeat of the enemy who retreated'.[89]

After this early victory, Raglan signalled his approval, lifting his hat 'to us as he rode past the regiment', recollected Robb. Congratulating the 42nd, the Duke of Cambridge said: 'Well done 42nd, you are a lot of bricks!' which gave the Regiment a new nickname for the duration of the campaign.[90] 'Lord Raglan came up presently and sent for me,' recorded Sir Colin Campbell, whereupon Campbell asked 'a great favour – that he would permit me to have the honour of wearing the Highland bonnet during the rest of the campaign, which pleased them very much'.[91] According to Wilkinson, the 42nd's Commanding Officer, Duncan Cameron, immediately added: 'with a *red* hackle in it'.[92] 'When Sir Colin's request was granted,' recounted McSally, 'the men set up a deafening cheer crying "Scotland forever" and "Ireland for longer" bawled an enthusiastic Irishman throwing his Feather Bonnet in the air, and yelling a "Harroo" that set everyone laughing.'[93] Raglan's dispatch home commended the Highland Brigade for advancing 'in admirable order and steadiness up the high ground', forcing the Russians 'completely to abandon the position they had taken such pains to defend and secure'.[94]

Once the senior officers had ridden past, the men could 'pile arms'. Supper consisted of beef with an extra half-ration of biscuits, ordered by Raglan, to compensate for their supplies, which had become sodden when crossing the Alma.[95] That evening, Lieutenant Montgomery wrote to his sister, describing their 'first victory' over the Russians and the 'very narrow escape' he had, when 'a shell burst close to me and a ball flew past my ear'.[96] Lieutenant John McLeod had only a scrap of paper on which to write to his mother: 'It is now pitch dark and I take advantage of the Adjutant's candle to scribble a few lines to let you know we have had a terrible engagement with the enemy who were posted very strongly on a range of hills, and that thank God we have escaped without any loss of officers and very few men killed.'[97] From the 42nd, seven private soldiers were killed; thirty-two soldiers and two sergeants were wounded.[98]

Russian losses were far greater: 'This battle field is exactly like pictures you see,' Wilkinson described to his sister, 'horses and men all dead in awful positions killed instantaneously, arms and shoulders torn off, men groaning, pots and pans and thousands of packs soon ransacked . . . you can't imagine how horrid the smell is. I have got quite accustomed to the horrors, dead being carried past me even now.'[99] 'What moved me most was a nice-looking young lad, about my own age,' Robb recorded, describing a wounded Russian. 'He waved his hand towards us. Tom Steele stepped out to him, gave him a drink out of his water keg, took off his knapsack and laid his head on it. The poor fellow took Tom's hand and kissed it. A short time after he died.'[100] Writing after the battle, McSally noted the effect 'on the tempers of the men'. Whereas normally in an argument 'the big man was apt to speak to a smaller one rather contemptuously . . . in the battle the big man found, that, however great his strength and determination to meet the enemy, he could not get one inch in front of the smallest man in the Regiment. He had therefore to respect him, and for long afterwards there was in the Regiment, a courtesy of intercourse most agreeable to experience.'[101]

The making of Campbell' s bonnet, combining the hackles of the three regiments in the Brigade, was entrusted to the 42nd's adjutant, Jock Drysdale. 'It was finally decided,' related historian Forbes, 'to have the upper third red for the 42nd, and the remaining two-thirds white at the bottom for the 79th and 93rd.' When it was ready, a brigade parade was ordered and Campbell rode into the square with his bonnet on. 'No formal signal was given but he was greeted with such volumes of cheering that both the English and French armies were startled into wonderment as to what was going on.'[102]

The Highland Brigade spent two nights on the heights of Alma. 'We have no tents; it is very cold at nights, sleeping in the open air but I think the cholera has gone,' Montgomery wrote home.[103] On the third day, they departed, 'leaving behind us a good many whose bones are still lying there as the only memorial of that great battle, the wounded being put on board of ship,' recorded Robb. 'With the exception of feeling regret for our helpless comrades, we were all in the best of spirits, and we were under the impression that we were to be in good winter quarters in Sebastopol, although we were marching over ground where there was no appearance of inhabitants or cultivation.'[104] After the defeat at Alma, lest the Russian army become encircled, Menshikov withdrew his troops, making sure to cut off the entrance to the inlet where the Russian fleet lay, by scuttling several ships.[105] The defence of Sebastopol was left in the hands of Vice Admiral Vladimir Kornilov, assisted by Menshikov's 'clever & energetic' engineer, Lieutenant Colonel Eduard Ivanovich Totleben.[106]

Meanwhile, instead of attacking Sebastopol from the north, Raglan agreed with the ailing Saint Arnaud, sick with cholera, to march the army south. This meant circumventing the city and losing the opportunity to attack Star Fort, arguably the most obvious point of entry into the city.[107] On the way, a brief encounter with the rear of a Russian division netted 'a vast quantity of ammunition and much valuable baggage', giving the troops the luxury of a diversion. Several wagons, loaded with flour and oatmeal, had been taken and so the soldiers were permitted to fall out and help themselves to as much oatmeal as they could carry. 'This was glorious news to us Scotchmen,' recollected Robb. 'In a short time we were more like millers than soldiers.'[108] But their progress was slow: 'only a few steps would be taken,' recorded Halkett, 'when a halt was necessary, it was exactly like what occurs in coming out of a crowded assembly – the least stop in front causes a block all the way back, & this went on for hours – all the time we were laden heavily with knapsack, blanket, greatcoat, & provisions in haversack, & I was so tired I could hardly get along.'[109]

Having crossed the Chernaya (Tchernaya) river and skirted around Sebastopol, the French and British armies found themselves marching through 'a perfect paradise; it seemed one immense garden; plums, apples, cherries in profusion, & on the ground, abundance of pumpkins, tomatoes, cabbages, and vines growing low & tied up to stakes, laden with ripe purple, & white grapes'.[110] While the French, now commanded by the deceased Saint Arnaud's successor, General François Canrobert, established their supply base below Sebastopol at Kamiesh Bay, the British took up position in a natural inlet further south frequented by the Venetians and Genoese in their maritime journeys to the Orient. 'To the front, a short distance off, there were steep heights, and on them was an ancient-like castle that had the appearance of being fortified,' recollected Robb. 'In a short time it was in our possession. We also took the town at the foot of the heights, the name of which will be long in dying out of history, namely, Balaclava.'[111]

Balaclava October 1854

When can their glory fade? Or the wild charge they made![112]

While the 93rd was left to guard Balaclava, the 42nd and 79th took up position on the high ground in front of Sebastopol. Since Campbell was in command at Balaclava, Lieutenant Colonel Duncan Cameron was given command of the Brigade, while Major George Cumberland took command of the Regiment.[113] 'As we were now before Sebastopol, along with the French, the heavy duty began,' noted Robb. While they waited for the siege guns to be landed at Balaclava, the troops began digging redoubts, gun batteries and trenches. 'Strong outlying pickets of the whole regiment were put out all around our position, and under fire from the long-range guns from the Russian ships in the bay and the forts.'[114] 'It was a disappointment to all to find that instead of an immediate assault, we were in for a regular siege – but no one thought it would hold out more than a few weeks,' wrote Halkett, who was observing thousands of Russian soldiers 'working like ants at the entrenchments, & not only they, but crowds of women & children, all carrying earth, wheeling barrows, & working away like anything'.[115]

Rations were poor. 'Tea was looked on as a treat in two ways, as the men that smoked would dry the leaves and smoke them, all the tobacco being done,' noted Robb. 'This was the time for real comradeship, for the duties were so hard and complicated that we might not see each other for days – the one on picket, the other on working or covering party duty. The one that happened to be in camp had to draw his comrade's rations, and be off on some duty before we would see him, but he would leave them at his place in the tent.'[116] 'I cannot describe how sick I am of the whole thing,' Wilkinson confided to his sister in late September, 'any man that says he likes it must tell a lie for to lie out all night in all weather on the ground and no tent, badly fed and then when you do fight, what can be more horrible than killing human nature.'[117]

On 17 October 1854, the artillery battle began. 'The 42nd was in the first parallel, the furthest off from the town, & the whole of the trenches were lined with troops, in case an assault being ordered should the Russian batteries be knocked to pieces. Never shall I forget that fire,' recalled Halkett, 'the air was filled with hurtling iron missiles, shells bursting in all directions, earth, gabions, & even men being sent flying into the air, as some heavy round shot tore its way through the shelter behind which the men were lying.'[118] 'We fall in at 4 a.m. and remain an hour under arms until daylight appears. They keep shelling at us all day but never come near enough,' Wilkinson told his sister. 'One hundred guns at Alma were bad enough but ourselves and enemy firing 400 guns at the same time have, as the papers say, beat the thunder. The thing is to sleep hard till they begin.'[119]

The Russians' first success was destroying two French batteries. British firepower then set off the magazine in one of the principal redoubts, the Malakoff, silencing most of the Russian guns and killing

Kornilov. His successor was Admiral Pavel Nakhimov, victor against the Turks at Sinope in 1853. Following the destruction of the French batteries, however, the planned infantry assault on the Malakoff did not take place, leaving later critics of the war to suggest that yet another opportunity for an early conquest had been missed.[120] After the first day's bombardment, 'all night, strong fatigue parties were working at the embrasures & repairing the havoc caused by the enemy,' recounted Halkett; 'the Russians were busy all night doing the same thing, & their batteries which, when we last saw them, were a heap of ruins, were next morning repaired with fresh earth, gabions, & new guns, & as good as ever – which made us begin to think we had a stiffer job before us than we expected.'[121]

Contrary to expectations back home, Sebastopol did not immediately fall. 'The people of England are in a terrible hurry to smash Sebastopol and one paper actually announces its fall on the 25th September or some day about that time, but here we are a month later and it has not fallen yet,' Montgomery complained on 22 October. 'It must be very tiresome for you having such a lot of contradictory accounts in the papers.' Yet he remained optimistic. 'This is the fifth day since our guns opened and report says that a very few more days will suffice, they cannot hold out and the mortality is very great whilst on our side it is very small.' He told his sister that he had not brushed his hair for a month. 'I am very uncomfortable and feel like a beast; a bed, even the small camp bed, would be a treat. We have our tents but no baggage so we lie like horses on straw.' With 'splendid weather and little rain', water was scarce, and what little they got 'very bad and dirty'.[122]

To add to their distress, cholera had returned: 'There was scarcely a day but we had more or less funerals to go to in our regiment, and the other regiments were as bad as us,' recalled Robb, describing how the chaplain, Reverend Campbell, 'offered up an impressive prayer at the grave, and would pray for the relations at home to receive the sad news with hope, and for grace and strength to those around the grave to do their duty as men, and that this dreadful conflict would soon be over.'[123]

Early on the morning of 25 October 1854, the Russian army counter-attacked, capturing two redoubts manned by the Turks at Balaclava. 'It so happened,' recollected Robb, 'that all our regiment was in camp, and we were expecting to get that day's rest, but the rations were scarcely served out when the words came – "Fall in; fall in, at once."'[124] Marching towards the plain of Balaclava, the 93rd was already in position 'and only supported by about two hundred weakly men, while before them was the enemy in overwhelming numbers in cavalry, artillery, and infantry'.[125] 'Sir Colin had already ridden off down to the plain to see what was going on,' Halkett recollected. 'When we arrived at the summit of the plateau over-looking the valley of Balaclava, the whole scene was spread out before us in a panorama – there were the whole Cavalry Division & the 93rd drawn up in a "thin red line" & great masses of Russian Cavalry out to the front, & as we looked, some regiments of Cossacks on small ponies advanced to the front, with evident intention to attack, & they were closely followed by other Regiments of Light Cavalry – we now observed our Heavy Cavalry begin to move, & the Scots Greys forming into line advanced towards the Russian Cavalry – as they approached, the Greys began to trot.'[126]

When they saw the Scots Greys, Robb recollected Major Cumberland calling out 'Good God, there's the Greys charging, and they are out of sight. Double 42nd; double.'[127] Robb continued: 'As we were coming down the heights, Sir Colin called out, as he saw us and the 79th, "Here come the Bricks." But we did not get the chance to prove ourselves bricks at that heat. Had we been there sooner, we would no doubt.'[128] Halkett took up the story: 'It was intensely exciting, as the Greys appeared to gallop completely over the Cossacks on their small horses, & they were tumbled about all over the ground, while swords were gleaming & lances thrusting in all directions.' With the 93rd standing fast, the 42nd continued marching 'to the scene of action & were soon drawn up in a line on the left of the 93rd. The heavy cavalry had by this time been engaged with the enemy, & were now returning after a brilliant charge in which they had put to rout a superior number of the enemy. I remember one Sgt of the Greys riding through our ranks with his leg smashed by a canon ball, & waving his hand to us saying "we gave it 'em hurrah for old Scotland" – and I heard Colonel Cameron say "splendid fellow".'[129]

Then came the charge of the Light Brigade, under the command of the Earl of Cardigan. 'They were ordered to recapture the guns abandoned by the Turks, the order was brought up at a gallop by Captain Louis Nolan 1st Hussars who was on Lord Cardigan's Staff, & who I believe had a great dislike to Cardigan.' According to Halkett, the order was to 'attack immediately' without being precise what to attack. 'So the Light Brigade started on its historical journey, with Captain Nolan riding immediately in advance – he was in the act of waving his sword as if to indicate the way, when a fragment of shell fired by the enemy struck him full in the chest – he was killed on the spot, but his horse turned & galloped back, the body still remaining erect in the saddle until shortly it fell to the ground among our own tents. The Light Brigade soon disappeared over the rising ground, & the actual charge could not be seen by us.'[130]

Even at the time, the soldiers realised that a terrible mistake had been made. Instead of charging to prevent the Russians carrying away the naval guns from the redoubts they had just captured from the Turks on the nearby Causeway Heights, as Raglan had intended, the Light Brigade had charged directly at the Russian army. Lieutenant Montgomery was on picket duty: 'The general report is that a mistake was made in the order, the cavalry were intended to charge and take some of the enemy's guns on the right of the position, which they could have easily done, but mistaking the order they charged the wrong place.'[131] Although, contrary to popular belief, the Brigade was not completely destroyed, it was severely mauled.[132] As the soldiers surveyed the carnage, 'awful' sights confronted them: 'The wounds were quite different to any we were accustomed to, as, being mostly inflicted by the cavalry swords, they were terrible to look at – men with an arm sliced off, or their head cut down to their shoulders – and a vast number of wounded in comparison with those killed.'[133] So terrible were their wounds that Robb recollected hearing the expression: 'Did Great Britain send out men to suffer like this?'[134]

The disaster at Balaclava marked the beginning of the winter campaign. 'The dismal time was now commenced,' Robb recollected, 'for with digging and picking in the daytime, and strong pickets at night, on poor rations, our clothing worn-out, and in a move of vermin, and the nearly worn-out bell tents to sleep in on the cold, bare ground, we were getting less in number every day. Diarrhoea was also making sad havoc among us.' If the weather was good, Robb described the bagpipes playing 'Johnnie Cope' and they had to turn out; if the weather was bad, they played 'Highland Laddie' and the men sat in their tents, ready to turn out. 'To the credit of the Commander-in-Chief, he allowed us two rations of rum a day now, and one more on picket or in the trenches.'[135] Prescient of the trench warfare to come sixty years later, Montgomery was observing what a 'fine science' military engineering was: 'the beautiful way these trenches are drawn out and the nicety with which the angles are placed so that you are in almost perfect safety when behind them'.[136] 'On duty at night it was very cold, but in the daytime the sun had some heat, and we could keep ourselves warm with the pick or spade, for the trenches were not finished along our position,' recollected Robb. 'Our duties were indeed hard, and our numbers were getting less every day. There was scarcely a day but we had more or less that died from it or some other trouble brought on by hardships and poor rations, while our clothes were in tatters.'[137]

With the frost setting in, the men relished the arrival of their baggage. 'I got several things out in the way of clean clothes, hair brushes, trousers,' Montgomery informed his sister, 'you must know I have had nothing on but my kilt since I landed; a few pots and pans for cooking and several little comforts in the way of pickles and preserves and to my inexpressible delight I rummaged out of my saddle bags a bottle of Cockburn and Campbell's sherry which was a treat. There are now however lots of shops set up and ships are arriving every day with wine, preserved meats, and everything that one can want.'[138] Others were less fortunate: 'we found that during the passage the sailors had broken open nearly all the trunks & taken anything they fancied mostly shoes & boots, the thing we most required,' recollected Halkett.[139]

To preserve the supply line from Balaclava harbour, Raglan ordered the Highland Brigade to the heights of the Balaclava valley, which meant it played no part in the next battle – at Inkerman – in early November. Watching events, Montgomery wrote enthusiastically: 'The 5th of November has been a memorable day in the History of England for the discovery of a desperate plot, it has now become memorable for the gallant defeat of a most desperate attack on our right flank in front of Sebastopol.' But, he said, it was 'attended with terrible loss, 138 officers killed and wounded 36 of whom are killed, several general officers are among the number, Sir George Cathcart is killed.'[140] 'The battle raged with great obstinacy for about three hours and the firing of musketry was very great,' John McLeod told his mother. Giving credit to the French, he described how they came up 'very opportunely and turned the tide of battle in our favour'.[141] 'I went up next day to see the field,' recalled Halkett, 'the whole plateau on the side next to the Inkerman Ridge was covered thick with dead, in some places lying one on top of the other, & the grass dark with coagulated blood.'[142]

The Russian defeat gave the British and French a commanding position on elevated ground on the north-eastern angle of the plateau before Sebastopol. To assist the defenders inside the fortress, the Russians began to move their troops into the city. Under instruction from Totleben, fortifications were extended around the main redoubts surrounding Sebastopol – the Redan, the Flagstaff Bastion and the Malakoff. As the Allies continued their siege works, Totleben ordered rifle pits to be dug, from where the Russians could snipe at the besiegers. In the weeks that followed, the Highland Brigade was in constant readiness against attack, spending nights in the trenches or in tents, with their muskets loaded.[143]

To compound the discomfort of the approaching winter, there was a particularly severe storm, as if 'the elements had proclaimed war against us', noted Robb. 'The wind was so strong that it tore up large trees from their roots. There was not a tent in the whole British line but was blown down.' In no time, the ground was 'a mire of mud and the trenches that we had made were washed away'.[144] The storm damaged the ships in the harbour, one of which held a supply of warm clothing for the troops, which was lost.[145] 'If we were bad before the storm we were a great deal worse after,' continued Robb. 'At night we had still to provide the outlying picket and the trench party, as the enemy was not a mile distant from us. False alarms were quite common at night, when all the men in the tents had to turn out and remain under arms till daylight.'[146]

'It is getting very cold,' Montgomery was writing at the end of November, 'so we are all digging holes in the ground and roofing them over which will be much warmer than tents. Won't we be like little rabbits all living under ground; you would scarcely know the fine soldiers you see in London out here, they are all so dirty and their clothes all torn and the poor horses are looking so miserable from cold and sometimes not getting enough to eat.'[147] Food for the officers appeared surprisingly plentiful, with consignments of sherry, port and salmon arriving from Constantinople. On one occasion, McLeod was describing a dinner of 'plum dough . . . our servants have become capital cooks, their apple dumplings and bubble and squeak are inimitable.' On another, he related how after a visit to Balaclava, they filled their pockets with carrots, turnips, onions and split peas as well as salt fish.[148]

The soldiers fared less well, and Robb recollected a letter from the Queen being read to the troops 'expressing her sorrow for us, and saying that she had wept over our woes and hardships, and that she had instructed her Ministers to see to our wants at once. Newspapers came telling us what the people were doing for us in getting warm clothing, etc,' but they took a long time to arrive. Since most of the transport animals had died, the Highland Brigade was charged with 'fatigue duty', carrying supplies of shot, shells and stores to the front. 'It was about seven or eight miles that they had to be taken, and up the steep heights and the bad roads,' recalled Robb.[149] 'The work was very irksome, & when the road, as it soon did, got into a perfect quagmire, it became a terrible duty – the soldiers, though they got extra pay for it, grumbled terribly. I heard one of our men say "I never joined to be turned into a d——d commissariat mule."'[150]

A makeshift hospital in a house at Kadikoi was crowded with patients, most of whom had diarrhoea or frostbite. All the men had to lie on was their greatcoats, with a louse-ridden blanket, using their knapsacks as pillows.[151] 'Oh may the hospital of the Black Watch never again be in such a state as it was at that time,' proclaimed Robb, who fell ill and was put on board a transport ship from Balaclava harbour to go to the hospital at Scutari. While he was there he was tended by a young Englishwoman, Florence Nightingale, thirty-four years old, who was making history by nursing the wounded and dying, '& to her system of organisation', remarked Halkett, 'many poor fellows owed their lives'.[152] News of the war, transmitted in William Howard Russell's vivid reports to *The Times*, was so shocking that the British public became angry at what appeared to be military incompetence which had left the soldiers ill and dying. 'During the past week 1,900 sick have been brought down from the Crimea,' Russell wrote from Scutari on Christmas Day. 'A few cases of wounded men occur among them, but the vast majority are dysenteric, and it gives at once an accurate and terrible conception of what campaigning is when one finds that two or three weeks of wet weather tell as strongly against the strength of our army as did the guns and battalions of the Czar at Inkermann or the Alma.'[153]

1855

At the beginning of 1855, Raglan was writing to Newcastle, explaining their difficulties: 'since the bad weather set in . . . thus circumscribed our progress in repairing batteries and platforms, bringing up Guns and warlike stores, and throwing forward new works, has been necessarily slow.'[154] On 29 January a motion to appoint a Select Committee to inquire into the conduct of the war was carried by a large majority in the House of Commons. Considering this to be a vote of no confidence, George Hamilton-Gordon, 4th Earl of Aberdeen, prime minister since 1852 and the man responsible for committing troops to the Crimea, resigned as did Newcastle. The new prime minister was Viscount Palmerston, the only person willing to accept the poisoned chalice which the Crimean War had become. 'A winter campaign is a fearful thing certainly, but government have certainly a great deal to answer for, they have shown a great want of forethought,' proclaimed Montgomery, now a captain, in one of his regular letters to his sister Helen. Even the philanthropic actions of those trying to help were criticised. 'The quantities of warm clothing, fur coats, buffalo robes arriving and being distributed is enormous, a great waste of money so many things are not wanted . . . A much more judicious choice of things also might have been made, more waterproof things are wanted and long boots, the latter however I hear have come but I also hear that a great many are altogether too small, some rascally contractor's work, what a disgrace!'[155]

The construction of wooden huts instead of tents provided better living quarters. Conditions in the hospital, which now had beds, had improved.[156] And, as winter turned to spring, the weather brightened, which meant better communications. A 'Grand Crimean Central Railway' had been laid, enabling supplies to be transported up to the siege lines. The Russians were also not idle. Having scuttled several ships in the harbour as blockships, Raglan was complaining that the Russians had now sunk 'three or four more ships of War', thereby increasing the 'impediments to the entrance of the harbour'.[157]

On 26 March, almost a year since war was declared, Montgomery was recording that there had been 'an armistice for a few hours up at the front on Saturday to bury the dead; while it lasted French, English and Russian officers mixed together and talked and joked away, the men also fraternized a little'.[158] But he was despondent: 'It's all very fine . . . they will never see Sebastopol taken if they don't send us out a sufficient force to invest the place. We are just as much besieged as they are, only we have the sea open to us and we get our supplies easier than they can as theirs must all come by land.'[159] On

Easter Sunday 1855 – 8 April – the Allies resumed their bombardment of Sebastopol.

Kertch

In early May, the order came to parade in line of marching order and go on board ship as part of a large expedition which included French troops: 'great excitement as to what was the object'.[160] Raglan's new plan was to cut off the Russian supply line from the mainland by taking control of the strait of Kertch (Kerch) leading into the Sea of Azoff (Azov), on the north-eastern rim of the Black Sea. Their destination was the port of Kertch and the respite of an expedition was welcome: 'we looked forward to doing something in the field, & felt that we had been looked upon by the rest of the army as a favoured lot, getting away from the monotony of the siege, & having a pleasant change.' To their disappointment, after only three days they were ordered to return to Balaclava.[161] As the men later learnt, the French were required back at Balaclava and so the expedition had been cancelled.

The following week, the Highland Brigade was ordered to form camp before Sebastopol. 'Every night at dusk, the trench party, consisting of about 200 men & 4 or 5 officers would be paraded in front of the centre of the Camp, all taking rations & water with them for 24 hours, & then as soon as it was dark, were marched off to take their places in the portion of the trenches assigned to them by the Engineers.'[162] After barely two weeks at the front, the Highland Brigade was again ordered to Balaclava harbour to board HMS *Leopard*, Robb recording how they were 'on best of terms with the crews and some of them did shake their feet well to our pipers'.[163]

'The scenery all along the coast was very fine,' observed Halkett; 'high cliffs & now & then, ravines running up from the shore, with thick fine woods & perhaps a villa half hid among the trees.'[164] At the entrance to the strait of Kertch, they could see batteries, armed with heavy guns, on each side '& a quantity of cavalry some little distance off drawn up'. Landing on 'a fine smooth sandy beach', Halkett recorded that they had a 'capital place' to camp, 'with short grass like a "links" and soon settled down to our rations round a camp fire'.[165] Beginning their march to Kertch, 'great caution was now taken in case of a surprise'. But there was no opposition. 'The bands of the regiments – who had brought their instruments were ordered to play, and it was very imposing & joyful, to hear the crash of the music & the roll of hundreds of drums of both the French & English, as we marched through the principal street,' Halkett continued. 'Capital shops there were, bakers, & confectioners with ices! Cigar shops, & all sorts of good things we saw as we passed along, the people all crowding the pavements & the house tops, & they were most astonished at the Highlanders & couldn't make them out at all.'[166] That night, the troops dined well: 'we had fresh meat & vegetables & iced champagne! for all the good houses had ice cellars, & we very soon made acquaintance with their wine cellars. No one was allowed to enter the town, & patrols were going about day & night to prevent plunder, but we, being outside, made free with the villas & the good things they contained.'[167]

The following day, together with the 93rd and a contingent of French, the 42nd was ordered to take Yenikale, east of Kertch, overlooking the Sea of Azoff. Yet again, their entry was unopposed, but when the troops were allowed to fall out 'a complete scene of anarchy prevailed,' with the French, according to Halkett, pillaging 'in all directions'. 'Some of our men were down in the town also, & I was ordered to go with a strong picket & fetch out any of our men who were there. We marched off at the double, as Colonel Cameron was furious at this outbreak, & especially at any of our men being mixed up in it.' To his dismay, Halkett encountered a soldier of the 42nd in one of the wine cellars, who had been shot dead. 'From what I gathered from the French soldiers, they were engaged in breaking open the cellar door, & one of their men was hammering it with the butt end of his Rifle, which went off & shot our man standing behind.'[168]

Their main work in Yenikale was to assist the Engineers to destroy the fortifications, 'which we blew up, and also to help to ship, on big rafts constructed for the purpose, the guns & mortars which were in the batteries – what we didn't carry away was thrown into the sea.'[169] They also burnt some of the offices and stores, 'only as it happened,' recollected Halkett, 'the wind got up and blew & fanned the flames till they caught the next buildings & so it went on till the principal streets were all in flames, & it could not be arrested till the whole town was a heap of ashes. I was on picket that night and the whole country was lit up like day, though we were six miles from it.'[170] In early June, they re-embarked for Balaclava, when 'it was whispered that there was to be a final attack made on Sebastopol on the 18th – Waterloo day'.[171]

Before Sebastopol

During their absence from Balaclava, the 42nd had left their belongings in a tent and the ponies 'tethered out . . . all the men's feather bonnets were piled up by companies in another marquee, as we didn't take them with us'.[172] But when they returned they found that the French battalion deputed to guard them 'had been riding our ponies all over the place, my little black pony "Dick" had his knees broke, and the French Guards had made our tents where all the feather bonnets were, into a guard tent, & made a bed of the bonnets! which were all as flat as pancakes; a regular "feather bed" they had – such a row the men made, & swore they would go to the Frenchmen's camp & punch their heads. But to show what an excellent headdress the feather bonnet is; being mounted upon a wire frame, & the feathers themselves not minding wet or squeezing, all we had to do, was to press out the wire into its shape, to put the bonnets out into the sun, to cockle up the plumes, & lo! they were just as good as ever.'[173]

Meanwhile, the shelling of Sebastopol continued. On 17 June, the 42nd marched up to the front. 'When we went into our trenches,' recollected Robb, 'they were full of men, and the shot, shell, and musket balls were coming thick, but everyone seemed to be in good spirits.'[174] At 5 o'clock next morning, while the French bombarded the Malakoff, the British launched an attack on the Redan, but the redoubts were more impregnable than expected and they suffered severe loss. 'However, we gained an important point – what was called the Quarries, if my memory does not fail me – and the French the Mamelon,' related Robb.[175] 'As for our attack on the Redan,' Montgomery wrote on 26 June, mindful that the 42nd in the 1st Division had been in the Reserve and spared the slaughter, 'it was a perfect piece of madness; it, I believe, was intended not to attack till the Malakoff was taken but some how or other there was a bungle and at it they went with the bravery of "Lions led by donkeys" as the Russian officers told us afterwards at the "play of truce" to bury the dead . . . Our loss was very great about 1400 killed & wounded.'[176] 'Such awful sights were to be seen at the burying that it is impossible for me to write them,' wrote Robb in his memoirs.[177]

As the attempt to lift the siege continued, the men heard that their Commander-in-Chief, Lord Raglan, was unwell '& no doubt the non success of the assault, which he hoped would give him Sebastopol, had weighed on him,' recollected Halkett. On 29 June, ill with cholera and dysentery, Raglan died aged sixty-six, 'to the great grief of the Allied Armies'.[178] His successor was Lieutenant General Sir James Simpson, who had arrived in the Crimea in February as chief of staff. Within days, the Russians lost Nakhimov, who was killed by a sniper while inspecting defences. Menshikov had already been replaced as Commander-in-Chief by Prince Mikhail Gorchakov, in command during the siege of Silistria. Meanwhile, Canrobert had disagreed with Raglan and resigned in May; his replacement was sixty-year-old Aimable Jean Jacques Pélissier, Marshal of France, who pursued the war with renewed determination.[179]

Throughout July, the 42nd was doing duty in the trenches. 'I always like to write a few lines before going into the Trenches as there is no saying what may happen before the departure of the next mail,' Captain Joseph Ross Grove wrote home. 'I go in tonight again for 24 hours.'[180] 'There were some nights worse than others, for now and again sorties were made. If we were on the advance trench a party of men had to go over the trench, and lie on the ground, and be ready to open fire, and then retire into the trench, then the line of trenches would open fire.'[181] One duty which Robb considered 'no joke' was to take down 'the shot and shell to the batteries through the open ground, exposed to all the fire that came out of Sebastopol, as we could not drag the wagon in the trenches'. 'To see those trenches,' he remarked, 'through the day would have made a good picture for an artist. Here would be a cluster of men, some singing songs, others telling stories, some firing off their rifles, others frying their pork on a shovel or boiling their coffee or tea.'[182]

During the siege, the Highland Brigade, including the 42nd, was posted to a new camp at Kamara, north of Balaclava. 'There was the finest scenery round about I ever saw, pretty green woods and brush-wood and the green plain, with a clear stream of water near by.'[183] On 7 August, the gunfire or 'the "feu d'enfer" as the Russians called it'[184] at the front seemed even louder. The following day, the Highland Brigade was ordered to march back to Sebastopol, where they went straight into the trenches. 'We kept up a sharp fire with our rifles,' recollected Robb.[185] That night a line of battleships was set on fire. 'I was in the trenches that night,' recollected Halkett, '& the whole surrounding scenery was lighted up, & as the ship contained a great supply of spirits, the blue flames cast a lugubrious light on the ramparts & the town.'[186] In mid-August, in an attempt to attack the Allies in the rear, the Russians crossed the Chernaya river, but were repulsed by a combined Sardinian and French force.

On 5 September the Allies began their sixth bombardment of Sebastopol. Over three hundred cannon fired several hundred thousand rounds at the beleaguered fortress and Russian casualties were in their thousands. Three days later the final assault began. 'On the morning of the 8th at daybreak the Russians were in great force manning their defences, with guns loaded with grape, expecting the assault, but it was not yet,' recalled Halkett. 'The furious cannonade still poured into them, & the fact of so many men being brought up to repel the assault, added greatly to the losses they had sustained. We on our side were also busy with the bombardment of the Redan

& other works in front of us, which were to be assaulted at the same time with the French.'[187] General Simpson had chosen the Light and 2nd Divisions to lead the attack, leaving the Highland Brigade in the Reserve 'in the 3rd parallel. In the last parallel were the 3rd & 4th Divisions.' The attack on Redan was partly a diversion to assist the French in taking the Malakoff, 'as their succeeding in taking the Malakoff would give us the key to Sebastopol'.[188]

At midday, the French began their assault 'like eager fox hounds'. But the Russians fought back and the battle was 'desperately bloody. Every inch was fought for, and taken and retaken over and over again. The French kept pouring in fresh Regts.' At length, as Halkett narrated, the Russian Commander-in-Chief, Prince Gorchakov, 'caused his troops to be withdrawn from what he saw was a hopeless struggle.'[189] Having earlier criticised the French, especially their pillaging 'right and left' at Kertch, McLeod commended their 'determined gallantry and unflinching courage' in taking the Malakoff.[190]

Watching the battle, Halkett found it so 'intensely exciting' that his attention was only brought back to what the British were doing 'by the sound of rapid rifle firing & the guns of the Redan opening with grape, showing that the English attack was now begun. We were not able to see the assaulting force leave the trenches from the configuration of the ground, but soon came the stretchers, one after the other laden with wounded and dying officers and men.'[191] The British Light and 2nd Divisions were not so successful in taking the Redan as the French were in taking the Malakoff. 'Suffering much from the heavy fire of round shot, grape, case & musketry, directed on them from every available point – the first arrivals passed into the work over the battered ramparts, but the rest lay down firing, instead of advancing – the supports from the reserves were obstructed by the number of wounded men & bearers, being brought back by the same route.'[192] The Highland Brigade had fifty-seven wounded and six killed. Duncan Cameron, acting as Brigadier General in command of the Brigade while Campbell commanded the Division, 'received a slight wound on the head from a splinter of a shell which did not compel him to leave the trenches'.[193]

Having failed to take the Redan, another assault was planned for the next day. 'I had just completed the posting of the advanced picquets and the occupation of the trenches,' noted Colin Campbell, 'when I was summoned to Head Quarters when I received instructions from the Commander of the Forces to make arrangements for an assault on the Redan by the Highlanders on the following day.'[194] At sunset, the Highland Brigade was moved down to the advanced trenches next to the Redan, ready for the assault. 'Although we all felt our great time had come for distinguishing the Brigade,' recollected Halkett, 'we could not disguise from ourselves that the fight would be a bloody one, and that our losses would be heavy.' As he estimated, the attack on the Redan had already cost 2,271 officers and men. Three generals were wounded. The French had lost 7,567 officers and men taking the Malakoff and other works; Russian casualties were even greater, having lost 12,913 officers and men and two generals. 'It was a frightful day for slaughter as between us, the total came to 22,751 killed and wounded!'[195]

Taking up position in the advanced trenches, they were served rum, cold pork and biscuit. 'After talking over the events of the day, we tried to get some rest, it is difficult in most circumstances to go to sleep when you will in all probability be killed on the following morning, but so tired out was I, that while thinking over all my people at home, & of the old place etc, I dropped off, & slept sound.' Halkett was woken in the middle of the night by 'the most tremendous explosion which lifted me off the ground, & I didn't know what had happened. Every man leapt to his feet, thinking an attack was being made.' In fact, the Russians were evacuating Sebastopol, blowing up the magazines: 'these explosions now followed each other in quick succession lighting up the night, & great fires broke out in Sebastopol which soon made the whole town & surrounding country as light as day.'[196]

As dawn broke, they saw the Russian garrison withdrawing across the harbour by a bridge of boats to the north. No one was left in the town except the sick and wounded.[197] As the British soon found, before the Russians retired from the Redan they were 'so humane as to dress many of our Wounded . . . and while apparently the

Magazines of every battery in its neighbourhood were exploded, that of the Redan was not fired, an omission which saved many wounded people from destruction.'[198] 'We could hardly realize that the great siege which had lasted 18 months, was brought to a termination,' recorded Halkett, '& that for a time at least, we could have respite from the continual trench work & ceaseless roar of the guns.' In the 'wildest of spirits' they marched back to Kamara. 'On our way back to the camp we met a regiment of the French Imperial Guard going down, & we mutually cheered each other frantically.'[199]

Together with two other officers, Halkett got a pass to enter Sebastopol. 'It was dangerous still as the enemy had arranged for the magazines to explode at long intervals, & one couldn't tell when a mine would go off.'[200] They also visited the Russian military hospital: 'it contained about 2000 desperately wounded men, who had lain there without aid, food or water, for two days. In one great long vaulted room, with beds placed close together, were 700 who had all undergone amputation, & who were all dead of their misery, lying in blood on their beds, or on the floor where they had writhed on to it. There were three English officers alive in this hospital, but they only lived to be carried back to our camp. They were severely wounded & captured at the assault.' In the days that followed, burying parties 'were hard at work in every direction, & pick & spades could be heard wherever one turned. The Russians sent over a flag of truce in the afternoon to enquire for their wounded.'[201]

As the men now realised, the buildings in the town they had been shelling had been 'magnificent; huge barracks, library, an opera house, the Admiralty etc, all built of the finest dressed stone, with gilded domes to the Churches, but now a mass of ruins. The docks were splendid, all of the finest workmanship & capable of dry docking the largest man of war. All these were afterwards blown up by our Engineers.' Halkett admitted that 'it must have been a fearful time, cooped up in the city during such fire as we kept upon it'.[202] Anticipating that the Russians could still stage a counter-attack, the Highland Brigade remained at Kamara. 'The troops lay accoutred every night and were under arms an hour before daybreak, till the winter was so far advanced that it was considered improbable that any movement would be made before winter set in, and during a great part of it, the whole army was employed erecting huts making roads, etc.'[203]

On 20 September, the first anniversary of the Battle of the Alma, the first distribution of medals for service in the Crimea was made. Colin Campbell described how the 'gallant soldiers' of the Highland Brigade, 'were the first to meet the Russians and defeat them upon their own territory':

> The fatigues and hardships of the last year are well known, and have greatly thinned our Ranks, since we scaled the Alma's Heights together, but happy am I to see so many faces around me who on that day by their courage, steadiness and discipline, so materially assisted in routing the Russian horde, from their vaunted impregnable position. To that day Scotchmen can look with pride (and Scotchmen are everywhere), for your deeds upon that day you received the marked encomiums of Lord Raglan, the thanks of your Queen and admiration of all. Scotchmen are proud of you. I too am a Scotchman and proud of the honor of Commanding so distinguished a Brigade and still prouder that through all the trying severities of winter, its incepant labours and decimating disease, in all your duties in trench and field you have still maintained the same unflinching courage and energy, which with your discipline, obedience and steadiness, in whatever circumstances you have been placed makes you so unrivalled (and none more so than the oldest Regiment in the Brigade) and your Commanders confident of success, however numerous and determined your foe.

Admitting that there were 'young soldiers' who had not been given a medal, he went on to say that they could soon 'win equal honours for many an Alma will yet be fought'. Mindful that the Russians had withdrawn from Sebastopol before the Highland Brigade had a chance to distinguish themselves, he said he felt positive that they would have 'gained renown'.[204]

The End of the Crimean War 1856

The fall of Sebastopol did not mark the immediate end of the Crimean War. Instead, while an armistice was negotiated, the Highland Brigade remained at Kamara, marching up to Sebastopol in parties 'for the purpose of seeing the place that had given us so much trouble'.[205] Compared with their first pitiable winter in 1854, the soldiers were well housed. 'The second Winter was a King to the first. We had every comfort, huts and warm clothing,' remarked Charles Wilson, promoted Corporal on 2 February 1856. Sergeant George Rankin, however, was complaining about having to parade on a Sunday. 'I wonder who the ministers who are sent out by government for the safety of men's souls, does not try to save the commander-in-chief[']s [soul] and tell him he is doing wrong in having such reviews on Sunday when there is time during the week for it.'[206]

On 2 March 1856, an Armistice was agreed to last for thirty days. 'A great cheer went up,' Wilson recalled.[207] Permitted to go as far as the river Chernaya, where a 'line of demarcation' separated the two armies, Robb described how, where the river was narrow, they could 'throw a small coin' to the Russian soldiers, 'and they would throw across some small article'.[208] 'I have been exploring all about our flank at Inkerman, where one could not go before as it drew down fire from the batteries on the opposite side,' Montgomery wrote home soon after the Armistice. 'There are several dead bodies of Russians still at the bottom of the Inkerman valley that could not be buried after the battle, as it was within the range of the Russian guns & you remember they fired on our burial parties.'[209]

When the men heard the treaty had been signed in Paris on 30 March 1856, salvos of guns were fired in celebration. As they prepared to depart, instructions were received that all the graveyards had to be enclosed, lest in time to come they were desecrated.[210] In early May, Sir Colin Campbell, who was returning to England, assembled the three regiments of the Highland Brigade at Kamara. Yet again, he saluted the men. 'Soldiers of the 42nd, 79th and 93rd! Old Highland Brigade! With whom I passed the early and perilous part of this War. I have now to take leave of you; in a few hours I shall be on board ship never to see you again as a body – a long Farewell! I am now old, and shall not be called to serve any more, and nothing will remain to me but the memory of my Campaigns and of the enduring, hard and generous soldiers with whom I have been associated, whose name and glory will long be kept alive in the hearts of our Countrymen.' Describing how they would be relating to their families the story of their 'immortal advance in that victorious echelon up the heights of Alma', he told the assembled officers and men that a pipe would never sound near him 'without carrying me back to those bright days when I was at your head and wore the bonnet you gained for me, and the honourable decorations on my breast many of which I owe to your conduct.– Brave Soldiers! Kind Comrades! Farewell.'[211]

On 15 June 1856, having spent two years in the Crimea, the 42nd Royal Highland Regiment embarked at Kamiesch to return home. After a passage of forty days they landed at Portsmouth and travelled straight to Aldershot, to be reviewed by Queen Victoria, who had taken such personal interest in the war. 'She was dressed in a scarlet tunic and a neat hat like a general's, and a broad gold sash over her shoulder,' recalled Robb. Once she had ridden along the line, 'all the royal Family saluting the colours as they passed them, we formed into column and marched past'. The following day, she inspected the regiments. 'When she came to our regiment, she was dressed as a plain lady, and went through our ranks and spoke to some of our officers.'[212] 'She had something to say to every man,' recollected Wilson, 'she had great respect for the Regiment, as she had our old Pipe Major Ross as her Piper and he was in Aldershot this day with her welcoming the Regiment back to England.'[213]

Brigaded with the 93rd at Dover, the soldiers 'were not altogether pleased', since they had expected to be sent to the land of 'oat cakes', recorded Private Walter Robertson. 'However, to obey is the first duty of a soldier and we had to console ourselves with the attractiveness of Kent.'[214] While the 93rd went into the Castle, the 42nd occupied the Citadel. 'It was very funny to find the extraordinary excitement caused by any one coming home from the Crimea,' Halkett wrote in his memoir. 'The eagerness to hear all about the campaign & if you had seen "so-&-so", as if one knew everyone in the Army, & the extraordinary hardships & sufferings of the previous winter, seemed to have caused wide sympathy with the soldiers, which we while out there could have no idea of, until we came home.' He was also struck by those in mourning. 'There were I suppose, very few, who had not some connection with those who had lost sons & husbands during the Campaign.'[215]

When the final reckoning was made, it was estimated that the Crimean War had taken over 120,000 French and British lives, most of whom died of illness. In comparison with the French, who lost an estimated 30,000 in battle and over 60,000 from disease, British casualties were considerably fewer: 2,755 were killed in action, 2,019 died of wounds and 16,323 died of sickness.[216] One officer and thirty-eight men of the 42nd were killed in action; 140 soldiers had been sent to England because of their wounds or ill-health; one officer and 226 men had died of sickness or their wounds.[217] Two men were recorded as having deserted.[218] The Russians had lost an estimated 450,00 men in action and from disease, the Turks losing a comparable number to the French.[219] The Crimean War signified a turning point in European relations. For the first time in hundreds of years, France and Britain had fought as allies. The expansion of the Tsarist Empire had been curtailed. What people most remembered was the ill-fated charge of the Light Brigade into 'the valley of death' immortalised by Alfred Lord Tennyson: '*Not tho' the soldier knew / Some one had blunder'd / ... Charging an army, while / All the world wonder'd*'.[220]

While Aberdeen's government had been blamed for 'sending an army into the field so badly provided for', Palmerston was criticised 'in making so easy terms with the Russians at the close after so much British blood and money had been wasted'.[221] After the war, the 42nd was reduced. Duncan Cameron and other officers were placed on half-pay from 10 November 1856, Cameron becoming Colonel of the Regiment in 1863. Of those whose accounts so vividly recreated their experiences, Halkett had transferred to a cavalry regiment, the 3rd King's Own Light Dragoons, on 3 January 1856.[222] He received lasting recognition for carrying the Queen's Colour at Alma, depicted in Robert Gibb's painting which showed Colin Campbell uttering the famous order: 'Forward 42nd!' Also identifiable is Viscount Forth, carrying the Regimental Colour, 'pitched in to' by Major Tulloch for not keeping in line. Having been wounded during the early stages of the war, he had retired from the Army in November 1854; noted as having a craving for alcohol, he committed suicide by poison in 1861.[223]

Montgomery retired in May 1857; Wilson remained with the Regiment, rising to the rank of sergeant in 1858, being reduced the following year.[224] Sergeant McSally and Privates Robb and Robertson remained with the Regiment. A further reduction was ordered on 12 March 1857. Some transferred to the 93rd to form part of a punitive expedition to China following an 'indignity' towards the British flag by the Governor of Canton, involving Britain in the 2nd Opium War. The ordeal of the British army and its allies in the Crimea was never to be forgotten. The 42nd Royal Highland Regiment received two new Battle Honours: *Alma* and *Sevastopol*.

18.

A Proper Style of Indian Warfare

Ye who may view this desert spot
When Battle fields shall be forgot
Know here the Forty Second fought.[1]

1856

The Indian Mutiny 1857

No sooner were the officers and soldiers of the 42nd Royal Highland Regiment established in their quarters at Dover than news came of a mutiny 'of the whole Native Army of Bengal, which arose *en masse*', sweeping all over India.[2] Disaffection had been building up amongst the Indian population both socially and economically. The Doctrine of Lapse – stating that if a feudal landowner died without a direct natural male heir, his property would become part of the East India Company – was deeply resented. There was also a growing fear that the British were trying to convert the Indians to Christianity.[3] Among the Indian soldiers, there was resistance to using cartridges greased with the lard of cows or pigs in the newly introduced Lee Enfield rifles.

On 10 May 1857, the general discontent broke out into open rebellion when the sepoys mutinied at Meerut, north-east of Delhi. Having captured Delhi, they made common cause with the eighty-two-year-old Mughal ruler, Bahadur Shah II, hailed as Emperor of Hindustan.[4] By September, British forces were once more in control of Delhi and Bahadur Shah had taken refuge within the city walls. The rebels then made for Lucknow, capital of the province of Oudh (Oude), recently annexed by Britain, according to the Doctrine of Lapse, and where anti-British feeling was running high. The European civilians and military took refuge in the Residency, which formed the focal point of their defence. During the first attack, in early July, the Commissioner, Sir Henry Lawrence, was killed.

At the same time, the Indian regiments at the garrison town of Cawnpore (Kanpur), under the command of General Sir Hugh Wheeler, rebelled. They were supported by Nana Sahib, the adopted heir of the deposed Peshwa or prime minister of the Maratha Confederacy, who had been exiled to nearby Bithoor (Bithur) after the Third Anglo-Maratha War in 1818. Resentful at being refused recognition as the Peshwa's natural heir, owing again to the Doctrine of Lapse, Nana Sahib threw in his lot with the rebels, declaring himself a vassal of Bahadur Shah.[5] For three weeks, the British contingent of over seven hundred men, women and children was besieged. On 23 June – the 100th anniversary of the Battle of Plassey, when the East India Company had defeated the Nawab of Bengal and his French allies – the rebel Indians made an all-out attack on Cawnpore. Already weakened by disease and hunger, and with dwindling medical supplies, Wheeler accepted Nana Sahib's offer of safe passage along the river to Allahabad.[6] As the Europeans were attempting to depart, firing broke out. In the confusion which followed, all the men were either killed or taken prisoner, including Wheeler. Together with several Indian soldiers who had remained loyal to the British they were later executed by the rebels. About 200 women and children were taken hostage. For two weeks they were confined in the local magistrate's house, known as the Bibighar (the house of the ladies), their numbers further depleted by cholera and dysentery due to poor sanitary conditions. In early July, as a British relieving force, commanded by General Henry Havelock, advanced from Allahabad, all the hostages were killed and their mutilated bodies thrown down a well.[7]

Nana Sahib, held accountable for the massacre, fled, leaving operations to be conducted by General Ramchandra Pandurang Tope, known as Tatya Tope.[8] On 16 July, Havelock recaptured Cawnpore. The siege of Lucknow was raised by Major General Sir James Outram in late September; with large numbers of sick and wounded in the city, instead of attempting to evacuate Lucknow, Outram enlarged the fortified area.[9] In Britain, the news of the mutiny and its atrocities was greeted with horrified indignation. When the Commander-in-Chief in India, General George Anson, died of cholera, Sir Colin Campbell was chosen as his successor. 'The 42nd was quartered in Dover, when he arrived about midnight to commence his journey,' recollected Sergeant Walter Robertson. 'The officers of that regiment which he knew so well welcomed him respectfully and affectionately, taking their farewell of him with three hearty cheers, never thinking they were soon to follow.'[10]

Departure to India 1857

Almost immediately after Campbell left for India, the Regiment was ordered to prepare for departure, its ranks supplemented by new recruits and volunteers from the 25th King's Own Borderers, making a complement of twelve companies. 'All was bustle and excitement,' recollected Private John Muir, who volunteered from the 25th, 'orderlys running hither and thither.' From Dover, the soldiers travelled to Portsmouth, where Muir 'donned for the first time the "garb of the old Gaul" the kilt, bonnet and feather'.[11] On 4 August Queen Victoria reviewed the Regiment. 'We marched past her in fours,' recollected Sandy Robb.[12] Once more, the Queen expressed her satisfaction at the 42nd Royal Highlanders, which she familiarly called 'my old friends'.[13]

For the journey to India, the 42nd travelled in convoy. 'We coaled 3 times on the voyage viz:- Cape Saint Vincent, Saint Simons Bay, and Point de Galle,' recorded John Muir on board the *Australian*.[14] Robb, on board the *James Baynes*, believed that he was 'never so well cared for as I was on board of that ship. We had as much good wholesome food as could put into us and a pint of porter every day for 120 days.' There was a 'fine' ship's library 'and a society gave us a present of some very good books, that I read with much enjoyment. Among them was a small volume by a soldier, on what he went through under Wellington in the Peninsula.'[15]

By mid-November the ships had reached Calcutta, taking up quarters at Fort William. 'We got our clothes washed and our land legs again,' related Robb, who noted that his company captain was William Baird, grandson of Sir David Baird, the famed 'hero of Seringapatam'.[16] On 11 November the Regiment was reviewed by the Governor-General, Viscount Canning, 'when our Colors were uncased for the first time in India'.[17] 'We marched off out of Fort William with about 600 men,' Wilkinson, in command of one contingent, wrote to his sister, 'and the papers say many a window was opened and a pretty face looked out to wish us luck. Well, my opinion was I never saw such dirty looking scoundrels in all my life.'[18]

Their destination was Allahabad. Travelling by boat up the Ganges river, and then by train to Raneegunj (Raniganj), about 120 miles from Calcutta, Sergeant Quibell Cooper found it 'a very dull place, we lay in straw huts and the jackals used to come into them by series during the night'.[19] As so often, cholera took away 'men who had gone through the whole of the Crimea', recollected Robb, who described how anyone who became sick had to get 'a comrade, or perhaps two, to wait upon him, and if possible, to keep the cramps from getting into his stomach, as well as to get the patient to drink as much brandy as he could – a job that was very difficult, because, although a man may be too fond of the liquor when he is all right, it is hard to get him to take any, or even to look at it, after he has taken cholera.'[20]

After Raneegunj, the onward journey was by bullock cart, four men travelling in the cart, while two men marched alongside. 'They went on night and day, only about two hours of a halt being allowed for getting our food cooked and ourselves refreshed. Our detachment was considerably weaker already on account of the deaths and the want of the men whom we had left behind recovering; and the cholera went along with us.'[21] On arrival in Allahabad the place 'was in great commotion'. The men were given tents and bedding, and camp followers who cooked for them; they then travelled on the short stretch of railway constructed upcountry from Allahabad to the camp, where 'we got our elephants and camels to carry our baggage. We were then in a proper style of Indian warfare.'[22]

Meanwhile, on 17 November a force under Sir Colin Campbell's command had relieved Lucknow for the second time. On this occasion, instead of trying to hold the city, Campbell evacuated it, making for Cawnpore. To oppose him, Tatya Tope was gathering a force of several thousand rebel soldiers, drawn mainly from nearby Gwalior, known as the 'Gwalior Contingent' and about 16,000 strong.[23] Hearing 'news of the state of affairs at Cawnpore', the headquarters and five companies of the 42nd were ordered to form an entrenched camp at Cheenee. In the early hours of 2 December a dispatch arrived from Campbell, with orders to make a forced march on Cawnpore. 'We left Cheenee at 8 p.m. the same day and reached Cawnpore by 12 noon on the 5th having done near 78 miles in less than three days, during the last twelve hours the men were much exhausted,' recounted Captain Richard Bayly. 'We were given short halts of from 4 to 5 minutes and lay down in the dust and were asleep at once.' As they were on the march, they passed a convoy of women and children, as well as the wounded who had been in the Lucknow siege, 'a sick and sorrowful company'.[24] A few hours after their arrival at Cawnpore, 'tho' terribly tired and foot sore', the soldiers were ordered to turn out again. 'We had not been in Cawnpore many minutes, when the order "stand to our Arms" was given.' After repelling the initial attack from the Indian rebels, 'we lay in our tents fully equipped ready to turn out at a moment's notice and on the following morning we struck our Tents.'[25]

Cawnpore December 1857

The battle for Cawnpore began on 6 December with a heavy cannonade against the rebels from inside the fort. The 42nd was brigaded with the 53rd, 93rd and the 4th Punjabis, under the command of thirty-seven-year-old Brigadier Adrian Hope, the youngest son of General John Hope, the 4th Earl of Hopetoun, Colonel of the Regiment between 1820 and 1823.[26] 'The whole was formed in battle array, the infantry in line flanked by cavalry, and the flying artillery in front being covered by the rifles in extended order,' related Sergeant Robertson. 'Our skirmishers advanced and "popped off" a great many of the enemy with the famous Enfield rifle. The artillery opening fire, threw them into great disorder; the lines of infantry gave them two or three volleys, then with a tremendous cheer they advanced hastily upon them, they were stunned and panic stricken and the quick, steady advance of the army made them tremble for their safety; our cavalry and field guns then went into them and mowed them down like grass.'[27]

During the battle, Lieutenant Colonel George Thorold had his horse shot from under him; undaunted, he 'sprang to his feet, and with his drawn sword in hand marched in front of the Regiment, during the remainder of the action and pursuit of the flying enemy'.[28] 'The fire was heavy in the extreme,' noted the Record of Service. 'The enthusiasm of the men was now indescribable, they rushed on, either crossing the bridge or fording the Canal, came upon the enemy's camp, and took some guns at the point of the bayonet.'[29] Pursuing the rebel Indians for fourteen miles, recorded Robertson, 'we made short work of the stragglers and dying (fires being lighted, their bodies were thrown on them in hundreds, as they prefer to die in the fire, we gave them their wish for once.)'[30]

So hurried was their adversaries' flight that they literally left 'their camp standing fires alight and dinners cooking', related Bayly. 'I was left with one company in charge of the captured camp and after posting half of my company in a ruined temple close by I proceeded to knock in the heads of numerous large casks of rum, the liquor quickly disappearing in the sand to the great distress of my company.' As he remarked, 'the collection of loot in this Camp was something wonderful, ladies silk and satin dresses, furniture, a General's cocked hat and gold laced forage cap.' Bayly particularly remembered seeing three drums 'with the legend emblazoned on them that they were taken by our 34th English Regiment from the 34th French Infantry; these drums I sent back to the 34th Regiment next day with my compliments.' At night they returned to Cawnpore, having captured seventeen guns. 'The courage and discipline of our men was remarkable, young lads who had never seen a shot before yet during the action and a long march not a man fell out nor complained of his hardships.'[31] Unable to find their tents in the dark, 'we were ordered by Sir Colin to pile arms and sleep in the open air all night'. Instead of tents, Campbell 'kindly ordered each man to be served a glass of grog'.[32]

Despite this immediate success, some rebels had escaped with their guns to neighbouring Bithoor, north of Cawnpore on the Ganges river. Believed to be the place where the Lord Brahma started the creation of the world, it was also where the deposed Peshwa and his adopted heir, Nana Sahib, had been exiled. Campbell therefore ordered Brigadier General James Hope Grant, who had marched from Delhi at the head of a force of cavalry and horse artillery, to go in pursuit. Having found Bithoor evacuated, Grant took a flying column of cavalry, light artillery and Hope's infantry brigade, including the contingent of the 42nd.[33] After marching all night, next morning they found the rebel Indians at the Serai Ghat ferry on the Ganges. 'They received our men with a heavy cannonade and tried to capture our guns with a charge of Cavalry but our horsemen soon drove them away,' leaving their carts stuck in sands on the river bank.[34]

After the rebel Indians had fled, the British took away fifteen guns 'and a large quantity of provisions, camp equipage and ammunition,' related Bayly. 'The sands about the ferry presented a most extraordinary spectacle covered as it was with dead and dying Rebels, horses and many very fine bullocks, many of these were slowly disappearing from sight in the Quicksands. Our men hastily shot a number and cut off great junks of beef before they finally disappeared.' Here they found their first Indian trophy in a cart 'that had almost disappeared from sight in the sand'. It was a large gong, belonging to Nana Sahib, which was 'unusually large and thick and possesses a most splendid tone that can be heard for many miles'.[35]

They destroyed Nana Sahib's palace at Bithoor and looked for treasure, 'a great quantity of which was found in a tank'.[36] 'Ways and means were at once taken to get the well emptied of water,' related Robb, 'a task that was not easily accomplished, for it was a large deep draw-well. . . . about twenty of us got hold of a rope and, running along together, we brought up a large bucketful of water. There were men down in the well fishing for the prize.'[37] 'It amounted to a great value, being chiefly gold and silver plate,' remarked Robertson.[38] But, although, as Muir recollected, Sir Colin had encouraged the men in their endeavours, their own share of the spoils was disappointing. 'Where this money went to I know not, but of this I am certain that very little came my way . . . I received prize money to the [amount] of about £3-10/.'[39]

Towards the end of December they were joined at Bithoor by the remaining companies of the 42nd which had arrived from Cawnpore under Wilkinson's command.[40] At Cawnpore, the men had availed themselves of the opportunity 'to stroll about,' remarked Robertson, '& look at the great "slaughter house" where the atrocious monster Nana Sahib & his arch-fiends committed so many inhuman deeds'.[41] In the days to follow, there were various alarms and excursions: 'When one night, as the camp was retiring to rest, and the piper had emptied his bag for the night, after playing "Donald Blue" an order came for us to get under arms,' recalled Robertson; 'immediately two regiments, viz the 42nd Highlanders and 53rd, with the 9th Lancers and Hodson's Horse, and some flying artillery, all under the command of Brigadier Adrian Hope, were ready.'[42] Their adversary was a force of Indians with six guns who had taken up position three miles from the town of Nihor in Rohilkand, intending to halt a siege train and capture it. 'We marched at 10 o'clock p.m. The whole night, the dew falling thick and fast more like rain than dew, and when morning dawned we were close upon their unsuspecting sentinels; the clouds of mist had hardly rolled away from the valleys, when the boom of a gun, and the whistling of a ball over our heads, put us on the "qui vive".'[43]

Although the British had lost the element of surprise, the rebels were no match for them. 'Our Bengal European cavalry started at a hard gallop, got up to them, and gave it them hot; they turned out their cavalry and the 42nd advanced to meet their grenadiers in "extended order"; they opened a fire upon their horsemen and tumbled a few of them off their horses. The enemy thought fit to retire, as their attack on our flank was frustrated and our army advancing at the charge, took six brass guns which were in splendid position, the 9th Lancers and Hodson's Horse went at them on the left flank and cut them off in sections.' William Hodson, in command of Hodson's Horse, narrowly escaped being killed 'and the field was ours. Our siege train moved down to Cawnpore unmolested, and the army rested for a while.'[44]

1857 – the year in which Britain had faced the most serious challenge to date to its authority in India – ended with the 42nd marching from Cawnpore in search of rebel Indians or 'Pandies' as they called them, after Mangal Pandey, who had fired the first shot of the Mutiny.[45] The weather made crossing the Ganges even harder. 'I suppose all my fellow-countrymen will understand what I mean by a wet and dry New Year,' recalled Sandy Robb. 'Then let me tell them the 42nd never had before or since such a wet New Year as they had in January 1858 . . . On we marched, the band playing "Come o'er the water Charlie".' Having waded only a short distance, they found they were up to their waists in water. 'It was a hard job for me to keep my rifle and ammunition dry. My height was only five feet and a half, and there were men there shorter than I was.'[46]

Since it was New Year's Day, the men were pleased to be given 'an extra glass of grog, free'.[47] As Robb was anxious to point out, although drunkenness in the Army had to be controlled, 'I say – Give the men grog after a march or an engagement. No matter how sorely they may be knocked up, it puts pluck into the men, and with a short rest they are as ready for work as ever.'[48] Their destination was Futtehgarh (Fatehgarh), 'situated in a district which is reckoned the finest part of India for growing grain and potatoes. Part of our regiment was camped on a potato field, and the potatoes were in their prime. These and other vegetables came in handy for our supper.'[49]

Lucknow March 1858

Despite their successes against the scattered enemy, the Governor-General, Viscount Canning, believed peace could not be fully restored until they had pacified the rebel stronghold of Oudh, which meant retaking Lucknow, evacuated by the British the previous November, and now occupied by the rebels.[50] At Alambagh, near Cawnpore, Campbell's army was organised into three divisions, supported by several thousand Nepalese soldiers and a cavalry division. 'Sir Colin Campbell (of course) being at its head,' recalled Robertson, 'every man thirsting for sweet revenge.'[51] 'We had pleasant cheery marches,' recollected Robb, 'and somehow, money was plentiful among us on account of the loot, and our pay which we could not get spent.'[52] As they neared Lucknow, they were ordered to ready their weapons, with the baggage animals kept in the rear to let the soldiers pass. 'The bugle sounded and off the whole army marched,' related Robertson, 'the pipers playing "the Campbells are coming" (this being literally true for Sir Colin Campbell was at our head) till the pipers thought proper to change tune.'[53]

Reaching Lucknow on 2 March, with a total force of 25,000 men, plus thousands of camp followers and 'a huge heterogeneous mass of elephants, camels and bullock carts', Campbell was facing an estimated 60,000 rebel Indians.[54] On 9 March the attack began. While one division, commanded by Outram, attacked from the north, the Infantry Brigade, under Hope's command, took up position near the Dilkusha Palace on the eastern side of the city. The first major objective was to take the military college of La Martiniere, fortified by a line of entrenchments. 'The 42nd led the attack, four Cos. of the left wing were thrown out in extended order,' related Captain John McLeod, commanding the light infantry company, 'followed by the Regiment in line at 80 paces – we had to cross an open space about 900 yards before we came to Martiniere. We went at the double, just as my Co. cleared the building behind which we were concealed, I got a shot in the foot from a spent ball, it did not hurt me and I went on. I was I think the first in at the Martiniere. The Sepoys bolted as we approached and the place was taken with little loss.'[55]

Following up their advantage, they occupied a village and embankment opposite the first line of works. But, as McLeod related, Hope ordered them to retire to the Martiniere, 'as it was not intended to advance beyond that point the first day; seeing our men retiring gave the Sepoys pluck and they salted us like fun.'[56] During the attack, twenty-year-old Lieutenant Francis Farquharson became the first member of the 42nd Royal Highland Regiment to receive the Victoria Cross 'for conspicuous bravery . . . in having led a portion of his company, stormed a bastion mounting two guns, and spiked the guns, by which the advanced position, held during the night of 9th of March, was rendered secure from the fire of Artillery'.[57]

The following day, they breached the wall of Banks's House – the residence of Major John Banks, who had briefly taken over from Henry Lawrence, before being shot by a sniper: 'the 42nd stormed it,' recorded Robertson, 'and the enemy kept up an obstinate resistance although the highlanders lined the parapets and kept up a hot fire upon the retiring enemy who now lined the walls of the covered ways and batteries of the Begum's Palace.'[58] Much to Robb's surprise, when his company, which had been on camp duty, approached Banks's House, he heard 'the bagpipes playing the Highland reel . . . We fell out, and when I went into this building three or four were dancing.'[59] Throughout the day, as McLeod continued: 'Captains of Companies were left to act a good deal according to circumstances.' Seeing that he could get a good position by breaking down a wall into a garden opposite the nearby Begum's Palace, McLeod organised some Punjabi sappers to smash it. 'On entering the garden, I found it a hotter place than I had bargained for.' Farquharson, the hero of yesterday's action, was severely wounded in the right arm, two soldiers were shot in the head. McLeod received a bullet which was stopped by the folds of his greatcoat. 'Curiously enough I was debating in my own mind that very morning whether I should carry my greatcoat with me.'[60]

The next objective on 11 April was the Begum's Palace, 'an extensive collection of gorgeous eastern palaces, elegant court yards, spacious halls, mirrored saloons, & tastefully laid our gardens'. It was 'strongly defended by a deep ditch, and guns placed in every available place; the streets were barricaded and the entrances were blocked up; heavy guns commanding all the roads'.[61] Once the walls had been breached, the soldiers were 'impatient to get loose'. As Robertson described, 'the walls were climbed, the ditches leaped and onwards we poured through the break for four hours. It was one awful scene of blood . . . nothing could withstand the desperate steel of the 42nd [and] 93rd Highlanders.' During the fighting William

Hodson, in command of Hodson's Horse, was fatally injured. 'The Highlanders supported him and he was carried back to the general quarters in Banks's House.'[62] Despite the ferocious onslaught, the 'tenacious' sepoys resisted 'not in hundreds but in swarms of thousands'.[63] Once the palace was taken, the sight defied description: 'for piles of men, lying as they had fallen, some already cold . . . even in death holding in their clenched hands their well used and bloody *talwars* and muskets with all the energy of their contracting muscles'.[64]

Meanwhile, McLeod and the light infantry company had been clearing some mud buildings nearby. 'Having cleared the position indicated, I observed to our right some men of the 93rd in difficulties at the head of a lane where four streets met. I went to their assistance.' Targeted by the rebels, 'they were mown down at every step'.[65] As McLeod withdrew, he was 'compelled to abandon the body of one of my men; we should have lost several men in endeavouring to carry it away'. The following day the dead man's feather bonnet 'was flying from one of the highest pinnacles of the Temple in their first line of defence. It hung there till brought down by a round shot from one of our guns.'[66]

'Daily we made such advances as the capture of the Begum's palace,' recorded Robertson, 'and in a few days the mighty Lucknow, the hope of the mutineers, the city of palaces and mosques was ours.'[67] During this time, the hangman, said Robb, was not idle. 'I saw about thirty prisoners at one place, and was told they were to be all hung. The hangman was there making them hold the rope till he would make the noose.'[68]

Nearly two weeks after the attack began, with the stronghold of the Kaisarbagh and the Residency recaptured, on 20 March, Robertson was recording that 'the last man of the enemy had left the town, the houses were locked up, the bazaars were closed, the streets empty, and not a human being to be seen save a few aged folk, who were only deserving of our pity; bands of Indians dogs prowled about the street taking advantage of the body of any unburied sepoy to satisfy the cravings of hungers, the houses and even the palaces were so defiled by the piles of dead that they smelt horribly, the pungent smell meeting you wherever you went into shelter from the rays of the meridian sun and almost suffocating you.'[69] Inevitably, the troops started to plunder: 'although there were severe restrictions against doing so, even the Hindoo temples ravaged for the metal of which the gods were made, everything of any value or which was worth taking away was removed and monopolised by the victorious army.'[70]

With British troops quartered throughout the town, in the aftermath of battle, 'soon light hearted Irishmen, kilted highlanders and boisterous John Bulls might have been heard singing old ballads and songs to the accompaniment of tom toms, drums, fifes and bugles in places where only princes were before allowed to walk; you could hear the loud chorus of Rory o' More issuing from the sacred chambers of the harems, such scenes becoming strangely out of place in Lucknow which then was literally a Golgotha.'[71]

For a while, the 42nd remained at the Dilkusha Palace recovering its strength. 'Swarms of flies by day, and mosquitos and bugs eat us alive at night,' McLeod complained to his brother.[72] But, although Lucknow had fallen, large numbers of rebel Indians had escaped and were joining forces with the local chiefs and Rajahs in neighbouring Rohilkand. A field force, under the command of General Robert Walpole, was ordered to go in pursuit. Brigadier Adrian Hope, 93rd, was in command of the 1st Brigade, made up of the three Highland Regiments, the 42nd, 79th and 93rd. A separate force was to advance from the north, and both were to converge on Bareilly, Rohilkand's capital.

As Wilkinson related, night marches during the campaign were a trial. 'Camels roaring outside and elephants, and tent pegs giving. You get up and your tent has to be packed, elephants loaded and camels. Bugles sound and you march off, after hearing 20 different lies about the enemy. Daylight appears, and you still go on in clouds of dust, cavalry dashing past you making dust so that you can eat it. Out comes the sun enough to bake you, and after 14 miles you arrive on a piece of ground 2 hours before your tent is pitched. If Field Officer you post your picquets, and visit them by night and day. If you are not shot, or fall down a well you come back to bed for about 4 hours, and again the same routine, sour bread and dust, no sugar, 9 servants that drive you wild, none being fit for anything.'

In early April, the 42nd marched out of Lucknow. 'We were all happy when the order was read that we were to march from Lucknow, and were sorry for the comrades we were leaving there in soldiers' graves,' recalled Sandy Robb.[73] 'Once more we were in the open country to go through long weary marches and to lose our energy under the heat of the Indian sun,' recollected Robertson, 'many had to leave the ranks on account of sickness brought on from an insatiable and continual desire for water.'[74] 'There are no roads but regular open country,' described Wilkinson, 'with here and there a Fort and village, then a lovely tope [wood] of trees, enormous and very green indeed. We halt now and then, and always march at 4 a.m. or earlier and in the dark, and about 9 a.m. arrive. All drink but few can eat, the sun the moment it rises begins to burn.'[75]

On the morning of 15 April they reached the fort of Ruhya, occupied by a 'mutinous' Rajah and which Walpole ordered the men to storm. 'We were formed in battle order by him about two miles from the fort, the infantry moving in column, with the battery in advance, the skirmishers being spread out in front of all,' recalled Robertson.[76] Before the siege guns arrived, the occupants opened 'a galling fire' on the skirmishers, 'every bullet having its billet'. The soldiers' 'fire though strong was entirely ineffective for the enemy never shewed themselves; the field guns also were too light for the length of the necessary throw'.[77] 'Of cover there was none except a ditch which alas! became the grave of many a gallant man,' related John Muir.[78]

After nearly two hours, the breaching guns arrived but, according to Robertson, Walpole's 'unstable mind' ordered them to be moved from the unguarded side of the fort: 'this movement gave time as well as encouragement to the enemy who no doubt were watching our unsteady manoeuvres.' While the guns were being shifted, 'all this time the highlanders in this exposed situation falling dead or wounded fast'.[79] The attempt to breach the fort's walls lasted for eight hours, during which 'the brave cool' Adrian Hope was shot through the heart, falling 'among the men he had so often led to battle'.[80] Eventually,

Walpole ordered a withdrawal. 'I never saw the 42nd in such a state of discontent,' Robb later wrote, 'and to complete our discomfiture it came on a heavy rain, and the band struck up the tune, "We will never march again"'[81] As they departed, Robertson recorded that they heard the occupants 'howling from their fort in triumph and sent 3 or 4 shots after us letting us know who was last in the field'.[82]

On reaching the camp, the doctors immediately started 'amputating, extracting balls and binding up wounds'.[83] Lest their adversaries attack in the middle of the night, strong pickets were posted, 'but there was no need for guarding against a surprise, for the enemy left the fort at midnight taking everything with them, and when we came to it on the next day we found nothing except four or five bodies smouldering on a heap of cinders.'[84] Orders were issued to the Brigade to parade in full dress for the burial of the dead, which included the 'beloved' Brigadier Adrian Hope. 'I chose the spot and saw the graves dug,' Wilkinson wrote home. 'Oh it was so sad marching down, bands playing Dead March the moon just rising. I walked by the Brigadier's body placed in white sheets and cottons.'[85] 'The beautiful Episcopalian funeral service was read, and our chaplain also had short services,' Robb recalled, adding that Reverend William Ross had often been under fire and 'did his very utmost to give Christian consolation to the dying and wounded'.[86]

'Well, fancy this disgrace to our swell Brigade never licked or mismanaged before,' commented Wilkinson to his sister, while marvelling that Walpole could have been 'such a fool' as to have ordered an attack without reconnoitring the fort.[87] 'It was a visible fact that the opposite side of the Fort to that on which he [Walpole] made the attack upon was defenceless not a wall not a ditch to oppose our progress,' related Robertson.[88] Describing the 'bitter feelings among the troops', *The Times*'s 'Special Correspondent' William Russell informed readers that: 'The attack was mismanaged – officers and men were uselessly sacrificed, and their loss was not avenged.'[89]

During the action, the 42nd lost two lieutenants. For 'conspicuous gallantry', three members of the 42nd received the Victoria Cross: Quarter Master Sergeant John Simpson, 'who had volunteered to go

20. *The Black Watch at Bay, Quatre Bras, 16 June 1815,* by W.B. Wollen. '*Shrieks and groans of men, the neighing of horses, and the discharge of musketry, rent the air, as men and horses mixed together in one heap of indiscriminate slaughter,*' wrote Sergeant James Anton.

21. *The Death of Lieutenant Colonel Robert Macara, Quatre Bras, 16 June 1815,* by S. Mitan. He was hit by a lance and died instantly.

22. *The Last March in Brigade of the 42nd, 79th and 93rd Highlanders from Dover Castle previous to their leaving for India, 1857*, by W. Burgess. '*All was bustle and excitement*,' recollected Private John Muir, 42nd, '*orderlys running hither and thither*'.

23. Left: Crimea veterans, Dover, 1856. Piper Muir, Privates Glen and Mackenzie and Colour Sergeant Gardner. The fashion for long beards was at its height. '*Now I am so proud of my moustache and beard you would not believe how the sun brings out one's beard*,' Captain Frederick Green Wilkinson informed his family from the Crimea.

24. Right: Diary of Private Archibald McIntosh. In India, the soldiers were encouraged to make use of a 'Regimental Garden'. The garden *'was divided into Rows, these rows are then divided among those of each Company who wish to cultivate a piece of ground, tools and all sorts of seeds are supplied on application to the Quarter Master'.*

25. Life in India by Ensign Francis Coleridge, 42nd, present at the battle of the Sarda river, warning his readers not to go out riding in the Himalayas *'without previously having got . . . a collar strap . . . and a crupper to your saddle . . . and satisfied yourself that your gaiters are strong'.*

26. *The Black Watch on parade at Floriana barracks, Valetta, Malta* by Paolo de Angelis. During the 'Long Peace', the 42nd spent several years in Malta as part of a 'Mediterranean routine'.

27. *The Wreck of the Birkenhead, 26 February 1852*, by Lance Culkin. '*Stand fast! I beg you,*' Captain Alexander Seton, RN, was recorded as saying, '*do not rush the boats carrying the women and children, you will swamp them*'. The 73rd lost two officers and fifty-four men.

28. *Colour Sergeant William Gardner winning his VC at Bareilly, India, 1858* for *'conspicuous and gallant conduct'.* By Orlando Norie.

29. *The Black Watch on the Sphinx, Egypt, 1883*, by Consalve Carelli. *'We were allowed to roam all over the place,'* Bandsman Spencer Barwood told his family in August 1883. *'We were quite done up, and had to take a couple of halts before we reached the top.'*

30. _Coming Down Stream_ by J. G. Keulemans: '*I have to go through another campaign*,' Lieutenant Colonel Robert Coveny told his family, '*we are to do most of the work in boats . . . made specially for the purpose.*'

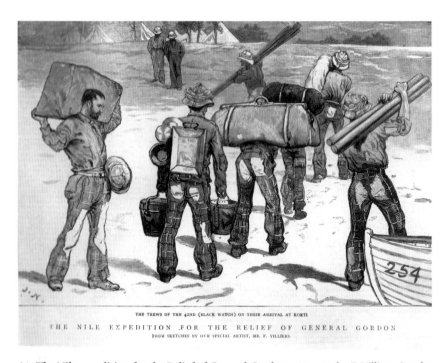

THE TREWS OF THE 42ND (BLACK WATCH) ON THEIR ARRIVAL AT KORTI

THE NILE EXPEDITION FOR THE RELIEF OF GENERAL GORDON
FROM SKETCHES BY OUR SPECIAL ARTIST, MR. F. VILLIERS

31. _The Nile expedition for the Relief of General Gordon, 1884–85_, by F. Villiers, *London Illustrated News*. '*All along the bank was the cargo piled up in allotments for the waiting boats,*' recorded Private John Gordon, '*meat, biscuits, tea, coffee, sugar, preserves, cheese.*'

32. *The Battle of Kirbekan, 1885, from a sketch by Lieutenant B. W. R. Usher,* '*There on top of that long razor back hill were lively mobs doing their wild war dance,*' recalled Private John Gordon, '*brandishing spears high over their heads.*'

33. Objects relating to The Black Watch's service in Egypt and the Sudan. After the Battle of Tel-el-Kebir in 1882, the British found the Eygptian camp stocked with provisions: '*camels, Arab steeds, and tents*'.

34. The Black Watch in traditional 'square' formation during training. *'They never broke our square'* said Lieutenant Colonel Robert Coveny after the Battle of Tamai.

35. Shoulder Belt Plate of the 42nd *c.* 1818–1830.

36. Badge of the 73rd, 1862–1881.

to an exposed point within forty yards of the parapet of the fort under heavy fire and carried back a Lieutenant and a Private, both of whom were seriously wounded'; Private James Davis, who offered to carry one of the 42nd lieutenants' bodies, performing 'this duty, of danger and affection under the very walls of the Fort'; and Lance Corporal Alexander Thompson, who volunteered to help bring back the body of another dead lieutenant in the 4th Punjab Rifles. Private Edward Spence would have been awarded the VC for volunteering with Thompson but he was wounded in the attempt and later died.[90] Having destroyed the fort of Ruhya – known for posterity as 'Walpole's folly' – the force continued upcountry, to be joined by Campbell, who arrived from Futtehgarh with reinforcements. 'Day after day,' Robertson narrated, they followed the Indian rebels, 'always close at their heels, often in coming into the very place they had occupied on the previous night, often finding smoking fires, and cakes of new baked bread.'[91]

Bareilly May 1858

Campbell's objective remained Bareilly, 'to which most of the army which had been defeated at Lucknow had retired' and where there was a large force of sepoys and rebel Indians, 'plenty of guns large and small and several thousand cavalry'.[92] On 5 May the attack began. As the mortars and siege artillery moved forward by road, the 42nd was covering the left flank of two batteries of field artillery, the right flank covered by the 93rd, while the 79th formed a second line. The cavalry was also advancing on the flanks and in front of the two batteries, with the sappers and miners moving forward along the road with the guns. 'In this splendid order we advanced till we came within sight of the enemy's position, they were hidden from view by trees which they had cut down and laid around them leaving spaces for the muzzles of the guns,' recorded Robertson. 'Almost immediately the enemy opened fire, the first round doing no harm but the second killing three men and one horse.'[93]

During the battle the 4th Punjab Rifles was forced to fall back into the ranks of the 42nd, pursued by 'mostly Ghazee fanatical Moosulmans' – who had 'maddened themselves' with bhang – a potent infusion of cannabis leaves and flowers – 'clothed in the religious green coloured garb'.[94] According to Robertson, the Regiment 'met the enemy with the bayonet and shot or cut down every man of them who had made the fatal advance against the Sikhs [i.e. 4th Punjabis]'.[95] In the midst of the fighting, three Ghazis succeeded in dragging Lieutenant Colonel Alexander Cameron off his horse, and were about to kill him when Colour Sergeant William Gardner stepped out from the ranks and bayoneted two of them; a third was killed by another soldier. Cameron escaped with only a light wound on his left wrist. For Gardner's 'conspicuous and gallant conduct' he was awarded the VC.[96] Throughout the day, Robertson recorded the Commander-in-Chief, Colin Campbell, as being 'the first man to pull a trigger, revolver and sword in hand; he encouraged and cheered us on till at last the hard fought battle was ours'.[97]

Having kept up 'a hot fire' on the fleeing rebels who took refuge in nearby villages, for the rest of the day the troops took shelter under the trees, 'the heat being very great and a dust storm blowing'.[98] 'They had left behind a great number of gun carriages, ready for use, and evidently had a foundry for casting guns somewhere, for there were several found lying about of all shapes and sizes as nearly finished as if from Europe,' related Robertson. 'Although the men had been commanded to take no prisoners, but to shoot down all that came within their reach, they brought in to head quarters droves of them, who had been captured armed and accoutred; they were shown no mercy, nor did they deserve any.'[99] That night the soldiers bivouacked on the battlefield, 'each man sleeping with his head at the foot of his rifle which stood stacked with two or three others in military order; the cavalry slept beside their horses and the artillerymen sought shelter under their gun carriages; on the next night we pitched camp in the beautiful suburbs of Bareilly.'[100]

'The taking of Bareilly,' noted John Muir, 'was practically the end of the Mutiny, at least its back was broken, and what remained to be done was merely the hunting down of the Mutineers.'[101] During the offensive, the 42nd had lost one private soldier; two officers were wounded, one sergeant and eleven soldiers.[102] Of special significance for the Regiment was that according to the recollections of Sergeant David Russell, the battle at Bareilly on 5 May 1858 was the last action in which the Colours were carried under fire.[103] For the next few months the Regiment remained encamped on the outskirts of Bareilly, 'rising early every morning to enjoy the cool morning breeze & a stroll among the ruined gardens of those whose wives & children once enjoyed their isolated but happy homes, but who now lay under the ruins of their villas'.[104] 'We all make the best of everything,' Wilkinson wrote to his sister, 'but really living in tents in May it is impossible, and miserable to spend ones days like this. *Any* country would be preferable. *No position* in my opinion can make up for it. Still one is doing ones duty, and if one survives it, one will be very glad indeed to have seen and done what we have, and got so many rupees.'[105]

In late May, Wilkinson was given command of the right wing of the Regiment and ordered to march north-west to Moradabad. 'I shall have great responsibility, and anxiety being separated from my Regiment,' he confided to his sister, recollecting Campbell's advice that he should always be alert: 'believing nothing and looking after sentries picquets etc of our men night & day'. It was 'curious', he said, that as soon as he was given a command 'I look at everything differently, I take greater interest, more zeal, and being occupied is everything, you forget the heat, as to hanging, killing, or blowing up from guns, positively I am already hardened, no sight I have not seen.' He also prided himself on the discipline and dress of the 42nd compared with the other regiments, the 79th and 93rd, where one man might wear a Bonnet, 'others a turban and so on, not half so tidy'.[106]

As the temperature rose in central India, the men were suffering from sunstroke, fever and diarrhoea. 'Every exertion was made to get them into temporary barracks but this was not effected until the middle of July just in time to escape the rains.'[107] At Moradabad, Wilkinson was doing his best to keep the men under his command 'as happy as we can', with races for men and officers. 'Our theatre is getting ready. Our latest amusement is putting up hurdles round the Bungalow and producing all our horses.'[108] Among those who fell ill 'was that fatherly officer, our [Lieutenant] Colonel, Alexander Cameron', who died on 9 August 1858.[109]

Meanwhile, having spent over ten years in South Africa, in April 1858 the 73rd Regiment had arrived directly in India. Like the 42nd, the soldiers occupied barracks in Fort William, 'where it was so unfortunate as to lose 28 men by cholera Fever'.[110] Unlike the 42nd, the Regiment saw comparatively little action and most of the time was spent in detachments, with individual companies posted along the Grand Trunk Road. By late July the headquarters, under the command of Lieutenant Colonel George Hankey Smith (in Pinckney's absence), was in Benares (Varanasi). Subsequently, the Regiment 'was employed on active service in the field on the Oude and Garrackpore Frontiers'. According to the Record of Service, 'on two or three occasions, detachments were engaged with the Rebel Sepoys'.[111]

In late September the 73rd marched to Lucknow, taking up barracks 'of a temporary and very unfurnished description' at Dilkusha. There the Regiment was inspected on Parade by Campbell, recently raised to the peerage as Baron Clyde of Clydesdale, who complimented the Regiment on 'its state and appearance'.[112] Moving around the countryside, the 73rd continued to be sent in detachments to relieve other regiments. In November, while travelling from Allahabad to Dinapore, the soldiers 'had to regret' the death from bronchitis of Lieutenant Colonel Pinckney – 'the soldier's friend' – 'his remains being interred in the cemetery at Ghazeepore'.[113]

Sarda River: 'Lawson's Men' January 1859

In late 1858, Walpole dispatched a column, commanded by Colonel Smythe, to guard the points of access on the Sarda river, bordering Oudh and Rohilkand. The detachment, consisting of one company of the 42nd, under the command of Captain William Lawson, a squadron of Indian cavalry and part of the newly raised Indian 'Kumaon' Regiment, made its way through the dense jungle to the banks of the Sarda river, where it was divided to guard the Maylah and Sissaya ghats.[114] 'It was nice soldiering there, as the duty was not hard,' remarked Robb. 'For some time we moved about in the jungle, camping here and there for perhaps two days at a time.'[115] At the same time, another detachment, commanded by Wilkinson, was sent to Madho Tanda, 'being a central position whence support might be sent in any direction required'.[116] 'I fear if the rains come on which they do at Xmas,' he remarked 'then we shall have fever, for when I am in the wet season it is deadly. We are all going to be vaccinated. The climate is lovely now, cricket match yesterday.'[117]

On the morning of 15 January 1859 a rebel Indian force crossed the Sarda at Maylah Ghat, three miles from Colonel Smythe's camp. To compound their difficulties, one half of Lawson's company was detached on picket duty with Ensign Francis Coleridge, 'and was so placed as to be cut off from the remainder of the force'. As noted in the Record of Service, 'the jungle was so dense, that the Cavalry could not act, the Kumaon Levies were all raw recruits who were with difficulty kept to their posts, so the fighting fell almost wholly to the lot of the 37 men under the command of Captain Lawson'.[118] Although Smythe sent for reinforcements, the detachment under Wilkinson's command at Madho Tanda was a day's march away. 'Late in the afternoon I remember Captain Lawson saying to us – "Well, lads, I fear we will have to do this ourselves,"' recollected Robb. Ordered to advance from the main body under Walpole's command, 'we fell into skirmishing order and fixed our bayonets . . . We were in the thick of the fight; and the natural quiet of a sultry Indian afternoon was broken by the quick rattle of musketry, the shrieks of wounded natives, and the stirring sounds of our Scottish cheers. I was in the centre of the party.'[119]

During the fight, Lawson was severely wounded in the groin. With Lieutenant Bayly wounded, the sergeant and two corporals killed, the action was left in the hands of the private soldiers. 'It was a scene of terrible excitement, and though it was not by any means my first taste of active warfare, I must confess that any courage

I displayed was in great measure the courage of despair.' In the midst of the battle, Robb related how another soldier, Duncan Millar, 'tore a medal off his chest', requesting Robb to send it to his mother if worst befell.[120] Unexpectedly, the detachment under Ensign Coleridge's charge arrived, having 'fought their way through the host of the enemy without a man of them being hurt'. As Robb surmised, the Indians thought greater reinforcements were coming and so fell back, enabling the soldiers to get into a better position. 'We remained on the defensive, but still kept up a brisk fire. Though our ranks were considerably thinned, we fought steadily on.'[121] To their relief, the arrival of reinforcements 'turned the tide of battle altogether in our favour – such of the enemy as could re-crossed the river in the dark and next morning nothing remained on the field but the dead and the dying, five small guns and some cattle belonging to the rebels.'[122] The following day, Wilkinson and his contingent reached Sissaya Ghat from Madho Tanda; 'and during the three days following the action upwards of 150 fugitives were picked up in the jungles'.[123]

Despite his fears, Private Duncan Millar had survived and received the Victoria Cross, as did another private soldier, Walter Cook. Their conduct, Walpole recorded, 'deserves to be particularly pointed out. At the time the fight was the severest, and the few men of the 42nd Regiment were skirmishing so close to the enemy (who were in great numbers), that some of the men were wounded by sword cuts, and the only officer [Lawson] with the 42nd was carried to the rear, severely wounded, and the Color-Sergeant was killed, these soldiers went to the front, took a prominent part in directing the Company, and displayed a courage, coolness, and discipline, which was the admiration of all who witnessed it.'

Later, the pipe tune 'Lawson's Men' was written to commemorate the incident.[124] According to Private David McAusland, writing to Robb in later life, there was another soldier, called Sanderson, who 'did his duty that day, and Duncan Millar walked away with the honours he should have got but this often happens in the service, as you have seen'.[125] Including Lawson, who died of his wounds, and Bayly, who was slightly wounded, a total of seventeen were killed and wounded. After the action, Clyde applauded the discipline of the soldiers 'who, cut off from their supports, had kept at bay a force of 2000 rebels for 10 hours in a dense jungle, conduct which, he said was beyond all praise'.[126]

Over the next few months the 42nd alternated between service on the Sarda river and at Bareilly.[127] Meanwhile a detachment of new recruits, which included seventeen-year-old Private Archibald McIntosh, had joined the Regiment. One of the first events McIntosh witnessed was a district court martial at Bareilly, 'held on a man of ours who was a Drummer . . . for "Disgraceful Conduct in stealing a Gold Ring the property of Sergeant Alexander Munro."' As McIntosh related, he was found guilty and sentenced to receive fifty lashes 'on the bare back to be administered in the usual way, he did cry at a fearfull rate, he was the first European I had seen flogged'.[128]

Peace in India 1859

'War is at an end,' Governor-General Canning proclaimed at a day of thanksgiving and prayer in July 1859. 'Rebellion is put down; the Noise of Arms is no longer heard where the enemies of the State have persisted in their last Struggle; the Presence of large Forces in the Field has ceased to be necessary.'[129] After a show trial, the last Mughal Emperor, Bahadur Shah II, was exiled to Burma, where he died in 1862. General Tatya Tope was captured and executed. Although there were numerous sightings of Nana Sahib, he never reappeared and was recorded as dying of fever in 1859 or as living as an ascetic in a cave in Uttar Pradesh until 1905.[130] Once hostilities were over, Clyde relinquished his position of Commander-in-Chief and returned home, dying aged seventy in 1863.

Between November 1857 and May 1859, the 42nd's casualties amounted to twenty officers and soldiers killed in action; 135 had died of wounds and disease and twenty-two were wounded.[131] During two years of insurrection, an estimated 11,000 British combatants had died, most of them through disease or sunstroke. No reliable sources exist but many thousands of sepoys and innocent civilians had been killed. Cities and towns across northern India had been destroyed. The uprising had generated a new policy embodied in the Government of India Act – correctly called An Act for the Better Government of India – which transferred ownership of the East India Company to the Crown. Henceforward the Governor-General would be Queen Victoria's representative and Viceroy. One of the first issues to be managed was the reorganisation of the army, providing for a British Army in India, or 'Indian Army', although regiments from Britain still carried out tours of duty. The 42nd was among those chosen to stay. In July, twenty-five men who had enlisted for ten years and whose terms of service had expired were sent home for discharge. Sixty-three men volunteered for the Bengal Artillery to fill the place of those discharged.

At the end of September 1859, while new barracks were being built in Bareilly, the 42nd shifted into a 'standing camp, we had 8 Men in each tent, and charpoys'. By Christmas, it had turned very cold. 'When we go to wash our face in the morning we have to break the ice.'[132] Much of the soldiers' time was spent mounting guard, either at the hospital, the jail or at the fort. In early February 1860, three companies of the Regiment were part of the escort accompanying Khan Bahadur Khan, rebel chief of the Rohilla Indians, to his execution. McIntosh who had often been on sentry duty, and used 'to have a chat with him in the native language', was clearly struck by the occasion. 'I was standing on the road-side when he passed, he was sitting in the cart erect and firm, his look to all was one of bitter hatred, defiance and scorn.'[133]

Having moved into their new barracks in May, the soldiers were encouraged to make use of the Regimental Garden, 'which is divided into Rows, these rows are then divided among those of each Company who wish to cultivate a piece of ground, tools and all sorts of seeds are supplied on application to the Quarter Master. A well is in the center with drains leading in to each piece of ground and each Company has a native gardener to look after the plants.'[134] As usual, 30 November – St Andrew's Day – was celebrated with a variety of Highland games, dancing, running and throwing, as well as 'Leaping, Vaulting with the pole, Hurdle Race, and Hitch and Kick . . . then we had Strathspey and Reel dancing, Sword Dance, and the Highland Fling'.[135]

On 1 January 1861, while at Bareilly, the 42nd was presented with new Colours by Lieutenant General Sir Hugh Rose, Clyde's successor as Commander-in-Chief in India, another veteran of the Crimean War. 'We marched past in slow and quick time and those who were spectators say that they never saw a Regiment in India March Past better,' recorded McIntosh, 'and few as well, and that the sight was the best they had seen.'[136]

'I do not ask you to defend the colors I have presented to you this day,' Rose began. 'It would be superfluous. You have defended them for nearly a hundred and fifty years with the best blood of Scotland. I do not ask you to carry these colors to the Front should you again be called into the Field. You have borne them round the world with success.' 'But,' he continued, 'I do ask the Officers and soldiers of this gallant and devoted regiment not to forget, because they are of ancient date, but to treasure in their memories the recollection of the brilliant deeds of arms of their forefathers and kinsmen, the scenes of which are inscribed on these colors. There is not a name on them which is not a study. There is not a name on them which is not connected with the most important events of the world's history or with the brightest pages of the military annals of England.'[137]

'The Old Colors were on parade for the last time,' observed McIntosh, 'and during the march past they hung mournfully to the poles as if they knew it was their last parade, many farewell glances were taken at them by those who had fought under them in the Crimea.'[138]

The 73rd Regiment had remained in India, having spent the final months of unrest at Dinapore and Berhampore.[139] In January 1861 orders were received to return to Britain. Before departing 334 privates transferred to the other regiments serving in the Bengal

Presidency; three soldiers joined the 42nd, now under the command of Lieutenant Colonel Edward Priestley, who had joined the Regiment in 1857.[140]

In March 1861, the 42nd left Bareilly; three companies were posted to Futtehgarh, the remainder to Agra. 'The weather is now very hot, almost intolerable, everything is burning hot, we can hardly wear any clothing, and are tormented almost to madness with Prickly heat, Bugs, Fleas and Mosquitoes, which put sleep out the question at night,' complained McIntosh. 'Then comes the Heat Winds, hot is only a mild name for them, but to know anything of them you must feel them, did you ever hold your face over a stove full of fire, and feel the rush of hot air that would almost choke you and burn your skin, well, hot winds are something like that, but coming in a stronger rush, it comes quietly at first, then burst in a roar scorching you, and shrivelling you up like a roasted pig, you feel as if some one had tightened the skin of your face, you feel as if an invisible flame was playing round your face and limbs, and making the skin crack.'[141] Outbreaks of cholera became so severe that the men were buried in groups. As during the Crimea, funerals were so frequent that no music was permitted, 'nor firing over the graves as the sound tended to depress the spirits of those in hospital and that place was full'. At the end of July the Regiment was sent for 'a change of air' to Secundra (Sikandar) Bagh. The heat was still 'very great' and it rained almost incessantly.[142]

Back in Agra, as a special mark of honour, Priestley informed the Regiment that 'Her Majesty has been graciously pleased to authorize the 42nd Highland Regiment being designated in addition to that title, the "Black Watch" by which name it was popularly known at, and for some time after the period of its being raised.' Priestley's Regimental Order went on to say that every soldier of The Black Watch 'who had the privilege of entering the canteen this evening is to have a ration of spirits gratis; but not in excess of the regulated allowance. The punishments of defaulters are remitted.'[143] Afterwards 'we were called to attention as the "Black Watch" and gave three cheers for the Queen'.[144] Henceforward, and with increasingly frequency, the name The Black Watch was used to refer to the Regiment. In time, it would be the only name by which the oldest Highland Regiment was known.

Mindful of the deaths from cholera, at the beginning of December the Regiment was sent to 'one of the finest stations in India',[145] Dugshai (Dagshai), in the foothills of the Himalayan mountains, which they reached by way of Umballa (Ambala) and Kalka in April 1862. 'Shortly after our arrival we were inspected by the Commander-in-Chief,' noted McIntosh, 'who gave us great praise for the manner in which we had done our drill, and the clean orderly state of the rooms.' Compared with life on the plains, the two years at Dugshai were enjoyable. 'We have a nice theatre here and a good company of Amateurs, we have also a good library with papers and all sorts of games.'[146] While at Dugshai, Queen Victoria commanded that *Lucknow* should be borne on the Colour of the Regiment.[147]

When the heat subsided, in October 1863 the Regiment was again marching south, this time to take part in 'a Camp of Exercise' in Lahore involving over 10,000 troops and presided over by General Rose, who noted the soldiers' 'smart and soldier-like appearance'.[148]

Four years after the end of the Indian Mutiny, the region which remained of continuing concern was the north-west frontier of India and the border area of neighbouring Afghanistan. Home to the Pashtun tribes, whose 'khels' resembled the clans of Scotland, the official frontier remained undefined. Nearly twenty-five years had passed since Britain's disastrous retreat from Afghanistan in 1842, but there was still the need to be vigilant.[149] In December 1863 the 42nd was ordered to make a forced march to Rawalpindi with the possibility of moving on to Peshawar if required. 'Such a miserable time we had in tents here especially Christmas Day, when it rained the whole day and night,' recorded Sergeant Quibell Cooper.[150] When the situation on the Frontier 'assumed a more favourable aspect', the Regiment returned to Dugshai, covering a distance of 800 miles 'by regular marches'.[151]

The following autumn, renewed concern about the Frontier meant that the 42nd was again ordered to Rawalpindi.[152] 'It will be some time before we get into barracks,' noted McIntosh on 14 December 1864, 'as they have to be whitewashed and cleaned out.'[153] While they waited, Cooper was recording that 'nothing extraordinary' happened to disturb 'the usual routine of a military life'.[154] One soldier who had gone home 'unfit for service' was Sandy Robb. Having completed his ten years' service in the Regiment and signed on for another ten years, he had an accident, losing the sight of one eye and strength in one side, and had to be invalided home.[155] In October the 42nd left Rawalpindi for Peshawar, 'which we don't care about as it is considered one of the most unhealthy places in India,' Cooper noted. 'During the winter the nights are very cold and very often in the morning there is ice on the water, we were visited also by several slight shocks of earthquakes at different times.'[156]

While the Frontier remained relatively quiet, throughout 1866 the soldiers had 'plenty of Brigade Field days'.[157] In the summer of 1867 there was another serious cholera epidemic. 'A Black day for the Black Watch,' Cooper observed.[158] 'The first man that took it was one of my Company,' McIntosh wrote in his diary. 'Another and another were seized shortly afterwards, taken to hospital and died in a few hours. By next morning we had lost 7 men and 2 children. God grant that this may not be such a scourge as we had in Agra.'[159] Four days later he was noting: '18 Men, 1 Woman, and 1 Child today, this was the worst day of all, it was heartrending to here [hear] the cries of agony of those in the cramps, but the poor fellows do not suffer long, the cramps go away and they depart in sleep.'[160]

In an attempt to stop the epidemic spreading, the Regiment moved from the cantonment to the plain, moving camp every second day, which 'had favourable consequences and the disease began to abate'. Having taken up quarters for the summer at the hill station of Cherat, 'in this very sickly season' deaths began again to take their toll.[161] The soldiers' main activity consisted of making roads during the cool of the day in the early morning. Misdemeanours still occurred. Sergeant William Whitson was found 'Drunk in Camp' and was reduced to the ranks. Private Pratt was court-martialled for

'Disgraceful Conduct in Stealing a Sheep from a Native', for which the punishment was 'Imprisonment with Hard Labour for 168 Days, to forfeit all his former service and claim to Good Conduct Pay and Pension on discharge'.[162] In contrast, Quarter Master Sergeant Thomas Torrance was honoured with a medal for his 'Long Service and Good Conduct'.[163] The Regiment was also unanimously praised for its endurance 'during this trying period' of the epidemic.[164]

After almost ten years in India, in October 1867 the 42nd began the return journey to England. From Cherat it was 'all downhill' to Nowshera. After a 'fine march' through Lahore and onwards, the Regiment travelled downriver on the Indus. On 30 November, 'this being Saint Andrews Day, the band played several Scotch Airs'.[165] By late January 1868 they had reached Bombay, sailing home via the Red Sea, where the Suez Canal was soon to be officially opened, shortening the journey by sea from Europe to Asia from four months to six weeks.

Before leaving Cherat, Private McIntosh had made one last visit to the graveyard for a 'Farewell Look at the Graves of those who have died up here, may they rest in peace. We have cut out their names on a rock with the dates of their death.'[166]

> The Black Watch – The Black Watch
> The Gallent Forty Twa
> Oh the name o' them
> And the Fame o' them
> Gangs ower the winds that blaw.[167]

19.

The Height of Empire

Yes home again, my gallant boys,
I'm but a Scottish lassie,
But ah that I had been with you,
The day you burned Coomassie![1]

1867

Home Duty 1868: the 42nd

In early 1868, the 42nd Royal Highland Regiment, The Black Watch, as the Regiment was now officially known, returned home after nearly a decade in India. 'We disembarked in Line of March Order and formed up in Line the Band playing "God save the Queen" then "Here's a health Bonnie Scotland to thee" and "Hurrah for the Highlands".'[2] Arriving in Portsmouth the soldiers took passage for Leith. Headquartered at Stirling Castle, with detachments at Perth and Dundee, the Regiment was armed with the new Snider breech-loading rifle.[3]

On 25 March, Lieutenant Colonel Edward Priestley died. Contrary to the official condolence describing him as 'a great favourite with the Regiment', Private McIntosh's opinion was that 'he was a very harsh stern old man and was regretted by very few men in the Regiment'.[4] Yet it was thanks to Priestley's recommendation that Sandy Robb had received a pension of nine pence a day for life.[5] Priestley's successor was John McLeod, 'a good man and well liked by the Regiment', who had prided himself on being the first to enter La Martiniere at Lucknow in 1858.[6] Promoted major during the attack on Lucknow, he had been a brevet lieutenant colonel since 1861, and had married Emily, Robert Henry Dick's niece, the daughter of his younger brother, Abercromby.[7] On 12 October 1868 the Regiment moved to Edinburgh Castle. 'There were very large crowds awaiting the arrival both at the Haymarket and Waverly Stations and, as the Regiment passed through the multitude, on its way to the Castle, it was greeted by a most enthusiastic reception, and tremendous cheering.'[8]

The Regiment's stay in Scotland was brief, and by November the soldiers were sailing around coastal Britain again to Portsmouth. Their destination was the military town of Aldershot, developed during the Crimean War. During The Black Watch's posting there, the Queen, together with members of the Royal Family, made one of her regular visits to watch manoeuvres: 'The various evolutions, which included an admirable sham fight, were gone through with even greater precision and skill than usual, the heavy rain having rendered the ground far more easy to manoeuvre on,' recorded the correspondent for a local newspaper. 'Of the infantry, the imposing appearance of The Black Watch (42nd Highlanders) with their dark plaid kilts, scarlet tunics, and plumed bonnets, excited universal admiration.'[9]

For the next eighteen months, the Regiment remained at Aldershot, taking part in exercises which remained standard military training into the next century. On 7 July 1871 new Colours were presented by Field Marshal, HRH the Duke of Cambridge, Commander-in-Chief of the British Army, Queen Victoria's cousin, under whom The Black Watch had served in the Crimea. It was, he said, 'the wish of the Regiment, that he should perform this important duty, and he had the greatest pleasure in doing so, from having been himself, connected with the Regiment in the Crimea, and knowing of its distinguished gallantry on all occasions.' He went on to trace the Regiment's history: 'in a very succinct manner to the time of the Peninsular War, from thence to the Crimea, of which time he spoke more feelingly of its gallant conduct. He alluded in very complimentary terms to the splendid charge of the Regiment at the Alma.' Finally, he praised the Regiment for always maintaining 'intact the purity of its colours, honouring those standards by their good and gallant conduct, and there never has been any doubt, as to its devotion to its Country and Sovereign'.[10] Lieutenant Colonel McLeod replied: 'It is no unmeaning ceremonial, in which we have been engaged, and solemn thoughts attend the reception of Emblems, which speak to us of the uncertain future.'[11]

In late September the 42nd moved to Raglan Barracks, Devonport; exercises were undertaken in the open spaces of Dartmoor. While The Black Watch remained in the south, in April 1872 a Memorial was unveiled in Dunkeld Cathedral. Dedicated to all who had fallen between 1739 and the end of the Indian Mutiny, it was sculpted in white marble by the renowned sculptor Sir John Steel, RSA, and depicted an officer mourning lost comrades on the battlefield, one of whom had the Colours clenched in his hand. As explained by Major Duncan Macpherson, who came from Devonport to unveil the monument, they had chosen Dunkeld Cathedral since it was close to where the Regiment had first mustered at Aberfeldy. During the ceremony, the Colours, carried in the Crimea and Indian Mutiny, were placed over the monument before being handed to the Cathedral to be hung in perpetuity.[12] In March 1873 the 42nd and the 79th Cameron Highlanders were linked in one Brigade, numbered the 57th, with Perth as its brigade depot, and the counties of Forfar, Perth and Fife included in the sub-district.[13]

The Ashanti War 1874

As Britain continued to assert its control over vast areas of Africa, British soldiers found themselves at war with the inhabitants of the Gold Coast, so called because of the large reserves of gold found in West Africa. Two wars had already been fought against the local Ashanti people, the dominant tribe in the region, whose ruler was known as the Asantehene, or Chief of the Ashantis. The 'Third Anglo-Ashanti' war broke out in 1873 following incursions into the Dutch Gold Coast, which Britain had recently purchased from the post-1815 re-constituted Kingdom of the Netherlands. Britain's adversary was the 'arrogant and vain' Asantahene, Kofi Karikari, and his army of several thousand warriors.[14] At the beginning of October 1873, Sir Garnet Wolseley, who had fought in the Crimea and India, still only forty years old, arrived to take up the post of Commander-in-Chief and Governor of the Gold Coast; his instructions were to make a punitive raid against the Ashantis' capital, Coomassie (Kumasi), in the heart of the West African jungle, having mustered support from the local tribes opposed to the Ashanti.

Wolseley's efforts to gain local support met with little success, and in October 1873 he was writing to request two infantry battalions of 'white troops' – the 2nd Battalion, Rifle Brigade, and the 23rd Fusiliers (The Royal Welsh Fusiliers) – together with a detachment of Royal Artillery and Royal Engineers. 'I have been shown how little reliance can be placed on even the best native troops in this bush fighting, where it is impossible to keep them under the immediate control of European officers,' he wrote in a dispatch to the War Office.[15] He also emphasised that there was no question of building a railway to transport the troops. 'The country which had been represented as being flat, is, so far as I have explored it, covered with rounded hills (mamelons) and intermediate deep ravines, so that the conditions as regards the laying down a railway are very different from those which I was led to expect.'[16]

To bolster his forces, Wolseley requested the services of another infantry battalion, the 42nd. To bring the Regiment up to full strength, it was supplemented by 126 men from the 79th: a 'very nice body of men,' commented a non-commissioned officer of the 42nd, '[they] seem anxious to fall into our way of doing things'.[17] In early December thirty officers and 652 men embarked from Portsmouth. 'Weather has been good since we started,' noted a 42nd non-commissioned officer, 'with light and favourable winds.'[18] In place of the now standard red hackle, the soldiers had a small red buckle fixed onto their regulation pith helmets: 'All seem rather proud of our distinguishing badge.'[19] 'The Armoury Sergeant goes on shore at 4.p.m.,' the 42nd NCO wrote in his diary, 'for the purpose of sharpening the men's swords, bayonets, with which they are being supplied to enable them to cut their way through the bush said to be very dense.' Initially Wolseley was planning to keep The Black Watch offshore in reserve and rely on West Indian troops, but since the West Indians needed the same rations as European troops and, having failed to gain sufficient local support, he changed his mind. On 18 December, he wrote to the War Office:

> When so splendid a battalion as the 42nd is ready to my hand, when
> I see the martial spirit which animates both officers and men, when
> I think of the vastly superior numbers of the enemy and see myself
> entirely deprived of the large force of native auxiliaries upon which
> I had counted, when I remember how vitally important it is that the

campaign should be short and decisive, I do not think that I should be acting wisely in keeping the 42nd Regiment at sea.[20]

Writing in his Journal, Wolseley noted that the '42nd is said to be in excellent order & to be by far the best of those Battalions sent out'.[21] He was also assuring his political superiors back home 'of my strong hope, bordering on conviction, that in about six weeks from the date of our crossing the Prah [river], I shall be able to embark the European troops, having suffered but little loss from the effects of the climate'.[22] In command of the Brigade was forty-seven-year-old Brigadier General Sir Archibald Alison. Having lost his left arm at Lucknow in 1857, he suffered uncomplainingly during the Ashanti campaign from abscesses on his remaining hand.[23]

Given the numerical superiority of an estimated 200,000 Ashanti warriors against Wolseley's 2,500 troops, his plan was to mount a multi-pronged advance. Lack of support from neighbouring tribes meant that, when the time came, his force was the only one to reach Coomassie. On 3 January 1874, the 42nd disembarked at Cape Coast. Henry Stanley, special correspondent for the *New York Herald* and one of a number of journalists reporting on the war, observed that 'they are mostly all young men of very good families, with cream-coloured complexions, light hair and whiskers, as if they had been turned out of one mould'.[24] Like the rest of Wolseley's army, rather than their kilts they were dressed in grey canvas trousers, the standard uniform prescribed for tropical warfare, with square-cut 'Norfolk' jackets. They were also given pocket filters, veils and respirators to help ward off fever, although they proved ineffectual.[25]

The following day, the British force began the 130-mile march into the African jungle, marvelling at the 'great variety of trees' and the 'many pretty birds and butterflies'. Although the road was 'pretty good', after a month at sea the 42nd soldiers found that they had not got their 'shore legs yet' and were feeling 'stiff at the ankles'.[26] 'The atmosphere is thick and vapoury, and in many places moisture is constantly dripping from the trees. Except where the ground has been cleared for camps and villages, the sun never penetrates, and at midday, in the forest, there is only the deeply gloom of twilight,' observed another soldier.[27] By 7 January they had reached Mansu, but there was another delay. En route, the porters, carrying the tons of biscuits, rice and supplies, including ammunition, deserted, whereupon '135 men of the gallant 42nd, under the command of Captain George Moore, volunteered to carry stores to Soota [Sutah] a march of 11 miles through dense forest. Some hand-barrows were hastily put together to carry the loads on, but these speedily coming to grief, the men took the 50 lb. boxes of rice on their heads and shoulders, and with this unaccustomed burden in such a climate marched the 11 miles in good style.' As noted by the 42nd NCO, they were paid '1s a day extra for it, and get a grog'.[28] Having performed this service, the soldiers returned to Mansu, but they were already suffering from the heat and humidity. At Prahsu on the Prah river – 'nearly as large as the Tay at Perth' – twenty-three men were left in hospital, ill with fever.[29]

On 26 January, having marched through 'a forest choked with a jungly under-bush', McLeod, in command of an advance guard, arrived at Borborassie. 'As they emerged into the clearing, [the soldiers] opened fire,' recorded Stanley. 'The surprise was complete, and an indiscriminate flying for shelter into the bush, and almost an immediate desertion of the village was the consequence.'[30] 'I estimate the killed of the enemy at 50,' McLeod wrote in his dispatch. 'Fifty-three Ashanti muskets were collected. Twelve kegs of powder, and the umbrella of [Chief] Essimanquatia were found in the village. It seems this old chief ran away just before the attack, and so narrowly escaped capture.' McLeod also acknowledged the 'valuable' services of his Staff Officer, Captain Francis Farquharson, who had already distinguished himself by receiving the first VC to be given to a member of the Regiment at Lucknow in 1858.[31] 'The attack on, and the capture of the village was effected with his [McLeod's] usual ability and vigour,' Sir Archibald Alison reported to the War Office.[32]

The main Ashanti force had taken up position on a hill overlooking a muddy ravine, near the town of Amoaful (Amoafo), blocking the approach to Coomassie. 'I hear that King Coffee is going to dispute our entry into Coomasie, and of course everybody is in great glee,' enthused the 42nd non-commissioned officer.[33] Wolseley therefore ordered the British force to approach in 'a large open square formation' with four columns, right, left, front and rear, so arranged that they could quickly close ranks, with the medical services and the headquarters within the square. Wolseley himself – the 'centre-piece of the procession' – was sitting on a cane chair, carried by 'four burly and practically naked Fantes'.[34] The 42nd, under Major Duncan Macpherson's command, was in the front column commanded by Alison; McLeod, who had rejoined the main army after Borborassie, was in command of the left column. 'At this slow pace we could but look listlessly on what we had often looked upon before,' remarked Stanley. 'There were no strong contrasting colours to relieve the wearied eye. Grey coats and white sun-helmets in front of us, grey coats and white helmets in rear of us; dense dark bush to the right, dense dark bush to the left; a strip of blue-grey sky above our heads.' Not having previously seen The Black Watch in fighting formation, Stanley 'improved the occasion to get a good look at them'.[35] 'Badly off for water; very small stream,' the 42nd non-commissioned officer was noting on 30 January.[36]

On the morning of 31 January 1874, with the pipers playing 'Hey, Johnnie Cope, are ye waking yet?', the Highlanders moved forward. 'After a little skirmish at Inganassie between the scouts and the men of the outpost, the 42d led the advance, without any native troops in its van, swept through the camp,' commented Winwood Reade, The Times's correspondent.[37] 'Reserving its fire until they encountered the enemy,' described Stanley, 'the Highlanders had continued advancing until they had penetrated about two hundred yards beyond the village [of Inganassie] when the concealed enemy suddenly revealed himself by driving into their faces from cleverly contrived ambuscades.'[38] 'This was a trying way for us, young soldiers, to get under fire,' recalled Private Ferguson. 'The Ashantees were swarming in advance on our flanks in thousands, and I almost felt my time was up, and that I was to be potted like a rabbit in cover.'[39] 'I now observed that the officer who always cried out "Advance!" was limping in evident pain,' noted Reade, 'It was Major Macpherson. He had been shot through the leg, and had tied it round with a handkerchief, but still bright-faced and smiling urged on the men.' 'We were in the midst of a semi-circle of hostile fire,' Alison related, 'and we hardly ever caught sight of a man. As company after company descended with their pipes playing into the ravine, they were almost immediately lost sight of in the bush.'[40]

Unfortunately, as the men were advancing, eager to return the Ashantis' fire, some of the British casualties were as a result of friendly fire. After more than four hours in action, the town of Amoaful, amounting to hundreds of huts constructed out of the branches of trees and plantain leaves, was in British possession. 'Thanks be to God, yesterday has been a brilliant affair,' Wolseley wrote in his Journal.[41] 'Nothing could have exceeded the admirable conduct of the 42nd Highlanders, on whom fell the hardest share of the work.'[42]

The battle against the Ashanti was not yet won, and their next stand was at Ordahsu. On 4 February, as the first rains were falling, and with supply lines cut by skirmishers in the rear, Wolseley's force advanced across the Ordah river. 'I advanced rapidly,' McLeod later wrote. '50 paces at a time, passing the skirmishing companies [on either side of the road] through each other. The enemy met us persistently, and at first men fell, but pressing steadily on his flanks with my skirmishers, and storming his ambuscades on the road, he gave way before us.'[43] During their advance, Captain George Moore – instrumental in organising the men to act as porters – and Lieutenant Andrew Wauchope, in command of a 'native' regiment of local Haussas, were wounded. But, as historian Rathbone Lowe remarked: 'Had the weapons and ammunition of the Ashantees been of a better description, many officers, who are the ornaments of the British Army, would have fallen beneath the heavy fire.' Even Wolseley 'narrowly escaped' with his life,[44] describing how his helmet and puggaree – the piece of cloth soldiers used to wrap around the crown of their sun helmets – had saved his 'old nut'.[45]

After some heavy fighting, the way was now open for Wolseley and the British troops to enter King Kofi's capital city – 'the town under the tree' – of Coomassie. 'Colonel McLeod, C.B., 42nd Highlanders, commanded the advanced guard during the march from the Adansi hills to Coomassie, conducting his operations with cool gallantry in the most skilful manner,' reported Wolseley in his dispatch. 'The forcing of all positions occupied by the enemy in our front devolved upon him, and I consider myself most fortunate in having had so able an officer to select for that very trying duty.'[46] As Alison witnessed: 'Without stop or stay, the 42nd rushed on cheering, their pipes playing, their officers to the front; ambuscade after ambuscade was successfully carried, village after village won in succession, till the whole Ashantees broke and fled in the wildest disorder down the pathway on their front to Coomassie.'[47] 'The Highlanders marched along at a rattling pace,' wrote *The Times*'s correspondent, Winwood Reade. 'At intervals of a mile or so, the foremost company came upon parties of Ashantees. Then we heard shots, and cheers "for Old Scotland," and the bagpipes played, and the whole regiment broke out into a double.'[48] 'Many fell wounded,' reported Wolseley, 'but nothing could stop them. The Ashantees seemed at last to realize this, for the shouting in front ceased for a moment as they fled in all directions in wild confusion.'[49]

Towards the late afternoon, the 42nd entered Coomassie, 'their pipers playing at their head'.[50] 'In the great main street hundreds of armed men were collected to observe the entry, yet not a single shot was fired,' related Wolseley's additional military secretary, Henry Brackenbury.[51] With the British troops formed in the main street, the assembled soldiers gave 'three cheers for Her Most Gracious Majesty, at the end of a most trying day's work'.[52] But the atmosphere was tense and there was no sign of King Kofi, who had fled into the jungle with his family. The following morning the soldiers awoke to find the city virtually deserted. Although several conciliatory messages had been received from the King, he did not return to sign the proposed peace treaty nor offer the 'hostages of rank' Wolseley was demanding. Anxious that the Ashanti were amassing in the jungle to counter-attack, and with the onset of heavy rains, Wolseley could wait no longer.

Before leaving, as 'a lasting mark of the British power',[53] the King's palace was destroyed, having been searched for what valuable items could be carried. 'Candles were scarce at Coomassie; and only four were available for the search, of which economy forbade that more than two should be alight at a time. By the light of these two candles the search began ... Box after box was opened and its contents hastily examined ... necklaces and bracelets of gold, Aggery beads, and coral ornaments of various descriptions ... silver-plate was carried off ... swords, gorgeous ammunition-belts, caps mounted in solid gold, knives set in gold and silver, bags of gold-dust and nuggets, carved stools mounted in silver.'[54] A surprising find was 'an oil painting of an anonymous English gentleman'. In addition, 'among rows of books in many languages' were some copies of the *Illustrated London News*.[55] More gruesome was a 'place of vultures ... a large open space, an acre or more in size' filled up with 'grinning skulls and fleshless bones ... and the whole mass living, writhing, with the worms that feast in corruption', a souvenir of past battles King Kofi had fought against his enemies.[56] Loaded with what treasure they could carry, Wolseley's army departed, the 42nd forming the rearguard, 'which did not retire till the town had been set on fire in every quarter, and the mines in the palace fired'.[57]

Their withdrawal came just in time. 'One stream, which when we had passed it on our march to Coomassie was scarcely three feet deep flowing between rather steep banks, had now apparently disappeared, and in its place was a sheet of water 200 yards wide, somewhere in the middle of which the stream must be,' recorded Brackenbury. The Ordah river was overflowing the bridge and was still rising. 'The carriers were made to go through the water with their bundles on their heads, while most of the white troops were passed over the bridge.' By the time the 42nd reached it, the bridge had given way and so the soldiers had 'to strip and wade or swim the river, their clothes being taken over by natives'.[58]

Having kept up their spirits during the fighting, according to a contemporary account, the soldiers of the 42nd 'began to droop very fast and by the time they reached the coast and took up their old quarters on board the *Sarmatian* at Cape Coast, their "ain mithers wudna hae kent them"'. To give them time to recover, the Royal Navy captain was ordered to go 'dead slow' on the return journey, 'with the object of gradually acclimatising the men for the colder region whither they were bound'. As the British troops returned home to Portsmouth, the excitement generated over the campaign was matched by an unprecedented euphoria in the press. 'The long-expected *Sarmatian*, with The Black Watch on board, arrived at Spithead last night at 11 o'clock,' reported the special correspondent for *The Scotsman*. 'The night being dark, no communication with the shore was possible, and so it was not till early this morning that Portsmouth learnt the good news [of the *Sarmatian*'s arrival].'[59]

When the Regiment disembarked, the soldiers received 'a hearty welcome'. Wolseley was recorded in the press as describing The Black Watch as 'the finest regiment I ever saw in action'.[60] 'Portsmouth has been joyously occupied in welcoming the homecoming soldiers and sailors from the Gold Coast,' enthused *The Graphic* newspaper. 'On Monday the *Sarmatian* came in with the 42nd Highlanders . . . these appear in much better condition than might have been expected.'[61] According to *The Scotsman*'s special correspondent, 'one extraneous advantage they possess in the matter of personal appearance . . . is that their kilts being on board they were able to get out of their measly-looking Ashantee uniform at Spithead, and sailed into Portsmouth harbour today in the bright scarlet uniform and tartan trews that comprise their ordinary uniform.'[62]

Of the three European Regiments, the 42nd had suffered the least amount of sickness but had the greatest mortality, 'chiefly due to gunshot wounds', recorded Brackenbury.[63] William Baird, General Sir David Baird's grandson, promoted brevet major in 1872, and wounded at Amoaful, died five weeks later on board ship. Francis Farquharson VC, commended by McLeod at Borborassie, and promoted brevet major in April 1874, died the following year in September 1875. Over one hundred men were wounded, including Lieutenant Colonel John McLeod and Major Duncan Macpherson, who had kept going 'by propping himself on a stick'.[64] Although most of the wounds were considered to be 'slight', some – such as the gunshot wound on the left side of the chest received by Private Thomas Pickard – were rated 'severe'.[65] Not till 'about a year' later did Lieutenant Andrew Wauchope, injured at Ordashu, have the bullet that wounded him extracted.[66]

Once more, the troops were to be reviewed by Queen Victoria, this time in Windsor Great Park, where it was announced that for 'skilfully leading his section through the bush for a whole day, although badly wounded early in the battle' Lance Sergeant Samuel McGaw was awarded the Victoria Cross.[67] Lieutenant Colonel John McLeod was to be knighted. 'The Review was held in the large open space between Queen Anne's Ride and the Long Walk . . . Her Majesty . . . drove in an open carriage drawn by four greys.'[68] *The Illustrated London News*, whose reporter was one of the several correspondents accompanying the Ashanti expedition, depicted the returning soldiers in their kilts, the illustration captioned 'the 42nd marching past the Queen'.[69] The Houses of Parliament gave a Vote of Thanks, regarded as the highest honour soldiers can receive 'next to the publicly expressed thanks of the Queen'.[70] There was 'some talk of a dinner to be given to the officers and men by the Corporation of the City of London'.[71]

The effusive praise heaped on the Regiment in the newspapers, combined with the ecstatic welcome, which outshone that given to the other infantry battalions, was exemplified by the sign in a printer's window on the 42nd's arrival in Portsmouth:

*We greet ye with Welcome,/English, Irish and Scotch,/
But a special glad Welcome, / To our gallant Black Watch.*[72]

Two years later, the Battle Honour *Ashantee* was granted.[73] The campaign, described as 'no child's play or insignificant warfare', was less important than the British public liked to think.[74] The Ashantis' defeat left a power vacuum and led to infighting among the lesser tribes. The eulogies heaped on Wolseley and his commanders hid the near-failure of the campaign, which could have been lost had the Ashantis been better armed or had the British force been caught by the approaching rains.[75] Although King Kofi eventually signed a 'Treaty of Peace', hostilities were resumed two decades later. A Fourth Anglo-Ashanti War was fought between 1894 and 1896, resulting in the incorporation of the Ashanti lands as part of the Gold Coast Colony in 1902 and the exile of the Ashanti leaders to the Seychelles. The Ashanti War was the only time The Black Watch fought in West Africa, but the memory of their exploits remained, recorded in another poetic offering:

> The Ashantees, when they saw the shanks of Jock McGraw,
> They turned aboot an' ran awa'.
> The rain may rain, an' the snaw may snaw,
> The wind may blaw, an' the cock may craw,
> But ye canna frichten Jock McGraw,
> He's the stoutest man in the Forty Twa.[76]

The Mediterranean Again: the 42nd: Malta 1874; Cyprus 1878

The Black Watch spent six months at Portsmouth before once more embarking for the Mediterranean. Their destination, on board HMS *Himalaya*, was Malta, where the Regiment had not served since 1847. Arriving in late November 1874, the posting on the island was for three years. As hot-weather dress, the soldiers wore red serges and white helmets instead of feather bonnets and doublets.[77] Compared with active service, life was dull, although in June 1877 the soldiers were equipped with the new improved Martini-Henry rifle, replacing the Snider.[78] While the Regiment was stationed in Malta, John McLeod handed over its command to Duncan Macpherson. Thirty years later McLeod became Colonel of the Regiment.

As Britain expanded its empire worldwide, foreign policy was still dominated by fears of Russian expansion. In Asia, Afghanistan remained a contested region in the 'Great Game' of strategic rivalry between Tsarist Russia and Imperial Britain, leading to a second

'Afghan War' in 1878; in the Balkan region, hostilities had again broken out between Russia and the Ottoman Empire, whose territorial integrity had been guaranteed by the Paris Peace Conference ending the Crimean War. With a Russian army at the gates of Constantinople, the Sultan of Turkey sued for an ignominious peace. According to the terms of the Treaty of San Stefano, signed on 3 March, Turkey agreed to the creation of an autonomous principality of Bulgaria. Fearful of Russia's growing influence in the region, on 1 April 1878 the new foreign secretary, Lord Salisbury, outlined Britain's position on the Eastern Question and began negotiations with Turkey, obtaining agreement that Britain could occupy the island of Cyprus, under Ottoman rule for over three hundred years. In return Turkey would receive assistance against further Russian encroachments on its soil as well as protection of Ottoman possessions in Asia. The Sultan also agreed to reform his administration, ensuring the safety of his non-Muslim subjects. On 25 May the Convention was signed.

At the same time, Salisbury had been negotiating with the Russians preparatory to a Conference of Great Powers, which met in Berlin in June 1878. Following the Russo-Turkish War, Britain, France and Germany, under the leadership of the German Chancellor, Otto von Bismarck, and in consultation with the Ottoman Turks, aimed at stabilising the Balkans. The more favourable terms negotiated by Russia with Turkey were reversed and the new autonomous Bulgaria was reduced in size. Although the Congress of Berlin was hailed as achieving peace in the region, the seeds of future conflict were sown, evidenced by the dissatisfaction of all the participants with the various provisions. Britain was, however, confirmed in its administration (although not sovereignty) of Cyprus.

Sir Garnet Wolseley was chosen as the first British High Commissioner and Commander-in-Chief of Cyprus, tasked with reforming land tax and the legal system. To occupy the island, an expeditionary force of some 10,000 men, including The Black Watch, was assembled. Having left Malta on board HMS *Himalaya* in mid-July 1878, the Regiment landed at Larnaca, one company disembarking at Kyrenia. The heat in midsummer was overwhelming and on 22 July, Samuel McGaw, VC, promoted sergeant after Ashanti, died of heat apoplexy 'on the line of march' to Camp Chiflik Pasha, where he was buried.[79]

Soon after McGaw's death, Wolseley was noting that six per cent of the British troops at Chiflik camp 'are now laid up with slight fevers common to the country . . . I have telegraphed for 6 more doctors to be sent here at once. It is a curious thing that the 42nd has double the number of sick men that the other regts. have, without any apparent reason, for the bulk of the men who are down were not in Ashanti.' As a result, Wolseley was planning to move the Regiment 'to another locality'.[80] Having moved them from Larnaca to the fort at Kyrenia, he reported that 'the 42nd . . . has now very few men on the sick list'.[81]

Despite an initial improvement, and with 'fine and enjoyable weather', in October Wolseley, who was 'wishing for a command in the event of an Afghan war', was again noting that 'strange to say our sick list is still very large, and the 42nd at Kyrenia especially still suffer from fever and the men who have suffered don't recover'.[82] Captain Andrew Scott-Stevenson's wife, Mary Esme, realised the cause of their ailments. 'Is it any wonder they got ill? They had no occupations, for it was too hot for parades; no recreations; nothing to do but lie dozing on their backs under the canvas, shifting their knapsacks now and again to save their heads being blistered.' She also attributed their frequent bouts in the hospital tent to boredom: '[they] most sensibly came to the conclusion that it was much better to be sick and sent to the cool hospital tent with plenty of luxuries, even beer and pipes than to lie idle in the shelterless tents.'[83]

By early November, after just over three months in Cyprus, Wolseley had decided to send the 42nd home. 'The men are listless and weak and evidently most depressed in spirits. I never saw a Corps so utterly demoralised. The [Lieutenant] Colonel, MacPherson, who has not, himself been unwell since he landed and who is generally so cheery and hopeful about his men, has lost heart. The men have no strength. They tumble down when in the ranks at each church parade on

Sunday. As a military unit the 42nd is useless.' Such criticism did not extend to the activities of Lieutenant Andrew Wauchope, who was put in charge of the district of Paphos, where he remained for two years as governor, his reputation for fairness being remembered by the inhabitants twenty years later. 'Even to this day his decisions in disputed land or water rights are relied on as *res judicata*,' wrote Wauchope's biographer in 1901.[84]

Once Wolseley's proposal to send the 42nd home was agreed by London, arrangements were made for embarkation.[85] On 19 November, the soldiers left on an Indian transport, the *Jumna*, for Gibraltar, briefly taking up quarters in the Buena Vista Barracks. In mid-June 1879 the Regiment embarked for England, landing at Cowes, on the Isle of Wight. In mid-August the 42nd was inspected by Queen Victoria, who expressed her approval at its appearance. For a year, the soldiers remained in the south, forming part of the Corps which marched to Windsor in July 1880 – yet again – to be reviewed by the Queen in Windsor Great Park. By 1881 the Regiment was back in Edinburgh – for the first time in twelve years.

There was a sequel to the Regiment's service in Cyprus. In June 1883, the *Cyprus Herald* reported that the government was proposing to level the graveyard at Chiflik where Sergeant McGaw was buried. His remains were disinterred and carefully conveyed to Kyrenia. Captain Andrew Scott-Stevenson, 'in the full uniform of the Black Watch', followed the coffin to a small cemetery above Kyrenia, where he was interred next to others who had died while the Regiment was in Cyprus. 'After the interment Mrs Scott-Stevenson decorated the grave with wreaths of passion flower and jasmine.' His body was later placed in a sarcophagus, visible today in the English cemetery in Kyrenia.[86]

Military Reform: the 73rd Perthshire Regiment

In August 1861, after fifteen continuous years away in South Africa and India, the 73rd arrived at Gravesend, 'from whence the men and officers were conveyed by coasting steamers to Plymouth'. The following year, after 'a long and honourable service of forty-four years', Lieutenant Colonel George Smith sold his commission, and was succeeded by Hugh Jones. In the same year, 1862, in 'consideration' of the Regiment having been embodied at Perth, Queen Victoria 'was graciously pleased to command' that in future the Regiment should be designated the 73rd Perthshire Regiment.[87] On 10 November 1862, new Colours were received; the old 'tattered and worn' Colours, which had seen service in South Africa and India, were hung in the Municipal Buildings of Perth, 'the County City of the Regiment'.[88] After postings in and around southern England, and having been equipped with the new more accurate Whitworth rifle, in 1864 the Regiment was sent to Dover 'for employment as a working party, under Royal Engineers supervision in the permanent fortifications' of the Dover garrison.[89] The following year, under the command of a new Lieutenant Colonel, Godfrey Burne, the 73rd was sent to Ireland.

The Regiment did not stay long. Over time, the number of Roman Catholics serving in the Regiment had increased. As part of a concerted policy to undermine British authority, supporters of the nationalist Fenian movement had been working to infiltrate British regiments and were believed to have achieved some success in the ranks of the 73rd.[90] Before such sentiment could act against the British government, in September 1866 the Regiment was ordered to prepare for immediate embarkation to Hong Kong, which Britain was later to lease as a Crown Colony for a period of ninety-nine years. Setting sail in November on board SS *Golden Fleece*, the journey, lasting six months, was unpleasant. 'We have 1005 souls on board & are a great deal too crowded,' complained Lieutenant William

Gordon to his mother. As usual, the women and children were worst off, 'poor things'.[91] Arriving in early March 1867, Gordon found that he did not 'dislike the look of the place'.[92] 'Every body wears uniform here, nothing else is seen.' Although 'English things' were highly-priced, 'flannel suits, coats for the climate, & solar Topees are not expensive. You can go any where in a chair for 10 cents (6d).'[93] After a pleasant eighteen-month posting, the Regiment embarked for Singapore and Galle in Ceylon, 'the right wing to be stationed at the former place and the left wing at the latter'.[94] After a few weeks in Singapore, the right wing joined the left wing in Ceylon.

Having spent five years in Ceylon, the 73rd Perthshire Regiment, now under the command of Lieutenant Colonel Wiseman Clarke, was ordered to return to India. Before the soldiers departed, Major General Renny, commanding troops in Ceylon, highlighted the fact that the Regiment had been divided among five stations during its service there 'with never more than 3 companies at headquarters at one time. A regiment so scattered generally deteriorates in efficiency and discipline but the separation has not effected the Regiment'.[95] Arriving from Colombo at Bombay in February 1874, as the 42nd Royal Highland Regiment, The Black Watch was celebrating the victory over the Ashantee, the 73rd's posting was Cawnpore, scene of so much bloodshed nearly twenty years previously. One of the Regiments first tasks was to take custody of a 'native alleged to be the famous "Nana of Bithoor" . . . this man was kept in the Regimental Cells under an officers Guard'.[96] When he turned out to be an imposter, he was handed to the civil authorities.[97]

In early December the Regiment was in Delhi as part of the 1st Brigade 1st Division, to prepare for the arrival in January 1876 of HRH the Prince of Wales, Prince Albert Edward of Wales, Queen Victoria's eldest son and heir, who had been touring India by train since November. In early January the British and Indian troops were reviewed by Lord Napier, Commander-in-Chief in India. As the 73rd was about to be dismissed, Napier, who was riding past, applauded its 'fine appearance'. On 12 January, a Grand Review of both British and Indian Regiments was held, when, in the uniform of a Field

Marshal, the Prince inspected the troops.[98] There were also military manoeuvres and a Cavalry Field Day when the Prince rode a charger. After the exercises, the 73rd left Delhi for the hill station at Subathu.[99]

By the end of 1877 the Regiment was in Lucknow, where it spent the next three years. Despite sickness, the 73rd was considered to be 'generally in very good order, which is due to attention bestowed upon it by its Lieutenant Colonel and the Officers in General'.[100] On 11 July 1877, Major James Barnes was formally appointed Lieutenant Colonel of the Regiment in place of Wiseman Clarke, who retired onto half-pay. Although not engaged on active service, deaths regularly occurred, either from illness or accident. Lieutenants James Bull and Andrew Parkinson both died after falling from their horses; others died from sunstroke, heat apoplexy, dysentery or cholera. On 18 September 1880 six men died from a 'great land-slip' at Naini Tal, in the foothills of the Himalayas, while attempting to rescue others. 'Their bodies were never found.'[101] Early in 1881, having received orders to return home, the Regiment left Lucknow by troop train for Bombay, embarking on board HMS *Malabar* on 20 January and arriving at Portsmouth a month later. Soon after-wards the Regiment was inspected by HRH Prince Edward of Saxe Weimar, General Officer Commanding Southern District, a cousin by marriage of Queen Victoria and who had fought in the Crimea.[102]

With The Black Watch and the 73rd Perthshire Regiment back in Britain, changes were taking place in the British Army affecting both regiments. After the Crimean War and the Indian Mutiny, a Royal Commission had been established in 1858 to assess not only instances of incompetence but also issues of manpower. Although the Commission had submitted its report in 1862, few changes were effected until, in 1868, Edward Cardwell, secretary of state for war, determined both to update and reform the British military estab-lishment. Flogging and other harsh disciplinary measures in peace-time were abolished. In 1870, the Army Enlistment (Short Service) Act was passed, designed to encourage men to serve for a shorter period than the statutory twelve years, but to remain on reserve with a modest payment in return for undertaking a short period of training each year.

The following year, the Regulation of the Forces Act 1871 was passed dividing the country into sixty-six brigade districts (later renamed Regimental Districts) based on the boundaries of the counties and their population density. All infantry regiments of the line would have two battalions, sharing a depot and a recruiting area. One battalion would serve overseas, while the other would remain at home for training. A militia in the related area could, in time of need, provide a third battalion. The senior twenty-five regiments already had two battalions, but The Black Watch had not had a second battalion since the Reserve in 1850. One recommendation was for the 42nd and 79th Cameron Highlanders, already associated in the 57th Brigade, to be brought together under the name of the Queen's Own Royal Highlanders, but the suggestion caused 'a touch of pain' to at least one reader of *The Times*. 'Surely the name of "the Black Watch" . . . is far better, and carries with it to Scotchmen, ay, and to Englishmen also, far nobler memories than can the new name of the Queen's Own Royal Highlanders,' complained a Ross-shire correspondent. 'To these and every other Highland regiment sweet memories are attached which would soon die out if their names were to be robbed in this fashion.'[103]

A Field Officer believed there was a 'crusade' in the War Office against maintaining *esprit de corps*, pointing out that although the civil servants might not understand the value of the distinctions in regimental dress, they were symbols 'which for regiments have a deep – we may almost say a holy – meaning to soldiers, for they commemorate or are associated with some gallant deeds which illustrate the history of a regiment'.[104] Another letter to *The Times* made an appropriate suggestion: 'Beginning with the 42d, who will not give up the red hackle, so gloriously won, nor willingly see it given to strangers, it seems only rational to bring back to its old second battalion, the 73d, which will doubtless be glad to resume the dress in which it gained its earliest honours and mess plates.'[105]

The decision to designate the 73rd as the 2nd Battalion marked the end of ninety-five years as a separate Regiment. 'The General requires,' stated Lieutenant General Curetow in his Farewell Order, 'before it leaves his command to record in Division Orders the high opinion he has of its efficiency in every respect. The Uniform good conduct of all ranks, their steadiness on Parade and smartness when off Duty have merited his warmest approval.'[106] In addition to changes in the organisation and uniform, all Regiments lost their numerical listings. 'The change of title for all Regiments will take effect from the 1st of July 1881 but the change of Uniform on the 1st April 1882 with the exception of the 73rd Regiment which will adopt its new uniform on the 1st July 1881.'[107] Having been known as the 42nd for over 130 years, the Regiment's name was changed to 'The Black Watch (Royal Highlanders)'.[108]

Between 1820 and 1881 the 42nd had spent thirty-six years on foreign service compared with twenty-one years on home service and five years on active service. During the same period, the 73rd had spent seventeen years on home service, and thirty-six years on foreign service with nine years on active service; for both regiments the time spent abroad was comparable to the other Highland Regiments. Between 1820 and 1872, with nearly three-quarters of the officers hailing from Scotland, the proportion remained the highest in the 42nd of all the kilted Regiments, compared with nineteen per cent from England and eight per cent from Ireland. Over half the men in the 73rd, which had temporarily lost its Highland name, were English, the remainder being made up of nearly twice as many Irish as Scots.[109] Throughout the nineteenth century, both Regiments had fought in some of the most testing environments across the world, from distant Australia and the freezing terrain of Canada to the rain-soaked landscape of Europe and the intense heat of southern Africa. The Regiment's next theatre of operations was Egypt and the Sudan, where the soldiers were to take part in some of the bloodiest fighting recorded in history.

20.

Land of the Pharaohs

With their bagpipes playing, and one ringing cheer,
And the 42nd soon did the trenches clear;
Then hand to hand they did engage,
And fought like tigers in a cage.[1]

1895

Egypt

On 21 July 1882, the 1st Battalion, The Black Watch was ordered to Egypt. The Regiment was to be equipped 'with dress suitable for tropical climate', recollected Private John Gordon, who had newly enlisted. Officers' mess silver and pictures were to be left behind, as well as 'feather bonnets, scarlet tunics, and other valuables'.[2] 'People knowing we were going to war, turned out in great numbers at every station to cheer us,' related Bandsman Spencer Barwood, whose young nephew, Arthur, was also in the Band.[3] Arriving at Albert Docks, Woolwich, they embarked on the troopship SS *Nepaul*, bound for Alexandria. In keeping with the new convention established by Cardwell's Reforms, while the 1st Battalion served abroad, the 2nd Battalion, under Lieutenant Colonel James Barnes's command, remained in Britain.[4]

Britain's involvement in Egypt – signalling The Black Watch's return to fight on the shores of North Africa for the first time in eighty years – was to protect Britain's interests in the Upper Nile and the Suez Canal.[5] Administrative control of Egypt was in the hands of the Khedive (Viceroy) Ismail Pasha, whose mounting debts had resulted in the sale of Egypt's share in the Suez Canal to Britain. British influence extended south to the vast expanse of the Sudan, over which Egypt had established sovereignty, on behalf of the Ottoman Empire. In 1873 Ismail had instated General Charles Gordon first as Governor of the Equatorial Province of Sudan and then as Governor-General of all Sudan.[6] Unfortunately, Gordon's attempt to end the slave trade proved disastrous economically; also upsetting to the locals was the impression that Gordon was embarking on a crusade against the Muslim Arabs. When, under pressure from the British government, Ismail abdicated in favour of his son Tawfiq Pasha in 1879, Gordon resigned.[7]

Tawfiq's rule was marked by rising disaffection; reacting against a law preventing the Egyptian peasantry from becoming officers in the Egyptian Army, Colonel Ahmed Urabi – known as Arabi Pasha, and founder of the Egyptian Nationalist Party in 1879 – protested against favouritism to the Turks. Bowing to pressure, Tawfiq repealed the law, but Arabi pressed for further reforms, including the creation of a parliamentary assembly and ridding the country of foreign influence.[8] In response to the unrest, having issued a 'Joint Note' in January 1882, pledging to preserve the Khedive's government, a combined Anglo-French fleet arrived in Alexandria in May. When the French withdrew, Britain was left as the sole European power opposing the Egyptian nationalists, who took control of Cairo. British presence also strengthened fears of a full-scale invasion, leading to even greater anti-European feeling. 'Reported riots in Alexandria, in which British subjects were killed, had been discussed on every street corner in Glasgow,' noted Private Gordon, referring to the 'massacre' of a number of Europeans in June 1882.[9] In early July, British warships started bombarding Alexandria, which Arabi Pasha had been fortifying. By the end of the month, the British Parliament had voted to send an expeditionary force to Egypt, under the supreme command of General Sir Garnet Wolseley.

Instead of attacking Cairo from Alexandria, Wolseley planned to surprise Arabi by taking the longer route from Ismailia along the Sweetwater Canal westwards, which meant securing the Suez Canal.[10] On 28 August, Arabi's forces challenged an inferior British brigade, commanded by Major General Sir Gerald Graham, near Kassassin, but the Household Cavalry's 'Moonlight Charge' forced the Egyptians back to their entrenched position at Tel-el-Kebir.[11] Meanwhile the 1st Battalion, The Black Watch, commanded by Lieutenant Colonel William Green, had reached Alexandria on 20 August. 'We landed about noon, pulled our baggage ashore, then devoured a huge pile of tropical fruit, an indescribable treat after twelve days of hardtack, salt beef and pork,' recalled Gordon. Travelling by train to Ramleh, the Regiment joined the Highland Brigade, which included the Highland Light Infantry, the Cameron Highlanders and the 1st Battalion, Gordon Highlanders, under the command of their former Brigade Commander in West Africa, Major General Sir Archibald

Alison. Gordon recollected his 'inspiring address on the historical reputation of our regiment, telling us he had had the honor of commanding the Black Watch before, on the Gold Coast, . . . and knew what it could do.'[12]

On 30 August, the Brigade left Ramleh, making the journey around the coast from Alexandria to Port Said, down the Suez Canal to Ismailia. From there, the line of march was westwards along the Sweetwater Canal, running parallel with the railway line. 'We commenced our march up to the front from Ismailia, through the desert, on a Saturday afternoon about 3.45, under most trying circumstances – a blazing sun over our heads and hot yielding sand under foot. We marched this way eleven miles,' related Captain Robert Coveny, 'having lost our way during the night in the desert; and, in our endeavours to find the direct route again, must have done an unnecessary two miles.'[13]

The following day, they marched until late afternoon. When they stopped for the night they had 'no tents, and simply stinking water from the canal to drink; we filtered it through pocket filters. It was something fearful sitting these hours in the sun; we made a sort of improvised tent with rifles and blankets, and that was all the shelter we had.' The next day they began another 'awful sunstroky, weary trudge', continued Coveny. 'My company was on rear guard that day. So you may imagine we had a rough time of it, looking after the poor fellows that fell out from the column. It nearly did for most of us.'[14] 'It was a dreary march, not a thing to be seen for miles but the dull, grey sand, knee deep too,' related Bandsman Barwood.[15] When they arrived in camp, Coveny described the men falling 'like logs when we piled arms and posted the company sentries for the night. I was never so done in my life; but, strange, after lying down on my back for about half-an-hour, I was quite refreshed.' Bivouacking under 'the star-lit sky of Egypt' was, he said, 'not a very great hardship'. At 5 a.m. they rose from their 'sandy beds' and marched to Kassassin, where they rested, 'prior to the impending attack on Tel-el-Kebir'.[16]

Tel-el-Kebir September 1882

On the morning of 12 September, Wolseley convened a 'Council of War', attended by the divisional and brigade commanders. As a result of their deliberations, he planned to make a night march, in order to assault Tel-el-Kebir at dawn. According to Coveny, Wolseley had decided that the Highland Brigade would 'bear the brunt of the business; at daylight tomorrow Arabi's position was to be carried at the point of the bayonet; the whole thing was to be a complete surprise, if possible, for the Egyptians'. At 6.30 in the evening they struck their tents, stowed them and their cooking utensils on transport wagons, 'and then the whole of the army fell in'.[17] To deceive Arabi Pasha and his numerically superior army, they left their campfires burning. 'This was a grave moment for us,' recollected Gordon, 'the gravest we had ever known. We realized now that before many hours we should be in the thick of a fight, exchanging death thrusts with the rebels. Our fate, as well as the enemy's was to be settled in a battle at Tel-el-Kebir.'[18]

The 1st Division was positioned on the right, with the Guards Brigade, commanded by Queen Victoria's third son, Prince Arthur, Duke of Connaught; on the left was the 2nd Division, which included the Highland Brigade. The artillery was in between the two divisions with the cavalry in the rear on the right flank. On the left, the Indian contingent marched with the Seaforth Highlanders. 'So you may imagine it must have cost Sir Garnet some thought to have arranged a night attack so that a force of those proportions should not get mixed,' observed Coveny in his letter home.[19] Trudging through the night, Private George Bedson recalled the 'grand sight' to see the two columns of the army advancing; 'they looked like two walls moving'.[20] 'Solemn, impressive, was that night march across the desert,' recollected Gordon.[21]

With only the sound of the horses' hoofs breaking the silence, they stopped briefly at a position called Nine-Gun Hill. 'We laid down at about 10.30, when a tot of rum (the second during the campaign) was served out to the men.' Continuing onwards, in the early hours of 13 September 'the word was quietly passed on, by companies, to get ready to march on to the attack'.[22] Each soldier, related Coveny, was carrying a hundred rounds of ammunition. During the march some mules broke loose, which threw back the left side of the column. 'This of course affected the centre and right of the attacking lines; and it took us a good half-hour to get better of the mistake; after this, the advance continued steadily on.' Wondering if perhaps the Egyptian sentries were all asleep, suddenly they saw some bright flashes in front. ' "Fix bayonets", quietly went down our line now. The bayonets had no sooner been fixed than the whole of the Egyptian line, about 100 yards in our front, seemed like a city suddenly lighted up with a continuous row of gas-jets; a deafening rattle of musketry – and a shower of Remington bullets hailed around us.'[23]

'On the order to charge we rushed forward to the sound of bagpipes,' recollected Gordon, 'cheering as loud as our lungs would allow, the most weird, unearthly noise imaginable.'[24] While the Gordon and Cameron Highlanders were plunging into a deep ditch before scrambling up the other side, The Black Watch, on the right, was cutting steps in the embankment. 'Our men,' described Private Donald Campbell, were 'half-mad to see their comrades falling before they were able to strike a blow; and whenever they got within reach of the enemy they fought like lions.'[25] 'Captain Wauchope . . . was among the first to enter the enemy's trenches, sword in hand,' recorded his biographer, William Baird.[26] 'The Highland blood was up,' related Coveny. 'In less than I have time to write from that last full stop, our supporting lines were in line, and joined in the attacking lines, and, with one yell, we went at those fellows with the bayonet. It was a regular company-officers' and soldiers' battle.' Just as they were storming the first entrenchment, Coveny got a bullet in his left shoulder. But he 'simply despised it' and continued 'bayoneting right and left around me. We drove them out, then they made for the last line, we pelting them with independent firing as they retreated. All this time we were exposed to a cross fire, and our poor chaps were dropping down a bit.'[27] When the Royal Horse Artillery guns came up, 'with a lusty cheer we opened our ranks to let them through,' recalled Gordon, 'and I can hear now their ringing "Scotland forever!"'[28] 'Arabi's army melted like snow before us.'[29]

Having put Arabi Pasha to flight, the British army took possession of the Egyptian camp, stocked with provisions: 'camels, Arab steeds, and tents', including Arabi's tent 'lined with amber and grey silk, and tons of ammunition'. As Coveny informed his family, their opponents had 'died very game, their bodies lying perfectly thick in the trenches'.[30] In a battle lasting barely an hour, an estimated two thousand Arabs had been killed, compared with British losses of fifty-seven soldiers. Three officers of the 42nd died. In addition, 'our Sergeant-Major [John McNeill], one of the handsomest and smartest fellows you could lay eyes on, was killed whilst hewing about him in a redoubt,' related Coveny.[31] 'His sense of justice in dealing with complaints brought before him commanded the respect of even those men he found to be in the wrong, while his wonderful human sympathy made him loved by every man from colonel to drummer boy,' observed Private Gordon.[32]

Commenting on the Highland Brigade's contribution at Tel-el-Kebir, the divisional commander, Lieutenant General Sir Edward Hamely, applauded the soldiers for having broken, 'under a tremendous fire, into the middle of the enemy's entrenchments' and having remained there 'in an arduous and dubious conflict for twenty minutes'. Having captured two miles of works and batteries, 'piercing the enemy's centre and loosening their whole system of defence', they had finished 'by taking the camp and the railway trains, and again assembling ready for any further enterprise'. The Scottish people, he said, 'may be satisfied with the bearing of those who represented them in the land of the Pharaohs'.[33]

After the battle, they entered the town of Tel-el-Kebir 'over a very Egyptian-looking bridge with tall iron pillars, topped with Sphinxes' heads very artistically modelled', recorded Coveny, who, having lost blood because of his injury, was given a horse to ride. Marching through melon and cornfields, bordered by date palms, the 'women and children, received us, cursing Arabi, and standing us coffee'.[34] While the rest of Wolseley's force went on to Cairo, The Black Watch was posted to Belbeis to guard the railway station. Without tents, they slept in their kilts. 'We had to wash our clothes and ourselves in the water that we drank,' Barwood narrated in the long letters he wrote to his family.[35] In his recollections, Gordon cited Rudyard Kipling's Barrack Room Ballad 'Oonts' to illustrate their boredom:

Wot makes the soldier's 'eart to penk, wot makes 'im to perspire?
It isn't standin' up to charge nor lyin' down to fire;
But it's everlastin' waitin' on a everlastin' road
For the commissariat camel an' 'is commissariat load.[36]

News of Arabi Pasha's surrender in Cairo meant an end to the desultory posting at Belbeis. 'After being nearly starved, we got the order to move to Cairo for the Review of the British Troops by the Khedive.'[37] In December Arabi Pasha was tried for 'rebellion' and sentenced to death; the sentence was later commuted and he was exiled to Ceylon.[38] Once restored as Khedive, Tawfiq Pasha confirmed British 'protection' of the Suez Canal, which lasted until 1954.

As part of the British 'Army of Occupation', The Black Watch temporarily occupied the city. With sickness affecting the troops, a number of regiments were ordered home, leaving the Highland Brigade in Cairo. Barwood 'felt the loss of the other Regiments, with them went all sport'.[39] On 21 November 1882 the Brigade moved into the Kasr-el-Nil barracks, 'which I can assure you we all felt a great boon ... The troops are quite healthy now and enjoy the place.'[40]

One diversion was visiting the Pyramids and the Sphinx, where the men were photographed. 'We were allowed to roam all over the place,' Barwood informed his family in August 1883. 'We were quite done up, and had to take a couple of halts before we reached the top.'[41] Outbreaks of cholera caused the Brigade to move to a camp in Suez and then inland to the 'Great Bitter Lake' before returning to Cairo. When the train stopped at Tel-el-Kebir – nearly a year after the battle – they visited the cemetery. 'I had a good walk round it, and saw a lot of graves where the Black Watch men were buried,' Barwood told his sister, Nellie.[42] Among them was 'poor Jimmy Banigan', related Arthur Barwood, 'the only Bandsman of ours that fell at Tel-el-Kebir'.[43]

El Teb February 1884

While the situation in Egypt remained peaceful, the Sudan was in turmoil. On 29 June 1881, Muhammad Ahmed bin Abd Allah, a Sufi Sheikh from the town of Dongola in northern Sudan, had proclaimed himself the 'Mahdi' or Messianic redeemer of the Islamic faith. Supporters of the Mahdi not only resented oppressive Turco-Egyptian rule but also Britain's military and economic presence. As his anti-European message spread, neighbouring tribes rallied to his cause. Among them were the Hadendowa, of the Beja tribe, led by Osman Ali, whose full beard gave him the name 'Digna'.[44] In November 1883, Mahdist forces armed with only spears and swords overwhelmed a superior force of Egyptians, led by a British officer, William Hicks, at Sheikan, extending the Mahdi's control to western Sudan.

With too few Egyptian troops in the Sudan to counter the rebellion, Prime Minister William Gladstone ordered an evacuation. In January, Gordon, who had just accepted an assignment in the Congo on behalf of King Leopold II of Belgium, was requested to return to the Sudan. Accompanied by Lieutenant Colonel Donald Stewart, he reached Khartoum in February. The Mahdist forces, however, were closing in, having overwhelmed a force of Egyptians, commanded by Valentine Baker, near the port of Suakin on the Red Sea at El Teb.[45] 'I suppose you have been startled a bit by the news from the country of Monsieur Mahdi et companie,' Coveny wrote home. 'I wish they would keep quiet. It is quite on the cards that a campaign takes place in the Soudan; and it won't be a very relishable one either, as those gents can fight and the heat is great down there.'[46]

Reluctantly – and under pressure from Queen Victoria – Gladstone agreed to send a British relief force, drawn from the garrisons in Egypt, Aden and India, to the now besieged garrison at Tokar, south of Suakin. Supported by cavalry and mounted infantry, the regiments were formed into two infantry brigades, under Major General Gerald Graham's command.[47] The Black Watch was positioned in the 2nd Infantry Brigade, together with the Yorks and Lancs (formerly the 65th), the Gordon Highlanders and a contingent of Royal Marine Light Infantry and a detachment from the Royal Navy.[48]

Travelling by train, they stopped again at Tel-el-Kebir, 'and,' Barwood told his sister, 'a good number of us took a few feathers out of our hackle and stuck them in our comrades graves.' At Suez, they embarked on troopships bound for the port of Trinkitat. 'On the night of the 21st February we landed. It was pitch dark, and the boats were guided by a lantern.'[49] But, as they now realised, the garrison at Tokar had already fallen without a fight. Instead of making a precipitate withdrawal, over the next few days Graham marshalled the army to march to 'Baker's Fort', three miles inland, erected by Baker shortly before his defeat by the Sudanese. 'The march was very difficult and tiring,' Barwood continued, 'here you would see one fellow fall, rifle and everything would sink under the mud.' On arrival, the men lay down to sleep. 'Bayonets were fixed, sentries posted etc. and in the formation of a British Square, we lay and slept.' In the early hours of the morning, 'a perfect deluge descended and nearly submerged us. We were not allowed to put on our coats, as that would necessitate the undoing of our packs,' related Barwood. The following morning, having had no breakfast since the wood was too wet to light, they marched for El Teb, where Osman Digna's forces were entrenched. 'Owing to the previous rain, the ground for the first two miles was very bad, and most difficult to get over; it took us all our time to keep in square.'[50]

When they reached El Teb, they found several thousand Arabs opposing them. Armed with Baker's field guns, captured in the previous battle, the Arabs at once opened fire on the approaching British force. The infantry were ordered to lie down, while the artillery and sailors, using their rapid-firing Gatling guns, 'soon silenced the enemy upsetting their guns', related Private Morrison. 'We continued to move steadily up to them, fighting our way, and succeeded in capturing their guns, and our artillery turning upon them soon made sad havoc.'[51] Having fought off a sword attack from the Hadendowas, the brigade commander, Major General John Davis, ordered the 42nd to charge. Confusion in the chain of command meant that they did not immediately do so. 'The officers seeing nothing to charge at and knowing the enemy were all hiding in holes just in their front,' Captain Andrew Scott-Stevenson later told his wife, 'quietly put themselves in the front of their companies and told our men not to move and take [their] command from the Colonel; our Brigadier [Davis], if he wanted the 42nd to charge should have told the Colonel so and he would have given us the command.'[52] From his perspective, Barwood understood what happened: 'Our men, knowing that the enemy were hidden in pits, hesitated and well for them that they did, for at that moment a regular rush was made by the enemy and was backed up by a shower of spears and rifle bullets.'[53] Having been ordered to advance, they eventually did so, with Jock, the Regimental dog, attacking 'the dervishes fiercely as enemies of Black Watch men'.[54]

In his report, Graham referred to the Royal Highlanders as being 'somewhat out of hand. I would, however, beg to observe that the ground was a most difficult one to move over, and that the desperate tenacity with which the enemy held a house on the right of the Royal Highlanders caused the men to form in an irregular manner so as to pour a converging fire on it.'[55] After just over three hours, the Mahdist forces withdrew. Thanks to their superior weaponry, British casualties were relatively light, with a total of thirty killed and 142 wounded out of a force of about 4,000.[56] One of the wounded 42nd officers was Captain Andrew Wauchope, who had been on horseback and 'a prominent figure in the fight'. Struck by a musket-shot, 'he was only saved from instant death by the friendly intervention of his binoculars, which were hanging by his side, the bullet striking the glass and smashing it to pieces'.[57] Coveny admitted having had a '*mauvais quart d'heure*', 'with the enemy's shell popping into the square. I never saw such fellows to fight as those Hadendowa Arabs; they know not what fear is in most cases.'[58]

As always, burying the dead was a necessary ritual. 'Our own dead were of course sought out first,' commented Barwood, 'and it was a pitiful sight to see them coming in, in twos and threes, some of them cut so fearfully as to be beyond recognition.' The Arabs too had suffered, some lying in pools of blood 'with their skulls cleft in two, others without arms, legs, and all manner of parts of their bodies'.[59] Coveny found the burials 'a fearful occupation. I had 100 men with me, and buried in about an hour's time 400 of those unfortunates. Another party before that had buried the same number; I think about 2,000 were buried there altogether at El-Teb.'[60]

Two companies of The Black Watch were assigned as part of the force sent to retake Tokar; 'my company, H,' related Coveny, 'was one of them. I never had such a hot march, bar the one to Tamanieb afterwards. I assure you I had hardly a kick left in me when we took up our position for attack opposite Tokar fort. Luckily I had a nip of brandy in my flask to give the machine impetus, but I did not use it, and when I heard the mounted infantry, 19th Hussars, firing on our flank, I got as right as the mail and gripped my old sword.' But, he said, 'that was the beginning and end of Tokar'. As they were approaching they saw a troop of horsemen riding towards them with a white flag, 'so we knew the garrison was all right'. The following day, they returned to El Teb, marching back with the evacuated Egyptians to Trinkitat, where the force re-embarked for Suakin.

Tamai – 'of terrible memory' – March 1884[61]

The Sudanese had withdrawn from El Teb, but they remained unvanquished. General Graham therefore decided to advance on Osman Digna's camp at Tamai, south of Suakin. One aspect of his preparations was criticising The Black Watch for its conduct at El Teb. 'Black Watch, I am a plain spoken man,' an astonished Scott-Stevenson recorded him as saying. 'And I must tell you I am not pleased with what you did at Teb the other day. You are young soldiers and I am as proud of the reputation of the regiment as any of you. Your officers are a magnificent and splendid body of men. Now I am going to give you another chance and assign you the post of honour in our front.'[62] Bandsman Barwood was surprised that Graham's remarks did not cause a greater reaction. 'We did not deserve it.'[63]

To limit the ill effects of the heat, with temperatures up to 110 degrees Fahrenheit (43 Celsius) in the shade, Graham ordered short marches in convoy. Despite these precautions, fifty men of The Black Watch fell out on the first day's march. 'No more water was to be had, the sand was getting thicker and the sun a good deal hotter,' remarked Barwood. Arriving at their advanced position on 12 March, on a minor hill overlooking Osman Digna's camp, it was too late to attack and so they began to build their zarebas – a cordon of prickly thorns, made from the available scrub – for protection at night. To the soldiers' dismay, Graham condemned The Black Watch's zareba as too big and ordered them to reconstruct it. Since dried black shrub could catch fire, they had to use green bush, which, related Barwood, was 'no easy job to get all green bush'.[64]

No sooner had they completed the task than about a thousand of Digna's forces arrived on the hills; 'the General called us to stand to arms, and called up two more guns,' continued Barwood. 'Seeing them firing as wildly,' Graham thought he might give them a 'taste' of the Gardiner gun, whose performance, Barwood maintained, had to be seen to be believed: 'when fired moderately it discharges 300 rounds per minute, its greatest speed being 500 per minute; a man has only to turn a handle like that of a street organ, and the shot flies from it with great velocity . . . the greatest distance they fire is about 2,000 yards, they kill at that distance. One gun is equal to about a whole Regiment of Martinis.'[65] The rapid firing soon dispelled their adversaries and the soldiers retired to their zareba for some rest, Scott-Stevenson later telling his wife that they were able to 'wash down' their rations with two magnums of Bell and Romnies champagne.[66] The soldiers had been given rum, and Barwood was horrified to find his 'fighting chum . . . insensibly drunk', which created 'an awful bother to get him to lie still and hold his tongue', later telling his sister that if any soldier made too much noise, he could be shot on the spot to silence him.[67]

Coveny was lying near Duncan McLeod, son of the Regiment's former Commanding Officer. 'The Osman Dignas were quite confident of a victory, they say, for the lady Hadendowas, amiable creatures, were actually on the hills ready to come down and mutilate us, if all had gone well for Master Osman that day.' Throughout the night their sleep was interrupted by the Sudanese firing into the camp, 'aided by a lovely full moon; their fire was wild; some unfortunates were hit, and one poor fellow killed in his sleep; a number of camels were hit. The bullets whistled and pinged and rushed through the air until about 3 o'clock, when the enemy all retired. I can never forget young Duncan that night with his calm face – "That one is pretty near, sir" he'd say, when one of those leaden messengers buried itself in the dust not three yards or so from our resting place.'[68]

Scott-Stevenson was equally tense. 'It was moonlight and a shower of bullets were going over the square,' he related to his wife. Ordered not to return the fire, it was 'very jumpy work being fired at for four hours . . . the bullets were whizzing very near our heads, and one struck a water tin between us, and another went thud into a folded blanket close to us. The Brigadier's horse was shot . . . I hated that night and was glad to see the day dawn.'[69] The next day, they ate breakfast, again under fire. 'This mixture,' recalled Gordon, 'bullets with breakfast, did not bother us much, our main object being to put in enough food to last through the fight.'[70]

To counter the Sudanese, Graham had ordered the two infantry brigades to form into two squares: 'One was to go to the right where the enemy were gathering and trying to drive [our allies] the Abyssinians back, the other (our division) was to go boldly to the enemy's front and so attract them from the other division.'[71] The 2nd Infantry Brigade, with The Black Watch, the Yorks and Lancs, Naval Brigade and Marines – whom the soldiers called Blue Jackets – forming one square, with their Abyssinian scouts, marched in what Graham had called the 'place of honour'. With his rebuke still in their minds, the mood of the Regiment was 'sticky'.[72]

Positioned on the left corner of the square with half of the Battalion facing the front and the other half on the left, with the Yorks and Lancs in a similar position on the right, they marched towards a gully where the Sudanese were making a stand. 'As we came on, the fire got hotter and the scouts cleared our front and fell back taking their wounded with them.'[73] Graham then ordered Lieutenant Colonel Green to signal to The Black Watch to charge. 'With a terrific yell of delight the gallant old 42nd went on expecting to crash every moment into a heavy crowd of niggers,' Scott-Stevenson wrote.[74] 'In giving us the command "Charge",' recorded Barwood, 'Graham evidently forgot to give the whole square the same command, and consequently [with] our Regiment running, whilst the others walked, we got about 200 yards ahead of the square, which left a wide gap, of course. The enemy seeing the gap, made for it, and poured in in thousands.'[75] By this stage they had reached a ravine, barely visible because of the smoke, where thousands more Sudanese lay hidden. 'The struggle developed into a wild hand-to-hand contest between swords, spears, crooked knives and boomerangs on the one side and bayonets on the other, a veritable hell,' Private Gordon recorded.[76]

Scott-Stevenson was in the thick of the fight: 'During the charge the machine guns drawn by the Naval Brigade were left a little behind and were unable to get into their place on the right corner of my company.' As he related, when Lieutenant Colonel Green saw that the Arabs were making for their right, 'he ordered me to wheel my right half and give them a flank fire . . . Two gatlings then came up and unlimbered among the left half of my company and I gave the word "protect the gatlings."'[77] Since 'a perfectly terrific fire' was going on, the smoke prevented Scott-Stevenson from seeing in front. 'To my horror on looking round behind, I saw crowds of Arabs at the gatlings, one was on the top of the gun and threw himself on me with a spear but it passed over my left shoulder and I hit him in the jaw with my right hand and sent him flying, another came at me from under the gun and I had just time to kick him in the mouth.' With no time to fire his revolver, Scott-Stevenson drew his claymore.[78]

While Scott-Stevenson was fighting off his attacker, the colour sergeant and two others were killed. 'We fell back crushed as it were by a weight and then my trusty claymore found its way to the hilt into several black devils. I clove a piece out of one of their heads just as one does an egg for breakfast and saw his white brain exposed. I was mad with rage and fury and had I not been a strong man I must have been thrown down and killed. I think God must have put a coat of armour on me that day.' Describing the battle to his wife, he related how 'it was a terrible, terrible fight', and how he was thinking of her and their daughter and whether he would 'be killed at once or die a lingering death'.[79] While Lieutenant Colonel Green was taking aim, his pistol misfired, giving time for his opponent to throw a stone at his head, which knocked off his sun helmet, 'and he was bareheaded under a burning sun, till gallant Norman MacLeod gave him his helmet and wrapped a cloth round his head'.[80] 'They are most awfully plucky,' Scott-Stevenson continued. 'I saw one man just dead & he was crawling towards us to kill a white man before he died. I took a splendid spear and killed a great many wounded men with it, it went into their hearts like lightning and their blood flowed out on the sand.'[81]

Attempting to retire with the other regiments, 'we found just as many in rear as we had in our front'. By this stage the 1st Infantry Brigade came into the action. 'As soon as the enemy heard their guns firing, they left us and made for these guns. This was just what we wanted for it gave us time to form up again.'[82] ' "Rally men! Rally lads!" being in the mouth of nearly every officer,' described Coveny, 'but we did not rally till we had retired about 200 or 300 yards, and then we gave it to those hordes of demons, and they scattered like deer.'[83] As the hand-to-hand fighting slackened, Stevenson looked around, expecting to see only himself standing, but remarkably, most of the Battalion was alive, although some were severely wounded. Major 'Charlie' Eden was 'as cool as if he was partridge shooting'.

Brevet Major Nicholas Brophy, who had been hit in the leg, was 'lame but pretending to be sound . . . Old Bob Coveny smiling with confidence and Norman MacLeod with his firm lips thirsting for more blood.' A young boy from Argyllshire, who had joined the Battalion the previous day, remained 'armed with a spear crying to be at the niggers again.'[84] Having routed the Sudanese, the two infantry brigades advanced to Osman Digna's camp, and the surviving Mahdist forces once more withdrew.

The memory of Tamai was so terrible that Coveny told his family: 'I detest bloodshed and fighting, and only go in for that slash all round work when it is an imperative necessity; on that day they were all round and amongst us like ants on and round an ant-hill, just as thick as they could be. They flew past brandishing their spears, but my time was taken up cheering on the lads to stand up and fight like men; and, after the first shock, how they responded to the call, and fought like splendid young fellows![85] Over two hundred had been killed or wounded. The Black Watch, in its exposed position, suffered the most casualties with sixty-one killed and thirty-three wounded.[86] Among the dead officers was Major Walker Aitken, who had been with the Regiment for over twenty years. 'Our loss was very grievous,' Graham reported, 'many brave men of the Royal Highlanders and York and Lancaster devoting themselves to certain death.'[87]

'After the battle was over,' related Stevenson, 'I was sent to bring in the dead 42nd men, oh!, the horrible sight, these horrible demons had cut and mutilated our poor fellows beyond recognition. I wish I had killed more now. If you had seen the camels bringing in our dead, three men on each side of a camel with their legs and arms dangling and their fingers hanging on by shreds of skin. It was awful.' 'I was one of the burial party,' recorded Gordon. 'In one long grave we laid eight sergeants and fifty-one men . . . heartbreaking was the task of arranging them side by side, just as they had fought. We spread their coats over them, covering the faces to protect them from the sand.'[88]

Writing to his family, Barwood described Tamai as 'the most terrible battle we have had this ten years . . . it was awful. You know I am in one of the three Companies that lost so heavily, and my section alone lost thirteen men out of twenty-four.'[89] Back at the zareba, Coveny described the sadness of realising that 'friends one had had one's cup of coffee with that morning [were] no more. I must say this kind of thing gives me a first class brand of a sickener of soldiering, but some of us must be soldiers.' Perhaps because the fighting had been so fierce, on behalf of the soldiers Coveny recorded that they were 'fearfully disgusted' at not being given a medal, with two clasps (for El Teb and Tamai): 'at least all of us old Egyptian campaigners of 1882 and the cholera time, and the last Soudan business'.[90]

For 'conspicuous bravery', twenty-year-old Black Watch Private Thomas Edwards, a member of one of the Naval Brigade's gun teams, responsible for carrying the gun's ammunition on mules, was awarded one of the two VCs given after Tamai. Seeing that both members of the crew of one gun had been killed, 'after bayoneting two Arabs, and himself receiving a wound with a spear, [he] rejoined the ranks with his mules and subsequently did good service in remaining by his gun throughout the action'.[91]

As those who fought came to realise, the battle became memorable less because of the outcome than for the portrayal of the Mahdists as having broken a British square, recorded by Rudyard Kipling in his Barrack Room Ballad 'Fuzzy-Wuzzy', published eight years later:

So 'ere's to you, Fuzzy-Wuzzy, at your 'ome in the Soudan;
You're a pore benighted 'eathen but a first-class fightin' man;
An' 'ere's to you, Fuzzy-Wuzzy, with your 'ayrick 'ead of 'air –
You big black boundin' beggar – for you broke a British square![92]

The claim that The Black Watch was responsible for the broken square was fiercely rejected by those present at the time. 'They never broke our square,' Coveny informed his family. The Black Watch, he said, had been ordered to charge 'and they did with a vengeance, but not without terrible loss'.[93] It was only after the action, Scott-Stevenson recorded, 'we found that when Graham ordered The Black

Watch to charge, he did not order the 65th [Yorks and Lancs] on our right to do the same, therefore when we got to the gully there was no square and the Arabs came in on our right . . . Who is to blame for this?'[94] 'At the moment of receiving the attack,' Graham later wrote in his report, 'the front face of the square of the 2nd Brigade was slightly disordered, owing to the gallant rush of the Royal Highlanders in charging the enemy to the top of the ravine. For this disorder I am to some extent personally responsible, as the charge took place under my eyes, and with my approval.'[95] For many years afterwards the Regiment was liable to be taunted with the assertion that their long spats were to remind them of the broken square.[96] 'A fight could be started in any pub in a garrison town where a Black Watch battalion, was stationed,' recorded Eric and Andro Linklater, 'simply by calling for "A pint of Broken Square."'[97]

Soon after Tamai, Graham ordered the British forces to advance on the village of Tamanieb, requiring another hot march. 'The firing opened at 7.30 and was brisk upon both sides,' reported the correspondent of *The New York Times*. 'The English cavalry and mounted infantry led the attack and drove the rebels from the rocks, dispersing them among the hills.'[98] 'The wells were occupied without any casualties and the village of Tamanieb consisting of about 300 huts was burned,' noted the Record of Service.[99]

The army then returned to Suakin. 'Our last march was the hardest we have had,' wrote Barwood. 'We were about thirty miles from Souakim and right into the mountains. First we would be on a high hill, then in a deep gully, then over large granite stones. I can assure you, we were just about done.'[100]

On 1 April, the weary soldiers embarked on board HMS *Orontes*, bound for Suez. Although Osman Digna was still at large, and Gordon was still in Khartoum, General Graham had received orders to withdraw from the Sudan. 'I can tell you I am very thankful to be back in Cairo,' Coveny wrote home, 'not that really it is much of a place, though we are housed in one of the old Ismail's palaces . . . but there is a certain amount of comfort here which did not at all exist during our two months in that awful Soudan.'[101] Coveny was also wishing he could go home. 'What a treat it would be if Australia were but 5,000 miles nearer to this land of Pharaoh.'[102] 'We had all we wanted of savages,' Private John Gordon recorded.[103]

The Nile Relief Expedition 1884–1885

Now like your own life is this tale of the Nile,
Its joys and its sorrows, my friend
Life's voyage you'll travel yet many a mile
Will you make the right port in the end?[104]

The British had prevailed through force of arms, but unlike Tel-el-Kebir, the battles against the Sudanese had not established Britain's supremacy in the region. When, in May, the town of Berber on the Nile fell General Gordon was left trapped in Khartoum. 'People talk of another campaign; of course there must be if General Gordon does not escape,' Coveny was writing in June, 'but bar buying camels and horses, nothing has been done yet in the way of preparation.'[105] After weeks of deliberation in London, involving financial wranglings about who should pay and discussions whether the longer Nile route should be taken, enabling supplies to be transported more easily, or the shorter more arduous one across the desert via Suakin, a relief force was assembled, under Wolseley's command. 'We boys felt that we knew him,' Private Gordon wrote of Wolseley, who had received a peerage for Tel-el-Kebir. 'What a tremendous responsibility rested on him now, to undertake a stupendous task so long deferred that success would be hardly short of miraculous.'[106]

'I have to go through another campaign, for Lord Wolseley wants us with him up the Nile for the Khartoum work,' Coveny wrote to his family, remarking that provided all went well, it would be 'a delightful way of seeing the Nile; and, I expect, very exciting, as we are to do most of the work in boats, as no doubt you have read, made specially for the purpose. I do not anticipate such foes to contend against as down in the Eastern Soudan, but I suppose we must have some fighting of some sort or the other, though I do not think, from all one hears, those fellows down in the Khartoum's direction will make much of a stand of it.'[107] Before embarking on the 1,500-mile journey from Cairo to Khartoum, Wolseley addressed The Black Watch. 'He told us he did not think there would be much fighting in this campaign, but there would be plenty of hard work; he said he expected us to show that we could work as we could fight, and added; "If fighting should become inevitable anywhere on the way, I know I have only to call on The Black Watch."'[108]

On 25 September 1884, the Nile Relief Expedition set out. Comprising some 5,400 soldiers, they travelled by train to Assuit; from there they went by Thomas Cook river steamer, towing four flat-bottomed barges filled with soldiers, to Assuan. 'It was lucky there was a strong wooden fence round the edge, otherwise some of us would have been crowded into the water,' recalled Private Gordon. 'At night, however, the steamers tied up at the bank where we were allowed, if there was no cultivation, to go ashore with our blankets and lie on the sand; it felt pretty good to have room to stretch at full length, kick or turn over.'[109] During the twelve-day journey a case of smallpox was discovered, which meant quarantining the Regiment when they reached Assuan. Another delay was caused by a shortage of coal. 'Nights we spent on the river bank, among bare rock,' recollected Gordon. 'Gloomy cold, they seemed'.[110]

To reach Khartoum, they had to navigate through numerous minor rapids and six major cataracts. 'I have often regretted,' Private Gordon later wrote, 'that in this most interesting region, wild, wonderful, the whole environment bearing the story of a buried humanity, the impressive significance, dependent on receptivity of mind, was lost on us.' A magnificent cataract, he said, was 'a fearful obstruction so steep near the top that to ascend it would be about as easy as to climb the side of a house, while what we saw in the boiling, foaming, roaring water at the base was crude, unharnessed power, ready to push aside anything encroaching on its wild freedom. Our word for it was "hellish."'[111]

At Wadi Halfa, before the second major cataract, they took possession of the specially constructed whaler boats, piloted by 'voyageur' French and English Canadians, and some Iroquois Indians. 'All along the bank was the cargo piled up in allotments for the waiting boats; meat, biscuits, tea, coffee, sugar, preserves, cheese,' noted Gordon.[112] Already a thousand miles from the Mediterranean, it was a further nine hundred miles to Khartoum. To encourage the men, Wolseley offered a prize of £100 for the quickest time to Korti, 350 miles away.

Before reaching Dongola, they had to pass through the third cataract, 'some twelve miles of rocky obstruction and rapids, and with many islands interspersed', signifying the division between Ancient Egypt and Ethiopia. Private Gordon did not consider it as bad as some of the minor cataracts through which they had come.[113] 'Our work has been more than we can put up with,' Barwood was writing to his sister in mid-December. 'Up to the waist in water every day and at all times of the day. Tugging boats with all our might, sometimes only to see the rope break or the nose of the boat give way and then several men go into the rapids, never to be found.' Describing the tattered state of their clothes, he related how some men had patched their trousers with bits of canvas, others with red handkerchiefs. 'To add to our misery, the flies here sting like bees; a small cut on your finger becomes a severe swelling.'[114] Travelling sometimes no more than a few miles a day, by Christmas Day, 'after hard pulling up stream', they reached the village of Argo Kadi: 'a pretty place, the birds all around warbling praise to their Maker'.[115] By late December it was 'very cold at night'.[116] 'Bed meant to us the softest place we could find among rocks,' recollected Gordon, 'often the top of a rock; sometimes I crept into a rift in a boulder, because it seemed a bit more cozy.'[117]

On 28 December Major Nicholas Brophy drowned 'through the capsizing of his boat when under sail by reason of a squall', his overcoat weighing him to the bottom. Honoured for Tel-el-Kebir, he had shown 'remarkable gallantry' at El Teb and Tamai, where he was wounded.[118] 'Strangely enough,' reported The Graphic newspaper, 'only a few days before he had, by his pluck and resource, saved a

Canadian baggage-boat, which, with its occupants, was in imminent peril.'[119]

On 3 January 1885 they reached Korti, The Black Watch being accorded second place in the race, with the Royal Irish the winners.[120] Here, Wolseley divided the force: the Desert Column, formed from the different regiments, including volunteers from The Black Watch,[121] was to undertake a rapid march across the desert, while the River Column, under the command of Major General William Earle, continued along the 'little known' route of the Nile above Korti, where the river makes 'its phenomenal bend and for a distance of about a hundred and sixty miles flows southerly instead of northerly, exactly opposite its usual course'.[122] At Hamdab, the men paraded 'in fatigue dress, side arms: General Earle inspected us'.[123] On 16 January Coveny was writing home describing the 'civility' of the locals, having conversed 'as far as my powers of Arabic allow, with several of the well-to-do natives and sheikhs'.[124] Having withstood the arduous journey, he was even expecting to be ordered to turn back, 'because I don't think these people care to trifle with England's power, and the tribes of Osman Digna got such a lesson when they came hand to hand with us at El Teb and Tamai; however, we must always be ready, and never under-rate.'[125] In early February, having passed the fourth cataract, they reached the ridge of Kirbekan, over-looking the Nile, only to find the Arabs assembled in force.

Kirbekan February 1885

On 10 February 1885 The Black Watch fought its last battle in the Sudan. 'True to their ancient tradition,' wrote the early twentieth-century historian Allan McAulay, 'to the skirl of the pipes and the sound of Highland cheering – they advanced with splendid steadi-ness, "scaled the rocks, and drove the enemy from their shelters."'[126] The reality was more challenging: 'There on top of that long razor back hill were lively mobs doing their wild war dance,' recalled Private Gordon, 'brandishing spears high over their heads, scooting back and forth among sheltering rocks, now in full view, again vanishing, like a lot of black devils in a game of hide and seek.'[127] Instead of making a frontal attack, Earle ordered what he hoped would be a surprise advance by skirting around towards the back of the ridge. 'By strategy we got nearer and nearer the enemy . . . when we reached the last advantage ground, there being only a ravine in front of us, we had the enemy hemmed in.'[128]

Transfixed by the fighting prowess of the 'brown-skinned savages', armed with 'nothing but a spear, a stick and not always a shield' against 'some of the best disciplined and most renowned troops' in the British Army, the *Daily News* correspondent described how two or three tried to force their way through a gap made in the right of the square 'by the unequal advance of the battalions'. But they were killed as soon as they entered the square, which was 'crushed inwards, not invaded – or, as it would be called, broken . . . And the Arabs [were] crushed in it because they fell with such swift suddenness upon the Highlanders and the 65th that the two latter, falling back in order to load and fire, became clubbed together.'[129] There was one notable fatality: Lieutenant Colonel Robert Charles Coveny, aged forty-three, was 'shot through the heart'; five soldiers were killed.[130] Andrew Wauchope, promoted brevet lieutenant colonel after El Teb, was severely wounded again, as were twenty-one soldiers. 'In the moment of victory', General Earle fell, his place as Commanding Officer taken by Major General Sir Henry Brackenbury.[131]

After Kirbekan, the River Column continued onwards, little knowing that their mission was now futile. On 23 February they reached Huella – 'destined to be the furthest point to which the expedition was to penetrate'.[132] The next day Brackenbury received a message from Wolseley, informing them that nearly a month previously – on 25 January – Khartoum had been stormed by Mahdist forces and Gordon killed. The Desert Column had reached Khartoum two days too late.[133] 'To be ordered to turn back now,' wrote Private Gordon, 'after we had battled with rapids and cataracts for about a hundred and forty miles from Hamdab to Huella and had reached a country practically free from rocks and with more or less cultivation on the banks, and where navigation from now on would be in clear water, was more than disappointing, it was infuriating.'[134] At midday on the 24 February, the expedition began 'its retrograde movement'. Although, by this stage, they were more experienced in handling the boats, the challenge now was to take them with the tide 'down the swift and broken waters'.[135]

By early March they had reached Abu Dom, where Brackenbury gave a final inspection, praising the River Column for being 'two thousand of the finest fighting men that it ever was man's lot to command'. The voyageurs also received recognition, without whom 'the ascent of the river if not impossible would have been far slower, without them the descent of the river would have been impossible'.[136] Brackenbury then returned to Cairo, leaving the 1st Battalion, The Black Watch in garrison, with a troop of Hussars and the Egyptian Camel Corps at Merawi. Disappointed at the outcome of the expedition, Wolseley's 'Special General Order to the Soldiers and Sailors of the Nile Expeditionary Force' informed them that the Queen had watched 'with deepest interest the doings of Her Sailors and Soldiers' and was wanting to express 'her admiration for your courage and your self devotion'. His concluding remarks confirmed that: 'a period of comparative inaction may now be expected, this army was not constituted with a view to undertaking the siege of Khartoum, and for the moment we must content ourselves with preparations for the autumn advance'.[137]

For the next two months, the 1st Battalion, The Black Watch remained at Merawi, guarding the line of telegraph wires and securing 'the fertile tract of country which is along both banks of the Nile to Korti'.[138] Not only were the soldiers occupying a part of the Sudan where it was thought no European troops could subsist during the hot season, but they had 'a meagre supply of tentage and none of the comforts generally considered to be essential for the preservation of health of British troops in a climate such as this'.[139] 'It is scorching here,' Barwood told his sister. 'All the stores are gone bad and we cannot depend on a piece of meat (such as it is) to keep for a couple of hours . . . if I want anything for breakfast, I have to pay at least 3/- for it; tea the same. Salt is as scarce as apples here.'[140] To guard against attack, the garrison was enhanced by the construction of huts and improvements to an old fort, called 'Fort St Andrew's' in honour of The Black Watch.[141] 'The only danger is being overwhelmed by numbers,' Barwood continued in his letter home; 'one thing that keeps them back is, the scarcity of food. They are starving and are selling their jewellery for grain.'[142]

In late May, the soldiers once more embarked on boats to return to Cairo. At Assuan they again travelled in Thomas Cook steamers to Assuit, where they boarded the train for Cairo. ' "Black Watch" has arrived in splendid condition,' Wolseley telegraphed London, having met the soldiers at the railway station, 'and looking the picture of military efficiency.'[143] By the end of June, they were back in the comfort of the Kasr-el-Nil barracks, which Barwood regarded as 'home'.[144] In July command of the 1st Battalion passed to Lieutenant Colonel Richard Bayly, who had recorded the finding of the regimental gong in India in 1857.

Of those whose accounts vividly described the challenges they faced, Coveny was dead; Scott-Stevenson was promoted brevet lieutenant colonel in July, colonel four years later, and died in 1892. Private John Gordon remained with the Battalion, as did Barwood, feeling that he had done his 'share' since he came to Egypt. In addition to the Battle Honours *Tel-el-Kebir, Egypt 1882, 1884, Kirbekan, Nile 1884–85*, which the Regiment received, and the 'Egypt' medal awarded by Queen Victoria, Khedive Tawfiq Pasha had issued a special 'Bronze Star' to all those who had fought on his behalf in Egypt.[145]

Britain continued its fight against the Sudanese until the end of the century. Although the Mahdi died a few months after Kirbekan, his successor, Kalifa Abdulla, remained hostile to Britain's presence and Osman Digna continued to fight on his behalf.[146] The Black Watch as a regiment played no further part in Britain's final attempt to control the Sudan and the victory at Omdurman in 1898, under the command of General Herbert Horatio Kitchener.[147] Having left Cairo on 1 May 1886 on board the SS *Poonah*, the 1st Battalion returned to Malta in May 1886, where it was inspected by Prince

Alfred, Duke of Edinburgh, Queen Victoria's second son, accompanied by his son Prince Alfred – Young Affie.[148] Among other recreational activities the soldiers enjoyed races and water sports, made possible by the purchase of some of the whale boats sold after the Nile Expedition.[149]

Time then 'rolled round' to New Year's Day 1887, 'which the Black Watch always celebrated with a grand dinner; company officers attended, and the men were allowed great latitude, but under the vigilant eyes of the Sergeants'.[150] On 9 June 1888, after nearly twenty-five years as Colonel of the Regiment, having already served for over a decade as Commanding Officer, Duncan Cameron died; his successor was General the Hon. Sir Robert Rollo, who had been commissioned into the Regiment in 1832. Soon afterwards, Bayly handed over command of the Battalion to William Gordon, of the former 73rd. Having been posted to Gibraltar in 1893, half the Battalion went to Mauritius, the other half to Cape Town. Before separating, the soldiers spent a month in Cairo at the familiar Kasr-el-Nil barracks. The Battalion was not reunited until it was sent to India in 1896.

Arriving in Bombay harbour, they occupied barracks in Subathu, Umballa and Benares. In 1897, the severe uprising of the tribes of the North-West Frontier – redolent of the Indian Mutiny – called for action in the Tirah. Although The Black Watch was not part of the force, Lieutenant Adrian Grant-Duff commanded the base depot in Peshawar, while Lieutenant Henry Holmes Sutherland was attached to the East Kent Regiment (the Buffs).[151] In 1898, Lieutenant Colonel Edward Grogan, wounded at Coomassie, took command. The final year of the nineteenth century was to be spent in 'Upper Burmah', but the order was cancelled, 'the Battalion being ordered to stand fast'.[152]

Throughout this period, the 2nd Battalion had remained in Scotland. In 1882 the Queen gave permission for the Regiment to bear 'on its Colours and Appointments, the words "South Africa" in commemoration of the Gallant behaviour of the 73rd Regiment' when engaged in operations in South Africa, during the years 1846–47, 1851–2–3.'[153] In December 1885 the 2nd Battalion was sent to Ireland. While it was stationed there, nearly a century after the battles against Tipu Sultan in Mysore, in 1889 the Queen again gave her approval for another Battle Honour, *Mysore*.[154]

In the same year, on 22 May, in front of a huge crowd at Oreman Park, in Belfast, new Colours were presented by the Queen's grandson, Prince Albert Victor of Wales, accompanied by his brother, the future George V. The Colours were the first to carry the new titles, 'The Black Watch, Royal Highlanders'; drawing attention to the recent re-amalgamation, the Prince said: 'It is a well known fact that the Black Watch is a household word throughout every part of England and her possessions. Both Battalions have greatly distinguished themselves in Campaigns in all parts of the Globe during the last century and were well worthy to be linked together in one great national Scottish Regiment.' Remarking that the Battalion had last been presented with Colours in 1862 – 'though it has not been the fortune of War for you to see so much active service during the last 10 years as your 1st Battalion' – he added that both Officers and men from the 2nd Battalion had been provided 'to take the place of those who had fallen'. In his reply, Lieutenant Colonel Alexander Kidston referred to the 'additional interest' which attached to the new Colours, 'as they are the first we have received since we were reunited to our old 1st Battalion'.[155]

When Kidston went on to half-pay in 1891, he was replaced as commanding officer by Major Howell Gunter. At the beginning of November 1891 Gunter agreed to exchange command of the 2nd Battalion with Lieutenant Colonel Arthur Goodall Wavell, The Norfolk Regiment, formerly the 9th. Wavell, who had been serving in India, wanted to return home with his wife and three small children.[156] This exchange began a tradition of service with The Black Watch by the Wavell family, which lasted four generations. Soon afterwards, the 2nd Battalion returned to Scotland, quartered first at Maryhill Barracks, Glasgow. One duty was providing the Guard of Honour at Balmoral for the state visit of the new Tsar of Russia,

Nicholas II, to Britain in 1894.[157] In August, Lieutenant Colonel Andrew Wauchope replaced Wavell, serving as Commanding Officer for four years, while the 2nd Battalion moved from Glasgow to Edinburgh and then York.

When, in 1899, hostilities broke out in South Africa with the Dutch-origin population, the Boers, reinforcements were required. In October the 2nd Battalion embarked for South Africa, where the soldiers were to form part of the Highland Brigade, commanded by Wauchope, promoted major general. By December, the Brigade was in action.

'The Forty-Second Never Dies!'

In 1887 – the year of Queen Victoria's golden jubilee – the town of Aberfeldy in Perthshire was *en fête*, 'the occasion being the unveiling of the memorial cairn erected in commemoration of the grand deeds of the famous Black Watch regiment' and situated close to Tay Bridge. 'Large numbers of the public were present,' reported *The Dundee Advertiser*, 'and the little town was thronged with such a crowd of holiday makers as it had never seen before.' On each of the four sides of the cairn 'surmounted by the figure of a Highlander in the original uniform of the gallant 42nd' was an inscribed tablet, celebrating the formation of the Regiment and the various engagements in which it had taken part since 1739.[158]

By the end of the century, 160 years had passed since the first muster on the banks of the river Tay in May 1740, near where the Highlander on top of the cairn still stands. During that time, thousands of men had fought and died, either in battle or through illness, with thousands more wounded, all eager for fortune and fame, as well as to preserve the honour of an illustrious name. By comparison a handful had deserted, gone missing or been killed accidentally. The Regiment had changed its listing from 43rd to 42nd, and its name several times, reverting to the name by which the independent companies from which it had been formed were known: The Black Watch. Additional battalions had been raised and disbanded as the calls of war dictated. There had been twelve distinguished Colonels of the 42nd Royal Highland Regiment, of whom the longest-serving was Lord John Murray, and numerous Lieutenant Colonels, commanding the various battalions. For nearly one hundred years the 2nd Battalion had been a separate Regiment – the 73rd – with a different Record of History, fourteen Colonels of the Regiment and seventeen Lieutenant Colonels, before being reunited with the 42nd as the 2nd Battalion. Men from Scotland, England, Ireland and Wales had fought on five continents in numerous campaigns, including epic wars – the Peninsular, Napoleonic and Crimean – requiring endurance and deprivation far beyond the comprehension of the soldier today.

The valiant actions against Britain's enemies during the last decades of the nineteenth century marked the end of the Victorian era of fighting. As the new century dawned, tensions were growing between the Great Powers of Europe which erupted into the First and Second World Wars. Fuelled by mass conscription and with a seemingly unlimited industrial capacity on all sides, the belligerents could equip armies with huge quantities of weapons and munitions of increasingly lethal capability. The battles fought across Europe, Africa and Asia in the twentieth and twenty-first centuries would challenge the British people and The Black Watch as never before.

> *The 'Forty-Second' never dies—*
> *It hath a regimental soul;*
> *Fond Scotia, weeping, filled the blanks*
> *Which Quatre Bras left in its roll.*
> *At Alma, at Sevastopol,*
> *At Lucknow, waved its bonnets blue!*
> *Its dark green tartan, who but knows?*
> *What heart but warms to 'Forty-Two!'*[159]

Appendix I

Colonels-in-Chief

His Majesty King George V, 3 September 1912–20 January 1936
Her Majesty Queen Elizabeth, the Queen Mother, 11 May 1937–30 March 2002
His Royal Highness Prince Charles, Duke of Rothesay, 1 July 2003 – 28 March 2006

Colonels of the 42nd

John, Earl of Crawford, 25 October 1739
Hugh, Lord Sempill, 14 January 1741
Lord John Murray, 25 April 1745
Sir Hector Munro, KB, 1 June 1787
George Gordon, Marquis of Huntly, GCB, PC, 3 January 1806
John, Earl of Hopetoun, GCB, 29 January 1820
The Rt Hon. Sir George Murray, GCB, GCH, 6 September 1823
Sir John Macdonald, GCB, 15 January 1844
Sir James Douglas, KCB, 10 April 1850
George, Marquis of Tweeddale, KT, 7 March 1862
Sir Duncan Alexander Cameron, GCB, 9 September 1863
Hon. Sir Robert Rollo, KCB, 9 June 1888
Sir John Chetham McLeod, GCB, 26 February 1907
Sir John Grenfell Maxwell, GCB, KCMG, CVO, DSO, 11 January 1914
Sir Archibald Rice Cameron, GBE, KCB, CMG, 21 February 1929
Sir Arthur Grenfell Wauchope, GCB, GCMG, CIE, DSO, 28 August 1940
Sir Archibald Percival Wavell, 1st Earl Wavell, PC, GCB, GCSI, GCIE, CMG, MC, 1 March 1946

Sir Neil Methuen Ritchie, GBE, KCB, DSO, MC, 24 May 1950
Neil McMicking, CB, CBE, DSO, MC, 19 June 1952
Robert Keith Arbuthnott, Viscount Arbuthnott, CB, CBE, DSO, MC, 31 March 1960
Henry Conyers Baker-Baker, DSO, MBE, 1 June 1964
Sir Bernard Edward Fergusson, Lord Ballantrae, KT, GCMG, GCVO, DSO, OBE, 1 June 1969
John Cassels Monteith, CBE, MC, 6 May 1976
Andrew Linton Watson, CB, 28 September 1981
Garry Charles Barnett, OBE, 28 September 1992
Sir Alistair Stuart Hastings Irwin, KCB, CBE, 28 September 2003

Colonels of the 73rd

Sir George Osborn, Bt, 18 April 1786
Sir William Medows, KB, 11 August 1786
Gerard Lake, 1st Viscount Lake, 2 November 1796
George Harris, 1st Lord Harris, GCB, 14 February 1800
Sir Frederick Adam, GCB, GCMG, 22 May 1829
William George Harris, 2nd Lord Harris, CB, KCH, 4 December 1835
Sir Robert Henry Dick, KCB, KCH, 10 June 1845
Sir John Grey, KCB, 3 April 1846
Sir Richard Goddard Hare Clarges, KCB, 18 May 1849
Robert Barclay Macpherson, CB, KH, 29 July 1852
Chesborough Grant Falconar, KH, 11 February 1857
Sir Michael Creagh, KH, 11 January 1860
Benjamin Orlando Jones, KH, 15 September 1860
Sir Henry Robert Ferguson-Davie, Bt 17 February 1865

Appendix II Victoria Cross

The following members of the Regiment have been awarded this decoration.

Indian Mutiny

Lieutenant Francis Edward Farquharson, Lucknow, 9 March 1858
Quarter Master John Simpson, Fort Ruhya, 15 April 1858
Lance Corporal Alexander Thompson, Fort Ruhya, 15 April 1858
Private James Davis, Fort Ruhya, 15 April 1858
Private Edward Spence, Fort Ruhya, 15 April 1858
Colour Sergeant William Gardner, Bareilly, 5 May 1858
Private Walter Cook, Sissaya Ghat, 15 January 1859
Private Duncan Millar, Sissaya Ghat, 15 January 1859

Ashanti War

Lance Sergeant Samuel McGaw, Amoaful, 31 January 1874

Egyptian Campaigns

Private Thomas Edwards, 1st Battalion, Tamai, 13 March 1884

First World War

Corporal John Ripley, 1st Battalion, Rue du Bois, 9 May 1915
Sergeant David Finlay, 2nd Battalion, Rue du Bois, 9 May 1915
Private Charles Melvin, 2nd Battalion, Istabulat, 21 April 1917
Lieutenant Colonel Lewis Pugh Evans, Zonnebeke, 4 October 1917

Select Bibliography

Unpublished sources

Alexander Turnbull Library, National Library of New Zealand, Wellington, New Zealand

Grant, Lieutenant John, Memoir, 1758–62

Black Watch Regimental Archive, Balhousie Castle, Perth, UK

Barwood, Bandsman Arthur Vincent, Diary on the Sudan and Nile Expeditions, 1882–5

Barwood, Bandsman Spencer Vincent, Letters to his family, 1882–5

Bayly, Lieutenant Colonel Richard Kerr, 'The Black Watch Gong', 1858

Bedson, Private George, Photograph Album

Bryson, Private John, Memoir, Crimean War and Indian Mutiny

Chronological Register of the Evidence bearing upon the Dress, Arms, Accoutrements and Colours, worn and carried by the 42nd (Royal Highland) The Black Watch Regiment, vol. I, 1725–1824, vol. II, c. 1820–90

Coleridge, Francis, 'Scrapbook of Her Majesty's XLII', Royal Highlanders, Album of Watercolours

Cooper, Sergeant Quibell, Diary, 1862–4

Coveny, Lieutenant Colonel Robert de Courcy, Diaries and Letters from Egypt and the Soudan, 1882–4 (also in the private collection of Major General Simon Willis, AM, CSC)

Dick, Major General Sir Robert, Letters and Papers, 1803–20

Drysdale, Lieutenant Colonel John, 'A Soldier's Life', Memoir/Diary, 1848–50, and Scrapbook, 1846–58

Gerard, Ensign George, Journal, 1814–15

Gibsone, Major Hugh Francis, Scrapbook containing sketches, photographs and notes, 1857–74

Gordon, Lieutenant William, Notes of a Voyage round the Cape (of Good Hope) from Ireland to China via Java in the *Golden Fleece*, November 1866 to March 1867

Grove, Joseph Ross, Letters, Crimea 1854–5

Gunn, Private James, Memoir, Peninsular and Waterloo Campaigns, 1809–15

Halford-Macleod, Ruari, Research Notes, covering the period 1758–63

Halkett, Sir Peter Arthur, 'My Recollections of a Military Life', 1851–88, written 1888–93, and Sketch Book

Huey, Ensign Alexander, 'The Voyage of the 73rd Regiment of Foot', 1809–11, Diary

Knyphausen, Lieutenant General Wilhelm von, Extract of a letter to Lord George Germaine, 1780

Lovat, Simon Fraser, Lord, Excerpts from letters to Lieutenant Colonel William Kennedy, Lieutenant Governor of Fort George, Inverness, Beaufort, 1739

McAusland, Private David, Memoir, 1848–60

McGregor, Charles, Diary 1794–1836, including description of the capture of Seringapatam (original diary and transcript)

McGregor, Malcolm, 'A Black Watch Who Was Who 1725–1881', a biographical record of the 1st and 2nd Battalions (Highland companies and the 42nd/73rd Foot) including Research Notes

McIntosh, Private Archibald Watt, Diary relating to service in India, 1858–67

McNiven, Lieutenant Colonel Thomas, Memoirs, 1795–1814

McSally, Sergeant Edward, 'The Royal Highlanders at Alma By one of them', 1854

Malcolm, Lieutenant John, Diary, 25 April to 18 June 1815

Montgomery, Captain Thomas Henry, Letters relating to the Crimean War, 1854–6

Old Rolls of Officers and Men, from papers in possession of 7th Duke of Atholl by whom they were placed at the disposal of the Regiment, 1890

Peters, H. William Robinson, Waterloo Veteran, memoir transcribed in 1978

Rankin, Sergeant George, Diary, 1856–8

Record of Issues of Clothing 1758–9, Quarter Master Adam Stewart

Record of Service of the 42nd, 1729–1873, and 1st Battalion 42nd, 1873–1939

Record of Service of the 73rd/2nd Battalion, The Black Watch, 1780–1909

Record of The Black Watch 1758–1763

Regimental and General Order Books, 42nd, 1785–93, 1804–5, 1806–8, 1814–18

Regimental Scrapbook, 1740–1917

Return of men who were killed and died of their wounds from 8 March 1801 to Embarkation 6 October 1801

Rich, Corporal John, 'Some Account of the Kaffir War', Memoirs and Diary, 1844–59, handwritten journal and edited transcript by Neville Mapham, 1990.

Robertson, Surgeon Andrew, Diary, Campaigns in the Low Countries, 1742–3

Robertson, Private Walter, Original diary, and two volumes (transcripts), Crimean War and Indian Mutiny, 1854–8

Ross, see Grove, Joseph Ross

Scott-Stephenson, Andrew, Letter to his wife, Mary Esme, 1882

Simpson, Private John, Memoir, 1795–1801

Smyth, Thomas B. (ed.), Officers of the 73rd 1786–1881, draft

State of the Rank and File and Numbers wanting to complete the Regiments of British Infantry up to the Establishment of 850 per Battalion at the beginning of February 1795

Stewart, Captain James, Orderly Book, vols 1–4, 18 February 1759 to 16 July 1759; 22 September 1759 to 3 August 1760; 6 April 1761 to 5 August 1761; 7 August 1761 to 6 November 1761

Stirling, Thomas, General Account of the British Attempts to Occupy the Illinois, transcribed from the Thomas Stirling Papers

Wheatley, John, Memoirs, 1817–37

Wilson, Charles Dunsmore, Memoirs of the Crimea, 1855

British Library

Bouquet, Colonel Henry, Papers

Campbell, Lieutenant Colonel John, Letter assigning his reasons for the surrender of Mangalore Fort to Tippoo Sa[h]ib, 4 February 1784

Macpherson, Laurence, 'A New Form of Prayer as used (since the battle of Fontenoy) by the British Troops in the Allied Army of Flanders', Compos'd by Laurence Macpherson, Chaplain to the Highland Regiment. Printed and Publish'd at the General Request of the Officers and Gentlemen in the British Corps. London: Printed for T. Lion, near St. Paul's MDCCXLV [1745]. , No. 65 – 1–8 in Tracts, 64–82, 1493c17.

Treaty of Peace with the Nabob Tippoo Sultaun Bahauder, 11 March 1784

James Hepburne Scott, private collection

Warrant for raising a company addressed to Colin Campbell of Skipness

Rules and Orders to be observed in recruiting the Right Honble the Earl of Crawford's Regiment of Foot, George Grant, Inverness, January 10th, 1740

Huntingdon Library, Pasadena, California, USA

Loudoun, the Papers of John Campbell 4th Earl

Macquarie University Library, Sydney, Australia

Antill, Henry, Journal of a Voyage to New South Wales 1809, Lachlan and Elizabeth Macquarie Archive, Macquarie University Library. www.library.mq.edu.au/digital/lema/1809/antill1809.html, original held in Mitchell Library, Sydney

Brownrigg, Governor Robert, Despatches, No. 73, 31 March 1814; No. 77, 17 August 1814, *Under A Tropical Sun*: www.library.mq.edu.au/digital/under/documents/1814 original held at National Archives of Sri Lanka

Campbell, John, unsigned letter, Pannang on the Malabar Coast,

22 Dec. 1782, Lachlan Macquarie, Memoranda & Related papers, original held in Mitchell Library, Sydney

Ceylon Government Gazette, 1 Feb. and 1 Nov. 1817, *Under a Tropical Sun*, www.library.mq.edu.au/digital/under/documents/

Wentworth, D'Arcy, correspondence, *Under a Tropical Sun*, www.library.mq.edu.au/digital/under/documents/, original held in Mitchell Library, Sydney

National Library of Scotland, Edinburgh, UK
Lundin, Richard, Narrative of the Shipwreck, & Surprising Adventures, in 1813, of Captain Richard Lundin, of Auchtermairney, Parish of Kennoway, Fifeshire, as related by himself

National Museums Scotland, Edinburgh, UK
Blantyre, 11th Baron, Journal of the Campaigns in Portugal and Spain in 1809–10, 1811 and 1812, from the Baird Papers

National Records of Scotland, Edinburgh, UK
Campbell of Barcaldine papers

Grant, Francis, letters, see Seafield family Muniments

Peebles, John, Original Diary, '13 Notebooks concerning military operations in America, 1776–1782'

Seafield family Muniments

Stirling Home Drummond Moray of Abercairny Muniments

Royal Green Jackets Museum, Winchester, UK
Wilkinson, Frederick Green, Letters to his family, 1854–8

The National Archives, London, UK
Abstracts of Grants of Land, 1764

Account of the Number of Forces, Officers included employed in North America, 24 October 1758

Advertisement concerning deserters, 29 July 1743

Advertisement for apprehending the Mutineers, 18 May 1743

Affray at Leith, 1779

Amherst Papers, Correspondence as Commander-in-Chief, North America

Amherst, Major General Jeffrey, Order for Drafting of the 2nd Battalion of Royal Highland Regiment into the First, 2 Oct. 1762

Campaigns, Battles, Ticonderoga

Commissions for a Regiment of Foot to be forthwith raised for His Majesty's Service, under the command of John Earl of Crawford

Correspondence between Commander-in-Chief and masters of vessels 1757–63

Court Martial, Report of the Proceedings, June 1743

Disbandment of 2nd Battalion 73rd, 7 April 1817

Distribution of the Forces under command of General Lord Raglan, GCB, Scutari, 10 May 1854

Embarkation Returns, New York, 19 Nov. 1761

Establishment of General and other Officers and Six Independent Companies of Foot in North Britain commencing the 24th of April 1725

Garrisons and Winter Quarters of His Majesty's Forces in North America under the command of His Excellency, Major General Amherst, Headquarters at New York, 15 December 1759

General Returns of the killed, wounded & missing of the Army commanded by Colonel J. Braithwaite during the Siege of Pondicherry, which ended on the 23rd of August 1793

His Majesty's 42nd or Royal Highland Regiment of Foot. Muster Rolls

Memorandum from the War Office, Harry Calvert, Adjutant General, Horse Guards 26 July 1816

Memorandum on the Dress Bonnet and Ostrich Feathers worn by Highland Regiments, Horse Guards 15 August 1828

Memorial for Captain Ja[me]s Drummond, Captain Colin Campbell, & Lieut Alex[ande]r McGregor, all of the 2nd Battalion, to Rt Hon. Sir George Yonge

Memorial of Lieutenant Colonel Charles Graham to Rt Hon. Sir George Yonge

Muster Rolls of 42nd Royal Highland Regiment of Foot commanded by Lord John Murray, I and II

102 Foot: New South Wales Corps

Order for Disbanding the 2nd Battn of Lord John Murray's Regt of Foot, and Orders and Instructions for Disbanding the 2nd Battn of Lord John Murray's Regt of Foot

Order for Drafting of the 2nd Battalion of Royal Highland Regiment into the First, 2 Oct. 1762

Order for Forming a Regt of Foot under the command of the Right Honourable John Earl of Crawford, dated 7 November 1739, TNA

Order for Putting a sentence in execution, 13 July 1743

Order for Recruiting the Highland Regiment of Foot, 1 September 1743

Order for the Establishment of the Regiment to 'commence and take place from the 25th day of October 1739'

Order to the Earl of Crawford to raise Voluntiers to compleat the Regt of Foot under his Command, 7 November 1739

Precis of the Ashanti Expedition, Intelligence Dept, Horse Guards, War Office, 13 April 1874

Return of Casualties at the Battle of Alma, 20 September 1854

Return of Commissioned, Non-commissioned Officers, etc., 28 March 1798

Return of Killed, Wounded & Missing, 24 January 1762, 27 January 1762

Return of Killed and Wounded in the two actions at Edge Hill near Bushy Run, 5 and 6 August 1763

Return of the 42nd and 77th Regiments, Carlisle, 13 July 1763

Return of the Loss sustained by the 42nd or Royal Highland Regiment in the action on 5 August 1763

Return of the Killed & Wounded of the British at the Siege of Nieuport, Ostend 1 November 1793

Return of the Killed, Wounded, and Missing of the Troops under the Command of Major General David Dundas at Geldermalsen, 5 January 1795

Return of the Killed, Wounded and Missing of the Army under the Command of General Sir Ralph Abercromby KB near Alexandria, 21 March 1801

Return of the Number of Killed, Wounded & Missing of the Army under the command of Lieut. General Lord Viscount Wellington KB in the action with the French Army commanded by Marshal Massena, . . . with the position of Busāco on 27 September 1810

Return of Killed, Wounded & Missing of the Army under the Command of His Excellency Field Marshal the Marquis of Wellington KG in the attack of the Enemy's Fortified position covering Toulouse on 10 April 1814

Royal Highland Regiment, Warrant for forming the 42nd Regt of Foot into two battalions with the title of Royal Highland Regt, 1758

State of the Rt Hon Lord Sempill's Highland Regt of Foot as Reviewed by General Wade on Finchley Common, 14 May 1743

State of the Troops in the Southern Department in 1763, signed by Major Allan Campbell

Statement of the Force composing the Grand Army under the Command of Lieutenant General Harris

Sterling, Captain [Thomas Stirling], Commanding a Detachment of the 42nd Regiment at Fort Chartres in the Illinois Country, Extract of a Letter to His Excellency General Gage, Fort Chartres, Oct. 18th, 1765

War Department In-Letters and Papers: selected

Published Works

Black Watch Regimental Library
Anon. (Rev. Mr Campbell), *The Behaviour and Character of Samuel Macpherson, Malcolm Macpherson and Farquhar Shaw*, Edinburgh, MDCCXLIII (1743)

Anon., *A Short History of the Highland Regiment*. Printed for Jacob

Robinson, London, 1743. Reprinted with Foreword by Col Paul P. Hutchison, Hope Farm Press, NY, 1963

The Black Watch Chronicle, T. & A. Constable, 1914

Chronology of the 42nd Royal Highlanders, The Black Watch from 1729 to 1905, 4th ed., printed for the Regiment, Berwick-on-Tweed, 1906

Ferguson, Adam, *Sermon preached in the Erse Language to his Majesty's First Highland Regiment of Foot*, commanded by Lord John Murray at their cantonment at Camberwell, on 18 December 1745, and translated by him into English for the Use of a Lady of quality in Scotland [Mary, the Dowager Duchess of Atholl], at whose Desire it is now published. London, printed for A. Millar, 1746

Forbes, Archibald, *The 'Black Watch': The Record of an Historic Regiment*, Cassell and Co. Ltd, 1st edition 1896, annotated with notes by Lieutenant Colonel Mackay Scobie

The Knock Notebook of 1731–1733. A relic of the New Independent Companies, owned by Mr James McArthur of Kirkmichael, Banffshire

Officers of The Black Watch, 1725 to 1986, ed. J.L.R. Samson, 1937, 2nd revised ed., Samson Books Ltd, 1989

The Red Hackle, selected issues

General

Allardyce, James (ed.), *Historical Papers Relating to the Jacobite Period 1699–1750*, New Spalding Club, Aberdeen, 1895

American Heritage Book of The Revolution, Editor-in-charge Richard M. Ketchum, American Heritage Publishing Co. Inc., 1958

Amherst, Jeffrey, *The Journal of Jeffrey Amherst, Recording the Military Career of General Amherst in America from 1758 to 1763*, ed. and with introduction and notes by J. Clarence Webster, The Ryerson Press, University of Chicago Press, 1931

And the River Rolled On . . . Two Hundred years on the Nashwaak, Nashwaak Bicentennial Association, 1984

Anon., *The Personal Narrative of a Private Soldier, Who Served in the*

Forty-Second Highlanders, for Twelve Years, during the Late War, London, 1821

Anon., *Memoir of Lieut-Col. John Campbell*, by a retired officer (Lt Col James Spens), Edinburgh, 1836

Anton, James, *Retrospect of A Military Life during the Most Eventful Periods of the Late Wars*, Edinburgh, 1841

Army Lists, selected issues

Baird, William, *General Wauchope*, T. and A. Constable, 1901

Beckett, Ian F.W. (ed.), *Wolseley and Ashanti, the Asante War Journal and Correspondence of Major General Sir Garnet Wolseley 1873–1874*, The History Press for the Army Records Society, 2009

Bevan, David, *Stand Fast*, Traditional Publishing, 2002

Bougainville, Louis Antoine de, *Adventure in the Wilderness, The American Journals of Louis Antoine de Bougainville, 1756–1760*, tr. and ed. Edward P. Hamilton, Norman, University of Oklahoma Press, 1964

Brackenbury, Henry, *The Ashanti War*, A Narrative prepared from the official documents by permission of Major General Sir Garnet Wolseley, in two volumes, Blackwood and Sons, 1874

Brittlebank, Kate, *Tipu Sultan's Search for Legitimacy: Islam and Kingship in a Hindu Domain*, OUP, 1995

Bulloch, John Malcolm, 'Lord Huntly's Black Watch Company', in *Territorial Soldiering in the North-East of Scotland during 1759–1914*, New Spalding Club, Aberdeen, 1914

Burt, Edmund, *Burt's Letters from the North of Scotland*, ed. Andrew Simmons, Birlinn, Edinburgh, 1998 (first published 1754)

Cannon, Richard, *Historical Record of the Forty-Second or The Royal Highland Regiment of Foot*, London, Parker, Furnivall and Parker, 1845

— *Historical Record of the Seventy-Third Regiment*, London, Parker, Furnivall and Parker, 1851

Carroon, Robert G. (ed.), see under Eddington and Stirling

Cavendish, Anne (ed.), *Cyprus 1878: The Journal of Sir Garnet Wolseley*, Cyprus Popular Bank Cultural Centre, Nicosia, 1991

Chamberlayne, John, *Magnae Notitia: or the Present State of Great Britain, in two parts*, printed for D. Midwinter, etc., London, 1726, 1735

Chronicles of the Families of Atholl and Tullibardine, III, collected and arranged by John, Seventh Duke of Atholl, privately printed, Ballantyne Press, Edinburgh, 1908

Clyde, Robert, *From Rebel to Hero*, Tuckwell Press, 1995

Colley, Linda, *Captives: Britain, Empire and the World 1600–1850*, Jonathan Cape, 2002

Constable's Miscellany of Original and Selected Publications in the Various Departments of Literature, Science, & the Arts, vol. XXVII, *Memorials of the Late War* vol. 1, Constable & Co. Edinburgh and Hurst, Chance & Co. London, 1828

Cornford, Leslie Cope, and Frank William Walker, *The Story of the Regiments: The Great Deeds of the Black Watch*, J.M. Dent & Sons, 1915

Cram, Duthie, Irwin and Taylor, *A Collection of Pipe Music of The Black Watch*, Balhousie Publications, 2011

Culloden Papers, 'comprising an extensive and interesting correspondence from the year 1625 to 1748', ed. H.R. Duff, T. Cadell & W. Davies, London, 1815

Cuneo, John R., *Robert Rogers of the Rangers*, Oxford University Press, 1959.

Currie, Jo, *Mull: The Island and Its People*, Birlinn Ltd, 2000

Dalrymple, William, *The Last Mughal*, Viking Penguin, 2006

David, Saul, *The Indian Mutiny 1857*, Viking, 2002

Davidson, Ian, 'Some Comments on the Traditional Historiography of The Black Watch, 1725–1815', *Journal of the Society for Army Historical Research*, vol. 84, 2006

— 'Pieces of Evidence Concerning the Origin and Early Years of the Black Watch', *Journal of the Society for Army Historical Research*, vol. 84, 2006

— 'The Black Watch, 1725–1815', *Journal of the Society for Army Historical Research*, vol. 84, 2006

— 'The Life and Works of H.D. MacWilliam (1859–1936)', *Journal of the Society for Army Historical Research*, vol. 86, 2008

Devine, T.M., *Scotland's Empire, 1600–1815*, Allen Lane, 2003

— *To the Ends of the Earth: Scotland's Global Diaspora 1750–2010*, Allen Lane, 2011

Dillon, Harry, and Peter Butler, *Macquarie: From Colony to Country*, Heinemann, Australia, 2010

Doddridge, Philip, *Some Remarkable Passages in the Life of the Hon. Colonel Gardiner, who was slain at the battle of Prestonpans*, Appendix, III, J. & J. Dundee, 1813

Dodgshon, Robert A., *From Chiefs to Landlords. Social and Economic Change in the Western Highlands, c 1493–1820*, Edinburgh University Press, 1998

Donaldson, William, *The Jacobite Song*, Aberdeen University Press, 1988

Duff, H.R. (ed.), see *Culloden Papers*

Dundas, David, 'Memorandum on the Capture of Havana', see Syrett

Eddington, James, 'Official Journal Kept by Lieut. Eddington', in Robert G. Carroon (ed.), *Broadswords and Bayonets*, The Society of Colonial Wars in the State of Illinois, 1984

Edwardes, Michael, *Battles of the Indian Mutiny*, Batsford, 1963

Esdale, Charles, *The Peninsular War*, Penguin Allen Lane, 2002

Fletcher, Ian, *Salamanca 1812: Wellington Crushes Marmont*, Osprey Publishing, 1997

Forbes, Archibald, *The 'Black Watch': The Record of an Historic Regiment*, Cassell and Co. Ltd, 1st edn 1896, 2nd edn 1910

Fraser, W., *In the Shadow of Cairngorm*, Inverness, 1900

Fry, Michael, *Scotland and the Americas*, John Carter Brown Library, 1995

— *The Scottish Empire*, Tuckwell Press, 2001

— *Wild Scots, Four Hundred Years of Highland History*, John Murray, 2005

Gardiner, Richard, Captain of Marines on board HMS *Rippon*, *An Account of the Expedition to the West Indies against Martinico, with the Reduction of Guadelupe, and Other the Leeward Islands; subject to the French King 1759*, London 1759

Gerard, George, Letters, *The Red Hackle*, 1932

Gordon, John, *My Six Years with The Black Watch, 1881–1887*, The Fort Hill Press, Boston, Mass., 1929

Groves, Lieutenant Colonel Percy, *Illustrated Histories of the Scottish Regiments, Book No. 1, The Black Watch, Royal Highlanders, 42nd Foot, 1729–1893.* Illustrated by Harry Payne, W. & A.K. Johnston, Edinburgh and London, 1893

Grubner, Ira D., see *John Peebles' American War*

Halford-Macleod, Ruari, *'When shall we see so fine a Regiment again?' The Early Officers of the Black Watch*, privately published, 1997

Harper, Marjory, *Adventurers and Exiles: The Great Scottish Exodus*, London, Profile Books, 2003

Henderson, Diana M., *Highland Soldier 1820–1920*, John Donald, 1989

Holmes, Richard, *Wellington: The Iron Duke*, Harper Collins, 2002

— *Redcoat: The British Soldier in the Age of Horse and Musket*, Harper Collins 2011

Howard, Philip, *The Black Watch*, Hamish Hamilton, 1968

Hutchison, Col Paul P., see Anon. *A Short History*

Hutton-Wilson, Guy, see Mackenzie, Lieutenant Donald

John Peebles' American War: The Diary of a Scottish Grenadier, 1776–1782, ed. Ira. D. Grubner, Army Records Society, Sutton Publishing Ltd, 1998

Kayle, Allan, *Salvage of the Birkenhead*, Southern Book Publishing, Johannesburg, 1990

Keltie, John S. (ed.), *A History of the Scottish Highlands, Highland Clans and Highland Regiments*, II, Fullarton & Co., 1875

— (ed.), *Historical Record of the 42nd Royal Highlanders (The Black Watch) from 1729 to 1881*, Thomas C. Jack, Edinburgh, 1887

Kilkeary, Bernard, see Samson, J. L.R.

Kirk[wood], Robert, *Through So Many Dangers: The Memoirs and Adventures of Robert Kirk*, ed. Ian McCulloch and Timothy Todish, Purple Mountain Press, 2004

Knox, Alfred, 'The Kaffir War of 1851', transcribed by H.L. Henchman, *Daily Dispatch*, East London, 1929

Knox, John, *An Historical Journal of the Campaign in North America for the Years 1757, 1758, 1759, and 1760: containing The Most Remarkable Occurrences of that Period; particularly The Two Sieges of Quebec, &c. &c.*, printed for the author, London, 1769

Konstam, Angus, *There Was a Soldier: First-Hand Accounts of the Scottish Soldier at War from 1707 to the Present Day*, Hachette Scotland, 2009

Laffin, John, *Scotland the Brave*, Cassell, London, 1963

Lagden, Alan, and Sly, John (ed.), *The 2/73rd at Waterloo*, privately published, 2nd ed., 1998

Lenman, Bruce, *The Jacobite Clans of the Great Glen, 1650–1784*, Scottish Cultural Press, 1984, 1995

Linklater, Eric and Andro, *The Black Watch*, Barrie & Jenkins Ltd, 1977

Lloyd, Alan, *Drums of Kumasi*, Longmans, 1964

Longford, Elizabeth, *Wellington: The Years of the Sword*, Weidenfeld & Nicolson, 1969

Lucas, Gould, 'Lucas's Account of the Wreck of the Birkenhead', *Africana Notes & News*, vol. 17, no. 6, June 1967

Lushington, the Rt Hon S.R., *The Life and Services of General Lord Harris, GCB*, John W. Parker, London, 1845

McCulloch, Ian Macpherson, *Sons of the Mountains, The Highland Regiments in the French & Indian War, 1756–1767*, vols I & II, Purple Mountain Press, 2006

Macfarlane, Charles, *Our Indian Empire: its History and Present State, from the Earliest Settlement of the British in Hindostan to the Close of the Year 1843*, Knight, 1844

McGuire, Thomas J., *Battle of Paoli*, Stackpole Books, PA, 2000

Macinnes, Allan I, *Clanship, Commerce and the House of Stuart, 1603–1788*, East Linton, Tuckwell Press, 1996

Mackenzie, Lieutenant Donald, *Merely a Memorandum: From Spain to Waterloo in Wellington's Army: The Personal Recollections of Lieutenant Donald Mackenzie, 42nd Royal Highland Regiment the*

Black Watch, compiled and edited by Guy Hutton-Wilson, Librario Publishing Ltd, 2005

Mackillop, Andrew, *'More Fruitful than the Soil': Army, Empire and the Scottish Highlands, 1715–1815*, East Linton, Tuckwell Press, 2000

Maclean, Fitzroy, *Bonnie Prince Charlie*, Weidenfeld & Nicolson, 1988

Macleod, Sergeant Donald, *Memoirs of the Life and Gallant Exploits of the Old Highlander*, introduction by J.G. Fyfe, reprint from original of 1791, Blackie & Son, 1933

McLeod, John Chetham, 'The Black Watch at Lucknow', *The Red Hackle*, 1935

— 'Unpublished Letters: A Scotsman in the Crimea', ed. Prof. R.F. Christian, Univ. of St Andrews, *The Red Hackle*, 1984–5

MacWilliam, H.D., *A Black Watch Episode 1731*, W. & A.K. Johnston, Edinburgh & London, 1908

— (ed.), *The Official Records of the Mutiny in The Black Watch*, Forester Groom & Co., London, 1910

— *The Black Watch Tartan*, The Northern Chronicle Office, Inverness, 1932

— 'The Origin of the Black Watch 1725–1739', *Celtic Monthly*, XXI, 1913, XXII, 1914

Malcolm, John, Esq. late of the 42d Regt., *Reminiscence s of a Campaign in the Pyrenees and South of France, in 1814*, in *Constable's Miscellany*, listed above

Mann, Michael, *A Particular Duty: The Canadian Rebellions 1837–1839*, Michael Russell, Salisbury, 1986

Mante, Thomas, *History of the Late War in America and the Islands of the West-Indies*, W. Strahan and T. Caldwell, London, 1772

Mathew, K.S., and S. Jeyaseela Stephen (ed.), *Indo-French Relations*, Pragati Publications, Delhi, 1999

Merolle, Vicenzo (ed.), *The Letters of Adam Ferguson*, vol. 1, *1745–1780*, with biographical introduction by Professor Jane Fagg, William Pickering, London, 1995

Miller, William, *The Ottoman Empire and its Successors, 1801–1927*, Cambridge University Press, 1936

Mitchell, Dugald, *A Popular History of the Highlands*, Paisley, 1900

More Culloden Papers, vol. III, *1725 to 1745*, ed. Duncan Warrand, Robert Carruthers & Sons, Inverness, 1927

Morris, Thomas, William, and William, Jun., *The Three Serjeants, or Phases of the Soldier's Life*, Effingham Wilson, London, 1858

Muir, John, 'The Indian Mutiny', Memoirs, *The Red Hackle*, 2008

Murray, A.K, *History of the Scottish Regiments of the British Army*, Thomas Murray & Son, Glasgow, 1862

Murray, C. de B., *Duncan Forbes of Culloden*, International Publishing Co. London, 1936

Murray, David, *Music of the Scottish Regiments*, Pentland Press, Edinburgh, 1994

Napier, Major General Sir W.F. P., *History of the War in the Peninsula and in the South of France from the year 1807 to the Year 1814*, VI, Thomas and William Boone, 1856

Nashwaak Families 1785–1885 See *And the River Rolled On . . .*

Newark, Tim, *Highlander: The History of the Legendary Highland Soldier*, Constable, 2009

Newton, Michael, *We're Indians Sure Enough: The Legacy of the Scottish Highlanders in the United States*, Saorsa Media, USA 2001

Pargellis, Stanley, *Lord Loudoun in North America*, Yale University Press, 1933

— *Military Affairs in North America 1748–1765*, Selected Documents from the Cumberland Papers in Windsor Castle, New York & London, 1936

Peebles, see *John Peebles*

Picken, Andrew, *The Black Watch*, 3 vols, ed. J.C. Picken, Richard Bentley, London, 1834

Pitt, William, *Correspondence when Secretary of State with Colonial Governors and Military and Naval Commissioners in America*, ed. Gertrude Selwyn Kimball, vols I and II, Macmillan, 1906

Pocock, Tom, *Battle for Empire: The Very First World War, 1756–63*, Caxton Editions, 2002

Prebble, John, *Culloden*, Secker & Warburg, 1961

— *The Highland Clearances*, Penguin Books Ltd, 1973

— *Mutiny*, Secker & Warburg, 1975

Rathbone Low, Charles, *A Memoir of Lieutenant General Sir Garnet J. Wolseley*, II, R. Bentley, 1878

Reade, Winwood, *The Story of the Ashantee Campaign*, Smith, Elder & Co., London, 1874

Report on American Manuscripts in the Royal Institution of Great Britain, vols I & II, HMSO, Mackie & Co., 1904 & 1906

Richards, Frederick B., 'The Black Watch at Ticonderoga and Major Duncan Campbell of Inverawe', An Excerpt from Volume X of the Proceedings of the New York State Historical Association. Reprinted Heritage Books Inc., Bowie, Maryland, 1999

Robb, Alexander, *Reminiscences of a Veteran, Late 6th Company, 42nd Highlanders (Black Watch)*, W. &. D.C. Thomson, Dundee, 1888

Robertson, James Irvine, *The First Highlander: Major-General David Stewart of Garth CB, 1768–1829*, Tuckwell Press, 1998

Rogers, Colonel H.C.B., *Wellington's Army*, Ian Allan, 1979

Rogers, Robert, *The Annotated and Illustrated Journals of Major Robert Rogers*, Timothy J. Todish, ed., Dublin, 1769, reprinted, Fleischmanns, New York, 2002

Rolt, Richard, *Memoirs of the Life of the Late Right Honourable John Lindesay: Earl of Craufurd*, Henry Koepp, 1753

Royle, Trevor, *The Great Crimean War, 1854–1856*, Abacus, 2000

— *The Black Watch*, Mainstream Publishing, 2006

Rutherfurd, John, 'An Episode in the Pontiac War, 1763 – An Unpublished Manuscript by Major Rutherfurd of the "Black Watch"', Transactions of the Canadian Institute, 1891–2

Salmond, J.B., *Wade in Scotland*, Moray Press, Edinburgh & London, 1934

Samson, J.L.R., 'A Ship's Sergeant-Major' (Bernard Kilkeary), *The Red Hackle*, December 1985

Scott-Moncrieff, Lesley (ed.), *The '45, To Gather an Image Whole*, Mercat Press, Edinburgh, 1988

Sharp, Percy, 'Women and Children First', *Reader's Digest*, January 1977

Simmons, Andrew, see Burt

Simpson, Peter, *The Independent Highland Companies, 1603–1760*, Edinburgh, 1996

Sly, John, see Lagden

Smelser, Marshall, *The Campaign for the Sugar Islands 1759: a study of amphibious warfare*, University of North Carolina Press, 1955

Spens, James, see Anon., *Memoir of Lieutenant Colonel John Campbell*

Spiers, Edward M., *The Victorian Soldier in Africa*, Manchester University Press, 2004

— *The Scottish Soldier and Empire, 1854–1902*, Edinburgh University Press, 2006

Stanley, H.M., *Coomassie and Magdala: The Story of Two British Campaigns in Africa*, Sampson Low, 1874

Stanley, Peter, *The Remote Garrison, The British Army in Australia 1788–1870*, Kangaroo Press, Sydney, 1986

Stewart, Major-General David (Stewart of Garth), *Sketches of the Character, Manners, and Present State of the Highlanders of Scotland; with Details of the Military Service of the Highland Regiments*, Constable & Co., Edinburgh, vol. 1, 1822, and vol. 2, 1822. 2nd edition 1822, 3rd edition 1825

Stirling, Thomas, *Broadswords and Bayonets*, ed. Robert G. Carroon, The Society of Colonial Wars in the State of Illinois, 1984

Syrett, David (ed.), *The Siege and Capture of Havana 1762*, Navy Records Society, 1970

Taylor, William, *The Military Roads in Scotland*, House of Lochar, Argyll, 1996

Thomson, Mowbray, *The Story of Cawnpore*, Richard Bentley, 1859

Timberlake, Lt Henry, *The Memoirs of Lt. Henry Timberlake: The Story of a Soldier, Adventurer, and Emissary to the Cherokees, 1756–1765*, ed. Duane H. King, Museum of the Cherokee Indian Press, North Carolina, 2007

Tullibardine, Marchioness of (ed.), *A Military History of Perthshire 1660–1902*, R.A. & J. Hay, 1908

Wallace, Col. R.F.H., 'Dress of The Black Watch', *The Red Hackle*, 1932–4

— 'Colours of The Black Watch', *The Red Hackle*, 1936–7

Warrand, Duncan (ed.), see *More Culloden Papers*

Wauchope, Arthur, *A Short History of The Black Watch (Royal Highlanders) 1725–1907*, Blackwood & Sons, Edinburgh, 1908

Westbrook, Nicholas (ed.), ' "Like Roaring Lions Breaking from their Chains": the Highland Regiment at Ticonderoga', *The Bulletin of the Fort Ticonderoga Museum*, vol. XVI, no. 1, 1998

Whitaker, Anne-Maree, *Joseph Foveaux: power and patronage in early New South Wales*, UNSW Press, 2000

Wilkin, Capt. W.H., *The Life of Sir David Baird*, George Allen & Co. Ltd, 1912

Wilson, *Commissary Wilson's Orderly Book: Expedition of the British and Provincial Army under Maj. Gen. Jeffrey Amherst, against Ticonderoga and Crown Point 1759*, Albany N.Y., 1857

Wolseley, see Beckett (ed.), Cavendish (ed.)

Journals and Newspapers

Africana Notes and News, 1967

The Army List of 1740, reprinted by The Society for Army Historical Research, 1931

Blackwood's Magazine, 1896

Bulletin of the Fort Ticonderoga Museum, vol. XVI, 1998, no. 1

Caledonian Mercury, selected issues

Celtic Monthly, vol. XXI, 1913, vol. XXII, 1914

The Edinburgh Review, 1896

The Garrison Gazette, selected issues

The Gentleman's Magazine, selected issues

History Today, 2002

The Illustrated London News, 1852, 1874

The Journal of the Society for Army Historical Research (*JSAHR*), selected issues

The Journal of Illinois History, Quarterly of the Illinois State Historical Library, vol. 2, no. 2, Summer 1999

The Kinross-shire Courier, 1874

The London Gazette, selected issues

The Reader's Digest, 1977
The Scots Magazine, selected issues
The Scotsman, selected issues
The Sydney Gazette and New South Wales Advertiser, selected issues
The Times, selected issues
Transactions of the Canada Institute, vol. III
Transactions of the Gaelic Society of Inverness, vol. LV 1986–8, Inverness, 1989

A note on early histories of The Black Watch

1743: the Anonymous *Short History* is the earliest history of The Black Watch.

1822: David Stewart of Garth published his *Sketches* in two volumes (revised in 1822 and 1825). Such was his reputation that his history has been used extensively by future historians who have copied his errors.

1838: James Browne, Advocate, *History of the Highlands and of the Highland Clans*.

1845: Richard Cannon, *A Historical Record of the Forty-Second or The Royal Highland Regiment of Foot* (as part of a series of Historical Records of the British Army comprising the History of every Regiment). The early narrative was directly taken from Browne's book, but supplemented with additional information up to 1844.

1862: A.K. Murray, *History of the Scottish Regiments in the British Army*, which included a section on the Forty-Second Foot, concluding with the Crimean War.

1875: J.S. Keltie edited an extensive *History of the Scottish Highlands, Highland Clans and Highland Regiments* in two volumes, with Part Third relating the History of the Highland regiments. The early text again repeated Browne's 1838 *History* with additions up to 1871 including the Crimean War and the Indian Mutiny, relying heavily on the Regimental Record of Service.

In the 1880s, a series of Historical Records of the 42nd Royal Highlanders from 1729 to 1874 (1874), from 1729 to 1881 (1881), and a Jubilee version from 1729 to 1887 (1887) was published by Thomas C. Jack. No author is cited, and again the text started with Browne's with supplementary material from the Regimental Record of Service.

1891: Lieutenant Colonel George Sandeman, 3rd Battalion, The Black Watch, wrote a short pamphlet drawn mainly from Stewart of Garth's *Sketches*.

1893: Lieutenant Colonel Percy Groves wrote an illustrated history.

1896: Archibald Forbes, *The Black Watch*. He used much of Stewart of Garth's narrative, repeating his errors, but with some rewording. The copy in the BWRL annotated by Lieutenant Colonel Mackay Scobie details some of Forbes's errors.

1908: *A Military History of Perthshire 1660–1902*, edited by the Marchioness of Tullibardine. The correct date for the raising of the Independent Companies was given as 1725.

1908: H.D. MacWilliam published *A Black Watch Episode of the Year 1731*, with relevant documents.

1908: Arthur Wauchope's *A Short History of The Black Watch* repeated earlier histories, making some factual errors, but giving an excellent account of the South African War in which he served.

1910: H.D. MacWilliam edited *The Official Records of The Black Watch Mutiny*, also correcting earlier factual errors.

In many contemporary accounts 'England' and 'English' is used even when, after 1707, the correct terminology would be to talk of 'Britain' and 'British'. To retain as much authenticity as possible, I have kept original spellings and avoided peppering the narrative with 'sic'!

Select Chronology

1707   Act of Union joining the Kingdoms of England and Scotland.

1714   Death of Queen Anne; accession of George I, great-grandson of James I of England and VI of Scotland.

1715   First Jacobite Uprising.

1717   Act disarming the Highlanders passed.

1718   Quadruple Alliance formed between England, France, Dutch Republic (of the United Netherlands) and Austria against Spain.

1721   Sir Robert Walpole becomes Prime Minister.

1725   Royal Warrant issued by George I to raise six independent companies in Scotland, the three larger ones to comprise a 'Captain, two Lieutenants, three Sergeants, three Corporalls, two Drummers, and sixty effective private Men'. The three smaller Companies consisted of one 'Lieutenant, One Ensign, Two Sergeants, Two Corporalls, One Drum[mer], and Thirty Effective Private Men' (WO 24/118,TNA).
        General George Wade appointed Commander-in-Chief of His Majesty's Forces, Castles, Forts, and Barracks in North Britain, &c.

1727   Death of George I; accession of his son, George II. Independent companies augmented.

1733   Opening of the Tay Bridge.

1739   Royal Warrant issued by George II to form the six Independent companies and four additional companies into a regiment of the British Army, numbered the 43rd in the Line of Foot.
        Whereas we have thought fit, that a Regt of Foot be forthwith formed under your command to consist of ten Companys, each to contain One Captain, One Lieutenant, one Ensign, three Sergeants, Three Corporals, Two Drummers and Seventy effective private Men, which said Regt shall be partly formed out of Our Six indept

Companys of Foot in the Highlands of North Britain; three of which are now commanded by Captains, and three by Captain Lieutenants. Our Will and Pleasure therefore is, that one sergeant, one corporal and Fifty private Men be forthwith taken out of the three Companys, commanded by Captains; and ten private Men only taken out of the three commanded by Captain Lieutenants, making One Hundred and Eighty private Men, who are to be equally distributed in the Four Companys hereby to be raised; And the three Sergeants and Three Corporals to be draughted as aforesaid, to be placed to such of the Four Companys as you shall judge proper.

(7 November 1739, WO 26/19, TNA)

John Lindsay, Earl of Crawford, appointed Colonel of the Regiment, which becomes known as Crawford's Highlanders or the Highland Regiment.

Captains of the new companies appointed.

John Wesley and George Whitefield begin religious revival of Anglican Church.

Britain at war with Spain.

1740　First muster of the Highland Regiment on the banks of the river Tay.

1741　Earl of Crawford replaced by Hugh, Lord Sempill as Colonel of the Regiment, now known as Sempill's Highlanders or the Highland Regiment.

1742　Spencer Compton, the Earl of Wilmington, becomes Prime Minister.

1743　Henry Pelham becomes Prime Minister; war of the Austrian Succession; Sempill's Highlanders ordered to London; some soldiers mutiny; trial, execution of three and deportation of remaining mutineers.

The Highland Regiment embarks for Flanders.

Battle of Dettingen 27 June.

1745　Battle of Fontenoy 11 May: soldiers of the Highland Regiment described as 'the Highland Furies'.

Lord John Murray appointed Colonel of the Regiment, known (until his death in 1787) as Murray's Highlanders.

Second Jacobite Uprising: Battle of Prestonpans 21 September. The Highland Regiment remains in the south of England, ordered to sail to North America, but is driven back by adverse winds, then ordered to the coast of France, then Ireland.

1746 Battle of Falkirk 17 January: death of Sir Robert Munro of Foulis, the Highland Regiment's first Lieutenant Colonel.

Battle of Culloden 16 April: defeat of the Jacobites.

Highlanders disarmed and forbidden to wear Highland dress, except those serving in a Highland Regiment.

1747 Regiment returns to England, then Flanders.

1748 Treaty of Aix-la-Chapelle signifies end of the war of the Austrian Succession.

Regiment returns to England, then Ireland.

1749 Regiment given numerical listing of 42nd in the Line of Foot, following the reduction of the former 42nd Regiment, Oglethorpe's.

George Frideric Handel's *Music for the Royal Fireworks* performed in Green Park, London, to celebrate the end of the war of the Austrian Succession.

1751 Royal Warrant confirming numerical listings; Regiment now known as the 42nd or still as The Highland Regiment.

1754 Thomas Pelham-Holles, Duke of Newcastle, becomes Prime Minister.

1755 General Braddock and British forces defeated on the Monongahela river near Fort Duquesne 9 July.

1756 William Cavendish, Duke of Devonshire, becomes Prime Minister.

French Indian Wars in North America.

42nd embarks for North America, landing in New York.

In India, over 100 British prisoners held by the Nawab of Bengal die of suffocation in guardroom, subsequently known as the 'Black Hole' of Calcutta.

1757   Newcastle's second term of office as Prime Minister.
        British victory at the Battle of Plassey in India.

1758   42nd's first engagement in North America at Fort Carillon,
        known as Ticonderoga 8 July. Death of Viscount Howe.
        By Royal Warrant dated 22 July, the title 'Royal' given to the
        Regiment, now known as the 42nd Royal Highland Regiment,
        also as 'Royal Highlanders'; a 2nd Battalion raised.
        Sovereign's and Regimental Colours presented, although no
        record remains indicating whether there was one stand or
        two.
        General Jeffrey Amherst appointed Commander-in-Chief in
        North America.

1759   2nd Battalion embarks for the West Indies; attack on
        Martinique; capture of Guadeloupe; 1st Battalion 42nd takes
        part in the capture of Ticonderoga and Crown Point; General
        James Wolfe killed during the successful capture of Quebec
        13 September.

1760   Death of George II; accession of his grandson, George III.
        Both Battalions involved in the capture of Montreal.

1762   John Stuart, Earl of Bute, becomes Prime Minister.
        The 42nd arrives in the West Indies; both battalions involved
        in the capture of Martinique and Havana, Cuba; Regiment
        returns to North America.
        Birth of Lachlan Macquarie, future Commanding Officer of
        73rd, Governor of New South Wales and 'father of Australia'.

1763   George Grenville becomes Prime Minister. Treaty of Paris.
        Proclamation Line.
        2nd Battalion 42nd disbanded. War against the Iroquois
        Confederacy known as Pontiac's War; 42nd involved in the
        Battle of Bushy Run at Edge Hill. General Thomas Gage
        appointed Commander-in-Chief of North America.

1764   Campaign under Colonel Bouquet to Muskingum river.
        Expedition under Captain Thomas Stirling to Fort de Chartres,
        the furthest west in North America soldiers of the 42nd ever
        serve.

1765 Charles Watson-Wentworth, Marquess of Rockingham, becomes Prime Minister.

1766 William Pitt, the Elder, Earl of Chatham, becomes Prime Minister.

1767 42nd leaves North America for Ireland.

1768 Augustus Fitzroy, Duke of Grafton, becomes Prime Minister. Death of James III, the Old Pretender.

Royal Warrant grants the Regiment the right to bear on the Colours under the King's cipher, St Andrew with the Latin motto of the Order of the Thistle, *Nemo me impune lacessit* (No one provokes me with impunity).

1770 Frederick, Lord North, becomes Prime Minister.

1771 Regimental Records damaged in a shipwreck off the Irish coast; some are lost.

1773 American colonists board tea ships in Boston harbour and empty the tea-chests into the sea – the event known as the Boston Tea Party.

1775 42nd returns to Scotland.

First fighting of the 'American War of Independence' at Lexington; Battle of Bunker Hill 17 June. George Washington appointed Commander-in-Chief of colonial forces, known as the 'Continental Army'.

1776 American Declaration of Independence 4 July.

The 42nd embarks for North America, landing at Staten Island. Battle of White Plains 28 October; attack on Fort Washington and Fort Lee.

Adam Smith publishes his magnum opus, *An Inquiry into the Nature and Causes of the Wealth of Nations.*

1777 American attack on the 42nd at Pisquatua. Battles of Brandywine river 11 September, Paoli Tavern 20/21 September, Germantown 4 October; British surrender at Saratoga 17 October.

1778 France recognises American independence. Battle of Monmouth 28 June.

1779   42nd engaged at Elizabeth Town; orders passed to raise a 2nd Battalion.

1780   British capture of Charleston; 2nd Battalion embodied at Perth: Colours presented.

1781   British surrender at Yorktown, Earl Cornwallis taken prisoner 19 October.
Hyder Ali becomes ruler of Mysore, invades the Carnatic in southern India.

1782   Rockingham's second term as Prime Minister but he dies in office; succeeded by William Petty-FitzMaurice, Earl of Shelburne.
British evacuation of Savannah; preliminary peace terms signed. 2nd Battalion 42nd arrives in India, engaged in Mysore Wars; death of Hyder Ali in December, succeeded by his son, Tipu Sultan.

1783   William Cavendish-Bentinck, Duke of Portland, becomes Prime Minister, succeeded by William Pitt the Younger, Britain's youngest Prime Minister, aged twenty-four.
Treaty of Versailles signed between Britain, France, Spain and the United States: independence of the United States of America recognised.
1st Battalion 42nd departs to Nova Scotia.
2nd Battalion 42nd under siege in Mangalore.

1784   Siege of Mangalore raised in January; 2nd Battalion 42nd becomes known as Mangaloris or Old Mangalores.

1785   New Colours presented to the 1st Battalion 42nd in Nova Scotia; later laid up in the House of Novar, Ross-shire.

1786   2nd Battalion 42nd becomes 73rd (Highland) Regiment of Foot; embodied at Dinapore in India; receives new Colours.
Cornwallis becomes Governor-General of India.

1787   Death of Lord John Murray, the 42nd's longest serving Colonel of the Regiment.
Arthur Wellesley, the future Duke of Wellington, commissioned in the 73rd as an ensign.

1788   Death of 'Bonnie Prince Charlie', the Young Pretender.

1789   French Revolution; storming of the Bastille.

George Washington becomes first President of the United States.

42nd returns to Britain from Nova Scotia.

1791   73rd engaged in renewed fighting against Tipu Sultan.

1792   The 'Terror' in France.

First Coalition of Austria, Prussia, Britain, Spain, Dutch Republic (of the United Netherlands) against France.

The 'Year of the Sheep': 42nd ordered to the north of Scotland to quell disturbances.

Treaty of Seringapatam signed with Tipu Sultan in India.

1793   Execution of Louis XVI and Marie Antoinette. France declares war against Britain and Dutch Republic.

42nd embarks for Flanders.

73rd march against French settlement of Pondicherry.

Sir John Shore becomes Governor-General of India.

1794   42nd returns to Britain, re-embarks for Flanders; remaining Regimental records lost.

1795   Formation of the Directory in France (until 1799).

Dutch Republic annexed by France, known as Batavian Republic.

42nd engaged in action at Geldermalsen; returns to Britain; parade at Royston and distribution of 'Red Hackles', Regiment departs for West Indies, only five companies arrive, the remaining five and headquarters later going to Gibraltar.

73rd leaves India to fight against Dutch in Ceylon.

1797   Five companies of the 42nd embark from West Indies for Gibraltar and are reunited with the Regiment.

George Washington succeeded by John Adams as President of the USA.

73rd returns to India from Ceylon.

1798   Battles of the Pyramids and the Nile; British victory at Aboukir Bay.

42nd engaged in capture of Minorca.

Second Coalition of Austria, Britain, Russia, Naples, Ottoman Empire, Papal States, Portugal against France.

The Earl of Mornington, Arthur Wellesley's brother, becomes Governor-General of India.

1799   Napoleon Bonaparte becomes First Consul of France (18 Brumaire) on 9 November.

Death of George Washington.

73rd engaged in the siege and capture of Seringapatam; death of Tipu Sultan, the 'Tiger of Mysore'.

1800   French victory against Austria in Italy at Battle of Marengo; 42nd leave Minorca for Gibraltar, Malta, then Bay of Marmorice.

1801   Act of Union uniting Great Britain (England and Scotland) with Ireland under the name of the United Kingdom of Great Britain and Ireland; Henry Addington succeeds Pitt as Prime Minister.

42nd arrives in Egypt. Battles of Aboukir and Alexandria; death of Sir Ralph Abercromby; Regiment returns to England; awarded badge of Sphinx superscribed Egypt.

1802   Treaty of Amiens; 42nd to Scotland; new Colours presented in Edinburgh, the first to bear the new distinction of the Sphinx superscribed Egypt; these Colours see the most continuous fighting of any stand and are later laid up in Balhousie Castle, Perth.

1803   Additional Forces Act. 2nd Battalion 42nd raised.

1804   Pitt's second term as Prime Minister.

1805   Third Coalition: Austria, Britain, Russia and Sweden against France.

British victory at Trafalgar on 21 October; death of Admiral Lord Nelson.

French victory against Austrians and Russians at Austerlitz on 2 December.

1st Battalion 42nd embarks for Gibraltar.

2nd Battalion 42nd embarks for Ireland.

73rd embarks for Britain, arrives 1806.

Cornwallis, now Marquess, becomes Governor-General of India, but dies soon after his arrival.

1806 Pitt dies in office; succeeded as Prime Minister by William Wyndham, Lord Grenville. Napoleon issues Berlin Decree on 21 November.

Fourth Coalition: Prussia, Russia, Saxony against France.

73rd Highland Regiment arrives in Britain from India.

1807 Duke of Portland's second term of office as Prime Minister. Act passed by Britain for the abolition of the slave trade. The Lord Minto becomes Governor-General of India. Treaty of Tilsit.

1808 French defeat at Vimeiro, Portugal 21 August; Convention of Cintra.

1st Battalion 42nd arrives in the Peninsula; retreat to Corunna under the command of Lieutenant General Sir John Moore.

73rd ordered to Australia; 2nd Battalion 73rd raised; new Colours received.

1809 Arrival of British army at Corunna; battle at Elvina 16 January, death of Sir John Moore.

1st Battalion 42nd returns to England and then embarks for Flanders.

Spencer Perceval becomes Prime Minister; descent of George III into madness and beginning of Regency period under his son, the future George IV.

Fifth Coalition: Austria and Britain against France.

Battle of Talavera 28 July in Spain: Arthur Wellesley becomes Viscount Wellington of Talavera.

2nd Battalion 42nd embarks for the Peninsula.

Lachlan Macquarie appointed Governor of New South Wales.

1st Battalion 73rd sails for Australia; 73rd gives up Highland dress.

1810 Battle of Busaco 27 September.

1811 Battle of Fuentes d'Onor 3–5 May.

1812 Robert Banks Jenkinson, Earl of Liverpool, becomes Prime

Minister after the assassination of Spencer Perceval. The first steam vessel plies on the river Clyde.

Battles of Ciudad Rodrigo and Salamanca 22 July; Wellington enters Madrid; failed British attempt on Burgos.

French invasion of and withdrawal from Russia, June to December.

1st Battalion 42nd returns to the Peninsula, 2nd Battalion 42nd returns to England.

1813   Sixth Coalition: Britain and Russia, joined by Austria, Prussia, Sweden and German States against France. Battle of Vittoria 21 June.

Siege of San Sebastian; Battle of Nivelle; Allied forces cross the Nive.

2nd Battalion 73rd's first military engagement at the Battle of Gorde.

French defeat at Leipzig (Battle of the Nations).

The Earl of Moira becomes Governor-General of India.

1814   Battles of Orthez 27 February and Toulouse 10 April.

Napoleon abdicates as Emperor and is exiled to Elba.

1st Battalion 42nd to Ireland.

2nd Battalion 42nd disbanded.

1st Battalion 73rd embarks for Ceylon from Australia.

Publication of Walter Scott's novel *Waverley*.

1815   Napoleon returns to France. Louis XVIII leaves Paris for Ghent.

Seventh Coalition: Austria, Britain, German States, Russia, Prussia, Sweden, against France.

Battles of Ligny, Quatre Bras 16 June and Waterloo 18 June. 42nd and 2nd Battalion 73rd fight at Quatre Bras and Waterloo; death of 42nd's commanding officer, Lieutenant Colonel Sir Robert Macara, at Quatre Bras.

Memorial cairn erected at Tor Alvic in his memory and of all those who fell in the Peninsular and Waterloo campaigns.

Napoleon abdicates as Emperor and is exiled to St Helena.

1st Battalion 73rd takes part in capture of Kandy, Ceylon.

42nd returns to Britain followed by 2nd Battalion 73rd.

1816 73rd (Highland) Regiment becomes known as 73rd Regiment of Foot.

1817 42nd to Ireland. Highland Society Vase presented to the Regiment.

2nd Battalion 73rd disbanded.

1818 42nd receives new Colours, although there is no record of their presentation and they saw no active service.

1820 Death of George III. Accession of his son, George IV.

1821 73rd ordered to return to Britain from Ceylon.

Death of Napoleon Bonaparte.

Lachlan Macquarie resigns as Governor of New South Wales.

1822 Army Order recognises the 42nd's exclusive right to wear the Red Hackle.

1823 Britain recognises independence of the South American republics.

73rd embarks for Ireland.

Lord Amherst becomes Governor-General of India.

1825 42nd leaves Ireland for Gibraltar.

1826 73rd ordered to Britain to quell disturbances in the north of England, returns to Ireland.

1827 George Canning becomes Prime Minister, but dies soon after taking office; succeeded by Frederick John Robinson, Viscount Goderich.

73rd receives new Colours at Waterford; leaves Ireland for Gibraltar.

1828 Arthur Wellesley, Duke of Wellington, becomes Prime Minister.

Lord William Bentinck becomes Governor-General of India.

1829 Emancipation of Catholics.

73rd embarks for Malta.

1830 Death of George IV; accession of his brother William IV.

Charles, Earl Grey, becomes Prime Minister.

First great railway between Liverpool and Manchester opened.

1832   Viscount Melbourne becomes Prime Minister.
       Parliamentary Reform Act, known as 'Great Charter of 1832',
       passed.
       42nd embarks for Malta.

1834   William Lamb, Viscount Melbourne, becomes Prime Minister
       but resigns and is briefly succeeded by Wellington then by
       Sir Robert Peel.
       73rd embarks for the Ionian Islands, 42nd follows.

1835   Melbourne's second term as Prime Minister.

1836   42nd returns to Scotland. Lord Auckland becomes Governor-
       General of India.

1837   Death of William IV; accession of his niece, Queen Victoria.

1838   42nd embarks for Ireland; 73rd embarks for service in Lower
       and Upper Canada.

1839   New Colours presented to the 42nd at Dublin. These Colours
       are the last to carry the same centre badges and Battle Honours
       and the XLII on top corners, later laid up in Dunkeld
       Cathedral.
       Beginning of the First Afghan War and First Opium War.

1840   'Penny postage' system introduced, fixing postage to 'a penny
       on all letters between all places in the United Kingdom'.
       42nd embarks for Ionian Islands.

1841   Peel's second term of office as Prime Minister.
       73rd arrives in Britain from Upper Canada: receives new
       Colours at Gosport.

1842   Lord Ellenborough becomes Governor-General of India.
       British withdrawal from Afghanistan; decimation of the army
       in the Khurd Kabul pass.
       Reserve Battalion 42nd raised in Scotland.
       42nd embarks for Malta with Reserve Battalion.

1844   Army Regulations alter the badge on the Queen's Colour to
       the Crown with the XLII in the centre. Battle Honours to be
       carried on the Regimental Colour.
       73rd embarks for Ireland.
       Sir Henry Hardinge becomes Governor-General of India.

1845   73rd departs for South Africa to fight in the amaXhosa Frontier
       Wars, waylaid in Montevideo, South America.
       Great Irish Potato Famine.
1846   Lord John Russell becomes Prime Minister.
       Death of Sir Robert Henry Dick, former Lieutenant Colonel
       of the 42nd and Colonel of the 73rd, at the Battle of Sobraon
       during the Sikh Wars in India.
       73rd arrives in South Africa from South America.
1847   42nd and Reserve stationed in Bermuda.
1848   Earl of Dalhousie becomes Governor-General of India.
1850   Reserve Battalion amalgamated with 1st Battalion 42nd.
1851   Great Exhibition at the Crystal Palace in London.
       42nd departs from Bermuda for Nova Scotia.
1852   Edward Smith-Stanley, Earl of Derby, becomes Prime Minister,
       succeeded by George Hamilton-Gordon, Earl of Aberdeen.
       Death of Duke of Wellington.
       Wreck of HMS *Birkenhead* off the coast of South Africa; from
       which the Birkenhead drill was established: 'woman and chil-
       dren first' (phrase adopted in 1860).
1853   42nd returns to England.
1854   Britain, France, Turkey declare war on Russia.
       42nd embarks for the Crimea; battles for the heights of Alma
       20 September and Balaclava: charge of the Heavy and Light
       Brigades 25 October; Battle of Inkerman 5 November.
1855   Aberdeen succeeded as Prime Minister by Henry John Temple,
       Viscount Palmerston. Fall of Sebastopol.
1856   42nd returns to Britain, based at Dover. Second Opium War
       (until 1860). Viscount Canning becomes Governor-General
       of India.
1857   Mutiny of Indian sepoys at Meerut, also known as First Indian
       War of Independence.
       42nd embarks for India; engaged in the battle of Cawnpore
       and at Bithur; the Regiment acquires the 'regimental gong'.
1858   Derby's second term of office as Prime Minister. Government
       of India Act; authority transferred from the East India

Company to the British Crown; Governor General becomes the Sovereign's representative or Viceroy.

42nd engaged in capture of Lucknow; battle of Bareilly; attack on Fort Ruhya 15 April; death of Brigadier Adrian Hope.

73rd embarks from South Africa for India.

1859   Palmerston's second term of office as Prime Minister.

Battle of the Sarda river; Maylah and Sissaya Ghats.

Peace in India established.

1861   Death of Prince Albert; Queen Victoria temporarily withdraws from public life.

New Colours presented to the 42nd at Bareilly (later laid up at the Royal Military College, Sandhurst); Regiment changes title to the 42nd Royal Highlanders, The Black Watch Regiment.

73rd returns to Britain.

1862   Royal Commission appointed to 'inquire into the condition of the Volunteer Force in Great Britain'.

Change of title of the 73rd to the 73rd (Perthshire) Regiment of Foot; receives new Colours at Plymouth.

Earl of Elgin becomes Viceroy of India.

1863   42nd involved in 'Camp Exercise' in Lahore, India.

1864   Sir John Lawrence becomes Viceroy of India.

73rd stationed in Ireland.

1865   Palmerston dies in office and Russell becomes Prime Minister.

1866   Derby's third term as Prime Minister.

73rd embarks for Hong Kong.

1867   Second Parliamentary Reform Act.

1868   Benjamin Disraeli becomes Prime Minister, followed by William Gladstone.

42nd arrives Britain from India, having travelled via Suez and Alexandria.

73rd stationed in Singapore and Ceylon.

1869   Suez Canal opened after ten years' construction.

1870   Army Enlistment (Short Services) Act; Education Act.

1871   Regulation of the Forces Act.

42nd posted to Devonport, then Dartmoor; new Colours presented to the Regiment.

1872 Ballot Act; Memorial to the fallen since 1739 unveiled at Dunkeld Cathedral; Colours which had been carried during the Crimean War and Indian Mutiny laid up at Dunkeld. Lord Northbrook becomes Governor-General and Viceroy of India.

1873 Ashanti War; 42nd embarks for West Africa.

1874 Disraeli's second term of office as Prime Minister; more social reforms enacted.
42nd disembarks on the Gold Coast; battles of Amoaful and Ordahsu; capture and burning of Coomassie; 42nd returns to England, embarks for Malta.
73rd arrives in India.

1876 73rd takes part in Grand Review in Delhi in front of the Prince of Wales. Lord Lytton becomes Viceroy of India.
Queen Victoria becomes Empress of India.

1878 Congress of Berlin; second British war in Afghanistan.
42nd posted to Cyprus, then Gibraltar.

1879 42nd returns to Britain.

1880 Gladstone's second term as Prime Minister.
First South African War against the Boer population.
Marquess of Ripon becomes Viceroy of India.

1881 73rd returns from India. Cardwell Reforms: amalgamation of the 42nd and 73rd to form the 1st and 2nd Battalions under the title The Royal Highlanders (The Black Watch).

1882 1st Battalion embarks for Egypt; battle of Tel-el-Kebir 13 September.

1883 Birth of the future Field Marshal Earl Wavell.

1884 Third Parliamentary Reform Act. Earl of Dufferin becomes Viceroy of India.
1st Battalion 42nd engaged in battles of El Teb 29 February and Tamai 13 March.

1885 Nile expedition to relieve General Charles Gordon in Khartoum; death of Gordon; Battle of Kirbekan 10 February.
2nd Battalion embarks for Ireland.

1886   Gladstone's third term as Prime Minister, succeeded by Robert Gascoyne-Cecil, Marquess of Salisbury.
       1st Battalion embarks for Malta.
1887   Queen Victoria's Golden Jubilee.
       Black Watch monument at Aberfeldy dedicated.
1888   Marquess of Lansdowne becomes Viceroy of India.
1889   World's Fair: the Eiffel Tower built, constituting the tallest man-made structure in the world for forty-one years.
       1st Battalion leaves Malta for Gibraltar.
       2nd Battalion receives new Colours in Belfast.
1892   Gladstone's fourth term as Prime Minister.
1893   1st Battalion arrives in Egypt; half battalion proceeds to Mauritius, half to South Africa.
1894   Archibald Primrose, Earl of Rosebery, becomes Prime Minister.
       Earl of Elgin becomes Viceroy of India.
1895   Salisbury's second term of office as Prime Minister.
       Jameson raid: Cecil Rhodes resigns as Prime Minister in South Africa.
1896   1st Battalion, reunited in Mauritius, embarks for India; 2nd Battalion stationed in Britain.
1897   Queen Victoria's Diamond Jubilee.
1899   1st Battalion ordered from India to Burma but move cancelled.
       Lord Curzon of Kedleston becomes Viceroy of India.
       Second South African War against the Boers begins.
       2nd Battalion leaves Britain for South Africa.

Notes

Abbreviations

Adm: Admiral; Bn: Battalion; Bt: Brevet; Capt: Captain; Col: Colonel; Cpl: Corporal; Gen: General; Lcpl: Lance Corporal Lt: Lieutenant; Maj: Major; NCO: Non-Commissioned officer; Pte: Private; RAdm: Rear Admiral; Sgt: Sergeant; VAdm: Vice Admiral.

BL: British Library, London
BWRA: Black Watch Regimental Archives
BWRL: Black Watch Regimental Library
BWRM: Black Watch Regimental Museum
CO: Colonial Office
JSAHR: *Journal of the Society for Army Historical Research*
MUL: Macquarie University Library
NLNZ: National Library of New Zealand
NLS: National Library of Scotland
NMS: National Museums Scotland
NRS: National Records of Scotland
TNA: The National Archives, London
WO: War Office

1. Raising the Regiment 1739

1. 'The Garb of Old Gaul', Sir Henry Erskine of Lava, Stirlingshire (*c.*1710–65), written *c.*1763.
2. Andrew Ross, The Historic Succession of The Black Watch, Tullibardine (ed.), *A Military History of Perthshire 1660–1902*, p. 28. He based his research on his earlier book, *Old Scottish Regimental Colours* (1885). Its importance was in refuting the claims of Stewart of Garth that 'independent companies' were

not formed until 1729/30. A King's Guard, consisting of a few 100 mounted troops, was raised in 1603 and two 'Highland Captaincies' of twenty men in 1624. The early companies varied in number and were frequently disbanded and re-raised. An early record is dated 3 Aug. 1667, when Charles II gave a commission under the Great Seal to John Murray, 2nd Earl of Atholl, whose family were staunch Royalists during the Civil War. In 1689 four independent companies were in existence, later increased to five. See Simpson, *The Independent Highland Companies, 1603–1760*, pp. 49, 52; Mitchell, *A Popular History of the Highlands*, p. 595; Davidson, 'The Black Watch, 1725–1815', *JSAHR*, 84, 2006, p. 225. The Royal Regiment (later Royal Scots, 1st Foot) raised in 1633 was a Lowland Regiment.

3. General George Wade (1673–1748), 'Report &c., Relating to the Highlands', quoted in Allardyce (ed.), *Historical Papers Relating to the Jacobite Period 1699–1750*, pp. 131–49.

4. Lovat's Memorial, quoted in Salmond, *Wade in Scotland*, pp. 27–31.

5. Wade, 'Report &c., Relating to the Highlands', quoted in Allardyce (ed.), *Historical Papers*, pp. 131–49; and see MacWilliam, *Official Records*, p. xxi.

6. Establishment of General and other Officers and Six Independent Companies of Foot in North Britain commencing the 24th of April 1725, dated 31 May 1725, WO 24/118, TNA. See Ross, 'Historic Succession', Tullibardine (ed.), *Military History of Perthshire 1660–1902*, pp. 48, 51. Forbes, *The 'Black Watch'*, p. 3, claims that it was his antecedent, Duncan Forbes of Culloden, who recommended the authorities in 1729 to raise independent companies. Stewart of Garth, *Sketches of the Character, Manners, and Present State of the Highlanders of Scotland*, II, 3rd ed., wrongly gives the date as 1729–30, p. 249. Wauchope, *A Short History of The Black Watch*, p. 4, says four were initially raised in 1725 'and the system proving an unqualified success, by 1729 two more companies had been embodied'. This is also an error which has been repeated by other historians. See Davidson, 'Pieces of Evidence Concerning the Origin and Early Years of the Black Watch (1)', Notes and Documents, 1781, *JSAHR*, 84, Spring 2006, pp. 65–7.

7. Forbes, *The 'Black Watch'*, p. 4. The Disarming Act was passed in 1717.

8. See 'Establishment of General and other Officers and Six Independent Companies of Foot in North Britain commencing the 24th of April 1725', dated 31 May 1725, WO 24/118, TNA. Stewart of Garth, *Sketches*, I, 3rd ed., pp. 248–9, wrongly states that the larger companies had 100 men and the smaller 70.

9. Stewart of Garth, *Sketches*, I, 3rd ed., p. 77. Stewart of Garth's narrative up to its conclusion in vol. II, p. 61, which ends with the Battle of Waterloo, is repeated almost verbatim in The Record of Service, 42nd, 1729–1873, pp. 1–173, BWRA 0079. For ease of reference, I have used Stewart of Garth.

10. Wade, quoted in MacWilliam, *The Black Watch Tartan*, pp. 5, 7. After exhaustive research, H.D. MacWilliam maintained that the Black Watch tartan was similar to the Campbells', although uniformity would have been gradual. Official 'Clan' tartans came after 1745.

11. H.D. MacWilliam, 'Origin of the Black Watch 1725–1739', *Celtic Monthly*, XXI, 1913, p. 85, states: 'Precisely at what date the designation arose is not likely to be ascertained now, but it was probably applied soon after the raising of the companies in 1725.' He quotes a letter dated 20 Dec. 1735 in which the companies are referred to as 'our Northern troops alias blak Watch'. See also Howard, *The Black Watch*, p. 11; Simpson, *The Independent Highland Companies*, p. 23.

12. Burt, *Burt's Letters from the North of Scotland*, Letter XIX, ed. Simmons, p. 201.

13. Letter, 3 Nov. 1725, quoted in MacWilliam, 'Origin of the Black Watch 1725–1739', *Celtic Monthly*, XXI, pp. 143–4.

14. Inverness, 15 Nov. (1728), quoted in Salmond, *Wade*, p. 90. Sir Henry Pelham, 5 May 1726, quoted in MacWilliam, 'Origin of the Black Watch 1725–1739', *Celtic Monthly*, XXI, p. 144.

15. Fort George pre-1746 is not to be confused with the Fort George built in a slightly different location after Culloden. Fort Augustus was formerly Kiliwhimin, renamed after 1715. Oliver Cromwell first saw the advantage of a series of forts on the line of the Great Glen as a method of controlling the Highlanders: Salmond, *Wade*, p. 43.

16. Duncan Forbes (1685–1747) to the Duke of Newcastle, Edinburgh, 18 Aug. 1726, Warrand (ed.), *More Culloden Papers*, III, p. 8.

17. Duncan Forbes to Charles Delafaye, Inverness, 2 Sept. 1726, ibid., p. 9.

18. The number of sergeants (serjeants) and corporals was increased and lieutenants in the smaller companies were promoted to the rank of captain lieutenant. There was also to be an extra drummer and sixty (instead of thirty) 'Effective Private Men'. See Warrant to Capt Lt Colin Campbell of Skipness, St James, 27 January 1726/7, James Hepburne Scott, private collection. See Ross, 'Historic Succession', Tullibardine (ed.), *Military History of Perthshire 1660–1902*, pp. 50–1. Source: War Office Estab. Books. Annual cost of £9,140. 17s. Taylor, *The Military Roads in Scotland*, 1996, p. 21.

19. *The Knock Notebook of 1731–1733*, a relic of the New Independent Companies, owned by Mr James McArthur of Kirkmichael, Banffshire, found in the farmhouse of Knock, p. 7. That the independent companies were stationed in the same barracks as at Ruthven in 1731 can be seen as an early step towards regimentation.

20. Forbes, *The 'Black Watch'*, p. 6.

21. Wade to Lord Islay, 1731, quoted in Taylor, *Military Roads in Scotland*, p. 22.

22. MacWilliam, *A Black Watch Episode 1731*, p. 9. His account includes exceptional contemporary records of a court martial.

23. MacWilliam, 'Origin of the Black Watch 1725–1739', *Celtic Monthly*, XXI, p. 183, citing Burt. Pipers were not officially listed until 1854; until then they were generally listed as drummers: see Ross, 'The Historic Succession of The Black Watch', Tullibardine (ed.), *Military History of Perthshire 1660–1902*, pp. 41–5. There is a mention of a 'pyper' in the 1730s *Knock Notebook*, p. 13. There was also Piper McDonald (Macdonnel) in the grenadier company –

one of the condemned mutineers in 1743. See Cram, Duthie, Irwin and Taylor, *A Collection of Pipe Music of The Black Watch*. Throughout history, pipers held an important position in the lives of soldiers, playing familiar tunes and raising their spirits before battle.

24. *Caledonian Mercury*, 8 Aug. 1732, Mf.N.776, NLS.
25. See MacWilliam, 'Origin of the Black Watch 1725–1739,' *Celtic Monthly*, XXII, 1914, p. 20. Also Andrew Mackillop, '*More Fruitful than the Soil*', p. 18, who describes how the independent companies often compounded local differences and increased tensions between the clans.
26. Lovat to Ludovick Grant, 30 July 1738, quoted in MacWilliam, 'Origin of the Black Watch 1725–1739', *Celtic Monthly*, XXII, p. 56.
27. Excerpts from letters from Simon, Lord Lovat to Lt Col William Kennedy, Lt Governor of Fort George, Inverness, Beaufort, 13 June 1739, BWRA 0389/L.
28. In 1731 Major Scipio Duroure, appointed by Wade in 1726 with responsibility for 'the care and command of the Highland Companies, in regard to their good order & discipline', had wanted 'to have the Hyland Companys regimented, and himself eyr Colonell, or Lieut-Coll.' James Grant, younger of Rothiemurchus, to Robert Grant of Tammore, 26 Nov. 1731, quoted in MacWilliam, 'Origin of the Black Watch 1725–1739', *Celtic Monthly*, XXI, p. 202. In 1728 Duncan Forbes had suggested raising four or five regiments to Lord Justice Clerk, quoted in Prebble, *Mutiny*, p. 33.
29. Anon., *A Short History of the Highland Regiment*, p. 18. Col Paul P. Hutchison (Foreword, 1963 ed.) describes the author as 'obviously a Sassenach of London', i.e. what the Scots called a Saxon, from the Gaelic *Sasunnuch*. War was declared on Spain on 3 Nov. 1739.
30. 'Our will and Pleasure therefore is that the Establishment for our Said Regiment do commence and take place from the 25th day of October 1739.' This order is dated 22 March 1739/40, in the thirteenth year of our reign, WO 24/186, TNA. As a Lowlander, Crawford was most probably chosen in order not to show a preference to one or other Highland clan.
31. John Lindsay, 20th Earl of Crawford (1702–1749). See Rolt, *Memoirs of the Life of the Late Right Honourable John Lindesay: Earl of Craufurd*, pp. 270–1. After his father died in 1713, Queen Anne maintained and educated the family. Forbes, *The 'Black Watch'*, p. 7.
32. Order for forming a Regt of Foot under the command of the Right Honourable John Earl of Crawford, dated 7 Nov. 1739, WO 26/19, p. 218, TNA. Note: the Volunteers to be raised *in any Country or Part of our Kingdom of Great Britain*.
33. Order to the Earl of Crawford to raise Voluntiers to compleat the Regt of Foot under his Command, dated 7 Nov. 1739, WO 26/19, p. 219, TNA. Also cited in Macwilliam (ed.), *Official Records of the Black Watch Mutiny*, p. xxxii. Stewart cites an almost identical order dated 25 October, which includes the words 'the men to be natives of that country and none other to be taken'.

Instead of 70 private men, the order which he reproduces states 100. See *Sketches*, I, 3rd ed. p. 252. See Prebble, *Mutiny*, p. 35, and McCulloch, *Sons of the Mountain*, I, p. xvi, who suggest that Stewart inserted the words out of loyalty to his Scottish heritage.

34. 'Commissions for a Regiment of Foot to be forthwith raised for His Majesty's Service, under the command of John Earl of Crawford . . .' (dated between 25 Oct. and 1 Nov. 1739), SP 44/181, p. 502, TNA.

35. Sir Robert Munro of Foulis (1684–1746), MP 1710–41. His mother, Jean, was Duncan Forbes's aunt and also enjoyed the Duke of Argyll's patronage. John Campbell of Carrick was a former independent company captain. See Rolt, *John Lindesay: Earl of Craufurd*, pp. 46–7, who relates how Crawford with some friends went into the garden of Mr Campbell senior and one of his friends was caught in a snare. 'This adventure was the foundation of an intimate friendship between the young earl of Craufurd and young Mr Campbell; which subsisted till the death of the latter.'

36. John Munro of Newmore (d. 1749); his father was George Munro of Newmore, who married Margaret, the sister of John and Duncan Forbes. Commissioned 19 May 1740; George Munro of Culcairn (d. 1746).

37. See Lenman, *The Jacobite Clans of the Great Glen 1650–1784*, p. 100.

38. 'Rules and Orders to be observed in recruiting the Right Honble the Earl of Crawford's Regiment of Foot, George Grant, Inverness, January 10th, 1740'. James Hepburne Scott, private collection.

39. In 1751 among those who enlisted, some occupations were: bookbinder, weaver, coppersmith, mason, fiddler, shoemaker, stocking weaver, 'Old Rolls of Officers and Men . . . 42nd Highlanders, Statistics of Companies', BWRA 0016/08 and 09.

40. Stewart of Garth, *Sketches*, I, 3rd ed., pp. 254–5. The sewn kilt was not in use until the 1790s.

41. Forbes, *The 'Black Watch'*, p. 10. See Davidson, 'Pieces of Evidence Concerning the Origin and Early Years of the Black Watch (2)', Notes and Documents, 1782. *JSAHR*, 84, Spring 2006, p. 68, who maintains that 'the impetus for the common tartan came from the companies acting as a unit'.

42. Stewart of Garth, *Sketches*, I, 3rd ed., p. 255, n. 'Tradition says that this fashion commenced in Montrose's army in the civil wars as a token of loyalty to the king, in distinction to the large and flat blue bonnets of the Covenanters and Puritans.' The border of white, red and green 'arranged in small squares to resemble the fess check' referred to by Stewart of Garth did not come in until later.

43. Stewart of Garth, *Sketches*, I, 3rd ed., p. 256. The Brown Bess musket was in use from 1722 to 1838 with minor variations. The bayonet was attached to the muzzle of the musket. Later the bayonet was fitted on the side of the rifle, effectively turning it into a spear.

44. Wye's Letter, verbatim, 15 January, *Caledonian Mercury*, 21 Jan. 1740,

Mf.N.776, NLS. Gregor MacGregor was promoted in another regiment. John Campbell (1717–58) served at Fontenoy and was killed at Ticonderoga. The date is generally given as shortly before the regiment marched south. Stewart of Garth, *Sketches*, I, 3rd ed., p. 258, and McCulloch, *Sons of the Mountains*, I, p. 102, and II, p. 23, put the date as 1743. MacWilliam, *The Black Watch Tartan*, p. 29, gives the correct date, 1740. A third soldier died on the way.

45. Allan McAulay, 'The First Battalion The Black Watch', Tullibardine (ed.), *Military History of Perthshire 1660–1902*, p. 57.

46. *Caledonian Mercury* does not record the muster and there is no official date. 12 May has been suggested but not sourced. The question was asked by a reader in the *JSAHR*, no. 74, Summer 1940, p. 122, but remains unanswered. On 19 May 1739 the independent company under Colin Campbell of Skipness had been ordered to assemble 'at Taybridge and places adjacent, on or before the ninth day of June next in order to be reviewed upon the eleventh': Warrant signed by Joshua Guest, Brigadier General Commander-in-Chief HM Forces in North Britain. James Hepburne Scott, private collection. See Forbes, *The 'Black Watch'*, p. 10; McAulay, 'The First Battalion The Black Watch', Tullibardine (ed.), *Military History of Perthshire, 1660–1902*, p. 56. See Clare Thomas and David Strachan. *Around Aberfeldy, A Brief History*, Perth & Kinross Trust, 2008.

47. Prebble, *Mutiny*, p. 37.

48. Hugh, 12th Lord Sempill (1688–1746).

49. See MacWilliam (ed.), *Official Records*, p. 44.

50. ibid., p. 1. Extract from letter Sir William Yonge, secretary at War, to Clayton, 29 July 1742.

51. Salic law was codified for governing the Salian Franks in the early Middle Ages. Its most important tenet is agnatic succession, excluding women from inheriting a throne.

52. Duncan Forbes to Clayton, 1742, *Culloden Papers*, no. CCCXC, pp. 360–1.

53. MacWilliam (ed.), *Official Records*, Letter III: The same to the same [Will. Yonge to Sempill], War Office, 5 March 1742/3, p. 2.

54. London *Daily Post*, 12 March 1743, quoted in MacWilliam (ed.), *Official Records*, p. xxxix.

55. MacWilliam (ed.), *Official Records*, p. xliii.

56. Anon., *Short History*, p. 32. The Regiment they met was The Royal Regiment, which had just returned from the West Indies.

57. ibid., pp. 19–20.

58. ibid., p. 1.

59. State of the Rt Honble Lord Sempill's Highland regt of Foot as Reviewed by General Wade on Finchley Common, the 14th May 1743, SP 41/14, TNA. The Surgeon, George (sometimes wrongly called James) Munro, was not of the Foulis clan. He is also not to be confused with Robert and George Munro's brother, Dr Duncan Munro, who died at Falkirk in 1746.

60. Anon., *The Behaviour and Character of Samuel Macpherson, Malcolm*

Macpherson and Farquhar Shaw, p. 8. This was an anonymous tract, written by Rev. Campbell; see MacWilliam, *Official Records*, p. xxiv), pp. 8–9.

61. Anon., *Behaviour and Character*, p. 10.
62. Prebble, *Mutiny*, p. 55.
63. Yonge to William Blakeney, no date, VI, Appendices, MacWilliam (ed.), *Official Records*, p. 217.
64. 'Advertisement for apprehending the Mutineers', 18 May 1743, War Office, WO 26/20, p. 26, TNA: 'and all such Persons as shall so apprehend any of the said Mutineers and Deserters shall receive forty shillings for each man over and above the Reward given by the said Act to such persons as shall apprehend Deserters.'
65. The mutineers included 13 MacGregors from Breadalbane or Balquhidder, 13 from Clan Cameron, 10 MacDonalds, 8 Frasers and some Stewarts, Macleans and Macintyres as well as men from the smaller clans of Atholl and 26 men from Clan Chattan, of whom 17 were Macphersons. See Prebble, *Mutiny*, p. 62.
66. *Caledonian Mercury*, 26 May 1743, Mf.N.776, NLS.
67. Anon., *Short History*, p. 46.
68. ibid., p. 50.
69. War Office, 9 June 1743, Phil Baker to Andrew Stone, Esq. SP 41/14, TNA.
70. Anon., *Short History*, p. 48. The narrative concludes before the verdict was given.
71. 'Report of the Proceedings of the Court Martial', June 1743, SP 41/14, TNA. And also quoted in MacWilliam (ed.), *Official Records*, pp. 209–10. There is an argument that some officers persuaded the men to 'confess', thereby confirming their guilt.
72. Peter Campbell was found guilty of desertion and sentenced to 1,000 lashes with a cat o' nine tails on his bare back, the sentence to be administered at 5 different times. MacWilliam (ed.), *Official Records*, p. 204. On p. lxxxviii he is called Patrick.
73. ibid., p. lxxxviii.
74. Letter, *Caledonian Mercury*, Monday, 13 June 1743. Mf.N.776, NLS.
75. Lord Carteret to the Duke of Newcastle, citing instruction by George II, quoted in MacWilliam (ed.), *Official Records*, p. xci.
76. Anon., *Behaviour and Character*, p. 20. Forbes, *The 'Black Watch'*, p. 19, incorrectly says they were executed on 12 July 1743.
77. 'Order for putting a sentence in execution', 13 July 1743, signed by Yonge, WO 26/20, p. 32, TNA.
78. MacWilliam (ed.), *Official Records*, p. cii.
79. ibid., p. ciii.
80. 'Warrants for incorporating thirty-eight men of Lord Sempill's Highland Regt into Brig Gen Oglethorpe's Regiment in Georgia'. See 'A Like Warrant for Incorporating Thirty-Eight Deserters of the Highland Regiment into Lt Gen Dalzell's Regiment of Foot, doing Duty in the Leeward Islands', W0 26/20, pp. 41, 42, TNA, p. 42. Figures in other sources vary.

81. 'Advertisement concerning deserters belong to Lord Sempill's Regiment', signed by Yonge, 29 July 1743, WO 26/20, p. 39, TNA.

82. 'Order for recruiting the Highland Regiment of Foot', 1 Sept. 1743, signed by Yonge, WO 26/20, p. 52, TNA.

83. Anon., *Short History*, p. 28.

84. ibid., p. 31.

85. Macleod, *Memoirs of the Life and Gallant Exploits of the Old Highlander*, p. 61. He wrote his memoirs in the third person.

86. Stewart of Garth, *Sketches*, I, 3rd ed., pp. 257–8.

87. ibid., p. 262.

88. ibid., p. 269. n.+.

89. Forbes, *The 'Black Watch'*, p. 14.

90. McAulay, 'The First Battalion The Black Watch', Tullibardine (ed.), *Military History of Perthshire 1660–1902*, p. 57.

91. Stewart of Garth, *Sketches*, I, 3rd ed., p. 269. There was a 4th print of Piper Donald McDonald, who was sent to join Lt Gen Dalzell's Regt in the Leeward Islands (not Georgia as stated in Eric and Andro Linklater, *The Black Watch*, p. 22, who spells his name MacDonnel, as spelt on contemporary prints); see MacWilliam (ed.), *Official Records*, p. 146, and 'Highlanders Incorporated into . . .', WO 26/20, pp. 47–53 & List of Prisoners Tried, SP 41/14, TNA. Capt John Munro gave Piper McDonald 'a particular good character'.

92. MacWilliam (ed.), *Official Records*, pp. v, vi.

93. Wye's Letter, verbatim, London, 21 May. *Caledonian Mercury*, 26 May, 1743, Mf.N.776, NLS.

94. Munro to Sempill, Greenwich, 21 May 1743, Letter XLVIII, MacWilliam (ed.), *Official Records*, pp. 43–4.

95. Anon., *Short History*, p. 48 (noted as Contemporary Pamphlet, by Scobie, annotated n. 2 in Forbes, *The 'Black Watch'*, p. 18). They embarked on 24 May 1743: 523 private men, 138 'wanting to compleat.' WO 30/43, p. 17, TNA.

96. Alan Ramsay, quoted in MacWilliam (ed.), *Official Records*, p. xxxiii.

2. Disastrous Fontenoy and the '45

1. Dugald Dhu, 'The Black Watch', An Historic Ode, *Written for Waterloo Day*, 1868, verse 1. At this stage the Highland Regiment was still listed as the 43rd.

2. See letter of Capt Philip Browne (to his family), Spire, 18 Sept. 1743 (O.S), Letter No. 28, *JSAHR*, V, no. 21, 1926, p. 100. Although he was not with the Highland Regiment, one can assume that conditions and complaints were the same.

3. Stewart of Garth, *Sketches*, I, 3rd ed., p. 272.

4. Elector Palatine (or of the Palatinate) quoted in Murray, *History of the Scottish*

Regiments of the British Army, p. 253. Charles IV Theodor (1724–99), who became Elector Palatine in 1742 and Duke of Bavaria in 1777 following the union of the Palatinate with Bavaria.

5. Halford-MacLeod, *'When shall we have so fine a regiment again?'* The early officers of the Black Watch, p. 44.

6. Capt John Munro of Newmore to Duncan Forbes, 26 August (O.S.) 1744, Warrand (ed.), *More Culloden Papers*, III, p. 209.

7. Duncan Campbell of Inverawe (1702–58). He had married Jean, the daughter of Colonel Alexander Campbell of Finab (also written Fonab), Captain of a pre-1717 independent company; Aeneas Mackintosh, b. 1701; Anne Farquharson Mackintosh (1723–87). Later referred to as a Jacobite spitfire, she reportedly rode around the glens using threats and a pistol to raise recruits for Prince Charles.

8. Lord John Murray (1711–87). He was the first son of the Duke of Atholl by his second marriage. Following the defection to the Jacobite cause of the Duke's elder son, Lord George Murray, the Duke brought his younger children up as supporters of the Hanoverians.

9. Forbes, *The 'Black Watch'*, p. 37.

10. John Campbell, Earl of Loudoun (1705–82), nephew of the former Commander-in-Chief, John Dalrymple, 2nd Earl of Stair, KT, PC (1673–1747).

11. Rev. Adam Ferguson (1723/4–1816). See Merolle (ed.), *The Letters of Adam Ferguson, 1745–80*, vol. 1, p. xxiii. Ferguson's father enjoyed the patronage of the Duke of Atholl. He was recommended by Lord John Murray's mother, the Dowager Duchess of Atholl, Lady Mary Ross. Gideon Murray was acting as Chaplain to the Earl of Stair.

12. Carlyle's *Autobiography*, p. 282, quoted in 'Adam Ferguson', *Edinburgh Review*, Jan. 1867, p. 62. Carlyle is wrong in saying that Murray was 'not more than twenty-two years of age'. He was thirty-four.

13. Forbes, *The 'Black Watch'*, p. 23. Prince William Augustus, Duke of Cumberland (1721–65), son of George II. He succeeded Field Marshal George Wade as C-in-C of the British army in 1744; Maurice Comte de Saxe (1696–1750) one of August II of Saxony's many illegitimate children. Bad weather and an action by the Royal Navy thwarted the attempt, but Charles and his supporters remained active, hopeful that France would openly favour the Stuart cause.

14. Orders by HRH the Duke of Cumberland, Anderlecht, 18 April 1745, *JSAHR*, V, no. 21, 1926, p. 108.

15. ibid., pp. 108, 109.

16. ibid., 19 April 1745, p. 109.

17. ibid., Hal Camp, 20 April 1745, p. 110.

18. ibid., 21 April 1745, p. 111. Before the British Calendar Act of 1751, Britain's use of the Julian calendar (O.S.) meant that it was eleven days behind the Gregorian calendar (N.S.) used in Europe. According to the Gregorian calendar, the battle of Fontenoy took place on 11 May rather than on 30 April as some contemporary sources indicate.

19. Stewart of Garth, *Sketches*, I, 3rd ed., p. 272.
20. Crawford says 'the grand army, if compleat, should have been composed of 51,660 men, but these were set down at 43,450.' Rolt, *John Lindesay: Earl of Craufurd*, p. 384.
21. Forbes, *The 'Black Watch'*, p. 23.
22. Wye's Letter, London, May 4. Since our Last arrived a Flanders Mail. A Letter from an Officer of Distinction at Ostend, 9th May [N.S.] to an eminent Merchant of this City, *Caledonian Mercury*, 7 May 1745, NLS.
23. Scobie annotated n. 1, in Forbes, *The 'Black Watch'*, p. 25. Rolt, *John Lindesay: Earl of Craufurd*, p. 390.
24. ibid., pp. 394–5. See also Stewart of Garth, *Sketches*, I, 3rd ed., p. 273.
25. Capt John Munro to Lord President Forbes, dated 2 May 1745 (O.S. – 13 May N.S.), *Culloden Papers*, no. CCXLIII, p. 200. Forbes's son John was with the Royal Regiment of Horse Guards – the Blues – and Munro wanted to tell his uncle that his son was 'in good health, having suffered nothing but the loss of his horse, who was shot in our retreat'.
26. Doddridge, *Some Remarkable Passages in the Life of the Hon. Colonel Gardiner*, Appendix, III, p. 241. See Stewart of Garth, *Sketches*, I, 3rd ed., pp. 281–2, who cites Doddridge. This is the first time the Colours of the Regiment were carried into battle. See Wallace, 'The Colours of the Black Watch', *The Red Hackle*, July 1936, p. 6.
27. Stewart of Garth, *Sketches*, I, 3rd ed., p. 282.
28. Macleod, *Memoirs*, p. 64.
29. See Stewart of Garth, *Sketches*, I, 3rd ed., p. 278, note.
30. Macleod, *Memoirs*, p. 64.
31. Capt John Munro to Lord President Forbes, dated 2 May 1745 (O.S. – 13 May N.S.), *Culloden Papers*, no. CCXLIII, p. 200.
32. ibid.
33. Stewart of Garth, *Sketches*, I, 3rd ed., p. 279.
34. Sir Walter Scott, *Miscellaneous Prose Works*, vol. xix, p. 331, quoted in *Memoirs of the Life of Sir Walter Scott*, J.G. Lockhart, Edinburgh, 1844, p. 483. Scott was a friend of Ferguson's son, Sir Adam Ferguson. See also Sir Walter Scott, review of the works of John Home, Esq. by Henry Mackenzie, *The Quarterly Review*, 36, June 1827, p. 196.
35. 'Church Parade'. Anon., *Blackwood's Magazine*, April 1896. See Stewart of Garth, *Sketches*, I, 3rd ed., pp. 281–2; Forbes, *The 'Black Watch'*, p. 32.
36. According to the Returns of Sempill's Regt of Foot dated 21 and 24 May 1743, no replacement chaplain was listed among the officers. SP 41/14, TNA. None of the early accounts of Ferguson's life mention the incident. Ferguson (letter 404) later wrote: 'I left Scotland in the summer of 1745, did not return till the year 1751.' Merolle (ed.), *Ferguson Letters*, p. ci, n. 8.
37. ibid., p. xxiv.
38. W. Skeoch Cumming (1864–1929). The painting is in the BWRM.
39. See Macpherson, 'A New Form of Prayer as used (since the battle of Fontenoy)

by the British Troops in the Allied Army of Flanders' in *Tracts*, 64–82, 1493c17, BL. It has not been possible to find out any information about Laurence Macpherson.

40. Story related by Forbes, *The 'Black Watch'*, p. 28. See also McAulay, 'The First Battalion The Black Watch', Tullibardine (ed.), *Military History of Perthshire 1660–1902*, p. 58.
41. Stewart of Garth, *Sketches*, I, 3rd ed., p. 284, note.
42. ibid., p. 285 & II, 3rd ed., Appendix I, p. ii.
43. Forbes, *The 'Black Watch'*, p. 28. A print, entitled 'A Hero of Fontenoy', is in Forbes, *The 'Black Watch'*, in BWRM added by Scobie opposite p. 28.
44. Paris, 26 May 1745, quoted in Stewart of Garth, *Sketches*, I, 3rd ed., p. 283.
45. Forbes, *The 'Black Watch'*, p. 33. See also Stewart of Garth, *Sketches*, I, 3rd ed., p. 278, n.
46. Ferguson to John Adam, 11 Sept. 1745, Merolle (ed.), *Letters*, Letter 1, p. 6. He became principal chaplain in April 1746 when Gideon Murray retired. His pay was increased to 6s 8d a day with an extra allowance of £3 15s for a 'bat-horse' to carry his baggage on campaign.
47. Tacksman of *Inbhir Chadain* ('Inverhadden', nr Kinlochrannoch), tr. Michael Newton, quoted in Newton, *We're Indians Sure Enough*, p. 34. A Tacksman was a leaseholder, the term applied particularly to a Highland tenant.
48. Loudoun escaped capture. Four companies of Loudoun's and one 'Additional' Company of the 43rd mustered only 185 men. See 'Jacobites at Heart', Scott-Moncrieff (ed.),*The '45, To Gather an Image Whole*, p. 125.
49. Aeneas Mackintosh, Return of Company, 29 Oct. 1745, Loudoun Papers LO 12078, Huntingdon Library, shows 3 officers, 3 sergeants, 2 corporals, 1 drummer and 10 private men. See also Ruari Halford-MacLeod, 'Everyone who has an intrigue hopes it should not be known', Lord Loudoun and Anne Mackintosh – An Intrigue of the "45"', *Transactions of the Gaelic Society of Inverness*, 1986–88, vol. LV, p. 264.
50. Stewart of Garth, *Sketches*, I, 3rd ed., p. 288; Forbes, *The 'Black Watch'*, p. 36.
51. Adam Ferguson, *Sermon preached in the Erse Language to his Majesty's First Highland Regiment of Foot*, pp. 7, 22.
52. Aeneas Mackintosh, Company Returns, 7 and 14 January 1746, Loudoun Papers LO 12078, Huntingdon Library; see also Halford-MacLeod, 'Intrigue of the "45"', *Transactions of the Gaelic Society of Inverness*, 1986–88, vol. LV, p. 265.
53. Dr Alasdair Maclean, 'Jacobites at Heart', Scott-Moncrieff (ed.), *The '45*, pp. 124–39.
54. Sir Harry Munro to Duncan Forbes, 22 Jan. 1746, *Culloden Papers*, CCCXI, p. 267.
55. *The Falkirk Herald*, 11 Nov. 1972, reprinted in *The Red Hackle*, Dec. 1972, p. 4.
56. Maclean, *Bonnie Prince Charlie*, p. 177. Halford-MacLeod, '*When shall we have so fine a regiment again?*', p. 71. See Dr Alasdair Maclean, 'Jacobites at Heart', Scott-Moncrieff (ed.), *The '45*, p. 130. There is some confusion as to whether

the warning came from Aeneas Mackintosh, fearful of the ignominy of having the Prince captured in his family home.

57. Newton, *We're Indians Sure Enough*, p. 32.

58. Act of Proscription. The punishment for conviction of a second offence was transportation.

59. *The Glasgow Journal*, 28 April 1746, quoted in Devine, *Scotland's Empire*, p. 308.

60. Forbes, *The 'Black Watch'*, p. 38.

61. Later Major General Allan Campbell (1723–94), Ensign in 43rd (later 42nd) 1744. In 1770 he transferred to the 36th Foot.

62. See John S. Gibson, 'The Summer's Hunting: Historiography of Charles Edward's escape'. Scott-Moncrieff (ed.), *The '45*, pp. 140–55.

63. Stewart of Garth, *Sketches*, I, 3rd ed., p. 294. 'The land forces amounted to nearly 8000 men.'

64. The former Spanish Netherlands, that region of the seventeen Dutch provinces which had remained loyal to Spain. At the end of the Spanish War of Succession in 1713 the territory was ceded to Austria and assumed the name of the Austrian Netherlands.

65. See C.T. Atkinson, 'A Flanders Sideshow: Hulst, 1747', *JSAHR*, XXII, no. 89, Spring 1944, pp. 205–212, and 'Military Memoirs of Lieutenant General the Hon. Charles Colville (21st Scots Fusiliers)', ed. J. O. Robson, *JSAHR*, XXVII, Summer 1949, pp. 70–8, XXVII, Autumn 1949, pp. 96–104, XXVII, Winter 1949, pp. 144–53, XXVIII, Spring 1950, pp. 2–12 and XXVIII, Summer 1950, pp. 70–8, *The Gentleman's Magazine*, XVII, 1747, for contemporary accounts.

66. 'Foreign History', May 1747, *Scots Magazine*, p. 238.

67. Lord John Murray, to His Grace, James, 2nd Duke of Atholl, May 1747, from Ellewortskyk in South Beveland, *Chronicles of the Families of Atholl and Tullibardine*, III, pp. 371–2. Stewart of Garth, *Sketches*, II, 3rd ed., Appendix I, p. ii, says 3 soldiers killed and 5 wounded at South Beveland. See *Scots Magazine*, May 1747, p. 238.

68. See C.T. Atkinson, 'A Flanders Sideshow: Hulst, 1747', *JSAHR*, XXII, no. 89, Spring 1944, pp. 210–1, who quotes contemporary sources: the British Consul, Charles Stuart and Colonel Yorke describing the 42nd's engagement at Bergen-op-Zoom. See Stewart of Garth, *Sketches*, I, 3rd ed., p. 299, who says the Regiment remained in Beveland, and Forbes, *The 'Black Watch'*, p. 39, who says the Regiment was not engaged at Bergen-op-Zoom. Ulrich Frederic Woldemar, Comte de Lowendahl (1700–55).

69. Cronstadt quoted in James Ferguson, 'Scots Brigade in Holland', *Scottish History Society*, vol. 35, 1899. See Halford-MacLeod, *'When shall we have so fine a regiment again?'*, p. 79.

70. See Atholl Roll, 1751, Atholl Papers, Bundle 253, Blair Castle in Halford-MacLeod, *'When shall we have so fine a regiment again?'*, p. 94 and 'Old Rolls of Officers and Men . . . The Black List Return of Men . . . who have had the disgrace of being whipped . . .', BWRA 0016/12.

71. C.T. Atkinson, 'A Flanders Sideshow: Hulst, 1747', *JSAHR*, XXII, no. 89, Spring 1944, p. 212.
72. Order for Disbandment & Instructions to disband the non-Commissioned officers and Private men upon their arrival at Rochester, Henry Fox, London 17 Nov. 1748, WO 26/21, p. 266, TNA.
73. H. Fox to Mr Pitt, War Office, 1 April 1749, WO 4/46, p. 115, TNA. 'So that each Company is to consist of 1 Captain, 1 Lieutenant, 1 Ensign, 2 Sergeants 2 Corporals, 1 Drummer and 29 effective private men and no more excepting the Grenadier Company which is to have 2 Lieutenants, instead of a Lieutenant & Ensign and likewise to reduce the Quarter Master to the said Regiment.' William Pitt, 1st Earl of Chatham (1708–78).
74. Edw. Lloyd to J. Cleveland, Esq, W[ar] O[ffice], 3 April 1749, WO 4/46, p. 116, TNA.
75. 1751, Royal Clothing Warrant, see Groves, *The Black Watch, Royal Highlanders*, p. 131; Forbes, *The 'Black Watch'*, p. 40. See also Wallace, 'The Colours of the Black Watch', *The Red Hackle*, July 1936, p. 6. 'There is no record of these colours or whether there was one stand or two.'
76. John Foulis (d. 1749) Lt Col John Campbell, 5th Duke of Argyll (1723–1806). Later Colonel, 54th Regiment; promoted General 1778, Field Marshal 1796.
77. Ferguson to Lord Findlater and Seafield (James Ogilvy, 5th Earl, Galway, 25 May, 1753, *Letters: 1745–1780*, ed. Merolle, p. 10. By Oct. 1754 Ferguson was writing from Groningen in the Netherlands and in Dec. from Leipzig and so was no longer with the Regiment.
78. Stewart of Garth, *Sketches*, I, 3rd ed., p. 302.
79. 'Old Rolls of Officers and Men . . ., Rolls of the 42nd Highlanders by Companies', 1751, BWRA 0016/11 and 12.
80. ibid. Stewart of Garth says that 'for many years no instance occurred of corporal punishment', *Sketches*, I, 3rd ed., p. 301.
81. Stewart of Garth, *Sketches*, I, 3rd ed., p. 301.
82. Rev. Percy Sumner, 'Notes on Regimental Uniforms, from the Irish Treasury Papers, 1713 to 1782', *JSAHR*, XIV, 1935, p. 217.
83. Francis Grant (1717–82). He and his brother Ludovic, the future Laird, were nephews of the Regiment's first major, George Grant, court-martialled for surrendering Inverness Castle and Fort George to the Jacobites. See Stewart of Garth, *Sketches*, I, 3rd ed., p. 305, n.*.
84. See Devine, *Scotland's Empire*, p. 309, and *To the Ends of the Earth*, p. 213.
85. Quoted in Murray, *History of the Scottish Regiments of the British Army*, p. 250.

3. Ticonderoga: The Utterance of the Dead

1. Anon., eighteenth-century poem tr. from Gaelic by Michael Newton, quoted in Newton, *We're Indians Sure Enough*, p. 110.
2. George Washington (1732–99), First President of the United States of America. Braddock's mistress was used for target practice and then eaten by the Indians. See Pocock, *Battle for Empire*, p. 91.
3. Royal Warrant, 'given at Our Court of St James 25th December 1755'. John Campbell, 4th Earl of Loudoun, Staff Officer in North America, 25 Dec. 1756 to 25 June 1757, WO 1/1, TNA. *Caledonian Mercury* gives date of 25 March 1756.
4. Pargellis, *Lord Loudoun in North America*, pp. 47–8.
5. James Maclagan, 'To the Highlanders Upon Departing for America', quoted in Newton, *We're Indians Sure Enough*, p. 127. In John Gilles's *Collection of Ancient and Modern Gaelic Poems and Songs*, Perth, 1786, the poem is cited as 'Anonymous'. Maclagan appears as the author in Patrick MacPhárlain's book of Gaelic poetry, *Co'-chruinneachadh de dh' orain agus de luinneagaibh thaghta Ghae'lach maille ris an treas duan de Sgeulachd na Tròidhe air a chuin an Gaelig o'n Ghrèugais, [etc., etc.]*, Stuibhart, 1813, p. 92. See Newton, *We're Indians Sure Enough*, p. 282, n. 55. Within two months some 2,000 Highlanders were mobilised; a total of 12,000 were involved by the end of the conflict: Newton, *We're Indians Sure Enough*, p. 103.
6. McCulloch, *Sons of the Mountains*, II, pp. 157, 158.
7. Robert Adam Letter, quoted in Fleming, *Robert Adam*, p. 201. Quoted in Merolle (ed.), *Correspondence of Adam Ferguson, I*, Biographical Introduction by Jane B. Fagg, p. xxv.
8. See ibid., pp. xxv, xxviii, xxix, and n. 22, p. cii, n. 51, p. ciii. Monthly Return of the following Corps of His Majesty's Services in North America, 24 March 1763, notes under Absent Officers: 'Chaplain Ferguson, never joined', f. 8, WO17/1489, TNA. Ferguson left the Church and accepted a chair as Professor of Natural Philosophy at Edinburgh University, later becoming Professor of Moral Philosophy and famed as 'the father of modern sociology'. See Alexander Broadie (ed.), *The Scottish Enlightenment*, Canongate Classic, 1997, p. 798. Robert Burns and Walter Scott met in Ferguson's house for the first and only time. The new chaplain appointed on 20 Dec. 1757 was James Stewart.
9. Francis Grant to Ludovic Grant, Modbury, 21 March 1746, GD 248/49/1, f. 31, NRS. Their father had recently died.
10. Maj Gen James Abercromby (1706–81) Commander-in-Chief in North America 1758.
11. Quoted in McCulloch, *Sons of the Mountains*, I, p. 6.
12. Louis-Joseph de Montcalm-Gozon, Marquis de Saint-Véran (1712–59), in command of the French regular troops in Canada.
13. Sir William Johnson (*c.*1715–74) He had learned the Mohawk language and

Iroquois customs. In Sept. 1755 he defeated Baron Dieskau, commanding French and Indian troops at the Battle of Lake George.

14. 'Plantation Affairs', *Scots Magazine*, Oct. 1756, XVIII, p. 520. Also known as the Five (later Six) Nations, whose members were the Mohawk, Oneida, Onondaga, Cayuga and Seneca. The sixth Nation was the Tuscarora.
15. *Pennsylvania Gazette*, 22 July 1756, quoted in McCulloch, *Sons of the Mountains*, I, p. 9.
16. 'Affairs in the plantations', *Scots Magazine*, XVIII, Nov. 1756, p. 559.
17. *Pennsylvania Gazette*, 5 Aug. and 12 Oct. 1756. See McCulloch, *Sons of the Mountains*, I, p. 10.
18. Loudoun to Cumberland, Albany, 20 Aug. 1756, quoted in Pargellis, *Military Affairs in North America*, pp. 223–5. See also Pargellis, *Lord Loudoun in North America*, p. 171.
19. Loudoun to Cumberland, Albany, 20 Aug. 1756, quoted in Pargellis, *Military Affairs*, pp. 223–5.
20. Francis Grant to Ludovic Grant, Albany, 1 Sept. 1756, GD 248/49/1 f. 9, NRS.
21. Diary of Capt Edward Wells (Connecticut Provincials), 25 Sept. 1756, quoted in McCulloch, *Sons of the Mountains*, I, p. 13. 'This observation constitutes the first reference to a Highland band performing in North America.'
22. Loudoun to Cumberland, Albany, 22 Nov. 1756 (concluded at New York, 26 Dec. 1756), quoted in Pargellis, *Military Affairs*, p. 264.
23. ibid.
24. Francis Grant to Ludovic Grant, Fort Edward Camp, 2 Nov. 1756, GD 248/49/1 f. 10, NRS.
25. Cumberland to Loudoun, from Court of St James, 2 Dec. 1756, quoted in Pargellis, *Military Affairs*, p. 254. (Flanderkins were those who had served in Flanders.) Additional 'supernumerary' recruits joined the 42nd, paid by the Royal Americans until vacancies in the 42nd arose. See Halford-MacLeod, *'When shall we have so fine a regiment again?' The early officers of the Black Watch, 1739–1765*, p. 107.
26. 'Distribution of the Troops in North America for the Winter, 1756', Cumberland Papers 46/129, quoted in McCulloch, *Sons of the Mountains*, I, p. 16.
27. Abercromby to Loudoun, Albany, 20 Dec. 1756, LO 2373, Loudoun Papers, Huntingdon Library.
28. In 1755 the French took Minorca. Admiral Byng was blamed, court-martialled and executed leading to the fall of Newcastle's government. William Pitt (the Elder), 1st Earl of Chatham PC (1708–78), paymaster general 1746, secretary of state for the southern dept 1756, prime minister 1766–8.
29. Loudoun to Pitt, New York, 25 April 1757, *Correspondence when Secretary of State*, I, p. 38.
30. ibid.

31. Francis Grant to Loudoun, 24 April 1757, LO 3342, Huntingdon Library; see McCulloch, *Sons of the Mountains*, I, p. 44. Maclagan's older brother, James, became chaplain of the 42nd in 1764. Gentleman Volunteers were enlisted private soldiers, but with sufficient education and appropriate background to become commissioned officers when the opportunity arose.

32. Francis Grant to Ludovic Grant, New York, 25 May 1757, GD248/49/1 f. 74, NRS.

33. Pargellis, *Loudoun in North America*, p. 237.

34. Stewart of Garth, *Sketches*, I, 3rd ed., p. 307, says 'the united force amounted to 10,500 men'.

35. Simon Fraser to Loudoun, 25 August 1757, Halifax Harbour, quoted in Colonel J.R. Harper, *The Fraser Highlanders*, Montreal, 1979, p. 42.

36. John Knox, *An Historical Journal of the Campaign in North America for the Years 1757, 1758, 1759, and 1760*, 22 July 1757, I, p. 18, Regiments included the 1st Bn 1st (Royals), 17th, 27th, 28th, 43rd, 46th and 55th. See also General Orders (May 7–Oct 19, 1757) July 3, 1757, LO 3576, Loudoun Papers, Huntingdon Library.

37. Knox, *Historical Journal*, 24–25 July 1757, I, p. 20, 1 Aug. 1757, I, p. 21. See General Orders, Halifax, 1 Aug. 1757 LO 3576, Loudoun Papers, Huntingdon Library. The 42nd was in the 2nd Brigade with the 17th, 46th and 2nd Bn 60th Royal Americans under Abercromby's command.

38. F.B. Richards, 'The Black Watch at Ticonderoga and Major Duncan Campbell of Inverawe', p. 11. Richards spent a decade researching the battles at Ticonderoga.

39. Forbes, *The 'Black Watch'*, p. 47. Numbers of dead were perhaps exaggerated for propaganda purposes.

40. Duke of Argyll to Duke of Atholl, 9 July 1757, quoted in *Chronicles of the Families of Atholl and Tullibardine*, III, p. 428.

41. Capt James Murray, later of Strowan (1734–94). Later Gen Sir Thomas Stirling of Ardoch (1733–1808). Born in Russia while his father, 3rd Baronet of Ardoch, was Admiral of the Russian Fleet and Governor of Cronstadt, Stirling joined the Scots (Dutch) Brigade aged thirteen and was in the garrison at Bergen-op-Zoom in 1747. McGregor, 'A Black Watch Who Was Who 1725–1881', Research Notes, 42nd, BWRA 0863/2. The Scots Brigade in Holland became known as Scots (or Scotch) Dutch Brigade because it was in the service of the States-General of the Netherlands. See McCulloch, *Sons of the Mountains*, II, p. 12.

42. Patrick Miller, Atholl Records, Bundle 259, quoted in Halford-MacLeod, '*When Shall We See So Fine a Regiment Again?*', p. 118.

43. Capt James Murray to (his brother) John Murray of Strowan (later 3rd Duke of Atholl 1729–65), 1 Dec. 1757, Youghall, in *Chronicles of the Families of Atholl and Tullibardine*, III, p. 433. Richards, 'The Black Watch at Ticonderoga', pp. 7–8, reproduces a letter from Loudoun to Pitt dated 1757, in which he discusses the arrival of the nine additional companies but this must be a mistake for 1758.

44. Ticonderoga comes from the Iroquois word tekontaró:ken meaning 'it is at the junction of two waterways' i.e. Lake George and Lake Champlain.
45. Loudoun to Cumberland, New York, 17 Oct. 1757, quoted in Pargellis, *Military Affairs*, pp. 400–2. See Amherst, *Journal*, p. 144, n. 120.
46. See Loudoun to Pitt, New York, 10 March 1758, quoted in Richards, 'The Black Watch at Ticonderoga', p. 8. (The letter is misdated 1757.)
47. Maj Duncan Campbell of Inverawe to John Campbell of Coichombie, Albany, 14 March 1758, quoted in Richards, 'The Black Watch at Ticonderoga', p. 38.
48. Robert Louis Stevenson, 'Ticonderoga: A legend of the West Highlands' (1887), based on a famous Scottish ghost story. See 'Inverawe and Ticonderoga', by Dean Stanley, from *Frazer's Magazine*, Oct. 1880, reprinted in *The Red Hackle*, July 1935.
49. Maj Duncan Campbell of Inverawe to John Campbell of Coichombie, Albany, 14 March 1758, quoted in Richards, 'The Black Watch at Ticonderoga', p. 38. See Halford-MacLeod, *'When shall we have so fine a regiment again?'*, pp. 111–12, for details of Duncan Campbell's attempt to sell his commission. See also *The Red Hackle*, May 2009, p. 8.
50. Lt Col Francis Grant, Memorial, quoted in Richards, 'The Black Watch at Ticonderoga', p. 14.
51. Abercromby to Pitt, 28 April 1758, New York, quoted in McCulloch, *Sons of the Mountains*, I, p. 65.
52. Account of the Number of Forces, Officers included employed in North America, 24 Oct. 1758 gives 16,674 rank & file, 18,929 Total Officers & Men, Establishment 23,023. In 1759 this figure was 27,330, WO17/1489, TNA.
53. Brig Gen George Augustus, 3rd Viscount Howe (*c.*1725–58). He had been Colonel of 3rd Bn 60th (Royal Americans), and was in command of the 55th. His grandmother was half-sister to George I.
54. See McCulloch, *Sons of the Mountains*, I, p. 86. Like Howe, Lt Gen Sir John Moore served in America and his experience was instrumental in founding the Light Infantry Brigade. See Pocock, *Battle for Empire*, p. 95.
55. Capt John Reid (1721–1807). He composed the music for the 'Highland March' written for two violins or flutes and a violoncello. Later, Sir Henry Erskine added the words and it became known as 'The Garb of Old Gaul' which remains the Slow March of The Black Watch. See David Murray, *Music of the Scottish Regiments*, 2nd ed, 2001, pp. 176–7 and Cram, Duthie, Irwin and Taylor, *A Collection of Pipe Music of The Black Watch*.
56. Quoted in McCulloch, *Sons of the Mountains*, I, p. 87.
57. Francis Grant to Ludovic Grant, Fort Edward, 16 June 1758, GD 248/49/1 f. 81, NRS.
58. Lt Kenneth Tolmie (1724–1809), from the Isle of Skye, was put in charge of the 42nd's detachment. He had some training as an engineer, perhaps acquired while serving in Flanders.
59. Capt James Murray to Mr Murray of Strowan, Albany, 19 July 1758, *Chronicles of the Families of Atholl and Tullibardine*, III, p. 438.

60. 'An unsuccessful attack at Ticonderoga', *Scots Magazine*, XX, Aug. 1758, p. 436.

61. McCulloch, *Sons of the Mountains*, I, p. 85. Piper Ewen (Owen/Evan/Ewan) McIntyre (d. 6 Aug. 1762 at the siege of Havana), from Skye, joined the Regiment in 1752 and was posted to the grenadier company on 10 April 1759. See Orderly Book of Capt James Stewart's Company (18/2/1759 – 16/7/1759), BWRA 0254: 'Ewen McIntyre pipper in the Grandr Compy is appointed pipper major and is this Day to Receive the Cloathing accordingly. Petter [?] McIntyre pipper in Captain McNiell Company is for the future to be on the footing of a Drum and to be subsisted accordingly.' See also Dr Willliam M. Forbes, PhD Ed., 'An Instrument of War', in McCulloch, *Sons of the Mountains*, II, pp. 164–7.

62. Abercromby to Pitt, Camp at Lake George, 12 July 1758, *Correspondence when Secretary of State*, I, p. 297. See also: 'An unsuccessful attack at Ticonderoga', *Scots Magazine*, XX, Aug. 1758, p. 436.

63. *Pennsylvania Gazette*, 27 July 1758. See McCulloch, *Sons of the Mountains*, I, p. 88.

64. Capt James Murray to Mr Murray of Strowan, Albany, 19 July 1758, *Chronicles of the Families of Atholl and Tullibardine*, III, p. 438.

65. Extract of letter from Maj Gen Abercromby to Mr Sec. Pitt, dated at the camp of Lake George 12 July 1758. 'An unsuccessful attack at Ticonderoga', *Scots Magazine*, XX, Aug. 1758, p. 436.

66. Abercromby to Pitt, Camp at Lake George, 12 July 1758. *Correspondence when Secretary of State*, I, p. 298.

67. Capt James Murray to Mr Murray of Strowan, Albany, 19 July 1758, *Chronicles of the Families of Atholl and Tullibardine*, III, p. 438.

68. Capt Hugh Arnot to Loudoun, Stillwater, 1 Aug. 1758, quoted in Westbrook (ed.),' "Like Roaring Lions Breaking from their Chains": the Highland Regiment at Ticonderoga', *The Bulletin of the Fort Ticonderoga Museum*, vol. XVI, no. 1, 1998, p. 28. Arnot was writing to his patron, the Earl of Loudoun.

69. Arnot, Journal, 7 July 1758, enclosed with his letter to Loudoun, Stillwater, 1 Aug. 1758, quoted in Westbrook (ed.), 'Like Roaring Lions', *Bulletin of Fort Ticonderoga*, p. 41.

70. Lt William Grant, 'Copy of a letter from North America', 17 Aug. 1758, Appendix, *Scots Magazine*, XX, 1758, pp. 698–9.

71. Arnot to Loudoun, Stillwater, 1 Aug. 1758, quoted in Westbrook (ed.), 'Like Roaring Lions', *Bulletin of Fort Ticonderoga*, p. 27.

72. Richards, 'The Black Watch at Ticonderoga', p. 19.

73. Arnot, Journal, 8 July 1758, enclosed with Abercromby's letter to Loudoun, Stillwater, 1 Aug. 1758, quoted in Westbrook (ed.), 'Like Roaring Lions', *Bulletin of Fort Ticonderoga*, p. 40 and n. 82. The 'Indian Halloo' was a psychological weapon. It was rumoured that not all Johnson's corps were Indians, but British soldiers painted and dressed as Indians.

74. Lt William Grant, 'Copy of a letter from North America', 17 Aug. 1758, Appendix, *Scots Magazine*, XX, 1758, pp. 698–9.

75. ibid.

76. ibid. See also Capt Allan Campbell to John Campbell, 11 July 1758, quoted in Westbrook (ed.), 'Like Roaring Lions', *Bulletin of Fort Ticonderoga*, p. 52.
77. Capt James Murray to Mr Murray of Strowan, Albany, 19 July 1758, *Chronicles of the Families of Atholl and Tullibardine*, III, p. 439.
78. Unidentified 55th Foot officer in *Scots Magazine*, XX, 1758, p. 439.
79. Lt William Grant, 'Copy of a letter from North America', 17 Aug. 1758, *Scots Magazine*, XX, 1758, pp. 698–9.
80. Louis Antoine de Bougainville, 8 July 1758, *Adventure in the Wilderness, American Journals, 1756–1760*, p. 233.
81. Captain Salah Barnard, quoted in Westbrook (ed.), 'Like Roaring Lions', *Bulletin of Fort Ticonderoga*, p. 18. See 'The Journal of Salah Barnard from the campaign of 1758'. www.files.usgwarchives.org/ma/franklin/bios/goodellg117gbs.txt.
82. Capt James Murray to Mr Murray of Strowan, Albany, 19 July 1758, *Chronicles of the Families of Atholl and Tullibardine*, III, p. 439.
83. Eighteenth-century Anon. poem, tr. from Gaelic by Michael Newton, quoted in Newton, *We're Indians Sure Enough*, p. 110.
84. Lt William Grant, 'Copy of a letter from North America', 17 Aug. 1758, Appendix, *Scots Magazine*, XX, 1758, pp. 698–9.
85. Capt Allan Campbell of Barcaldine to 'Dr Broyr.' (Dear Brother), Camp at Lake George, 11 July 1758, GD87/1/82, NRS. See also Westbrook (ed.), 'Like Roaring Lions', *Bulletin of Fort Ticonderoga*, p. 51.
86. Lt William Grant, 'Copy of a letter from North America', 17 Aug. 1758, Appendix, *Scots Magazine*, XX, 1758, pp. 698–9.
87. ibid.
88. See 'A Legend of Argyll', by Robert Louis Stevenson, reprinted in Richards, 'The Black Watch at Ticonderoga', p. 34. Stevenson calls Campbell Cameron. See Francis Parkman, *Montcalm and Wolfe*, Little, Brown and Co., 1884 and the lively account by Lt Gen Sir Alistair Irwin given at a Ticonderoga Banquet, New York, reproduced in *The Red Hackle*, May 2009.
89. Tullibardine (ed.), *Military History of Perthshire 1660–1902*, p. 59, gives the figures of 314 killed and 333 wounded (total 647). Stewart of Garth, *Sketches*, II, 3rd ed., Appendix No. I, p. ii, says 316 killed and 333 wounded (total 649), as does Richards, 'The Black Watch at Ticonderoga', p. 52. It is not clear how many died of their wounds. Between July and Oct. seventy were taken off the pay-roll. See 'A Record of The Black Watch 1758–1763', BWRA 0395.
90. Eighteenth-century Anon. poem translated from Gaelic by Michael Newton, quoted in Newton, *We're Indians Sure Enough*, p. 110.
91. Lt William Grant, 'Copy of a letter from North America', 17 Aug. 1758, *Scots Magazine*, XX, 1758, Appendix, pp. 698–9.
92. Maj Gen Abercromby to Lord Barrington, Lake George, 12 July 1758, Campaigns, Battles, etc. Ticonderoga, WO 1/,1, f. 198, pp. 395, 455, TNA.
93. Extract of letter from Maj Gen Abercromby to Mr Sec. Pitt, camp of Lake George, July 12, 1758. 'An unsuccessful attack at Ticonderoga', *Scots Magazine*, XX, Aug. 1857, p. 437.

94. Bougainville, *American Journals*, p. 236.

95. Bougainville, Mémoir pour le Ministre de Marine, 17 janvier 1759, Rapport de l'Archiviste de la Province de Québec pour 1932–1933, quoted in McCulloch, *Sons of the Mountains*, I, p. 103.

96. *The Gentleman's Magazine*, 1758, p. 446. Figures for the British army: 17,550; French army: 4,236. Casualty rate of British was 11% compared with French casualty rate of 13%. McCulloch, *Sons of the Mountains*, p. 105.

97. Tulliken's Report, 13, Lee Narratives, quoted in McCulloch, *Sons of the Mountains*, I, p. 105.

98. Warrant for forming the 42nd Regt of Foot into two battalions with the title of Royal Highland Regt, signed by Lord Barrington, 1758, WO 26/23, p. 418, TNA. Each bn was to have 1,000 private men. It is not clear why the title Royal was given at this time. The Royal Archives, Windsor hold archives only from the reign of George III in 1760 onwards. Miss Pam Clark, Registrar, Sept. 2011.

99. See 'A Record of The Black Watch 1758–1763'. BWRA 0389/H–I. As noted, pipers were normally listed as drummers and the grenadier company had had a piper-major since augmentation. The back date for raising the 2nd Bn was 25 June 1758.

100. Capt Francis MacLean (1717–81). Major 'in the Army' 25 March 1759. In 1761 he was promoted in the 97th Foot.

101. William Murray, younger of Lintrose (1737–77). Ensign in 34th Foot, 1755; joined 42nd as capt 1758; to 27th as lt col in 1777.

102. Lord John Murray to James, 2nd Duke of Atholl, London, 22 July 1758, *Chronicles of the Families of Atholl and Tullibardine*, III, p. 442. One captain, Robert Arbuthnot, died before the Company embarked, and he was replaced by Capt David Haldane of Aberuthven (*c.*1722–?1777). Stewart of Garth, *Sketches*, I, 3rd ed., p. 330, mistakenly says Arbuthnot died of fever in 1759. The 2nd Bn's surgeon was Robert Drummond (*c.*1730–*c.*1788), who received his commission on 5 Aug. 1758. He fell ill in Havana but survived. Before exchanging to half-pay 24 Oct. 1763, he was administering to the sick of both battalions on Long Island.

103. Newark, *Highlander: The History of the Legendary Highland Soldier*, p. 95, says that bagpipes were not banned. 'Contrary to popular myth the playing of Highland bagpipes was not prohibited after Culloden'; see J.G. Gibson, *Traditional Gaelic Bagpiping*, Edinburgh NMS Publishing, 1998. The 1746 Disarming Act was repealed in 1782.

104. John Grant (b.1741), Journal, pp. 25–6, MS Copy Micro 491, Alexander Turnbull Library, NLNZ. He was born in Dec. and so would have been sixteen when he raised the company.

105. John Grant, Journal, p. 26, MS Copy Micro 491, Alexander Turnbull Library, NLNZ.

106. Forbes, *The 'Black Watch'*, p. 160.

107. Record of Issues of Clothing by Quartermaster Adam Stewart, Account of Cloathing &c furnished by William Sandeman at Perth for the 7 companys

of the Royal Highland Regiment (undated), BWRA 0253. Sandeman acted as the Regiment's general agent in Perth. See also 'A Record of The Black Watch 1758–1763'. BWRA 0389/H-I.

108. Record of Issues of Clothing by Quartermaster Adam Stewart, Account of Cloathing, Glasgow 13 Nov. 1758, BWRA 0253.

109. ibid. See also 'A Record of The Black Watch 1758–1763'. BWRA 0389/H-I. No record exists of the 2nd Bn being issued with its own stand of Colours.

110. John Grant, Journal, p. 28, MS Copy Micro 491, Alexander Turnbull Library, NLNZ.

111. Capt James Murray to Mr Murray of Strowan, Albany, 17 Aug. 1758, *Chronicles of the Families of Atholl and Tullibardine*, III, p. 443.

112. Francis Grant to Ludovic Grant, New York, 27 November 1758, GD 248/49/1, f. 82, NRS.

113. Orderly Book of Captain James Stewart's Company (18-2-59–16-7-59), Regimental Orders, New York, 3 March 1759, BWRA 0254.

114. ibid., New York, 15 March 1759.

115. ibid., New York, 20 March 1759.

116. ibid., New York, 21 March 1759.

117. Annual Register, 13 March 1759, see also Steve Brummell, 'Home from the Wars', *History Today*, March 2002, p. 41. *Westminster Review*, quoted by Scobie, annotated n. in Forbes, The *'Black Watch'*.

118. 'Affairs in Scotland', *Scots Magazine*, XXI, 1759, p. 213. A similar account is given in the *Westminster Review*, Scobie's annotated footnote in Forbes, The *'Black Watch'*.

4. Clipping the Wings of the French

1. Capt Allan Campbell to Duncan Campbell of Glenure, Ticonderoga, 27 July 1759, GD170/1067, f. 244A, NRS.

2. Smelser, *The Campaign for the Sugar Islands 1759*, p. 19. Maj Gen Peregrine Thomas Hopson (d. 1759). First recorded military appointment was as a Lt in 1703; in 1759 he would have been in his seventies.

3. Maj Gen Hon. John Barrington (*c.*1722–64).

4. Later Admiral Sir John Moore KB (1719–79). Capt Richard Gardiner, *An Account of the Expedition to the West Indies . . . 1759*, 8 Jan., p. 10, says they were reinforced by 200 Royal Highlanders. He is wrongly listed as Major Richard Gardiner in the British Library integrated catalogue, reference: 1197.i.15. Although not 42nd, I have used his account to supplement John Grant's journal.

5. '12 flat bottomed boats, of a new construction, were launched at Portsmouth to be employed in landing the troops on the enemy's coast. They carry 63 men each, are rowed with 12 oars, and draw not above two feet [of water].'

Historical Chronicle, May 1758, Wednesday 17 [May], *The Gentleman's Magazine*, XXVIII, 1758, p. 242. Hopson to Pitt, Basseterre, in the Island of Guadeloupe, 30 Jan. 1759, Pitt, *Correspondence when Secretary of State*, II, p. 21.

6. Gardiner, *West Indies*, 16 [Jan.], p. 13.
7. ibid., p. 14. Fort Royal is frequently referred to as Port Royal.
8. 'Journal of an officer' enclosed in a letter from Hopson to Pitt, Basse Terre, Guadaloupe, 30 Jan. 1759. Pitt, *Correspondence when Secretary of State*, II, p. 27. Kept as an independent force, the 2nd Bn was under the command of Bt Maj Charles Anstruther, 26th Foot.
9. Gardiner, *West Indies*, 17 Jan., p. 15.
10. 'Journal of an officer', enclosed in a letter from Hopson to Pitt, Basse Terre, Guadaloupe, 30 Jan. 1759. Pitt, *Correspondence when Secretary of State*, II, p. 28.
11. Haldane's 'proceedings', Newcastle Papers, quoted in Smelser, *Sugar Islands*, p. 49.
12. Gardiner, *West Indies*, 17 Jan., p. 15. It was common for writers at the time to refer to the troops as 'English' even though they should have been called 'British'. See also entries by historian, Thomas Mante.
13. Lt George Leslie (*c.*1735–62) wounded storming Morne Tartenson in 1759 and 1762; by 17 Aug. he had died of his wounds and fever at Havana.
14. Gardiner, *West Indies*, 17 Jan., p. 16.
15. Smelser, *Sugar Islands*, p. 74.
16. See Gardiner, *West Indies*, 22 [Jan.], p. 22.
17. Moore to Pitt, Guadalupe, 30 January 1759, Pitt, *Correspondence when Secretary of State*, p. 30. See also 'Expedition and Martinico and Guadalupe', *Scots Magazine*, XXI, 1759, p. 93.
18. Smelser, *Sugar Islands*, p. 89, citing William Matthew Burt, King's fiscal agent to Newcastle, 30 Jan. 1759, Add. MSS. 32887, f. 410, Newcastle Papers.
19. Gardiner, *West Indies*, 24 Jan., p. 29.
20. ibid., p. 31.
21. ibid., 25 [Jan.], p. 31.
22. See ibid., 4 [Feb.], p. 35.
23. Lt Alexander MacLean to Lord John Murray (extract), Guadeloupe, 4 March 1759, *Chronicles of the Families of Atholl and Tullibardine*, III, p. 451. Alexander Maclean (*c.*1740–62). Promoted a Major in Keith and Campbell's Highlanders, he was killed at Burcker Muhl in Germany, 21 Sept. 1762. Francis MacLean died in the West Indies in 1762.
24. Gardiner, *West Indies*, 4 [Feb.], p. 35.
25. Hopson to Pitt, Basse Terre, in the Island of Guadeloupe, 30 January 1759, Pitt, *Correspondence when Secretary of State*, II, pp. 24–5.
26. Dominica was established by the French in 1715.
27. Lord John Murray to Duke of Atholl, London, 29 May 1759, *Chronicles of the Families of Atholl and Tullibardine*, III, p. 451.
28. John Grant, Journal, pp. 29–30, MS Copy Micro 491, Alexander Turnbull

Library, NLNZ. Grant was obviously not privy to the discussions. McCulloch, *Sons of the Mountains*, I, p. 148, says Clavering heard about their state of equipment from the company captains.

29. Gardiner, *West Indies*, 6 [Feb.], p. 36.
30. John Grant, Journal, p. 30, MS Copy Micro 491, Alexander Turnbull Library, NLNZ. Some reports say attack on 14 Feb., not 13.
31. ibid., p. 31.
32. ibid., p. 32.
33. ibid.
34. ibid., pp. 32–3.
35. ibid., p. 37.
36. Gardiner, *West Indies*, 14 [Feb.], p. 37.
37. Barrington to Pitt, Basse Terre, Guadeloupe, 2 March 1759, Pitt, *Correspondence when Secretary of State*, II, pp. 46–7. See Smelser, *Sugar Islands*, pp. 105–7 for more details.
38. John Grant, Journal, pp. 35–6, MS Copy Micro 491, Alexander Turnbull Library, NLNZ,
39. ibid., p. 37.
40. Barrington to Pitt, Basse Terre, Guadeloupe, 2 March 1759, Pitt, *Correspondence when Secretary of State*, II, p. 46–7.
41. Smelser, *Sugar Islands*, p. 108. Stewart of Garth, *Sketches*, II, 3rd ed., Appendix No. I, p. ii, says ten killed and thirty-two wounded from the 42nd. Only the 38th Foot had more casualties.
42. Gardiner, *West Indies*, 1 March, p. 40. The *Spy* sloop sailed on 6 March for England with news of Hopson's death.
43. John Charles St Clair, d. May 1762, Robert Robertson d. Nov. 1759, McGregor, 'A Black Watch Who Was Who 1725–1881', Research Notes, BWRA 0863/2.
44. John Grant, Journal, p. 40, MS Copy Micro 491, Alexander Turnbull Library, NLNZ.
45. ibid., p. 41.
46. Gardiner, *West Indies*, 16 [April], p. 47.
47. Letters from Guadeloupe, quoted in Stewart of Garth, *Sketches*, I, 3rd ed., p. 330 n.*.
48. Gardiner, *West Indies*, 10 [May], p. 61.
49. John Grant, Journal, p. 42, MS Copy Micro 491, Alexander Turnbull Library, NLNZ.
50. Return sent to Maj General Amherst said there were 507 men left. Amherst, *The Journal of Jeffrey Amherst*, 19 [July 1759], p. 141. Actual figure was 193.
51. Lord John Murray to Duke of Atholl, London, 29 May 1759, *Chronicles of the Families of Atholl and Tullibardine*, III, p. 451.
52. Gardiner, *West Indies*, 7 [June], p. 63. Gardiner returned to England with Barrington.

53. Together with the 1st, 17th, 27th, 55th and 77th Regiments of regulars, 80th light armed infantry and provincials, plus Rangers and Indians.
54. Orderly Book of Capt James Stewart's Company (18/2/1759–16/7/1759), Evening Regimental Orders, New York, 5 May 1758, BWRA 0254. The 4 Orderly Books from Feb. 1759 to Nov. 1761 give an exceptional view of the life of the Regiment. See Wallace, 'The Black Watch in 1761', *The Red Hackle*, Jan., April, July, Oct. 1935, reprinted in *JSAHR*, vol. XXX, no. 121, Spring 1952, pp. 8–19, 44. James Stewart of Urrard (*c.*1727–*c.*1790) joined the 42nd as Capt July 1757, wounded at Ticonderoga and left the Regiment in 1762.
55. Stewart, Orderly Book, Regimental Orders, New York, 7 May 1758, BWRA 0254.
56. ibid., Albany Camp, 18 May 1759.
57. Amherst, *Journal*, 17 [May 1759], p. 110.
58. ibid., 7 [June 1759], p. 116.
59. Wilson, Orderly Book, General Orders, Fort Edward, 17 June 1759, p. 31.
60. General Orders, quoted in Knox, *An Historical Journal*, 8 June 1759, p. 367.
61. ibid.
62. Amherst, *Journal*, 17 [June 1759], p. 122.
63. ibid., 11 [July 1759], p. 133. Capt Allan Campbell to Duncan Campbell of Glenure, Ticonderoga, 27 July 1759, GD170/1067, f. 244, NRS. See Amherst to Campbell, 18 June 1759, WO 1/5, p. 131, TNA.
64. Stewart, Orderly Book, After Orders, Lake George Camp, 27 June 1759, BWRA 0254.
65. Richards, 'The Black Watch at Ticonderoga', p. 30, says 14,500. McCulloch's source is the Return, p. 152, n. 42.
66. Amherst to the Hon. [Lieutenant Governor of New York] James DeLancey, Camp before Ticonderoga, 24 July 1759, f. 63 (p. 125), Amherst Papers, XXX, Correspondence between the Commander-in-Chief and the Government of New York, March 1756–Nov. 1763, WO 34/30, TNA. He wrote another detailed letter to DeLancey, Camp at Ticonderoga, 27 July 1759, quoted in Richards, 'The Black Watch at Ticonderoga', p. 31. This letter is not in the series of letters in WO 34/30, TNA.
67. Capt James Murray to Mr Murray of Strowan, Camp at the Lines of Burning Theanderoga, 27 July 1759, *Chronicles of the Families of Atholl and Tullibardine*, III, p. 452.
68. ibid.
69. Capt Allan Campbell to Duncan Campbell of Glenure, Ticonderoga, 27 July 1759, GD170/1067, f. 244, NRS.
70. Amherst to DeLancey, Camp at Ticonderoga 27 July 1759, quoted in Richards, 'The Black Watch at Ticonderoga', p. 31.
71. Capt Alexander Campbell, Ticonderoga, 27 July 1759, Campbell Letters and Papers, GD87/1/87, NRS. Statistics: Stewart of Garth, *Sketches*, II, 3rd ed., Appendix No. I, p. ii; during the campaign in July and August, 3 private soldiers were killed, 1 Sgt and 4 soldiers wounded.

72. Wilson, Orderly Book, Parole, Gage, Ticonderoga, 29 July 1759, p. 104.
73. Capt Allan Campbell to Duncan Campbell of Glenure, Ticonderoga, 27 July 1759, GD170/1067, f. 244A, NRS.
74. John Grant, Journal, p. 42, MS Copy Micro 491, Alexander Turnbull Library, NLNZ.
75. ibid., p. 43. Townsend died on 25 July 1759, having been hit by a cannon ball.
76. Record of Issues of Clothing by Quarter Master Adam Stewart, Albany, 3 Aug. 1759, BWRA 0253.
77. John Grant, Journal, p. 44, MS Copy Micro 491, Alexander Turnbull Library, NLNZ.
78. Amherst, *Journal*, 1 [Aug. 1759], p. 149. After a nineteen-day siege, Fort Niagara had also fallen to the British on 26 July.
79. A detachment of 40 men was sent to join the 1st Bn. H.B. Eaton, 'Lieutenant General Patrick Sinclair, An Account of His Military Career', *JSAHR*, LVI, 1978, p. 129.
80. John Grant, Journal, pp. 44–5, MS Copy Micro 491, Alexander Turnbull Library, NLNZ.
81. ibid., p. 46.
82. ibid., p. 47.
83. ibid., p. 48.
84. ibid., p. 51.
85. Amherst to DeLancey, Camp at Crown Point, 5 Aug. 1759, f. 65 (p. 129), Amherst Papers, WO 34/30, TNA.
86. Stewart, Orderly Book (22/9/1759–3/8/1760), BWRA 0225. Stewart's entries give a detailed description of the works undertaken.
87. John [Mac]Gregor (*c.*1725–*c.*1800). He went on half-pay in 1763 when the 2nd Bn was reduced, but returned as a Lt in 42nd to fight in the American War.
88. Stewart, Orderly Book, 30 Sept. 1759, BWRA 0225.
89. Thomas Mante, *History of the Late War in America*, p. 218, gives this as the reason. Amherst obviously also wanted information.
90. Mante, *History of the Late War in America*, p. 218.
91. Amherst, *Journal*, 12 [Sept. 1759], p. 168. Rogers, *The Annotated and Illustrated Journals of Major Robert Rogers*, p. 71. Robert Rogers (1731–95). Eight Gentleman Volunteers from the 42nd attended the Robert Rogers Training School. They were Alexander Robertson, John Robertson, William Frazier, senior, Andrew Ross, William Frazier, junior, John Graham [Graeme], Angus Campbell and Charles Menzies.
92. Mante, *Late War in America*, p. 219.
93. The memoir written by Robert Kirkwood (under the name Robert Kirk), published in 1775, is a rare eyewitness account of this controversial expedition. The earlier part borrowed extensively from an earlier French traveller, Baron de Lahontan's *New Voyages in North America*, written in the late seventeenth century. His later memoirs appear authentic but not always reliable.

See Kirk[wood], *Through So Many Dangers: The Memoirs and Adventures of Robert Kirk*. Kirkwood had spent nearly a year as a prisoner of the Shawnee, before escaping. He had also deserted from the British army and been pardoned.

94. Kirk[wood], *Memoirs*, p. 65.
95. Amherst, *Journal*, 19 [Sept. 1759], p. 170.
96. Rogers, quoted in Cuneo, *Robert Rogers of the Rangers*, p. 106.
97. Mante, *Late War in America*, p. 221. He says the party was reduced from 220 to 142 men.
98. Kirk[wood], *Memoirs*, p. 66.
99. Mante, *Late War in America*, p. 222. See also Amherst, *Journal*, 7 [Nov. 1759], p. 188.
100. Kirk[wood], *Memoirs*, pp. 67–8.
101. Mante, *Late War in America*, pp. 223–4. See Kirkwood, *Memoirs*, ed. note, p. 68. George Campbell (*c.*1738–62) Ensign 31 Jan. 1756; lt 1758 serving with 80th Foot (Gage's Light Infantry). He died at Martinique. The raid is referred to as the 'raid that destroyed the savage Abenaki Nation forever', but as the 'Rogers Massacre' by the Abenaki survivors.
102. On 8 Nov. 1759 Amherst, who had sent an officer of the Rangers to assist the party, noted that he returned having 'brought in four Indians, two Rangers, . . . two young Squaws, and a young Indian boy. They were loaded with wampum & fine things they took at St Francis', *Journal*, p. 189. This appears to have been a rare incident of cannibalism due to extreme conditions, although other incidents, unreported, may have happened.
103. Stewart, Orderly Book, Camp at Crown Point, 2 Oct. 1759, BWRA 0255. Later increased to twenty-six boats.
104. ibid., 10 Oct. 1759.
105. ibid., Orders for Passing Lake Champlain.
106. Detailed instructions given in Stewart, Orderly Book, BWRA 0255.
107. ibid., Crown Point, 11 Oct. 1759. Some men of the 42nd undertook the duties of seamen; having either grown up in coastal towns or near the Highland lochs, they were often experienced sailors.
108. ibid., Orders for passing Lake Champlain. These were the 17th, 27th and 55th. The 77th was with the 42nd.
109. Amherst, *Journal*, 11, 12 [Oct. 1759], pp. 179–80. Alexander Mackay (*c.*1740–72). See also Amherst to DeLancey, Esq, Camp at Crown Point, 18 Oct. 1759, f. 88 (p. 175), WO 34/30, TNA. Forbes, *The 'Black Watch'*, p. 69, says an officer and twenty men were captured.
110. Amherst, *Journal*, 13 & 14 [Oct. 1759], pp. 180–1.
111. Amherst to DeLancey, Esq, Camp at Crown Point, 18 Oct. 1759, Amherst Papers, WO 34/30, f. 88 (p. 175), TNA.
112. Mante, *Late War in America*, p. 219.
113. Amherst, *Journal*, 19 [Oct. 1759], p. 183.
114. ibid., 21 [Oct. 1759], p. 183.

115. ibid., 10 [Nov. 1759], p. 189.

116. Garrisons and Winter Quarters of His Majesty's Forces in North America under the command of His Excellency, Major General Amherst, Headquarters at New York, 15 Dec. 1759, WO 17/1489. TNA. Five Companies were at Fort Edward, individual companies at Halfway Brook, Fort Miller, Saratoga, Stillwater and Halfmoon. See Amherst, *Journal*, 28 [Nov.1759], p. 194.

117. John Grant, Journal, p. 52, MS Copy Micro 491, Alexander Turnbull Library, NLNZ.

118. ibid., p. 56.

119. Capt James Murray to Mr Murray of Strowan, Albany, 11 June 1760, *Chronicles of the Families of Atholl and Tullibardine*, III, p. 461.

120. Mr Murray of Strowan to (his uncle) Duke of Atholl, Kinloch, 1 Sept. 1759, ibid., p. 454.

5. Reduction of the Universe 1760–1762

1. Lt Sandy Farquharson, to Mr Murray of Strowan, 2 Feb. 1762, on board the *Bird* transport, Fort Royal Bay, Martinique, *Chronicles of the Families of Atholl and Tullibardine*, III, p. 491.

2. John Grant, Journal, p. 56, MS Copy Micro 491, Alexander Turnbull Library, NLNZ.

3. Stewart, Orderly Book, Camp at Ontario, 16 July 1760, BWRA 0255.

4. ibid., 17 July 1760.

5. ibid., General After Orders (undated but probably 16 July).

6. ibid., Camp at Ontario, 16 July 1760.

7. 42nd Foot 2nd Battalion 1759–83, WO 12/5553, TNA. See also H. B. Eaton, 'Lieutenant General Patrick Sinclair, An Account of His Military Career', *JSAHR*, LVI, 1978, p. 130. The Onondagas were original members of the Iroquois Confederacy.

8. Correspondence between Commander-in-Chief and masters of vessels 1757–63, WO 34/60 f. 127, and various officers in charge of vessels on the lakes 1760–63, WO 34/65, f. 149, TNA. Richard Sinclair was commissioned as an ensign in July 1758, promoted lt on 27 July 1759. He was later put in command of the *Mohawk* and remained at Fort William Augustus. He left the 42nd in 1761.

9. John Grant, Journal, p. 59, MS Copy Micro 491, Alexander Turnbull Library, NLNZ, says that 'one thousand' Indians returned home because they had not been allowed to scalp the prisoners. This is an exaggeration since there were only 706 Indians present. It is more likely that 100 left. See H.B. Eaton, 'Lieutenant General Patrick Sinclair, An Account of His Military Career', *JSAHR*, LVI, 1978, pp. 128–33.

10. John Grant, Journal, p. 61, MS Copy Micro 491, Alexander Turnbull Library,

NLNZ. He says they rowed forty miles on the first day.

11. Amherst, *Journal*, 2 [Sept. 1760], pp. 242–3.
12. Thomas Stirling to William Stirling, 9 Sept. 1760, Camp at Montreal, GD 24/1/458, f. 1, NRS. It is possible that they are also referring to the Manitou rapids seven miles upstream.
13. Capt Alexander Reid (younger son of Baron Reid, brother of John) to Baron Reid of Straloch, Mont Real, 9 Sept. 1760, *Chronicles of the Families of Atholl and Tullibardine*, III, p. 478.
14. Amherst to Pitt, Camp of Montreal, 8 Sept. 1760, Pitt, *Correspondence when Secretary of State*, II, p. 329. Previously he says 'on the 31st I sat [set] out, rowed twenty four miles, and camped on Isle au Chat, the Rapides were more frightfull than dangerous. Sept 1st. I passed the long Saut, marched covering Partys.'
15. John Grant, Journal, p. 61, MS Copy Micro 491, Alexander Turnbull Library, NLNZ. The river did not become navigable until 1958 with the construction of the St Lawrence Seaway.
16. Amherst, *Journal*, 4 [Sept. 1760], p. 244.
17. John Grant, Journal, p. 62, MS Copy Micro 491, Alexander Turnbull Library, NLNZ.
18. Amherst, *Journal*, 8 [Sept. 1760], p. 247.
19. Lt Alexander Farquharson to Mr Jacob Feneik, Camp at Montreal 16 Sept. 1760, BWRA 0401.
20. Capt Alexander Reid to Baron Reid, Mont Real, 9 Sept. 1760, *Chronicles of the Families of Atholl and Tullibardine*, III, p. 478.
21. Major John Reid to Baron Reid, Camp at Montreal, 10 Sept. 1760, ibid., p. 479.
22. See McCulloch, *Sons of the Mountains*, II, p. 15.
23. Thomas Stirling to William Stirling, Camp at Montreal, 9 Sept. 1760, GD 24/1/458, f. 1, NRS.
24. John Grant, Journal, p. 63, MS Copy Micro 491, Alexander Turnbull Library, NLNZ.
25. Lt Alexander Farquharson to Mr Jacob Feneik, Camp at Montreal, 16 Sept. 1760, BWRA 0401.
26. John Grant, Journal, p. 64, MS Copy Micro 491, Alexander Turnbull Library, NLNZ. Grant says they celebrated the King's birthday on 9 Nov., although it was on 10 Nov. Writing in later life, Grant perhaps got the date wrong and the celebration was on the correct date!
27. ibid., pp. 64–5.
28. ibid., p. 65.
29. Amherst, *Journal*, 17 [Jan. 1761], p. 264.
30. At the time a commonly used expression in the Regiment to describe what in the British Army today would be referred to as rifle companies.
31. Stewart, Orderly Book (4/4/1761–5/8/1761), Montreal, 19 April 1761, BWRA 0256.
32. ibid., Montreal, 26 April 1761. It was the custom in the Army to make the previous year's coat into a waistcoat.

33. John Grant, Journal, p. 66, MS Copy Micro 491, Alexander Turnbull Library, NLNZ.
34. Stewart, Orderly Book, Montreal, 28 May 1761, BWRA 0256.
35. ibid., Montreal, 30 May 1761. This order would appear to be an early effort to regiment what had become a profusion of different colours. It was also becoming common practice to decorate the knitted bonnet with feathers, no doubt influenced by the headdress of the North American Indians. In time the bonnet became entirely covered with feathers and given extra height by being attached to a light 'cage'. These feathers were different from the wearing of a distinctive set of feathers as a 'hackle'.
36. ibid., Montreal 3 June 1761.
37. ibid.
38. ibid., 4 June 1761. It appears the 2nd Bn left before the 1st Battalion.
39. Stewart, Orderly Book, Regimental Order, 4 June 1761, BWRA 0256.
40. ibid., Camp at St Jones (John's), 10 June 1761.
41. John Grant, Journal, p. 66, MS Copy Micro 491, Alexander Turnbull Library, NLNZ.
42. Stewart, Orderly Book, General Orders, Crown Point, 13 June 1761, BWRA 0256.
43. ibid., Regimental Order, 16 June 1761.
44. ibid., Crown Point, 24 June 1761.
45. ibid., Crown Point, 17 June 1761, 'Two setts of Muster Rolls to be made immediately'. Muster rolls were in use until the end of the nineteenth century.
46. ibid., 19 June 1761.
47. ibid., Camp at Crown Point, 27 June 1761.
48. ibid., 18 June 1761.
49. ibid., Regimental Orders, Crown Point, 25 June 1761.
50. ibid., Regimental Orders, 27 June 1761.
51. ibid., 19 June 1761.
52. ibid., Camp at Crown Point, 27 June 1761.
53. ibid., Crown Point, 1 July 1761.
54. John Grant, Journal, p. 67. Alexander Turnbull Library, NLNZ, MS Copy Micro 491. Against this comment, has been added: '(see Last of Mohicans)'. This indicates that the Journal must have been written after publication in 1826 of James Fenimore Cooper's *The Last of the Mohicans*. He also calls Saratoga 'as yet a bloodless field', i.e. before 1777, p. 68.
55. Stewart, Orderly Book (6/7/1761–5/11/1761), General Order, 10 July 1761, BWRA 0257.
56. ibid., Regimental Order, 12 July 1761.
57. Col. R.F. H. Wallace, 'The Black Watch in 1761: from Montreal to New York', *The Red Hackle*, July 1935, p. 21.

58. John Grant, Journal, p. 60, MS Copy Micro 491, Alexander Turnbull Library, NLNZ.
59. ibid., p. 60, says they arrived 'the later end of June'. The 1st Bn arrived on 25 July.
60. Stewart, Orderly Book, Watson's Ferry, 25 July 1761, BWRA 0257.
61. John Grant, Journal, p. 60, MS Copy Micro 491, Alexander Turnbull Library, NLNZ. Stewart, Orderly Book, Staten Island 31 July 1761, BWRA 0257.
62. Maj Gen Robert Monckton (1726–82). 1st Brigade commanded by William Haviland, 2nd Brigade by Francis Grant, including 42nd, 76th & 77th. The other two Brigades were commanded by Sir William Rufane and Lord Rollo. The 5th Brigade was commanded by Hunt Walsh.
63. Embarkation Returns, New York, 19 Nov. 1761, Figures for 1st Bn 688, 2nd Bn 657. The total force number coming from New York was 6,667, WO 1/5, p. 417, TNA.
64. John Grant, Journal, p. 70, MS Copy Micro 491, Alexander Turnbull Library, NLNZ.
65. ibid., p. 71.
66. ibid.
67. General Orders, 1 Jan. 1762, Bridgetown, Barbados, quoted in McCulloch, Sons of the Mountains, I, p. 271.
68. John Grant, Journal, p. 71, MS Copy Micro 491, Alexander Turnbull Library, NLNZ.
69. Hunt Walsh, Martinique, 31 Jan. 1762, Capture of Martinique, WO 1/19, f. 154 (p. 293), TNA. He was probably writing to Col Monckton, 17th Foot; he mentions General Monckton in the letter.
70. Forbes, The 'Black Watch', p. 72.
71. Hunt Walsh, 31 Jan. 1762, Capture of Martinique, f. 154 (p. 294), WO 1/19, TNA.
72. John Grant, Journal, pp. 76–7, MS Copy Micro 491, Alexander Turnbull Library, NLNZ.
73. Quoted in Forbes, The 'Black Watch', p. 72.
74. Lt Alexander Farquharson, on board the Bird transport in Fort Royal Bay off the Island of Martinique, 2 Feb. 1762, Chronicles of the Families of Atholl and Tullibardine, III, pp. 491–2.
75. Capt James Murray to Mr Murray of Strowan, ps. to Farquharson's letter, ibid., p. 492.
76. Stewart of Garth, Sketches, I, 3rd ed., p. 194. He served as an ensign in the 77th (Duke of Atholl's) Highlanders, which Murray later raised. Return of Killed, Wounded & Missing, 24 Jan. 1762, lists 1 capt, 1 lt 1 sgt 5 rank & file killed, 1 maj, 1 capt (Murray), 3 lts, 3 sgts, 1 drummer and 44 rank & file wounded; 27 Jan. 1762: 1 rank & file killed, 2 wounded, WO 17/1489, TNA.
77. 'General John Reid', in Tullibardine (ed.), Military History of Perthshire 1660–1902, pp. 387–95. Statistics from Stewart of Garth, Sketches, II, Appendix 1, p. ii, and see p. 354.

78. James Stewart's Orderly Books end on 5 Nov. 1761. James Abercromby (*c*.1740–1804).

79. John Grant, Journal, pp. 76–7, MS Copy Micro 491, Alexander Turnbull Library, NLNZ.

80. Anon. poem, tr. Michael Newton, quoted in Newton, *We're Indians Sure Enough*, p. 111.

81. Forbes, *The 'Black Watch'*, p. 74.

82. George Keppel, 3rd Earl of Albemarle, KG, PC (1724–70).

83. John Grant, Journal, pp. 84–5, MS Copy Micro 491, Alexander Turnbull Library, NLNZ. Already 39 of the 1st Bn and 99 of the 2nd Bn were sick. Abstract of the General Return of HM's forces under the command of Lt Gen. Lord Albemarle, quoted in Syrett (ed.), *The Siege and Capture of Havana 1762*, p. 126.

84. John Grant, Journal, p. 85, MS Copy Micro 491, Alexander Turnbull Library, NLNZ says 24 ships of the line, 36 frigates and 400 transports and10,000 troops but statistics vary. Thomas Mante (*c*.1730–85), *History of the Late War in America*, pp. 409, 410, says a total force of 11,353, with 22 ships of the line, 20 frigates, plus transports, supply and hospital ships, as well as ships for 'negroes, horses and baggage for the general officers', making a total of over 200 ships. Monthly Return, 31 March 1762, gives total number of rank & file from 23 regiments as 11,791; statistics for the 42nd in ten companies: 1st Bn: 588 Rank & File; 2nd 557 Rank and File; only the 76th in two Bns supplied more men, WO17/1489, TNA. Mante describes himself as 'assistant engineer' but little is known about him. Stewart of Garth does not give much information on the Regiment's activities.

85. Captain David Dundas, 'Memorandum on the Capture of Havana', in Syrett (ed.), *Siege and Capture of Havana*, p. 315. Written in 1800 'it is thought they [the recollections] are not incorrect', Syrett (ed.), p. 326.

86. John Grant, Journal, p. 85, MS Copy Micro 491, Alexander Turnbull Library, NLNZ.

87. ibid., p. 86.

88. ibid.

89. Dundas, 'Memorandum', quoted in Syrett (ed.), *Siege and Capture of Havana*, p. 315.

90. See Pocock, *Battle for Empire*, p. 207.

91. Dundas, 'Memorandum', quoted in Syrett (ed.), *Siege and Capture of Havana*, pp. 316–17.

92. Will of Alexander Farquharson, *Felicity* transport, 6 June 1762. Farquharson's diary was from 6 May to 6 June 1762. The 1762 *Almanac* is now in the Rare Book Dept of the New York Public Library. See Syrett (ed.), *Siege and Capture of Havana*, p. 163; Pocock, *Battle of Empire*, p. 202. James Thomson (1700–1748), *The Seasons*, printed for A. Hamilton, London 1793. The quotation is from 'Spring', p. 13. He also wrote the lyrics for *Rule Britannia*.

93. See Mante, *Late War in America*, p. 419.

94. Under the command of Gen William Howe, who had served under Wolfe in

Quebec. Later 5th Viscount Howe, and Commander-in-Chief, North America 1775–8.

95. John Grant, Journal, p. 86, MS Copy Micro 491, Alexander Turnbull Library, NLNZ.

96. Dundas, 'Memorandum', quoted in Syrett (ed.), *Siege and Capture of Havana*, p. 317.

97. Mante, *Late War in America*, p. 421.

98. Dundas, 'Memorandum', quoted in Syrett (ed.), *Siege and Capture of Havana*, p. 316.

99. ibid., pp. 316–17.

100. Mante, *Late War in America*, p. 422.

101. John Grant, Journal, p. 86, MS Copy Micro 491, Alexander Turnbull Library, NLNZ.

102. ibid., p. 87.

103. ibid., p. 88.

104. ibid.

105. Don Luis (de) Velasco, see *New York Times*, 6 Feb. 1903. http://query. nytimes.com/mem/archive-free. Don Juan de Prado Malleza Portocarrero y Luna (1716–?1770). See *Confession de Mariscal de Campo Don Juan de Prado*, Madrid, 1763, Library of Congress OCLC 38096822.

106. See Syrett (ed.), *Siege and Capture of Havana*, p. xxviii.

107. Prado, Diary, 1 July 1762, quoted in Syrett (ed.), *Siege and Capture of Havana*, p. xxviii.

108. Mante, *Late War in America*, p. 426.

109. ibid., p. 430.

110. 'Return of the Surgeons', 21 July 1762, quoted in McCulloch, *Sons of the Mountains*, I, p. 280.

111. See Mante, *Late War in America*, pp. 432–3. Forbes, *The 'Black Watch'*, p. 81, says '80 feet deep and forty wide'.

112. See Stewart of Garth, *Sketches*, I, 3rd ed., p. 359, and Forbes, *The 'Black Watch'*, pp. 81–2.

113. Mante, *Late War in America*, p. 440. No date but after 22 July and before 30 July.

114. ibid., pp. 441–2. See Forbes, *The 'Black Watch'*, p. 82, who says Lt Col James Grant led the Highlanders across the breach. But he must mean Francis Grant, who had transferred out of the Regiment on 9 July 1762. Stewart of Garth, *Sketches*, I, 3rd ed., p. 359, says Lt Col James Stewart commanded the assault. Capt Charles Forbes of Auchernach (1730–94), 2nd Bn 1st Foot, is credited with leading 'The Forlorn Hope' across the narrow ridge. He joined the 2nd Bn 42nd 'in place of' John Small, who was promoted Capt on 15 Aug. 1762, reduced on half-pay in 1763, later joining the 66th Foot. Source: McGregor,

'A Black Watch Who Was Who, 1725–1881', Research Notes, 42nd, BWRA 0683/2.

115. Forbes, The 'Black Watch', p. 83.

116. John Grant, Journal, p. 89, MS Copy Micro 491, Alexander Turnbull Library, NLNZ. Grant does not mention El Morro and so he was presumably engaged in siege operations against Havana.

117. ibid., pp. 90–1.

118. ibid., p. 92. Grant's Journal ends here. He left the 42nd in 1764 and his Journal ended up in New Zealand. He is perhaps related to Dr John Johnson, New Zealand's first Colonial Surgeon, whose son was called John Grant Johnson.

119. Mante, Late War in America, p. 458, says 12 Aug. Dundas. 'Memorandum', quoted in Syrett (ed.), Siege and Capture of Havana, p. 322, says 13 Aug., with full possession taken on 14 Aug.

120. Mante, Late War in America, p. 460. Forbes, The Black Watch, p. 85, says total 1,657 lost (345 killed, 640 wounded, 672 died through sickness).

121. Mante, Late War in America, p. 461. Mante is obviously referring to British casualties.

122. 'A Letter from a Gentleman in New York to his Friend in London', Feb. 1763, Letters from New York, The Gentleman's Magazine, Feb. 1763. Statistics from Stewart of Garth, Sketches, II, Appendix I, p. ii: 6 soldiers killed, 12 soldiers and 1 drummer/piper wounded in the fighting. Forbes, The Black Watch, p. 85, says 'twelve men killed and wounded'.

123. Albemarle to Pocock, 8 August 1762, quoted in Syrett (ed.), Siege and Capture of Havana, p. 281.

124. He was succeeded as Piper Major by Peter (Patrick) McIntyre. Lachlan Johnston also known as John Laughlin.

125. Mante, Late War in America, p. 463.

126. Albemarle to Amherst, Headquarters, near Havana, 18 August 1762, quoted in Syrett (ed.), Siege and Capture of Havana, p. 293.

127. Figures: 5,366 men, of whom 4,708 had died from disease, compared with 273 who were killed in action and 246 who had died of their wounds. General Return of Officers, Sergeants, Drum[me]rs, Rank and File killed, died by wounds, died by sickness, deserted, and missing from the 7 June to 18 October, Havana, dated 18 Oct. quoted in Syrett (ed.), Siege and Capture of Havana, p. 305.

128. Mante, Late War in America, p. 464.

129. See Stewart of Garth, Sketches, I, 3rd ed., p. 360, Syrett (ed.), Siege and Capture of Havana, p. xxxiv. Battle Honours were granted in Army Order 295 in 1909. Wallace, 'The Colours of The Black Watch', The Red Hackle, July 1936, p. 8.

130. J. Boswell's London Journal 1762–1763, with Introduction and Notes by Frederick A. Pottle, William Heinemann Ltd, 1951, p. 146.

131. Edmund Burke, quoted in Forbes, The 'Black Watch', p. 85.

132. Anon. poem, declaring 'immortal fame for the Black Watch', tr. by Michael Newton, quoted in Newton, We're Indians Sure Enough, pp. 111–12.

6. Every Tree is Become an Indian

1. Rev. James Maclagan, 'To the Highlanders Upon Departing for America', tr. by Michael Newton, quoted in Newton, *We're Indians Sure Enough*, p. 125.
2. Sir Jeffery Amherst, Order for Drafting of the 2nd Battalion of Royal Highland Regiment into the First, 2 Oct. 1762, Amherst Papers, vol. XCIII, WO 34/93, p. 3, TNA.
3. Allan Campbell of Barcaldine was one of those appointed an additional company captain in 1757 and so was an officer of the 2nd Bn. Being reduced on half-pay meant having a reduced salary but with the opportunity to return to full pay when a suitable opportunity presented itself. Officers and men could sometimes spend years on half-pay.
4. See Order for Disbanding the 2nd Battn of Lord John Murray's Regt of Foot, and Orders and Instructions for Disbanding the 2nd Battn of Lord John Murray's Regt of Foot, Signed by His Majesty's Command W. Ellis to Lord John Murray, 11 March 1763, p. 118, to Gordon Graham, 11 March 1763, pp. 119–22, WO 26/26. 'Whereas our intention is only to pay off at present and clear the non commissioned Officers and pruivate Men of our said Battalion,' i.e. Commissioned officers not disbanded. See also W. Ellis to Rt Hon. Henry Fox, indicating the same, 11 March 1763, WO 4/71, p. 395, TNA.
5. List of officers of the 2nd Battn of the Royal Highland Regiment Reduced at Guildford the 18th March 1763, WO 34/95, p. 4, TNA.
6. 'The Official Journal Kept by Lt Eddington or the Surgeon', in Carroon (ed.), *Broadswords and Bayonets*, pp. 103–4. James Eddington (1739–1802) also written as Eddingstone; authorship is not confirmed, but the journal could not have been written by the Surgeon, Alex Potts, since he did not accompany the expedition. Authorship has also been attributed to the Surgeon's Mate, James Murdoch or Lt John Smith. For simplicity, I am attributing authorship to Eddington in the narrative. See *Broadswords and Bayonets*, p. 46, and Kirk[wood], *Through So Many Dangers: The Memoirs and Adventures of Robert Kirk*, ed. McCulloch and Toddish, who refer to it as the Smith – Eddington – Murdoch – Journal [SEMJ], p. 101. Chief Pontiac or Obwandiyag (*c.*1720–69). The reference to the 'English' was in common use, obviously meaning British.
7. Eddington/ Surgeon, Official Journal, in Carroon (ed.), *Broadswords and Bayonets*, p. 105.
8. Rutherfurd's Narrative – 'An Episode in the Pontiac War, 1763', *Transactions of the Canada Institute*, vol. III, pp. 233, 237, Major Thomas Rutherfurd (1746–1830). See Colley, *Captives: Britain, Empire and the World 1600–1850*, pp. 193–5.
9. Lt Col Henry Bouquet (1719–65). Of French Huguenot descent, born in Switzerland, he had begun his career aged seventeen in the Netherlands. He

had come to North America to take command of the 1st Bn 60th Foot, The Royal Americans. Lt General Sir Edward, Hutton, 'Henry Bouquet: a Biographical Sketch', 1911. Original in Royal Green Jackets Museum.

10. Amherst to Bouquet, New York, 6 June 1763, WO 34/41, p. 189, TNA. In correspondence both Amherst and Bouquet agreed to give the Indians blankets infected with smallpox. See 'History of Colonel Henry Bouquet and the Western Frontiers of Pennsylvannia, 1747–1764', collected and edited by Mary C. Darlington, 1911?. Typescript manuscript.

11. Amherst to Bouquet, New York, 12 June 1763, WO 34/41, p. 191, TNA.

12. ibid.

13. ibid., 19 June 1763, WO 34/41, p. 201, TNA. See also letters Amherst to Bouquet, 14, 16 and 18 June, 1783, WO 34/41, pp. 193, 199, TNA.

14. Bouquet to Amherst, 29 June 1763, Carlisle, Bouquet Papers, Add. MSS 21634, folio 308, BL.

15. See Return of the 42nd and 77th Regiments, Carlisle the 13th July 1763, & State of the Troops in the Southern Department, signed by Major Allan Campbell, WO 34/40, pp. 621 & 623, TNA. Campbell listed 147 fit for duty present, twenty-one sick, 137 gone forward with a total of 284 rank and file fit for duty.

16. Allan Campbell to Amherst, Bedford, 27 July 1763, Amherst Miscellaneous Correspondence, WO 34/95, p. 2, TNA. Amherst received the letter on 6 August and answered it next day.

17. Timberlake, *The Memoirs of Lt. Henry Timberlake*, p. 79. He was a third-generation American, born in 1730.

18. Bouquet to Amherst, Camp at Edge Hill, 5 Aug. 1763, WO 34/40, p. 645, TNA. See also Bouquet to Amherst, 5 Aug. 1763, Camp at Edge Hill, 26 Miles from Fort Pitt, Bouquet Papers, Drafts of Letters, 1760–1764, Add. MSS 21653, p. 199. BL.

19. Bouquet to Amherst, Camp at Edge Hill, 26 miles from Fort Pitt, 5 Aug. 1763, WO 34/40, pp. 645–7 TNA. See also Bouquet to Amherst, 5 Aug. 1763, Camp 26 Miles from Fort Pitt, Bouquet Papers, Drafts of Letters, 1760–1764. Add. MSS 21653, p. 201, BL.

20. Bouquet to Amherst, Camp at Edge Hill, 26 miles from Fort Pitt, 5 Aug. 1763, WO 34/40, pp. 645–7, TNA.

21. Bouquet to Amherst, Camp at Bushy Run, 6 August 1763, WO 34/40, pp. 649–51, TNA. See also Bouquet Papers, Drafts of Letters 1760–1764, Add. MSS. 21653, f. 203, BL.

22. Return of Killed and Wounded in the two actions at Edge Hill near Bushy Run, 5 and 6 August 1763, WO 34/40, p. 653, TNA. 42nd losses: One capt, 1 lt, 1 sgt, 1 corporal and 25 rank and file killed; 1 capt, 1 lt, 2 sgts, 3 corporals, 1 drummer and 27 men wounded compared with the 77th (5 soldiers killed, 7 wounded) or the 60th (6 killed, 4 wounded). Totals: 50 killed, 60 wounded, 5 missing.

23. Return of the Loss sustained by the 42nd or Royal Highland Regiment in the

action of the 5th August 1763, WO 34/40, TNA, p. 681. Signed by Allan Campbell, with additional note by Col Henry Bouquet 'given under my hand at Fort Pitt, 14 August 1763'.

24. Amherst to Major Wilkins, or Officer Commanding at Niagara, New York, 20 Aug. 1763, WO 34/23, pp. 266–7, TNA.

25. Amherst to the Honble Lt Governor Colden, New York, 26 Aug. 1763, Amherst Papers, WO 34/30, p. 503, TNA.

26. Amherst to Bouquet, New York, 25 Aug. 1763, Amherst Papers, WO 34/41, p. 243, TNA.

27. Bouquet to Campbell, 12 Aug. 1763, Fort Pitt, Bouquet Papers, Drafts of Letters, 1760–64, Add. MSS. 21653, p. 207, BL.

28. Bouquet to Amherst, Fort Pitt, 26 Aug. 1763, WO 34/40, p. 661. He said that only 245 men in the 42nd and 77th were fit for duty.

29. Amherst to Bouquet, New York, 7 Aug. 1763, WO 34/41, pp. 235–6, TNA. Given the disappointment of some lieutenants who would have to be reduced, provision was made for them to remain in any vacant ensign's position, on an ensign's pay, on the understanding they would succeed to the first vacant lieutenancy.

30. Amherst to Bouquet, New York, 7 Aug. 1763, WO 34/41, p. 235, TNA. The order says two 'contingent' men.

31. Amherst to Bouquet, New York, 7 Aug. 1763, WO 34/41, p. 238, TNA.

32. See His Majesty's 42nd Royal Highland Regiment of Foot. Muster Rolls, WO 12/5478, I, p. 96, TNA. He was entertained from the 77th on 25 Oct. 1763 and admitted into the 42nd in March 1778.

33. Bouquet to Amherst, Fort Pitt, 11 Aug. 1763, WO 34/40, p. 658; Amherst to Bouquet, New York, 25 Aug. 1763, WO 34/41, p. 243, TNA.

34. Peebles to Bouquet, Fort Pitt, 29 Sept. 1763, Bouquet Papers, Add. MSS. 21649, folio 366, BL. Amherst granted his request.

35. Allan Campbell to Amherst, [Fort Ligonier], 17 Aug. 1763, Amherst Miscellaneous Correspondence, WO 34/95, p. 103, TNA.

36. Amherst to Campbell, New York, 31 Aug. 1763, Amherst Papers, WO 34/41, TNA, p. 247. 'Immediately on receipt of yours of the 17th inst. I sent to Lt Colonel Reid . . .'

37. See Reid to Amherst, undated (1763), in which he describes having to settle his personal affairs and offering to resign, WO 34/95, p. 5; Campbell to Amherst, Fort Bedford, 8 Oct. 1763. WO 34/95, pp. 206–7, TNA.

38. http://www.ushistory.org/declaration/related/proc63.htm.

39. Pressure was immediately exerted to move the line further west. Further treaties with the Indians in 1768 and 1770 opened up present-day West Virginia and Kentucky to British settlement.

40. Kirk[wood], *Memoirs and Adventures*, p. 95.

41. On 30 June 1765 Maclagan had 'not yet joined'. A new surgeon was also needed since David Hepburn had resigned on 15 April 1764; see Muster Rolls, WO 12/5478, I, p. 101.

42. Kirk[wood], *Memoirs and Adventures*, p. 96. He wrongly suggested the force numbered 2,000 and that they set out on 1 July.

43. ibid., p. 96.

44. Colley, *Captives*, pp. 196–7.

45. See Stirling, 'General Account of the British Attempts to Occupy the Illinois', Thomas Stirling Papers, Fragment of letter, envelope 2, folio 2, BWRA 0398; transcribed as Stirling, Personal Journal, in Carroon (ed.), *Broadswords and Bayonets*, pp. 17–18. Although the French were bound by the terms of the Treaty to hand over the garrisons and forts, given the residue of hostility from the Indians, the situation remained fluid, hence the idea of taking both French and Indians by surprise.

46. Between 1763 and 1765, the British made nine unsuccessful attempts to establish control of the Illinois country. See 'The Stirling Expedition, Journal of Illinois History', p. 90, and Stirling, Personal Journal, in Carroon (ed.), *Broadswords and Bayonets*, p. 20. This expedition was led by the Superintendent of Indian Affairs, William Johnson's deputy, George Croghan. Croghan was taken prisoner by Kickapoo and Mascouten Indians, and robbed of the gifts he was bringing. 'He himself would have been burnt had not the French Commandant sent a belt in the French King's name to save him.' The expedition included eight volunteers from the 42nd.

47. Lt James Rumsay (Rumsay) (*c*.1740–177?/*c*.1800). He was commissioned in an Independent Company of Free Negroes, 6 Feb. 1762, in the West Indies, later transferring to the 77th and then the 42nd. See McGregor, 'A Black Watch Who Was Who 1725–1881', Research Notes, 73rd, BWRA 0683/3.

48. Stirling, Personal Journal, Carroon (ed.), *Broadswords and Bayonets*, p. 26. See also 'The Stirling Expedition', *Journal of Illinois History*, p. 91.

49. See Benson J. Lossing, *The Pictorial Fieldbook of the Revolution*, 2 vols, New York, 1859 and 1860, and Kirk[wood], *Memoirs and Adventures*, p. 101.

50. Stirling, Personal Journal, in Carroon (ed.), *Broadswords and Bayonets*, p. 26 (Stirling, 'General Account', folio 3/2, BWRA 0398).

51. Stirling, Personal Journal, Carroon (ed.), *Broadswords and Bayonets*, pp. 26, 42. 'Having the surgeon's mate with me, I made him occasionally mark down in my Journal (which I regularly kept) everything that we saw remarkable as well as the bearings of the river.' The original manuscript was lost.

52. Stirling, Personal Journal, Carroon (ed.), *Broadswords and Bayonets*, p. 26 (Stirling, 'General Account', folio 3/4 BWRA 0398). Eddington/ Surgeon, Official Journal, describes him as falling into the river when he was 'endeavouring to push the Battoe he was in off a large Rifft [reef]', Carroon (ed.), *Broadswords and Bayonets*, p. 49. This view was endorsed by Kirk[wood], *Memoirs and Adventures*, p. 102.

53. Stirling, Personal Journal, in Carroon (ed.), *Broadswords and Bayonets*, p. 27 (Stirling, 'General Account', folio 3 /4–5, BWRA 0398).

54. ibid., p. 28 (Stirling General Account, folio 3/5, BWRA 0398).

55. Kirk[wood], *Memoirs and Adventures*, p. 101.

56. Eddington/ Surgeon, Official Journal, Sunday Augt 25th [1765], in Carroon (ed.), *Broadswords and Bayonets*, p. 50.

57. Stirling, Personal Journal, in Carroon (ed.), *Broadswords and Bayonets*, p. 32 (Stirling 'General Account', folio 3/8, BWRA 0398).

58. Kirk[wood], *Memoirs and Adventure*, p. 103. (Could this be the origin of the music-hall joke which tells how a Scotsman out hunting in Canada, on seeing his first moose, says to his guide: 'If yon's a mouse, I'd hate to see a rat.'?)

59. Stirling, Personal Journal, in Carroon (ed.), *Broadswords and Bayonets*, pp. 34, 36 (Stirling 'General Account', folio 3/ 10–12, BWRA 0398).

60. Corn Cob (meaning Chief) to Stirling, quoted in ibid., pp. 40–1 (Stirling, 'General Account', folio 3/16 BWRA 0398).

61. ibid., p. 41 (Stirling, 'General Account', folio 3/16, BWRA 0398).

62. Kirk[wood], *Memoirs and Adventures*, pp. 107–8.

63. ibid., p. 108, says Stirling and the main party arrived before Rumsey.

64. Eddington/ Surgeon, Official Journal, Thursday Octr. 10th, in Carroon (ed.), *Broadswords and Bayonets*, p. 83.

65. Extract of a Letter from Captain Sterling, Commanding a Detachment of the 42nd Regiment at Fort Chartres in the Illinois Country; to His Excellency General Gage, Dated Fort Chartres 18 Oct., 1765, pp. 17–23, WO 1/7, TNA. Distance was 1,081 miles, departed 24 Aug. arrived 9 Oct. 1765.

66. Kirk[wood], *Memoirs and Adventures*, p. 108.

67. Stirling to Gage, Fort Chartres, 18 Oct. 1765, p. 21, WO 1/7, TNA.

68. Kirk[wood], *Memoirs and Adventures*, p. 111.

69. Eddington/Surgeon, Official Journal, in Carroon (ed.), *Broadswords and Bayonets*, pp. 94–5.

70. ibid., 21 [Dec. 1765], p. 97.

71. ibid., 25 [Dec. 1765], p. 98.

72. Kirk[wood], *Memoirs and Adventures*, p. 113. He remembered incorrectly that they arrived on 1 Jan. 1766. He also incorrectly states that it took them fifteen rather than twenty days.

73. Eddington/ Surgeon, Journal, in Carroon (ed.), *Broadswords and Bayonets*, p. 109.

74. ibid., p. 110.

75. ibid., p. 113.

76. Forbes, *The 'Black Watch'*, Scobie's annotated note, p. 87.

77. Eddington/Surgeon, Journal, in Carroon (ed.), *Broadswords and Bayonets*, p. 105.

78. Rev. James Maclagan, 'To the Highlanders Upon Departing for America', tr. by Michael Newton, quoted in Newton, *We're Indians Sure Enough*, p. 126.

79. Cadwallader Colden, Esq., Lt Governor, New York, 11 July 1764, Abstracts of Grants of Land, CO/5/1134, II, pp. 235a.

80. Halford-MacLeod, *'When shall we have so fine a regiment again?'*, p. 197. Susanna Alexander was the daughter of James Alexander, surveyor-general of New York and New Jersey.

81. Kirk[wood], *Memoirs and Adventures*, p. 116. 42nd Regiment Return, Cork, Ireland, 3 Sept. 1767, quoted in McCulloch, *Sons of the Mountains*, I, p. 346.

82. *Virginia Gazette*, sent by 'A Pennsylvanian' from Philadelphia, 30 July (1767), 'as a tribute due to the worthy officers, and brave men, of the Royal Highland regiment', to *Scots Magazine*, XXIX, Nov.1767, pp. 605–6.

83. Forbes, *The 'Black Watch'*, p. 92. The Duke of Atholl, Lord John Murray's half-brother, died in 1764 and John Murray of Strowan, James Murray's brother, succeeded to the Dukedom.

84. Forbes, *The 'Black Watch'*, p. 92. This is the first mention of the badge and motto of the Order of the Thistle being used. It was the order of chivalry most associated with Scotland. See Wallace, 'The Colours of the Black Watch', *The Red Hackle*, July 1936, p. 8. The original stands were destroyed by fire in 1841.

85. Stewart of Garth, *Sketches*, I, 3rd ed., p. 372. There is no information as to how they came by ostrich feathers in Ireland, or what colour they were.

86. Dr Jackson's European Armies, quoted in Stewart of Garth, *Sketches*, I, 3rd ed., p. 372.

87. Stewart of Garth, *Sketches*, I, 3rd ed., p. 372. This was clearly a sporran.

88. See McCulloch, *Sons of the Mountains*, II, p. 131, who says that in 1758–9 the musket barrels were cut down to 42 inches to make them lighter and easier to carry through the woods.

89. Stewart of Garth, Preface to the 1st edition, *Sketches*, I, p. vi, 2nd ed., p. vi.

90. Stewart of Garth, *Sketches*, I, 3rd ed., p. 376.

91. ibid., p. 377. See n.*: Of the soldiers 931 were Highlanders, 74 Lowland Scotch, 5 English (in the band), 1 Welsh and 2 Irish.

92. Quoted in McAulay, 'The First Battalion The Black Watch', Tullibardine (ed.), *Military History of Perthshire 1660–1902*, p. 59.

93. Stewart of Garth, *Sketches*, I, 3rd ed., p. 375.

94. General James Adolphus Ougthon (1720–80), Colonel of the 31st, quoted in ibid., p. 377; Forbes, *The 'Black Watch'*, p. 97.

95. Rev. James Maclagan, 'To the Highlanders Upon Departing for America', tr. Michael Newton, quoted in Newton, *We're Indians Sure Enough*, p. 126.

7. America: the War of Independence

1. *John Peebles' American War: The Diary of a Scottish Grenadier, 1776–1782*, ed. Ira. D. Gruber, p. 74. John Peebles (1739–1824). His diary is exceptional because it describes not only the major battles but also army life and appears to be the only account written by an officer serving in the 42nd. The original Peebles' Diary, '13 Notebooks concerning military operations in America, 1776–1782', and (microfilm MFilP/GD21/492) is in NRS.

2. Lt Col Charles Graham, Memorial to Rt Hon. Sec at War, 6 June 1785, quoted in Cannon, *Historical Record of the Forty-Second*, p. 85 n.*.

3. *The American Heritage Book of the Revolution*, p. 46.

4. William Howe (1729–1814) 5th Viscount, Sir Henry Clinton (1730–95), John Burgoyne (1722–92). Richard, Lord Howe (1726–1799) 4th Viscount.

5. Lord George Germaine (1716–85), formerly Lord George Sackville. He took the name of his deceased wife.

6. By the end of what became known as the 'American War of Independence', 18 regiments had been raised in the Highlands, consisting of over 20,000 fighting men. Michael Newton, *We're Indians Sure Enough*, p. 112.

7. *John Peebles' American War*, 17 April 1776, p. 24.

8. Raised in Scotland by Simon Fraser after the 78th was disbanded a decade previously.

9. See Forbes, *The 'Black Watch'*, p. 100. They were exchanged and rejoined the 42nd in 1778.

10. See *John Peebles' American War*, Thursday 13 June, p. 35, for what happened to some of the 71st.

11. Declaration of Independence, 4 July 1776, quoted in Merill Jensen, *The Founding of a Nation: A History of the American Revolution, 1763–1776*, OUP, 1968, p. 688. See http://www.connecticutsar.org/articles/king_georges_head.htm.

12. Cannon, *Historical Record of the Forty-Second*, p. 81.

13. Under the command of Lt Col Thomas Musgrave. When he was wounded he was succeeded by Lt Col (later Gen) Robert Abercromby GCB (1740–1827). He died aged eighty-seven, the oldest general in the British army. His elder brother was the renowned Sir Ralph Abercromby (1734–1801).

14. Cannon, *Historical Record of the Forty-Second*, p. 81.

15. Newark, *Highlander*, p. 63; Stewart of Garth, *Sketches*, I, 3rd ed., p. 410.

16. Charles, 2nd Earl (later 1st Marquess) Cornwallis (1738–1805).

17. The Germans included Hessians and Waldeckers from the principality of Waldeck. See Millard, H. Wright, *Nova Scotia Waldeckers: German Mercenaries Who Fought in the American Revolutionary War and Settled in Nova Scotia in 1783*, privately published, 2003. Lieutenant General Wilhelm von Knyphausen (1716–1800). Hugh Percy, 2nd Duke of Northumberland (1742–1817). He did not get along with Howe and resigned his commission in 1777.

18. See Stewart of Garth, *Sketches*, II, 3rd ed., Eighty-Fourth or Royal Highland Emigrant Regiment, pp. 208–13. Mary Beacock Fryer, *Allan Maclean, Jacobite General*, Dundurn Press, Toronto, 1987. By 1782 only 25% of the enlisted men were Scots: Newton, *We're Indians Sure Enough*, p. 48.

19. Later Maj Gen Lachlan Macquarie (1762–1824), Lt Col 73rd 1805–9, Governor of New South Wales (1809–1821).

20. Gen Israel Putnam (1718–90) sometimes credited with having made the memorable injunction: 'Don't fire until you can see the whites of their eyes.'

21. www.rootsweb.ancestry.com//~nbnorthu/vets.htm. No diary entry for Peebles and so he is not the author.

22. William Alexander (1726–83), 'Lord Stirling', not to be confused with the family of Thomas Stirling of Ardoch. William Alexander was exchanged for Loyalist Montfort Browne, Governor of West Florida, captured in March 1776.

23. Forbes, *The 'Black Watch'*, p. 103.

24. Stewart of Garth, *Sketches*, I, 3rd ed., pp. 383–4, n.*.

25. Forbes, *The 'Black Watch'*, p. 104.

26. Stewart of Garth, *Sketches*, I, 3rd ed., p. 384, n.+. See II, 3rd ed., Appendix I, p. ii. Ensign Alexander Mackenzie died of his wounds.

27. *John Peebles' American War*, Octr. 28th, p. 59. Peebles' Diary (original) cites G[eneral] O[rders]. Head Qtrs New York Island. 8 Oct. 1776: 'The two 71st Grenadier Companys of the 4th Battn Grenadiers being very sickly are to join their Regt. The 42nd Grenadiers Company of said Battn will join the 3rd Battn of Grenadiers under the command of Major Marsh & Major Stuart.' MFilP/GD21/492, NRS.

28. ibid., Octr. 28th, p. 59.

29. Stewart of Garth, *Sketches*, I, 3rd ed., p. 385, n.*. Stewart adds: 'Such being the opinion entertained of the regiment, it forms a ready solution of the alacrity with which young men in those days joined a body of troops they thought so brave and invincible.'

30. *John Peebles' American War*, Saturday Novr. 2d, 1776, p. 60. Peebles' Diary (original) MFilP/GD21/492, NRS.

31. Stewart of Garth, *Sketches*, I, 3rd ed., p. 386.

32. *John Peebles' American War*, Novr. 16. Attack of Ft. Washington, p. 63.

33. Stewart of Garth, *Sketches*, I, 3rd ed., p. 386; Forbes, *The 'Black Watch'*, p. 105.

34. Stewart of Garth, *Sketches*, I, 3rd ed., p. 387, n.*. One sergeant, 10 privates killed; 2 lts, 4 sgts, 66 privates wounded.

35. *American Heritage Book of the Revolution*, p. 188.

36. Stewart of Garth, *Sketches*, I, 3rd ed., p. 387.

37. ibid., pp. 387–8.

38. *John Peebles' American War*, Novr. 17th., p. 64, Peebles Diary (original), 17 Nov..(1776) MFilP/GD21/492, NRS.

39. *John Peebles' American War*, Sunday 8th. Decr., p. 70.

40. ibid., Wednesday 11th. Decr., p. 71.

41. ibid., Wednesday 25th. Decr. Xmass, p. 74.

42. Stewart of Garth, *Sketches*, I, 3rd ed., p. 388.

43. ibid., and Forbes, *The 'Black Watch'*, p. 106, both give the date of 22 Jan. 1777.

44. *John Peebles' American War*, Friday 3d Janry, (1777), p. 77.

45. Stewart of Garth, *Sketches*, I, 3rd ed., p. 389.

46. ibid., p. 390. Also in *The Highlanders in America*, John Patterson MacLean, Southern History Association, 1900, p. 335.

47. Extract of a letter from New York, 3 April 1777, in *Caledonian Mercury*, Edinburgh, Wednesday 4 June 1777, Mf.N.776, NLS.

48. Stewart of Garth, *Sketches*, I, 3rd ed., p. 391.

49. *John Peebles' American War*, Saturday 10 May, p. 111 counts 3 sgts, 6 rank and file killed, 2 sgts & 15 wounded '- of the Enemy about 30 found dead in different places & 28 taken prisoners.'

50. Stewart of Garth, *Sketches*, I, 3rd ed., p. 391, gives figures of 3 sgts and 9 private soldiers killed; 3 sgts and 30 private soldiers wounded; Capt Duncan Macpherson 'slightly' wounded. In Appendix I, II, p. ii, he says 35 rank and file wounded. Other sources vary.

51. Stewart of Garth, *Sketches*, I, 3rd ed., pp. 391–2, n.*; Forbes, *The 'Black Watch'*, p. 108.

52. *John Peebles' American War*, Saturday 10 May [1777], p. 111.

53. Stewart of Garth, *Sketches*, I, 3rd ed., p. 392. Stewart of Garth does not mention the relationship in his *Sketches*. William left the Regiment in 1777, returning as Capt in 1782.

54. Wednesday 21st. [May] fine day; *John Peebles' American War*, p. 113. He was promoted Capt Lt Oct. 1777, Capt Aug. 1778.

55. 'New arrangement 24th June 1777', Peebles' Diary (original), MFilP/GD21/492, NRS. The 42nd were in the 3rd Brigade with the 15th, 44th and 17th. Charles, Ist Earl Grey, KB, PC (1729–1807). Stewart of Garth, *Sketches*, I, 3rd ed., p. 393.

56. *American Heritage Book of the Revolution*, p. 250.

57. *John Peebles' American War*, Monday 25th. Augt., p. 128.

58. Details from Plans relating to the Progress of the Royal Army, private collection.

59. *John Peebles' American War*, Thursday 11th. Septr., p. 133.

60. Howe to Lord Germaine, German Town, 10 Oct. 1777, CO 5/236, p. 148, TNA.

61. Stewart of Garth, *Sketches*, I, 3rd ed., p. 395; Forbes, *The 'Black Watch'*, p. 111. Of those companies in the light brigade 4 privates killed, 2 sgts and 15 privates wounded.

62. Howe to Germaine, German Town, 10 Oct. 1777, CO 5/236, p. 149, TNA. Figures of at least 53 killed, 163 known casualties, given in McGuire, *Battle of Paoli*, p. 215.

63. James Murray, *An Impartial History of the War in America*, vol. 2, pp. 271–2, Robeson, 1783, quoted in McGuire, *Battle of Paoli*, p. 125. See also C.T. Atkinson to A.P. Wavell, 29 September 1934, BWRA 0389.

64. Capt John Andre, letter to unknown recipient, German Town, Sepr. 28, 1777, p. 50, quoted in McGuire, *Battle of Paoli*, p. 125.

65. Boatner, Mark, *Cassell's Biographical Dictionary of the American War of Independence 1763–1783*, 1973, p. 829.

66. *John Peebles' American War*, Friday 26th. Septr., p. 138.

67. ibid., Saturday 4th. Octr., p. 140.

68. Howe to Lord Germaine, German Town, 10 Oct. 1777, CO 5/236, TNA, pp. 152–3.
69. *John Peebles' American War*, Monday 20th [Oct.], p. 144.
70. ibid., Monday 1st. Decr., p. 152.
71. Stewart of Garth, *Sketches*, I, 3rd ed., n.*, p. 397.
72. *John Peebles' American War*, Philad[elphi]a. Janry. 30th 1778, p. 161.
73. ibid., Tuesday 3d. [Feb.], p. 162; [undated] January 1778, p. 161.
74. Formed by Robert Rogers, they were the successors of the Rangers formed during the French–Indian wars.
75. *John Peebles' American War*, Thursday 26th Febry., pp. 165–6.
76. ibid., Monday 4th [May], p. 178.
77. ibid., Monday 18th [May], pp. 181–3.
78. ibid., Wednesday 27th [May], p. 184.
79. *Correspondence of Adam Ferguson*, I, Biographical Introduction, p. li; Ferguson was a friend of George Johnstone, a member of the Commission.
80. *John Peebles' American War*, Wednesday 10th June, p. 188.
81. ibid., Thursday 18th [June], p. 189.
82. ibid., Saturday 27th June, p. 193.
83. ibid., Sunday 28th June a fight, p. 194.
84. ibid., Saturday 5th Septr., p. 214.
85. Stewart of Garth, *Sketches*, I, 3rd ed., p. 400.
86. *John Peebles' American War*, Wednesday 28th [Oct.], p. 228.
87. ibid., Saturday 31st [Oct.], p. 229.
88. ibid., Monday 23d [Nov.], cold, p. 233.
89. ibid., Monday 7th Decr., p. 238.
90. ibid., 2d. May, p. 259. Inhabitants of Newton published an address to Lt Col Stirling. Peebles was quartered with the Grenadiers about 100 miles from the Regiment.
91. ibid., Tuesday 12th [Jan. 1779], p. 243.
92. ibid., Friday 22d [Jan.], p. 244.
93. ibid., Monday 1st Febry., p. 245.
94. ibid., Friday 26th, p. 250, and Thursday 11th [March], p. 252.
95. Forbes, *The 'Black Watch'*, says this was 'in the summer', p. 113. Source: *Officers of The Black Watch, 1725–1986*, p. 94.
96. *John Peebles' American War*, Sunday 25th; Tuesday 27th [April 1779], pp. 257–8.
97. ibid., Wednesday 19th [May] p. 260, and Peebles' Diary (original), MFilP/GD21/492, NRS.
98. ibid., Sunday 23d May, p. 261, and Peebles' Diary (original), MFilP/GD21/492, NRS.
99. ibid., Saturday 4th July, Peebles' Diary (original), MFilP/GD21/492, NRS.

100. ibid., Saturday, 17th July, and, 4 August, Peebles' Diary (original), MFilP/GD21/492, NRS.
101. Stewart of Garth, *Sketches*, I, 3rd ed., p. 401; *John Peebles' American War*, Thursday 28th Octr. [1779], p. 303.
102. *John Peebles' American War*, Thursday 18th [Nov.], p. 309.
103. See Scheer and Ranking, *Rebels and Redcoats*, World Publishing Co., Cleveland, 1957.
104. Record of Service, 42nd, 2nd Battalion, Now 73rd Regiment (handwritten Army book, 1780–1907), BWRA 0005. See also Raising of 2nd Battalion (then 73rd) BWRA 0395/R, and Amherst to Charles Jenkinson, Whitehall, 30 July 1779, WO 1/616, p. 329, TNA.
105. Stewart of Garth, *Sketches*, I, 3rd ed., p. 403.
106. 'Affray at Leith', Capt James Innes, 71st (commanding additional companies of Highlanders at Stirling) to Rt Hon Charles Jenkinson, Secretary of War, Edinburgh, 21 April 1779, WO 1/1004, TNA. Fencibles (from 'defensible') were Army regiments raised from local volunteers commanded by regular Army officers.
107. Forbes, *The 'Black Watch'*, pp. 114–16. See also Stewart of Garth, *Sketches*, I, 3rd ed., p. 402.
108. *John Peebles' American War*, Thursday 26th [Aug.] 1779, p. 289.
109. See chapter 9: The East Indies and the Tiger of Mysore.
110. Extract of a Letter from Lt Gen Knyphausen to Lord George Germaine, dated New York, 27 March 1780, Regimental Scrapbook 1740–1917, BWRA 0313.
111. ibid.
112. *John Peebles' American War*, Friday 12th May 1780, p. 372.
113. Stewart of Garth, *Sketches*, I, 3rd ed., p. 407 n.*. Stewart of Garth's statistics vary compared with what he records in his narrative and Appendix No. I, p. ii. Here he says nine privates were killed but in the Appendix, twelve.
114. *John Peebles' American War*, Sunday 18 June 1780, p. 388.
115. Paul Pace, *Kilts & Courage, the Story of the 42nd Royal Highland Regiment in the American War for Independence 1776–1783*, cited on http://greensleeves.typepad.com/berkshires/2008/06/whatever-happen.html. *John Peebles' American War*, p. 497, describes Stirling as being present at the dinner on 30 Nov. 1781. He returned to Britain in Dec. 1781.
116. http://www.myrevolutionarywar.com/battles/800623.htm.
117. *John Peebles' American War*, Wednesday 21 June, p. 389.
118. Stewart of Garth, *Sketches*, I, 3rd ed., p. 407 Forbes, *'The Black Watch'*, p. 119.
119. *John Peebles' American War*, 12th. Octr, 1781, p. 482. Prince William Henry (1765–1837), later William 1V and known as the 'Sailor King'.
120. Lawrence James, *The Rise and Fall of the British Empire*, Abacus, 1995, p. 118. The song was written in 1643 when Oliver Cromwell insisted Christmas should be a solemn occasion.

121. *John Peebles' American War*, 30 Nov. 1781, p. 497.

122. ibid., 16 Dec. 1781, p. 500; Tuesday, 25th, Xmass, 1781, p. 501.

123. ibid., Thursday 10th. Janry, 1782, p. 503.

124. ibid., Monday 21st. Janry. 1782, p. 503.

125. ibid., Saturday 2d. Febry. 1782, p. 506. Cornwallis was exchanged with Henry Laurens (1724–1792), merchant and political leader who had been captured at sea and imprisoned in the Tower of London.

126. By the terms of the Quebec Act, the province's territory was expanded to take over part of the Indian Reserve, including much of modern-day Ontario, Ohio, Michigan, Illinois, Wisconsin and parts of Minnesota.

127. *John Peebles' American War*, Friday 8th [Feb. 1782], p. 507. As was common at the time, they had a matrimonial contract. See GD21/159 and MFilP/GD21/492. NRS.

128. ibid., Saturday Morning, 2d. March, pp. 510–11.

129. Peebles' Diary (original), MFilP/GD21/492, NLS. This entry marks the end of Peebles' diary.

130. Later Lt Gen Charles Graham (*c.*1740–1798), wounded at St Vincent 1796. Appointed Lt Col on 28 April 1782. Graham's record remaining unsurpassed until Robert Henry Dick in the early nineteenth century.

131. Forbes, *The 'Black Watch'*, p. 120. This is probably an exaggeration of the 42nd's good behaviour!

132. ibid., p. 121. There were other desertions, for example when 42nd first arrived in North America in 1756, and as *Peebles' American Diary* illustrates court martials were often held for a variety of misdemeanours. See also Stewart of Garth, *Sketches*, I, 3rd ed., p. 408.

133. See Stewart of Garth, *Sketches*, II, 3rd ed., Appendix No. I, p. ii. *Sketches*, I, 3rd ed., p. 409, gives figures of 83 killed, 286 wounded.

134. Muster Roll 42nd Royal Highland Regiment 1780–84, BWRA 0013.

135. Lt Dugald Campbell (d. 1810). As the Surveyor, he obtained a substantial lot of 584 acres. See *And the River Rolled On . . .*, Nashwaak Bicentennial Association, 1984, pp. 70–1, in which Margaret Pugh describes the fortunes of the 42nd. Nova Scotia was partitioned on 16 Aug. 1784 and the province of New Brunswick was created.

136. *And the River Rolled On . . .* as n. 135 above.

137. Orderly Book, Montreal, 30 May 1761, BWRA 0256.

138. See Stewart of Garth, *Sketches*, II, 3rd ed., Fraser's Highlanders, p. 132. See also chapter 8, the section on Geldermalsen. The 71st's recently appointed Colonel, Thomas Stirling – the 42nd's former Lt Col – exchanged to half-pay, becoming Colonel of the 41st in 1790. When James Murray of Strowan died, Stirling bought his estate. He later succeeded to the baronetcy of Ardoch when his older brother William died in 1799. See McCulloch, *Sons of the Mountains*, II, pp. 11–12.

139. Maj Gen John Campbell, Halifax, Nova Scotia, 1 Jan. 1785, quoted in *Historical Record of the Forty-Second Foot*, pp. 81–4; original BWRA 0011 (BWRA 0209).

This stand of Colours is the oldest belonging to the Regiment which is still preserved. See Wallace, 'The Colours of the Regiment', *The Red Hackle*, July 1936, p. 8.

140. HQ Halifax, 30 Oct. 1785, General Order Book 1785–1793, BWRA 0012.

141. ibid., 21 Jan. 1786.

142. ibid., 15 March 1786.

143. War Office 10 March 1785, Signed by His Majesty's command, George Yonge, BWRA 0012.

144. HQ Halifax, 1 June 1786, General Order Book 1785–1793, BWRA 0012.

145. ibid., 3 June 1786.

146. Adjutant Generals Office 10 April 1786, General Orders for the Infantry, 8 July 1786, BWRA 0012.

147. Stewart of Garth, *Sketches*, I, 3rd ed., p. 412, gives his date of death as 1 June 1787 but he is confusing the date with the new Colonel's appointment.

148. ibid., p. 412, note. David Stewart of Garth (1768–1829). He had been on half-pay having served with the Atholl Highlanders (77th Duke of Atholl's) raised by James Murray of Strowan. The 77th was disbanded after a mutiny at Portsmouth, the men having heard they were to be sent to India. Murray later raised the 78th (renumbered the 72nd), which became the Seaforth Highlanders. See biography in McCulloch, *Sons of the Mountains*, II, pp. 11–12. Chaplain James Mclagan retired and was replaced by George Watson. General Order Book, 1785–1793, Headquarters Quebec, War Office Promotions, 17 March 1788, BWRA 0012.

149. Sir Hector Munro (1726–1805), son of Hugh Munro of Novar; Samson (ed.), *Officers of The Black Watch, 1725 to 1986*, p. 13 states he was Munro of Foulis (correctly given as of Novar on p. 79). The two clans separated in the fifteenth century.

150. Stewart of Garth, *Sketches*, I, 3rd ed., p. 413.

151. Duncan Kennedy, tr. Michael Newton, in Newton, *We're Indians Sure Enough*, p. 150.

8. Revolutionary Wars

1. James Hogg, 'Donald M'Donald', quoted in Donaldson, *The Jacobite Song*, p. 92.

2. Stewart of Garth, *Sketches*, I, 3rd ed., p. 413. He says fourteen years but the Regiment departed in 1776 and returned in 1789 – hence thirteen years. Cannon, *Historical Record of the Forty-Second*, p. 86.

3. Cannon, *Historical Record of the Forty-Second*, p. 86. Geo. Yonge to Sir Hector Munro (undated but probably May) 1790, General Order Book, 1785–1793, BWRA 0012.

4. Geo. Yonge to Sir Hector Munro, War Office 29 May 1790, General Order Book, 1785–1793, BWRA 0012.

5. Wm Fawcet, Adjutant General, to Lt Col Graham, 13 May 1790, General Order Book, 1785–1793, BWRA 0012. This compared with regulations stipulated when the Regiment was raised of height five foot seven inches, and men not to be older than twenty-five.

6. George Gordon, Marquess of Huntly, GCB, PC (1770–1836). Later 5th Duke of Gordon. He was commissioned on 25 Jan. 1791, taking the place of Capt Alexander Grant, who exchanged onto half-pay.

7. See John Malcolm Bulloch, 'Lord Huntly's Black Watch Company', in *Territorial Soldiering in the North-West of Scotland during 1759–1914*, pp. 129, 139. The caricature was in 1792. In 1794 the 92nd Gordon Highlanders were raised. They took the Black Watch tartan, adding a yellow stripe because they were 'gey', i.e. self-important. See Donaldson, *The Jacobite Song*, p. 92. In 1789 Prince George – the future George IV – had worn Highland dress at a masquerade ball.

8. Effective Size Record of Companies of the 42nd or Royal Highland Regiment of Foot, Edinburgh Castle, 6 Sept. 1791, BWRA 0008. Stewart of Garth, *Sketches*, I, 3rd ed., p. 415, calls them 'a fine band of Highlanders'.

9. Wm. Fawcett, Adj Gen, General Orders, 14 Jan. 1792, BWRA 0012.

10. Cannon, *Historical Record of the Forty-Second*, p. 86. See also Stewart of Garth, *Sketches*, I, 3rd ed., p. 416.

11. Stewart of Garth, *Sketches*, I, 3rd ed., pp. 416–17 and n.*. See Prebble, *The Highland Clearances*, pp. 41–2; Erich Richard, *A History of The Highland Clearances*, v. 2, Taylor & Francis, 1985, p. 96.

12. George Yonge to Major Grant, Hector Munro, Colonel of the 42nd Regt of Foot, 19 Jan. 1793, BWRA 0012. Augmentation of 1 sgt, 1 drummer and 17 private men.

13. Effective Size Roll, April 1793, BWRA 0008. Each Company had 80 to 90 private men.

14. Stewart of Garth, *Sketches*, I, 3rd ed., p. 419.

15. Prince Frederick, Duke of York and Albany (1763–1827) was the founder of Sandhurst Military College.

16. Lt Gen Sir Charles Grey to Rt Hon. Henry Dundas, Ostend, 29 Oct. 1793, pp. 433–4, 30 Oct. 1793, WO 1/167, p. 437, TNA.

17. Return of the killed & wounded of the British at the Siege of Nieuport, Ostend, 1 Nov. 1793, WO 1/167, p. 519, TNA (which replaces the Return dated 30 Oct. 1793, WO 1/167, p. 445, TNA).

18. Stewart of Garth, *Sketches*, I, Preface to the 1st ed., quoted in 2nd ed., pp. vi–vii.

19. The belief that pages of the missing history were found in the library of The Royal United Services Institution (later Institute for Defence Studies), in London in 1913 proved wrong, since the manuscript ended in 1819, after the transports were captured. Entries also cited Stewart of Garth, who published his history in 1822. Although RUSI sources state that the documents were returned to the 1st Bn, there is no record of them in the BWRA. See *The Times*, 22

Oct. 1913, *Black Watch Chronicle*, 1914, pp. 92–3, and *RUSI Journal*, Oct. 1913, pp. 1278–9.

20. Cannon, *Historical Record of the Forty-Second*, p. 90; see Stewart of Garth, *Sketches*, I, 3rd ed., p. 422.

21. Lt Gen Sir Ralph Abercromby KB (1734–1801). He had been on half-pay for a decade, but when France declared war on Britain he had resumed active service. His brother was Robert Abercromby, under whom the 42nd had served in North America in 1776.

22. Later the Duke of Wellington. See chapter 9: The East Indies and the Tiger of Mysore, for details of his early life. See also Garry David Willis, *Wellington's First Battle: combat at Boxtel 15 September 1794*, Caseshot Publishing, 2011.

23. Stewart of Garth, *Sketches*, I, 3rd ed., p. 424. Forbes, *The 'Black Watch'*, p. 133.

24. Stewart of Garth, *Sketches*, I, 3rd ed., p. 424.

25. Sgt Rowland Cameron, 'Account of the manner in which the Red Hackle was gained in January 1795'. A true copy signed by John Drysdale, Major 42nd Record of Service, 42nd, 1729–1873, pp. 248–56, BWRA 0079 and in BWRA 0016/02. Six soldiers of the 42nd were wounded and one drummer. Return of Killed, Wounded & Missing of the British Troops, under the Command of Maj Gen David Dundas, at the attack of Tuyl, 30 Dec. 1794, WO 1/172, f. 31, TNA.

26. Sgt Rowland Cameron, 'Account of the manner . . .', cited above, n. 25.

27. Andrew Dowie eyewitness account, 30 March 1845. A true copy signed by John Drysdale, Major 42nd, Record of Service, 42nd, 1729–1873, BWRA 0079.

28. Sgt Rowland Cameron, 'Account of the manner . . .', cited above, n. 25.

29. Andrew Dowie's eyewitness account, cited above, n. 27. Stewart of Garth does not record this version of events, although he must have been present at the time, neither does Forbes, *The 'Black Watch'*, nor Cannon, *Historical Record of the Forty-Second*.

30. Keltie (ed.), *A History of the Scottish Highlands, Highland Clans and Highland Regiments*, II, p. 361.

31. Dundas to Lt Gen Harcourt commanding the British Troops at Doorn, Buren, 6 Jan. 1795, WO 1/172, f. 97, TNA.

32. Return of the Killed, Wounded, and Missing of the Troops under the Command of Major General David Dundas at Geldermalsen, 5 January 1795, WO 1/172, f. 101, TNA. In addition to the private soldier killed, Lt Colin Lamont and seven private soldiers were wounded. In early Feb. Maj Gen H.E. Fox relieved Dundas 'in consequence of his indisposition'. Fox to Harcourt, Head Quarters Rheine, 11 Feb. 1795, WO 1/172 ff. 338–9, TNA.

33. Stewart of Garth, *Sketches*, I, 3rd ed., p. 426.

34. Harcourt, from Doorn, 9 Jan. 1795 (the letter is incorrectly dated 1794 – a common mistake at the beginning of a New Year), WO 1/172, f. 93, TNA.

35. Stewart of Garth, *Sketches*, I, 3rd ed., p. 427.

36. 'State of the Rank & File and Numbers wanting to complete the Regiments of British Infantry up to the Establishment of 850 p[er] Bn at the beginning of February 1795', WO 1/617, f. 553, TNA.

37. Stewart of Garth, *Sketches*, I, 3rd ed., p. 426.

38. See chapter 9: The East Indies and the Tiger of Mysore.

39. Sergeant Rowland Cameron, 'Account of the manner . . .', cited above, n. 25. Cameron's suggestion that the wearing of a red plume was taken away from the 11th Light Dragoons also appears incorrect, since photographs in the early nineteenth century show officers of that regiment wearing both red and white plumes.

40. McAulay, 'The First Battalion The Black Watch', in Tullibardine (ed.), *Military History of Perthshire 1660–1902*, p. 60. It is not clear why vulture feathers in particular were chosen. Black and Griffon vultures were quite common in Spain and the Eastern Mediterranean, but not in Britain.

41. Linklater, *The Black Watch*, p. 42. As the authors concede, Stewart of Garth also failed to mention the parade at Royston. See also 'The Origins of The Red Hackle', *The Red Hackle*, April 1982, p. 11.

42. See Stewart of Garth, *Sketches*, I, 3rd ed., p. 255; John Grant, Journal, MS Copy Micro 491, Alexander Turnbull Library, NLNZ; Orderly Book, Montreal, 30 May 1761, BWRA 0256. See also chapters 7 and 15. 'Red Hackle Day' was agreed at the formation of the Black Watch Association in 1919. Although the battle commenced on 4 January 1795, the Return of Killed etc. is dated 5 January 1795.

43. Later Brigadier Gen William Dickson of Kilbucho, d. 8 May 1815. Ensign 1780; he took command of the Regiment on 1 Sept. 1795 before departing for the West Indies.

44. Stewart of Garth, *Sketches*, I, 3rd ed., p. 429. See Wallace, 'The Dress of The Black Watch, III, 1790–1797', *The Red Hackle*, July 1932, p. 7.

45. Stewart of Garth, *Sketches*, I, 3rd ed., p. 430, n.

46. Cannon, *Historical Record of the Forty-Second*, p. 93. 16,000 Infantry, 500 Cavalry.

47. Simpson, Memoir, p. 1, BWRA 0229. The journal was presented to the BWRA by Capt J. Simpson of New South Wales, Australia (Simpson's great-great grandson), on 26 Oct. 1965. *The Red Hackle*, Dec. 1965, p. 4.

48. Simpson, Memoir, p. 203, BWRA 0229.

49. Wallace, 'The Dress of the Black Watch 1790–1797, III, 1790–1797', *The Red Hackle*, July 1932, p. 9. 'We are not told what happened to the duck pantaloons and round hats of the Gibraltar companies, but probably they resumed their Highland dress in the interval before re-embarkation.' See also Stewart of Garth, *Sketches*, I, 3rd ed., p. 433.

50. Stewart of Garth, *Sketches*, I, 3rd ed., p. 435. The five companies would have been under the command of the senior major, James Stewart, promoted 21 Oct. 1795.

51. Lieutenant General Sir John Moore KB (1761–1809).

52. Simpson, Memoir, pp. 5–6, BWRA 0229.

53. ibid., p. 7.

54. Cannon, *Historical Record of the Forty-Second*, p. 95.

55. Simpson, Memoir, p. 10, BWRA 0229. Cannon, *Historical Record of the Forty-Second*, implies they all landed on the same day, 26 April, see p. 95.
56. Simpson, Memoir, p. 13, BWRA 0229.
57. Stewart of Garth, *Sketches*, II, 3rd ed., Appendix, No. 1, p. iii.
58. Simpson, Memoir, p. 22, BWRA 0229.
59. Cannon, *Historical Record of the Forty-Second*, p. 95.
60. Simpson, Memoir, pp. 22–3, BWRA 0229.
61. ibid., pp. 24–6.
62. Stewart of Garth, *Sketches*, I, 3rd ed., Appendix No. 1, p. iii. Forbes, *The 'Black Watch'*, p. 154.
63. Cannon, *Historical Record of the Forty-Second*, p. 96.
64. Stewart of Garth, *Sketches*, I, 3rd, p. 447, n.*. Also quoted in Cannon, *Historical Record of the Forty-Second*, p. 96.
65. Cannon, *Historical Record of the Forty-Second*, p. 97.
66. Simpson, Memoir, p. 27, BWRA 0229.
67. Cannon, *Historical Record of the Forty-Second*, p. 97. See also Stewart of Garth, *Sketches*, I, 3rd ed., p. 446, n.*. He refers to him as 'Colonel', but Graham was a Major General.
68. Stewart of Garth, *Sketches*, I, 3rd ed., pp. 448–9. See also J.E. Caulfield, *One Hundred Years' History of the Second Battalion, West India Regiment, from date of raising, 1795–1895*, London, 1899, pp. 13–14, who repeats the story almost verbatim but does not mention Stewart of Garth's involvement.
69. Simpson, Memoir, pp. 28–32, BWRA 0229.
70. ibid., p. 35.
71. ibid., p. 36.
72. Stewart of Garth, *Sketches*, I, 3rd ed., p. 450. He was promoted at the end of June 1796.
73. Simpson, Memoir, p. 38, BWRA 0229.
74. ibid., pp. 42–3.
75. ibid., p. 67. The British force including German mercenaries was between 7,000 and 13,000.
76. ibid., pp. 68–70.
77. ibid., pp. 71–2.
78. Stewart of Garth, *Sketches*, I, 3rd ed., p. 451. He says 264 officers and 12,387 died between May 1796 and June 1797.
79. Simpson, Memoir, p. 72, BWRA 0229. Cannon, *Historical Record of the Forty-Second*, p. 99, says that 'a greater number of transfers were received than the casualties of the two preceding years amounted to, and the five companies embarked complete in numbers and free of illness'. Stewart of Garth, *Sketches*, says the number of men received from the 79th 'exceeded the casualties of the two preceding years, making the detachment stronger than when they embarked at Portsmouth in October 1795': I, 3rd ed., p. 453.
80. Simpson, Memoir, pp. 75–6, BWRA 0229.
81. ibid., pp. 84, 85: 'for which we were paid 9d every night after our work was

done'. See Wallace, 'The Dress of the Black Watch, III, 1790–1797', *The Red Hackle*, July 1932, p. 9, who suggests they would have 'received a complete new outfit of Highland clothing' at Hillsea before re-embarkation.

82. Wallace, 'The Dress of the Black Watch, III, 1790–1797, *The Red Hackle*, July 1932, p. 9. See Cannon, *Historical Record of the Forty-Second*, p. 99.

83. Return of Commissioned, Non-commissioned Officers, etc. 28 March 1798, CO 91/40, p. 77, TNA.

84. Charles O'Hara to His Grace The Duke of Portland, Gibraltar, 29 Dec. 1798, CO 91/40 (no page no.), TNA. General Charles O'Hara (1740–1802). The son of General James O'Hara and his Portuguese mistress, he fought in the American War and the Napoleonic Wars, surrendering to Washington at Yorktown in 1781 and Napoleon in France in 1793. William Bentinck, 3rd Duke of Portland (1738–1809), formerly Prime Minister in 1783 and again 1807–9. No record exists of the response!

85. Stewart of Garth, *Sketches*, I, 3rd ed., p. 454.

86. Simpson, Memoir, p. 86, BWRA 0229.

87. ibid., pp. 87–9. The other Regiments were the 28th, 58th and 90th.

88. Stewart of Garth, *Sketches*, I, 3rd ed., p. 455.

89. Simpson, Memoir, p. 92, BWRA 0229.

90. ibid., p. 93.

91. Cannon, *Historical Record of the Forty-Second*, p. 100. See also Stewart of Garth, *Sketches*, I, 3rd ed., p. 456.

92. Simpson, Memoir, pp. 96–7, BWRA 0229.

93. ibid., p. 97.

94. Stewart of Garth, *Sketches*, I, 3rd ed., p. 455. Later Lt Gen Sir Hildebrand Oakes (1754–1822). He was wounded at Alexandria in 1801.

95. Simpson, Memoir, p. 98, BWRA 0229.

96. ibid., pp. 99–101.

97. Traditional Song.

9. The East Indies and the Tiger of Mysore

1. Regimental Ballad of the Old 73rd, quoted in Tullibardine (ed.), *A Military History of Perthshire 1660–1902*, p. 85. One out of nine verses.

2. Lt Col Norman MacLeod (1754–1801). Other regiments: were the 8th, 9th, 20th and 47th.

3. Anon. (Lt Col James Spens), *Memoir of Lieutenant Colonel John Campbell by a retired officer*, p. 17. James Spens (1761–1840), Ensign 1778, Lt 1780, Capt 1783, Maj 73rd 1791, Bt Lt Col 1795, Lt Col Sept. 1795, retired by sale Aug. 1798. McGregor, A Black Watch Who Was Who 1725–1881, Research Notes, 42nd, BWRA 0863/2.

4. Anon. (Spens), *Memoir, John Campbell*, p. 23. Commodore George Johnstone

(1730–87); Gen Sir William Medows KB (1738–1813), Col 89th Regiment. Lt John Oswald, d. 1793. He did not see active service in India, but sold his commission and returned home overland. A supporter of the ideals of the French Revolution, he went to France, where he and his two sons were killed. Stewart of Garth, *Sketches*, II, 3rd ed., p. 215 n.

5. Anon. (Spens), *Memoir, John Campbell*, p. 19. Maj Patrick Graeme had been commissioned as an ensign into the Regiment in 1772 and was wounded at Fort Washington in 1776.

6. ibid., p. 21.

7. Later Lt Col John Campbell of Stonefield (1753–84). Campbell's first cousin, Elizabeth, later married Lachlan Macquarie. Research Notes, Robin Walsh, 2011.

8. Cannon, *Historical Record of the Seventy-Third Regiment*, p. 6. Khasa Chamaraja Wodeyar (Krishnaraja Vodeyar); Hyder (Haider) Ali (*c*.1722–82).

9. There were four Anglo-Mysore Wars: 1767–9; 1780–4 (which was widened when the British declared war on the Dutch in 1781); 1789–92; 1799.

10. Tipu (Tipoo) Sahib Tipu Sultan (*c*.1750–99). Ruler of Mysore 1782–99. He was named after the Sufi saint Tipu Mastan Auliya, and Fateh Ali after his grandfather Fath Muhammed. See Kate Brittlebank, *Tipu Sultan's Search for Legitimacy*, p. 23.

11. Later Gen Sir David Baird (1757–1829). The 42nd served under his command at Corunna in 1809, see chapter 12.

12. Macfarlane, *Our Indian Empire: Its History and Present State, from the Earliest Settlement of the British in Hindostan to the Close of the Year 1843*, p. 197.

13. Anon. (Spens), *Memoir, John Campbell*, p. 29.

14. ibid.

15. ibid., p. 32.

16. Letter [unsigned] but obviously by John Campbell, Pannang [Panianj] on the Malabar Coast, 30 leagues to the Southward of Tillicherry, 24th Decr. 1782, Lachlan Macquarie, Memoranda & Related papers, 22 Dec. 1808 – 14 July 1823. Original held in Mitchell Library, Sydney, ML A772 f.210. Anon (Spens), *Memoir, John Campbell*, p. 33.

17. Letter [unsigned] as in n. 16 above.

18. Cannon, *Historical Record of the Seventy-Third*, p. 8, says that forces 'led by Monsieur Lally at the head of his Europeans' took part in the battle. This is not Thomas Lally, the French officer of Irish descent, who fought in India in the 1750s, was arrested in France, accused of treason and executed in 1766 but Henri-François-Pierre-Charles de Motz de la Lallé, the French mercenary who had joined Hyder Ali's service in 1779. He was killed in 1790 but his men retained the name 'Lallé's parti' or corps. See Jean Marie Lafont, 'Observations on the French Military Presence,' in Indo-French Relations, ed. K.S.. Mathew and S.J. Stephen, p. 203 and Brittlebank, *Tipu Sultan's Search for Legitimacy*, p. 22.

19. Col Norman MacLeod, General Order 29 Nov. 1782, quoted in Anon. (Spens), *Memoir, John Campbell*, pp. 35–6.

20. Cannon, *Historical Record of the Seventy-Third*, p. 9. Hyder Ali had died in early December of a carbuncle. Tipu was crowned Sultan on 29 Dec. 1782.

21. Anon. (Spens), *Memoir, John Campbell*, p. 38. See Dodsley's *Annual Register* for 1783, p. 91.

22. Anon. (Spens), *Memoir, John Campbell*, p. 41. There were claims that 400 women, bleeding with their wounds, were stripped of their jewels and raped, p. 40.

23. ibid., p. 42.

24. See Appendix to Dodsley's *Annual Register* for 1783, p. 286. Anon. (Spens), *Memoir, John Campbell*, p. 42 n.*.

25. Anon. (Spens), *Memoir, John Campbell*, p. 45.

26. ibid., p. 47. Spens says 140,000 fighting men, including 60,000 cavalry, 30,000 infantry soldiers, irregulars, a Bn of about 600 Frenchmen, a further corps of European (French, Dutch, Portuguese) infantry and dismounted cavalry. Colonel David Charpentier de Cossigny (d. 1801) became Governor-General of French India 1785–7.

27. Anon. (Spens), *Memoir, John Campbell*, p. 48. See also *An account of the gallant defence at Mangalore in the East Indies*, John Rogerson Wolsey, Bathurst, 1786.

28. Anon. (Spens), *Memoir, John Campbell*, p. 50. Promoted capt on 24 May 1783 no doubt in succession to a deceased officer. Macfarlane, *Our Indian Empire*, p. 200, says 700 British and about 3,000 Indian sepoys.

29. Anon. (Spens), *Memoir, John Campbell*, p. 44. A powerful and warlike people, the Maratha defeat at the Battle of Panipat in 1761 by the Afghan ruler, Ahmed Shah Abdali, had halted their expansion north. But although in decline, the individual semi-autonomous states comprising the Maratha Confederacy retained their power until the nineteenth century.

30. ibid., p. 50.

31. ibid., p. 51. See Walter Biggar Blaikie, '2nd Battalion The Black Watch', in Tullibardine (ed.), *Military History of Perthshire 1660–1902*, p. 80, who does not seem to know that the horse was eaten!

32. Wilkin, *The Life of Sir David Baird*, p. 17.

33. Anon. (Spens), *Memoir, John Campbell*, p. 58.

34. Macfarlane, *Our Indian Empire*, p. 201.

35. Anon. (Spens), *Memoir, John Campbell*, p. 51.

36. Macfarlane, *Our Indian Empire*, p. 201.

37. 'King of histories', quoted in Colonel Wilks, 'Sketches of the South of India', quoted in Macfarlane, *Our Indian Empire*, p. 201, n.*.

38. Anon. (Spens), *Memoir, John Campbell*, p. 52.

39. General Return of His Majesty's Troops belonging to the Mangalore Garrison Present at Tillecherry 11 Feb. 1784, copy of original 'Return', in Anon. (Spens), *Memoir, John Campbell*, opposite p. 70. Eight officers and fifty-five soldiers of the detachments of the 98th, 100th and 102nd had survived, as well as twelve artillery officers and four civilians.

40. Anon. (Spens), *Memoir, John Campbell*, p. 53. The Peace of Paris was signed

in Sept. 1783, ratified in 1784. Letter from Colonel Campbell assigning his reasons for the surrender of Mangalore Fort to Tippoo Sa[h]ib dated 4th February 1784, pp. 41–43; Treaty of Peace with the Nabob Tippoo Sultaun Bahauder, p. 56–64, IOR/H/Misc/684, BL.

41. Anon. (Spens), *Memoir, John Campbell*, p. 63. Note, p. 64.

42. ibid., p. 65.

43. ibid., p. 63, n.

44. See Stewart of Garth, *Sketches*, II, 3rd ed., pp. 222–5.

45. Memorial of Lt Colonel Charles Graham to Rt Hon. Sir George Yonge, WO 71/11, pp. 272–9, TNA. Memorials sent by Sir George Yonge to Sir Charles Gould, Judge Advocate General, 6 June 1785, pp. 271–84, 325, TNA.

46. Memorial for Captain Ja[me]s Drummond, Captain Colin Campbell, & Lt Alex[ande]r McGregor, all of the 2nd Battalion to Rt Hon. Sir George Yonge, WO 71/11, pp. 280–4. Memorial sent by Sir George Yonge to Sir Charles Gould, Judge Advocate General, 6 June 1785, pp. 280–4, TNA.

47. Judge Advocate General and Board of Officers, Monday 20 June 1785, WO 71/11, p. 312, TNA.

48. George Yonge to Judge Advocate General, War Office, 6 July 1785, WO 71/11, p. 325, TNA.

49. W.O. 18 April 1786, signed Geo. Yonge to Campbell in Nova Scotia, WO 4/335, p. 51, TNA. See also W.O. 26 April 1786, WO 4/296, p. 66, TNA, and War Office, 18 April 1786, General Order Book 1785–1793, BWRA 0012. (It was not uncommon for duplicate documents to be sent by different pacquets. Another suggestion to send home the officers and NCOs and draft the privates into other non-Highland Regiments serving in India was resisted by MacLeod: 'My own Company are all of my own name and Clan, and, if I return to Europe without them I shall be effectually banished from my own home.' See Clyde, *From Rebel to Hero*, p. 160; Frank Adam, *The Clans, Septs and Regiments of the Scottish Highlands*, Edinburgh, 1934, pp. 307–8.

50. Sir George Osborn, d. 1818.

51. Record of Service, 73rd, p. 15, BWRA 0005. It has been wrongly stated that the tartan worn by the 73rd was known as the MacLeod of Harris tartan adopted by Maj Gen John (Mackenzie), Lord MacLeod. This related to the earlier 73rd, raised in 1777 and which became the 71st in 1786.

52. Later Field Marshal Arthur Wellesley, 1st Duke of Wellington, KG, KP, GCB, GCH, PC, FRS (1769–1852), quoted in Longford, *Wellington: the Years of the Sword*, p. 22.

53. Wellington disowned the story when questioned by his friend John Wilson Croker in 1850. Despite his denial, the story 'has been repeated as fact in every subsequent biography of the Duke': Longford, *Wellington*, p. 23. See Tullibardine (ed.), *Military History of Perthshire 1660–1902*, p. 81.

54. Lushington, *Life and Services of General Lord Harris*, p. 106.
55. ibid., p. 107.
56. Gen Sir Robert Abercromby GCB (1740–1827). When he died he was the oldest general in the British army.
57. Record of Service, 73rd, p. 12, BWRA 0005.
58. ibid., p. 13.
59. ibid., pp. 13–14.
60. General Returns of the killed, wounded & missing of the Army commanded by Colonel J. Braithwaite during the Siege of Pondicherry, which ended on the 23rd of August 1793, WO 1356, f. 25, TNA.
61. Return of Killed and Wounded of the Forces Commanded by Colonel Stuart during the Siege of the Fort of Trincomallee, August 29th, 1795, WO 1/356, f. 133, TNA. Combined figures for wounded 72nd and 73rd amounted to eight (1 capt, 1 sgt and 6 soldiers).
62. Record of Service, 73rd, p. 15, BWRA 0005.
63. Gerard Lake, later Viscount, d. 1808. Appointed on 2 Nov. 1796.
64. Cannon, *Historical Record of the Seventy-Third*, p. 10 n.
65. Longford, *Wellington*, p. 54, says the first letter signed 'Arthur Wellesley' was dated 19 May 1798.
66. Nizam Asaf Jan II (1734–1803).
67. Later General George Harris, 1st Baron Harris GCB (1746–1829). He was given local rank of Lieutenant General. Lushington, *General Lord Harris*, p. 106.
68. Sir John Coape Sherbrooke (1764–1830). He later became Governor of British North America, i.e. Canada. Cannon, *Historical Record of the Seventy-Third*, p. 16. See 'Statement of the Force composing the Grand Army under the Command of Lieutenant General Harris', WO 1/357, f. 285, TNA. The total force numbered 21,649.
69. Cannon, *Historical Record of the Seventy-Third*, p. 17.
70. War Department In-Letters and Papers: of the French Wars period 1797–1809, Camp 3rd May 1799, WO 1/357, f. 293, TNA. With orders like these it is surprising that anything happened!
71. Sir David Baird was commanding the 71st or Macleod's Highlanders (which became the Highland Light Infantry). Since it had previously been numbered the 73rd, it is sometimes assumed that he was commanding the newly raised 73rd (former 2nd Bn 42nd), Tullibardine (ed.), *Military History of Perthshire 1660–1902*, p. 82, n. 1.
72. McGregor, Diary, 4 May 1799, p. 52, BWRA 0685. The diary was found by Col. Alban Wilson DSO, 1st Bn, 8th Gurkhas, in a Hindu temple at Manipore in 1891. Wilson kept it until 1917, when he presented it to Col A.G. Wauchope and officers of 2nd Bn The Black Watch in remembrance of campaigning days together. The diary is now in the BWRA 0755 (typescript BWRA 0685). It is referred to as 'Captain McGrigor's Diary', but his name is spelt McGregor in the Army List; he was not a Captain until he joined the 90th Regiment in

1801. Confusingly, he talks about 'my friend Captain McGrigor of the Cavalry' in the narrative.

73. McGregor, Diary, 4 May 1799, pp. 52–3, BWRA 0685.
74. Cannon, *Historical Record of the Seventy-Third*, p. 18.
75. In the Black Watch Regimental Museum, Balhousie Castle.
76. Cannon, *Historical Record of the Seventy-Third*, p. 20.
77. McGregor, Diary, 14 June 1799, p. 57, BWRA 0685. £1 = 2.5 pagodas. 100,000 pagodas would be the equivalent of £40,000.
78. ibid.
79. Horse Guards, 24 June 1818, Harry Calvert, Adjutant General, WO 3/68, p. 152, WO 3/383, p. 326, TNA. Also given to the 19th Lancers, 22nd (late 25th) Light Dragoons, 12th, 33rd, 74th, 75th, 77th and 94th Foot.
80. McGregor, Diary, 30 June 1799, p. 57, BWRA 0685. He ruled for over seventy years until his death in 1868.
81. Cannon, *Historical Record of the Seventy-Third*, p. 20.
82. McGregor, Diary, 6 Sept. 1799, p. 63, BWRA 0685.
83. ibid., 30 Nov. 1800, p. 74.
84. ibid., 11 Feb. 1800, p. 73.
85. ibid., 11 Feb. 1800, p. 73.
86. ibid., 17 March 1800, p. 75.
87. ibid., 9 April 1800, p. 77, & 12 April 1800, p. 78.
88. ibid., 29 June 1800, p. 86.
89. ibid., 18 July 1800, p. 91.
90. ibid., 21 July 1800, p. 92.
91. ibid., 10 Sept. 1800, p. 99.
92. Holmes, *Wellington: The Iron Duke*, p. 65. Salabut died of cholera in 1822.
93. McGregor, Diary, 10 Sept. 1800, pp. 99–100, BWRA 0685.
94. ibid., 24 Oct. 1800, p. 104.
95. ibid., 11 May 1801, p. 117.
96. Major James MacDonald: McGregor, A Black Watch Who Was Who 1725–1881, Research Notes, 73rd, BWRA 0683/3. He was dismissed from the service 15 Oct. by sentence of a G[rand] C[ourt] Martial].
97. McGregor, Diary, 26 Dec.1801, p. 128, BWRA 0685.
98. ibid., 16 March 1802, p. 132. Dr Mien (Mein) joined the 73rd as surgeon on 3 May 1800. See Thomas B. Smyth, Officers of the 73rd 1786–1881, draft and McGregor, A Black Watch Who Was Who 1725–1881, Research Notes, 73rd, BWRA 0683/3.

10. Egypt: the Honours of Battle 1801

1. Quoted in Cannon, *Historical Record of the Forty-Second*, p. 120.
2. Lt Gen. H.E. Fox to Brig. Gen. Stewart, quoted in ibid., p. 101 n.*.

3. Simpson, Memoir, p. 118, BWRA 0229.
4. Cannon, *Historical Record of the Forty-Second*, p. 101.
5. Stewart of Garth, *Sketches*, I, 3rd ed., p. 458.
6. Simpson, Memoir, pp. 114–15, BWRA 0229.
7. Stewart of Garth, *Sketches*, I, 3rd ed., p. 459.
8. Simpson, Memoir, pp. 115–16, BWRA 0229.
9. ibid., pp. 117–18.
10. ibid., p. 121.
11. Cannon, *Historical Record of the Forty-Second*, p. 102. See Stewart of Garth, *Sketches*, I, p. 461, for statistics: he says the force was 'in all 13,234 men and 630 artillery. Deducting about 300 sick, the efficient force was 12,334.' The 'enemy' were estimated at 32,000 'independently of several thousand native auxiliaries'.
12. Lt Gen Sir John Moore KT (1761–1809). Like Viscount Howe in North America, he realised the importance of 'light infantry'.
13. Simpson, Memoir, p. 122, BWRA 0229.
14. Cannon, *Historical Record of the Forty-Second*, p. 103.
15. Simpson, Memoir, p. 124, BWRA 0229.
16. Cannon, *Historical Record of the Forty-Second*, p. 103.
17. Simpson, Memoir, p. 126, BWRA 0229.
18. Cannon, *Historical Record of the Forty-Second*, p. 103; Forbes, *The 'Black Watch'*, p. 170.
19. Stewart of Garth, *Sketches*, II, 3rd ed., Appendix, p. iii.
20. See Lachlan Macquarie Biography, http://www.lib.mq.edu.au/lmr/biography. Promoted major in 1804, Charles Macquarie never recovered from his head wound and retired from the Army in 1811. The name was spelt Macquarrie but changed by the two brothers to Macquarie, 'so that it resembled the name of the chiefs of MacQuarrie, yet remained distinctive', Currie, *Mull: The Island and Its People*, p. 245.
21. Stewart of Garth, *Sketches*, I, 3rd ed., p. 469, n.*.
22. Simpson, Memoir, p. 126, BWRA 0229.
23. ibid., pp. 126–7.
24. Forbes, *The 'Black Watch'*, p. 174.
25. Simpson, Memoir, p. 129, BWRA 0229.
26. Stewart of Garth, *Sketches*, II, Appendix, p. iii, says 1 field officer, 1 captain, 1 subaltern and 4 soldiers wounded. Other sources: 3 sgts, 1 drummer and 23 soldiers.
27. Simpson, Memoir, pp. 129–30, BWRA 0229.
28. ibid., p. 132.
29. ibid., p. 133.
30. Cannon, *Historical Record of the Forty-Second*, p. 106.
31. Orders by General Menou to the French army 20 March 1801, found in the pocket of the Adjutant General of the French army who was killed in the field, in Simpson, Memoir, p. 153, BWRA 0229. General Abdullah Jacques-

François de Menou, Baron de Boussay (1750–1810).

32. Simpson, Memoir, p. 136, BWRA 0229. At Alexandria the 28th gained the privilege of wearing the 'back badge' because the men had stood back to back to observe the French from both directions.

33. ibid., p. 138.

34. ibid., pp. 137–9.

35. Cannon, *Historical Record of the Forty-Second*, p. 106.

36. Simpson, Memoir, pp. 140–2, BWRA 0229.

37. ibid., p. 142.

38. ibid., pp. 143–4. Stirling was in command because Dickson was wounded on 13 March 1801.

39. ibid., p. 145. Out of 650, an estimated 250 survived. Stewart of Garth, *Sketches*, I, p. 479, says about 200 surrendered.

40. Simpson, Memoir, p. 146, BWRA 0229, makes the point: 'The left wing and such of the right wing as were Employd in destroying the Invincibles . . . had returned to their place in the line before the cavalry made the charge.'

41. ibid., p. 148. According to Private Andrew Dowie, the 42nd did not know that the French Grenadiers were called 'Invincibles' until after the Regiment returned to England. Instead they were known as 'Bonaparte's Bons Grenadiers', Forbes, *The 'Black Watch'*, p. 194.

42. See Groves, *Illustrated Histories of the Scottish Regiments, Book No. 1, The Black Watch, Royal Highlanders, 42nd Foot, 1729–1893*, p. 11: 'General Moore ordered the regiment to advance before its formation was completed.'

43. Sir Ralph Abercromby, quoted in Cannon, *Historical Record of the Forty-Second*, p. 107.

44. The standard was hung in the Royal Chapel, Whitehall, London, but its whereabouts are currently unknown. Cannon, *Historical Record of the Forty-Second Foot*, p. 109 n.*. See Forbes, *The 'Black Watch'*, for his account of what happened to Anthony Lutz, also 'The Invincible Standard', BWRA 0016/03..

45. Simpson, Memoir, p. 148, BWRA 0229.

46. ibid., p. 152.

47. ibid., p. 151.

48. ibid., pp. 154–5. (1082 rank and file killed, 10 officers, 9 sgts 224 wounded.)

49. Return of the Killed, Wounded and Missing of the Army under the Command of General Sir Ralph Abercromby KB near Alexandria 21 March 1801, WO 1/345, f. 149, TNA. See also Stewart of Garth, *Sketches*, II, 3rd ed., App. No. I, iii. Total of 42nd killed on 8, 13 and 21 March: ninety-three officers and soldiers.

50. Stewart of Garth, *Sketches*, I, 3rd ed., p. 492 n.*.

51. ibid., p. 486.

52. Simpson, Memoir, pp. 154–5, BWRA 0229. Abercromby died on 28 March 1801.

53. Stewart of Garth, *Sketches*, I, 3rd ed., p. 487.

54. Maj Gen Hely-Hutchinson, Camp 4 miles from Alexandria, 1 April 1801, to Rt Hon. Henry Dundas, one of His Majesty's Principal Secretaries of State, WO 1/345, f. 143-4; see also Cannon, *Historical Record of the Forty-Second Foot*, p. 111.

55. General Orders of the British Army after the engagement, Camp in front of Alexandria, 21 March 1801, in Simpson, Memoir, BWRA 0229.

56. ibid., pp. 157–9.

57. Hely-Hutchinson, Camp 4 miles from Alexandria, 3 April 1801, to Dundas, WO 1/345. f. 151, TNA.

58. Simpson, Memoir, p. 165, BWRA 0229.

59. ibid., p. 166.

60. ibid., p. 167.

61. Hely-Hutchinson, Camp 4 miles from Alexandria, 20 April 1801, to Dundas, WO 1/345, f. 207, TNA..

62. Simpson, Memoir, p. 169, BWRA 0229.

63. ibid., pp. 170–1.

64. ibid., pp. 173–6.

65. ibid., pp. 176–7.

66. ibid., pp. 218–20.

67. ibid., pp. 225–6.

68. ibid., p. 228.

69. ibid., pp. 240–1.

70. ibid., pp. 247–8.

71. ibid., p. 249.

72. ibid., pp. 253–5.

73. List of men who were killed & died of their wounds from 8th March 1801 (the day of landing in Egypt) to Embarkation 6th Oct. 1801, A/C of Deceased Men, BWRA 0025. Stewart of Garth says 88 killed, 491 wounded.

74. Simpson, Memoir, pp. 263–4, BWRA 0229.

75. ibid., p. 284. Simpson's memoir ends here.

76. John Erly, died in Brighton, Aug. 1844.

77. Henry Addington, 1st Viscount Sidmouth, PC (1757–1844), Prime Minister 1801–4. Pitt had resigned as prime minister on 14 March 1801, ostensibly for reasons of ill-health but primarily because of his dispute with George III over Catholic emancipation.

78. Stewart of Garth, *Sketches*, I, 3rd ed., p. 509.

79. Cannon, *Historical Record of the Forty-Second*, p. 115. See also Wallace, 'The Colours of the Black Watch', *The Red Hackle*, July 1936, p. 8: the new Colours also saw the 'hardest and most continuous fighting of any stand'.

80. Lt Gen Vyse, quoted in Cannon, *Historical Record of the Forty-Second*, p. 116.

81. Forbes, *The 'Black Watch'*, p. 163. He points out that, unlike other regiments,

the 42nd was not 'solicitous for honours on its colours'. Battle honours for Guadaloupe 1759, Havannah and North America 1763–64 were awarded in 1909.

82. See Wallace, 'The Colours of the Black Watch', *The Red Hackle*, July 1936, p. 8.

83. Meeting of the Highland Society of Scotland, 12 Jan. 1802, quoted in Forbes, *The 'Black Watch'*, p. 202. Cannon, *Historical Record of the Forty-Second*, p. 114 n.*. The Highland Society pledged itself to preserve the traditional life of the Highlands in the face of continuing land clearances and agricultural change. Newark, *Highlander: The History of the Legendary Highland Soldier*, p. 96. Stewart of Garth, *Sketches*, I, 3rd ed., p. 505. See also Keltie (ed.), *A History of the Scottish Highland, Highland Clans and Highland Regiments*, II, pp. 399–400; Keltie (ed.), *Historical Record of the 42nd Royal Highlanders (The Black Watch) from 1729 to 1881*, p. 374.

84. Stewart of Garth, *Sketches*, I, 3rd ed., p. 506. Sir John Sinclair (1754–1835), politician.

85. ibid., p. 510.

86. ibid., p. 511.

87. Record of Service, 42nd, 1729–1873, p. 90, BWRA 0079, See also Stewart of Garth, *Sketches*, I, 3rd ed., pp. 512–13 who explains the significance of recruiting by ballot with service confined to Britain and Ireland unless they volunteered for the regular army 'on a certain bounty'. Also in Forbes, *The 'Black Watch'*, p. 205.

88. See Charles John Fedorak, *Henry Addington, Prime Minister, 1801–1804. Peace, War and Parliamentary Politics*, The University of Akron Press, 2002, Ohio, p. 165. Prior to these initiatives the regular Army stood at 132,000.

89. *Personal Narrative of a Private Soldier, Who Served in the Forty-Second Highlanders, for Twelve Years, during the Late War*, p. 12. The book is taken from a series of letters written by a private who calls himself 'John' (p. 87), known to the publisher since their school days and with whom the publisher corresponded. Although the original letters he wrote from Spain were lost, the publisher assured future readers that in editing the letters he wrote from recollection, he had 'only taken such liberties as the grammatical functions of an editor usually warrant. Beyond this licence, I have rarely ventured to alter the original composition of the writer, either by curtailing or adding to the text.' Preface, p. xi.

90. Anon., *Personal Narrative of a Private Soldier*, p. 13. There is no record of presentation of Colours to the 2nd Bn which would have been carried throughout the 2nd Battalion's service in the Peninsular War. See Wallace, 'The Colours of The Black Watch', *The Red Hackle*, July 1936, p. 8.

91. Anon., *Personal Narrative of a Private Soldier*, p. 14.

92. Regimental Orders, Headquarters, Colchester, 28 May 1804, General Order Book, BWRA 0018.

93. Regimental Orders, Weely [barracks], 31 May 1804, Record of Service, 42nd, 1729–1873, BWRA 0079.

94. James Gunn, Memoir, Peninsular and Waterloo Campaigns, 1809–15 (type-script), p. 5, BWRA 0233. An incomplete edited typescript is referenced BWRA 0215. He wrote the memoir for his grandson James sixty-four years later. I have alternated between the two versions, using, where possible, what is most original. He is not to be confused with another James Gunn who enlisted in 1759.

95. Record of Service, 42nd, 1729–1873, p. 90, BWRA 0079; Forbes, The 'Black Watch', p. 205.

96. Capt Walpole to the Earl of Dalkeith (Dec. 1808). He went on a tour of Ireland with Blantyre. See GD 224/31/16/18, NRS.

97. Robert, 11th Baron Blantyre, Lt Col 2nd Bn 42nd 1804–13; accidentally killed in Brussels 1830.

98. Anon., Personal Narrative of a Private Soldier, p. 16.

99. ibid., p. 18.

100. ibid., p. 19.

101. ibid., p. 20.

102. ibid., p. 21.

103. Anton, Retrospect of a Military Life, pp. 32–3. Linklater, The Black Watch, p. 55 describes the loss of the pig-tail as taking place in 1805.

104. This was the Third Coalition, which Pitt had worked to bring together. It fell apart after Napoleon's victories at Austerlitz in 1805, Jena in 1806. The war of the Fourth Coalition started in 1806 with a declaration of war by Prussia; it ended with the Peace of Tilsit in 1807.

105. Stewart of Garth, Sketches, I, 3rd ed., p. 518 n.*.

106. Anon., Personal Narrative of a Private Soldier, p. 34.

107. ibid., p. 41.

108. ibid.

11. Australia: a Place So Little Known

1. Excerpt from 'The Distracted Jockey's Lamentation', a well known traditional song mentioned frequently between 1793 and 1815 in the context of regiments leaving home for war. See Nicholas Potts, 'Over the Hills and Far Away', The Garrison Gazette, Autumn 2010, http://73rdregiment.tripod.com.

2. Record of Service, 73rd, gives the number of 512, p. 26, BWRA 0005.

3. Lachlan Macquarie (1762–1824). He became lt col of the 73rd on 30 May 1805, in succession to Hon. George St John, lt col 28 Aug. 1801 d. 27 May 1804, PROB[ate] 31/981/664–6, TNA. Macquarie started his military service with the 84th Highland Emigrants, raised by his cousin, Allan Maclean. After joining the 77th, he was posted to India and fought at Seringapatam. McGregor, 'A Black Watch Who Was Who 1725–1881', Research Notes, 73rd, BWRA 0863/3.

4. Later General George Harris, 1st Baron Harris GCB (1746–1829). Colonel of the 73rd 1800–29.

5. Henry Colden Antill (1779–1852), Journal of a Voyage to New South Wales 1809, Lachlan & Elizabeth Macquarie Archive, MUL, www.library.mq.edu.au/digital/lema/1809/antill1809.html. Antill began his journal on 7 Nov. 1810, for his sister Eliza and another lady, Mary. He annotated it on 28 Dec. 1849. It is not clear why the 73rd was posted so soon after returning home, nor what the precise policy in allocating regiments for service abroad was, although this was probably determined by which regiment was considered fit and up to strength.

6. H.V. Evatt, *Rum Rebellion, A Study of the Overthrow of Governor Bligh by John Macarthur and the New South Wales Corps*, Angus and Robertson, 1865, p. 77.

7. See Michael Duffy, *Man of Honour: John Macarthur*, Macmillan Australia, Sydney, 2006, for the causes of the struggle for power between the government and private entrepreneurs.

8. Later Lt Gen Sir Miles Nightingall (1768–1829). He had served as military secretary during Cornwallis's Viceroyalty in India. He had just returned from serving in the Peninsula.

9. Antill, Journal of a Voyage, Lachlan & Elizabeth Macquarie Archive, MUL, pp. 6–7.

10. ibid., p. 8.

11. ibid.

12. William George Harris, 2nd Baron Harris KCH (1782–1845). Later Col of the 73rd 1835–45 (succeeded by Sir Robert Henry Dick 1845–6). His wife was Robert Dick's sister, Eliza, See Cannon, *Historical Record of the Seventy-Third*, p. 64.

13. Record of Service, 73rd, p. 27, BWRA 0005. The Bn was placed on the Establishment on 24 Dec. 1808.

14. ibid.

15. Lagden and Sly (ed.), *The 2/73rd at Waterloo*, p. xi. See WO 3/196, Horse Guards, 11 April 1809, p. 306, TNA, and WO 3/47, Horse Guards 15 June 1809, p. 349, TNA. Same for the 72nd, 74th, 75th, 91st and 94th Regiments; see Cannon, *Historical Record of the Seventy-Third*, p. 24, n.

16. See M. H. Ellis, *Lachlan Macquarie*, Angus and Robertson, 1973, p.167.

17. See Antill, Journal of a Voyage, Lachlan & Elizabeth Macquarie Archive, MUL, pp. 10–13. Paraphrased history makes it appear that Macquarie was appointed to succeed Bligh.

18. Lt Col Maurice Charles O'Connell (1768–1848).

19. Antill, Journal of a Voyage, Lachlan & Elizabeth Macquarie Archive, MUL, p. 17. The accompanying anonymous editorial notes of Ensign Alexander Huey's diary assessed: *Dromedary* 368 soldiers, 54 women, 41 children, 10 officers; *Hindustan* 602 soldiers, p.1, BWRA 0232. Also at www.nla.gov.au/apps/doview/nla.aus-vn1991851-p.pdf

20. Ensign Alexander Huey, Diary, p. 2, BWRA 0232. With sixty volunteers from the 'Veteran Battalions', the 73rd comprised ten companies, with fifty-four sgts, twenty-two drummers and 1,000 private soldiers. Record of Service, 73rd, p. 28, BWRA 0005.
21. Huey, Diary, pp. 2–3, BWRA 0232.
22. Antill, Journal of a Voyage, Lachlan & Elizabeth Macquarie Archive, MUL, p. 18.
23. Ship's Standing Orders, Huey, Diary, p. 2, BWRA 0232. See also BWRA 0415.
24. Antill, Journal of a Voyage, Lachlan & Elizabeth Macquarie Archive, MUL, p. 19.
25. ibid., p. 20.
26. Huey, Diary, p. 3, BWRA 0232.
27. ibid., p. 4.
28. Antill, Journal of a Voyage, Lachlan & Elizabeth Macquarie Archive, MUL, p. 27.
29. Huey, Diary, p. 6, BWRA 0232.
30. ibid., p. 7.
31. Antill, Journal of a Voyage, Lachlan & Elizabeth Macquarie Archive, MUL, pp. 29–30.
32. ibid., p. 31.
33. ibid., p. 35. 100 oranges for two pence, Huey, Diary, p. 10.
34. Huey, Diary, p. 10.
35. ibid.
36. João VI the Merciful (1767–1826), third son of Maria I Francisca the Pious (1734–1816).
37. Huey, Diary, p. 10, BWRA 0232.
38. ibid., p. 11.
39. ibid., p. 10. An earlier detachment of the 73rd, sailing from Cork reached New South Wales on 14 Aug. 1809 on board the convict transport ship *Boyd*: *The Sydney Gazette and New South Wales Advertiser*, 20 Aug. 1809, http://trove.nla.gov.au/ndp/del/page/6555/.
40. Antill, Journal of a Voyage, Lachlan & Elizabeth Macquarie Archive, MUL, p. 40.
41. ibid., p. 45.
42. Huey, Diary, p. 15, BWRA 0232.
43. Antill, Journal of a Voyage, Lachlan & Elizabeth Macquarie Archive, MUL, p. 43. Huey, Diary, p. 16, said they had 120 sheep, all consumed by 24 Oct. having left South Africa on 13 Oct.
44. Huey, Diary, p. 16, BWRA 0232.
45. ibid., p. 17.
46. ibid., p. 18.
47. ibid.

48. ibid., p. 20.
49. Antill, Journal of a Voyage, Lachlan & Elizabeth Macquarie Archive, MUL, p. 51.
50. ibid., p. 58.
51. Huey, Diary, p. 21, BWRA 0232. See Stanley, *The Remote Garrison: The British Army in Australia 1788–1870*, p. 25.
52. *The Sydney Gazette and New South Wales Advertiser*, Sunday 7 Jan. 1810. http://trove.nla.gov.au/ndp/del/page/6595. Sydney Cove was called 'Werrong' in the language of the Cadigal clan of the Eora aboriginal people, the traditional owners of the area, and is the site of the present-day Sydney Harbour Bridge and Opera House.
53. Huey, Diary, p. 22, BWRA 0232. There is a debate about whether or not the New South Wales Corps was already a Regiment of the line prior to being given the number 102, and hence whether the 73rd was the 'first' British regiment to serve in Australia. Robin Walsh to the author, Sept. 2010.
54. Huey, Diary, p. 23, BWRA 0232.
55. Stanley, *The Remote Garrison*, p. 26.
56. *The Sydney Gazette and New South Wales Advertiser*, Sunday 14 Jan. 1810, http://trove.nla.gov.au/ndp/del/page/6598.
57. See www.theaustralian.com.au/news/arts/lachlan-macquarie/story-e6frg8n6-1225922181253. Catholic emancipation was in 1829. Believers in transubstantiation affirm that the bread of the Mass becomes the body of Christ.
58. Huey, Diary, p. 23, BWRA 0232.
59. ibid.
60. ibid., p. 24.
61. See New South Wales Corps, 102 Foot, WO 25/1342, p. 219, TNA. The bulk of the men transferred on 24 April 1810.
62. 'The Macquaries' Servants' from the Old Government House website, *The Garrison Gazette*, ed. Dave Sanders, Spring 2009, http://73rdregiment.tripod.com/id14.html.
63. John Dunn, 'The Royal Veterans', *The Garrison Gazette*, Spring 2007.
64. Ron Ray, 'Sir Maurice Charles O'Connor', *The Garrison Gazette*, Summer 2009–2010.
65. Ron Ray, 'Mary Bligh O'Connor (O'Connell)', *The Garrison Gazette*, Summer 2009–2010.
66. Huey's diary resumes on 29 October 1810 and ends mid-journey on 18 Feb. 1811. The last part of the diary was lost.
67. 'The History of the 1st Battalion 73rd Regiment of Foot 1809–1815', *The Garrison Gazette*, Summer 2008–2009.
68. 'The 73rd in New South Wales 1810–1814', sent by Colonel Donald Ramsey, Scots College, Sydney, *The Red Hackle*, Dec. 1985, p. 12. It seems these meetings marked the origin of the Sydney Turf Club. See also *Military Forces in New South Wales, An Introduction Part 1, 1788–1904*, ed. Ralph, Sutton, Ken Thompson and Bill Storey, The Army Museum Sydney

Foundation, 3rd ed., pp. 8–9. By 1810 the number of horses listed in the colony had increased to 203.

69. 'The Records of the Colonial Secretary – 73rd Regiment', *The Garrison Gazette*, Winter 2009.

70. See Ida Lee (Mrs Charles Bruce Marriott), *The Coming of the British to Australia 1788 to 1829*, Longmans, Green and Co., 1906, p. 72.

71. 'The History of the 1st Battalion 73rd Regiment, of Foot 1809–1815', *The Garrison Gazette*, Summer 2008–2009.

72. Francis Greenway (1777–1837). He was emancipated following building of the Macquarie Lighthouse. From 1966–88 Greenway's face appeared on the Australian $10 note, making him probably the only convicted forger in the world to be so honoured.

73. Andrew Thompson (1773–1810). Thompson left Macquarie a quarter of his considerable real and personal estate.

74. See also Christopher Allen, 'The Governor: Lachlan Macquarie, 1810 to 1821, *The Australian* http://www.theaustralian.com.au/news/arts/lachlan-macquarie/story-e6frg8n6-122592218125318, Sept. 2010.

75. Stanley, *Remote Garrison*, p. 26.

76. *The Sydney Gazette and New South Wales Advertiser*, 1 June 1811.

77. Headquarters, Sydney, Monday, 9 March 1812. *The Sydney Gazette and New South Wales Advertiser*, 14 March 1812.

78. Stanley, *Remote Garrison*, p. 26.

79. David Beswick, 'The Girl From Liverpool and the Scottish Soldier'. He died in 1819. *The Garrison Gazette*, Autumn 2007.

80. Stanley, *Remote Garrison*, p. 28.

81. 'The History of the 1st Battalion 73rd Regiment, of Foot 1809–1815', *The Garrison Gazette*, Summer 2008–2009.

82. Government and General After Orders, Headquarters, Sydney, *The Sydney Gazette and New South Wales Advertiser*, Saturday, 17 July 1813. The sentences were light and the court martial obviously biased in favour of the offenders. Macquarie did not interfere with the court's decision but chose to lecture the Regiment.

83. Major General Lachlan Macquarie, General Orders, 17 March 1814, quoted in Cannon, *Historical Record of the Seventy-Third*, p. 26. See also 'The 73rd in New South Wales 1810–1814', Colonel Donald Ramsey, Scots College, Sydney, *The Red Hackle*, Dec. 1985, p. 12.

84. For Antill's account of a journey across the Blue Mountains in 1815, see: http://www.library.mq.edu.au/digital/lema/1815/antill1815.html.

85. Antill retired from the Army in 1821.

86. Capt. Richard Lundin (1791–1832) *Narrative of a Shipwreck & Surprising Adventures, in 1813 . . .*, pp. 1–2, APS. 1.81.30, NLS.

87. Geoffrey Bolton, 'Australia's First Statesman', *The Weekend Australian Review*, 24–25 July 2010, p. 21.

88. Graham Davidson, John Hirst and Stuart MacIntyre, *The Oxford Companion*

to Australian History, OUP, 1998, p. 406. www.theaustralian.com.au/news/arts/ lachlan-macquarie/story-e6frg8n6-1225922181253, 18 Sept. 2010.

89. Lt D'Arcy Wentworth Jnr (1793–1861) to D'Arcy Wentworth Snr, Colombo, 3 July 1814, Wentworth Papers, vol. 1. Original held in Mitchell Library Sydney (ML Ref.: A755; ff. 3–6). Transcript prepared by Robin Walsh, MUL, *Under a Tropical Sun* http://www.lib.mq.edu.au/digital/under/documents/

90. Governor Robert Brownrigg to Earl Bathurst, Secretary of State, Government House, Aripo, 31 March 1814 (Despatch No. 73), National Archives of Sri Lanka: 5/7/85–6. Letterbook copy of original sent to London. Transcript prepared by Robin Walsh, MUL, *Under a Tropical Sun* http://www.lib. mq.edu.au/digital/under/documents/.

91. Wentworth Jnr to Wentworth Snr, Colombo, 3 July 1814, Wentworth Papers, vol. 1. Original held in Mitchell Library Sydney (ML Ref: A755; ff. 3–6). Transcript prepared by Robin Walsh, MUL, *Under a Tropical Sun* http://www.lib.mq.edu.au/digital/under/documents/.

92. ibid.

93. ibid. Atkins was discharged on 10 June 1817.

94. Brownrigg to Earl Bathurst, Secretary of State. King's House, Colombo, 17 August 1814 (Despatch No. 77), National Archives of Sri Lanka: 5/7/104–9. Letterbook copy of original sent to London. Transcript prepared by Robin Walsh, as in n. 90.

95. ibid.

96. ibid.

97. Cannon, *Historical Record of the Seventy-Third*, p. 25.

98. The remainder embarked on the brig *Kangaroo*, reaching Colombo on 19 August 1815. Cannon, *Historical Record of the Seventy-Third*, p. 27.

99. Wentworth Jnr to Wentworh Snr, Camp Ballangaddie, 30 January 1815, as in n. 91. Record of Service, 73rd, pp. 32–3, BWRA 0005.

100. ibid., p. 33.

101. See chapter 14: 1815.

102. Morris, *The Three Serjeants*, p. 166. This is William Morris giving his account.

103. ibid., p. 167.

104. Record of Service, 73rd, p. 34, BWRA 0005.

105. ibid., pp. 34–5. See Morris, *Three Serjeants*, p. 167.

106. Morris, *Three Serjeants*, p. 168.

107. ibid., p. 169.

108. Cannon, *Historical Record of the Seventy-Third*, p. 30. Lt John Maclaine (*c.* 1792–1818).

109. *Ceylon Governmental Gazette* 1 Feb and 1 Nov. 1817. Transcript prepared by Robin Walsh, MUL, *Under a Tropical Sun*.

110. www.adb.online.anu.edu.au/biogs/A020128b.html. William Thomas Lyttleton (1786?–1839), wrongly listed in the Army Lists as 'W.H.'

111. Jarred Ray and Ron Ray, 'Some History Relevant to the 73rd Regiment of Foot', *The Garrison Gazette*, Spring 2009. Baxter's grave is no longer visible.

Author's visit to Parramatta, Nov. 2011 and Robin Walsh to the author, Dec. 2011. When the 73rd left Australia, Whalan transferred to the 46th.

112. Michael Massey Robinson, Laureate Ode on New Year's Day, 1820. Quoted in Ellis, *Lachlan Macquarie*, p. 164.

12. The Peninsular Wars

1. Dugald Dhu, 'The Black Watch', An Historic Ode, *written for Waterloo Day*, 1868, verse 2.
2. Jean-Andoche Junot, 1st Duc d'Abrantes (1771–1813).
3. Joseph-Napoleon Bonaparte (1768–1844). William Cavendish Bentinck, 3rd Duke of Portland (1738–1809).
4. Gunn, Memoir, Peninsular and Waterloo Campaigns, 1808–15, pp. 6–7, BWRA 0215 (edited), 0233 (unedited). See n. 94, chapter 10 above.
5. The preliminary armistice was signed by Wellesley; the Convention by his superiors Sir Harry Burrard and Sir Hew Dalrymple. It was regarded as a humiliation for Britain. All three men were recalled and an inquiry held. Although acquitted, Burrard and Dalrymple were diplomatically retired.
6. Anon., *Personal Narrative of a Private Soldier*, p. 45.
7. Gunn, Memoir, p. 9, BWRA 0215.
8. Stewart of Garth, *Sketches*, I, 3rd ed., p. 522. Vol. I finished with the death of Sir John Moore, vol. II ends with Waterloo and end of the Napoleonic Wars.
9. Anon., *Personal Narrative of a Private Soldier*, pp. 47–8. The 1st Bn 42nd was brigaded in the 1st Division under the command of Hon. Lieutenant General Sir John Hope, 92nd, under Baird's command.
10. ibid., pp. 50–1.
11. Gunn, Memoir, p. 10, BWRA 0215.
12. Nicolas Jean-de-Dieu Soult, Marshal General of France (1769–1851). Created Marshal in 1804 for distinguished service. See Stewart of Garth, *Sketches*, I, p. 526: The British army consisted of 26,311 infantry and 2,450 cavalry.
13. Anon., *Personal Narrative of a Private Soldier*, p. 56.
14. Cannon, *Historical Record of the Forty-Second*, p. 119.
15. Gunn, Memoir, p. 12, BWRA 0215.
16. ibid., p. 13.
17. Anon., *Personal Narrative of a Private Soldier*, p. 59.
18. Gunn, Memoir, p. 16, BWRA 0215/0233.
19. Anon., *Personal Narrative of a Private Soldier*, p. 62.
20. ibid., pp. 64–5.
21. Gunn, Memoir, p. 18, BWRA 0215/0233.
22. ibid.
23. Anon., *Personal Narrative of a Private Soldier*, p. 68.
24. ibid., p. 69.

25. Sir John Moore's last dispatch to the Rt Hon. Lord Castlereagh, Corunna, 13 January 1809, p. 213, published in *Constable's Miscellany of Original and Selected Publications in the Various Departments of Literature, Science, & the Arts*, vol. XXVII, *Memorials of the Late War*, vol. 1. See also S.P.G. Ward, 'Some Fresh Light on the Corunna Campaign', *JSAHR*, XXVIII, no. 115, Autumn 1950, p. 125.

26. Anon., *Personal Narrative of a Private Soldier*, p. 75.

27. M.R. Howard, 'Medical aspects of Sir John Moore's Corunna Campaign, 1808–1809', *Journal of the Royal Society of Medicine*, vol. 84, May 1991, p. 300.

28. Anon., *Personal Narrative of a Private Soldier*, pp. 75–6.

29. ibid., p. 77.

30. Gunn, Memoir, p. 21, BWRA 0215.

31. Anon., *Personal Narrative of a Private Soldier*, p. 83.

32. Maj Gen James Stirling, Musselburgh, 30 March 1830, quoted in Cannon, *Historical Record of the Forty-Second*, Appendix, p. 197. This letter was written to the Editor of *The Edinburgh Magazine* to correct the account given in Cannon's *Historical Record* at pp. 119–20, which states 'from some misapprehension' that the 42nd retired from the battle of Corunna. He also insisted that Moore only addressed the 42nd once with the words 'Highlanders, remember Egypt!' Gunn says that Baird said the words: 'Calmly Forty second, one volley, Charge, Remember Egypt.' – p. 23, BWRA 0233.

33. Cannon, *Historical Record of the Forty-Second*, p. 120.

34. Anon., *Personal Narrative of a Private Soldier*, p. 83.

35. ibid., p. 84.

36. Maj Gen James Stirling, Musselburgh, 30 March, 1830, quoted in Cannon, *Historical Record of the Forty-Second*, p. 197.

37. Hope to Baird, on board HMS *Audacious*, off Corunna 18th Jan[uar]y 1809, enclosed in Baird's letter to Castlereagh, HMS *Ville de Paris* – at Sea, 18 January 1809. Because of his severe wound he had asked Hope for his report of the battle, WO 1/236, p. 512, TNA. Also published in *Constable's Miscellany . . .*, vol. XXVII, *Memorials of the Late War* vol. I, pp. 220–8.

38. Anon., *Personal Narrative of a Private Soldier*, p. 85.

39. Hope to Baird, on board HMS *Audacious*, off Corunna 18 Jan[uar]y 1809, WO 1/236, p. 512, TNA.

40. Gunn, Memoir, p. 24, BWRA 0233.

41. Anon., *Personal Narrative of a Private Soldier*, p. 86.

42. Maj Gen James Stirling, Musselburgh, 30 March 1830, quoted in Cannon, *Historical Record of the Forty-Second*, p. 197.

43. Anon., *Personal Narrative of a Private Soldier*, p. 88.

44. ibid., p. 87.

45. Gunn, Memoir, p. 25, BWRA 0233.

46. Hope to Baird, on board HMS *Audacious*, off Corunna, 18 Jan[uar]y 1809, WO 1/236, pp. 513, 514, TNA.

47. Lt Gen Hope, quoted in Cannon, *Historical Record of the Forty-Second*, pp. 121–2.

48. Stewart of Garth, *Sketches*, II, Appendix, p. iii. *Chronology of the 42nd Royal Highlanders, The Black Watch from 1729 to 1905*, p.11, states 215 Officers and Men killed and wounded.

49. Cannon, *Historical Record of the Forty-Second*, p. 122. See also Linklater, *The Black Watch*, p. 62, who say 35 killed, 111 wounded, 99 men marked 'missing in Spain'.

50. To the Lt General the Marquis of Huntly, Horse Guards, 3 March 1812, WO 3/55, p. 320; see also WO 3/203, p.127, TNA.

51. Anon., *Personal Narrative of a Private Soldier*, p. 95.

52. Gunn, Memoir, p. 27, BWRA 0233.

53. Anon., *Personal Narrative of a Private Soldier*, p. 97.

54. Gunn, Memoir, p. 28, BWRA 0215.

55. Anon., *Personal Narrative of a Private Soldier*, p. 98.

56. ibid., p. 99. The new lt col was John Farquharson, who had joined the Regiment as a lt in 1787. Promoted lt col in March 1808, Stirling had remained in command.

57. ibid., p. 100.

58. ibid., p. 104.

59. Gunn, Memoir, p. 29, BWRA 0233.

60. ibid., p. 30.

61. Macara to Dick, Canterbury, 1 March 1810, Dick Papers, BWRA 0276/07. Four months later a third of the force which had taken part in the Walcheren Expedition was still unfit for service. See Rogers, *Wellington's Army*, p. 22.

62. Anon., *Personal Narrative of a Private Soldier*, pp. 109–10.

63. Gunn, Memoir, p. 30, BWRA 0215.

64. Anon., *Personal Narrative of a Private Soldier*, p. 108.

65. Statement of the Services of Major Robert Henry Dick, Dick Papers, BWRA 0276/11.

66. In June, Wellesley had organised the army into one cavalry division and four infantry divisions, of two brigades each. The 42nd was in the 1st Division, commanded by Lt Gen Sherbrooke, in Brig Gen Cameron's Brigade, consisting of the 24th, 42nd and 61st.

67. Don Gregorio Garcia de la Cuesta (1741–1811), described by historian Philip Guedalla as 'the embodiment of Spain at its very worst – old, proud, incompetent and ailing' (quoted in Holmes, *The Iron Duke*, p. 133).

68. Blantyre, Journal of the Campaigns in Portugal and Spain in 1809–1810, 1811 and 1812, p. 3, M.1995.54.2, NMS.

69. ibid., p. 7.

70. ibid., pp. 12, 13. By end Oct., out of 665 men, 478 were recorded as fit for duty, 188 were in hospital. General Monthly Return of the troops stationed in Spain and Portugal, 25 October 1809, Monthly returns, WO 17/1264, TNA.

71. Blantyre, Journal, p. 15, M.1995.54.2, NMS. Those fit for duty had fallen to

344, out of a complement of 608 men, while 245 were in hospital. General Monthly Return of the troops stationed in Spain and Portugal, 25 Dec. 1809, Monthly returns, WO 17/1264, TNA.

72. Blantyre, Journal, p. 27, M.1995.54.2, NMS.

73. John Swanson to Major Dick, Belin(?), 23 May 1810, Dick Papers, BWRA 0276/12:2. Maj Gen Sir Robert Henry Dick of Tulliemet, KCB, KCH (1785/6– 1846) was appointed junior major in 1808 when the Bn was serving in Ireland. His father, Dr William Dick, was surgeon in the service of the East India Company. See Tullibardine (ed.), *Military History of Perthshire 1660–1902*, p. 497, n. 8. In Cameron's absence, Blantyre frequently took command of the Brigade.

74. Blantyre, Journal, p. 28, M.1995.54.2, NMS.

75. ibid., p. 29.

76. ibid., pp. 37–8.

77. Return of the Number of Killed, Wounded & Missing of the Army under the command of Lieutenant General Lord Viscount Wellington KB in the action with the French Army commanded by Marshal Massena . . . with the position of Busãco on 27 Sept. 1810, Head Quarters Coimbra 30 Sept. 1810, pp. 638–9, WO 1/245, TNA.

78. See Wallace, 'The Colours of the Black Watch', *The Red Hackle*, July 1936, p. 8.

79. Blantyre, Journal, pp. 40–1, M.1995.54.2, NMS.

80. ibid., p. 44.

81. Dr Dick to 'my Dearly Beloved Robert', 14 Jan. 1811, Dick Papers, BWRA 0276/03.

82. Dr Dick to 'my Dearest Robert', from Hertford St, Mayfair, 28 January 1811, Dick Papers, BWRA 0276/03.

83. Blantyre, Journal, p. 50, M.1995.54.2, NMS.

84. Statement of the Services of Major Robert Henry Dick, & Summary of Dick's Service from March 1804 until Fuentes de Honores, with references to his battle service at Maida, Eygpt and Portugal. Unsigned and undated, probably written in mid-1811. Dick Papers, BWRA 0276/11.

85. Blantyre, Journal, p. 52, M.1995.54.2, NMS.

86. ibid.

87. ibid., p. 53.

88. ibid., pp. 56–7.

89. ibid., p. 59.

90. ibid.

91. ibid., pp. 60–1.

92. ibid., p. 62; Stewart of Garth, *Sketches*, II, 3rd ed., Appendix No. 1, p. iii.

93. Cannon, *Historical Record of the Forty-Second*, p. 126. See Horse Guards 22 Dec. 1817, WO 3/67, p. 324, TNA.

94. Dr Dick to Major Dick, 27 May 1811, Dick Papers, BWRA 0276/03.

95. Blantyre, Journal, p. 63, M.1995.54.2, NMS.

96. ibid., p. 66.

97. ibid., pp. 73–4.

98. ibid., p. 75.

99. Mackenzie, *Merely a Memorandum: The Personal Recollections of Lieutenant Donald Mackenzie*, compiled and edited by Guy Hutton-Wilson, p. 63.

100. Anon., *Personal Narrative of a Private Soldier*, p. 116.

101. Blantyre, Journal, p. 79, M.1995.54.2, NMS.

102. ibid., p. 81. General Auguste de Marmont (1774–1852).

103. Dr Dick to Major Dick, No. 8 Hertford Street, Mayfair, 25 Feb. 1812, BWRA 0276/03. See Return of Killed, Wounded and Missing of the Army under the Command of His Excellency General Lord Viscount Wellington KB [at Ciudad Rodrigo] between the 15th and the 19th Days of January 1812, Head Quarters Gallegos, 21 January 1812, WO 1/253, pp. 107, 132, TNA.

104. Cannon, *Historical Record of the Forty-Second*, p. 126; & Blantyre, Journal, p. 81, M.1995.54.2, NMS.

105. Blantyre, Journal, pp. 84, 85, M.1995.54.2, NMS.

106. Dr Dick to Major Dick, 25 April 1812, BWRA 0276/03.

107. Longford, *Wellington*, p. 265.

108. Mackenzie, *Merely a Memorandum*, p. 64.

109. ibid., p. 66.

110. Gunn, Memoir, p. 30, BWRA 0233. Figure was 1,160. Included in the Highland Brigade were the 71st and 92nd.

111. See Blantyre to Dick, Lisbon, 15 May 1812, who assures him that Macara 'will not be long in your way'. The correspondence gives an interesting insight into purchase and ambition, Dick Papers, BWRA 0276/04.

112. Wellington, quoted in Linklater, *The Black Watch*, p. 63.

113. Mackenzie, *Merely a Memorandum*, p. 70.

114. Gunn, Memoir, p. 32, BWRA 0233.

115. Mackenzie, *Merely a Memorandum*, p. 72.

116. ibid., pp. 72–3.

117. ibid.

118. ibid., p. 73. Salamanca was not granted as a Battle Honour until 1951.

119. Wallace, 'The Colours of the Black Watch', *The Red Hackle*, July 1936, p. 8; Return of the Killed, Wounded and Missing of the Allied Army under the command of His Excellency General the Earl Wellington KB in the battle near Salamanca on the 22nd day of July 1812, Head Quarters Flores de Avelas 15th July 1812, p. 143, WO 1/155, TNA. Stewart of Garth, *Sketches*, II, 3rd ed., Appendix I, p. iii. French statistics from David Gates, *The Spanish Ulcer: a History of the Peninsular War*, Da Capo Press, 2001, p. 358.

120. Mackenzie, *Merely a Memorandum*, p. 74.

121. ibid., p. 75.
122. ibid., p. 76.
123. Gunn, Memoir, p. 32, BWRA 0215.
124. ibid.
125. Anon., *Personal Narrative of a Private Soldier*, p. 147.
126. Mackenzie, *Merely a Memorandum*, p. 77.
127. Gunn, Memoir, p. 33, BWRA 0215. Gunn mistakes the storming of the castle for the taking of the hornwork fortifying the hill of San Miguel 300 yards from the castle.
128. Mackenzie, *Merely a Memorandum*, p. 78.
129. ibid.
130. ibid.
131. Supplement to *The London Gazette*, 3 October 1812, BWRA 0276/11.
132. Anon., *Personal Narrative of a Private Soldier*, p. 143.
133. ibid., p. 151.
134. ibid., pp. 154–5.
135. Mackenzie, *Merely a Memorandum*, p. 78.
136. ibid., p. 79.
137. See Stewart of Garth, *Sketches*, II, 3rd ed., Appendix I, p. iii. Also Cannon, *Historical Record of the Forty-Second*, p. 129. Private John says the 42nd lost upwards of 200 excellent soldiers: Anon., *Personal Narrative of a Private Soldier*, p. 154.
138. Anon., *Personal Narrative of a Private Soldier*, p. 145.
139. ibid., pp. 146–7.
140. ibid., p. 156.
141. Mackenzie, *Merely a Memorandum*, p. 81.
142. Anon., *Personal Narrative of a Private Soldier*, p. 159.
143. ibid., p. 161.
144. ibid., p. 162.
145. Mackenzie, *Merely a Memorandum*, p. 82.
146. ibid., p. 83.
147. ibid.
148. Anon., *Personal Narrative of a Private Soldier*, p. 174.
149. ibid., pp. 171–2.
150. ibid., pp. 180–2. Lt Alexander Dickenson, commissioned as an ensign in 1810; shot by McMorran in 1812.
151. Lt Innes, quoted in Linklater, *The Black Watch*, p. 66.
152. Anon., *Personal Narrative of a Private Soldier*, p. 183.
153. The Highland Brigade, commanded by Brig Gen Sir Denis Pack, included the 9th East Norfolk, 79th Cameron Highlanders, 91st Argyll Highlanders and one company of 60th Royal Rifle Corps. In the 9th there was a young Lt Colin Campbell, under whom the 42nd later served in the Crimea and the Indian Mutiny.
154. Gunn, Memoir, p. 35, BWRA 0233.

155. Anon., *Personal Narrative of a Private Soldier*, p. 184.
156. Macara to Dick, commanding 2nd Bn, in Inverness, from Camp before Pampeluna, 12 July 1813, Dick Papers, BWRA 0276/07. Dick, promoted brevet lt col in Oct. 1812 had taken over temporarily from Blantyre, who had gone on half-pay.
157. ibid.
158. Mackenzie, *Merely a Memorandum*, p. 86.
159. Gunn, Memoir, p. 37, BWRA 0233. The treasure included gold bars, jewellery and works of art, including paintings by Velazquez. Mackenzie, *Merely a Memorandum*, p. 87.
160. Anon., *Personal Narrative of a Private Soldier*, p. 187.
161. Mackenzie, *Merely a Memorandum*, p. 87. The defeat at Vittoria encouraged Austria to enter the war against France.
162. Stewart of Garth, *Sketches*, II, 3rd ed., p. 28. San Sebastian fell on 31 Aug. After a four month siege, Pampeluna fell on 31 Oct. 1813.
163. Mackenzie, *Merely a Memorandum*, p. 88.
164. Gunn, Memoir, p. 38, BWRA 0233.
165. ibid.
166. ibid., p. 39. Mackenzie, *Merely a Memorandum*, p. 90, records a similar episode in a field of peas.
167. Mackenzie, *Merely a Memorandum*, p. 88.
168. Stewart of Garth, *Sketches*, II, 3rd ed., p. 29.
169. Mackenzie, *Merely a Memorandum*, p. 91.
170. ibid.
171. John Home to Dick, camp near Maya, 22 Aug. 1813, Dick Papers, BWRA 0276/12:2.
172. ibid.
173. John Malcolm, Esq., late of the 42d Regt., *Reminiscences of a Campaign in the Pyrenees and South of France, in 1814* (dated Edinburgh, 1 Dec. 1827), p. 247 (in *Constable's Miscellany . . .*, vol. XXVII), *Memorials of the Late War*, vol. 1. His account begins on p. 235 of the *Miscellany*. Ensign 1807, lt 1809. See also his unpublished diary, BWRA 0220.
174. Anton, *Retrospect of a Military Life*, p. 35.
175. Malcolm, *Reminiscences*, p. 251.
176. ibid., p. 252.
177. ibid., p. 253.
178. ibid., p. 254.
179. Marshal Soult; see Malcolm, *Reminiscences*, p. 262.
180. See Horse Guards 22 Dec 1817, WO 3/67, p. 324, TNA.
181. Morris, *Three Serjeants*, p. 9. Thomas, b. 1795, by trade a gunmaker, promoted corporal 17 Oct. 1815. Transferred to 1st Bn in 1817, remained with Depot Company in Britain. Discharged 20 Nov. 1818. William, b. 1793, also transferred to 1st Bn in 1817 and went to Trincomalee in Sept. 1817. Promoted sgt 1818, discharged 1820, re-enlisted in 63rd in 1827. William Junior was a

colour sgt in the 63rd and served in the Crimea. Their account was mainly written by Thomas. The Swedes were commanded by Crown Prince Bernadotte, one of Napoleon's trusted generals but who was induced to change sides.

182. Morris, *Three Serjeants*, p. 7.

183. ibid., pp. 9–10.

184. ibid., p. 11.

185. ibid., p. 12.

186. ibid., p. 13.

187. Maj Gen Samuel Gibbs to Bathurst, Stralsund, 3 Sept. 1813, War Department In-Letters and Papers: of the French Wars period, WO 1/422, f. 53, TNA; Morris, *Three Serjeants*, p. 14. General Ludwig von Wallmoden-Gimborn (1769–1862).

188. Lt Col Harris, quoted in Morris, *Three Serjeants*, p. 15. For full complement, see Bernhard Schwertfeger, *Geschichte der Königlich Deutschen Legion 1803–1816*, Hanover & Leipzig, 1907. http://www.cgsc.edu/CARL/nafziger/813IIH.pdf.

189. Morris, *Three Serjeants*, p. 16. He continued: 'When the British Colours were exhibited, the French troops fancied that not only we but the majority of the red coats were English'. See Lagden and Sly, *The 2/73rd at Waterloo*.

190. Morris, *Three Serjeants*, p. 16.

191. ibid., p. 18.

192. ibid., p. 19.

193. Gibbs to Bathurst, Stralsund, 22 Oct. 1813, WO 1/422, f. 121, TNA.

194. Morris, *Three Serjeants*, p. 25.

195. Memorandum, Horse Guards, 21 Nov. 1813, WO 1/199, f. 37, TNA. It was initially proposed that the 2nd Bn 73rd would be brigaded with the 25th, 33rd and 54th under the command of Maj Gen Gibbs. Later the composition of the Brigade under Gibbs was altered to include the 35th, 52nd and a provisional bn of the 95th Rifles as well as the 2 Bn 73rd.

196. Morris, *Three Serjeants*, p. 28.

197. ibid., p. 29.

198. ibid., p. 36.

199. Lt Gen Graham to Bathurst, Head Quarters Merxem, 6 Feby 1814, WO 1/199, ff. 569, 573, TNA.

13. The Road to Toulouse 1813–1814

1. George Gerard, Journal, British Camp, 15 April 1814, BWRA 0116/01.

2. Malcolm, *Reminiscences of a Campaign in the Pyrenees and South of France 1814*, p. 291.

3. Malcolm, *Reminiscences*, p. 257.

4. Anton, *Retrospect of a Military Life*, p. 63.

5. ibid., p. 64.

6. Malcolm, *Reminiscences*, p. 259.

7. ibid., p. 263.

8. Mackenzie, *Merely a Memorandum*, p. 91.

9. Malcolm, *Reminiscences*, p. 266.

10. Anton, *Retrospect of a Military Life*, pp. 68–9. Daniel Defoe's *Robinson Crusoe* was published in 1719.

11. Cannon, *Historical Record of the Forty-Second*, p. 131. The 1st Bn 42nd was in the 1st or Highland Brigade with the 79th and 91st Regiments, commanded by Major General Sir Denis Pack, supported by the 11th, 32nd, 37th and 61st Regiments. See Anton, *Retrospect of a Military Life*, p. 80.

12. Anton, *Retrospect of a Military Life*, pp. 69–70.

13. Malcolm, *Reminiscences*, p. 267.

14. Mackenzie, *Merely a Memorandum*, p. 92.

15. Gunn, Journal, pp. 41–2, BWRA 0215.

16. Malcolm, *Reminiscences*, p. 268.

17. Anton, *Retrospect of a Military Life*, pp. 72, 73.

18. Stewart of Garth, *Sketches*, II, 3rd ed., App. I, p. iii.

19. Anton, *Retrospect of a Military Life*, pp. 76–7.

20. Malcolm, *Reminiscences*, p. 268.

21. Anton, *Retrospect of a Military Life*, p. 78.

22. Gunn, Memoir, pp. 39–40, BWRA 0215.

23. Malcolm, *Reminiscences*, p. 269.

24. Anton, *Retrospect of a Military Life*, p. 81.

25. ibid., p. 82.

26. Malcolm, *Reminiscences*, p. 271.

27. ibid.

28. Anton, *Retrospect of a Military Life*, p. 85. 'A soldier's blanket is their shroud; no sculptured stone marks the spot, or records their name, but it is impressed on our remembrance, from which death only can efface it.'

29. Thomas McNiven, Memoirs, 1795–1814, p. 51, BWRA 0035.

30. Mackenzie, *Merely a Memorandum*, p. 93.

31. Anton, *Retrospect of a Military Life*, p. 89.

32. Malcolm, *Reminiscences*, p. 277.

33. Anton, *Retrospect of a Military Life*, pp. 92, 93. Ten (Anton, p. 86, says 11) soldiers were killed; a sgt and 15 soldiers wounded. Stewart of Garth, *Sketches*, II, 3rd ed., App. I, p. iii, says 2 officers killed, 11 soldiers wounded at the Passage of the Nive.

34. Stewart of Garth, *Sketches*, II, 3rd ed., p. 43.

35. Mackenzie, *Merely a Memorandum*, p. 94.

36. Anton, *Retrospect of a Military Life*, pp. 96, 97.

37. ibid., p. 97.

38. ibid., pp. 99–100.

39. McNiven, Memoirs, BWRA 0035. There are no further page numbers in his Memoirs.

40. ibid.

41. ibid.

42. ibid.

43. Mackenzie, *Merely a Memorandum*, p. 94. The army numbered approximately 44,000.

44. Anton, *Retrospect of a Military Life*, p. 102.

45. Gunn, Memoir, pp. 46–7. BWRA 0215.

46. Mackenzie, *Merely a Memorandum*, p. 96.

47. ibid.

48. Anton, *Retrospect of a Military Life*, p. 105. Lt John Innes, ensign 1804, killed at Orthez, 27 Feb. 1814.

49. Stewart of Garth, *Sketches*, II, 3rd ed., Appendix No. I, p. iii.

50. Anton, *Retrospect of a Military Life*, p. 106.

51. ibid.

52. ibid., p. 117.

53. Malcolm, *Reminiscences*, p. 287.

54. Stewart of Garth, *Sketches*, II, 3rd ed., p. 50.

55. Anton, *Retrospect of a Military Life*, pp. 120–1.

56. Anon., *Personal Narrative of a Private Soldier*, p. 243.

57. See Mackenzie, *Merely a Memorandum*, p. 98.

58. George Gerard, Journal, British Camp, 8 April 1814, BWRA 0116/01. Gerard's aunt was Mrs Moyes of Forglen Manse, by Turiff, Aberdeen. He had a brother Arthur and his cousin was Mrs Allardyce. See also 'Letters of Ensign Gerard', *The Red Hackle*, Jan. 1932, pp. 13–14.

59. Malcolm, *Reminiscences*, p. 291.

60. Gerard, Journal, British Camp, 9 April 1814, BWRA 0116/01.

61. Anton, *Retrospect of a Military Life*, pp. 121–2.

62. Malcolm, *Reminiscences*, p. 292.

63. Anon., *Personal Narrative of a Private Soldier*, p. 249.

64. Malcolm, *Reminiscences*, p. 292.

65. Gunn, Memoir, p. 48, BWRA 0215 (edited) /0233.

66. Gerard, Memoir, Heights above Toulouse, 11 April 1814, BWRA 0016/01.

67. Malcolm, *Reminiscences*, p. 293.

68. Gerard, Journal, Heights above Toulouse, 11 April 1814, BWRA 0016/01.

69. Malcolm, *Reminiscences*, p. 293.

70. Anon., *Personal Narrative of a Private Soldier*, pp. 251–3.

71. Anton, *Retrospect of a Military Life*, p. 123.
72. Gerard, Journal, Heights above Toulouse, 11 April 1814, BWRA 0016 .01.
73. Anon., *Personal Narrative of a Private Soldier*, pp. 251–3.
74. Anton, *Retrospect of a Military Life*, pp. 125–6.
75. Mackenzie, *Merely a Memorandum*, p. 99.
76. Malcolm, *Reminiscences*, pp. 299–300.
77. Anton, *Retrospect of a Military Life*, p. 131.
78. ibid., p. 126.
79. Gerard, Journal, Heights above Toulouse, 11 April 1814, BWRA 0116/01.
80. ibid.
81. ibid.
82. Cannon, *Historical Record of the Forty-Second*, p. 133.
83. British commander, public dispatch, Cannon, *Historical Record of the Forty-Second*, p. 134.
84. Gerard says 414 out of 529 men were killed or wounded. Journal, Heights above Toulouse, 11 April 1814, BWRA 0016/01. According to the Return of Killed, Wounded & Missing of the Army under the Command of His Excellency Field Marshal the Marquis of Wellington KG in the attack of the Enemy's Fortified position covering Toulouse on the 10th day of April 1814, 413 men of the 1st Bn 42nd were killed, wounded or missing. WO 1/203, f. 125, TNA. This compares with 297 wounded and killed at Burgos and 649 wounded and killed at Ticonderoga. Stewart of Garth, *Sketches*, II, 3rd ed., Appendix No. I, p. iii gives the correct statistics for killed (47 soldiers killed, 4 officers, 3 sgts), but not for wounded.
85. Gerard, Journal, British Camp, 15 April 1814, BWRA 0116/01.
86. ibid., 16 April 1814.
87. Anton, *Retrospect of a Military Life*, p. 139.
88. Gerard, Journal, British Camp, 16 April, BWRA 0116/01.
89. ibid.
90. Anton, *Retrospect of a Military Life*, p. 127, says '436 of inferior rank killed or wounded, 20 officers, one sgt major'.
91. Gerard, Journal, Heights above Toulouse, 11 April 1814, BWRA 0016/01.
92. McNiven, Memoirs, BWRA 0035. After several months being cared for by a French family, he left Toulouse on 19 June 1814.
93. Gerard, Journal, British Camp, 15 April 1814, BWRA 0116/01.
94. Anon., *Personal Memoir of a Private Soldier*, p. 256.
95. Gerard, Journal, 17 April 1814, BWRA 0116/01.
96. Gerard, Journal, Cantonments, 19 April 1814, BWRA 0016/01.
97. McNiven, Memoirs, BWRA 0035.
98. *Peninsula* (which included both battalions of the 42nd) was granted in 1815, Harry Calvert, Adjutant General, Horse Guards, 6 April 1815, WO 3/160, p. 239, TNA; *Toulouse* in 1816. Calvert, 26 July 1816, WO 3/161, p. 369. TNA. *Fuentes d'Honor, Pyrenees, Nivelle, Nive* and *Orthes* in 1817: to Lt Gen The

Marquis of Huntly from Calvert, Horse Guards 22 Dec. 1817, WO 3/67, p. 324, TNA. See Wallace, 'The Colours of the Black Watch', *The Red Hackle*, July 1936, p. 8. *Busaco* was granted in 1910; *Salamanca* in 1951, see Army Order 136/51, printed in *The Red Hackle*, Jan. 1952, p.2.

99. McNiven, Memoirs, BWRA 0035.

100. Anton, *Retrospect of a Military Life*, p. 146.

101. Anon., *Personal Narrative of a Private Soldier*, p. 262.

102. Louis XVIII (1755–1824).

103. *The Times*, Tuesday, 12 April 1814.

104. Anton, *Retrospect of a Military Life*, p. 150.

105. Gunn, Memoir, p. 49, BWRA 0215.

106. Anon., *Personal Narrative of a Private Soldier*, p. 264.

107. Anton, *Retrospect of a Military Life*, p. 151.

108. ibid.

109. Lt Gen Graham to Bathurst, Head Quarters Merxem, 6 Feby 1814, WO 1/199, ff. 569, 573, TNA. One lt, 2 sgts, 2 drummers and 27 soldiers from the 73rd were wounded; 3 men killed. Return of Killed, Wounded and Missing of the Army ... in the attack upon the village of Merxem on the morning of the 2nd Feb. 1814. WO 1/199, f. 581, TNA.

110. Morris, *Three Serjeants*, p. 69.

111. ibid., p. 72.

112. ibid., p. 73.

113. ibid.

114. Blantyre to Dick, from Erskine, 9th Sept. 1814, Dick Papers, BWRA 02767/04.

115. Stewart of Garth, *Sketches*, II, 3rd ed., Appendix No. I, p. iii. Wounded 1,280, but his figures for Toulouse were inaccurate.

116. Mrs Allardyce, on the death of her 'dear' cousin, George Gerard, 1815. *The Red Hackle*, Jan. 1932 p.14.

14. 1815

1. Dugald Dhu, 'The Black Watch', An Historic Ode, *Written for Waterloo Day*, 1868, verse 3.

2. Morris, *Three Serjeants*, p. 75.

3. Mackenzie, *Merely a Memorandum*, p. 112.

4. Anton, *Retrospect of a Military Life*, pp. 172–3.

5. William Frederick, Prince of Orange (1792–1849).

6. See Longford, *Wellington: The Years of the Sword*. Napoleon's army numbered approximately 122,000 men as well as the Imperial Guard. Note: Belgium was still part of the United Kingdom of the Netherlands.

7. Gerard to his sister, Mrs (Keturah) Simmie, Rothiemay, Banffshire, from Brussels, 13 June 1815, Letters of Ensign Gerard, *The Red Hackle*, Jan. 1932, p. 13.

8. Anton, *Retrospect of a Military Life*, p. 170.

9. Diary of Lt John Malcolm (concerning the period 25 April to 18 June 1815, with description of Quatre Bras), handwritten copy, p. 2, BWRA 0220.

10. Gerard, Journal, Ghent, 26 May 1815, BWRA 0016/01.

11. Anton, *Retrospect of a Military Life*, p. 173.

12. Malcolm, Diary (handwritten), pp. 4–5, BWRA 0220.

13. Gerard, Journal, Ghent, 26 May 1815, BWRA 0016/01.

14. Gerard to his sister, Mrs (Keturah) Simmie, 13 June 1815, Letters of Ensign Gerard, *The Red Hackle*, Jan. 1932, p. 14.

15. Gerard, Journal, Brussels 28 May 1815, BWRA 0016/01.

16. *Paul's Letters to his Kinsfolk*, printed by James Ballantyne and Co. for Archibald Constable and Co., Edinburgh; and Longman, Hurst, Rees, Orme and Brown and John Murray, London 1816. Quoted in Cannon, *Historical Record of the Forty-Second*, p. 140 n.*. Walter Scott was among the first civilians to visit Waterloo after the battle. His letters, written under a fictitious name, gave a detailed history of the battle based on eyewitness accounts.

17. Anton, *Retrospect of a Military Life*, p. 179.

18. Gerard, Journal, Brussels, 28 May 1815, BWRA 0016/01.

19. ibid., 1 June 1815.

20. ibid., 8 June 1815. There were two more entries on 9 and 13 June describing the use of dogs as draught animals and the houses in Brussels. Excerpts from his Journal were published in *The Red Hackle*, April 1963, pp. 55–6.

21. Gerard to his sister, Mrs (Keturah) Simmie, 13 June 1815. Letters of Ensign Gerard, *The Red Hackle*, Jan. 1932, p. 13.

22. Quoted in Morris, *Three Serjeants*, p. 92.

23. Longford, *Wellington*, p. 416. Mackenzie, *Merely a Memorandum*, p. 113, calls her the Duchess of Gordon.

24. Mackenzie, *Merely a Memorandum*, p. 113.

25. Gunn, Memoir, p. 51, BWRA 0233.

26. Forbes, *The 'Black Watch'*, p. 262. Stewart of Garth's account is brief, since 'so much has been already said and written, and that so recently, that every part is fresh in the memory of all'. *Sketches*, II, 3rd ed., p. 38. The Record of Service, 42nd, 1729–1873, BWRA 0079, is equally brief. Keltie (ed.), *A History of the Scottish Highlands, Highland Clans and Highland Regiments*, II, gives a short narrative. See also Holmes, *Wellington: the Iron Duke*, p. 226; Longford, *Wellington: The Years of the Sword*, pp. 413–17.

27. Maj General Sir Denis Pack (c.1772–1823). The 9th Brigade also included a Bn of the 1st Royals, the 44th and 92nd Regiments. Pack had been wounded eight times in the Peninsular Wars.

28. Malcolm, Diary, pp. 7, 8, BWRA 0220.

29. Major General Colin Halkett GCB, GCH, GCTE (1774–1856). His younger brother was General Hugh Halkett, under whom the 73rd had served at Gorde. He was also present in the Peninsula, and at Waterloo was in command of the 3rd Hanoverian Brigade in Lt Gen Sir Henry Clinton's 2nd Division. Also in the 5th Brigade were the 2nd Battalions of the 30th, 69th and 33rd.

30. Morris, *Three Serjeants*, pp. 88–9.
31. ibid., p. 90.
32. ibid., pp. 90–1.
33. ibid., p. 91.
34. ibid., p. 92.
35. Wellington had promised assistance to Blücher, but 'urgent operational necessity' at Quatre Bras meant that he failed to give it. Holmes, *Wellington*, p. 232.
36. Anton, *Retrospect of a Military Life*, p. 182.
37. Mackenzie, *Merely a Memorandum*, p. 116.
38. Anton, *Retrospect of a Military Life*, p. 182.
39. ibid., p. 183.
40. Forbes, *The 'Black Watch'*, p. 265.
41. Anton, *Retrospect of a Military Life*, p. 183. This is mentioned by several sources as grain, rye or corn.
42. ibid., p. 185.
43. ibid.
44. ibid., pp. 185–6.
45. Capt Siborne, 'History of the Campaign of 1815', quoted in Cannon, *Historical Record of the Forty-Second Foot*, p. 144 n.*.
46. 'A letter from a gallant officer of the Royal 42d Highlanders', Edinburgh News, *Caledonian Mercury*, Saturday, 1 July 1815, NLS.
47. Huntly wrote to Dick: 'Poor Davidson I regret; he was a good & brave man.' 11 Aug. 1815, Dick Papers, BWRA 0276/05.
48. Anton, *Retrospect of a Military Life*, p. 187.
49. Mackenzie, *Merely a Memorandum*, p. 117.
50. Anton, *Retrospect of a Military Life*, p. 187.
51. ibid., p. 188.
52. ibid.
53. Morris, *Three Serjeants*, p. 94.
54. Anton, *Retrospect of a Military Life*, p. 187. There was some debate about whether the 73rd went into the woods at Bossu. In Jan. 1845, Harris told historian William Siborne, who was conducting interviews for his history of Waterloo, that the Regiment did not enter the wood, but 'took up ground a little to the right of where it had been at that moment' – quoted in Lagden and Sly, *2/73rd*, pp. xxvi–xxvii. The 69th was the only Regiment to lose the King's Colour.
55. Morris, *Three Serjeants*, p. 95. The Duke of Brunswick was wounded twice and then killed.
56. Jean-Baptiste Drouet, Comte d'Erlon (1765–1844). Like Ney, he transferred allegiance to the House of Bourbon then back to Napoleon. Had fought in the Peninsula.
57. Anton, *Retrospect of a Military Life*, p. 194.

58. Gerard, Journal, St Jean de Luz, 11 March 1814, BWRA 0116/01. See Letters of Ensign Gerard, *The Red Hackle*, Jan. 1932, p. 14.
59. A total of 298 killed and wounded. See Stewart of Garth, *Sketches*, II, Appendix No. 1, p. iii. Casualties are comparable to those at Burgos. Forbes, *The 'Black Watch'*, p. 273, names Lt Gordon as George instead of Robert. His statistics differ from those of Stewart of Garth. See also Anton's statistics, *Retrospect of a Military Life*, p. 194.
60. Malcolm, Diary (handwritten), p. 10, BWRA 0220. His diary finished describing his passage to Antwerp on the evening of 18 June, having missed fighting at Waterloo.
61. Anton, *Retrospect of a Military Life*, p. 194. The soldier's name was Smyth Fyfe.
62. Morris, *Three Serjeants*, p. 95.
63. ibid., p. 97.
64. Cannon, *Historical Record of the Forty-Second*, p. 144. He also commended the 28th, 78th and 92nd Regiments, the Bn of Hanoverians and the Brunswick Corps. Stewart of Garth, *Sketches*, II, 3rd ed., p. 61.
65. William Mudford, *An Historical Account of the Campaign in the Netherlands in 1815, under His Grace the Duke of Wellington, and Marshal Prince Blücher*, printed for Henry Colburn, 1817, quoted in Cannon, *Historical Record of the Forty-Second*, p. 142. His detractors criticised him for being a government tool.
66. Mackenzie, *Merely a Memorandum*, p. 117.
67. Morris, *Three Serjeants*, p. 98. Joseph William Strachan. McGregor, List of Officers, 73rd, BWRA 0683/3.
68. Morris, *Three Serjeants*, p. 99.
69. Mackenzie, *Merely a Memorandum*, p. 118.
70. Morris, *Three Serjeants*, p. 99.
71. Anton, *Retrospect of a Military Life*, p. 201.
72. Morris, *Three Serjeants*, p. 100.
73. ibid., pp. 100–1. Major Archibald John McLaine (1778–1815). Ensign 1794, lt 1796, capt 1804, maj 1812. He was a cousin of Lachlan Macquarie.
74. Dugald Dhu, The Black Watch, An Historic Ode, *Written for Waterloo Day*, 1868. See also Lagden and Sly, *2/73rd at Waterloo*, Appendix iv, Regimental Song, p. 267.
75. Morris, *Three Serjeants*, p. 102.
76. Anton, *Retrospect of a Military Life*, p. 199.
77. Morris, *Three Serjeants*, p. 105.
78. ibid., p. 99.
79. Anton, *Retrospect of a Military Life*, p. 200.
80. The issue of when the Battle of Waterloo began has been a subject of much debate. See W.H. Fitchett, 'King-making at Waterloo', in *Deeds that Won the Empire, Historic Battle Scenes*, 2006 (1897), http://www.gutenberg.org/files/19255/19255-h/19255-h.htm#chap1900.

81. Morris, *Three Serjeants*, p. 107.
82. ibid., pp. 107–8.
83. ibid., p. 107.
84. ibid., p. 108.
85. ibid., p. 109.
86. Lt Gen Sir Thomas Picton GCB (1758–1815). He had served in the Peninsula as commander of the 3rd Division.
87. Anton, *Retrospect of a Military Life*, pp. 202–3. Major General Sir William Ponsonby's 2nd 'Union' Brigade was so called because it comprised the 'Scots' Greys, an Irish regiment, the 6th Inniskilling and the English 1st Regiment, The Royals. The 1st and 2nd Brigades were under the overall command of the Earl of Uxbridge, later 1st Marquess of Anglesey KG, GCB, GCH (1768–1854). This is the famous charge depicted in Lady Elizabeth Butler's painting, showing the Gordon Highlanders holding on to the stirrups of the Scots Greys, so eager were they to enter the battle.
88. Anton, *Retrospect of a Military Life*, p. 203.
89. ibid., p. 205.
90. Morris, *Three Serjeants*, p. 109.
91. ibid. Morris describes this so well that I assume it is true! See Holmes, *Wellington: The Iron Duke*, who describes the same thing happening at Quatre Bras: 'the nearest battalion was the 92nd Highlanders', p. 231.
92. Morris, *Three Serjeants*, p. 112.
93. ibid. This was Robinson.
94. ibid.
95. ibid., p. 113.
96. Mackenzie, *Merely a Memorandum*, pp. 118–19.
97. ibid., p. 119.
98. Holmes, *Wellington: The Iron Duke*, p. 247.
99. Capt Garland to William Siborne, 4 Dec. 1834, quoted in Lagden and Sly, *2/73rd*, p. 76. He had served in the Peninsular campaigns in the 30th Regiment. He is obviously writing later, because Lt Col Harris became Lord Harris on the death of his father in 1829.
100. Morris, *Three Serjeants*, p. 114,
101. ibid., p. 113.
102. Marshal Ney, quoted in John Booth, *The Battle of Waterloo: Containing the Accounts Published by Authority, British and Foreign, and Other Relative Documents, with Circumstantial Details, Previous and After the Battle, from a Variety of Authentic and Original Sources*, 2nd ed. 1815, printed for J. Booth and T. Ergeton; Military Library, Whitehall, pp. 73–4.
103. Anton, *Retrospect of a Military Life*, p. 207. This is a rather romantic version of the charge. Gunn gives very little detail, as does Mackenzie.
104. Gunn, Memoir, p. 52, BWRA 0233.
105. Morris, *Three Serjeants*, p. 115.
106. ibid., p. 116.

107. Mackenzie, *Merely a Memorandum*, p. 119.
108. Morris, *Three Serjeants*, pp. 122–3. It was common to strip the bodies of dead men for their clothes, shoes, etc.
109. www.britishbattles.com/waterloo/waterloo-june-1815.htm.
110. Stewart of Garth, *Sketches*, II, 3rd ed., Appendix No. 1, p. iii. Forbes, *The 'Black Watch'*, p. 273, counts six officers and thirty-nine rank and file wounded.
111. Blantyre to Dick, comm. 42nd R.H. Regmt with the Duke of Wellington's Army, [in] France from Erskine, 6 July 1815. He was promoted on 18 June 1815. Warrant, Dick Papers, BWRA 0276/11.
112. Lagden and Sly, *2/73rd*, Appendix III, p. 266. This is the most authoritative account of the 73rd's role. Statistics are for Quatre Bras and Waterloo, although the 73rd suffered most of their casualties and fatalities at Waterloo.
113. Morris, *Three Serjeants*, p. 115. in 1889 Archibald Maclaine's remains were removed to Evere, noth-east of Brussels where, with others, they were re-interred beneath a monument erected to the memory of those in the British Army who fell in the Waterloo campaign. See Lagden and Sly, *2/73rd*, pp. 146–7.
114. ibid., p. 114 n.*.
115. ibid., p. 115.
116. Lagden and Sly, *2/73rd at Waterloo*, p. 94. Before being wounded he was knocked off his horse and received severe contusions from the bursting of a shell. Morris, *Three Serjeants*, p. 95, describes how he took the initiative in forming the company into a square when the Company Commander failed to do so.
117. Morris, *Three Serjeants*, p. 124. See also p. 124 n.*, where Morris corrects himself. During the Great Exhibition Robinson came to London and visited Morris. See *Fleetwood Chronicle* obituary notice of 15 October 1880, reproduced in *Carlisle Patriot*, 15 Oct, 1880, in H. Peters, *William Robinson, Waterloo Veteran*, typescript 1978, BWRA 0560.
118. See John D. Ellis, 'An Exemplary Soldier The Reverend George Rose', *The Red Hackle*, May 2001, pp. 16–17.
119. Later Lt Maurice Shea (1794–1892). *Montreal Daily Star*, 9 Feb. 1892. Regimental Scrapbook, 2nd Battalion, BWRA 0447. See also Lagden and Sly, *2/73rd*, pp. 205–9.
120. Morris, *Three Serjeants*, p. 123.
121. Blantyre to Lt Col Sir Henry Dick, Erskine 6 July 1815, Dick Papers, BWRA 0276. Napoleon surrendered to the British and was exiled to the South Atlantic island of St Helena, where he died six years later.
122. *Journal de l'Empire*, quoted in *Caledonian Mercury*, Courier Extraordinary of Monday morning, Monday 3 July 1815, Mf.N.776, NLS. Louis XVIII remained King of France until 1824, the last French monarch to die a King.
123. Morris, *Three Serjeants*, p. 124.
124. Gunn, Memoir, pp. 53–4, BWRA 0233.
125. Huntly to Dick, 11 Aug. 1815, Dick Papers, BWRA 02767/05. A Memorial cairn to Macara's memory and those who fell in the Peninsular and Waterloo campaigns was erected on the hill of Tor Alvic on the Duke of Richmond's

estate of Kinrara by the Marquis of Huntly on 16 August 1815, see Groves, *Black Watch*, p. 27, n. 1.

126. Cannon, *Historical Record of the Forty-Second*, p. 147.
127. Morris, *Three Serjeants*, p. 129.
128. Gunn, Memoir, p. 54, BWRA 0233.
129. ibid., p. 55.
130. Mackenzie, *Merely a Memorandum*, p. 155. After the Napoleonic Wars, Donald Mackenzie married and left the Army, setting up home in Edinburgh. He died in 1838.
131. Gunn, Memoir, p. 55, BWRA 0233.
132. Morris, *Three Serjeants*, p. 132.
133. ibid., p. 135.
134. ibid., p. 137.
135. ibid., p. 140.
136. Disbandment of 2nd Battalion 73rd, H. Calvert to General the Marquis of Hastings, H. Guards, 7 April 1817. WO 3/66, TNA, p. 311: effective on 4 May 1817 'the Officers at home to be placed on Half Pay from 25th June next, those who are serving with the other Battalions abroad, will be allowed full Pay until their arrival in this Country, with the usual advance of two months pay from the period of their arrival'.
137. Morris, *Three Serjeants*, p. 140.
138. Deputy Adjutant General to all Regiments, Horse Guards 14 Dec. 1815, WO 3/161, p. 52, TNA.
139. Lagden and Sly, *2/73rd*, p. lxi; Cannon, *Historical Record of the Seventy-Third*, p. 53.
140. The Military General Service Medal (MGSM) commemorating earlier battles was authorised in 1847 and issued only to survivors living at that time.
141. William Morris did not add to the account given by his brother Thomas. Instead he wrote: 'As the progress and result of our operations on the continent have been already recorded, my brother and myself having undergone the same fatigues, the same hardships and dangers, being always up with the regiment; the same narrative, therefore, answers for both.' *Three Serjeants*, p. 161.

15. The Long Peace

1. Poem quoted in Diary of Pte David McAusland (bandsman), p. 56, BWRA 0179. Author unknown.
2. Gunn, Memoir, p. 57, BWRA 0215/0233. His account ends with Waterloo.
3. Anton, *Retrospect of a Military Life*, pp. 241–2. He does not omit to say that the hospitality they received was so great that by the time they reached the barracks they were 'groping or sprawling their way down the High Street. No lives were lost, though many a bonnet and kilt changed owners, and not a few disappeared entirely,' p. 243.

4. ibid., pp. 246–7, The first Army Dress Regulations published for general use were issued in 1822. See Wallace, 'The Dress of The Black Watch, Part V, 1816–1856', *The Red Hackle*, January 1933, p. 15.

5. Forbes, *The 'Black Watch'*, p. 276.

6. Anton, *Retrospect of a Military Life*, p. 248. A number of societies demanding reforms were established. Penalties for dissent were severe.

7. John Wheatley, Memoirs, *The Red Hackle*, April 1922, p. 4. See also full transcription by Thomas B. Smyth, BWRA 0429.

8. Keltie (ed.), *Historical Record of the 42nd Royal Highlanders (The Black Watch) from 1729 to 1874, Part Third*, p. 399. Cannon, *Historical Record of the Forty-Second Foot*, p. 148.

9. The vase is one of the main exhibits at the Black Watch Regimental Museum at Balhousie Castle, Perth.

10. Wheatley, Memoirs, *The Red Hackle*, April 1922, p. 4. His 'reminiscences . . . thrown together entirely from recollection' over fifty years later give an excellent picture of a soldier's daily activities.

11. 'An Exemplary Soldier The Reverend George Rose', *The Red Hackle*, ed. note, May 2001, p. 17. He was appointed band sgt. He died in 1873.

12. See Wheatley, Memoirs, *The Red Hackle*, October 1922, p. 7.

13. Wheatley, Memoirs, *The Red Hackle*, April 1922, p. 4.

14. ibid.

15. ibid., p. 6.

16. Record of Service, 42nd, 1729–1873, p. 125, BWRA 0079.

17. Keltie (ed.), *Historical Record of the 42nd Royal Highlanders (The Black Watch) from 1729 to 1874, Part Third*, p. 400.

18. Stewart of Garth, *Sketches*, I, Preface, 1st ed., 24 April 1821, quoted in 2nd ed., p. ix. His account became the celebrated *Sketches of the Character, Manners, and Present State of the Highlanders of Scotland*, in two volumes, first published in two editions in 1822, with a third edition in 1825.

19. Wheatley, Memoirs, *The Red Hackle*, April 1922, p. 6.

20. ibid., p. 7.

21. ibid.

22. These Colours in use between 1818 and 1839 would have been the first stand to carry the new battle honours granted for the Peninsular and Waterloo campaigns. See Wallace, 'The Colours of The Black Watch', *The Red Hackle*, July 1936, p. 9.

23. Wheatley, Memoirs, *The Red Hackle*, July 1922, p. 4. Anton, *Military Life*, says there were thirteen in the burned-down house.

24. Wheatley, Memoirs, *The Red Hackle*, July 1922, p. 6.

25. ibid.

26. Anton, *Retrospect of a Military Life*, p. 266.

27. Wheatley, Memoirs, *The Red Hackle*, July 1922, p. 7.

28. ibid.

29. ibid.

30. Anton, *Retrospect of a Military Life*, p. 271.
31. Wheatley, Memoirs, *The Red Hackle*, July 1922, p. 8. There is a painting in the BWR Museum called *The Dublin Guard*.
32. Anton, *Retrospect of a Military Life*, p. 273.
33. Regimental Order Book, 1815–1820, Dublin 20 June 1819, p. 25, BWRA 0009/2.
34. General Order, 17 September 1807, Regimental Order Book, 1815–1820, Dublin, 9 November 1819, p. 56, BWRA 0009/2.
35. Anton, *Retrospect of a Military Life*, p. 275.
36. Details from Forbes, *The 'Black Watch'*, p. 274. John Hope, 4th Earl of Hopetoun (1765–1823). Appointed second-in-command in the Peninsula in 1813, he was promoted to the rank of general in 1819. Although Stewart of Garth revised his *Sketches* in 1822 and again in 1825, for the rest of the century the main printed record is Forbes.
37. Lt Col Henry Dick to Earl of Hopetoun, from Richmond Barracks, 6 March 1820, Dick Papers, BWRA 0276/10.
38. Wheatley, Memoirs, *The Red Hackle*, July 1922, p. 9.
39. Wallace, 'The Dress of The Black Watch', continued, *The Red Hackle*, October 1931, p. 5.
40. Wheatley, Memoirs, *The Red Hackle*, July 1922, p. 11.
41. ibid., October 1922, p. 3.
42. The Statutes at Large, &c. Anno Regni GEORGII IV. First introduced in 1796, the act imposed the death penalty (replaced by transportation for life in 1807) on people who administered what was known as 'illegal oaths'. It allowed the government to proclaim specific districts as disturbed, impose a curfew and suspend trial by jury, and gave magistrates sweeping powers. The act was in force 1796–1802, 1807–10, 1812–14 and 1822–5.
43. Wheatley, Memoirs, *The Red Hackle*, October 1922, p. 5.
44. ibid.
45. ibid., p. 7.
46. 'Memorandum for the Officer Commanding the 78th Regiment', signed H. Torrens, Horse Guards 20 August 1822. A similar Memorandum to the above was addressed to the Officer Commanding the 79th, 92nd and 93rd Regiments, Regimental Letters, WO 3/398, TNA. See Wallace, 'The Dress of The Black Watch, Part V, 1816–1856', *The Red Hackle*, January 1933, p. 16. See chapter 7.
47. Dick to Stirling, 8 Sept. 1822. He is obviously referring to the French Grenadiers. Stirling to Dick, undated, BWRA 0536/1, reprinted in *The Red Hackle*, April 1982, p. 11. See also commentary by Lt Col David Arbuthnot 1982. It is likely that the true origins of the Red Hackle will never be established, being based more on serendipity than on a specific incident or order. The Red Hackle is now made of hens' feathers, dyed red, imported from India. Major Ronnie Proctor, 2009.
48. Anton, *Retrospect of a Military Life*, p. 305.
49. Cannon, *Historical Record of the Forty-Second*, p. 150.
50. Wheatley, Memoirs, *The Red Hackle*, Jan. 1923, p. 5.

51. Record of Service, 73rd, p. 35, BWRA 0005. Cannon, *Historical Record of the Seventy-Third*, pp. 32–3.

52. Wheatley, Memoirs, p. 135, BWRA 0429. The New Land Pattern was in use from 1802; the New Light Infantry Land Pattern from 1811. Both weighed over 10 lbs. Maj Gen Sir George Murray GCB, GCH (1772–1846) had served as Wellington's Quarter Master General in the Peninsula, but when Napoleon escaped from Elba he was in Canada and missed fighting at Waterloo. Between 1828 and 1830 he was secretary of state for war and the colonies, MP for Perth 1824–32 and 1834–5. It is believed that he chose to name the new city of Perth in Western Australia after his birthplace, Perth, Scotland. Hopetoun had died in Paris.

53. Record of Service, 73rd, p. 37, BWRA 0005. See Wallace, 'The Colours of The Black Watch,' *The Red Hackle*, Oct. 1936, p. 6, for minor discrepancy over the date. 1827 is correct.

54. Wheatley, Memoirs, pp. 136–7, BWRA 0429.

55. Anton, *Retrospect of a Military Life*, p. 321.

56. Wheatley, Memoirs, p. 138, BWRA 0429.

57. Anton, *Retrospect of a Military Life*, pp. 325–6.

58. Wheatley, Memoirs, pp. 139–40, BWRA 0429. Wheatley was on leave in Scotland in 1826–7, so there is no information in his diary for that period of life in Gibraltar.

59. Anton, *Retrospect of a Military Life*, p. 335.

60. Forbes, *The 'Black Watch'*, p. 276.

61. Anton, *Retrospect of a Military Life*, p. 336.

62. Wheatley, Memoirs, p. 155, BWRA 0429.

63. Anton, *Retrospect of a Military Life*, p. 338.

64. Wheatley, Memoirs, p. 157, BWRA 0429.

65. Anton, *Retrospect of a Military Life*, pp. 340, 342. It is not known precisely what the epidemic was – most probably yellow fever.

66. Cannon, *Historical Record of the Forty-Second*, p. 151.

67. Record of Service, 73rd, p. 38, BWRA 0005 and see Cannon, *Historical Record of The Seventy-Third*, p. 34.

68. Cannon, *Historical Record of The Seventy-Third*, p. 35. Lieutenant Governor General Sir George Don, GCB, order dated 2 December 1829.

69. See H. Torrens, 'Memorandum on the Dress Bonnet and Ostrich Feathers worn by Highland Regiments', 15 Aug. 1828, in response to letter from the secretary of state, 30 May 1828, WO 3/257.

70. Wheatley, Memoirs, Gibraltar, 1829, p. 162, BWRA 0429.

71. ibid., p. 164.

72. ibid., p. 165.

73. ibid., p. 168.

74. ibid., p. 186. Fraser of Milford received two years' pay as a capt and a permanent pension as lt for his wounds. McGregor, 'A Black Watch Who Was Who 1725–1881', Research Notes, 42nd, BWRA 0683/2.

75. Wheatley, Memoirs, Gibraltar, 1831, p. 190, BWRA 0429.

76. ibid., Malta, 1832, p. 192. See also Cannon, *Historical Record of the Forty-Second*, p. 151.

77. Major General Maurice Charles O'Connell, 25 August 1830, quoted in Cannon, *Historical Record of the Seventy-Third*, p. 37.

78. Lt Col James McNair, formerly 52nd (Oxfordshire) Regiment of Foot.

79. Rt Hon. Sir Frederick Adam, GCB, GCMG, appointed 22 May 1829.

80. Wheatley, Memoirs, Malta, 1832, p. 192, to Corfu, 1834, p. 193, BWRA 0429.

81. Anton, *Retrospect of a Military Life*, pp. 245, 360. His *Military Life* was published in 1841 in second edition. He first wrote it in rhyme, his 'illiterate vanity' making him think what he had written was poetry; when he realised this was not so, he burnt his rhyming journal and reconstructed it in prose! He received 2s 1d a day pension, dying in Edinburgh in 1863. He also received a Good Conduct Medal with Gratuity.

82. Record of Service, 73rd, p. 134, BWRA 0005. Wheatley, Memoirs, Corfu, p. 194, BWRA 0429. It later became the Greek Theological College.

83. Wheatley, Memoirs, Corfu, p. 195, BWRA 0429.

84. ibid., Corfu, pp. 195–6.

85. ibid., Corfu, p. 196.

86. ibid., Corfu, p. 197.

87. ibid., Corfu, p. 201.

88. ibid., Corfu, 1835, p. 201. Forbes, *The 'Black Watch'*, p. 275, says he took command on 23 Oct. 1835.

89. Wheatley, Memoirs, Corfu, 1835, p. 201, to Corfu, 1836, p. 201a, BWRA 0429.

90. Cannon, *Historical Record of the Forty-Second*, p. 152.

91. Wheatley, Memoirs, pp. 203–4, BWRA 0429.

92. ibid., p. 202.

93. ibid., p. 205.

94. Queen Victoria (1819–1901). She ascended the throne in 1837 and became the longest-reigning monarch to date, ruling for sixty-three years and seven months.

95. John Drysdale, Diary, 'A Soldier's Life', BWRA 0214. He enlisted aged twenty on 28 June 1836. Quotations from the original. The diary has since been transcribed by Thomas B. Smyth, Archivist, BWRA.

96. Drysdale, Diary, BWRA 0214.

97. Later Field Marshal Sir Edward Blakeney PC (Ire) GCB, GCH (1778–1868). Quoted in Record of Service, 42nd, 1729–1873, BWRA 0079. See Wallace, 'The Colours of the Black Watch', *The Red Hackle*, July 1936, p. 9. This was the stand carried at Alma and the last to be carried into battle.

98. Drysdale, Diary, BWRA 0214.
99. ibid.
100. ibid.
101. ibid.
102. Lt Col Sir Duncan Alexander Cameron GCB, d. 1888. George Johnstone went onto half-pay in Sept. 1843.
103. Rt Hon. Sir George Murray (undated), quoted in Cannon, *Historical Record of the Forty Second*, p. 157.
104. Drysdale, Diary, BWRA 0214.
105. ibid.
106. ibid. Six women were permitted for every 100 men, but 'no care is taken of them'.
107. Cannon, *Historical Record of the Forty-Second*, Wheatley's annotated note, p. 158. He concludes the *Historical Record* in 1844.
108. Drysdale, Diary, BWRA 0214.
109. McAusland, Memoir, 1848–60, p. 2, BWRA 0179.
110. Governor, Capt Charles Elliot, RN, 3 June 1851, quoted in Record of Service, 42nd, 1729–1873, p. 158, BWRA 0079.
111. Traditional Song. The Broomie Law is a stretch of land running along the north bank of the Clyde, Glasgow.

16. Frontier Wars

1. Gould Lucas (1832–1914) to his father, Cape Town, 20 March 1852. See S. O'Byrne, 'Lucas's Account of the Wreck of the Birkenhead', *Africana Notes & News*, vol. 17, no. 6, June 1967, pp. 254–61. Lucas's original letter to his father appears to have been lost. The account reproduced as 'as near as possible a copy' written on 17 Feb. 1905. Birkenhead File, Regimental Archivist.
2. Quoted in Mann, *A Particular Duty: The Canada Rebellions 1837–1839*, p. 24.
3. Record of Service, 73rd, p. 49, BWRA 0005.
4. Mann, *A Particular Duty*, p. 111.
5. Record of Service, 73rd, p. 49, BWRA 0005.
6. ibid., p. 51.
7. ibid., pp. 52–3.
8. Corporal John Rich, Memoirs, 1844–1859, p. 3, BWRA 0033. The events relating to service in South Africa were transcribed from Rich's handwritten memoirs by Neville Mapham in 1990 titled 'Some Account of the Kaffir War', held in BWRL. After some pages the handwritten account becomes illegible and I have used the typescript. The detachment included the 45th on board the *Apollo*.
9. Rich, Memoirs, p. 4, BWRA 0033.
10. William Gore Ouseley, British diplomat, writer and painter (1797–1866).
11. Having brokered the independence of Uruguay, a former province of Argentina,

Britain retained an active interest in the continuing power struggle between rival Uruguayan factions.

12. Vander Meulen 73rd Regiment commanding the Troops at Montevideo to the Military Secretary, Montevideo, 28 March 1846, WO 1/598, f. 242, TNA. Lt Col Charles Vander Meulen (1791–1856). He had been with the Regiment since 1838.

13. ibid., ff. 243–4.

14. Vander Meulen to Lt Gen Fitzroy Somerset KCB, 13 April 1846, WO 1/598, ff. 247–8, TNA. Somerset, the future 1st Baron Raglan, was Military Secretary to the Duke of Wellington until his death in 1852.

15. Rich, Memoirs, pp. 4–5, BWRA 0033.

16. Later Lt Gen Sir John Grey (1772–1856), removed to 5th Fusiliers 1849. He had served in the Peninsula and was twice wounded at Ciudad Rodrigo.

17. The monument was erected 'at the behest of the officers serving under him and friends in the East India Company in Bengal'. Inscription on monument, Dunkeld Cathedral.

18. Vander Meulen to Lt Gen Fitzroy Somerset KCB, 18 April 1846, WO 1/598, ff. 251–4, TNA.

19. Vander Meulen to the Adjutant General (Lt Gen Sir John Macdonald), Montevideo, 4 May 1846, WO 1/598, ff. 263–5, TNA.

20. Wellington to Gladstone, Horse Guards 11 June 1846 (enclosing Vander Meulen's letters dated 28 March, 13 and 18 April 1846), WO 1/598, f. 235, TNA. Wellington is probably referring to Sir William Macnaghten (1793–1841), British political agent in Kabul.

21. Rich, Memoirs, p. 6, BWRA 0033.

22. King Mgolombane Sandile Ngqika (1820–78); killed in 9th Frontier War. Maqoma (1798–1873).

23. Record of Service, 73rd, p. 58, BWRA 0005. Out of the 5,475 British troops stationed between the Keiskamma and Kei rivers, the 73rd constituted 526 rank and file. Return of the Troops at the Cape on the 1st March 1847, WO 1/441, f. 655, TNA.

24. Lt Col. William Eyre (1805–59), Lt Col. of the Regiment 1847–54. Not to be confused with his elder brother Henry, who joined the 73rd and was promoted Lt Col. in 1843. Maj later Lt Col. Frederick Pinckney (1806–59). See McGregor, 'A Black Watch Who Was Who 1725–1881', Research Notes, 73rd, BWRA 0683/3.

25. Record of Service, 73rd, p. 60, BWRA 0005.

26. ibid., p. 62.

27. ibid., p. 64.

28. Rich, 'Some Account of the Kaffir War', p. 1 (tr. Mapham) or Memoirs, p. 7, BWRA 0033. Rich calls the Ngqikas by their other name, 'Gaikas'. His account ends in March 1853.

29. Rich, 'Some Account of the Kaffir War', tr. Mapham, p. 1.

30. ibid., p. 2.

31. ibid.

32. ibid.

33. ibid., p. 3. The Cape Mounted Riflemen had been formed in 1793 by the Dutch. Briefly called the Corps of Free Hottentots, after Britain took possession of the Colony the Corps was divided into mounted and infantry; when the infantry was disbanded in 1827 the corps became known as Cape Mounted Riflemen.

34. Rich, 'Some Account of the Kaffir War', tr. Mapham, p. 4.

35. Record of Service, 73rd, p. 56, BWRA 0005.

36. Knox, Diary, transcribed by H.L. Henchman, quoted in 'The Kaffir War of 1851', *Daily Dispatch*, East London, 9 Feb. 1929, BWRA 0395 K–L. Knox wrote four diaries; the first entry was in Feb. 1851 and the last in May 1852.

37. ibid.

38. ibid.

39. ibid.

40. ibid.

41. Knox, Diary, tr. Henchman, quoted in 'The Kaffir War of 1851', *Daily Dispatch*, East London, 4 March 1929, BWRA 0395 K–L.

42. Rich, 'Some Account of the Kaffir War', tr. Mapham, p. 56.

43. ibid., p. 31.

44. ibid., p. 32.

45. ibid.

46. ibid., p. 33.

47. ibid., 18 July 1851, p. 35.

48. Knox, Diary, quoted in 'The Kaffir War of 1851', as cited in n. 41 above.

49. Gould Lucas to his father, Cape Town, 20 March 1852, S. O'Byrne, 'Lucas's Account of the Wreck of the Birkenhead', *Africana Notes & News*, vol. 17, no. 6, June 1967, pp. 255–6. Birkenhead File, BWRL.

50. Capt Percy Sharp, 'Women and Children First', *Reader's Digest*, Jan. 1977, p. 98. See also 'The Wreck of the Troopship Birkenhead, 26th February 1852', BWRA 0395/B. 'That sealed the doom of the Birkenhead. The water rushed in through the gaping hole in her bows and the forward bulkhead gave way and the engine room was flooded.'

51. Bernard Kilkeary, quoted in 'A Ship's Sergeant-Major', J.L.R.S[ampson], *The Red Hackle*, Dec. 1985, p. 12. Bernard Kilkeary (1827–1907) wrote his account in 1906. He is wrongly listed as Kilberry in the Record of Service, 73rd, BWRA 0005, and in *Illustrated London News*, 10 April 1852, p. 287. Maj Edward Wright, 91st, in the *Illustrated London News* says the women and children were put in the care of the Master's assistant, Mr Richards, and does not mention Kilkeary.

52. Seton, 74th Highlanders, quoted in Captain Percy Sharp, 'Women and Children First', *Reader's Digest*, Jan. 1977, pp. 100, 101, Birkenhead File, BWRL.

53. Gould Lucas to his father, as cited in n. 49 above.

54. Lucas remained in Natal until ordered on active service to India. He returned

to South Africa, retiring to North Wales in May 1914. Kilkeary completed thirteen years with the 73rd and spent a further twenty years with the auxiliary forces; see 'Death of Mr Bernard Kilkeary', *Tyrone Courier*, Thursday, 21 Nov. 1907, Birkenhead File, BWRL.

55. 'A Ship's Sergeant-Major', J.L.R.S[ampson], *The Red Hackle*, Dec. 1985, p. 12.
56. Gould Lucas to his father, as cited in n. 49 above.
57. ibid.
58. 'Fatal Wreck of Her Majesty's Steamer', *Illustrated London News*, 10 April 1852, p. 287. Numbers are disputed; no record remains of the servants, like the unfortunate Collins, on board. Maj Edward Wright, 91st, says total loss of men was nine officers and 339 men, besides the crew; *Illustrated London News*, 10 April 1852, p. 287.
59. Record of Service, 73rd, BWRA 0005, lists fifty-three privates killed and two lts. Bevan, *Stand Fast*, p. 184, 171 lists fifty-four private soldiers and two lts from the 73rd out of 436 who perished from a total of 643 on board at Danger Point. In 1983 Dr Allan Kayle obtained the permit to salvage the *Birkenhead* from the National Monuments Council in South Africa. Numerous artefacts were salvaged, including coins, a spoon, a buckle and bottle stop belonging to the 73rd, now in the BWRM, together with two claret jugs, reportedly taken by a corporal's wife, presented to the Regiment by Maj Gen Sir John Grey, Col of the 73rd 1846–9. A large pay packet was rumoured to be on board, but Kayle noted, 'the legendary gold eluded us': *Salvage of the Birkenhead*, Southern Book Publishers, 1990, p. 124.
60. Knox, Diary, 17 March 1852, tr. Henchman, quoted in 'The Kaffir War of 1851', 4 March 1929, *Daily Dispatch*, East London, BWRA 0395 K–L.
61. Knox, Diary, 11 May 1852, tr. Henchman, cited in ibid.
62. Record of Service, 73rd, p. 65, BWRA 0005.
63. ibid.
64. Rich, 'Some Account of the Kaffir War', Memoirs, 29 Oct. 1852, tr. Mapham, p. 63.
65. ibid., 19 Nov. 1852, p. 64.
66. ibid., 2 Dec. 1852, p. 65.
67. Knox, Diary, tr. Henchman, quoted in 'The Kaffir War of 1851', *Daily Dispatch*, East London, 4 March 1929, BWRA 0395 K–L.
68. Rich, 'Some Account of the Kaffir War', Memoirs, 19–21 Dec. 1852, tr. Mapham, p. 67.
69. Knox, Diary, tr. Henchman, quoted in 'The Kaffir War of 1851', *Daily Dispatch*, East London, 4 March 1929, BWRA 0395 K–L.
70. Head Quarter Camp, General Order No. 103, Plaatberg 22 Dec. 1852, Record of Service, 73rd, p. 68, BWRA 0005.
71. Rich, 'Some Account of the Kaffir War', Memoirs, 29 Oct. 1852, tr. Mapham, p. 64.

72. Cathcart, General Order, 14 March 1853, Grahams Town, quoted in Record of Service, 73rd, p. 69, BWRA 0005.

73. Record of Service, 73rd, p. 72, BWRA 0005.

74. Halkett, 'My Recollections of a Military Life', June 1851, written 1889–93, vol. I, no. 2, p. 78, BWRA 0031. Ensign 20 May 1853, Lt, 18 Aug. 1854, Capt, 7 Sept. 1855, 3rd Light Dragoons 1856, retired by sale May 1858. *Officers of The Black Watch* incorrectly gives his previous Regiment as the 71st.

75. Halkett, 'Military Life', vol. 1, no. 2, p. 78, BWRA, 0031.

76. ibid., p. 79. This was Sir Duncan Cameron GCB, Lt Col of the Regiment since 5 Sept.1843.

77. ibid., pp. 82–4.

78. ibid., pp. 83–4.

79. ibid., p. 87. This was Sir Francis Scott KCB, commissioned as an Ensign on 24 Nov.1852. Promoted Bt Lt Col for the Ashanti war, 1874.

80. ibid., pp. 88–9.

17. Invading the Crimea

1. W.S. Daniel, 'The Highlanders' "War-Cry" at Alma', from Lt John Drysdale, Scrap Book, BWRA 0861. The Crimean War is also called the Russian War and the Eastern War.

2. Frederick Green Wilkinson to his sister, Matilda, 3 March 1854, D1269, RGJ (Rifles) Museum. He transferred to the 42nd as a captain in 1851.

3. Alexander Robb, *Reminiscences of a Veteran, Late 6th Company, 42nd Highlanders (Black Watch)*, p. 2.

4. Private Walter Robertson, Diary (copy), p. 1, BWRA 1022/2. Attested for the 42nd, Aberdeen, 21 Nov. 1851. Aged 18. Embarked at Portsmouth on 22 May to join the Eastern Army; sgt 1855, reduced to private 1856, served in Indian Mutiny, promoted corporal 1858, lance sgt 1859, sgt 1860, reduced to private 1861, discharged time expired 29 Oct. 1862.

5. Robb, *Reminiscences*, p. 7.

6. Halkett, 'My Recollections of a Military Life', I, no. 2, pp. 3–4, BWRA 0031.

7. ibid., p. 7. By this stage the Russians had withdrawn from Moldavia and Wallachia, but the attack on Sinope at the end of Nov. 1853 provided the *casus belli*.

8. ibid., pp. 8–9. Two skeleton companies were left behind for further recruiting. The Regiment's complement was 944.

9. George Armand Furse, *Military Expeditions Beyond the Seas*, vol. 1, William Clowes & Sons Ltd, 1897, p. 203.

10. Lt Thomas Henry Montgomery to his sister, Mrs Helen Mackenzie, *Hydaspes*, 31/05/1854, BWRA 0231. He signs himself Henry.

11. Halkett, 'Military Life', I, no. 2, p. 15, BWRA 0031.

12. ibid., pp. 16–17.
13. John Chetham McLeod (later Maj Gen Sir John McLeod, KCB), 'Unpublished Letters: A Scotsman in the Crimean War', ed. Prof. R.F. Christian, Univ. of St Andrews, *The Red Hackle*, Aug. 1984, p. 8. McLeod wrote 'some 65 letters between June 1854 and May 1856 . . . on 300 sheets of closely written notepaper'. The letters are in the possession of his grandson, Major Norman McLeod, of Monimail, Fife.
14. McLeod, 'A Scotsman in the Crimean War', *The Red Hackle*, Aug. 1984, p. 8.
15. Robb, *Reminiscences*, p. 9.
16. ibid., p. 10.
17. Wilkinson to Matilda, Off Varna Bay, 14 May 1854, D1269, f. 6, RGJ (Rifles) Museum. He has confused the month. They landed at Varna on 15 June 1854.
18. Robb, *Reminiscences*, p. 10.
19. Record of Service, 42nd, 1729–1873, p. 165, BWRA 0079.
20. Sir Colin Campbell (1792–1863), 1st Baron Clyde GCB, KSI. His grandfather chose the losing side in the '45 and his estates were confiscated. Campbell, born Macliver, was brought up by his mother's brother, Lt John Campbell, and took the name Campbell.
21. See 'Distribution of the Forces under command of General Lord Raglan, GCB, Scutari, 10th May 1854', WO 1/368, p. 43, TNA.
22. Robb, *Reminiscences*, p. 12.
23. Halkett, 'Military Life', I, no. 2, pp. 30–1, BWRA 0031.
24. Robb, *Reminiscences*, p. 14.
25. Montgomery to Mrs Helen Mackenzie, 13/07/1854, BWRA 0231. On 10 July 1854 Raglan wrote to Newcastle informing of their arrival. WO1/368, p. 137, TNA.
26. Montgomery to Mrs Helen Mackenzie, 13/07/1854, BWRA 0231.
27. Robb, *Reminiscences*, p. 12. Marshal Armand-Jacques Leroy de Saint Arnaud (1801–1854).
28. Montgomery to Mrs Helen Mackenzie, Camp Varna, 21/06/1854, BWRA 0231.
29. Halkett, 'Military Life', I, no. 2, p. 36, BWRA 0031.
30. Wilkinson to 'My dear Mama', Camp Varna, Saturday 17 May [sic] 1854, D1269, f. 9, RGJ (Rifles) Museum. The date should be June.
31. Montgomery to Mrs Helen Mackenzie, Camp Varna, 21/06/1854, BWRA 0231.
32. Robb, *Reminiscences*, p. 15.
33. Wilkinson to 'Caro Fratello' (his brother Henry), Camp Alydene [sic] 8 July 1854, D1269, f. 27, RGJ (Rifles) Museum.
34. Montgomery to Mrs Helen Mackenzie, Camp Alladyne, 8/07/1854, BWRA 0231.
35. ibid., Camp Alladyne, 17/07/1854.
36. Halkett, 'Military Life', I, no. 2, p. 52, BWRA 0031.
37. Robb, *Reminiscences*, p. 16. He calls it Geikjiler; Montgomery calls it Genezeklar. Wilkinson calls it Givenckler.

39. McLeod, 'A Scotsman in the Crimean War', *The Red Hackle*, Aug. 1984, p. 10.

40. Montgomery to Mrs Helen Mackenzie, from Camp Galata[bourna] near Varna, 23/08/1854, BWRA 0231.

41. Wilkinson to 'My Dearest Mama', Camp Varna, 17 Aug. 1854, D1269, f. 43, RGJ (Rifles) Museum.

42. Wilkinson to his brother (Henry), Camp Galata Buono [*sic*] 23 Aug. 1854, D1269, RGJ (Rifles) Museum.

43. McLeod, 'A Scotsman in the Crimean War', *The Red Hackle*, Aug. 1984, p. 10. Record of Service, 42nd, 1729–1873, p. 167, BWRA 0079.

44. Wilkinson to 'My Dear Mama', Varna Bay, Aug. 30th 1854, D1269, ff. 52–3, RGJ (Rifles) Museum.

45. Montgomery to Jack, on board the steamship *Emeu* off Varna, 1 & 2/09/1854, BWRA 0231.

46. Robb, *Reminiscences*, p. 18.

47. Wilkinson to 'My dearest Mama', *Emeu* steamer, Varna Bay, 5 Sept. 1854, D1269, ff. 61–2, RGJ (Rifles) Museum.

48. Wilkinson to 'My dearest Matilda', *Emeu* steamer, the middle of the Black Sea, Friday, 5 Sept. 1854, D1269, f. 59, RGJ (Rifles) Museum.

49. Halkett, 'Military Life', I, no. 2, p. 64, BWRA 0031.

50. Record of Service, 42nd, 1729–1873, p. 167–8, BWRA 0079. Approximate no. of forces: 37,000 French, 27,000 British, 7,000 Turks. Miller, *The Ottoman Empire and its Successors 1801–1927*, p. 226. It is believed that the tradition of playing the 'Crimean Long Reveille', consisting of seven tunes, may have started the first morning the Highland Regiments spent on Russian soil. The Long Reveille continued to be played on the 15th day of each month, watched by all officers junior to the adjutant, as a reminder of their responsibilities. See Cram, Duthie, Irwin and Taylor, *A Collection of Pipe Music of The Black Watch*.

51. Robb, *Reminiscences*, p. 19.

52. Montgomery to Mrs Helen Mackenzie, Crimea, 18/09/1854, BWRA 0231.

53. Halkett, 'Military Life', I, no. 2, pp. 66–7, BWRA 0031.

54. Private John Bryson, Memoir, Crimean War and Indian Mutiny, typescript, no page number, BWRA 0218/2.

55. Montgomery to Mrs Helen Mackenzie, Crimea, 18/09/1854, BWRA 0231.

56. W.S. Daniel, 'The Highlanders' "War-Cry" at Alma', from Drysdale Scrap Book, BWRA 0861.

57. Fitzroy Somerset, 1st Baron Raglan GCB, PC (1788–1855). He had distinguished himself in the Peninsula and lost his right arm at Waterloo.

58. McSally, 'The Royal Highlanders at Alma By one of them', p. 1, BWRA 0640/1, no. 2 copy, p. 1; also BWRA 0016/05.

59. Montgomery to Mrs Helen Mackenzie, written on the field of the Alma, 21/09/1854.

60. Robb, *Reminiscences*, p. 23.

675

61. Halkett, 'Military Life', I, no. 2, pp. 80–1, BWRA 0031. Promoted Lt on 18 Aug. 1854.
62. ibid., p. 82.
63. McSally, 'Royal Highlanders at Alma', no. 2 copy, p. 2, BWRA 0640/1.
64. Charles Dunsmore Wilson, Memoirs of the Crimea, 1855, typescript, BWRA 0218/1, handwritten BWRA 0393. He joined the 42nd in Aug. 1851, colour sgt 1859, reduced 1862 and discharged 1867.
65. McSally, 'Royal Highlanders at Alma', no. 2 copy, p. 2, BWRA 0640/1. Prince Alexander Sergeyevich Menshikov (1787–1869), a veteran of the Napoleonic Wars.
66. Bryson, Memoir, BWRA 0218/2.
67. Record of Service, 42nd, 1729–1873, p. 169, BWRA 0079.
68. McSally, 'Royal Highlanders at Alma', no. 2 copy, p. 2, BWRA 0640/1.
69. Wilkinson to 'My dearest Mama', Banks of the Alma, 21 Sept. 1854, D1269, f. 66, RGJ (Rifles) Museum.
70. McSally, 'Royal Highlanders at Alma', no. 2 copy, p. 3, BWRA 0640/1.
71. Montgomery to Mrs Helen Mackenzie, 21/09/1854, written on the field of the Alma, BWRA 0231.
72. McSally, 'Royal Highlanders at Alma', no. 2 copy, p. 4, BWRA 0640/1.
73. Raglan to Newcastle, Head Quarters, Kutscha river, 23 Sept. 23, 1854, WO 1/369, p. 381, TNA.
74. McSally, 'Royal Highlanders at Alma', no. 2 copy, p. 4, BWRA 0640/1.
75. Halkett, 'Military Life', I, no. 2, p. 85, BWRA 0031.
76. Cornford and Walker, The Story of the Regiments: The Great Deeds of the Black Watch, p. 120. Wilkinson describes Campbell as saying 'Forward, Highlanders' before they crossed the river. Banks of the Alma, 21 Sept. 1854, D1269, f. 67, RGJ (Rifles) Museum.
77. McSally, 'Royal Highlanders at Alma', no. 2 copy, p. 6, BWRA 0640/1. Record of Service, 42nd, 1729–1873, says they advanced 'in the most perfect order and steadiness', BWRA 0079.
78. Lt Montgomery to Mrs Helen Mackenzie, written on the field of the Alma, 21/09/1854, BWRA 0231.
79. McSally, 'Royal Highlanders at Alma', no. 2 copy, p. 7, BWRA 0640/1.
80. Halkett, 'Military Life', p. 90. George Henry Charles Francis Malcolm Drummond, Viscount Forth (1834–61), son of the 5th Earl of Perth, ensign 4 Nov. 1853. He died young, classified as a dipsomaniac, see Oxford DNB.
81. Related by McSally, 'Royal Highlanders at Alma', no. 2 copy, p. 7, BWRA 0640/1.
82. Robb, Reminiscences, p. 25.
83. McSally, 'Royal Highlanders at Alma', no. 2 copy, p. 7, BWRA 0640/1.
84. ibid., p. 8.
85. ibid., p. 9.
86. Halkett, 'Military Life', I, no. 2, p. 98, BWRA 0031.
87. McSally, 'Royal Highlanders at Alma', no. 2 copy, p. 12, BWRA 0640/1.
88. Record of Service, 42nd, 1729–1873, p. 171, BWRA 0079.

89. Montgomery to Mrs Helen Mackenzie, written on the field of the Alma, 21/09/1854, BWRA 0231.

90. McSally, 'Royal Highlanders at Alma', no. 2 copy, p. 11, BWRA 0640/1.

91. Sir Colin Campbell, quoted in Forbes, *The 'Black Watch'*, p. 282.

92. Wilkinson, Banks of the Alma, 21 Sept. 1854, D1269, f. 67, RGJ (Rifles) Museum.

93. McSally, 'Royal Highlanders at Alma', no. 2 copy, p. 12, BWRA 0640/1.

94. Raglan to His Grace the Duke of Newcastle, secretary for war, from Head Quarters, Kutscha river, 23 Sept. 1854, WO 1/369, p. 381, TNA.

95. McSally, 'Royal Highlanders at Alma', no. 2 copy, p. 12, BWRA 0640/1.

96. Montgomery to Mrs Helen Mackenzie, written on the field of the Alma, 21/09/1854, BWRA 0231.

97. McLeod, 'A Scotsman in the Crimean War', *The Red Hackle*, Dec. 1984, p. 12.

98. Return of Casualties at the Battle of Alma, 20 Sept. 1854, WO 1/370, pp. 51, 73, TNA, which corrected provisional figures in Return of Casualties which occurred in Action on the River Alma, Crimea 20 Sept. 1854, WO 1/369, p. 415, TNA. Original strength was '700 bayonets'. Record of Service, 42nd, 1729–1873, BWRA 0079, says thirty-six were wounded, two of whom later died.

99. Wilkinson to 'Dearest Matilda', Alma Camp, 22 Sept. 1854, D1269, f. 69, RGJ (Rifles) Museum.

100. Robb, *Reminiscences*, p. 28.

101. McSally, 'Royal Highlanders at Alma', no. 2 copy, p. 13, BWRA 0640/1.

102. Forbes, *The 'Black Watch'*, p. 283.

103. Montgomery to Mrs Helen Mackenzie, 21/09/1854, written on the field of the Alma, BWRA 0231.

104. Robb, *Reminiscences*, p. 32.

105. Miller, *The Ottoman Empire and its Successors, 1801–1927*, p. 228.

106. Halkett, 'Military Life', I, no. 2, p. 157, BWRA 0031. Eduard Ivanovich Totleben (1818–1884), a Baltic German military engineer in the Imperial Russian Army. Halkett described him as being 'omnipresent'.

107. Saint Arnaud was blamed by British historians for insisting that the Allied armies marched south, which meant losing the opportunity to attack Sebastopol when it was weak. See Miller, *The Ottoman Empire and its Successors, 1801–1927*, p. 230 and Andrew D. Lambert, *The Crimean War: British grand strategy against Russia 1854–56*, p. 125-6, Manchester University Press ND, 1990.

108. Robb, *Reminiscences*, p. 35.

109. Halkett, 'Military Life', I, no. 2, pp. 127–8, BWRA 0031.

110. ibid., p. 130.

111. Robb, *Reminiscences*, p. 37. General François Canrobert (1809–1895).

112. Alfred Lord Tennyson, FRS (1809–92), Poet Laureate, 'The Charge of the Light Brigade' published in *The Examiner*, 9 Dec. 1854.

113. Maj George Cumberland joined the 42nd from half-pay as a lt in 1829; promoted Maj in 1850.

114. Robb, *Reminiscences*, p. 38.

115. Halkett, 'Military Life', I, no. 2, pp. 140–1, BWRA 0031.

116. Robb, *Reminiscences*, p. 39.

117. Wilkinson to 'Dearest Matilda', Balaclava camp, 28 Sept. 1854, D1269, f. 74, RGJ (Rifles) Museum.

118. Halkett, 'Military Life', I, no. 2, p. 154, BWRA 0031.

119. Wilkinson to Dearest Matilda, '7th or 8th October 1854 (I really don't know which there are so many opinions)', D1269, f. 77, RGJ (Rifles) Museum. Wilkinson again seems not to know what date it is and would appear to be using the Julian calendar since Russia did not adopt the Gregorian calendar until 1918 when Wednesday 31 Jan. was followed by 14 Feb. 1918. Soon afterwards Wilkinson fell ill and was invalided home.

120. This was due to the state of the French army after the destruction of their batteries. If the Malakoff had been stormed the belief persisted that it would have fallen and also the city. Admiral Pavel Nakhimov (1802–1855).

121. Halkett, 'Military Life', I, no. 2, pp. 156–7, BWRA 0031.

122. Montgomery to Mrs Helen Mackenzie, Camp before Sebastopol, 22/10/1854, BWRA 0231.

123. Robb, *Reminiscences*, p. 41.

124. ibid., p. 43.

125. ibid., p. 44.

126. Halkett, 'Military Life', I, no. 2, p. 160, BWRA 0031.

127. Robb, *Reminiscences*, p. 44.

128. ibid., pp. 44–5.

129. Halkett, 'Military Life', I, no. 2, pp. 161–2, BWRA 0031.

130. ibid., pp. 162–4.

131. Montgomery to Mrs Helen Mackenzie, Balaclava, 28/10/1843, BWRA 0231.

132. 156 men killed or taken prisoner, 122 wounded. Only 195 horses remaining, 335 horses killed or had to be destroyed. See Calthorpe, Somerset John Gough, *Letter from Headquarters: Or, The Realities of the War in the Crimea, by an Officer on the Staff*, John Murray, London (1857), p. 132. Since the 42nd were not involved, it is beyond the scope of this narrative to discuss the issue in detail. Lord Lucan, commander of both the Light and Heavy Brigades, blamed Raglan; Cardigan blamed Lucan. Raglan also blamed Lucan, while Nolan was dead and could not give his version of events.

133. Halkett, 'Military Life', I, no. 2, p. 165, BWRA 0031.

134. Robb, *Reminiscences*, p. 45.

135. ibid., pp. 46–7. Linklater, *The Black Watch*, p. 99, says that Cameron 'allowed no drink in the Regiment'!

136. Montgomery to Mrs Helen Mackenzie, Balaclava Heights, 07/11/1854, BWRA 0231.

137. Robb, *Reminiscences*, p. 48.

138. Montgomery to Mrs Helen Mackenzie, Balaclava Heights, 07/11/1854, BWRA 0231.

139. Halkett, 'Military Life', I, no. 2, p. 147, BWRA 0031.

140. Montgomery to Mrs Helen Mackenzie, Balaclava Heights, 07/11/1854, BWRA 0231.

141. McLeod to his mother, Camp at Balaclava, 7 November 1854, in 'A Scotsman in the Crimean War', *The Red Hackle*, Dec. 1984, p. 12.

142. Halkett, 'Military Life', I, no. 2, pp. 178–9, BWRA 0031.

143. McLeod, 'A Scotsman in the Crimean War', *The Red Hackle*, Dec. 1984, p. 13.

144. Robb, *Reminiscences*, p. 49.

145. Record of Service, 42nd, 1729–1873, p. 175, BWRA 0079.

146. Robb, *Reminiscences*, p. 50.

147. Montgomery to Lilly, Balaclava Heights, 28/11/1854, BWRA 0231.

148. McLeod to his family, 23 Nov. 1854. 'A Scotsman in the Crimean War', *The Red Hackle*, Dec. 1984, pp. 13–14. He was promoted Capt in Jan. 1855 without the need to purchase a Company.

149. Robb, *Reminiscences*, pp. 51–2.

150. Halkett, 'Military Life', I, no. 2, p. 171, BWRA 0031. See also Record of Service, 42nd, 1729–1873, BWRA 0079.

151. Robb, *Reminiscences*, p. 53.

152. ibid. Also Halkett, 'Military Life', I, no. 2, p. 218, BWRA 0031.

153. 'The Sick and Wounded Fund', From our own correspondent, Scutari, Dec. 25, *The Times*, Saturday Jan. 6 1855, p. 8. Another correspondent was Thomas Chenery, see Royle, *Great Crimean War*, p. 246.

154. 'Despatches from Lord Raglan': Raglan to His Grace the Duke of Newcastle, Before Sebastopol, 2 Jan. 1855, WO 1/370, pp. 588–91, TNA.

155. Montgomery to Mrs Helen Mackenzie, Balaclava Heights, 18/01/1855, BWRA 0231.

156. Robb, *Reminiscences*, p. 59.

157. Raglan to Lord Panmure (later the Earl of Dalhousie), secretary of state for war, Before Sebastopol, 27 Feb. 1855, WO 1/371, pp. 627–8, TNA.

158. Montgomery to Mrs Helen Mackenzie, Balaclava Heights, 26/03/1855, BWRA 0231.

159. Montgomery to Graham, Balaclava Heights, 26 March 1855, BWRA 0231.

160. Halkett, 'Military Life', I, no. 2, p. 221, BWRA 0031.

161. ibid., vol. II, p. 3 (p. 1 of typescript), BWRA 0032.

162. ibid., II, p. 5.

163. Robb, *Reminiscences*, p. 61.

164. Halkett, 'Military Life', II, p. 12, BWRA 0032.

165. ibid., II, p. 15, BWRA 0032. State of the Troops embarked under command of Lt Gen. Sir George Brown gives a total of 127 Officers and 2,602 men with 905 horses, (of which 42nd: 18 officers, 631 men and 12 horses), WO 1/374, p. 519, TNA.

166. Halkett, 'Military Life', II, pp. 17–19, BWRA 0032.

167. ibid., pp. 20–1.

168. ibid., pp. 22–4. Robb, *Reminiscences*, p. 65, relates the same story, saying that

the man was shot in the head, not the heart, as Halkett says. His name was Barney O'Neil.

169. Halkett, 'Military Life', II, pp. 30–1.

170. ibid., p. 32.

171. Robb, *Reminiscences*, p. 68.

172. Halkett, 'Military Life', II, p. 33, BWRA 0032.

173. ibid., pp. 34–5.

174. Robb, *Reminiscences*, p. 68.

175. ibid.

176. Montgomery to Mrs Helen Mackenzie, Camp before Sebastopol, 25 & 26/06/1855, BWRA 0231.

177. Robb, *Reminiscences*, p. 69.

178. Halkett, 'Military Life', II, p. 84, BWRA 0032. Raglan's body was transported back to England.

179. Lt Gen James Sir James Simpson (1792–1868). Prince Mikhail Dmitrievich Gorchakov (1793–1861), Menshikov was dismissed in Feb. 1855 for incompetence; Marshal Aimable Jean Jacques Pélissier (1794–1864). After the Crimea, he took the title 1st Duc de Malakoff.

180. Joseph Charles Ross Grove to My dearest [illegible], Before Sebastopol, Aug. 15th, 1855, BWRA 0393/4, promoted capt 17 July 1855. He changed his name to Ross after leaving the Army in 1887.

181. Robb, *Reminiscences*, p. 70.

182. ibid., p. 72.

183. ibid., pp. 72, 73.

184. Halkett, 'Military Life', II, p. 110, BWRA 0032.

185. Robb, *Reminiscences*, p. 75.

186. Halkett, 'Military Life', II, p. 110, BWRA 0032.

187. ibid., pp. 110–11.

188. ibid., p. 112. Simpson was criticised for using the Light and 2nd Divisions since the soldiers were 'raw' recruits. The distance between French lines and the Malakoff was much closer than the distance between the British lines and the Redan; this partly accounts for the French success compared with British failure.

189. Halkett, 'Military Life', II, pp. 114–15, BWRA 0032.

190. McLeod, 'A Scotsman in the Crimean War', *The Red Hackle*, Dec. 1984, pp. 13–14.

191. Halkett, 'Military Life', II, pp. 114–15, BWRA 0032.

192. ibid., II, p. 115.

193. Campbell to Maj Gen Sir Richard Airey, Quarter Master General, from Camp Comara, 9 Sept.1855, WO 1/379, p. 471, TNA.

194. ibid.

195. Halkett, 'Military Life', II, p. 117.

196. ibid., pp. 118–20.

197. Record of Service, 42nd, 1729–1873, p. 180–1, BWRA 0079.

198. Campbell to Maj Gen Sir Richard Airey, Quarter Master General, from Camp Comara, 9 Sept. 1855, WO 1/379, p. 472, TNA.
199. Halkett, 'Military Life', II, p. 121, BWRA 0032.
200. ibid., p. 122.
201. ibid., p. 124.
202. ibid., p. 125. The siege lasted from 5 Oct. 1854, the day the soldiers broke ground at the start of the siege, until 8 Sept. 1855.
203. Record of Service, 1729–1873, p. 181, BWRA 0079.
204. Lt Gen Sir Colin Campbell, 19 Sept. 1855, quoted in Record of Service, 1729–1873, pp. 181–2, BWRA 0079.
205. Robb, *Reminiscences*, p. 77.
206. Rankin, Diary, 24 Feb. 1856, BWRA 0200.
207. Wilson, Memoirs of the Crimea, typescript, BWRA 0218/1, (handwritten, BWRA 0393).
208. Robb, *Reminiscences*, p. 80.
209. Montgomery to Helen, Camp Kamara, Monday 17 [March 1856], BWRA 0213.
210. Rankin, Diary, 5 April 1856, BWRA 0200.
211. Lt Gen Sir Colin Campbell, Camp Kamara, 9 May 1856, handwritten letter in Record of Service, 1729–1873, inserted between pp. 183 and 184, BWRA 0079. Also quoted in Robb, *Reminiscences*, Appendix, p. 123.
212. Robb, *Reminiscences*, p. 84.
213. Wilson, Memoirs of the Crimea, typescript, BWRA 0218/1, (handwritten Memoir, BWRA 0393).
214. Robertson, Diary (copy), p. 23, BWRA 1022/2
215. Halkett, 'Military Life', II, p. 146 (p. 43 typescript), BWRA 0032.
216. Paul Kerr et al., *The Crimean War*, Boxtree, 1997, p. 178. See Trevor Royle, *The Great Crimean War, 1854–1856*; John Shelton Curtiss, *Russia's Crimean War*, Duke University Press, 1979, pp. 459–60.
217. Forbes, 'The Black Watch', p. 285. *Chronology of the 42nd Royal Highlanders, The Black Watch from 1729 to 1905*, p. 17, gives same statistics. Record of Service, 42nd 1729–1873, p. 186, BWRA 0079 makes the comparison between the 850 soldiers who embarked in May 1854 and who increased by 453 during the two-year period, making a total of 1,305, and the 765 who returned in July 1856.
218. Record of Service, 42nd, 1729–1873, p. 186, BWRA 0079.
219. See Curtiss, *Russia's Crimean War*, pp. 470–1.
220. Tennyson, 'The Charge of the Light Brigade', published in *The Examiner*, 9 Dec. 1854.
221. Robb, *Reminiscences*, p. 45.
222. Halkett, 'Military Life', II, pp. 149–50, BWRA 0032.
223. Robert Gibb RSA (1845–1932). *Alma: Forward the 42nd*, painted in 1889, is in the Kelvingrove Art Gallery and Museum, Glasgow.
224. Charles Wilson wrote no further memoir. In Feb. 1858 he was promoted lance

sgt, then sgt, reduced to private in May 1859; transferred to Bengal Artillery 1860, discharged 1861 when the Indian Army was transferred to the Crown.

18. A Proper Style of Indian Warfare

1. 'The Battle of the Sarda River', Bengal, by Sergeant John Thompson, quoted in Private David McAusland, Memoir, p. 157, BWRA 0179.
2. Record of the Service, 42nd, 1729–1873, p. 188, BWRA 0079. The Indian Mutiny is also known as the First War of Independence, the Revolt of 1857, the Sepoy Mutiny, the 1857 Uprising, and India's First Nationalist Uprising. Sepoys were equivalent to private soldiers; they were known as sowars in the cavalry units.
3. See Dalrymple, *The Last Mughal*, pp. 22–3.
4. Bahadur Shah II (1775–1862).
5. Nana Sahib, born Dhondu Pant (1824–59/1905?). After the Cawnpore massacre, he disappeared and was believed to have fled to Nepal.
6. Maj General Sir Hugh Wheeler KCB (1788–1857). His son, Lt Gordon Wheeler, was decapitated by a roundshot, which greatly unnerved Wheeler senior..
7. The massacre at Cawnpore is the subject of much debate regarding who gave the order and whether it was in retaliation for brutality perpetrated by the British against Indian villagers. After Cawnpore was retaken the captured rebels were themselves severely punished. Only four men survived, two dying soon afterwards. See *The Story of Cawnpore*, published in 1859, written by one of the survivors, Capt Mowbray Thomson, 53rd Native Infantry.
8. Ramchandra Pandurang Tope (1814–59), known as Tantya or Tatya Tope.
9. Later Lt Gen Sir James Outram, GCB, KSI (1803–63). He had long experience in India and had been responsible for the British annexation of Oudh.
10. Robertson, Diary, Book 3, p. 33, BWRA 1022/3. (There are three books. Book 1 is the original diary, Books 2 and 3 are transcripts.) The position of C-in-C India was held by Maj Gen Patrick Grant until Campbell's arrival.
11. Memoirs of John Muir (1825–1903), 'The Indian Mutiny', *The Red Hackle*, May 2008, p. 23. He took his discharge as a private soldier in 1862.
12. Robb, *Reminiscences*, p. 87.
13. Record of the Service, 42nd, 1729–1873, p. 189, BWRA 0079.
14. Memoirs of John Muir, 'The Indian Mutiny', *The Red Hackle*, May 2008, p. 23. The two contingents were commanded by Lt Col George Thorold, who had joined the 42nd from the 92nd on 28 July 1857. and Lt Col Frederick Wilkinson. Lt Col Alexander Cameron came out separately.
15. Robb, *Reminiscences*, p. 87. It is possible this was private soldier John's Anonymous 'personal narrative', published in 1821.

16. Robb, *Reminiscences*, pp. 88–9. Robertson does not give much information on his activities.

17. Sergeant Quibell Cooper, Diary, BWRA 0212. Companies present: 1, 3, 8, 9, 10; the others arrived in stages throughout November. The early part of the journal appears to have been copied from an earlier diary, the latter part appears to have been written contemporaneously. In Jan. 1949, D.C. Browning, a friend or associate of Cooper's son, Colin, living in Oxford and who donated the library to the BWRA, noted that the Diary appears to be a 'fair copy of some document or documents'. Charles, Viscount Canning (later 1st Earl) KG, GCB, PC (1812–1862).

18. Wilkinson to his sister, 'My dearest Matilda', 29 Nov. 1857, Runnigunge, 150 miles North of Calcutta, D1270, ff. 6–7, RGJ (Rifles) Museum.

19. Cooper, Diary, BWRA 0212.

20. Robb, *Reminiscences*, pp. 89–90.

21. ibid., p. 90.

22. ibid., p. 93.

23. Cooper's statistic, Diary, BWRA 0212.

24. Bayly, 'The Black Watch Gong', written at Auberge-de-Baviers, 22 May 1888, BWRA 0016/06.

25. Cooper, Diary, BWRA 0212.

26. Brigadier Adrian Hope (1821–58). Because of his father's connection with the Regiment, and his own personality, he was much 'beloved'.

27. Robertson (copy), Book 2, p. 38, BWRA 1022/2.

28. Record of Service, 42nd, 1729–1873, p. 196, BWRA 0079. Margin note.

29. Record of Service, 42nd, 1729–1873, p. 196, BWRA 0079.

30. Robertson (copy), Book 2, pp. 38–9, BWRA 1022/2.

31. Bayly, 'The Black Watch Gong', BWRA 0016/06.

32. Memoirs of John Muir, 'The Indian Mutiny', *The Red Hackle*, May 2008, p. 23.

33. Lt Gen James Hope Grant. He had fought at the Battle of Sobraon, during which the 42nd's former Lt Col, Sir Henry Dick, was killed.

34. Record of Service, 42nd, 1729–1873, p. 197, BWRA 0079.

35. Bayly, 'The Black Watch Gong', BWRA 0016/06. Bayly added: 'and [the gong] has since its capture accompanied the Regiment everywhere'. *Officers of The Black Watch, 1725–1986* states that Bayly was wounded at Seria Ghat on 9 Dec. 1858; he was in fact wounded in 1859 on the Sarda river. The gong is still in daily use as part of The Black Watch routine.

36. Record of Service, 42nd, 1729–1873, BWRA 0079.

37. Robb, *Reminiscences*, p. 94.

38. Robertson, Diary (copy), Book 2, p. 39, BWRA 1022/2.

39. Memoirs of John Muir, 'The Indian Mutiny', *The Red Hackle*, May 2008, p. 23.

40. Companies 2, 4, 5, 6, 7 under command of Maj Frederick Green Wilkinson. Lt Col Cameron and Maj Priestley, who had been in Calcutta, had joined

headquarters on 12 Dec. Before the battle for Lucknow in March, Wilkinson hurt his leg and did not take part.

41. Robertson, Diary, Book 2, p. 42, BWRA 1022/2.

42. ibid., p. 40.

43. ibid., pp. 40–1.

44. ibid., p. 42.

45. Mangal Pandey (1827–57) was an Indian soldier in the 34th Bengal Native Infantry who effectively fired the first shot of the Mutiny, when on 29 March 1857 he fired at (but missed) a British officer. He was caught and sentenced to death.

46. Robb, *Reminiscences*, pp. 94–5. According to the Record of Service, 42nd, 1729–1873, BWRA 0079, they were supposed to destroy some boats but the mission failed.

47. Record of Service, 42nd, BWRA 0079.

48. Robb, *Reminiscences*, p. 97.

49. ibid., p. 98.

50. Edwardes, *Battles of the Indian Mutiny*, p. 125.

51. Robertson, Diary (copy), Book 2, p. 44, BWRA 1022/2.

52. Robb, *Reminiscences*, p. 103.

53. Robertson, Diary, (copy), Book 2, p. 46, BWRA 1022/2.

54. Memoirs of John Muir, 'The Indian Mutiny', *The Red Hackle*, May 2008, p. 24.

55. McLeod, 'The Black Watch at Lucknow', John McLeod to his brother Capt 'Bill' McLeod, Lucknow, 29 March 1858, quoted in *The Red Hackle*, July 1935, pp. 29–30.

56. ibid. See also Sir Colin Campbell, 'The Capture of Lucknow', Camp La Martiniere, Lucknow, March 22, 1858, *The Scotsman*, 26 May 1858, Mf.N3, NLS.

57. Lt Francis Farquharson (1837–1875). *The London Gazette*, 21 June 1859, no. 22278, p. 2420. www.london-gazette.co.uk/issues/22278/pages/2420. The Victoria Cross was introduced during the Crimean War.

58. Robertson, Diary (copy), Book 2, p. 51, BWRA 1022/2. Major John Banks, the Civil Commissioner who took over when Henry Lawrence was killed.

59. Robb, *Reminiscences*, p. 109.

60. McLeod, 'The Black Watch at Lucknow', as cited above, n. 55.

61. Robertson, Diary (copy), Book 2, pp. 46, 50, BWRA 1022/2.

62. ibid., pp. 47–9, BWRA 1022/2, but I have retained the original version (BWRA 1022/1), which is sometimes richer. For instance, in the copy, instead of 'never scarce to be seen in time of war by the actors on that tragic stage', the copied version reads: 'are only too often seen by soldiers and sailors'. Hodson was renowned for having killed the Emperor Bahadur's sons in Delhi at the outbreak of the mutiny.

63. Robertson, Diary (copy), Book 2, pp. 52–3, BWRA 1022/2. It was estimated that the palace was held by 'some 5,000 rebels': Edwardes, *Indian Mutiny*, p. 131.

64. Robertson, Diary (copy), Book 2, pp. 55–6, BWRA 1022/2.

65. ibid., p. 57.

66. McLeod, 'The Black Watch at Lucknow' (as cited above, n. 55), p. 30. Muir says the dead officer was Robert Holmes: Memoirs of John Muir, 'The Indian Mutiny', *The Red Hackle*, May 2008, p. 23.

67. Robertson, Diary, Book 2 (copy), p. 59, BWRA 1022/2.

68. Robb, *Reminiscences*, p. 111.

69. Robertson, Diary, Book 2 (copy), pp. 63–4, BWRA 1022/2. The city was declared cleared of rebels on 21 March.

70. ibid., p. 64.

71. ibid., pp. 64–5. John Bull: the personification of a British middle class man. Rory o' More: Irish jig.

72. McLeod, 'The Black Watch at Lucknow' (cited above, n. 55), p. 30.

73. Robb, *Reminiscences*, p. 111.

74. Robertson, Diary (copy), Book 2, pp. 67–8, BWRA 1022/2.

75. Wilkinson to My Dearest Maude, March 30 (April 1st), [1858], Mooleh Mahal. Palace of P–, D1270, f.15–16, Wilkinson to My dearest Matilda, Camp near Sandhu, 20 miles from Futtehghar (Fateghar), Oude April 20th, 1858 awfully . . . hot, D1270, f. 18, RGJ (Rifles) Museum.

76. Robertson, Diary (copy), Book 3, p. 1, BWRA 1022/3. Ruhya, also called Roer or Rhodamow.

77. ibid., pp. 3 and 2, BWRA 1022/3.

78. Memoirs of John Muir, 'The Indian Mutiny', *The Red Hackle*, May 2008, p. 25.

79. Robertson, Diary (copy), Book 3, p. 3, BWRA 1022/3. When a captain of the 42nd 'expostulated with Walpole on the needless exposure of the men', he was told to do his duty and reinforcements would be sent 'when he thought fit', p. 3.

80. ibid., p. 4.

81. Robb, *Reminiscences*, p. 112.

82. Robertson, Diary (copy), Book 3, p. 5, BWRA 1022/3.

83. ibid., p. 6.

84. ibid.

85. Wilkinson to My dearest Matilda, Camp near Sandhu, 20 miles from Futtehghar, Oude, April 20th, 1858 awfully . . . hot, D1270, f. 20, RGJ (Rifles) Museum.

86. Robb, *Reminiscences*, p. 113.

87. Wilkinson to My dearest Matilda, Camp near Sandhu, 20 miles from Futtehghar, Oude April 20th, 1858 awfully . . . hot, D1270, f. 20, RGJ (Rifles) Museum. He was observing events from a nearby mound with an advance guard.

88. Robertson, Diary (copy), Book 3, p. 5, BWRA 1022/3.

89. 'The British Army in India', *The Times*'s Special Correspondent (William Howard Russell), reprinted in *The Scotsman*, Saturday, 5 June 1858, Mf.N3, NLS.

90. Quarter Master John Simpson VC (1826–84); Private James Davis, VC

(1835–93). Lance Corporal Alexander Thompson VC (1824–80), Edward Spence (1837–58) was awarded the VC posthumously in 1907. The deceased officer carried back by Davis was Lt Alfred Jennings Bramley, wounded with McLeod during the siege of Lucknow. The other Lieutenant carried by Simpson was Charles Douglas who died of his wounds. See *The London Gazette*, May 27, 1859, no. 22268, p. 2106 www.london-gazette.co.uk/issues/22268/pages/2106.

91. Robertson, Diary (copy), Book 3, pp. 10–11, BWRA 1022/3.

92. ibid.

93. ibid., pp. 13–14.

94. ibid., p. 17.

95. ibid., p. 16.

96. William Gardner VC, (1821–97). The citation for Gardner's VC refers to 'three Fanatics' and describes how Gardner was 'in the act of attacking the third' when he was shot by a soldier of another regiment; see letter from Captain Macpherson, 42nd, to Lt Col Cameron, *The London Gazette*, no. 22176, p. 3903. http://www.london-gazette.co.uk/issues/22176/pages/3903. Forbes, *The 'Black Watch'*, p. 296, spells his name Gardiner. See Record of Service, 42nd, 1729–1873, p. 208, BWRA 0079.

97. Robertson, Diary, (copy), Book 3, pp. 18–19, BWRA 1022/3.

98. ibid., p. 19. Record of Service, 42nd, 1729–1873, p. 208, BWRA 0079.

99. Robertson, Diary (copy), Book 3, p. 20, BWRA 1022/3. Throughout the Indian Mutiny, feeling against the rebel Indians ran very high and this attitude is typical. Punishments included strapping captured Indians to the mouths of cannons and blowing them to pieces.

100. ibid., pp. 20, 21.

101. Memoirs of John Muir, 'The Indian Mutiny', *The Red Hackle*, May 2008, p. 25.

102. Statistics from Record of Service, 42nd, 1729–1873, p. 208, BWRA 0079. Forbes, *The 'Black Watch'*, p. 296, counts twelve soldiers wounded.

103. See Wallace, 'The Colours of The Black Watch', *The Red Hackle*, July 1936, p. 9.

104. Robertson, Diary (copy), Book 3, pp. 24–5, BWRA 1022/3. He ends his diary with a 'Farewell to Sir Colin Campbell'.

105. Wilkinson to My dearest Matilda, Camp Bareilly, 12 May 1858, D1270, f. 24, RGJ (Rifles) Museum.

106. ibid., 12 (13) May 1858, D1270, ff. 25–6.

107. Record of Service, 42nd, 1729–1873, p. 209, BWRA 0079.

108. Wilkinson to My dearest Matilda, Aug. 7 [1858], Moradabad, D1270, f. 35, RGJ (Rifles) Museum.

109. Robb, *Reminiscences*, p. 114. Record of Service, 42nd, 1729-1873, says he died

on 9 Aug. He was succeeded by Lt Col Edward Priestley on 10 Aug. 1858. Since the Regiment operated in wings, command also devolved onto George Thorold and Frederick Wilkinson.

110. Record of Service, 73rd, p. 74, BWRA 0005.
111. ibid., pp. 74–5. In Feb. 1859, Pinckney rejoined the Regiment and resumed command.
112. ibid. And see *The London Gazette*, no. 22171, 6 August 1858, p. 3667.
113. ibid., p. 76. Description of a 'soldier's friend' given by Colonel George Hankey Smith, who became Lieutenant Colonel.
114. Ghats, i.e. steps providing access to the river. Newspaper (unnamed), Regimental Scrapbook 1740–1917, BWRA 0313.
115. Robb, *Reminiscences*, p. 115.
116. Record of Service, 42nd, 1729–1873, p. 210, BWRA 0079.
117. Wilkinson to Caro Fratello [Henry], Madho Tanda. Dec. 8th [1858], D1270, f. 44, RGJ (Rifles) Museum.
118. Capt William Lawson, enlisted 1837, commissioned Ensign 1854, Capt 10 Aug. 1858, died 18 Aug. 1859. Record of Service, 42nd, 1729–1873, p. 210, BWRA 0079.
119. Robb, *Reminiscences*, p. 117.
120. ibid.
121. ibid., p. 118. Ensign Francis Coleridge, (1838–1923); transferred to 25th Foot as a lieutenant in December 1859, becoming a celebrated artist. His 'Scrapbook of Her Majesty's XLII Royal Highlanders' (Album of Watercolours) is BWRA 0428.
122. Record of Service, 42nd, 1729–1873, p. 211, BWRA 0079.
123. ibid.
124. Lawson's pipe tune by Pipe-Major David Muir. Walter Cook VC (1834–c.1864). Duncan Millar VC (1824–81), *The London Gazette*, 21 June 1859, no. 22278, p. 2420. www.london-gazette.co.uk/issues/22278/pages/2420.
125. David McAusland from Paisley to Alexander Robb (undated), *Reminiscences*, p. 128.
126. Quote in newspaper (unnamed), Regimental Scrapbook 1740–1917, BWRA 0313.
127. Record of Service, 42nd, 1729–1873, p. 212, BWRA 0079. It was now under Lt Col Edward Priestley's command following Cameron's death in August 1858.
128. Private A.W. McIntosh, (handwritten) Diary, vol. 1, p. 156, BWRA 0421. He enlisted on 4 Jan. 1858.
129. Viscount Canning, Governor-General, quoted in Saul David, *The Indian Mutiny*, p. 375. The day of thanksgiving and prayer was on 28 July after operations in Oudh had finished. Canning described India as being in 'a state of peace' on 8 July 1858.
130. Saul David, *The Indian Mutiny*, pp. 372–3, says Nana Sahib almost certainly died of fever in 1859. In his book on the Maharastrian saint, *Brahmachaitanya*

Shree Gondhavalekar Maharaj, Charitra & Vaagmay, Professor K.V. Belsare suggests that he died aged eighty-one, having lived in a cave near Sitapur, Uttar Pradesh.

131. *Chronology of the 42nd Royal Highlanders, The Black Watch from 1729 to 1905*, p. 18, BWRL.

132. McIntosh, Diary, vol. 1, pp. 159, 160, BWRA 0421.

133. ibid., pp. 165, 167.

134. ibid., p. 173.

135. ibid., pp. 176, 177.

136. ibid., pp. 178–9.

137. Record of Service, 42nd, 1729–1873, BWRA 0079. See McIntosh, Diary, pp. 181–6, BWRA 0421.

138. McIntosh, Diary, New Year's Day, 1861, p. 178, BWRA 0421. They were later hung in Dunkeld Cathedral, see chapter 19.

139. Record of Service, 73rd, p. 78, BWRA 0005. The 73rd had three Colonels of the Regiment in swift succession: on 11 Jan. 1860 Sir Michael Creagh, KH replaced Chesborough Grant Falconer, KH; when he died he was replaced by Benjamin Orlando Jones, KH. He died in 1865 and was replaced by Lt Gen Sir Henry Robert Ferguson Davie.

140. Record of Service, 73rd, p. 79, BWRA 0005. Wilkinson took command of the Regimental Depot 27 Sept. 1861.

141. McIntosh, Diary (July 1861), vol. 1, pp. 249–50, BWRA 0421.

142. ibid., pp. 251–2. He says at one time 450 men out of seven companies were unfit for duty. The three companies at Futtehgarh (Fategarh) suffered less, with six deaths, of which four were from cholera, during the twelve-month period.

143. Priestley, Regimental Order, Agra, 12 Sept. 1861, Record of Service, 42nd, 1729–1873, BWRA 0079 (General Orders, Horse Guards, 20 June 1861). See Forbes, *The 'Black Watch'*, p. 297.

144. McIntosh, Diary (21 Sept. 1861), vol. 1, p. 263, BWRA 0421.

145. ibid.

146. ibid., p. 286.

147. Queen Victoria, 3 Sept. 1863, Record of Service, 42nd, 1729–1863, p. 223, BWRA 0079.

148. Record of Service, 42nd, 1729–1873, p. 221, BWRA 0079. Gen Sir Hugh Rose, later Field Marshal the Lord Strathnairn, GCB, GCSI (1801–85).

149. ibid., p. 222. The Durand Line, demarcating a still-contested frontier between Afghanistan and British India (later Pakistan), was effected in 1893.

150. Cooper, Diary, 19 [Dec. 1863], at Rawal Pindee, BWRA 0212.

151. Record of Service, 42nd, 1729–1873, p. 222, BWRA 0079.

152. ibid., p. 224, BWRA 0079.

153. McIntosh, Diary, 14 Dec. 1864, vol. 1, p. 352 (last entry in this volume), BWRA 0421.

154. Cooper, Diary, 14 [Dec. 1864], at Rawal Pindee, BWRA 0212. He was appointed colour sgt on 1 April 1864.

155. Robb, *Reminiscences*, p. 121. He was discharged in 1865. His *Reminiscences of a Veteran* was published in 1888.
156. Cooper, Diary (30 Oct. 1865), BWRA 0212.
157. Cooper, Diary, BWRA 0212.
158. ibid., 20 May 1867.
159. McIntosh, Diary, 20 May 1867, vol. 2, p. 175, BWRA 0421.
160. ibid., p. 177.
161. See ibid., pp. 180–4. Out of 674 men, during the first twelve days of the epidemic, sixty-six died plus two women and four children. *Chronology of the 42nd Royal Highlanders*, p. 19, says from 20 May to 17 Oct. 1867 two officers and eighty-six non-commissioned officers and men died.
162. As recorded by McIntosh, Diary, vol. 2, 3 June [1867], p. 185, and on the 16th day [of their march from Cherat] Saturday 9th [Nov. 1867], p. 225, BWRA 0421. See also Records of the Sergeants, p. 74, BWRA 0261.
163. McIntosh, Diary, vol. 2, 23rd [Sept. 1867], p. 206, BWRA 0421.
164. ibid., 13th [Sept. 1867], p. 198.
165. ibid., 30th [Nov. 1867], p. 208.
166. ibid., 13th [Oct. 1867], p. 208. Traces of the graves can still be seen at Cherat.
167. Traditional Song.

19. The Height of Empire

1. Anon. in the style of William McGonagall (1825–1902), quoted in Linklater, *The Black Watch*, p. 124.
2. McIntosh, Diary, vol. 2, 26th Thursday [March 1868], p. 257, BWRA 0421.
3. 42nd Order Book, quoted in Wallace, 'The Dress of The Black Watch, VI, 1857–80', *The Red Hackle*, April 1933, p. 8.
4. McIntosh, Diary, vol. 2, 26th Thursday [March 1868], Diary, p. 259, BWRA 0421. McIntosh gave both the official opinion of Priestly in Regimental Morning Orders, Stirling Castle, 26 March 1868, pp. 259–61, and his own, p. 259. Linklater, *The Black Watch*, p. 111, attributed the official opinion as though it were McIntosh's. McIntosh (1840–1903) received his discharge on 16 April 1868 with a 'very good character', having served 10 Years, 3 Months and 12 Days 'good service' of which 9 Years and 6 Months was foreign service in India.
5. Robb, *Reminiscences*, p. 121. He was discharged in 1865.
6. McIntosh, Diary, vol. 2, 26th Thursday [March 1868], p. 259, BWRA 0421.
7. Dick Papers, BWRA 0276/19. McGregor, 'A Black Watch Who Was Who 1725–1881', Research Notes, 42nd, BWRA 0683/2.
8. Record of Service, 42nd, 1729–1873, p. 234, BWRA 0079.
9. Newspaper report (undated), Regimental Scrapbook 1740–1917, BWRA 0313.
10. Record of the Service of the 42nd, 1729–1873, p. 236, BWRA 0079.

11. ibid., p. 237.
12. *The Scotsman*, 3 April 1872. The Colours are still there. Visit by the author, 8 Aug. 2011.
13. Record of the Service, 42nd, 1729–1873, p. 237, BWRA 0079 'in accordance with General Order No. 18 issued on 14/17 March 1873, and under the provisions of Section 104 of the Mutiny Act'. This area became the Regimental Recruiting area from 1881 to 2006. The 73rd was linked with the 90th. See Army List 1877, pp. 286, 325, 319, 336.
14. Stanley, *Coomassie and Magdala: The Story of Two British Campaigns in Africa*, p. 145. See also Rathbone Low, *A Memoir of Lieutenant General Sir Garnet J. Wolseley*, II, pp. 86–212.
15. Wolseley to War Office, Government House Cape Coast, 7 Oct. 1873, f. 85, & Cape Coast Castle, 13 Oct. (no. 39) & 15 Oct. 1873, f. 94 and Confidential Report, p. 46, WO 33/26, TNA.
16. Wolseley to War Office, from Government House Cape Coast, 7 Oct. 1873, f. 85, WO 33/26, TNA.
17. 'The Ashantee War. Diary of a Non-Commissioned Officer of the 42D Regiment', Frid, Dec. 5, *Kinross-shire Courier*, 28 March 1874, p. 2. Statistic from Linklater, *The Black Watch*, p. 122.
18. 'The Ashantee War. Diary of a Non-Commissioned Officer of the 42D Regiment', Frid, Dec. 5, *Kinross-shire Courier*, 28 March 1874, p. 2.
19. ibid., Sun. Dec. 14.
20. Wolseley to Rt Hon. Secretary of State for War, War Office, 18 Dec. 1873, WO 33/26, f. 130, TNA.
21. Wolseley Journal, 19 Dec., Beckett (ed.), *Wolseley and Ashanti, the Asante War Journal and Correspondence of Major General Sir Garnet Wolseley 1873–1874*, p. 276.
22. Wolseley to Rt Hon. Secretary of State for War, War Office, 18 Dec. 1873, WO 33/26, f. 130, TNA.
23. Later Lt Gen Sir Archibald Alison (1826–1907). He had served in the Crimea and was on the expedition to Kertch. He had served as military secretary to Colin Campbell in India but lost his left arm during the second relief of Lucknow 1857 and was invalided home. See Oxford DNB.
24. Stanley, *Coomassie and Magdala*, p. 103.
25. Wallace, 'The Dress of The Black Watch, Part VI, 1857–1880', *The Red Hackle*, April 1933, p. 8.
26. 'The Ashantee War. Diary of a Non-Commissioned Officer of the 42D Regiment', 3 Jan. 1874 & Mon. 5 Jan., *Kinross-shire Advertiser*, 4 April 1874, pp. 2–3. See also *The Times*, 7 March 1874, p. 9.
27. 'The Black Watch. Twenty-Two Years' Experience in the 42D Highlanders', (York) *Evening Press*, 8 Nov. 1895, p. 2, quoted in Spiers, *The Scottish Soldier and Empire, 1854–1902*, p. 29 and n. 18.
28. Letter to the Editor, *The Times*, 9 March 1874, p. 7. 'The Ashantee War. Diary of a Non-Commissioned Officer of the 42D Regiment', Sat. 10 Jan., *Kinross-*

shire Advertiser, 4 April 1874, p. 2. He gives statistics of 181 men volunteering and 143 men doing the carrying.

29. 'The Ashantee War. Diary of a Non-Commissioned Officer of the 42D Regiment', Wed. 21 Jan. 1874, *Kinross-shire Advertiser*, 4 April 1874, p. 2.
30. Stanley, *Coomassie and Magdala*, p. 187.
31. Lt Col McLeod, CB, to Chief of the Staff, Gold Coast, Camp Quar-Man, 30 Jan. 1874, f. 147, WO 33/26, TNA.
32. Brig Gen Sir A. Alison to Chief of Staff, Gold Coast, Amoaful, 1 Feb. 1874, f. 147, WO 33/26, TNA.
33. 'The Ashantee War. Diary of a Non-Commissioned Officer of the 42D Regiment', Mon. 26 Jan. 1874, *Kinross-shire Advertiser*, 4 April 1874.
34. Lloyd, *Drums of Kumasi*, p. 107. Statistic from Rathbone Low, *Wolseley*, II, p. 165.
35. Stanley, *Coomassie and Magdala*, pp. 192, 194.
36. 'The Ashantee War. Diary of a Non-Commissioned Officer of the 42D Regiment', Fri. Jan. 30, *Kinross-shire Advertiser*, 4 April 1874. This was his last diary entry.
37. 'The Ashantee War, From our special correspondent', *The Times*, 17 March 1784, p. 11. See Reade, *The Story of the Ashantee Campaign*, pp. 312–13, 317–19. Reade was *The Times*'s correspondent. Linklater, *The Black Watch*, p. 123, gives incorrect date of 2 Feb.
38. Stanley, *Coomassie and Magdala*, p. 197.
39. 'A Stirlingshire Soldier's Account of the War', p. 6; see also 'The Black Watch. Twenty-Two Years' Experience', quoted in Spiers, *The Scottish Soldier and Empire*, p. 31.
40. Alison, quoted in Rathbone Low, *A Memoir of Sir Garnet J. Wolseley*, II, p. 167.
41. Wolseley Journal, Beckett (ed.), *Wolseley and Ashanti*, p. 380.
42. Maj Gen Sir Garnet Wolseley to War Office, Head Quarters Amoaful, 1 Feb. 1874, f. 141, WO 33/26, TNA. See also his report in *The Times*, 7 March 1874, p. 9. 'The brunt of the attack, as is evident from the casualties, fell upon the front column, and more particularly upon the 42d Highlanders.' Reade, *The Ashanti Campaign*, p. 313, says '105 men were wounded and 2 killed; 9 officers were wounded, and one of them Major Baird, afterwards died.'
43. McLeod, quoted in Linklater, *The Black Watch*, pp. 123–4.
44. Rathbone Lowe, *Wolseley*, II, p. 182.
45. Wolseley Journal, 4 Feb. 1874, Beckett (ed.), *Wolseley and Ashanti*, p. 386. Lt Edward Grogan (later Brig Gen CB, CBE), wounded at Coomassie; Lt Andrew Wauchope (later Maj Gen CB, CMG). He was killed in 1899 at Magersfontein.
46. Wolseley to War Office, Coomassie, 5 Feb. 1874, WO 33/26, f. 141, TNA.
47. Alison, quoted in Rathbone Low, *Wolseley*, II, p. 183.
48. Reade, *The Ashanti Campaign*, p. 342.
49. Sir Garnet Wolseley, quoted in Laffin, *Scotland the Brave*, p. 122.

50. 'The Advance on Coomassie', Special Military Correspondent, Coomassie, 5 Feb. 1874, *The Scotsman*, Monday, 9 March 1874, Mf.N3, NLS.

51. Brackenbury, *The Ashanti War*, p. 223. Later Gen Sir Henry Brackenbury, GCB, KCSI (1856–1904). He was Wolseley's Additional Military Secretary.

52. Precis of the Ashanti Expedition, Intelligence Dept, Horse Guards, War Office, 13 April 1874, f. 182, WO 33/26, TNA.

53. 'Burning of Coomassie, Return of the Troops', Colonial Office, 7 March 1874, *The Scotsman*, Monday, 9 March 1874, Mf 3, NLS. See Alan Lloyd, *Drums of Kumasi*, pp. 141–4.

54. Brackenbury, *The Ashanti War*, pp. 240–1.

55. Lloyd, *Drums of Kumasi*, p. 143.

56. Brackenbury, *The Ashanti War*, pp. 242–3. Rathbone Lowe, *Wolseley*, II, p. 190.

57. Maj Gen Sir Garnet Wolseley to War Office, Agemmum, 7 Feb. 1874, f. 143, WO 33/36, TNA.

58. Brackenbury, *The Ashanti War*, II, pp. 245.

59. 'The Ashantee Expedition, Reception of 42D Highlanders', From our Special Correspondent, Portsmouth, *The Scotsman*, Monday, 9 March 1874, Mf.N3, NLS.

60. 'The Ashantee Expedition', Portsmouth, *The Scotsman*, 23 March 1874, Mf.N3, NLS.

61. *The Graphic* 1874, Regimental Scrapbook 1740–1917, BWRA 0313.

62. 'The Ashantee Expedition, Reception of 42D Highlanders', From our Special Correspondent, Portsmouth, *The Scotsman*, Monday, 9 March 1874, Mf.N3, NLS. 540 rank and file 28 officers, arrived at Portsmouth on 23 March, having sailed on 27 Feb. Precis of the Ashanti Expedition, Intelligence Dept, Horse Guards, War Office, 13 April 1874, f. 188, WO 33/26, TNA.

63. Brackenbury, *The Ashanti War*, p. 341. Six died from gunshot wounds, Table II – Casualties, p. 342. Record of Service, 42nd, p. 23, 1873–1939, notes 688 embarked on board the *Sarmatian*, 568 disembarked on 23 March 1874.

64. Lloyd, *Drums of Kumasi*, p. 108.

65. 'The Ashantee War', Army Headquarters, Coomassie, 5 Feb. 1874, *The Scotsman*, Tuesday, 10 March 1874, Mf.N3, NLS.

66. Wauchope had acted as commander of one of the local regiments raised, Russell's Regiment of Haussas: Baird, *General Wauchope*, p. 57.

67. 'Sergeant Samuel McGaw, VC – 131 Years On', *The Red Hackle*, May 2010, p. 19.

68. Rathbone Low, *Wolseley*, II, p. 216.

69. *Illustrated London News*, 11 April 1874, p. 337.

70. See 'The History of the Ashantee War', *The Times*, 31 March 1874.

71. *The Graphic* 1874, Regimental Scrapbook 1740–1917, BWRA 0313.

72. 'Reception of Troops from the Gold Coast', *Hampshire Telegraph and Sussex Chronicle*, 21 March 1874, p. 7, quoted in Spiers, *The Scottish Soldier and Empire*, p. 34.

73. Authority dated Horse Guards, War Office, 28 October 1876, Record of Service, 42nd, 1873–1939, BWRA 0080.

74. 'The Ashantee War', Cape Coast, *The Scotsman*, Thursday, 19 March 1874, Mf.N3, NLS.

75. Reade, *The Ashanti Campaign*, p. 412: 'if the Ashantees had been armed with the Snider it would have gone badly with us.'

76. Lance Sergeant Samuel McGaw. The award of the VC gave rise to the song 'The Stoutest Man in the Forty Twa', quoted in Linklater, *The Black Watch*, p. 124. His name is misspelt McGraw in the song, and there is no evidence he was 'stout'! After the Ashanti campaign, Pipe Major John McDonald wrote the tune 'The Black Watch march to Coomassie' and became known as Coomassie John.

77. Wallace, 'The Dress of The Black Watch, VI, 1857–1880', *The Red Hackle*, April 1933, p. 10.

78. Record of Service, 42nd, 1873–1939, p. 29, BWRA 0080.

79. Cavendish (ed.), *Cyprus, 1878, The Journal of Sir Garnet Wolseley*, p. 10 n. 1.

80. ibid., Saturday 10 Aug. 1878, p. 42. See Major A.G. Harfield, 'British Military Presence in Cyprus in the 19th Century', *JSAHR*, LVI, 1978, pp. 160–70. Record of Service, 42nd, 1873–1939, BWRA 0800, says one officer and fifty-eight soldiers invalided with malaria.

81. Cavendish (ed.), *Cyprus, 1878, The Journal of Sir Garnet Wolseley*, Thursday 22 Aug. 1878, p. 49.

82. ibid., Thursday 3 Oct. 1878, pp. 98–9. Wolseley described Maj Gen William George Elphinstone, who had commanded the army in 1839–42 during the 1st Afghan War, as 'about as useful as an old applewoman whom the Horse Guards might have picked up upon the parade in front of their windows.'! Elphinstone died in 1842, aged sixty.

83. Mary Esme Scott-Stevenson, *Our Home in Cyprus*, S.I.1880, quoted in Cavendish (ed.), *Cyprus, 1878, The Journal of Sir Garnet Wolseley*, p. 57 n. 1.

84. Baird, *General Wauchope*, p. 60. He remained in Cyprus until 1880 and was assisted by Lt Alexander Gordon Duff.

85. Cavendish (ed.), *Cyprus, 1878, The Journal of Sir Garnet Wolseley*, Sunday 10 Nov. 1878, p. 129. Wolseley described the 71st as being 'furious' at the 42nd leaving, since they expected to go home before the 42nd.

86. See *The Red Hackle*, May 2010, p. 19. Four Privates are also buried there, and four at Paphos. See Baird, *General Wauchope*, p. 61, who says that Wauchope was responsible for removing McGaw's remains to Kyrenia.

87. Record of Service, 73rd, pp. 80–1, BWRA 0005.

88. ibid., p. 85. There is no record of actual presentation of the Colours in 1862. The old Colours were destroyed when the Municipal Buildings caught fire in 1895. Wallace, 'The Colours of the Black Watch', *The Red Hackle*, Oct. 1936, p. 6 wrongly says the Town Hall, as does the Record of Service. See Wauchope, *Short History*, p. 82, and *The Scotsman*, 24 Jan. 1895.

89. ibid., p. 87. The Whitworth cost four times as much as the Enfield and was only used for trial purposes.

90. A.J. Semple, 'The Fenian Infiltration of the British Army', *JSAHR*, LII, no. 211, Autumn 1977, pp. 133–60. See also Henderson, *Highland Soldier*, p. 218.

91. Lt (later Col) William Gordon, Notes of a voyage round the Cape (Good Hope) from Ireland to China via Java in the full rigged ship 'Golden Fleece' Nov. 1866 to March 1867, conveying 73rd, to his mother, Mrs Charlotte Gordon. BWRA 0395/G (see also BWRA 0127/2). He was commissioned into the 73rd as an ensign in 1861.

92. Gordon to his mother, p. 27, BWRA 0395/G.

93. ibid., p. 31.

94. Record of Service, 73rd, p. 92, BWRA 0005.

95. ibid., p. 99.

96. ibid., p. 101.

97. See K.V. Belsare, *Brahmachaitanya Shree Gondhavalekar Maharaj*.

98. Record of Service, 73rd, p. 104, BWRA 0005. William Howard Russell, Hon. Private Secretary to HRH The Prince Wales, *The Prince of Wales' Tour – A Diary in India, with some accounts of the visits . . .*, illustr. Sydney P. Hall, Sampson Low, Marston, Searle, London 1877.

99. Record of Service, 73rd, pp. 104–5, BWRA 0005.

100. Lt Gen Chamberlain, 27 March 1878, quoted in Record of Service, 73rd, p. 112, BWRA 0005.

101. Record of Service, 73rd, p. 114, BWRA 0005. Celebrated as the 'great land-slip', 1880: 151 people were buried. Since 2007, 18 Sept. is celebrated as 'Clean up Nainital Day'.

102. Prince William August Edward of Saxe-Weimar-Eisenach KP, GCB, GCH, GCVO, PC (1823–1902). His sister Adelaide was married to William IV. Record of Service, 73rd, p. 116, BWRA 0005.

103. Regimental Titles, *The Times*, 8 Sept. 1880, p. 10, and Letter to the Editor, *The Times*, 15 Sept. 1880, p. 10.

104. Letter to the Editor, *The Times*, 18 Nov. 1880, p. 6.

105. ibid. See Henderson, *Highland Soldier 1820–1920*, p. 217, for argument that the amalgamation of the 73rd with the 42nd was done purposely: 'the question has to be raised as to whether their Fenian leanings resulted directly in their being linked to and consumed by entirely loyal and primarily Protestant Scottish regiments.'

106. Record of Service, 73rd, p. 115, BWRA 0005.

107. ibid., pp. 116–17. The listing was as follows: 1st Bn 42nd, 2nd Bn 73rd, 3rd Bn Royal Perthshire Militia, 4th Bn not yet formed. There were six volunteer Bns: 1st, 2nd, 3rd Forfarshire, 1st, 2nd Perthshire, 1st Fifeshire. Source: Army List, Dec. 1882. In 1887 they were renamed and as a result of reforms in 1908 the Volunteers became the Territorial Force.

108. Record of Service, 42nd, 1873–1939, p. 35, BWRA 0080.

109. Henderson, *Highland Soldier*, pp. 163–5, 91. 42nd: 73% Scots, 19% English, 8% Irish; 73rd: 55% English, 29% Irish, 15% Scots.

20. Land of the Pharaohs

1. William McGonagall (1825–1902), 'The Battle of Tel-el-Kebir', verse 11, quoted in D. Phillips, *McGonagall and Tommy Atkins*, 1986, p. 89. Acclaimed as the worst poet in British history, his poems were popular because of the comic effect of how bad they were!

2. Private John Gordon, *My Six Years with the Black Watch, 1881–1887*, p. 21.

3. Bandsman Spencer V[incent]. Barwood (1859–1938), Book III, The Nile Campaign, Letters to his family, (N[ellie], E[mmy], Min, Tom) Cairo, 1 Dec. 1882, p. 1, BWRA 0203/1. His nephew, Arthur V. Barwood, was also a bandsman and is often mentioned in his uncle's account. See Arthur V. Barwood Diary on the Sudan, BWRA 0203/2, the Nile Expedition, BWRA 0203/3. He did not take part in the Sudan campaign, and remained at Wadi Halfa during the Nile Relief Expedition, employed as a clerk. He fell ill with enteric fever.

4. Lt Colonels: James Barnes 1–11 July 1881; Hastings D'Oyly Farrington until 11 July 1882; Thomas Warren until 29 January 1887.

5. There is a debate whether Britain's invasion was to protect the Suez Canal from Arabi's 'anarchist' forces, as argued by Robinson and Gallagher, *Africa and the Victorians*, Palgrave Macmillan, 1982, or – as argued by A.G. Hopkins, 'The Victorians and Africa: A Reconsideration of the Occupation of Egypt, 1882', *Journal of African History*, vol. 27, no. 2, p. 372 – to safeguard British investments in Egypt and gain popularity for the government of William Gladstone FRS, FSS (1809–98), prime minister 1868–74, 1880–5, 1886, 1892–4.

6. Ismail Pasha, the Magnificent (1830–95). By decree in 1876, the Khedivate of Egypt became virtually independent of the Sublime Porte. Maj Gen Charles Gordon CB (1833–85). Known as 'Chinese Gordon' for his service in China, he had come to the Khedive's attention while inspecting British cemeteries in the Crimea.

7. Tawfik (Tewfik) Pasha (1852–92).

8. Col Ahmed Urabi (Orabi), aka Arabi Pasha (1841–1911). Minister of War under the Khedive; he effectively deposed him when hostilities broke out against the British.

9. Gordon, *My Six Years with the Black Watch*, p. 21.

10. An earlier attempt to reach Cairo from Alexandria had failed.

11. General Sir Gerald Graham, VC, GCB, GCMG (1831–99). He was awarded the VC for gallantry during the Crimean War.

12. Gordon, *My Six Years with the Black Watch*, pp. 38–9.

13. Capt (promoted Maj 29 Sept. and later Bt Lt Col) Robert de Courcy Coveny (1842–85). Letter, written when going home wounded after Tel-el-Kebir, 28 Sept. 1882, *Diaries and Letters*, p. 5, BWRA 0204, and in the private collection of Maj Gen Simon Willis, AM, CSC, Coveny's great-grand nephew. Correspondence 15 March 2011.

14. Coveny, Letter, 28 Sept. 1882, *Diaries and Letters*, p. 5, BWRA 0204.
15. Barwood, Dear N[ellie], Cairo, Egypt, 1 Dec.1882, p. 9, BWRA 0203/1 (part of a long letter divided into chapters).
16. Coveny, Letter, 28 Sept. 1882, *Diaries and Letters*, p. 6, BWRA 0204.
17. ibid. See Spiers, *The Victorian Soldier in Africa*, and *The Scottish Soldier and Empire, 1854–1902*, for additional contemporary accounts published in local newspapers.
18. Gordon, *My Six Years with the Black Watch*, p. 50. British: 17,000, Egyptians 25,000 approximately.
19. Coveny, Letter, 28 Sept. 1882, *Diaries and Letters*, p. 7, BWRA 0204.
20. Private George Bedson, 'A Private Soldier's Description of the Battle of Tel-el-Kebir', *Staffordshire Advertiser*, 7 Oct. 1882, quoted in Spiers, *The Victorian Soldier in Africa*, p. 87.
21. Gordon, *My Six Years with the Black Watch*, p. 51.
22. Coveny, Letter, 28 Sept. 1882, *Diaries and Letters*, p. 7, BWRA 0204.
23. ibid. See also Contemporary Letter from Brig Gen Goodenough, 'The Battle of Tel-el-Kebir', ed. Brig Gen H. Biddulph, CB CMG, DSO, *JSAHR*, XIX, no. 75, Autumn 1940, pp. 160–2.
24. Gordon, *My Six Years with the Black Watch*, pp. 52, 55. See also Sergeant John Gordon, 'The Egyptian Campaign of 1882', *The Black Watch Chronicle*, 1914, pp. 75–91.
25. Private Donald Campbell, Black Watch. See 'The Battle of Tel-el-Kebir (By a 42D Highlander)', (Edinburgh) *Daily Review*, 5 Oct. 1882, p. 5, quoted in Spiers, *The Victorian Soldier in Africa*, p. 88.
26. Baird, *General Wauchope*, p. 78.
27. Coveny, Letter, 28 Sept. 1882, *Diaries and Letters*, p. 8, BWRA 0204.
28. Gordon, *My Six Years with the Black Watch*, p. 54.
29. Coveny, Letter, 28 Sept. 1882, *Diaries and Letters*, p. 8, BWRA 0204.
30. ibid.
31. ibid.
32. Gordon, *My Six Years with the Black Watch*, p. 58. Of the total force, 382 were wounded and thirty missing: Spiers, *The Victorian Soldier in Africa*, p. 90. Of these six officers and thirty-seven men belonged to The Black Watch: Forbes, *The 'Black Watch'*, p. 304.
33. 'The Charge of the Highland Brigade at Tel-el-Kebir, 13 Sept. 1882,' Lt Gen Sir Edward Hamley KCB in *The Nineteenth Century* for Dec. 1882, Regimental Scrapbook 1740–1917, BWRA 0313. There was initial disappointment in Wolseley's dispatch, which was rumoured to have 'heaped praise' on the Guards, under the command of Prince Arthur, Duke of Connaught, Queen Victoria's son, instead of on those who had fought in the front line. Wolseley wanted a peerage and pension and was writing to please the Queen. See Spiers, *The Victorian Soldier in Africa*, pp. 92–3, and *The Scottish Soldier and Empire*, p. 80.
34. Coveny, Letter, 28 Sept. 1882, *Diaries and Letters*, p. 8, BWRA 0204.

35. Barwood, Dear N[ellie] 2 Dec. 1882, p. 15, BWRA 0203/1.

36. Kipling, 'Oonts', *Barrack Room Ballads*, quoted in Gordon, *My Six Years with The Black Watch*, p. 63. An 'oont' is a camel.

37. Barwood, Dear N[ellie] 2 Dec. 1882, p. 15, BWRA 0203/1.

38. Arabi Pasha returned to Egypt in 1901, dying in 1911.

39. Barwood, Dear N[ellie] Kasr-el-Nil, 10 Jan. 1883, p. 21, BWRA 0203/1.

40. ibid., pp. 21–2, BWRA 0203/1.

41. Barwood to Ben, Kasr-el-Nil, Cairo, 4 Aug. 1883, p. 22 (duplicate page), BWRA 0203/1. See photograph album of Sergeant Maj George Bedson, BWRA. Enlisted April 1882, corporal 1884; lance sgt, sgt Dec. 1885. He left the Army in 1911, but aged fifty-three he responded to Kitchener's call, serving as Regimental Sergeant Major of the 9th Bn.

42. Barwood, Dear N[ellie], Kasr-el Nil, Cairo, 5 Sept. 1883, p. 43, BWRA 0203/1.

43. A.V. Barwood, Diary, dated July–Sept. 1883, p. 1, BWRA 0203/2.

44. Osman Ali or Digna (*c.*1836–1926).

45. Valentine Baker (1827–87), known as 'Baker Pasha' for his services to the Ottomans.

46. Coveny, Letter, 10 Feb.1884, *Diaries and Letters*, p. 9, BWRA 0204.

47. Graham later received the thanks of Parliament, and was promoted lt general.

48. They were equipped with Gardiner and Gatling guns patented by American Dr Richard J. Gatling in 1861, first used in the American Civil War, then in the Franco-Prussian War. It was one of the best-known early rapid-fire weapons and a forerunner of the modern machine gun.

49. Barwood, Dear N[ellie], Station Hospital, Book II, The Soudan Campaign, Cairo, 9 May 1884, pp. 51, 53, BWRA 0203/1.

50. ibid., Cairo, 9 May 1884, pp. 57, 58. The firewood was too wet to make a fire, so they could not boil water for tea.

51. Private Morrison, 'Letter from a Soldier of the Black Watch', p. 2, quoted in Spiers, *The Victorian Soldier*, p. 103.

52. Capt Andrew Scott-Stevenson to his wife, Mary Esme, Camp Suakine, 16 March 1884, p. 2 handwritten photocopy (pp. 1–20), BWRA 0641/1, type-script BWRA 0758. Excerpts were published in *The Red Hackle*, April 1970, ed. by Lt Col V.E.O. Stevenson-Hamilton, p. 46.) Scott-Stevenson was not present but heard what had happened from his fellow subalterns. Later Gen Sir John Davis, KCB (d. 1901).

53. Barwood to his sister, N[ellie], Station Hospital, Cairo, 9 May 1884, p. 60, BWRA 0203/1.

54. Gordon, *My Six Years with The Black Watch*, p. 360. Throughout the Regiment's history, pets became 'genuine' members of the Regiment. Space prevents me from going into detail!

55. Graham to secretary of state for war, Camp, Tokar, 2 March 1884, WO 33/42, TNA.

56. Spiers, *The Victorian Soldier*, p. 105.

57. Baird, *General Wauchope*, p. 91. Wauchope and other wounded were taken to Trinkitat and put on board ship for Suez. He did not rejoin the Battalion until April, and so was not present at Tamai.
58. Coveny, Letter, 9 June 1884, after El Teb, *Diaries and Letters*, p. 10, BWRA 0204.
59. Barwood, Dear E[mmy], Kasr-el-Nil, 8 July 1884, p. 62, p. 64, BWRA 0203/1.
60. Coveny, Letter, 9 June 1884, after El Teb, *Diaries and Letters*, p. 11, BWRA 0204.
61. ibid.
62. Scott-Stevenson to his wife, Camp Suakine, 16 March 1884, p. 2, BWRA 00641/1. Stevenson believed the proper chain of command had not been observed.
63. Barwood to Dear E[mmy], Kasr-el-Nil, 30 Aug. 1884, p. 69, BWRA 2030/1.
64. ibid., p. 70.
65. ibid., 14 Sept. 1884, p. 75.
66. Scott-Stevenson to his wife, Camp Suakine, 16 March 1884, p. 5, BWRA 0641/1.
67. Barwood, to Dear E[mmy], Kasr-el-Nil, 14 Sept. 1884, p. 77, BWRA 0230/1.
68. Coveny, Letter, 9 June 1884, after El Teb, *Diaries and Letters*, p. 124, BWRA 0204.
69. Scott-Stevenson to his wife, Camp Suakine, 16 March 1884, p. 6, BWRA 0641/1.
70. Gordon, *My Six Years with The Black Watch*, p. 115.
71. Barwood to Dear E[mmy], Kasr-el-Nil, 22 Sept. 1884, p. 80, BWRA 0203/1.
72. Lt Col William Green, quoted in Linklater, *The Black Watch*, p. 127.
73. Scott-Stevenson to his wife, 16 March 1884, pp. 8–9, BWRA 0641/1.
74. ibid, p. 10. He calls it a gully, Barwood says ravine.
75. Barwood to E[mmy], Kasr-el-Nil, 22 Sept. 1884, p. 81, BWRA 0203/1. He continues that the Blue Jackets 'strove manfully' to recapture the six guns 'but a good many of them were cut down'. In his report Graham says that the Royal Highlanders distinguished themselves 'by the gallant manner in which they cheered and charged up to the edge of the ravine; but at this moment a more formidable attack came from another direction, and a large body of natives, coming in one continuous stream charged with reckless determination . . . The Brigade fell back in disorder, and the enemy captured the guns of the Naval Brigade, which, however, were blocked by Officers and men, who stood by them to the last.' Graham to secretary of state for War, Camp, Suakin, 15 March 1884, WO 33/42, p. 305, TNA.
76. Gordon, *My Six Years with The Black Watch*, p. 117.
77. Gatling gun, see n. 48 above; Scott-Stevenson to his wife, 16 March 1884, p. 13, BWRA 0641/1.
78. ibid. This would be his broadsword.
79. ibid., p. 14.
80. ibid., p. 16. Lt Norman MacLeod of Dalvey was wounded at El Teb and again at Tamai.
81. ibid., p. 18. The spears are in the BWRM, Balhousie Castle, Perth.
82. Barwood to Dear E[mmy], Kasr-el-Nil, 22 Sept. 1884, pp. 81–2, BWRA 0203/1.

83. Coveny, Letter, 9 June 1884, after El Teb, *Diaries and Letters*, p. 12, BWRA 0204.

84. Scott-Stevenson to his wife, 16 March 1884, p. 17, BWRA 0641/1.

85. Coveny, Letter, 9 June 1884, after El Teb, *Diaries and Letters*, p. 11, BWRA 0204.

86. Scott-Stevenson says '65 men and nearly all our sergeants', p. 19. Record of Service, 42nd, 1873–1939, p. 53, BWRA 0080, says 42nd killed: 1 officer, 8 sgts, 1 drummer, 50 privates; wounded: 3 officers 1 sgt, 3 corporals, 22 soldiers.

87. Graham to secretary of state for war, 15 March 1884, WO 33/42, p. 308, TNA.

88. Gordon, *My Six Years with The Black Watch*, p. 119.

89. Barwood to Dear E[mmy] (undated but after Kasr-el-Nil, 24 Aug. 1884), p. 183, BWRA 0231/1.

90. Coveny, Letter, 9 June 1884, after El Teb, *Diaries and Letters*, pp. 12–13: 'we, that is, the 60th, 42nd, 75th, some RA's and RE's, get no medal for fighting for the Egyptians in the Soudan, while the remainder of the force en route from India, like the 10th Hussars, 65th, and 89th, and RE's and RA's get a medal for the same thing.' BWRA 0204.

91. Private Thomas Edwards (1863–1953), *The London Gazette*, 21 May 1884. Tamai, Sudan, 13 March 1884. Awarded on 21 May 1884. His VC is in BWRM, Balhousie Castle, Perth.

92. Rudyard Kipling (1865–1936), 'Fuzzy-Wuzzy', *Barrack Room Ballads* (1892). He was referring particularly to the Hadendowa tribe because of the way they kept their hair.

93. Coveny, Letter, 9 June 1884, after El Teb, *Diaries and Letters*, p. 11, BWRA 0204. Graham to secretary of state for war [Marquess of Hartingdon, later Duke of Devonshire], 14 March 1884: 'I deeply regret losses, mainly caused by 2nd Brigade square being broken by charge of enemy,' Correspondence relative to the Expedition to Suakin, WO 33/42, p. 263, TNA.

94. Scott-Stevenson to his wife, 16 March 1884, p. 1, BWRA 0641/1.

95. Graham to secretary of state for war, 15 March 1884, WO 33/42, p. 307, TNA.

96. This is clearly not true, since photographs of The Black Watch before 1884 show square-cut spats!

97. Linklater, *The Black Watch*, p. 127.

98. 'Another British Victory', Suakin, 27 March 1884, *New York Times*, 28 March 1884.

99. Record of Service, 42nd, 1873–1939, p. 54, BWRA 0080.

100. Barwood to Dear E[mmy], [Kasr-el-Nil, 24 Aug. 1884], p. 184, BWRA 0203/1.

101. Coveny, Letter, 9 June 1884, after El Teb, *Diaries and Letters*, p. 10, BWRA 0204.

102. ibid., p. 13.

103. Gordon, *My Six Years with The Black Watch*, p. 126.

104. A.V. Barwood, 'The Nile Expedition', poem composed by 'my esteemed friend' Francis Freeman, Band, 56th, Essex Regt, Cairo, Egypt, Feb. 1885, p. 21, BWRA 0203/3.

105. Coveny, Letter, 9 June 1884, after El Teb, *Diaries and Letters*, p. 13, BWRA 0204.

106. Gordon, *My Six Years with The Black Watch*, p. 132.

107. Coveny, Letter, 15 Sept. 1884, *Diaries and Letters*, p. 14, BWRA 0204.

108. Gordon, *My Six Years with The Black Watch*, p. 135.

109. ibid., p. 136.

110. ibid., p. 140.

111. ibid., p. 150.

112. ibid., p. 143.

113. ibid., p. 160.

114. Barwood to Dear E[mmy], Dal, 13 Dec. 1884, p. 125, BWRA 0203/1.

115. Coveny, Diary entry 25 Dec. 1884, *Diaries and Letters*, p. 22, BWRA 0204. He kept his diary from 25 Nov. at Wadi Halfa until 9 Feb. 1885 near El Kirbekan.

116. ibid., 27 Dec. 1884.

117. Gordon, *My Six Years with The Black Watch*, p. 151.

118. Maj Nicholas Brophy. Ensign March 1865, lt 1869, capt 1878. Record of Service, 42nd, 1873–1939, p. 65, BWRA 0080; Gordon, *My Six Years with the Black Watch*, p. 156.

119. *The Graphic* (undated, probably Jan. 1885), Regimental Scrapbook 1740–1917, BWRA 0313.

120. Gordon, *My Six Years with The Black Watch*, p. 163.

121. ibid., p. 169. From eight companies, one officer, one sgt, one corporal.

122. ibid., p. 173. He added that the distance from Korti to Metemmeh by river is 400 miles, while the desert route is about 180 miles.

123. Coveny, Diary entry 12 Jan. 1885, *Diaries and Letters*, p. 24, BWRA 0204.

124. Coveny, Letter, 16 Jan. 1885, *Diaries and Letters*, p. 15, BWRA 0204.

125. ibid., p. 16.

126. Allan McAulay, 'The First Battalion The Black Watch', in Tullibardine (ed.), *Military History of Perthshire 1660–1902*, p. 64.

127. Gordon, *My Six Years with The Black Watch*, p. 182.

128. ibid., pp. 183–4.

129. *Daily News*, 1 April 1885, Regimental Scrapbook 1740–1917, BWRA 0313.

130. Record of Service, 42nd, 1873–1939, p. 68, BWRA 0080. The section was written after publication of Brackenbury's account in 1885.

131. Forbes, *The 'Black Watch'*, p. 305: his statistics. See Baird, *General Wauchope*, p. 100.

132. Record of Service, 42nd, 1873–1939, p. 69, BWRA 0080.

133. ibid., pp. 69–70.

134. Gordon, *My Six Years with The Black Watch*, p. 221.

135. Record of Service, 42nd, 1873–1939, p. 70, BWRA 0080.

136. Gen Brackenbury, quoted in ibid., p. 73.

137. Special General Order, Gen Lord Wolseley, quoted ibid., p. 74A.

138. ibid., p. 74.

139. ibid., pp. 74–75A.
140. Barwood to Dear E[mmy], Abu Dom, 17 May 1885, pp. 138, 140, BWRA 0203/1.
141. Record of Service, 42nd, 1873–1939, p. 74, BWRA 0080. Barwood describes it as an 'old fort' which they altered.
142. Barwood to Dear E[mmy], Abu Dom, 17 May 1885, p. 140, BWRA 0203/1.
143. Record of Service, 42nd, 1873–1939, p. 76, BWRA 0080. Also Forbes, *The 'Black Watch'*, p. 305. Forbes's account concludes at the end of the Sudanese campaign.
144. Barwood, to Dear Emm[y], Kasr-el-Nil, 1 July 1885, p. 142, BWRA 0203/1. He does not mention Kirbekan.
145. ibid., 12 July 1885, p. 159. Barwood left the Regiment in Nov. 1886, having served twelve years and forty-four days. John Gordon joined a mounted infantry detachment to strengthen the Frontier Field Force at Wadi Halfa. He returned to Cairo in April 1886. See *My Six Years with The Black Watch*, pp. 334–56. By Royal Assent, recipients were permitted to wear the Khedive's Bronze Star when in uniform. There were a number of bars for the Egypt medal and one bar for the Bronze Star.
146. Osman Digna was captured in 1900 and sent as a prisoner to Rosetta, where he remained for eight years. He died in 1926.
147. Andrew Wauchope, promoted maj gen, was a member of the expedition.
148. Record of Service, 1873–1939, p. 79, BWRA 0080. The Duke of Edinburgh was appointed honorary Colonel of 3rd Battalion, Royal Perthshire Militia, Perth. He had served with the 1st Bn in the Mediterranean 'and gained the love and esteem of every one'. Lt Col Kidston, quoted in Record of Service, The Black Watch, 2nd Bn, pp. 130–1, BWRA 0005.
149. Baird, *General Wauchope*, p. 107.
150. Gordon, *My Six Years with The Black Watch*, p. 358.
151. Record of Service, 42nd, 1873–1939, p. 91, BWRA 0080. Later Lt Col Adrian Grant-Duff, killed in action commanding 1st Bn, Sept. 1914. Later Lt Col Henry Holmes Sutherland, DSO (d. 1940).
152. ibid., p. 92.
153. General Order no. 252 (1882), quoted in Record of Service, The Black Watch, 2nd Bn, p. 129, BWRA 0005.
154. Army Order No. 136, March 1889, quoted in ibid., p. 130.
155. HRH Prince Albert Victor and Lt Col. Kidston, quoted ibid., pp. 130–1. Kidston says 'after a separation of over one hundred years'. It was ninety-five years from 1786 to 1881. Albert died in 1892 and so his brother, George, became King (and Colonel-in-Chief of The Black Watch 1912–1936). See Wallace, 'The Colours of The Black Watch', *The Red Hackle*, Oct. 1936, p. 6.
156. Record of Service, The Black Watch, 2nd Bn, p. 140, BWRA 0005.
157. Wauchope, *A Short History of The Black Watch (Royal Highlanders)*, p. 83. The Tsar was married to Queen Victoria's granddaughter.

158. *The Dundee Advertiser*, 14 Nov. 1887, p. 3, Regimental Scrapbook 1740–1917, BWRA 0313. It is suggested that the Highlander is Farquhar Shaw, one of the 1743 mutineers. See Clare Thomas and David Strachan, *Around Aberfeldy*, Perth & Kinross Trust, 2008. As noted in *The Dundee Advertiser*, 'The attitude is, however, different from that of the well-known portrait of Farquhar Shaw.'
159. Dugald Dhu, The Black Watch, An Historic Ode, *Written for Waterloo Day*, 1868, verse 4.

Index